America's Top-Rated Cities: a Statistical Handbook

Volume IV
Eastern Region

1998
6th Edition

Rhoda Garoogian, *Managing Editor*
Andrew Garoogian, *Research Editor*
Patrice Walsh Weingart, *Assistant Editor*

Universal Reference Publications

America's Top-Rated Cities: A Statistical Handbook 1998
ISBN 1-881220-38-7 (4 volume set)
ISBN 1-881220-40-0 (Vol. 1 - South)
ISBN 1-881220-41-9 (Vol. 2 - West)
ISBN 1-881220-42-7 (Vol. 3 - Central)
ISBN 1-881220-43-5 (Vol. 4 - East)

Printed and bound in the United States of America.

Preface

This revised and expanded 1998 edition of *America's Top-Rated Cities* is intended to provide the user with a current and concise statistical profile of 76 "top" U.S. cities with populations over 100,000, based on latest census data and/or current estimates. These cities, selected on the basis of their rankings in various surveys (*Money, Fortune, Entrepreneur, Home Office Computing, Site Selection* and others) were found to be the "best" for business and/or living, during 1997.

There are now four regional guides in the series: Southern, Western, Central and Eastern. Designed with ease of use in mind, each handbook is arranged alphabetically by city and divided into two sections: the business environment and the living environment. Rankings and evaluative comments follow a brief overview. Information is then presented under such topics as cost of living, finances, taxes, population, employment and earnings, commercial real estate, education, major employers, media, crime, climate and more. Where appropriate, comparisons with Metropolitan Statistical Areas (MSA) and U.S. figures are included.

There is also a section listing Chambers of Commerce, economic development groups, and State Departments of Labor/Employment Security, that the reader may wish to contact for further information.

In addition to material provided by public/private agencies/organizations, numerous library sources were also consulted. Also utilized were various web sites on the Internet. Tables and charts are properly cited with the appropriate reference to the source of the data. Those tables which are based on the 1990 Census of Population & Housing: Summary Tape File 3C contain sample data to represent the total population.

Although every effort has been made to gather the most current and most accurate information, discrepancies may occur due to the changing nature in the way private and governmental agencies compile and interpret statistical data.

Information in previous editions should not be compared with data in this edition since some historical and forecast data have been revised.

The *America's Top-Rated Cities* series has been compiled for individuals considering relocating, business persons, general and market researchers, real estate consultants, human resource personnel, urban planners as well as students and others who use public, school, academic and special libraries.

The editors wish to thank all of those individuals who responded to our requests for information. Especially helpful were the many Chambers of Commerce, economic development organizations, labor market information bureaus and city school districts. Their assistance is greatly appreciated.

The mission of Universal Reference Publications is to develop a series of comprehensive but reasonably priced statistical reference handbooks about America's "best" cities. Towards that end we have also published *America's Top-Rated Smaller Cities, Health & Environment in America's Top-Rated Cities* and *Crime in America's Top-Rated Cities*.

We welcome your comments and suggestions for improving the coverage and presentation of data in future editions of these handbooks.

The Editors

Table of Contents

Allentown, Pennsylvania

Baltimore, Maryland

Boston, Massachusetts

Bridgeport, Connecticut

Charlotte, North Carolina

Cincinnati, Ohio

Cleveland, Ohio

Durham, North Carolina

Greensboro, North Carolina

Lexington, Kentucky

New York, New York

Norfolk, Virginia

Philadelphia, Pennsylvania

Pittsburgh, Pennsylvania

Raleigh, North Carolina

Richmond, Virginia

Stamford, Connecticut

Washington, D.C.

Worcester, Massachusetts

Comparative Statistics

Allentown, Pennsylvania

Background

In 1735 William Allen, a merchant and later mayor of Philadelphia, bought a parcel of land on the Lehigh River in eastern Pennsylvania about 60 miles northwest of Philadelphia. He initially used the land as a hunting and fishing retreat, but in 1762 he designed a town to be built on the property. Originally called Northampton, the town became the Lehigh County seat in 1812. In 1838 its name was changed to Allentown in honor of its founder.

Located amid large zinc, iron ore, and limestone deposits, Allentown developed an iron industry (1847) and a cement industry (1850) for which it is still known today. With the Lehigh River and the completion of the Lehigh Canal, Allentown became a distribution center for goods produced in the area. Today with its fellow cities Bethlehem and Easton, Allentown is the third partner in a large urban industrial complex. The city has a number of manufacturing industries within its environs including; trucks, electrical equipment and appliances, machinery and tools, textiles, clothing, shoes and cigars.

The industrial side of Allentown is balanced by the beautiful countryside that surrounds it. On the edge of town is the wildfowl refuge of the Trexler Memorial Park. Ten miles northwest of the city is located the Trexler-Lehigh County Game Preserve, home to buffalo, elk and deer. Surrounding it all is the famous "Pennsylvania Dutch Country." Hex signs on barns and colorful Amish quilts hung to dry on outdoor clotheslines dot the beautiful and fertile farmland. Providing the city with corn, wheat, orchard fruits and livestock, the "Pennsylvania Dutch Country" also contributes to another of Allentown's industries - processed foods.

But Allentown has more to offer than industry to provide jobs and beautiful countryside to provide food for both body and soul. The city has a long and proud tradition of higher education. Four colleges and one university can be found within the city limits. Muhlenberg College was founded in 1848 and Cedar Crest College for Women was founded in 1868. In 1912 the Allentown Campus of Pennsylvania State University was opened, and the Allentown College of St. Francis de Sales and Lehigh Carbon Community College were founded in 1964 and 1966 respectively.

Allentown's long history can be seen in many of its buildings. On the corner of Hamilton and Church Streets is the Liberty Bell Shrine. Located in the Victorian Gothic building of the Zion Reformed Church built in 1888, the shrine contains a replica of the original Liberty Bell. During the Revolutionary War the Liberty Bell was brought to Allentown and hidden in the church previously on the site, to protect it from the British. Trout Hall, a colonial Georgian building built in 1770 by James Allen, son of the city's founder, houses the Lehigh County Historical Society which maintains a museum of state and local history.

If the modern day is more to your liking, you can pick up a book at the large public library, view the local museum of fine arts, take in a play at the civic theater or listen to the local symphonic orchestra. There is something for everyone in Allentown.

The weather in Allentown is generally mild. Seasonal snowfall is quite variable. Snowfalls producing 10 inches or more occur once every two years. Flooding is frequently a threat, but the area is seldom subject to destructive storms.

General Rankings and Evaluative Comments

- Allentown was ranked #152 out of 300 cities by *Money's* 1997 "Survey of the Best Places to Live." Criteria used: health services, crime, economy, housing, education, transportation, weather, leisure and the arts. The city was ranked #170 in 1996 and #207 in 1995. *Money, July 1997; Money, September 1996; Money, September 1995*

- *Ladies Home Journal* ranked America's 200 largest cities based on the qualities women care about most. Allentown ranked 16 out of 200. Criteria: low crime rate, good public schools, well-paying jobs, quality health and child care, the presence of women in government, proportion of women-owned businesses, size of the wage gap with men, local economy, divorce rates, the ratio of single men to single women, whether there are laws that require at least the same number of public toilets for women as men, and the probability of good hair days. *Ladies Home Journal, November 1997*

- Allentown was ranked #101 out of 219 cities in terms of children's health, safety, and economic well-being. Criteria: total population, percent population change, birth rate, child immunization rate, infant mortality rate, percent low birth weight infants, percent of births to teens, physician-to-population ratio, student-to-teacher ratio, dropout rate, unemployment rate, median family income, percent of children in poverty, violent and property crime rates, number of juvenile arrests for violent crimes as a percent of the total crime index, number of days with pollution standard index (PSI) over 100, pounds toxic releases per 1,000 people and number of superfund sites. *Zero Population Growth, Children's Environmental Index 1997*

- According to *Working Mother,* "The situation in this state is a mixed bag: Ratios and training requirements are quite good, but child care centers and family child care homes rarely get surprise inspection visits, and there's no statewide resource & referral (R&R) system to help parents find care. But change is in the works. The state is using some of its federal money to create an R&R network this year, and legislation is pending to require unannounced inspections. Both would be welcome developments.

  As we went to press, parents and child advocates here were responding to Governor Tom Ridge's latest budget proposal. He says he's made the largest-ever increase in child care funds—$68 million. But nearly all of that is federal money, the governor allotted only $1 million in new state funds for child care aid to parents in low-income jobs. Meanwhile, 11,700 children needing subsidized care are on a waiting list, and the state has a budget surplus of nearly $500 million!" *Working Mother, July/August 1997*

Business Environment

STATE ECONOMY

State Economic Profile

"Pennsylvania's economy is steadily improving....The revival is broad-based, with Pennsylvania's largest industries—services, retail trade, and manufacturing, all improving....

Last year, Pennsylvania lowered its business costs by enacting several business tax cuts and reforming the workers compensation system. This year, a healthy fiscal situation in Pennsylvania has led to a state budget that includes a 3.7% increase in state spending during fiscal 1998 and another $167 million in tax cuts.

Philadelphia's convention center has created an estimated 6,200 jobs and significantly boosted the hotel and retail markets in the metro area since it opened in 1993. For Philadelphia's hotels, the convention center has meant more business, with the occupancy rate increasing to 70% from 64% prior to the convention center's opening. Because of strong demand, at least four more hotel projects are planned for downtown Philadelphia. A one-half percent sales tax increase will be used to partially finance the expansion of Pittsburgh's convention center. If approved, the $300 million project will significantly expand the center's exhibit, meeting and parking space, while also adding over 50 hotel rooms.

A relatively high rate of consumer spending (retail sales grew by 9% in Pennsylvania and by only 5% in the U.S. last year), in combination with below average income growth, is leading to surging personal bankruptcy filings in pennsylvania. Personal bankruptcy filings increased by 44% in the state last year, compared to 29% at the national level.

With a high cost of doing business, poor demographic trends, and strong union activity, Pennsylvania will have difficulty attracting new and growing industries to replace its aging manufacturers. Pennsylvania will underperform the nation in both the near and long term." *National Association of Realtors, Economic Profiles: The Fifty States, July 1997*

IMPORTS/EXPORTS

Total Export Sales

Area	1993 ($000)	1994 ($000)	1995 ($000)	1996 ($000)	% Chg. 1993-96	% Chg. 1995-96
MSA[1]	1,273,865	1,371,116	1,492,805	1,477,243	16.0	-1.0
U.S.	464,858,354	512,415,609	583,030,524	622,827,063	34.0	6.8

Note: (1) Metropolitan Statistical Area - see Appendix A for areas included
Source: U.S. Department of Commerce, International Trade Association, Metropolitan Area Exports: An Export Performance Report on Over 250 U.S. Cities, October 1997

Imports/Exports by Port

Type	Cargo Value			Share of U.S. Total	
	1995 (US$mil.)	1996 (US$mil.)	% Change 1995-1996	1995 (%)	1996 (%)
Imports	0	0	0	0	0
Exports	0	0	0	0	0

Source: Global Trade Information Services, WaterBorne Trade Atlas 1997

CITY FINANCES

City Government Finances

Component	FY92 ($000)	FY92 (per capita $)
Revenue	81,981	777.02
Expenditure	72,152	683.86
Debt Outstanding	82,039	777.57
Cash & Securities	85,894	814.11

Source: U.S. Bureau of the Census, City Government Finances: 1991-92

City Government Revenue by Source

Source	FY92 ($000)	FY92 (per capita $)	FY92 (%)
From Federal Government	0	0.00	0.0
From State Governments	6,460	61.23	7.9
From Local Governments	100	0.95	0.1
Property Taxes	20,101	190.52	24.5
General Sales Taxes	0	0.00	0.0
Selective Sales Taxes	21	0.20	0.0
Income Taxes	5,453	51.68	6.7
Current Charges	13,540	128.33	16.5
Utility/Liquor Store	9,487	89.92	11.6
Employee Retirement[1]	11,909	112.87	14.5
Other	14,910	141.32	18.2

Note: (1) Excludes "city contributions," classified as "nonrevenue," intragovernmental transfers.
Source: U.S. Bureau of the Census, City Government Finances: 1991-92

City Government Expenditures by Function

Function	FY92 ($000)	FY92 (per capita $)	FY92 (%)
Educational Services	0	0.00	0.0
Employee Retirement[1]	5,588	52.96	7.7
Environment/Housing	18,120	171.74	25.1
Government Administration	8,945	84.78	12.4
Interest on General Debt	3,118	29.55	4.3
Public Safety	16,106	152.65	22.3
Social Services	2,951	27.97	4.1
Transportation	5,097	48.31	7.1
Utility/Liquor Store	7,922	75.09	11.0
Other	4,305	40.80	6.0

Note: (1) Payments to beneficiaries including withdrawal of contributions.
Source: U.S. Bureau of the Census, City Government Finances: 1991-92

Municipal Bond Ratings

Area	Moody's	S & P
Allentown	A3	n/a

Note: n/a not available; n/r not rated
Source: Moody's Bond Record, 2/98; Statistical Abstract of the U.S., 1997; Governing Magazine, 9/97, 3/98

POPULATION

Population Growth

Area	1980	1990	% Chg. 1980-90	July 1996 Estimate	% Chg. 1990-96
City	103,758	105,090	1.3	102,211	-2.7
MSA[1]	635,481	686,688	8.1	614,304	-10.5
U.S.	226,545,805	248,765,170	9.8	265,179,411	6.6

Note: (1) Metropolitan Statistical Area - see Appendix A for areas included
Source: 1980/1990 Census of Housing and Population, Summary Tape File 3C; Census Bureau Population Estimates

Population Characteristics

Race	City					MSA[1]	
	1980		1990		% Chg. 1980-90	1990	
	Population	%	Population	%		Population	%
White	97,610	94.1	90,482	86.1	-7.3	649,880	94.6
Black	3,176	3.1	5,316	5.1	67.4	13,456	2.0
Amer Indian/Esk/Aleut	125	0.1	82	0.1	-34.4	716	0.1
Asian/Pacific Islander	726	0.7	1,522	1.4	109.6	7,282	1.1
Other	2,121	2.0	7,688	7.3	262.5	15,354	2.2
Hispanic Origin[2]	5,294	5.1	11,822	11.2	123.3	28,383	4.1

Note: (1) Metropolitan Statistical Area - see Appendix A for areas included; (2) people of Hispanic origin can be of any race
Source: 1980/1990 Census of Housing and Population, Summary Tape File 3C

Ancestry

Area	German	Irish	English	Italian	U.S.	French	Polish	Dutch
City	36.3	11.0	5.8	7.9	1.9	1.7	4.3	3.8
MSA[1]	40.6	14.4	8.9	11.5	2.3	2.1	5.7	5.0
U.S.	23.3	15.6	13.1	5.9	5.3	4.2	3.8	2.5

Note: Figures are percentages and include persons that reported multiple ancestry (eg. if a person reported being Irish and Italian, they were included in both columns); (1) Metropolitan Statistical Area - see Appendix A for areas included
Source: 1990 Census of Population and Housing, Summary Tape File 3C

Age

Area	Median Age (Years)	Age Distribution (%)						
		Under 5	Under 18	18-24	25-44	45-64	65+	80+
City	33.7	7.2	21.9	11.3	31.9	18.0	17.0	4.1
MSA[1]	35.3	6.7	23.2	9.7	31.7	20.1	15.2	3.2
U.S.	32.9	7.3	25.6	10.5	32.6	18.7	12.5	2.8

Note: (1) Metropolitan Statistical Area - see Appendix A for areas included
Source: 1990 Census of Population and Housing, Summary Tape File 3C

Male/Female Ratio

Area	Number of males per 100 females (all ages)	Number of males per 100 females (18 years old+)
City	88.8	85.6
MSA[1]	93.3	90.2
U.S.	95.0	91.9

Note: (1) Metropolitan Statistical Area - see Appendix A for areas included
Source: 1990 Census of Population, General Population Characteristics

INCOME

Per Capita/Median/Average Income

Area	Per Capita ($)	Median Household ($)	Average Household ($)
City	12,822	25,983	31,177
MSA[1]	14,995	32,667	39,258
U.S.	14,420	30,056	38,453

Note: all figures are for 1989; (1) Metropolitan Statistical Area - see Appendix A for areas included
Source: 1990 Census of Population and Housing, Summary Tape File 3C

Household Income Distribution by Race

Income ($)	City (%)					U.S. (%)				
	Total	White	Black	Other	Hisp.[1]	Total	White	Black	Other	Hisp.[1]
Less than 5,000	5.3	4.0	10.2	20.1	19.2	6.2	4.8	15.2	8.6	8.8
5,000 - 9,999	11.2	10.8	11.0	17.6	15.7	9.3	8.6	14.2	9.9	11.1
10,000 - 14,999	9.8	9.8	10.3	8.8	8.7	8.8	8.5	11.0	9.8	11.0
15,000 - 24,999	21.7	21.8	18.0	22.4	23.9	17.5	17.3	18.9	18.5	20.5
25,000 - 34,999	18.0	18.1	23.5	12.4	12.9	15.8	16.1	14.2	15.4	16.4
35,000 - 49,999	18.9	19.4	18.3	12.9	13.6	17.9	18.6	13.3	16.1	16.0
50,000 - 74,999	10.7	11.3	5.8	5.1	5.1	15.0	15.8	9.3	13.4	11.1
75,000 - 99,999	2.7	2.9	2.6	0.3	0.4	5.1	5.5	2.6	4.7	3.1
100,000+	1.8	2.0	0.5	0.4	0.5	4.4	4.8	1.3	3.7	1.9

Note: all figures are for 1989; (1) people of Hispanic origin can be of any race
Source: 1990 Census of Population and Housing, Summary Tape File 3C

Effective Buying Income

Area	Per Capita ($)	Median Household ($)	Average Household ($)
City	15,238	30,984	37,439
MSA[1]	17,641	38,744	46,159
U.S.	15,444	33,201	41,849

Note: data as of 1/1/97; (1) Metropolitan Statistical Area - see Appendix A for areas included
Source: Standard Rate & Data Service, Newspaper Advertising Source, 2/98

Effective Household Buying Income Distribution

Area	% of Households Earning						
	$10,000 -$19,999	$20,000 -$34,999	$35,000 -$49,999	$50,000 -$74,999	$75,000 -$99,000	$100,000 -$124,999	$125,000 and up
City	17.7	26.5	19.5	17.1	4.4	1.3	1.3
MSA[1]	14.0	22.3	19.8	22.3	8.1	2.5	2.4
U.S.	16.5	23.4	18.3	18.2	6.4	2.1	2.4

Note: data as of 1/1/97; (1) Metropolitan Statistical Area - see Appendix A for areas included
Source: Standard Rate & Data Service, Newspaper Advertising Source, 2/98

Poverty Rates by Race and Age

Area	Total (%)	By Race (%)				By Age (%)		
		White	Black	Other	Hisp.[2]	Under 5 years old	Under 18 years old	65 years and over
City	12.9	8.8	31.2	41.6	39.8	25.8	22.0	9.7
MSA[1]	7.2	6.0	24.1	31.6	33.3	11.8	10.2	8.0
U.S.	13.1	9.8	29.5	23.1	25.3	20.1	18.3	12.8

Note: figures show the percent of people living below the poverty line in 1989. The average poverty threshold was $12,674 for a family of four in 1989; (1) Metropolitan Statistical Area - see Appendix A for areas included; (2) people of Hispanic origin can be of any race
Source: 1990 Census of Population and Housing, Summary Tape File 3C

EMPLOYMENT

Labor Force and Employment

Area	Civilian Labor Force			Workers Employed		
	Dec. '95	Dec. '96	% Chg.	Dec. '95	Dec. '96	% Chg.
City	51,604	52,185	1.1	48,990	49,717	1.5
MSA[1]	302,419	306,021	1.2	289,822	294,120	1.5
U.S.	134,583,000	136,742,000	1.6	127,903,000	130,785,000	2.3

Note: Data is not seasonally adjusted and covers workers 16 years of age and older; (1) Metropolitan Statistical Area - see Appendix A for areas included
Source: Bureau of Labor Statistics, http://stats.bls.gov

Unemployment Rate

Area	1997											
	Jan.	Feb.	Mar.	Apr.	May	Jun.	Jul.	Aug.	Sep.	Oct.	Nov.	Dec.
City	6.3	6.5	6.4	6.5	6.7	6.4	6.5	6.1	6.2	5.6	5.5	4.7
MSA[1]	5.3	5.3	5.2	5.1	5.2	5.2	5.4	5.1	5.0	4.5	4.3	3.9
U.S.	5.9	5.7	5.5	4.8	4.7	5.2	5.0	4.8	4.7	4.4	4.3	4.4

Note: Data is not seasonally adjusted and covers workers 16 years of age and older; All figures are percentages; (1) Metropolitan Statistical Area - see Appendix A for areas included
Source: Bureau of Labor Statistics, http://stats.bls.gov

Employment by Industry

Sector	MSA[1]		U.S.
	Number of Employees	Percent of Total	Percent of Total
Services	82,600	30.8	29.0
Retail Trade	46,900	17.5	18.5
Government	31,700	11.8	16.1
Manufacturing	56,800	21.2	15.0
Finance/Insurance/Real Estate	13,200	4.9	5.7
Wholesale Trade	11,400	4.3	5.4
Transportation/Public Utilities	15,500	5.8	5.3
Construction/Mining	10,000	3.7	5.0

Note: Figures cover non-farm employment as of 12/97 and are not seasonally adjusted; (1) Metropolitan Statistical Area - see Appendix A for areas included
Source: Bureau of Labor Statistics, http://stats.bls.gov

Employment by Occupation

Occupation Category	City (%)	MSA[1] (%)	U.S. (%)
White Collar	54.6	55.6	58.1
Executive/Admin./Management	8.5	10.5	12.3
Professional	12.6	13.4	14.1
Technical & Related Support	4.0	4.0	3.7
Sales	11.3	11.1	11.8
Administrative Support/Clerical	18.1	16.5	16.3
Blue Collar	29.8	31.0	26.2
Precision Production/Craft/Repair	11.0	12.5	11.3
Machine Operators/Assem./Insp.	10.0	9.4	6.8
Transportation/Material Movers	4.1	4.3	4.1
Cleaners/Helpers/Laborers	4.8	4.8	3.9
Services	14.9	12.2	13.2
Farming/Forestry/Fishing	0.7	1.2	2.5

Note: figures cover employed persons 16 years old and over; (1) Metropolitan Statistical Area - see Appendix A for areas included
Source: 1990 Census of Population and Housing, Summary Tape File 3C

Occupational Employment Projections: 1994 - 2005

Occupations Expected to have the Largest Job Growth (ranked by numerical growth)	Fast-Growing Occupations (ranked by percent growth)
1. Registered nurses	1. Electronic pagination systems workers
2. Systems analysts	2. Personal and home care aides
3. Waiters & waitresses	3. Systems analysts
4. Cashiers	4. Computer engineers
5. Salespersons, retail	5. Home health aides
6. Nursing aides/orderlies/attendants	6. Human services workers
7. Teachers aides, clerical & paraprofess.	7. Computer scientists
8. General managers & top executives	8. Manicurists
9. Home health aides	9. Physical therapists
10. Child care workers, private household	10. Residential counselors

Projections cover Pennsylvania.
Source: U.S. Department of Labor, Employment and Training Administration, America's Labor Market Information System (ALMIS)

Average Wages

Occupation	Wage	Occupation	Wage
White-Collar Occupations	$/Hour	**Blue-Collar Occupations**	$/Hour
Accountants/Auditors	15.49	Assemblers	15.39
Bookkeepers	11.35	Carpenters	12.53
Cashiers	8.06	Electricians	18.34
Clerks, General Office	10.62	Groundskeepers, except farm	8.39
Clerks, Order	12.29	Hand Packers/Packagers	8.79
Computer Programmers	16.56	Helpers/Mechanics/Repairers	12.61
Computer Systems Analysts	22.73	Machinists	14.05
Data Entry Keyers	9.30	Mechanics, Automobile	12.32
Drafters	15.45	Plumbers/Pipefitters/Steamfitters	19.05
Electrical/Electronic Tech.	14.53	Printing Press Operators	11.96
Engineers, Mechanical	22.34	Roofers	15.01
Managers, Medicine/Health	24.79	Truck Drivers	12.01
Managers, Financial	28.49	Welders/Cutters	16.78
Nurses, Licensed Practical	14.11	**Service Occupations**	
Nurses, Registered	19.42	Cooks	8.72
Receptionists	9.15	Guards	8.79
School Teachers, Secondary	32.39	Janitors/Cleaners	10.38
Secretaries	11.80	Maids	7.03
Social Workers	13.25	Police/Detectives	16.38
Typists	10.47	Waiters/Waitresses	3.21

Note: Figures are for May-June 1996 and cover the Allentown-Bethlehem-Easton Metropolitan Statistical Area (see Appendix A for areas included).
Source: Bureau of Labor Statistics, COMP2000 Pilot Survey, October 1996

TAXES

Major State and Local Tax Rates

State Corp. Income (%)	State Personal Income (%)	Residential Property (effective rate per $100)	Sales & Use State (%)	Sales & Use Local (%)	State Gasoline (cents/ gallon)	State Cigarette (cents/ 20-pack)
9.99	2.8	n/a	6.0	None	25.9[a]	31

Note: Personal/corporate income tax rates as of 1/97. Sales, gasoline and cigarette tax rates as of 1/98; (a) Rate is comprised of 12 cents excise and 13.9 cent motor carrier tax
Source: Federation of Tax Administrators, www.taxadmin.org; Washington D.C. Department of Finance and Revenue, Tax Rates and Tax Burdens in the District of Columbia: A Nationwide Comparison, June 1997; Chamber of Commerce

Total Taxes Per Capita and as a Percent of Income

Area	Per Capita Income ($)	Per Capita Taxes ($)			Taxes as Pct. of Income (%)		
		Total	Federal	State/ Local	Total	Federal	State/ Local
Pennsylvania	26,194	9,229	6,216	3,013	35.2	23.7	11.5
U.S.	26,187	9,205	6,127	3,078	35.2	23.4	11.8

Note: Figures are for 1997
Source: Tax Foundation, Web Site, www.taxfoundation.org

COMMERCIAL REAL ESTATE

Office Market

Class/ Location	Total Space (sq. ft.)	Vacant Space (sq. ft.)	Vac. Rate (%)	Under Constr. (sq. ft.)	Net Absorp. (sq. ft.)	Rental Rates ($/sq.ft./yr.)
Class A						
CBD	1,705,052	483,260	28.3	20,000	-218,760	12.50-15.50
Outside CBD	5,228,265	530,860	10.2	188,000	11,200	16.50-21.00
Class B						
CBD	n/a	n/a	n/a	n/a	n/a	10.00-15.50
Outside CBD	n/a	n/a	n/a	n/a	n/a	14.00-16.00

Note: Data as of 10/97 and covers Allentown; CBD = Central Business District; n/a not available;
Source: Society of Industrial and Office Realtors, 1998 Comparative Statistics of Industrial and Office Real Estate Markets

"During 1998 office development projects in the Allentown area will be determined by preleasing criteria. Consolidation in the health care field in Allentown has led to the formation of several large medical practices. These groups will be in the market for facilities that are a minimum of 50,000 sq. ft. Our SIOR reporters expect both new construction and rental rates to increase moderately during 1998. The expansion in the local economy should be strong enough to lift absorption to the point where vacancy rates decline slightly. Part of this absorption will come from several local tenants now located in high-tech business incubator facilities who should be ready to graduate into office facilities of their own." *Society of Industrial and Office Realtors, 1998 Comparative Statistics of Industrial and Office Real Estate Markets*

Industrial Market

Location	Total Space (sq. ft.)	Vacant Space (sq. ft.)	Vac. Rate (%)	Under Constr. (sq. ft.)	Net Absorp. (sq. ft.)	Lease ($/sq.ft./yr.)
Central City	3,174,770	853,675	26.9	n/a	-58,675	2.75-3.25
Suburban	25,525,230	3,067,053	12.0	2,900,000	4,672,718	2.75-4.50

Note: Data as of 10/97 and covers Allentown-Bethlehem-Easton (Lehigh Valley); n/a not available
Source: Society of Industrial and Office Realtors, 1998 Comparative Statistics of Industrial and Office Real Estate Markets

"At the end of 1997 a total of 2.9 million sq. ft. of additional space was under construction. All of this space was build-to-suit, high-cube design. Additional construction during 1998 will likely be build to suit as well. Very few developers in the area are interested in purely speculative construction. However, some developers will build facilities that are larger than the requirements of a primary build-to-suit tenant. The strength of the industrial real estate market in the Allentown area is expected to carry through into 1998. Our SIOR reporters anticipate additional increases in absorption during 1998, particularly in warehouse/distribution and High-Tech/R&D space. Sales and lease prices are also expected to increase as are the dollar volumes of sales and leasing." *Society of Industrial and Office Realtors, 1998 Comparative Statistics of Industrial and Office Real Estate Markets*

COMMERCIAL UTILITIES

Typical Monthly Electric Bills

Area	Commercial Service ($/month)		Industrial Service ($/month)	
	12 kW demand 1,500 kWh	100 kW demand 30,000 kWh	1,000 kW demand 400,000 kWh	20,000 kW demand 10,000,000 kWh
City	n/a	n/a	n/a	n/a
U.S.	162	2,360	25,590	545,677

Note: Based on rates in effect July 1, 1997; n/a not available
Source: Edison Electric Institute, Typical Residential, Commercial and Industrial Bills, Summer 1997

TRANSPORTATION

Transportation Statistics

Avg. travel time to work (min.)	17.7
Interstate highways	I-78
Bus lines	
In-city	Lehigh & Northampton TA (LANTA)
Inter-city	4
Passenger air service	
Airport	Lehigh Valley International
Airlines	9
Aircraft departures	9,003 (1995)
Enplaned passengers	390,431 (1995)
Rail service	No Amtrak Service
Motor freight carriers	49
Major waterways/ports	None

Source: OAG, Business Travel Planner, Summer 1997; Editor & Publisher Market Guide, 1998; FAA Airport Activity Statistics, 1996; Amtrak National Time Table, Northeast Timetable, Fall/Winter 1997-98; 1990 Census of Population and Housing, STF 3C; Chamber of Commerce/Economic Development 1997; Jane's Urban Transport Systems 1997-98; Transit Fact Book 1997

Means of Transportation to Work

Area	Car/Truck/Van		Public Transportation			Bicycle	Walked	Other Means	Worked at Home
	Drove Alone	Car-pooled	Bus	Subway	Railroad				
City	70.4	14.0	3.3	0.0	0.0	0.4	8.7	0.9	2.2
MSA[1]	77.9	12.6	1.2	0.0	0.0	0.2	4.9	0.7	2.4
U.S.	73.2	13.4	3.0	1.5	0.5	0.4	3.9	1.2	3.0

Note: figures shown are percentages and only include workers 16 years old and over; (1) Metropolitan Statistical Area - see Appendix A for areas included
Source: 1990 Census of Population and Housing, Summary Tape File 3C

BUSINESSES

Major Business Headquarters

Company Name	1997 Rankings	
	Fortune 500	Forbes 500
Air Products & Chemicals	340	-
PP&L Resources	472	-

Note: Companies listed are located in the city; Dashes indicate no ranking
Fortune 500: companies that produce a 10-K are ranked 1 - 500 based on 1996 revenue
Forbes 500: private companies are ranked 1 - 500 based on 1996 revenue
Source: Forbes 12/1/97; Fortune 4/28/97

HOTELS & MOTELS

Hotels/Motels

Area	Hotels/ Motels	Rooms	Luxury-Level Hotels/Motels		Average Minimum Rates ($)		
			♦♦♦♦	♦♦♦♦♦	♦♦	♦♦♦	♦♦♦♦
City	14	1,431	0	0	67	82	n/a
Airport	3	369	0	0	n/a	n/a	n/a
Total	17	1,800	0	0	n/a	n/a	n/a

Note: n/a not available; Classifications range from one diamond (budget properties with basic amenities) to five diamond (luxury properties with the finest service, rooms and facilities).
Source: OAG, Business Travel Planner, Summer 1997

CONVENTION CENTERS

Major Convention Centers

Center Name	Meeting Rooms	Exhibit Space (sf)
Days Inn Conference Center	9	9,424

Source: Trade Shows Worldwide 1997

Living Environment

COST OF LIVING

Cost of Living Index

Composite Index	Housing	Utilities	Groceries	Health Care	Trans-portation	Misc. Goods/ Services
103.0	98.0	116.6	107.9	93.6	101.7	103.5

Note: U.S. = 100; Figures are for the Metropolitan Statistical Area - see Appendix A for areas included
Source: ACCRA, Cost of Living Index, 1st Quarter 1997

HOUSING

Median Home Prices and Housing Affordability

Area	Median Price[2] 3rd Qtr. 1997 ($)	HOI[3] 3rd Qtr. 1997	Afford-ability Rank[4]
MSA[1]	103,000	76.3	45
U.S.	127,000	63.7	–

Note: (1) Metropolitan Statistical Area - see Appendix A for areas included; (2) U.S. figures calculated from the sales of 625,000 new and existing homes in 195 markets; (3) Housing Opportunity Index - percent of homes sold that were within the reach of the median income household at the prevailing mortgage interest rate; (4) Rank is from 1-195 with 1 being most affordable
Source: National Association of Home Builders, Housing Opportunity Index, 3rd Quarter 1997

It is projected that the median price of existing single-family homes in the metro area will increase by 7.7% in 1998. Nationwide, home prices are projected to increase 6.6%.
Kiplinger's Personal Finance Magazine, January 1998

Average New Home Price

Area	Price ($)
MSA[1]	134,900
U.S.	133,782

Note: Figures are based on a new home with 1,800 sq. ft. of living area on an 8,000 sq. ft. lot; (1) Metropolitan Statistical Area - see Appendix A for areas included
Source: ACCRA, Cost of Living Index, 1st Quarter 1997

Average Apartment Rent

Area	Rent ($/mth)
MSA[1]	564
U.S.	563

Note: Figures are based on an unfurnished two bedroom, 1-1/2 or 2 bath apartment, approximately 950 sq. ft. in size, excluding all utilities except water; (1) Metropolitan Statistical Area - see Appendix A for areas included
Source: ACCRA, Cost of Living Index, 1st Quarter 1997

RESIDENTIAL UTILITIES

Average Residential Utility Costs

Area	All Electric ($/mth)	Part Electric ($/mth)	Other Energy ($/mth)	Phone ($/mth)
MSA[1]	125.94	–	–	17.85
U.S.	110.19	56.83	45.14	19.36

Note: (1) (1) Metropolitan Statistical Area - see Appendix A for areas included
Source: ACCRA, Cost of Living Index, 1st Quarter 1997

HEALTH CARE

Average Health Care Costs

Area	Hospital ($/day)	Doctor ($/visit)	Dentist ($/visit)
MSA[1]	470.00	36.75	55.80
U.S.	385.60	47.34	59.26

Note: Hospital - based on a semi-private room. Doctor - based on a general practitioner's routine exam of an established patient. Dentist - based on adult teeth cleaning and periodic oral exam; (1) Metropolitan Statistical Area - see Appendix A for areas included
Source: ACCRA, Cost of Living Index, 1st Quarter 1997

Distribution of Office-Based Physicians

Area	Family/Gen. Practitioners	Specialists		
		Medical	Surgical	Other
MSA[1]	145	340	320	245

Note: Data as of 12/31/96; (1) Metropolitan Statistical Area - see Appendix A for areas included
Source: American Medical Assn., Physician Characteristics & Distribution in the U.S., 1997-1998

Hospitals

Allentown has 3 general medical and surgical hospitals, 1 psychiatric, 1 rehabilitation. *AHA Guide to the Healthcare Field 1997-98*

EDUCATION

Public School District Statistics

District Name	Num. Sch.	Enroll.	Classroom Teachers[1]	Pupils per Teacher	Minority Pupils (%)	Current Exp.[2] ($/pupil)
Allentown City SD	23	15,042	694	21.7	n/a	n/a
Parkland SD	10	6,830	347	19.7	n/a	n/a
Salisbury Township SD	4	1,802	109	16.5	n/a	n/a

Note: Data covers the 1995-1996 school year unless otherwise noted; (1) Excludes teachers reported as working in school district offices rather than in schools; (2) Based on 1993-94 enrollment collected by the Census Bureau, not the enrollment figure shown in column 3; SD = School District; ISD = Independent School District; n/a not available
Source: National Center for Education Statistics, Common Core of Data Survey; Bureau of the Census

Educational Quality

School District	Education Quotient[1]	Graduate Outcome[2]	Community Index[3]	Resource Index[4]
Allentown City	108.0	66.0	110.0	148.0

Note: Nearly 1,000 secondary school districts were rated in terms of educational quality. The scores range from a low of 50 to a high of 150; (1) Average of the Graduate Outcome, Community and Resource indexes; (2) Based on graduation rates and college board scores (SAT/ACT); (3) Based on the surrounding community's average level of education and the area's average income level; (4) Based on teacher salaries, per-pupil expenditures and student-teacher ratios.
Source: Expansion Management, Ratings Issue 1997

Educational Attainment by Race

Area	High School Graduate (%)					Bachelor's Degree (%)				
	Total	White	Black	Other	Hisp.[2]	Total	White	Black	Other	Hisp.[2]
City	69.4	71.4	65.8	41.7	41.8	15.3	16.0	9.6	8.1	5.0
MSA[1]	74.1	74.6	71.0	55.9	50.0	17.7	17.7	12.5	20.8	8.5
U.S.	75.2	77.9	63.1	60.4	49.8	20.3	21.5	11.4	19.4	9.2

Note: figures shown cover persons 25 years old and over; (1) Metropolitan Statistical Area - see Appendix A for areas included; (2) people of Hispanic origin can be of any race
Source: 1990 Census of Population and Housing, Summary Tape File 3C

School Enrollment by Type

Area	Preprimary				Elementary/High School			
	Public		Private		Public		Private	
	Enrollment	%	Enrollment	%	Enrollment	%	Enrollment	%
City	857	57.4	635	42.6	12,733	87.4	1,833	12.6
MSA[1]	7,056	54.8	5,827	45.2	91,613	88.3	12,092	11.7
U.S.	2,679,029	59.5	1,824,256	40.5	38,379,689	90.2	4,187,099	9.8

Note: figures shown cover persons 3 years old and over;
(1) Metropolitan Statistical Area - see Appendix A for areas included
Source: 1990 Census of Population and Housing, Summary Tape File 3C

School Enrollment by Race

Area	Preprimary (%)				Elementary/High School (%)			
	White	Black	Other	Hisp.[1]	White	Black	Other	Hisp.[1]
City	76.7	6.7	16.6	22.7	74.2	8.0	17.8	23.6
MSA[2]	93.6	1.6	4.8	5.7	91.2	3.1	5.6	7.2
U.S.	80.4	12.5	7.1	7.8	74.1	15.6	10.3	12.5

Note: figures shown cover persons 3 years old and over; (1) people of Hispanic origin can be of any race; (2) Metropolitan Statistical Area - see Appendix A for areas included
Source: 1990 Census of Population and Housing, Summary Tape File 3C

SAT/ACT Scores

Area/District	1996 SAT				1996 ACT	
	Percent of Graduates Tested (%)	Average Math Score	Average Verbal Score	Average Combined Score	Percent of Graduates Tested (%)	Average Composite Score
Allentown	n/a	464	472	936	n/a	n/a
State	71	492	498	990	6	21.0
U.S.	41	508	505	1,013	35	20.9

Note: Math and verbal SAT scores are out of a possible 800; ACT scores are out of a possible 36
Caution: Comparing or ranking states/cities on the basis of SAT/ACT scores alone is invalid and strongly discouraged by the The College Board and The American College Testing Program as students who take the tests are self-selected and do not represent the entire student population. 1996 SAT scores cannot be compared to previous years due to recentering.
Source: Pennsylvania Department of Education, 1996; American College Testing Program, 1996; College Board, 1996

Classroom Teacher Salaries in Public Schools

District	B.A. Degree		M.A. Degree		Ph.D. Degree	
	Min. ($)	Max ($)	Min. ($)	Max. ($)	Min. ($)	Max. ($)
Allentown	32,000	49,409	35,600	57,853	38,300	61,252
Average[1]	26,120	39,270	28,175	44,667	31,643	49,825

Note: Salaries are for 1996-1997; (1) Based on all school districts covered
Source: American Federation of Teachers (unpublished data)

Higher Education

Two-Year Colleges		Four-Year Colleges		Medical Schools	Law Schools	Voc/ Tech
Public	Private	Public	Private			
1	2	0	2	0	0	8

Source: College Blue Book, Occupational Education 1997; Medical School Admission Requirements, 1998-99; Peterson's Guide to Two-Year Colleges, 1997; Peterson's Guide to Four-Year Colleges, 1997; Barron's Guide to Law Schools 1997

MAJOR EMPLOYERS

Major Employers

Air Products & Chemical	Lehigh Valley Hospital
Pennsylvania Power & Light	Sacred Heart Hospital of Allentown
Sacred Heart Health Care System	Morning Call
Allentown Osteopathic Medical Center	Fieldcrest Cannon Sure Fit

Note: companies listed are located in the city
Source: Dun's Business Rankings 1997; Ward's Business Directory, 1997

PUBLIC SAFETY

Crime Rate

Area	All Crimes	Violent Crimes				Property Crimes		
		Murder	Forcible Rape	Robbery	Aggrav. Assault	Burglary	Larceny -Theft	Motor Vehicle Theft
City	7,063.5	5.7	46.5	304.6	261.9	1,435.9	4,431.9	577.0
Suburbs[1]	2,918.6	1.2	15.2	56.5	147.1	442.0	2,095.4	161.3
MSA[2]	3,632.3	2.0	20.6	99.2	166.9	613.2	2,497.7	232.9
U.S.	5,078.9	7.4	36.1	202.4	388.2	943.0	2,975.9	525.9

Note: Crime rate is the number of crimes per 100,000 pop.; (1) defined as all areas within the MSA but located outside the central city; (2) Metropolitan Statistical Area - see Appendix A for areas incl.
Source: FBI Uniform Crime Reports 1996

RECREATION

Culture and Recreation

Museums	Symphony Orchestras	Opera Companies	Dance Companies	Professional Theatres	Zoos	Pro Sports Teams
5	2	1	1	2	0	0

Source: International Directory of the Performing Arts, 1996; Official Museum Directory, 1998; Chamber of Commerce/Economic Development 1997

Library System

The Allentown Public Library has one branch, holdings of 219,000 volumes and a budget of $1,876,176 (1995-1996). The Parkland Community Library has no branches, holdings of 59,427 volumes and a budget of $183,889 (1994-1995). *American Library Directory, 1997-1998*

MEDIA

Newspapers

Name	Type	Freq.	Distribution	Circulation
The East Penn Press	n/a	1x/wk	Area	5,860
Morning Call	n/a	7x/wk	Area	134,348

Note: Includes newspapers with circulations of 500 or more located in the city; n/a not available
Source: Burrelle's Media Directory, 1998 Edition

AM Radio Stations

Call Letters	Freq. (kHz)	Target Audience	Station Format	Music Format
WAEB	790	General	N/S/T	n/a
WYNS	1160	General	M	Country
WTKZ	1320	General	S/T	n/a
WHOL	1600	Hisp/Relig	M/N/S/T	Christian/Spanish

Note: Stations included broadcast in the Allentown metro area; n/a not available
Station Format: E = Educational; M = Music; N = News; S = Sports; T = Talk
Source: Burrelle's Media Directory, 1998 Edition

FM Radio Stations

Call Letters	Freq. (mHz)	Target Audience	Station Format	Music Format
WXLV	90.3	General	E/M/N	Classic Rock
WMUH	91.7	General	M/N/S	n/a
WZZO	95.1	General	M	AOR
WFMZ	100.7	n/a	M/N	Easy Listening
WAEB	104.1	General	M	Adult Contemporary

Note: Stations included broadcast in the Allentown metro area; n/a not available
Station Format: E = Educational; M = Music; N = News; S = Sports; T = Talk
Music Format: AOR = Album Oriented Rock; MOR = Middle-of-the-Road
Source: Burrelle's Media Directory, 1998 Edition

Television Stations

Name	Ch.	Affiliation	Type	Owner
WBPH	60	n/a	Commercial	Sonshine Family Television Inc.
WFMZ	69	n/a	Commercial	Maranatha Broadcasting

Note: Stations included broadcast in the Allentown metro area
Source: Burrelle's Media Directory, 1998 Edition

CLIMATE

Average and Extreme Temperatures

Temperature	Jan	Feb	Mar	Apr	May	Jun	Jul	Aug	Sep	Oct	Nov	Dec	Ann
Extreme High (°F)	72	76	84	93	97	100	105	100	99	90	81	72	105
Average High (°F)	35	38	48	61	71	80	85	82	75	64	52	39	61
Average Temp. (°F)	28	30	39	50	60	70	74	72	65	54	43	32	52
Average Low (°F)	20	22	29	39	49	58	63	62	54	43	34	24	42
Extreme Low (°F)	-12	-7	-1	16	30	39	48	41	31	21	11	-8	-12

Note: Figures cover the years 1948-1990
Source: National Climatic Data Center, International Station Meteorological Climate Summary, 3/95

Average Precipitation/Snowfall/Humidity

Precip./Humidity	Jan	Feb	Mar	Apr	May	Jun	Jul	Aug	Sep	Oct	Nov	Dec	Ann
Avg. Precip. (in.)	3.2	3.0	3.5	3.8	4.2	3.6	4.3	4.4	3.9	2.9	3.8	3.6	44.2
Avg. Snowfall (in.)	9	9	6	1	Tr	0	0	0	0	Tr	1	6	32
Avg. Rel. Hum. 7am (%)	77	76	75	75	78	79	82	86	88	86	82	79	80
Avg. Rel. Hum. 4pm (%)	62	57	51	48	52	52	52	55	57	56	60	64	55

Note: Figures cover the years 1948-1990; Tr = Trace amounts (<0.05 in. of rain; <0.5 in. of snow)
Source: National Climatic Data Center, International Station Meteorological Climate Summary, 3/95

Weather Conditions

Temperature			Daytime Sky			Precipitation		
5°F & below	32°F & below	90°F & above	Clear	Partly cloudy	Cloudy	0.01 inch or more precip.	0.1 inch or more snow/ice	Thunder-storms
6	123	15	77	148	140	123	20	31

Note: Figures are average number of days per year and covers the years 1948-1990
Source: National Climatic Data Center, International Station Meteorological Climate Summary, 3/95

AIR & WATER QUALITY

Maximum Pollutant Concentrations

	Particulate Matter (ug/m^3)	Carbon Monoxide (ppm)	Sulfur Dioxide (ppm)	Nitrogen Dioxide (ppm)	Ozone (ppm)	Lead (ug/m^3)
MSA[1] Level	65	3	0.035	0.024	0.11	0.08
NAAQS[2]	150	9	0.140	0.053	0.12	1.50
Met NAAQS?	Yes	Yes	Yes	Yes	Yes	Yes

Note: (1) Metropolitan Statistical Area - see Appendix A for areas included; (2) National Ambient Air Quality Standards; ppm = parts per million; ug/m^3 = micrograms per cubic meter; n/a not available
Source: EPA, National Air Quality and Emissions Trends Report, 1996

Pollutant Standards Index

In the Allentown MSA (see Appendix A for areas included), the Pollutant Standards Index (PSI) exceeded 100 on 0 days in 1996. A PSI value greater than 100 indicates that air quality would be in the unhealthful range on that day. *EPA, National Air Quality and Emissions Trends Report, 1996*

Drinking Water

Water System Name	Pop. Served	Primary Water Source Type	Number of Violations in Fiscal Year 1997	Type of Violation/ Contaminants
Allentown City Bureau of Water	105,200	Surface	None	None

Note: Data as of January 16, 1998
Source: EPA, Office of Ground Water and Drinking Water, Safe Drinking Water Information System

Allentown tap water is alkaline, hard and not fluoridated.
Editor & Publisher Market Guide, 1998

Baltimore, Maryland

Background

No one industry dominates Baltimore. But many industries have one thing in common: Baltimore's port and facilities. These facilities provide companies in its municipal area access to domestic and international markets. Baltimore's port is the second or third largest by volume in the United States. It also has the advantage of being 150 miles closer to the Midwest than other eastern U.S. port cities. With its easily accessible harbor, reached via a 42-foot deep main canal from Chesapeake Bay, and its renowned stable work force, Baltimore is truly an economy based upon maritime trade.

The city was founded in 1729 and named for the Barons Baltimore, who established the colony of Maryland in the early 17th century.

Since Baltimore's founding, much of its history has revolved around its maritime presence. In 1812, composer Francis Scott Key wrote *The Star Spangled Banner*, while watching an unsuccessful bombardment of the city by the British, from a warship. During World War I, the city's economy due to a need for ships and other industrial products.

There remains a wealth of history, however that is not related to its ships or the sea. Baltimore is the site of the first Roman Catholic Cathedral in the country, the Basilica of the Assumption of the Blessed Virgin Mary, which was designed by Benjamin H. Latrobe. It was the site of the first telegraph line in the United States. Among its more famous institutions are Johns Hopkins University, several medical colleges, and such schools as the Peabody Conservatory of Music and the Maryland Institute College of Art.

Despite the urban decay experienced during the 1950's, 60's, and 70's, reconstruction of many of its old areas, such as Inner Harbor, and the construction of new complexes, such as the Charles Center, are bringing people back to Baltimore.

The Baltimore waterfront area is being redeveloped into a retail and entertainment district. The historic power plant complex located in the heart of the Inner Harbor is undergoing massive renovation and the first two anchor tenants, Hard Rock Cafe (opened in July 1997) and Barnes & Noble (opening this fall) represent the kind of national force not much in evidence along the downtown waterfront redevelopment district. Indeed when Barnes & Noble opens "it will be the largest retailer in downtown Baltimore." *New York Times 8/3/97*

Celebrating its 200th birthday this year, Baltimore has also earmarked $500 million to fund more projects including Port Discovery, a Disney-designed children's museum set to open in 1998. In additional the Inner Harbor is also home to the Orioles at Camden Park, and just to the south a new stadium will be home to the National Football League Ravens (should be ready for the 1998 season.

The region is subject to frequent changes in weather although the mountains to the west and the bay and ocean to the east produce a more equable climate compared with other locations farther inland at the same latitude.

In the summer, the area is under the influence of the high pressure system commonly known as the "Bermuda High" which brings warm, humid air. In general, the humidity tends to be high year round. In winter it snows frequently mixed with rain and sleet, but seldom remains on the ground for more than a few days. Rainfall distribution is rather uniform throughout the year, but the summer and early fall receives the most precipitation. Hurricanes and severe thunderstorms are confined to this time of year as well, but rarely have hurricanes caused widespread damage.

General Rankings and Evaluative Comments

- Baltimore was ranked #156 out of 300 cities by *Money's* 1997 "Survey of the Best Places to Live." Criteria used: health services, crime, economy, housing, education, transportation, weather, leisure and the arts. The city was ranked #91 in 1996 and #113 in 1995. *Money, July 1997; Money, September 1996; Money, September 1995*

- *Ladies Home Journal* ranked America's 200 largest cities based on the qualities women care about most. Baltimore ranked 110 out of 200. Criteria: low crime rate, good public schools, well-paying jobs, quality health and child care, the presence of women in government, proportion of women-owned businesses, size of the wage gap with men, local economy, divorce rates, the ratio of single men to single women, whether there are laws that require at least the same number of public toilets for women as men, and the probability of good hair days. *Ladies Home Journal, November 1997*

- Baltimore was ranked #212 out of 219 cities in terms of children's health, safety, and economic well-being. Criteria: total population, percent population change, birth rate, child immunization rate, infant mortality rate, percent low birth weight infants, percent of births to teens, physician-to-population ratio, student-to-teacher ratio, dropout rate, unemployment rate, median family income, percent of children in poverty, violent and property crime rates, number of juvenile arrests for violent crimes as a percent of the total crime index, number of days with pollution standard index (PSI) over 100, pounds toxic releases per 1,000 people and number of superfund sites. *Zero Population Growth, Children's Environmental Index 1997*

- Baltimore is among the 20 most livable cities for gay men and lesbians. The list was divided between 10 cities you might expect and 10 surprises. Baltimore was on the cities you wouldn't expect list. Rank: 8 out of 10. Criteria: legal protection from antigay discrimination, an annual gay pride celebration, a community center, gay bookstores and publications, and an array of organizations, religious groups, and health care facilities that cater to the needs of the local gay community. *The Advocate, June 1997*

- *Conde Nast Traveler* polled 37,000 readers in terms of travel satisfaction. Cities were ranked based on the following criteria: people/friendliness, environment/ambiance, cultural enrichment, restaurants and fun/energy. Baltimore appeared in the top thirty, ranking number 18, with an overall rating of 63.5 out of 100 based on all the criteria. The cities were also ranked in each category separately. Baltimore appeared in the top 10 based on restaurants, ranking number 6 with a rating of 78.3 out of 100. *Conde Nast Traveler, Readers' Choice Poll 1997*

- *Yahoo! Internet Life* selected "America's 100 Most Wired Cities & Towns". 50 cities were large and 50 cities were small. Baltimore ranked 24 out of 50 large cities. Criteria: Internet users per capita, number of networked computers, number of registered domain names, Internet backbone traffic, and the per-capita number of Web sites devoted to each city. *Yahoo! Internet Life, March 1998*

- According to *Working Mother,* "Like officials in many states, those in Maryland found themselves under severe pressure to make budget cuts. Yet even while the over-all state budget declined for the first time since the Depression, child care funding increased by $1 million last year.

  Nevertheless, advocates fear the state will still have trouble meeting the growing demand for child care. 'In two years, as more people are moved off welfare, we fear we won't have enough money or space to provide child care for everyone who needs it,' says Sandy Skolnik, executive director of the Maryland Committee for Children.

  Maryland has been ahead of most other states in providing extensive child care resource and referral services—and it continues to be a pioneer in this area. Data on child care providers is now being computerized; the Maryland Committee for Children is working to make special software available in a variety of settings from libraries to businesses to government offices. (Maryland is among the 10 best states for child care.)" *Working Mother, July/August 1997*

Business Environment

STATE ECONOMY

State Economic Profile

"The Maryland legislature approved a 10% cut in income taxes by reducing tax rates and increasing personal deductions, in an attempt to make the state more competitive with neighboring jurisdictions. The impact of this cut will be minimal for several reasons: competition from lower cost states in the South; an anticipated slowdown in the exodus of Washington D.C. residents as the Congress reforms the city; and concerns that the tax cut may be temporary, because of state budget problems.

Maryland's plan to control hospital prices will force price freezes or cuts in about half of its hospitals. If these rate freezes are implemented, additional cost cutting measures may turn this average performing industry into a loser.

The Congressional budget compromise places strict limits on nominal discretionary spending that will result in roughly a 10% decline in real spending by 2002. Maryland has the greatest exposure to these cuts, from both federal jobs in Maryland and Maryland residents who commute to Washington D.C. In addition to direct federal employees, many consulting and business services firms in Suburban Maryland rely on federal contracts. However, the likelihood of all of these cuts actually occurring is small because the most serious cuts occur in the out-years of the budget, while experience has shown that only the first year or two of a seven-year budget are implemented without significant change.

Because of its overexposure in defense and federal government employment, Maryland has underperformed the U.S. economy for the past decade....Maryland is poorly ranked for long-term growth." *National Association of Realtors, Economic Profiles: The Fifty States, July 1997*

IMPORTS/EXPORTS

Total Export Sales

Area	1993 ($000)	1994 ($000)	1995 ($000)	1996 ($000)	% Chg. 1993-96	% Chg. 1995-96
MSA[1]	1,783,407	1,868,968	2,209,168	2,110,417	18.3	-4.5
U.S.	464,858,354	512,415,609	583,030,524	622,827,063	34.0	6.8

Note: (1) Metropolitan Statistical Area - see Appendix A for areas included
Source: U.S. Department of Commerce, International Trade Association, Metropolitan Area Exports: An Export Performance Report on Over 250 U.S. Cities, October 1997

Imports/Exports by Port

Type	Cargo Value			Share of U.S. Total	
	1995 (US$mil.)	1996 (US$mil.)	% Change 1995-1996	1995 (%)	1996 (%)
Imports	12,240	11,536	-5.75	3.13	3.01
Exports	8,422	7,892	-6.29	3.68	3.33

Source: Global Trade Information Services, WaterBorne Trade Atlas 1997

CITY FINANCES

City Government Finances

Component	FY94 ($000)	FY94 (per capita $)
Revenue	2,135,033	3,036.64
Expenditure	1,728,616	2,458.60
Debt Outstanding	1,232,157	1,752.49
Cash & Securities	2,231,273	3,173.52

Source: U.S. Bureau of the Census, City Government Finances: 1993-94

City Government Revenue by Source

Source	FY94 ($000)	FY94 (per capita $)	FY94 (%)
From Federal Government	57,575	81.89	2.7
From State Governments	833,052	1,184.84	39.0
From Local Governments	47,721	67.87	2.2
Property Taxes	483,428	687.58	22.6
General Sales Taxes	0	0.00	0.0
Selective Sales Taxes	46,281	65.83	2.2
Income Taxes	125,858	179.01	5.9
Current Charges	103,920	147.80	4.9
Utility/Liquor Store	60,312	85.78	2.8
Employee Retirement[1]	220,003	312.91	10.3
Other	156,883	223.13	7.3

Note: (1) Excludes "city contributions," classified as "nonrevenue," intragovernmental transfers.
Source: U.S. Bureau of the Census, City Government Finances: 1993-94

City Government Expenditures by Function

Function	FY94 ($000)	FY94 (per capita $)	FY94 (%)
Educational Services	616,590	876.97	35.7
Employee Retirement[1]	108,608	154.47	6.3
Environment/Housing	269,309	383.04	15.6
Government Administration	102,340	145.56	5.9
Interest on General Debt	82,648	117.55	4.8
Public Safety	256,080	364.22	14.8
Social Services	67,451	95.94	3.9
Transportation	93,650	133.20	5.4
Utility/Liquor Store	59,595	84.76	3.4
Other	72,345	102.90	4.2

Note: (1) Payments to beneficiaries including withdrawal of contributions.
Source: U.S. Bureau of the Census, City Government Finances: 1993-94

Municipal Bond Ratings

Area	Moody's	S & P
Baltimore	A1	A

Note: n/a not available; n/r not rated
Source: Moody's Bond Record, 2/98; Statistical Abstract of the U.S., 1997; Governing Magazine, 9/97, 3/98

POPULATION

Population Growth

Area	1980	1990	% Chg. 1980-90	July 1996 Estimate	% Chg. 1990-96
City	786,775	736,014	-6.5	675,401	-8.2
MSA[1]	2,199,531	2,382,172	8.3	2,474,118	3.9
U.S.	226,545,805	248,765,170	9.8	265,179,411	6.6

Note: (1) Metropolitan Statistical Area - see Appendix A for areas included
Source: 1980/1990 Census of Housing and Population, Summary Tape File 3C; Census Bureau Population Estimates

Population Characteristics

Race	City					MSA[1]	
	1980		1990		% Chg. 1980-90	1990	
	Population	%	Population	%		Population	%
White	346,692	44.1	287,933	39.1	-16.9	1,710,510	71.8
Black	430,934	54.8	435,619	59.2	1.1	615,218	25.8
Amer Indian/Esk/Aleut	2,170	0.3	2,373	0.3	9.4	6,653	0.3
Asian/Pacific Islander	4,898	0.6	7,982	1.1	63.0	41,870	1.8
Other	2,081	0.3	2,107	0.3	1.2	7,921	0.3
Hispanic Origin[2]	7,638	1.0	6,997	1.0	-8.4	28,538	1.2

Note: (1) Metropolitan Statistical Area - see Appendix A for areas included; (2) people of Hispanic origin can be of any race
Source: 1980/1990 Census of Housing and Population, Summary Tape File 3C

Ancestry

Area	German	Irish	English	Italian	U.S.	French	Polish	Dutch
City	13.9	9.3	5.4	3.5	2.6	1.2	3.9	0.8
MSA[1]	28.5	17.2	13.2	6.1	3.3	2.5	5.5	1.6
U.S.	23.3	15.6	13.1	5.9	5.3	4.2	3.8	2.5

Note: Figures are percentages and include persons that reported multiple ancestry (eg. if a person reported being Irish and Italian, they were included in both columns); (1) Metropolitan Statistical Area - see Appendix A for areas included
Source: 1990 Census of Population and Housing, Summary Tape File 3C

Age

Area	Median Age (Years)	Age Distribution (%)						
		Under 5	Under 18	18-24	25-44	45-64	65+	80+
City	32.5	7.7	24.5	11.1	32.9	17.9	13.7	3.0
MSA[1]	33.3	7.4	24.2	10.2	34.6	19.4	11.7	2.4
U.S.	32.9	7.3	25.6	10.5	32.6	18.7	12.5	2.8

Note: (1) Metropolitan Statistical Area - see Appendix A for areas included
Source: 1990 Census of Population and Housing, Summary Tape File 3C

Male/Female Ratio

Area	Number of males per 100 females (all ages)	Number of males per 100 females (18 years old+)
City	87.7	83.1
MSA[1]	93.5	90.2
U.S.	95.0	91.9

Note: (1) Metropolitan Statistical Area - see Appendix A for areas included
Source: 1990 Census of Population, General Population Characteristics

INCOME

Per Capita/Median/Average Income

Area	Per Capita ($)	Median Household ($)	Average Household ($)
City	11,994	24,045	31,415
MSA[1]	16,596	36,550	44,405
U.S.	14,420	30,056	38,453

Note: all figures are for 1989; (1) Metropolitan Statistical Area - see Appendix A for areas included
Source: 1990 Census of Population and Housing, Summary Tape File 3C

Household Income Distribution by Race

Income ($)	City (%)					U.S. (%)				
	Total	White	Black	Other	Hisp.[1]	Total	White	Black	Other	Hisp.[1]
Less than 5,000	11.7	6.9	15.8	16.0	13.7	6.2	4.8	15.2	8.6	8.8
5,000 - 9,999	11.6	10.4	12.6	11.3	7.5	9.3	8.6	14.2	9.9	11.1
10,000 - 14,999	9.5	9.1	9.9	8.3	11.0	8.8	8.5	11.0	9.8	11.0
15,000 - 24,999	18.7	18.0	19.3	16.3	16.9	17.5	17.3	18.9	18.5	20.5
25,000 - 34,999	15.7	16.4	15.1	16.2	16.0	15.8	16.1	14.2	15.4	16.4
35,000 - 49,999	15.9	17.3	14.6	14.7	19.0	17.9	18.6	13.3	16.1	16.0
50,000 - 74,999	11.3	13.6	9.3	12.2	11.3	15.0	15.8	9.3	13.4	11.1
75,000 - 99,999	3.2	4.1	2.3	3.0	2.5	5.1	5.5	2.6	4.7	3.1
100,000+	2.4	4.2	0.9	2.0	2.1	4.4	4.8	1.3	3.7	1.9

Note: all figures are for 1989; (1) people of Hispanic origin can be of any race
Source: 1990 Census of Population and Housing, Summary Tape File 3C

Effective Buying Income

Area	Per Capita ($)	Median Household ($)	Average Household ($)
City	12,562	25,842	33,519
MSA[1]	17,224	39,446	46,329
U.S.	15,444	33,201	41,849

Note: data as of 1/1/97; (1) Metropolitan Statistical Area - see Appendix A for areas included
Source: Standard Rate & Data Service, Newspaper Advertising Source, 2/98

Effective Household Buying Income Distribution

Area	% of Households Earning						
	$10,000 -$19,999	$20,000 -$34,999	$35,000 -$49,999	$50,000 -$74,999	$75,000 -$99,000	$100,000 -$124,999	$125,000 and up
City	18.9	24.2	16.6	13.6	3.7	1.1	1.3
MSA[1]	12.5	21.4	20.2	22.7	8.4	2.5	2.5
U.S.	16.5	23.4	18.3	18.2	6.4	2.1	2.4

Note: data as of 1/1/97; (1) Metropolitan Statistical Area - see Appendix A for areas included
Source: Standard Rate & Data Service, Newspaper Advertising Source, 2/98

Poverty Rates by Race and Age

Area	Total (%)	By Race (%)				By Age (%)		
		White	Black	Other	Hisp.[2]	Under 5 years old	Under 18 years old	65 years and over
City	21.9	12.6	27.9	25.2	21.5	34.3	32.5	19.3
MSA[1]	10.1	5.4	23.2	10.8	11.5	15.3	14.4	11.6
U.S.	13.1	9.8	29.5	23.1	25.3	20.1	18.3	12.8

Note: figures show the percent of people living below the poverty line in 1989. The average poverty threshold was $12,674 for a family of four in 1989; (1) Metropolitan Statistical Area - see Appendix A for areas included; (2) people of Hispanic origin can be of any race
Source: 1990 Census of Population and Housing, Summary Tape File 3C

EMPLOYMENT

Labor Force and Employment

Area	Civilian Labor Force			Workers Employed		
	Dec. '95	Dec. '96	% Chg.	Dec. '95	Dec. '96	% Chg.
City	319,737	318,809	-0.3	297,220	293,955	-1.1
MSA[1]	1,311,035	1,299,373	-0.9	1,251,836	1,238,084	-1.1
U.S.	134,583,000	136,742,000	1.6	127,903,000	130,785,000	2.3

Note: Data is not seasonally adjusted and covers workers 16 years of age and older; (1) Metropolitan Statistical Area - see Appendix A for areas included
Source: Bureau of Labor Statistics, http://stats.bls.gov

Unemployment Rate

Area	1997											
	Jan.	Feb.	Mar.	Apr.	May	Jun.	Jul.	Aug.	Sep.	Oct.	Nov.	Dec.
City	7.8	7.9	7.8	7.7	8.2	9.2	8.5	8.3	10.7	8.7	8.4	7.8
MSA[1]	5.2	5.4	5.1	4.9	5.1	5.7	5.4	5.0	5.7	5.2	5.0	4.7
U.S.	5.9	5.7	5.5	4.8	4.7	5.2	5.0	4.8	4.7	4.4	4.3	4.4

Note: Data is not seasonally adjusted and covers workers 16 years of age and older; All figures are percentages; (1) Metropolitan Statistical Area - see Appendix A for areas included
Source: Bureau of Labor Statistics, http://stats.bls.gov

Employment by Industry

Sector	MSA[1]		U.S.
	Number of Employees	Percent of Total	Percent of Total
Services	394,300	33.2	29.0
Retail Trade	216,100	18.2	18.5
Government	213,000	17.9	16.1
Manufacturing	101,000	8.5	15.0
Finance/Insurance/Real Estate	73,300	6.2	5.7
Wholesale Trade	64,700	5.4	5.4
Transportation/Public Utilities	59,100	5.0	5.3
Construction	65,900	5.5	4.5
Mining	200	0.0	0.5

Note: Figures cover non-farm employment as of 12/97 and are not seasonally adjusted; (1) Metropolitan Statistical Area - see Appendix A for areas included
Source: Bureau of Labor Statistics, http://stats.bls.gov

Employment by Occupation

Occupation Category	City (%)	MSA[1] (%)	U.S. (%)
White Collar	56.1	64.5	58.1
Executive/Admin./Management	10.0	14.8	12.3
Professional	13.3	15.8	14.1
Technical & Related Support	4.2	4.4	3.7
Sales	8.8	11.5	11.8
Administrative Support/Clerical	19.8	17.8	16.3
Blue Collar	24.9	22.1	26.2
Precision Production/Craft/Repair	9.3	10.7	11.3
Machine Operators/Assem./Insp.	6.4	4.3	6.8
Transportation/Material Movers	4.7	3.9	4.1
Cleaners/Helpers/Laborers	4.6	3.3	3.9
Services	18.3	12.4	13.2
Farming/Forestry/Fishing	0.7	1.0	2.5

Note: figures cover employed persons 16 years old and over; (1) Metropolitan Statistical Area - see Appendix A for areas included
Source: 1990 Census of Population and Housing, Summary Tape File 3C

Occupational Employment Projections: 1992 - 2005

Occupations Expected to have the Largest Job Growth (ranked by numerical growth)	Fast-Growing Occupations (ranked by percent growth)
1. Registered nurses	1. Respiratory therapists
2. General office clerks	2. Travel agents
3. Janitors/cleaners/maids, ex. priv. hshld.	3. Paralegals
4. Truck drivers	4. Physical therapists
5. Nursing aides/orderlies/attendants	5. Recreational therapists
6. General managers & top executives	6. Home health aides
7. Salespersons, retail	7. Interviewing clerks, exc. personnel
8. Cashiers	8. Surgical technologists
9. College & university faculty	9. Occupational therapists
10. Receptionists and information clerks	10. Medical assistants

Projections cover Baltimore City.
Source: Maryland Labor Market Information, Baltimore City, Planning for Today - Looking Toward Tomorrow

Average Wages

Occupation	Wage	Occupation	Wage
Professional/Technical/Clerical	$/Week	**Health/Protective Services**	$/Week
Accountants III	755	Corrections Officers	536
Attorneys III	1,267	Firefighters	643
Budget Analysts III	798	Nurses, Licensed Practical II	531
Buyers/Contracting Specialists II	662	Nurses, Registered II	731
Clerks, Accounting III	448	Nursing Assistants II	308
Clerks, General III	389	Police Officers I	630
Computer Operators II	461	**Hourly Workers**	$/Hour
Computer Programmers II	597	Forklift Operators	12.48
Drafters II	500	General Maintenance Workers	10.01
Engineering Technicians III	644	Guards I	6.62
Engineering Technicians, Civil III	558	Janitors	7.04
Engineers III	922	Maintenance Electricians	17.19
Key Entry Operators I	305	Maintenance Electronics Techs II	17.96
Personnel Assistants III	497	Maintenance Machinists	16.58
Personnel Specialists III	749	Maintenance Mechanics, Machinery	16.10
Secretaries III	509	Material Handling Laborers	11.17
Switchboard Operator-Receptionist	348	Motor Vehicle Mechanics	14.43
Systems Analysts II	861	Shipping/Receiving Clerks	11.52
Systems Analysts Supervisor/Mgr II	-	Tool and Die Makers	18.51
Tax Collectors II	534	Truckdrivers, Tractor Trailer	13.94
Word Processors II	447	Warehouse Specialists	12.70

Note: Wage data includes full-time workers only for 5/95 and cover the Metropolitan Statistical Area (see Appendix A for areas included). Dashes indicate that data was not available.
Source: Bureau of Labor Statistics, Occupational Compensation Survey

TAXES

Major State and Local Tax Rates

State Corp. Income (%)	State Personal Income (%)	Residential Property (effective rate per $100)	Sales & Use State (%)	Sales & Use Local (%)	State Gasoline (cents/ gallon)	State Cigarette (cents/ 20-pack)
7.0	2.0 - 5.0	2.42	5.0	None	23.5	36

Note: Personal/corporate income tax rates as of 1/97. Sales, gasoline and cigarette tax rates as of 1/98.
Source: Federation of Tax Administrators, www.taxadmin.org; Washington D.C. Department of Finance and Revenue, Tax Rates and Tax Burdens in the District of Columbia: A Nationwide Comparison, June 1997; Chamber of Commerce

Total Taxes Per Capita and as a Percent of Income

Area	Per Capita Income ($)	Per Capita Taxes ($) Total	Federal	State/ Local	Taxes as Pct. of Income (%) Total	Federal	State/ Local
Maryland	29,297	10,474	7,044	3,431	35.8	24.0	11.7
U.S.	26,187	9,205	6,127	3,078	35.2	23.4	11.8

Note: Figures are for 1997
Source: Tax Foundation, Web Site, www.taxfoundation.org

Estimated Tax Burden

Area	State Income	Local Income	Property	Sales	Total
Baltimore	2,430	1,215	3,600	425	7,670

Note: The numbers are estimates of taxes paid by a married couple with two kids and annual earnings of $65,000. Sales tax estimates assume they spend average amounts on food, clothing, household goods and gasoline. Property tax estimates assume they live in a $225,000 home.
Source: Kiplinger's Personal Finance Magazine, June 1997

COMMERCIAL REAL ESTATE

Office Market

Class/ Location	Total Space (sq. ft.)	Vacant Space (sq. ft.)	Vac. Rate (%)	Under Constr. (sq. ft.)	Net Absorp. (sq. ft.)	Rental Rates ($/sq.ft./yr.)
Class A						
CBD	8,118,308	956,121	11.8	62,000	704,170	15.00-28.00
Outside CBD	12,663,509	1,336,690	10.6	617,949	276,643	14.50-21.00
Class B						
CBD	5,705,481	1,592,761	27.9	0	121,566	8.00-16.00
Outside CBD	12,717,732	999,740	7.9	0	205,697	13.00-16.50

Note: Data as of 10/97 and covers Baltimore; CBD = Central Business District; n/a not available;
Source: Society of Industrial and Office Realtors, 1998 Comparative Statistics of Industrial and Office Real Estate Markets

"The local economy has been expanding slowly for the last five years and this expansion is expected to continue during 1998. With suburban vacancy rates reasonably low approximately 737,800 sq. ft. of office space has been proposed for 1998 spread among Anne Arundel, Howard, and Baltimore counties. Our SIOR reporter expects a moderate increase in both absorption and construction. However, net absorption is not expected to keep pace with the additional space coming to the market and vacancy rates are expected to increase outside of the central business district." *Society of Industrial and Office Realtors, 1998 Comparative Statistics of Industrial and Office Real Estate Markets*

Industrial Market

Location	Total Space (sq. ft.)	Vacant Space (sq. ft.)	Vac. Rate (%)	Under Constr. (sq. ft.)	Net Absorp. (sq. ft.)	Gross Lease ($/sq.ft./yr.)
Central City	37,350,000	8,400,000	22.5	50,000	-150,000	3.00-5.00
Suburban	105,000,000	10,900,000	10.4	2,750,000	900,000	3.00-7.50

Note: Data as of 10/97 and covers Baltimore; n/a not available
Source: Society of Industrial and Office Realtors, 1998 Comparative Statistics of Industrial and Office Real Estate Markets

"During 1998, the level of speculative development is not expected to be as high as it was during 1997. However, the space which was under construction at the end of 1997 will be completed and the competitive pressures on lease prices will intensify. These pressures are unlikely to affect manufacturing space but lease prices for warehouse distribution space and High-Tech/R&D space could decline by as much as five percent. The modest slowing in the economy is not expected to lead to additional declines in absorption. The near term outlook for sales prices in the area is basically flat. Sales prices in the suburban market during 1997 were well above the cost of new construction. The combination of sales prices above construction costs and new space coming on-line at a faster pace than absorption is not the typical mix of factors leading to increases in sales prices." *Society of Industrial and Office Realtors, 1998 Comparative Statistics of Industrial and Office Real Estate Markets*

Retail Market

Shopping Center Inventory (sq. ft.)	Shopping Center Construction (sq. ft.)	Construction as a Percent of Inventory (%)	Torto Wheaton Rent Index[1] ($/sq. ft.)
47,132,000	0	0.0	13.01

Note: Data as of 1997 and covers the Metropolitan Statistical Area - see Appendix A for areas included; (1) Index is based on a model that predicts what the average rent should be for leases with certain characteristics, in certain locations during certain years.
Source: National Association of Realtors, 1997-1998 Market Conditions Report

"Baltimore's retail sector has stagnated over the past few years. The area's retail rent index has remained in the $13.00 per square foot range, which is slightly lower than the South's average of $13.79 per square foot. One major reason is a decline in new residents to the area due to the loss of high-paying defense-related and banking jobs. Population growth has declined to 0.4% per year over the past two years. Weak income growth, ranking near the bottom nationally, will continue to hinder the prospect of any new retail developments in the near future." *National Association of Realtors, 1997-1998 Market Conditions Report*

COMMERCIAL UTILITIES

Typical Monthly Electric Bills

Area	Commercial Service ($/month)		Industrial Service ($/month)	
	12 kW demand 1,500 kWh	100 kW demand 30,000 kWh	1,000 kW demand 400,000 kWh	20,000 kW demand 10,000,000 kWh
City	151	2,978	31,985	665,046
U.S.	162	2,360	25,590	545,677

Note: Based on rates in effect July 1, 1997
Source: Edison Electric Institute, Typical Residential, Commercial and Industrial Bills, Summer 1997

TRANSPORTATION

Transportation Statistics

Avg. travel time to work (min.)	26.0
Interstate highways	I-70; I-83; I-95; I-97
Bus lines	
In-city	Maryland MTA, 805 vehicles
Inter-city	7
Passenger air service	
Airport	Baltimore-Washington International
Airlines	14
Aircraft departures	75,981 (1995)
Enplaned passengers	5,665,813 (1995)
Rail service	Amtrak; Metro/Light Rail
Motor freight carriers	160
Major waterways/ports	Chesapeake Bay; Port of Baltimore

Source: OAG, Business Travel Planner, Summer 1997; Editor & Publisher Market Guide, 1998; FAA Airport Activity Statistics, 1996; Amtrak National Time Table, Northeast Timetable, Fall/Winter 1997-98; 1990 Census of Population and Housing, STF 3C; Chamber of Commerce/Economic Development 1997; Jane's Urban Transport Systems 1997-98; Transit Fact Book 1997

A survey of 90,000 airline passengers during the first half of 1997 ranked most of the largest airports in the U.S. Baltimore-Washington International ranked number 10 out of 36. Criteria: cleanliness, quality of restaurants, attractiveness, speed of baggage delivery, ease of reaching gates, available ground transportation, ease of following signs and closeness of parking. *Plog Research Inc., First Half 1997*

Means of Transportation to Work

Area	Car/Truck/Van		Public Transportation			Bicycle	Walked	Other Means	Worked at Home
	Drove Alone	Car-pooled	Bus	Subway	Railroad				
City	50.9	16.8	19.3	1.6	0.4	0.2	7.4	1.7	1.6
MSA[1]	70.9	14.2	6.2	0.8	0.3	0.2	4.0	1.1	2.3
U.S.	73.2	13.4	3.0	1.5	0.5	0.4	3.9	1.2	3.0

Note: figures shown are percentages and only include workers 16 years old and over; (1) Metropolitan Statistical Area - see Appendix A for areas included
Source: 1990 Census of Population and Housing, Summary Tape File 3C

BUSINESSES

Major Business Headquarters

Company Name	1997 Rankings	
	Fortune 500	Forbes 500
Baltimore Gas & Electric	429	-
USF&G	389	-

Note: Companies listed are located in the city; Dashes indicate no ranking
Fortune 500: companies that produce a 10-K are ranked 1 - 500 based on 1996 revenue
Forbes 500: private companies are ranked 1 - 500 based on 1996 revenue
Source: Forbes 12/1/97; Fortune 4/28/97

Fast-Growing Businesses

According to *Fortune*, Baltimore is home to one of America's 100 fastest-growing companies: Sylvan Learning Systems. Companies were ranked based on three years' earnings-per-share growth using least squares analysis to smooth out distortions. Criteria for inclusion: public companies with sales of least $50 million. Companies that lost money in the most recent quarter, or ended in the red for the past four quarters as a whole, were not eligible. Limited partnerships and REITs were also not considered. *Fortune, 9/29/97*

Baltimore was ranked #6 out of 24 (#1 is best) in terms of the best-performing local stocks in 1996 according to the Money/Norby Cities Index. The index measures stocks of companies that have headquarters in 24 metro areas. *Money, 2/7/97*

Women-Owned Businesses: Number, Employment, Sales and Share

Area	Women-Owned Businesses in 1996				Share of Women-Owned Businesses in 1996	
	Number	Employment	Sales ($000)	Rank[2]	Percent (%)	Rank[3]
MSA[1]	73,300	128,600	16,516,900	26	37.9	17

Note: (1) Metropolitan Statistical Area - see Appendix A for areas included; (2) Calculated on an averaging of number of businesses, employment and sales and ranges from 1 to 50 where 1 is best; (3) Ranges from 1 to 50 where 1 is best
Source: The National Foundation for Women Business Owners, 1996 Facts on Women-Owned Businesses: Trends in the Top 50 Metropolitan Areas, March 26, 1997

Women-Owned Businesses: Growth

Area	Growth in Women-Owned Businesses (% change from 1987 to 1996)				Relative Growth in the Number of Women-Owned and All Businesses (% change from 1987 to 1996)			
	Num.	Empl.	Sales	Rank[2]	Women-Owned	All Firms	Absolute Difference	Relative Difference
MSA[1]	82.6	92.1	156.5	43	82.6	60.8	21.8	1.4:1

Note: (1) Metropolitan Statistical Area - see Appendix A for areas included; (2) Calculated on an averaging of the percent growth of number of businesses, employment and sales and ranges from 1 to 50 where 1 is best
Source: The National Foundation for Women Business Owners, 1996 Facts on Women-Owned Businesses: Trends in the Top 50 Metropolitan Areas, March 26, 1997

Minority Business Opportunity

Baltimore is home to three companies which are on the Black Enterprise Industrial/Service 100 list (largest based on gross sales): Stop Shop Save Food Markets (supermarkets); La-Van Hawkins Urban City Foods, LLC (Burger King fast foods); Community Foods Inc. T/A Super Pride Markets (supermarkets). Criteria: 1) operational in previous calendar year; 2) at least 51% black-owned; 3) manufactures/owns the product it sells or provides industrial or consumer services. Brokerages, real estate firms and firms that provide professional services are not eligible. *Black Enterprise, July 1997*

HOTELS & MOTELS

Hotels/Motels

Area	Hotels/ Motels	Rooms	Luxury-Level Hotels/Motels		Average Minimum Rates ($)		
			♦♦♦♦	♦♦♦♦♦	♦♦	♦♦♦	♦♦♦♦
City	38	7,152	1	0	63	133	255
Airport	18	2,656	0	0	n/a	n/a	n/a
Suburbs	34	4,658	0	0	n/a	n/a	n/a
Total	90	14,466	1	0	n/a	n/a	n/a

Note: n/a not available; Classifications range from one diamond (budget properties with basic amenities) to five diamond (luxury properties with the finest service, rooms and facilities).
Source: OAG, Business Travel Planner, Summer 1997

CONVENTION CENTERS

Major Convention Centers

Center Name	Meeting Rooms	Exhibit Space (sf)
The Conference Center at Sheppard Pratt	5	n/a
Hyatt Regency Baltimore	20	19,849
Omni Inner Harbor Hotel Baltimore	25	20,600
Stouffer-Harbor Place	n/a	18,606
USF&G Mount Washington Conference Center	12	n/a

Note: n/a not available
Source: Trade Shows Worldwide 1997

Living Environment

COST OF LIVING

Cost of Living Index

Composite Index	Housing	Utilities	Groceries	Health Care	Trans-portation	Misc. Goods/ Services
98.4	95.4	108.7	98.7	97.9	100.5	97.7

Note: U.S. = 100
Source: ACCRA, Cost of Living Index, 3rd Quarter 1997

HOUSING

Median Home Prices and Housing Affordability

Area	Median Price[2] 3rd Qtr. 1997 ($)	HOI[3] 3rd Qtr. 1997	Afford-ability Rank[4]
MSA[1]	135,000	67.3	111
U.S.	127,000	63.7	–

Note: (1) Metropolitan Statistical Area - see Appendix A for areas included; (2) U.S. figures calculated from the sales of 625,000 new and existing homes in 195 markets; (3) Housing Opportunity Index - percent of homes sold that were within the reach of the median income household at the prevailing mortgage interest rate; (4) Rank is from 1-195 with 1 being most affordable
Source: National Association of Home Builders, Housing Opportunity Index, 3rd Quarter 1997

It is projected that the median price of existing single-family homes in the metro area will increase by 8.1% in 1998. Nationwide, home prices are projected to increase 6.6%.
Kiplinger's Personal Finance Magazine, January 1998

Average New Home Price

Area	Price ($)
City	133,476
U.S.	135,710

Note: Figures are based on a new home with 1,800 sq. ft. of living area on an 8,000 sq. ft. lot.
Source: ACCRA, Cost of Living Index, 3rd Quarter 1997

Average Apartment Rent

Area	Rent ($/mth)
City	495
U.S.	569

Note: Figures are based on an unfurnished two bedroom, 1-1/2 or 2 bath apartment, approximately 950 sq. ft. in size, excluding all utilities except water
Source: ACCRA, Cost of Living Index, 3rd Quarter 1997

RESIDENTIAL UTILITIES

Average Residential Utility Costs

Area	All Electric ($/mth)	Part Electric ($/mth)	Other Energy ($/mth)	Phone ($/mth)
City	–	65.23	45.47	22.01
U.S.	109.40	55.25	43.64	19.48

Source: ACCRA, Cost of Living Index, 3rd Quarter 1997

HEALTH CARE

Average Health Care Costs

Area	Hospital ($/day)	Doctor ($/visit)	Dentist ($/visit)
City	536.60	44.00	53.60
U.S.	392.91	48.76	60.84

Note: Hospital - based on a semi-private room. Doctor - based on a general practitioner's routine exam of an established patient. Dentist - based on adult teeth cleaning and periodic oral exam.
Source: ACCRA, Cost of Living Index, 3rd Quarter 1997

Distribution of Office-Based Physicians

Area	Family/Gen. Practitioners	Specialists		
		Medical	Surgical	Other
MSA[1]	400	2,185	1,509	1,548

Note: Data as of 12/31/96; (1) Metropolitan Statistical Area - see Appendix A for areas included
Source: American Medical Assn., Physician Characteristics & Distribution in the U.S., 1997-1998

Hospitals

Baltimore has 16 general medical and surgical hospitals, 2 psychiatric, 2 orthopedic, 1 chronic disease, 1 other specialty, 2 children's other specialty. *AHA Guide to the Healthcare Field 1997-98*

According to *U.S. News and World Report,* Baltimore has 4 of the best hospitals in the U.S.: **Johns Hopkins Hospital**, noted for AIDS, cancer, cardiology, endocrinology, gastroenterology, geriatrics, gynecology, neurology, ophthalmology, orthopedics, otolaryngology, pediatrics, psychiatry, pulmonology, rehabilitation, rheumatology, urology; **University of Maryland Medical System**, noted for AIDS, gastroenterology, neurology, orthopedics, urology; **Sheppard and Enoch Pratt Hospital**, noted for psychiatry; **Greater Baltimore Medical Center**, noted for gynecology. *U.S. News and World Report, "America's Best Hospitals", 7/28/97*

EDUCATION

Public School District Statistics

District Name	Num. Sch.	Enroll.	Classroom Teachers[1]	Pupils per Teacher	Minority Pupils (%)	Current Exp.[2] ($/pupil)
Baltimore City Pub Sch System	180	109,980	6,047	18.2	85.7	5,471

Note: Data covers the 1995-1996 school year unless otherwise noted; (1) Excludes teachers reported as working in school district offices rather than in schools; (2) Based on 1993-94 enrollment collected by the Census Bureau, not the enrollment figure shown in column 3; SD = School District; ISD = Independent School District; n/a not available
Source: National Center for Education Statistics, Common Core of Data Survey; Bureau of the Census

Educational Quality

School District	Education Quotient[1]	Graduate Outcome[2]	Community Index[3]	Resource Index[4]
Baltimore City	63.0	52.0	55.0	81.0

Note: Nearly 1,000 secondary school districts were rated in terms of educational quality. The scores range from a low of 50 to a high of 150; (1) Average of the Graduate Outcome, Community and Resource indexes; (2) Based on graduation rates and college board scores (SAT/ACT); (3) Based on the surrounding community's average level of education and the area's average income level; (4) Based on teacher salaries, per-pupil expenditures and student-teacher ratios.
Source: Expansion Management, Ratings Issue 1997

Educational Attainment by Race

Area	High School Graduate (%)					Bachelor's Degree (%)				
	Total	White	Black	Other	Hisp.[2]	Total	White	Black	Other	Hisp.[2]
City	60.7	64.4	57.3	72.5	66.7	15.5	23.5	8.6	32.7	25.3
MSA[1]	74.7	78.2	63.0	80.4	79.7	23.1	26.2	12.0	39.5	30.6
U.S.	75.2	77.9	63.1	60.4	49.8	20.3	21.5	11.4	19.4	9.2

Note: figures shown cover persons 25 years old and over; (1) Metropolitan Statistical Area - see Appendix A for areas included; (2) people of Hispanic origin can be of any race
Source: 1990 Census of Population and Housing, Summary Tape File 3C

School Enrollment by Type

Area	Preprimary				Elementary/High School			
	Public		Private		Public		Private	
	Enrollment	%	Enrollment	%	Enrollment	%	Enrollment	%
City	7,935	67.4	3,830	32.6	102,104	85.5	17,364	14.5
MSA[1]	25,147	55.8	19,929	44.2	320,507	86.2	51,108	13.8
U.S.	2,679,029	59.5	1,824,256	40.5	38,379,689	90.2	4,187,099	9.8

Note: figures shown cover persons 3 years old and over;
(1) Metropolitan Statistical Area - see Appendix A for areas included
Source: 1990 Census of Population and Housing, Summary Tape File 3C

School Enrollment by Race

Area	Preprimary (%)				Elementary/High School (%)			
	White	Black	Other	Hisp.[1]	White	Black	Other	Hisp.[1]
City	34.8	63.7	1.4	1.4	26.1	72.4	1.5	1.1
MSA[2]	73.5	24.2	2.4	1.6	64.4	32.6	3.0	1.5
U.S.	80.4	12.5	7.1	7.8	74.1	15.6	10.3	12.5

Note: figures shown cover persons 3 years old and over; (1) people of Hispanic origin can be of any race; (2) Metropolitan Statistical Area - see Appendix A for areas included
Source: 1990 Census of Population and Housing, Summary Tape File 3C

SAT/ACT Scores

Area/District	1997 SAT				1997 ACT	
	Percent of Graduates Tested (%)	Average Math Score	Average Verbal Score	Average Combined Score	Percent of Graduates Tested (%)	Average Composite Score
Baltimore CSD	n/a	407	425	832	n/a	19.6
State	64	507	507	1,014	11	20.7
U.S.	42	511	505	1,016	36	21.0

Note: Math and verbal SAT scores are out of a possible 800; ACT scores are out of a possible 36
Caution: Comparing or ranking states/cities on the basis of SAT/ACT scores alone is invalid and strongly discouraged by the The College Board and The American College Testing Program as students who take the tests are self-selected and do not represent the entire student population.
Source: Baltimore Public Schools, Research & Evaluation, 1997; American College Testing Program, 1997; College Board, 1997

Classroom Teacher Salaries in Public Schools

District	B.A. Degree		M.A. Degree		Ph.D. Degree	
	Min. ($)	Max ($)	Min. ($)	Max. ($)	Min. ($)	Max. ($)
Baltimore	24,684	34,229	26,049	36,621	29,106	40,910
Average[1]	26,120	39,270	28,175	44,667	31,643	49,825

Note: Salaries are for 1996-1997; (1) Based on all school districts covered
Source: American Federation of Teachers (unpublished data)

Higher Education

Two-Year Colleges		Four-Year Colleges		Medical Schools	Law Schools	Voc/ Tech
Public	Private	Public	Private			
3	1	4	8	2	2	23

Source: College Blue Book, Occupational Education 1997; Medical School Admission Requirements, 1998-99; Peterson's Guide to Two-Year Colleges, 1997; Peterson's Guide to Four-Year Colleges, 1997; Barron's Guide to Law Schools 1997

MAJOR EMPLOYERS

Major Employers

Abacus Corp. (building cleaning)	Baltimore Gas & Electric
Baltimore Sun	Bell-Atlantic Maryland
Charlestown Community (real estate)	First National Bank of Maryland
USF&G Corp. (insurance)	Franklin Square Hospital Center
Greater Baltimore Medical Center	Johns Hopkins Bayview Medical Center
Johns Hopkins Hospital	Sinai Hospital of Baltimore
St. Agnes Health Care	St. Joseph Medical Center
Union Memorial Hospital	Maryland Casualty Co.
University of Maryland Medical System	Harbor Hospital Center
Bethship (shipbuilding)	Alex Brown & Sons (security brokers)

Note: companies listed are located in the city
Source: Dun's Business Rankings 1997; Ward's Business Directory, 1997

PUBLIC SAFETY

Crime Rate

Area	All Crimes	Violent Crimes				Property Crimes		
		Murder	Forcible Rape	Robbery	Aggrav. Assault	Burglary	Larceny -Theft	Motor Vehicle Theft
City	12,001.2	45.8	89.5	1,450.6	1,136.9	2,066.0	5,656.0	1,556.4
Suburbs[1]	5,023.2	3.7	27.1	207.2	400.9	817.8	3,110.5	456.0
MSA[2]	7,026.9	15.8	45.0	564.3	612.2	1,176.2	3,841.4	772.0
U.S.	5,078.9	7.4	36.1	202.4	388.2	943.0	2,975.9	525.9

Note: Crime rate is the number of crimes per 100,000 pop.; (1) defined as all areas within the MSA but located outside the central city; (2) Metropolitan Statistical Area - see Appendix A for areas incl.
Source: FBI Uniform Crime Reports 1996

RECREATION

Culture and Recreation

Museums	Symphony Orchestras	Opera Companies	Dance Companies	Professional Theatres	Zoos	Pro Sports Teams
31	2	1	2	7	1	2

Source: International Directory of the Performing Arts, 1996; Official Museum Directory, 1998; Chamber of Commerce/Economic Development 1997

Library System

The Enoch Pratt Free Library has 27 branches, holdings of 2,400,320 volumes and a budget of $21,954,748 (1996-1997). *American Library Directory, 1997-1998*

MEDIA

Newspapers

Name	Type	Freq.	Distribution	Circulation
The Baltimore Afro-American	Black	1x/wk	Local	15,000
Baltimore Chronicle	General	1x/mo	Local	28,000
Baltimore Jewish Times	Religious	1x/wk	Local	20,000
Baltimore Messenger	General	1x/wk	Local	15,738
Baltimore Times	General	1x/wk	Local	32,000
Catholic Review	General	1x/wk	Area	69,300
City Paper	Alternative	1x/wk	Area	91,000
Daily Record	General	6x/wk	State	18,000
East Baltimore Guide	General	1x/wk	Local	40,000
The Enterprise	General	1x/wk	Local	30,000
Every Wednesday	Black	1x/wk	Area	40,000
Northeast Times Booster	General	1x/wk	Local	20,000
Northeast Times Reporter	General	1x/wk	Local	19,000
Owings Mills Times	n/a	1x/wk	Local	34,000
The Perry Hall & Parkville Avenue	General	1x/wk	Local	40,000
Rooster-Greater Towson Edition	n/a	2x/mo	Local	30,000
Rooster-Northeast Edition	General	2x/mo	Local	30,000
The Sun	General	7x/wk	Area	320,986
Towson Times	General	1x/wk	Local	38,261

Note: Includes newspapers with circulations of 10,000 or more located in the city; n/a not available
Source: Burrelle's Media Directory, 1998 Edition

AM Radio Stations

Call Letters	Freq. (kHz)	Target Audience	Station Format	Music Format
WCAO	600	General	M/N	Christian
WCBM	680	General	T	n/a
WBMD	750	General	M	Christian
WBGR	860	General	M	Christian
WAMD	970	General	M/N/S	Oldies
WOL	1010	General	N/T	n/a
WOLB	1010	n/a	N/T	n/a
WBAL	1090	General	N/S/T	n/a
WITH	1230	General	M/T	Christian
WWIN	1400	General	M	Christian
WKDB	1570	General	E	n/a
WJRO	1590	Religious	E/M/T	Adult Standards/Christian

Note: Stations included broadcast in the Baltimore metro area; n/a not available
Station Format: E = Educational; M = Music; N = News; S = Sports; T = Talk
Source: Burrelle's Media Directory, 1998 Edition

FM Radio Stations

Call Letters	Freq. (mHz)	Target Audience	Station Format	Music Format
WJHU	88.1	General	M/N/S	Classical/Jazz
WEAA	88.9	General	M/N/S	Adult Contemporary/Big Band/Easy Listening/Jazz/Oldies/
WTMD	89.7	Alternative	M/N	Adult Contemporary
WBJC	91.5	n/a	M/N	Classical
WERQ	92.3	Black	M/N/S	Contemporary Top 40/Urban Contemporary
WPOC	93.1	General	M/N/S	Country
WRBS	95.1	Religious	M/N/S	Christian
WWIN	95.9	n/a	M	Urban Contemporary
WIYY	97.9	n/a	M	AOR
WGRX	100.7	General	M/N/S	Country
WLIF	101.9	General	M	Adult Contemporary
WXYV	102.7	General	M/N/S	Urban Contemporary
WOCT	104.3	n/a	M	Adult Contemporary
WWMX	106.5	n/a	M/N/S	Adult Contemporary

Note: Stations included broadcast in the Baltimore metro area; n/a not available
Station Format: E = Educational; M = Music; N = News; S = Sports; T = Talk
Music Format: AOR = Album Oriented Rock; MOR = Middle-of-the-Road
Source: Burrelle's Media Directory, 1998 Edition

Television Stations

Name	Ch.	Affiliation	Type	Owner
WMAR	2	ABC	Commercial	Scripps Howard Broadcasting
WBAL	11	NBC	Commercial	The Hearst Corporation
WJZ	13	CBS	Commercial	Westinghouse Broadcasting Company
WMPT	22	PBS	Public	State of Maryland
WHSW	24	HSN	Commercial	Silver King Communications Inc.
WCPB	28	PBS	Public	State of Maryland
WWPB	31	PBS	Public	State of Maryland
WGPT	36	PBS	Public	State of Maryland
WBFF	45	Fox	Commercial	Sinclair Broadcast Group
WNUV	54	UPN	Commercial	Glencairn Communications
WFPT	62	PBS	Public	State of Maryland
WMPB	67	PBS	Public	State of Maryland

Note: Stations included broadcast in the Baltimore metro area
Source: Burrelle's Media Directory, 1998 Edition

CLIMATE

Average and Extreme Temperatures

Temperature	Jan	Feb	Mar	Apr	May	Jun	Jul	Aug	Sep	Oct	Nov	Dec	Ann
Extreme High (°F)	75	79	87	94	98	100	104	105	100	92	86	77	105
Average High (°F)	41	44	53	65	74	83	87	85	79	68	56	45	65
Average Temp. (°F)	33	36	44	54	64	73	77	76	69	57	47	37	56
Average Low (°F)	24	26	34	43	53	62	67	66	58	46	37	28	45
Extreme Low (°F)	-7	-3	6	20	32	40	50	45	35	25	13	0	-7

Note: Figures cover the years 1950-1990
Source: National Climatic Data Center, International Station Meteorological Climate Summary, 3/95

Average Precipitation/Snowfall/Humidity

Precip./Humidity	Jan	Feb	Mar	Apr	May	Jun	Jul	Aug	Sep	Oct	Nov	Dec	Ann
Avg. Precip. (in.)	2.9	3.0	3.5	3.3	3.7	3.7	3.9	4.2	3.4	3.0	3.2	3.3	41.2
Avg. Snowfall (in.)	6	7	4	Tr	Tr	0	0	0	0	Tr	1	4	21
Avg. Rel. Hum. 7am (%)	72	71	71	71	77	79	80	83	85	83	78	74	77
Avg. Rel. Hum. 4pm (%)	56	53	48	47	52	53	53	55	55	54	55	57	53

Note: Figures cover the years 1950-1990; Tr = Trace amounts (<0.05 in. of rain; <0.5 in. of snow)
Source: National Climatic Data Center, International Station Meteorological Climate Summary, 3/95

Weather Conditions

Temperature			Daytime Sky			Precipitation		
10°F & below	32°F & below	90°F & above	Clear	Partly cloudy	Cloudy	0.01 inch or more precip.	0.1 inch or more snow/ice	Thunder-storms
6	97	31	91	143	131	113	13	27

Note: Figures are average number of days per year and covers the years 1950-1990
Source: National Climatic Data Center, International Station Meteorological Climate Summary, 3/95

AIR & WATER QUALITY

Maximum Pollutant Concentrations

	Particulate Matter (ug/m³)	Carbon Monoxide (ppm)	Sulfur Dioxide (ppm)	Nitrogen Dioxide (ppm)	Ozone (ppm)	Lead (ug/m³)
MSA[1] Level	75	4	0.028	0.027	0.13	0.03
NAAQS[2]	150	9	0.140	0.053	0.12	1.50
Met NAAQS?	Yes	Yes	Yes	Yes	No	Yes

Note: (1) Metropolitan Statistical Area - see Appendix A for areas included; (2) National Ambient Air Quality Standards; ppm = parts per million; ug/m³ = micrograms per cubic meter; n/a not available
Source: EPA, National Air Quality and Emissions Trends Report, 1996

Pollutant Standards Index

In the Baltimore MSA (see Appendix A for areas included), the Pollutant Standards Index (PSI) exceeded 100 on 4 days in 1996. A PSI value greater than 100 indicates that air quality would be in the unhealthful range on that day. *EPA, National Air Quality and Emissions Trends Report, 1996*

Drinking Water

Water System Name	Pop. Served	Primary Water Source Type	Number of Violations in Fiscal Year 1997	Type of Violation/ Contaminants
Baltimore City	1,600,000	Surface	None	None

Note: Data as of January 16, 1998
Source: EPA, Office of Ground Water and Drinking Water, Safe Drinking Water Information System

Baltimore tap water is alkaline, very soft and fluoridated.
Editor & Publisher Market Guide, 1998

Boston, Massachusetts

Background

Who would think that Boston, a city founded upon the Puritan principles of hard work, plain living, sobriety, and unyielding religious conviction would find it in her to perform such a radical act as to throw tea overboard from a ship?

The answer to that question lies in the wealth upon which Boston grew: ship trading. Because Boston sea captains reaped more profits than English ones in molasses from the West Indies, mahogany from Honduras, and slaves from Guinea, jealous England decided to impose additional taxes upon her colonial subjects. The unpopular Stamp Tax and Molasses Tax aroused resentment amongst Boston citizens against its mother country. In defiance against any more taxes, Samuel Adams led the Sons of Liberty, to throw a precious cargo of tea, so dear to the English, overboard. Events catapulted, and you know the rest: a shot was "heard 'round the world" in Concord, and the American Revolution began.

After the Revolution, Boston continued to grow into the Yankee capital that it is today. "Boston Brahmins" (a reference to the highest social caste in India) such as Isabella Stewart Gardiner, brought artistic cache to the city; while "thinkers" such as Louisa May Alcott, Ralph Waldo Emerson, and Henry David Thoreau contributed significant ideas to the classrooms of many Liberal Arts schools.

As the largest city in New England, Boston has been recognized not only as a leading educational, cultural and medical center but also as an area for high technology and electronics research.

Boston's weather is influenced by three factors: 1) its latitude places it in the path of both tropical and polar air masses; 2) it lies near several tracks frequented by low pressure storms so that the weather fluctuates from fair to cloudy to stormy conditions; 3) its east-coast location on the ocean has a moderating influence on temperature extremes.

Hot summer afternoons are relieved by sea breezes. In winter the severity of cold waves is often reduced by the proximity of the relatively warm ocean.

General Rankings and Evaluative Comments

- Boston was ranked #23 out of 300 cities by *Money's* 1997 "Survey of the Best Places to Live." Criteria used: health services, crime, economy, housing, education, transportation, weather, leisure and the arts. The city was ranked #69 in 1996 and #75 in 1995. *Money, July 1997; Money, September 1996; Money, September 1995*

- Boston appeared on *Fortune's* list of "North America's Most Improved Cities" Rank: 3 out of 10. The selected cities satisfied basic business-location needs and also demonstrated improvement over a five- to ten-year period in a number of business and quality-of-life measures.

  "Despite being three decades shy of its 400th birthday, this city that holds dear its peculiar mix of Brahmin blood and working-class pride suddenly has found new energy.

  Boston's renaissance can be summed up in two words—mutual funds. Almost a fourth of the country's mutual fund assets...are managed in Massachusetts, with the vast majority in Boston....

  Boston is also giving Silicon Valley a run for its money as a mecca for technology and venture capital, thanks to its unparalleled network of 68 colleges and universities. No other American city benefits from such a concentration of brainpower....

  If you need hard evidence that Boston has bounced back, look no further than the booming real estate market. Three years ago the vacancy rate downtown was 15%; today it stands at 5%....

  In terms of scope, nothing in the city rivals the $10 billion infrastructure project under way....The first stage of the project, a new tunnel connecting Logan Airport to the highway, opened in 1995. When the Big Dig is completed in 2008, the North End will be reconnected to the rest of the city and much of the reclaimed area will be devoted to open space.

  Another important change: Boston's violent crime is now at its lowest since 1973....

  People have confidence in Boston once again, and it shows. New residents are arriving, and onetime city dwellers are returning from the suburbs...." *Fortune, 11/24/97*

- *Ladies Home Journal* ranked America's 200 largest cities based on the qualities women care about most. Boston ranked 44 out of 200. Criteria: low crime rate, good public schools, well-paying jobs, quality health and child care, the presence of women in government, proportion of women-owned businesses, size of the wage gap with men, local economy, divorce rates, the ratio of single men to single women, whether there are laws that require at least the same number of public toilets for women as men, and the probability of good hair days. *Ladies Home Journal, November 1997*

- Boston is among "The Best Places to Raise a Family". Rank: 9 out of 301 metro areas. Criteria: low crime rate, low drug and alcohol abuse, good public schools, high-quality health care, a clean environment, affordable cost of living and strong economic growth.

  "Downtown, office towers sit hard by historic sites such as Paul Revere's house. Some 3.25 million people live in the surrounding metro area, populating city neighborhoods and suburbs that each have a distinct personality. And the area's abundance of private schools and colleges earned Boston especially high ratings in these categories." *Reader's Digest, April 1997*

- Boston was ranked #124 out of 219 cities in terms of children's health, safety, and economic well-being. Criteria: total population, percent population change, birth rate, child immunization rate, infant mortality rate, percent low birth weight infants, percent of births to teens, physician-to-population ratio, student-to-teacher ratio, dropout rate, unemployment rate, median family income, percent of children in poverty, violent and property crime rates, number of juvenile arrests for violent crimes as a percent of the total crime index, number of days with pollution standard index (PSI) over 100, pounds toxic releases per 1,000 people and number of superfund sites. *Zero Population Growth, Children's Environmental Index 1997*

- The Villages at Great Hill, located 40 miles north of Boston, is among America's best retirement communities. Criteria: communities must have state-of-the-art facilities, newly built homes for sale, and give you the most value for your money in every price range. Communities must also welcome newcomers of all races and religions. *New Choices, July/August 1997*

- Boston is among the 20 most livable cities for gay men and lesbians. The list was divided between 10 cities you might expect and 10 surprises. Boston was on the cities you would expect list. Rank: 8 out of 10. Criteria: legal protection from antigay discrimination, an annual gay pride celebration, a community center, gay bookstores and publications, and an array of organizations, religious groups, and health care facilities that cater to the needs of the local gay community. *The Advocate, June 1997*

- Boston appeared on *Travel & Leisure's* list of the world's best cities. Rank: 20 out of 25. Criteria: activities/attractions, culture/arts, people, restaurants/food, and value. *Travel & Leisure, September 1997*

- *Conde Nast Traveler* polled 37,000 readers in terms of travel satisfaction. Cities were ranked based on the following criteria: people/friendliness, environment/ambiance, cultural enrichment, restaurants and fun/energy. Boston appeared in the top thirty, ranking number 9, with an overall rating of 69.1 out of 100 based on all the criteria. The cities were also ranked in each category separately. Boston appeared in the top 10 based on cultural enrichment, ranking number 2 with a rating of 87.2 out of 100. Boston appeared in the top 10 based on restaurants, ranking number 7 with a rating of 76.7 out of 100. *Conde Nast Traveler, Readers' Choice Poll 1997*

- *Yahoo! Internet Life* selected "America's 100 Most Wired Cities & Towns". 50 cities were large and 50 cities were small. Boston ranked 7 out of 50 large cities. Criteria: Internet users per capita, number of networked computers, number of registered domain names, Internet backbone traffic, and the per-capita number of Web sites devoted to each city. *Yahoo! Internet Life, March 1998*

- *Reader's Digest* non-scientifically ranked the 12 largest U.S. metropolitan areas in terms of having the worst drivers. The Boston metro area ranked number 2. The areas were selected by asking approximately 1,200 readers on the *Reader's Digest* Web site and 200 interstate bus drivers and long-haul truckers which metro areas have the worst drivers. Their responses were factored in with fatality, insurance and rental-car rates to create the rankings. *Reader's Digest, March 1998*

- Boston appeared on *Sales & Marketing Management's* list of the 20 hottest domestic markets to do business in. Rank: 4 out of 20. America's 320 Metropolitan Statistical Areas were ranked based on the market's potential to buy products in certain industries like high-tech, manufacturing, office equipment and business services, as well as population and household income growth. The study had nine criteria in all.

  "With good reason, Boston employs 115,000 people in the high-tech sector: Digital Equipment Corporation and Raytheon Company are Boston's two largest public companies."Boston has its share of other industries: healthcare, tourism, finance, and education."But why would a high-tech start-up business choose snowy Boston over sunny San Jose?...Boston's advantage lies with the supporting systems that are already in place. There are law firms that specialize in patenting and established venture capitalists with good investment records. And with 32 colleges and universities in the area, Boston has the brainpower for technology development....

  With mountains and the ocean just a short drive away and great cultural institutions in the city, Boston is appealing to new businesses...." *Sales & Marketing Management, January 1998*

- Gillette, headquartered in Boston, is among the "100 Best Companies to Work for in America." Criteria: trust in management, pride in work/company, camaraderie, company responses to the Hewitt People Practices Inventory, and employee responses to their Great Place to Work survey. The companies also had to be at least 10 years old and have a minimum of 500 employees. *Fortune, January 12, 1998*

- Beth Israel Deaconess Medical Center, John Hancock Mutual Life Insurance Co., and Hill, Holliday, Connors, Cosmopulos, Inc., headquartered in Boston, are among the "100 Best Companies for Working Mothers." Criteria: pay compared with competition, opportunities for women to advance, support for child care, flexible work schedules and family-friendly benefits. *Working Mother, October 1997*

- According to *Working Mother,* "Governor William Weld proposed increasing spending by $23 million this year, which would bring the total child care spending in Massachusetts to $283 million by 1998. Such funding is badly needed in the face of ever-increasing demand for child care across the state.

  The state also allocated $25 million to improve salaries for caregivers in many child care programs, a move that should help reduce turnover in centers. Other states should follow this example.

  As long as they hire an assistant, family child care providers here will soon be able to take in up to four more children (for a total of 10). This move increases the supply of care and also boosts its quality. In effect, the new assistants will improve the adult-to-child ratio in many homes. (Massachusetts is among the 10 best states for child care.)" *Working Mother, July/August 1997*

Business Environment

STATE ECONOMY

State Economic Profile

"...house prices have hit new highs in many areas and income growth is above the national average. The state's economy is strongest in the greater Boston area and markedly weaker, but strengthening, in western Massachusetts....

One of the largest new growth industries for the state is telecommunications, which has added more than 34,000 new jobs in the last three years. Internet-related companies alone have created nearly 30,000 new jobs since 1993, while telecommunications manufacturing, which includes network switching and fiber-optic devices, among others, created another 33,000 jobs. Of course, a good part of this growth is being offset by the continued downsizing of traditional telephone companies.

Construction is currently one of Massachusetts's fastest growing industries. Single-family permits issued rose nearly 15% in the first quarter of 1997, while multifamily permits rose a blistering 440%. While single-family activity is expected to moderate in the face of rising mortgage rates, the outlook for multifamily activity is very promising. Massachusetts' strong economy will increase household formation rates and decrease housing affordability. Rising rents will motivate developers to build additional units, and local towns have removed rent controls and anti-development laws.

Massachusetts has successfully replaced the shrinking minicomputer and defense industries with vibrant growth industries, such as money management, software, computer networking, Internet products, biotechnology, and business services. In addition, the state has enacted regulatory and tax reforms that have eased the state's high cost of doing business. Massachusetts' economy would be an even stronger performer if the state's migration flows and population growth were more favorable...." *National Association of Realtors, Economic Profiles: The Fifty States, July 1997*

IMPORTS/EXPORTS

Total Export Sales

Area	1993 ($000)	1994 ($000)	1995 ($000)	1996 ($000)	% Chg. 1993-96	% Chg. 1995-96
MSA[1]	6,472,471	7,095,349	7,902,660	8,715,804	34.7	10.3
U.S.	464,858,354	512,415,609	583,030,524	622,827,063	34.0	6.8

Note: (1) Metropolitan Statistical Area - see Appendix A for areas included
Source: U.S. Department of Commerce, International Trade Association, Metropolitan Area Exports: An Export Performance Report on Over 250 U.S. Cities, October 1997

Imports/Exports by Port

Type	Cargo Value			Share of U.S. Total	
	1995 (US$mil.)	1996 (US$mil.)	% Change 1995-1996	1995 (%)	1996 (%)
Imports	3,022	3,655	20.97	0.77	0.95
Exports	614	516	-15.89	0.27	0.22

Source: Global Trade Information Services, WaterBorne Trade Atlas 1997

CITY FINANCES

City Government Finances

Component	FY94 ($000)	FY94 (per capita $)
Revenue	2,048,866	3,704.14
Expenditure	1,927,067	3,483.94
Debt Outstanding	1,115,253	2,016.27
Cash & Securities	2,009,932	3,633.76

Source: U.S. Bureau of the Census, City Government Finances: 1993-94

City Government Revenue by Source

Source	FY94 ($000)	FY94 (per capita $)	FY94 (%)
From Federal Government	56,173	101.56	2.7
From State Governments	753,445	1,362.15	36.8
From Local Governments	2,360	4.27	0.1
Property Taxes	654,945	1,184.07	32.0
General Sales Taxes	0	0.00	0.0
Selective Sales Taxes	27,486	49.69	1.3
Income Taxes	0	0.00	0.0
Current Charges	215,595	389.77	10.5
Utility/Liquor Store	88,635	160.24	4.3
Employee Retirement[1]	155,692	281.48	7.6
Other	94,535	170.91	4.6

Note: (1) Excludes "city contributions," classified as "nonrevenue," intragovernmental transfers.
Source: U.S. Bureau of the Census, City Government Finances: 1993-94

City Government Expenditures by Function

Function	FY94 ($000)	FY94 (per capita $)	FY94 (%)
Educational Services	509,205	920.59	26.4
Employee Retirement[1]	190,606	344.60	9.9
Environment/Housing	215,673	389.92	11.2
Government Administration	51,962	93.94	2.7
Interest on General Debt	51,730	93.52	2.7
Public Safety	294,926	533.20	15.3
Social Services	319,299	577.26	16.6
Transportation	64,422	116.47	3.3
Utility/Liquor Store	54,043	97.70	2.8
Other	175,201	316.75	9.1

Note: (1) Payments to beneficiaries including withdrawal of contributions.
Source: U.S. Bureau of the Census, City Government Finances: 1993-94

Municipal Bond Ratings

Area	Moody's	S & P
Boston	A1	A+

Note: n/a not available; n/r not rated
Source: Moody's Bond Record, 2/98; Statistical Abstract of the U.S., 1997; Governing Magazine, 9/97, 3/98

POPULATION

Population Growth

Area	1980	1990	% Chg. 1980-90	July 1996 Estimate	% Chg. 1990-96
City	562,994	574,283	2.0	558,394	-2.8
MSA[1]	2,805,911	2,870,650	2.3	3,263,060	13.7
U.S.	226,545,805	248,765,170	9.8	265,179,411	6.6

Note: (1) Metropolitan Statistical Area - see Appendix A for areas included
Source: 1980/1990 Census of Housing and Population, Summary Tape File 3C; Census Bureau Population Estimates

Population Characteristics

Race	City					MSA[1]	
	1980		1990		% Chg. 1980-90	1990	
	Population	%	Population	%		Population	%
White	396,635	70.5	361,513	63.0	-8.9	2,503,373	87.2
Black	126,438	22.5	146,695	25.5	16.0	208,075	7.2
Amer Indian/Esk/Aleut	1,455	0.3	1,865	0.3	28.2	5,245	0.2
Asian/Pacific Islander	16,298	2.9	30,457	5.3	86.9	94,285	3.3
Other	22,168	3.9	33,753	5.9	52.3	59,672	2.1
Hispanic Origin[2]	36,068	6.4	59,692	10.4	65.5	122,999	4.3

Note: (1) Metropolitan Statistical Area - see Appendix A for areas included; (2) people of Hispanic origin can be of any race
Source: 1980/1990 Census of Housing and Population, Summary Tape File 3C

Ancestry

Area	German	Irish	English	Italian	U.S.	French	Polish	Dutch
City	5.9	22.4	6.7	10.5	1.8	2.8	3.0	0.6
MSA[1]	8.5	29.0	14.1	16.9	2.7	5.6	4.0	0.9
U.S.	23.3	15.6	13.1	5.9	5.3	4.2	3.8	2.5

Note: Figures are percentages and include persons that reported multiple ancestry (eg. if a person reported being Irish and Italian, they were included in both columns); (1) Metropolitan Statistical Area - see Appendix A for areas included
Source: 1990 Census of Population and Housing, Summary Tape File 3C

Age

Area	Median Age (Years)	Age Distribution (%)						
		Under 5	Under 18	18-24	25-44	45-64	65+	80+
City	30.2	6.2	19.1	17.3	36.8	15.3	11.5	2.9
MSA[1]	33.3	6.4	20.8	12.4	35.1	18.9	12.9	3.1
U.S.	32.9	7.3	25.6	10.5	32.6	18.7	12.5	2.8

Note: (1) Metropolitan Statistical Area - see Appendix A for areas included
Source: 1990 Census of Population and Housing, Summary Tape File 3C

Male/Female Ratio

Area	Number of males per 100 females (all ages)	Number of males per 100 females (18 years old+)
City	91.4	90.3
MSA[1]	92.0	89.2
U.S.	95.0	91.9

Note: (1) Metropolitan Statistical Area - see Appendix A for areas included
Source: 1990 Census of Population, General Population Characteristics

INCOME

Per Capita/Median/Average Income

Area	Per Capita ($)	Median Household ($)	Average Household ($)
City	15,581	29,180	37,907
MSA[1]	19,288	40,491	50,478
U.S.	14,420	30,056	38,453

Note: all figures are for 1989; (1) Metropolitan Statistical Area - see Appendix A for areas included
Source: 1990 Census of Population and Housing, Summary Tape File 3C

Household Income Distribution by Race

Income ($)	City (%)					U.S. (%)				
	Total	White	Black	Other	Hisp.[1]	Total	White	Black	Other	Hisp.[1]
Less than 5,000	8.0	6.3	10.5	15.3	12.6	6.2	4.8	15.2	8.6	8.8
5,000 - 9,999	12.5	11.3	15.1	15.2	17.1	9.3	8.6	14.2	9.9	11.1
10,000 - 14,999	7.4	7.2	7.5	8.3	9.7	8.8	8.5	11.0	9.8	11.0
15,000 - 24,999	15.8	14.6	18.7	18.6	20.2	17.5	17.3	18.9	18.5	20.5
25,000 - 34,999	14.6	14.5	14.9	13.9	14.0	15.8	16.1	14.2	15.4	16.4
35,000 - 49,999	16.2	17.0	15.0	13.3	13.4	17.9	18.6	13.3	16.1	16.0
50,000 - 74,999	15.3	16.6	13.0	10.7	9.1	15.0	15.8	9.3	13.4	11.1
75,000 - 99,999	5.4	6.4	3.3	2.8	2.4	5.1	5.5	2.6	4.7	3.1
100,000+	4.8	6.1	1.9	1.8	1.4	4.4	4.8	1.3	3.7	1.9

Note: all figures are for 1989; (1) people of Hispanic origin can be of any race
Source: 1990 Census of Population and Housing, Summary Tape File 3C

Effective Buying Income

Area	Per Capita ($)	Median Household ($)	Average Household ($)
City	17,607	34,523	44,905
MSA[1]	18,900	42,850	50,561
U.S.	15,444	33,201	41,849

Note: data as of 1/1/97; (1) Metropolitan Statistical Area - see Appendix A for areas included
Source: Standard Rate & Data Service, Newspaper Advertising Source, 2/98

Effective Household Buying Income Distribution

Area	% of Households Earning						
	$10,000 -$19,999	$20,000 -$34,999	$35,000 -$49,999	$50,000 -$74,999	$75,000 -$99,000	$100,000 -$124,999	$125,000 and up
City	15.1	20.1	16.5	18.7	8.1	3.1	3.0
MSA[1]	12.1	18.3	18.1	23.6	10.5	3.8	3.6
U.S.	16.5	23.4	18.3	18.2	6.4	2.1	2.4

Note: data as of 1/1/97; (1) Metropolitan Statistical Area - see Appendix A for areas included
Source: Standard Rate & Data Service, Newspaper Advertising Source, 2/98

Poverty Rates by Race and Age

Area	Total (%)	By Race (%)				By Age (%)		
		White	Black	Other	Hisp.[2]	Under 5 years old	Under 18 years old	65 years and over
City	18.7	13.9	24.2	32.0	33.9	27.9	28.3	15.3
MSA[1]	8.3	6.3	21.7	23.4	28.4	12.1	11.5	9.2
U.S.	13.1	9.8	29.5	23.1	25.3	20.1	18.3	12.8

Note: figures show the percent of people living below the poverty line in 1989. The average poverty threshold was $12,674 for a family of four in 1989; (1) Metropolitan Statistical Area - see Appendix A for areas included; (2) people of Hispanic origin can be of any race
Source: 1990 Census of Population and Housing, Summary Tape File 3C

EMPLOYMENT

Labor Force and Employment

Area	Civilian Labor Force			Workers Employed		
	Dec. '95	Dec. '96	% Chg.	Dec. '95	Dec. '96	% Chg.
City	289,851	295,561	2.0	279,622	285,759	2.2
MSA[1]	1,779,891	1,816,012	2.0	1,727,884	1,765,991	2.2
U.S.	134,583,000	136,742,000	1.6	127,903,000	130,785,000	2.3

Note: Data is not seasonally adjusted and covers workers 16 years of age and older; (1) Metropolitan Statistical Area - see Appendix A for areas included
Source: Bureau of Labor Statistics, http://stats.bls.gov

Unemployment Rate

Area	1997											
	Jan.	Feb.	Mar.	Apr.	May	Jun.	Jul.	Aug.	Sep.	Oct.	Nov.	Dec.
City	4.4	4.0	4.1	3.9	4.1	4.5	4.4	4.7	4.6	3.7	3.8	3.3
MSA[1]	3.8	3.5	3.6	3.3	3.3	3.6	3.4	3.5	3.6	2.9	3.0	2.8
U.S.	5.9	5.7	5.5	4.8	4.7	5.2	5.0	4.8	4.7	4.4	4.3	4.4

Note: Data is not seasonally adjusted and covers workers 16 years of age and older; All figures are percentages; (1) Metropolitan Statistical Area - see Appendix A for areas included
Source: Bureau of Labor Statistics, http://stats.bls.gov

Employment by Industry

Sector	MSA[1]		U.S.
	Number of Employees	Percent of Total	Percent of Total
Services	762,800	38.9	29.0
Retail Trade	324,500	16.6	18.5
Government	232,000	11.8	16.1
Manufacturing	225,400	11.5	15.0
Finance/Insurance/Real Estate	160,500	8.2	5.7
Wholesale Trade	111,300	5.7	5.4
Transportation/Public Utilities	84,400	4.3	5.3
Construction	58,000	3.0	4.5
Mining	500	0.0	0.5

Note: Figures cover non-farm employment as of 12/97 and are not seasonally adjusted; (1) Metropolitan Statistical Area - see Appendix A for areas included
Source: Bureau of Labor Statistics, http://stats.bls.gov

Employment by Occupation

Occupation Category	City (%)	MSA[1] (%)	U.S. (%)
White Collar	66.2	70.2	58.1
Executive/Admin./Management	14.5	16.6	12.3
Professional	18.2	19.6	14.1
Technical & Related Support	4.4	4.5	3.7
Sales	9.4	11.4	11.8
Administrative Support/Clerical	19.7	18.1	16.3
Blue Collar	16.0	16.9	26.2
Precision Production/Craft/Repair	6.4	8.2	11.3
Machine Operators/Assem./Insp.	4.1	3.7	6.8
Transportation/Material Movers	2.8	2.5	4.1
Cleaners/Helpers/Laborers	2.7	2.5	3.9
Services	17.3	12.2	13.2
Farming/Forestry/Fishing	0.4	0.7	2.5

Note: figures cover employed persons 16 years old and over; (1) Metropolitan Statistical Area - see Appendix A for areas included
Source: 1990 Census of Population and Housing, Summary Tape File 3C

Occupational Employment Projections: 1994 - 2005

Occupations Expected to have the Largest Job Growth (ranked by numerical growth)	Fast-Growing Occupations (ranked by percent growth)
1. Systems analysts	1. Systems analysts
2. Registered nurses	2. Computer scientists
3. Salespersons, retail	3. Personal and home care aides
4. General managers & top executives	4. Home health aides
5. Janitors/cleaners/maids, ex. priv. hshld.	5. Human services workers
6. Waiters & waitresses	6. Electronic pagination systems workers
7. Home health aides	7. Manicurists
8. Cashiers	8. Computer engineers
9. Nursing aides/orderlies/attendants	9. Physical therapy assistants and aides
10. Computer engineers	10. Economists

Projections cover Massachusetts.
Source: U.S. Department of Labor, Employment and Training Administration, America's Labor Market Information System (ALMIS)

Average Wages

Occupation	Wage	Occupation	Wage
Professional/Technical/Clerical	$/Week	**Health/Protective Services**	$/Week
Accountants III	803	Corrections Officers	-
Attorneys III	1,441	Firefighters	639
Budget Analysts III	791	Nurses, Licensed Practical II	-
Buyers/Contracting Specialists II	695	Nurses, Registered II	-
Clerks, Accounting III	491	Nursing Assistants II	-
Clerks, General III	438	Police Officers I	638
Computer Operators II	466	**Hourly Workers**	$/Hour
Computer Programmers II	647	Forklift Operators	-
Drafters II	494	General Maintenance Workers	11.95
Engineering Technicians III	705	Guards I	8.04
Engineering Technicians, Civil III	574	Janitors	9.08
Engineers III	995	Maintenance Electricians	19.10
Key Entry Operators I	380	Maintenance Electronics Techs II	16.48
Personnel Assistants III	522	Maintenance Machinists	16.90
Personnel Specialists III	814	Maintenance Mechanics, Machinery	17.42
Secretaries III	581	Material Handling Laborers	-
Switchboard Operator-Receptionist	402	Motor Vehicle Mechanics	17.52
Systems Analysts II	964	Shipping/Receiving Clerks	-
Systems Analysts Supervisor/Mgr II	1,419	Tool and Die Makers	17.66
Tax Collectors II	-	Truckdrivers, Tractor Trailer	14.71
Word Processors II	497	Warehouse Specialists	-

Note: Wage data includes full-time workers only for 6/96 and cover the Metropolitan Statistical Area (see Appendix A for areas included). Dashes indicate that data was not available.
Source: Bureau of Labor Statistics, Occupational Compensation Survey, 11/96

TAXES

Major State and Local Tax Rates

State Corp. Income (%)	State Personal Income (%)	Residential Property (effective rate per $100)	Sales & Use		State Gasoline (cents/ gallon)	State Cigarette (cents/ 20-pack)
			State (%)	Local (%)		
9.5[a]	5.95[b]	1.37	5.0	None	21	76

Note: Personal/corporate income tax rates as of 1/97. Sales, gasoline and cigarette tax rates as of 1/98; (b) A 12% rate applies to interest, capital gains and dividends; (a) Rate includes a 14% surtax, as does the following: an additional tax of $2.60 per $1,000 on taxable tangible property (or net worth allocable to state for intangible property corporations). Minimum tax is $456
Source: Federation of Tax Administrators, www.taxadmin.org; Washington D.C. Department of Finance and Revenue, Tax Rates and Tax Burdens in the District of Columbia: A Nationwide Comparison, June 1997; Chamber of Commerce

Total Taxes Per Capita and as a Percent of Income

Area	Per Capita Income ($)	Per Capita Taxes ($)			Taxes as Pct. of Income (%)		
		Total	Federal	State/ Local	Total	Federal	State/ Local
Massachusetts	31,617	11,027	7,600	3,427	34.9	24.0	10.8
U.S.	26,187	9,205	6,127	3,078	35.2	23.4	11.8

Note: Figures are for 1997
Source: Tax Foundation, Web Site, www.taxfoundation.org

Estimated Tax Burden

Area	State Income	Local Income	Property	Sales	Total
Boston	3,162	0	3,150	425	6,737

Note: The numbers are estimates of taxes paid by a married couple with two kids and annual earnings of $65,000. Sales tax estimates assume they spend average amounts on food, clothing, household goods and gasoline. Property tax estimates assume they live in a $225,000 home.
Source: Kiplinger's Personal Finance Magazine, June 1997

COMMERCIAL REAL ESTATE

Office Market

Class/ Location	Total Space (sq. ft.)	Vacant Space (sq. ft.)	Vac. Rate (%)	Under Constr. (sq. ft.)	Net Absorp. (sq. ft.)	Rental Rates ($/sq.ft./yr.)
Class A						
CBD	36,008,441	1,015,613	2.8	0	1,172,716	34.00-48.00
Outside CBD	58,654,919	3,138,447	5.4	2,450,300	183,798	28.00-35.00
Class B						
CBD	3,807,099	133,838	3.5	0	195,882	26.00-32.00
Outside CBD	3,152,887	227,365	7.2	0	288,936	20.00-27.00

Note: Data as of 10/97 and covers Boston; CBD = Central Business District; n/a not available;
Source: Society of Industrial and Office Realtors, 1998 Comparative Statistics of Industrial and Office Real Estate Markets

"During 1998 the Boston economy is expected to continue to expand with financial services and technology firms among the strongest sectors. However, the growth in Boston's economy will be tempered by shortages of both labor and office space. The space crunch will lead to renovations in the central business district. Our SIOR reporter notes new developments at 10 Saint James Avenue om the Back Bay, the World Trade Center East, Prudential on Huntington, and the Landmark Center for a total of two million sq. ft. of space. In the suburban markets, several developers will have speculative projects under construction in 1998 but these properties represent a very small proportion of the projected needs. Vacancy rates will continue to decline as a consequence." *Society of Industrial and Office Realtors, 1998 Comparative Statistics of Industrial and Office Real Estate Markets*

Industrial Market

Location	Total Space (sq. ft.)	Vacant Space (sq. ft.)	Vac. Rate (%)	Under Constr. (sq. ft.)	Net Absorp. (sq. ft.)	Lease ($/sq.ft./yr.)
Central City	n/a	n/a	n/a	n/a	n/a	n/a
Suburban	47,500,000	6,175,000	13.0	0	1,925,000	4.00-4.50

Note: Data as of 10/97 and covers Boston; n/a not available
Source: Society of Industrial and Office Realtors, 1998 Comparative Statistics of Industrial and Office Real Estate Markets

"Although shortages developed across the board in the industrial market during 1997, the overall vacancy rate was still high enough to discourage speculative construction in 1998. Slightly more than six million sq. ft. of space was vacant during the latter part of 1997. While firms may have difficulty locating space in the submarket they prefer during 1998, developers, and more importantly lenders, will likely wait out the year before speculative construction reappears in the market. The near term outlook for the industrial real estate market in the

Boston area is bright. The combination of shortages and strong leasing activity during 1998 will likely lead to increases in lease prices on the order of one to five percent. Sales prices during 1997 were lower than several other markets leading to the conclusion that there is a good deal of room for sales prices to increase during 1998." *Society of Industrial and Office Realtors, 1998 Comparative Statistics of Industrial and Office Real Estate Markets*

Retail Market

Shopping Center Inventory (sq. ft.)	Shopping Center Construction (sq. ft.)	Construction as a Percent of Inventory (%)	Torto Wheaton Rent Index[1] ($/sq. ft.)
61,005,000	1,036,000	1.7	15.18

Note: Data as of 1997 and covers the Metropolitan Statistical Area - see Appendix A for areas included; (1) Index is based on a model that predicts what the average rent should be for leases with certain characteristics, in certain locations during certain years.
Source: National Association of Realtors, 1997-1998 Market Conditions Report

"Since 1992, the Boston retail rent index has improved 35% and is higher than the Northeast average of $14.30 per square foot. The area has benefitted from a net influx of new residents and an unemployment rate that has fallen below 4.5%.The strong economy has provided small retailers the opportunity to move to better locations or open new space. Shopping centers are becoming an increasingly attractive investment because intense competition for office space has investors looking for alternatives. Rents in the Boston area are expected to rise above 5% per year through the year 2000." *National Association of Realtors, 1997-1998 Market Conditions Report*

COMMERCIAL UTILITIES

Typical Monthly Electric Bills

Area	Commercial Service ($/month)		Industrial Service ($/month)	
	12 kW demand 1,500 kWh	100 kW demand 30,000 kWh	1,000 kW demand 400,000 kWh	20,000 kW demand 10,000,000 kWh
City	304	4,667	35,370	828,777
U.S.	162	2,360	25,590	545,677

Note: Based on rates in effect July 1, 1997
Source: Edison Electric Institute, Typical Residential, Commercial and Industrial Bills, Summer 1997

TRANSPORTATION

Transportation Statistics

Avg. travel time to work (min.)	24.9
Interstate highways	I-90; I-93; I-95
Bus lines	
In-city	Massachusetts Bay TA, 980 vehicles
Inter-city	12
Passenger air service	
Airport	Logan International
Airlines	37
Aircraft departures	164,745 (1995)
Enplaned passengers	10,507,611 (1995)
Rail service	Amtrak; Metro/Light Rail
Motor freight carriers	500+
Major waterways/ports	Boston Harbor; Port of Boston

Source: OAG, Business Travel Planner, Summer 1997; Editor & Publisher Market Guide, 1998; FAA Airport Activity Statistics, 1996; Amtrak National Time Table, Northeast Timetable, Fall/Winter 1997-98; 1990 Census of Population and Housing, STF 3C; Chamber of Commerce/Economic Development 1997; Jane's Urban Transport Systems 1997-98; Transit Fact Book 1997

A survey of 90,000 airline passengers during the first half of 1997 ranked most of the largest airports in the U.S. Logan International ranked number 34 out of 36. Criteria: cleanliness, quality of restaurants, attractiveness, speed of baggage delivery, ease of reaching gates, available ground transportation, ease of following signs and closeness of parking. *Plog Research Inc., First Half 1997*

Means of Transportation to Work

Area	Car/Truck/Van Drove Alone	Car/Truck/Van Car-pooled	Public Transportation Bus	Public Transportation Subway	Public Transportation Railroad	Bicycle	Walked	Other Means	Worked at Home
City	40.1	10.5	13.6	13.2	1.0	0.9	14.0	4.5	2.2
MSA[1]	65.8	9.8	5.4	5.9	1.4	0.5	6.5	2.0	2.6
U.S.	73.2	13.4	3.0	1.5	0.5	0.4	3.9	1.2	3.0

Note: figures shown are percentages and only include workers 16 years old and over; (1) Metropolitan Statistical Area - see Appendix A for areas included
Source: 1990 Census of Population and Housing, Summary Tape File 3C

BUSINESSES

Major Business Headquarters

Company Name	1997 Rankings Fortune 500	1997 Rankings Forbes 500
Bank of Boston	233	-
Connell Limited Partnership	-	141
Fidelity Investments	-	28
Fleet Financial Group	186	-
Gillette	152	-
International Data Group	-	81
John Hancock Mutual Life Ins.	168	-
Liberty Mutual Insurance Group	126	-
State Street Boston	477	-
Unicco Service Company	-	403

Note: Companies listed are located in the city; Dashes indicate no ranking
Fortune 500: companies that produce a 10-K are ranked 1 - 500 based on 1996 revenue
Forbes 500: private companies are ranked 1 - 500 based on 1996 revenue
Source: Forbes 12/1/97; Fortune 4/28/97

Fast-Growing Businesses

Boston is home to one of *Business Week's* "hot growth" companies: Transition Systems. Criteria: sales and earnings, return on capital and stock price. *Business Week, 5/26/97*

According to Deloitte & Touche LLP, Boston is home to two of America's 100 fastest-growing high-technology companies: The Counsell Group and Art Technology Group. Companies are ranked by percentage growth in revenue over a five-year period. Criteria for inclusion: must be a U.S. company developing and/or providing technology products or services; company must have been in business for five years with 1992 revenues of at least $50,000. *Deloitte & Touche LLP, January 7, 1998*

Boston was ranked #14 out of 24 (#1 is best) in terms of the best-performing local stocks in 1996 according to the Money/Norby Cities Index. The index measures stocks of companies that have headquarters in 24 metro areas. *Money, 2/7/97*

Women-Owned Businesses: Number, Employment, Sales and Share

Area	Women-Owned Businesses in 1996 Number	Employment	Sales ($000)	Rank[2]	Share of Women-Owned Businesses in 1996 Percent (%)	Rank[3]
MSA[1]	112,100	217,600	29,477,500	15	34.9	41

Note: (1) Metropolitan Statistical Area - see Appendix A for areas included; (2) Calculated on an averaging of number of businesses, employment and sales and ranges from 1 to 50 where 1 is best; (3) Ranges from 1 to 50 where 1 is best
Source: The National Foundation for Women Business Owners, 1996 Facts on Women-Owned Businesses: Trends in the Top 50 Metropolitan Areas, March 26, 1997

Women-Owned Businesses: Growth

Area	Growth in Women-Owned Businesses (% change from 1987 to 1996)				Relative Growth in the Number of Women-Owned and All Businesses (% change from 1987 to 1996)			
	Num.	Empl.	Sales	Rank[2]	Women-Owned	All Firms	Absolute Difference	Relative Difference
MSA[1]	58.5	60.6	80.2	50	58.5	43.4	15.1	1.3:1

Note: (1) Metropolitan Statistical Area - see Appendix A for areas included; (2) Calculated on an averaging of the percent growth of number of businesses, employment and sales and ranges from 1 to 50 where 1 is best
Source: The National Foundation for Women Business Owners, 1996 Facts on Women-Owned Businesses: Trends in the Top 50 Metropolitan Areas, March 26, 1997

Minority Business Opportunity

Boston is home to one company which is on the Black Enterprise Industrial/Service 100 list (largest based on gross sales): Grimes Oil Co. Inc. (petroleum products distributor). Criteria: 1) operational in previous calendar year; 2) at least 51% black-owned; 3) manufactures/owns the product it sells or provides industrial or consumer services. Brokerages, real estate firms and firms that provide professional services are not eligible. *Black Enterprise, July 1997*

Small Business Opportunity

According to *Forbes*, Boston is home to one of America's 200 best small companies: Transition Systems. Criteria: companies must be publicly traded, U.S.-based corporations with latest 12-month sales of between $5 and $350 million. Earnings must be at least $1 million for the 12-month period. Limited partnerships, REITs and closed-end mutual funds were not considered. Banks, S&Ls and electric utilities were not included. Forbes, November 3, 1997

HOTELS & MOTELS

Hotels/Motels

Area	Hotels/ Motels	Rooms	Luxury-Level Hotels/Motels		Average Minimum Rates ($)		
			♦♦♦♦	♦♦♦♦♦	♦♦	♦♦♦	♦♦♦♦
City	36	10,886	3	1	94	182	256
Airport	4	1,314	0	0	n/a	n/a	n/a
Suburbs	95	14,703	1	0	n/a	n/a	n/a
Total	135	26,903	4	1	n/a	n/a	n/a

Note: n/a not available; Classifications range from one diamond (budget properties with basic amenities) to five diamond (luxury properties with the finest service, rooms and facilities).
Source: OAG, Business Travel Planner, Summer 1997

Boston is home to one of the top 100 hotels in the world according to *Travel & Leisure*: Four Seasons. Criteria: value, rooms/ambience, location, facilities/activities and service. *Travel & Leisure, September 1997*

CONVENTION CENTERS

Major Convention Centers

Center Name	Meeting Rooms	Exhibit Space (sf)
Bayside Expo Center	17	240,000
Boston Garden	n/a	n/a
Boston Park Plaza Castle Exposition & Conference Center	35	17,280
The Executive Ctr. at the Sheraton Boston Hotel & Towers	10	1,276
The Exec. Conf. Ctr. at the World Trade Center of Boston	24	120,000
John B. Hynes Veterans Memorial Convention Center	38	193,000
John Hancock Conference Center	12	n/a
World Trade Center-Boston	24	120,000

Note: n/a not available
Source: Trade Shows Worldwide 1997

Living Environment

COST OF LIVING

Cost of Living Index

Composite Index	Housing	Utilities	Groceries	Health Care	Trans-portation	Misc. Goods/ Services
138.5	194.5	143.4	110.2	135.8	121.6	108.5

Note: U.S. = 100; Figures are for the Metropolitan Statistical Area - see Appendix A for areas included
Source: ACCRA, Cost of Living Index, 3rd Quarter 1997

HOUSING

Median Home Prices and Housing Affordability

Area	Median Price[2] 3rd Qtr. 1997 ($)	HOI[3] 3rd Qtr. 1997	Afford-ability Rank[4]
MSA[1]	151,000	67.5	109
U.S.	127,000	63.7	–

Note: (1) Metropolitan Statistical Area - see Appendix A for areas included; (2) U.S. figures calculated from the sales of 625,000 new and existing homes in 195 markets; (3) Housing Opportunity Index - percent of homes sold that were within the reach of the median income household at the prevailing mortgage interest rate; (4) Rank is from 1-195 with 1 being most affordable
Source: National Association of Home Builders, Housing Opportunity Index, 3rd Quarter 1997

It is projected that the median price of existing single-family homes in the metro area will increase by 7.0% in 1998. Nationwide, home prices are projected to increase 6.6%. *Kiplinger's Personal Finance Magazine, January 1998*

Average New Home Price

Area	Price ($)
MSA[1]	264,200
U.S.	135,710

Note: Figures are based on a new home with 1,800 sq. ft. of living area on an 8,000 sq. ft. lot; (1) Metropolitan Statistical Area - see Appendix A for areas included
Source: ACCRA, Cost of Living Index, 3rd Quarter 1997

Average Apartment Rent

Area	Rent ($/mth)
MSA[1]	1,106
U.S.	569

Note: Figures are based on an unfurnished two bedroom, 1-1/2 or 2 bath apartment, approximately 950 sq. ft. in size, excluding all utilities except water; (1) Metropolitan Statistical Area - see Appendix A for areas included
Source: ACCRA, Cost of Living Index, 3rd Quarter 1997

RESIDENTIAL UTILITIES

Average Residential Utility Costs

Area	All Electric ($/mth)	Part Electric ($/mth)	Other Energy ($/mth)	Phone ($/mth)
MSA[1]	–	78.09	73.33	22.47
U.S.	109.40	55.25	43.64	19.48

Note: (1) (1) Metropolitan Statistical Area - see Appendix A for areas included
Source: ACCRA, Cost of Living Index, 3rd Quarter 1997

HEALTH CARE

Average Health Care Costs

Area	Hospital ($/day)	Doctor ($/visit)	Dentist ($/visit)
MSA[1]	649.00	69.00	74.00
U.S.	392.91	48.76	60.84

Note: Hospital - based on a semi-private room. Doctor - based on a general practitioner's routine exam of an established patient. Dentist - based on adult teeth cleaning and periodic oral exam; (1) Metropolitan Statistical Area - see Appendix A for areas included
Source: ACCRA, Cost of Living Index, 3rd Quarter 1997

Distribution of Office-Based Physicians

Area	Family/Gen. Practitioners	Specialists		
		Medical	Surgical	Other
Metro Area[1]	470	4,192	2,300	3,294

Note: Data as of December 31, 1996; (1) Essex, Middlesex, Norfolk, Plymouth and Suffolk Counties
Source: American Medical Assn., Physician Characteristics & Distribution in the U.S., 1997-1998

Hospitals

Boston has 12 general medical and surgical hospitals, 2 psychiatric, 1 eye, ear, nose and throat, 1 rehabilitation, 3 chronic disease, 2 other specialty, 1 children's general, 2 children's other specialty. *AHA Guide to the Healthcare Field 1997-98*

According to *U.S. News and World Report,* Boston has 8 of the best hospitals in the U.S.: **Dana-Farber Cancer Institute**, noted for cancer; **Massachusetts General Hospital**, noted for AIDS, cancer, cardiology, endocrinology, gastroenterology, geriatrics, gynecology, neurology, orthopedics, otolaryngology, pediatrics, psychiatry, pulmonology, rheumatology, urology; **Brigham & Women's Hospital**, noted for AIDS, cardiology, endocrinology, gastroenterology, geriatrics, gynecology, neurology, orthopedics, pulmonology, rheumatology, urology; **Beth Israel Hospital**, noted for AIDS, cardiology, endocrinology, gastroenterology, geriatrics, gynecology, neurology, orthopedics, pulmonology, rheumatology, urology; **New England Deaconness Hospital**, noted for AIDS, endocrinology, geriatrics; **Spaulding Rehabilitation Hospital**, noted for rehabilitation; **Children's Hospital**, noted for pediatrics; **Massachusetts Eye & Ear Infirmary**, noted for ophthalmology; *U.S. News and World Report, "America's Best Hospitals", 7/28/97*

Beth Israel Deaconess Medical Center; Brigham & Women's Hospital are among the 100 best-run hospitals in the U.S.
Modern Healthcare, January 5, 1998

EDUCATION

Public School District Statistics

District Name	Num. Sch.	Enroll.	Classroom Teachers[1]	Pupils per Teacher	Minority Pupils (%)	Current Exp.[2] ($/pupil)
Boston School District	123	63,293	n/a	n/a	82.2	7,782
City on a Hill CS	1	65	n/a	n/a	n/a	n/a
Renaissance Charter Sch	1	615	n/a	n/a	n/a	n/a

Note: Data covers the 1995-1996 school year unless otherwise noted; (1) Excludes teachers reported as working in school district offices rather than in schools; (2) Based on 1993-94 enrollment collected by the Census Bureau, not the enrollment figure shown in column 3; SD = School District; ISD = Independent School District; n/a not available
Source: National Center for Education Statistics, Common Core of Data Survey; Bureau of the Census

Educational Quality

School District	Education Quotient[1]	Graduate Outcome[2]	Community Index[3]	Resource Index[4]
Boston	70.0	61.0	84.0	64.0

Note: Nearly 1,000 secondary school districts were rated in terms of educational quality. The scores range from a low of 50 to a high of 150; (1) Average of the Graduate Outcome, Community and Resource indexes; (2) Based on graduation rates and college board scores (SAT/ACT); (3) Based on the surrounding community's average level of education and the area's average income level; (4) Based on teacher salaries, per-pupil expenditures and student-teacher ratios.
Source: Expansion Management, Ratings Issue 1997

Educational Attainment by Race

Area	High School Graduate (%)					Bachelor's Degree (%)				
	Total	White	Black	Other	Hisp.[2]	Total	White	Black	Other	Hisp.[2]
City	75.7	81.5	66.7	55.8	52.8	30.0	36.7	14.0	20.3	13.9
MSA[1]	83.7	85.4	70.7	68.0	58.8	33.1	34.1	17.9	33.9	18.2
U.S.	75.2	77.9	63.1	60.4	49.8	20.3	21.5	11.4	19.4	9.2

Note: figures shown cover persons 25 years old and over; (1) Metropolitan Statistical Area - see Appendix A for areas included; (2) people of Hispanic origin can be of any race
Source: 1990 Census of Population and Housing, Summary Tape File 3C

School Enrollment by Type

Area	Preprimary				Elementary/High School			
	Public		Private		Public		Private	
	Enrollment	%	Enrollment	%	Enrollment	%	Enrollment	%
City	3,504	56.5	2,698	43.5	58,244	77.2	17,231	22.8
MSA[1]	27,026	49.3	27,803	50.7	331,757	85.6	55,619	14.4
U.S.	2,679,029	59.5	1,824,256	40.5	38,379,689	90.2	4,187,099	9.8

Note: figures shown cover persons 3 years old and over;
(1) Metropolitan Statistical Area - see Appendix A for areas included
Source: 1990 Census of Population and Housing, Summary Tape File 3C

School Enrollment by Race

Area	Preprimary (%)				Elementary/High School (%)			
	White	Black	Other	Hisp.[1]	White	Black	Other	Hisp.[1]
City	50.0	37.8	12.2	11.7	39.1	42.1	18.8	17.4
MSA[2]	88.2	6.8	5.1	3.7	80.9	11.0	8.2	6.6
U.S.	80.4	12.5	7.1	7.8	74.1	15.6	10.3	12.5

Note: figures shown cover persons 3 years old and over; (1) people of Hispanic origin can be of any race; (2) Metropolitan Statistical Area - see Appendix A for areas included
Source: 1990 Census of Population and Housing, Summary Tape File 3C

SAT/ACT Scores

Area/District	1997 SAT				1997 ACT	
	Percent of Graduates Tested (%)	Average Math Score	Average Verbal Score	Average Combined Score	Percent of Graduates Tested (%)	Average Composite Score
Boston PS	60	433	412	845	n/a	n/a
State	80	508	508	1,016	6	21.6
U.S.	42	511	505	1,016	36	21.0

Note: Math and verbal SAT scores are out of a possible 800; ACT scores are out of a possible 36
Caution: Comparing or ranking states/cities on the basis of SAT/ACT scores alone is invalid and strongly discouraged by the The College Board and The American College Testing Program as students who take the tests are self-selected and do not represent the entire student population.
Source: Boston Public Schools, Office of Research, Assessment & Evaluation, 1997; American College Testing Program, 1997; College Board, 1997

Classroom Teacher Salaries in Public Schools

District	B.A. Degree		M.A. Degree		Ph.D. Degree	
	Min. ($)	Max ($)	Min. ($)	Max. ($)	Min. ($)	Max. ($)
Boston	30,770	46,997	32,889	49,723	37,283	55,332
Average[1]	26,120	39,270	28,175	44,667	31,643	49,825

Note: Salaries are for 1996-1997; (1) Based on all school districts covered
Source: American Federation of Teachers (unpublished data)

Higher Education

Two-Year Colleges		Four-Year Colleges		Medical Schools	Law Schools	Voc/ Tech
Public	Private	Public	Private			
1	6	2	18	3	4	20

Source: College Blue Book, Occupational Education 1997; Medical School Admission Requirements, 1998-99; Peterson's Guide to Two-Year Colleges, 1997; Peterson's Guide to Four-Year Colleges, 1997; Barron's Guide to Law Schools 1997

MAJOR EMPLOYERS

Major Employers

Bank of Boston
Brigham & Women's Hospital
Fleet Financial Group
John Hancock Mutual Life
Liberty Mutual Fire Insurance
New England Medical Center Hospitals
State Street Bank & Trust
Affiliated Publications
New England Telephone & Telegraph
Blue Cross & Blue Shield of Massachusetts
Children's Hospital
Globe Newspaper
Liberty Mutual
FMR Corp. (brokers)
St. Elizabeth's Medical Center
Stone & Webster Engineering
Dana-Farber Cancer Institute

Note: companies listed are located in the city
Source: Dun's Business Rankings 1997; Ward's Business Directory, 1997

PUBLIC SAFETY

Crime Rate

Area	All Crimes	Violent Crimes				Property Crimes		
		Murder	Forcible Rape	Robbery	Aggrav. Assault	Burglary	Larceny -Theft	Motor Vehicle Theft
City	8,092.2	10.7	74.9	628.0	943.1	914.4	3,843.1	1,678.0
Suburbs[1]	2,941.7	1.3	16.6	61.7	295.6	534.4	1,667.6	364.4
MSA[2]	3,768.2	2.8	26.0	152.6	399.5	595.3	2,016.7	575.2
U.S.	5,078.9	7.4	36.1	202.4	388.2	943.0	2,975.9	525.9

Note: Crime rate is the number of crimes per 100,000 pop.; (1) defined as all areas within the MSA but located outside the central city; (2) Metropolitan Statistical Area - see Appendix A for areas incl.
Source: FBI Uniform Crime Reports 1996

RECREATION

Culture and Recreation

Museums	Symphony Orchestras	Opera Companies	Dance Companies	Professional Theatres	Zoos	Pro Sports Teams
18	3	3	3	3	1	4

Source: International Directory of the Performing Arts, 1996; Official Museum Directory, 1998; Chamber of Commerce/Economic Development 1997

Library System

The Boston Public Library has 26 branches, holdings of 6,319,206 volumes and a budget of $n/a. Note: n/a means not available. *American Library Directory, 1997-1998*

MEDIA

Newspapers

Name	Type	Freq.	Distribution	Circulation
Bay State Banner	Black	1x/wk	Local	10,500
Boston Chinese News	Asian	1x/wk	Regional	10,000
Boston Globe	General	7x/wk	Regional	466,000
The Boston Herald	General	7x/wk	Regional	285,335
Your Style	n/a	1x/wk	n/a	210,759
Boston Phoenix	General	1x/wk	State	135,000
The Christian Science Monitor	General	5x/wk	National	87,257
The Daily Free Press	n/a	5x/wk	Campus	community & alumni
East Boston Times-Free Press	General	1x/wk	Local	15,500
El Mundo	Hispanic	1x/wk	Local	35,000
The Episcopal Times	Religious	8x/yr	Regional	40,000
The Fenway News	General	1x/mo	Local	11,000
In News Weekly	n/a	1x/wk	Local	21,000
The Jewish Advocate	Religious	1x/wk	Local	27,500
La Semana	Hispanic	1x/wk	Regional	10,000
Post-Gazette	General	1x/wk	Local	15,900
South End News	General	1x/wk	Local	18,500

Note: Includes newspapers with circulations of 10,000 or more located in the city; n/a not available
Source: Burrelle's Media Directory, 1998 Edition

AM Radio Stations

Call Letters	Freq. (kHz)	Target Audience	Station Format	Music Format
WECB	640	General	M/N/S	Alternative
WTBU	640	General	M/N/S	Alternative
WRKO	680	General	T	n/a
WEEI	850	General	S	n/a
WBPS	890	General	M/N/S/T	Christian/R&B/Spanish/Urban Contemporary
WROL	950	General	M/T	Christian
WBZ	1030	General	N/T	n/a
WILD	1090	Black	M/N/S	Urban Contemporary
WRCA	1330	n/a	M	Spanish
WXKS	1430	General	M/N/T	Adult Contemporary/Adult Standards/R&B/Urban Contemporary
WNTN	1550	n/a	M/T	MOR
WUNR	1600	n/a	M/N/S/T	Spanish

Note: Stations included broadcast in the Boston metro area; n/a not available
Station Format: E = Educational; M = Music; N = News; S = Sports; T = Talk
Music Format: AOR = Album Oriented Rock; MOR = Middle-of-the-Road
Source: Burrelle's Media Directory, 1998 Edition

FM Radio Stations

Call Letters	Freq. (mHz)	Target Audience	Station Format	Music Format
WMBR	88.1	General	M	n/a
WERS	88.9	General	M/N/S	n/a
WGBH	89.7	General	E/M/N	Classical/Jazz
WBUR	90.9	General	M/N/S/T	Jazz
WUMB	91.9	General	E/M/T	Big Band/MOR/Jazz
WFPB	91.9	General	M/N	Big Band/Jazz
WBPR	91.9	n/a	M/N	Jazz
WBOS	92.9	n/a	M	AOR
WEGQ	93.7	n/a	M	Classic Rock
WHRB	95.3	General	M/N/S	Alternative/Classical/Country/Jazz/Urban Contemporary
WSJZ	96.9	General	M/N	Jazz
WBMX	98.5	n/a	M	Adult Contemporary
WKLB	99.5	General	M/N	Country
WZLX	100.7	General	M/N/S	Classic Rock
WCRB	102.5	General	M/N/S	Classical
WODS	103.3	General	M	Oldies
WBCN	104.1	General	M/N	AOR/Alternative
WRBB	104.9	General	M/N/S	Alternative/Christian/Jazz/R&B/Urban Contemporary
WROR	105.7	General	M	Country
WMJX	106.7	n/a	M/N/S	Adult Contemporary

Note: Stations included broadcast in the Boston metro area; n/a not available
Station Format: E = Educational; M = Music; N = News; S = Sports; T = Talk
Music Format: AOR = Album Oriented Rock; MOR = Middle-of-the-Road
Source: Burrelle's Media Directory, 1998 Edition

Television Stations

Name	Ch.	Affiliation	Type	Owner
WGBH	n/a	n/a	n/a	n/a
WSBK	n/a	UPN	n/a	n/a
WGBH	2	PBS	Public	WGBH Educational Foundation
WBZ	4	CBS	Commercial	Westinghouse Broadcasting Company
WCVB	5	ABC	Commercial	The Hearst Corporation
WHDH	7	NBC	Commercial	WHDH-TV, Inc.
WCEA	19	SUR	Commercial	WCEA-TV
WNBU	21	n/a	Commercial	BUCI Television
WSBK	38	n/a	Commercial	UPN
WGBX	44	PBS	Public	WGBH Educational Foundation
WLVI	56	WB	Commercial	Tribune Broadcasting Co.
WMFP	62	n/a	Commercial	Shop at Home Inc.
WABU	68	n/a	Commercial	BUCI Television

Note: Stations included broadcast in the Boston metro area
Source: Burrelle's Media Directory, 1998 Edition

CLIMATE

Average and Extreme Temperatures

Temperature	Jan	Feb	Mar	Apr	May	Jun	Jul	Aug	Sep	Oct	Nov	Dec	Ann
Extreme High (°F)	72	70	85	94	95	100	102	102	100	90	83	73	102
Average High (°F)	36	38	46	56	67	76	82	80	73	63	52	41	59
Average Temp. (°F)	30	31	39	48	58	68	74	72	65	55	45	34	52
Average Low (°F)	22	23	31	40	50	59	65	64	57	47	38	27	44
Extreme Low (°F)	-12	-4	1	16	34	45	50	47	37	28	15	-7	-12

Note: Figures cover the years 1945-1990
Source: National Climatic Data Center, International Station Meteorological Climate Summary, 3/95

Average Precipitation/Snowfall/Humidity

Precip./Humidity	Jan	Feb	Mar	Apr	May	Jun	Jul	Aug	Sep	Oct	Nov	Dec	Ann
Avg. Precip. (in.)	3.8	3.6	3.8	3.7	3.5	3.1	2.9	3.6	3.1	3.3	4.4	4.1	42.9
Avg. Snowfall (in.)	12	12	8	1	Tr	0	0	0	0	Tr	1	8	41
Avg. Rel. Hum. 7am (%)	68	68	69	68	71	72	73	76	79	77	74	70	72
Avg. Rel. Hum. 4pm (%)	58	57	56	56	58	58	58	61	61	59	61	60	59

Note: Figures cover the years 1945-1990; Tr = Trace amounts (<0.05 in. of rain; <0.5 in. of snow)
Source: National Climatic Data Center, International Station Meteorological Climate Summary, 3/95

Weather Conditions

Temperature			Daytime Sky			Precipitation		
5°F & below	32°F & below	90°F & above	Clear	Partly cloudy	Cloudy	0.01 inch or more precip.	0.1 inch or more snow/ice	Thunder-storms
4	97	12	88	127	150	253	48	18

Note: Figures are average number of days per year and covers the years 1945-1990
Source: National Climatic Data Center, International Station Meteorological Climate Summary, 3/95

AIR & WATER QUALITY

Maximum Pollutant Concentrations

	Particulate Matter (ug/m³)	Carbon Monoxide (ppm)	Sulfur Dioxide (ppm)	Nitrogen Dioxide (ppm)	Ozone (ppm)	Lead (ug/m³)
MSA[1] Level	80	5	0.037	0.031	0.11	n/a
NAAQS[2]	150	9	0.140	0.053	0.12	1.50
Met NAAQS?	Yes	Yes	Yes	Yes	Yes	n/a

Note: (1) Metropolitan Statistical Area - see Appendix A for areas included; (2) National Ambient Air Quality Standards; ppm = parts per million; ug/m³ = micrograms per cubic meter; n/a not available
Source: EPA, National Air Quality and Emissions Trends Report, 1996

Pollutant Standards Index

In the Boston MSA (see Appendix A for areas included), the Pollutant Standards Index (PSI) exceeded 100 on 0 days in 1996. A PSI value greater than 100 indicates that air quality would be in the unhealthful range on that day. *EPA, National Air Quality and Emissions Trends Report, 1996*

Drinking Water

Water System Name	Pop. Served	Primary Water Source Type	Number of Violations in Fiscal Year 1997	Type of Violation/ Contaminants
Boston Water & Sewer Commiss.	551,675	Purchased surface	1	Failure to filter

Note: Data as of January 16, 1998
Source: EPA, Office of Ground Water and Drinking Water, Safe Drinking Water Information System

The Metropolitan Water District (combined sources, Quabbin Reservoir and Wachusett Reservoir) supplies municipal Boston and the ABC City Zone. Water is soft and slightly acid. *Editor & Publisher Market Guide, 1998*

Bridgeport, Connecticut

Background

Bridgeport is the largest city in Connecticut and the seat of Fairfield County. Located in the southwestern section of the state, Bridgeport is 60 miles northeast of New York City. With an excellent harbor on Long Island Sound and at the mouth of the Pequonnock River, the town was settled in 1639 and originally called Newfield and later Stratfield. In 1800 it was incorporated and renamed Bridgeport in honor of the first drawbridge across the Pequonnock River.

From its agrarian beginnings, Bridgeport soon grew into an industrial center proving its motto "Industria Crecimus" (By Industry We Thrive). Holding a special place in United States industrial history, it was here that Elias Howe built his first sewing machine, E.P. Bullard invented the vertical turret lathe, Lucien Warner developed a low-priced corset and the American Gramophone Company (later the Columbia Phonograph Company) produced the first gramophones. Today the town produces a wide array of commodities from consumer goods to electrical and transportation equipment, plastics, machine tools and automotive parts. Connecticut's chief manufacturing city, Bridgeport has also become a leading banking center for New England.

There is much to recommend Bridgeport from its past history to its present-day persona. The Barnum Museum and the annual Barnum Festival pays tribute to a former resident and past mayor of Bridgeport, P.T. Barnum. Once the winter headquarters of the Barnum and Bailey Circus, Bridgeport was also the hometown of a famous Barnum attraction, General Tom Thumb. The city is further indebted to the famous showman who donated the land for Seaside Park which overlooks Long Island Sound. With the landscape designed by Fredrick Law Olmstead (the landscape designer of New York City's Central Park), Seaside Park is one of the most beautiful of New England's beaches. It is only one of the 36 parks within the Bridgeport city limits.

Also within the city limits is Connecticut's only zoo. The Beardsley Zoo is located on a 30 acre site with more than 200 animals, ranging from bison to a rare Siberian tiger. Or if you prefer indoor entertainment, visit the Discovery Museum which houses hands-on exhibits for kids of all ages, a planetarium, the Challenger Center, the Wonder Workshop and an Art Exhibition Center. In nearby Stratford, the American Shakespeare Festival Theater presents the works of the great bard.

Educational opportunities abound in Bridgeport. The University of Bridgeport boasts of a student-faculty ratio of 11:1. Other educational institutions include Sacred Heart University, the Bridgeport Engineering Institute and famous Yale University is in nearby New Haven.

All in all, Bridgeport is a great city to enjoy all that New England has to offer.

The city lies within a terrain that is of glacial origin, rising in a rolling, mostly wooded manner, to the foothills of the Berkshires, 30 miles to the north and northwest. Temperatures during the fall and winter months are moderated because of the proximity of Long Island Sound. One of the hazards along the coastal area is the flooding of low-lying areas.

General Rankings and Evaluative Comments

- Bridgeport was ranked #130 out of 300 cities by *Money's* 1997 "Survey of the Best Places to Live." Criteria used: health services, crime, economy, housing, education, transportation, weather, leisure and the arts. The city was ranked #168 in 1996 and #264 in 1995. *Money, July 1997; Money, September 1996; Money, September 1995*

- *Ladies Home Journal* ranked America's 200 largest cities based on the qualities women care about most. Bridgeport ranked 93 out of 200. Criteria: low crime rate, good public schools, well-paying jobs, quality health and child care, the presence of women in government, proportion of women-owned businesses, size of the wage gap with men, local economy, divorce rates, the ratio of single men to single women, whether there are laws that require at least the same number of public toilets for women as men, and the probability of good hair days. *Ladies Home Journal, November 1997*

- Bridgeport was ranked #169 out of 219 cities in terms of children's health, safety, and economic well-being. Criteria: total population, percent population change, birth rate, child immunization rate, infant mortality rate, percent low birth weight infants, percent of births to teens, physician-to-population ratio, student-to-teacher ratio, dropout rate, unemployment rate, median family income, percent of children in poverty, violent and property crime rates, number of juvenile arrests for violent crimes as a percent of the total crime index, number of days with pollution standard index (PSI) over 100, pounds toxic releases per 1,000 people and number of superfund sites. *Zero Population Growth, Children's Environmental Index 1997*

- Bridgeport appeared on *Sales & Marketing Management's* list of the 20 hottest domestic markets to do business in. Rank: 7 out of 20. America's 320 Metropolitan Statistical Areas were ranked based on the market's potential to buy products in certain industries like high-tech, manufacturing, office equipment and business services, as well as population and household income growth. The study had nine criteria in all.

  "This small area in Connecticut is most attractive as a consumer market, because of its wealthy population. The market's median household effective buying income is the highest in the country....Businesses have thrived off this wealth and moved to this area, because of its rich economy." *Sales & Marketing Management, January 1998*

- According to *Working Mother,* "Connecticut remains a leader among the states on the child care front. Even with a tight state budget the governor and state lawmakers have pledged $10 million in new funds for early education. This means as many as 2,500 children will now have access to prekindergarten programs in four school districts.

  The governor is also committed to establishing many more child care programs across the state by the year 2000. Caregiver training and more pre-K programs are high on the agenda, according to advocate Jude Carroll of the Connecticut Association for Human Services. As we went to press, state lawmakers had just passed a bill to pay a higher rate to caregivers who meet NAEYC training requirements—giving them incentive to meet these higher standards.

  Despite these impressive strides, however, the state has taken a step back, drastically cutting funds for inspecting child care facilities. As a result, centers will merely be required to 'register' with the state, rather than meet stricter licensing standards, and child care facilities will no longer be inspected on a regular basis, unless they receive a complaint. (Connecticut is among the 10 best states for child care.)" *Working Mother, July/August 1997*

Business Environment

STATE ECONOMY

State Economic Profile

"Consistent positive signs are appearing in Connecticut's economy for the first time in a decade. Connecticut's growth is buoyed by the strong national economy, the vibrant expansion in neighboring Massachusetts, and by the strong performance of the state's major growth industry, gaming. Another important factor in the state's expansion is the lessening drag from Connecticut's former growth industries, primarily defense, aircraft, and insurance....

...Fairfield County is profiting from Wall Street's boom times and should benefit from the pending cut in capital gains tax....

Financial services has been one of the state's weakest industries since the decade began, but the outlook is brightening. Even as it continues to shrink in Hartford, financial services, particularly money management, is a promising growth industry for Fairfield. Several large money management boutiques, made up of expatriates from large New York City investment banks, have set up shop in Fairfield County.

Stronger employment growth, rising state tax revenues, the prospect of tax cuts, lower out-migration, and the emergence of new growth industries all bode well for the state's long-term outlook. Nonetheless, the hurdles to faster growth in Connecticut are still considerable. These include the state's very high cost of doing business and still-high defense exposure. Connecticut's economy will remain one of the slowest growing over the forecast horizon." *National Association of Realtors, Economic Profiles: The Fifty States, July 1997*

IMPORTS/EXPORTS

Total Export Sales

Area	1993 ($000)	1994 ($000)	1995 ($000)	1996 ($000)	% Chg. 1993-96	% Chg. 1995-96
MSA[1]	1,125,870	918,847	952,929	788,587	-30.0	-17.2
U.S.	464,858,354	512,415,609	583,030,524	622,827,063	34.0	6.8

Note: (1) Metropolitan Statistical Area - see Appendix A for areas included
Source: U.S. Department of Commerce, International Trade Association, Metropolitan Area Exports: An Export Performance Report on Over 250 U.S. Cities, October 1997

Imports/Exports by Port

Type	Cargo Value			Share of U.S. Total	
	1995 (US$mil.)	1996 (US$mil.)	% Change 1995-1996	1995 (%)	1996 (%)
Imports	103	125	21.27	0.03	0.03
Exports	29	20	-30.90	0.01	0.00

Source: Global Trade Information Services, WaterBorne Trade Atlas 1997

CITY FINANCES

City Government Finances

Component	FY92 ($000)	FY92 (per capita $)
Revenue	345,733	2,473.07
Expenditure	369,769	2,645.00
Debt Outstanding	203,269	1,454.01
Cash & Securities	61,537	440.18

Source: U.S. Bureau of the Census, City Government Finances: 1991-92

City Government Revenue by Source

Source	FY92 ($000)	FY92 (per capita $)	FY92 (%)
From Federal Government	5,764	41.23	1.7
From State Governments	149,409	1,068.74	43.2
From Local Governments	0	0.00	0.0
Property Taxes	140,900	1,007.88	40.8
General Sales Taxes	0	0.00	0.0
Selective Sales Taxes	0	0.00	0.0
Income Taxes	0	0.00	0.0
Current Charges	26,971	192.93	7.8
Utility/Liquor Store	0	0.00	0.0
Employee Retirement[1]	0	0.00	0.0
Other	22,689	162.30	6.6

Note: (1) Excludes "city contributions," classified as "nonrevenue," intragovernmental transfers.
Source: U.S. Bureau of the Census, City Government Finances: 1991-92

City Government Expenditures by Function

Function	FY92 ($000)	FY92 (per capita $)	FY92 (%)
Educational Services	146,744	1,049.68	39.7
Employee Retirement[1]	0	0.00	0.0
Environment/Housing	33,875	242.31	9.2
Government Administration	10,488	75.02	2.8
Interest on General Debt	17,677	126.45	4.8
Public Safety	42,237	302.13	11.4
Social Services	38,474	275.21	10.4
Transportation	2,108	15.08	0.6
Utility/Liquor Store	0	0.00	0.0
Other	78,166	559.13	21.1

Note: (1) Payments to beneficiaries including withdrawal of contributions.
Source: U.S. Bureau of the Census, City Government Finances: 1991-92

Municipal Bond Ratings

Area	Moody's	S & P
Bridgeport	Baa2	n/a

Note: n/a not available; n/r not rated
Source: Moody's Bond Record, 2/98; Statistical Abstract of the U.S., 1997; Governing Magazine, 9/97, 3/98

POPULATION

Population Growth

Area	1980	1990	% Chg. 1980-90	July 1996 Estimate	% Chg. 1990-96
City	142,546	141,686	-0.6	137,990	-2.6
MSA[1]	438,557	443,722	1.2	443,637	-0.0
U.S.	226,545,805	248,765,170	9.8	265,179,411	6.6

Note: (1) Metropolitan Statistical Area - see Appendix A for areas included
Source: 1980/1990 Census of Housing and Population, Summary Tape File 3C; Census Bureau Population Estimates

Population Characteristics

Race	City					MSA[1]	
	1980		1990		% Chg. 1980-90	1990	
	Population	%	Population	%		Population	%
White	100,805	70.7	83,124	58.7	-17.5	372,585	84.0
Black	29,871	21.0	37,753	26.6	26.4	45,704	10.3
Amer Indian/Esk/Aleut	286	0.2	303	0.2	5.9	611	0.1
Asian/Pacific Islander	1,241	0.9	3,019	2.1	143.3	5,923	1.3
Other	10,343	7.3	17,487	12.3	69.1	18,899	4.3
Hispanic Origin[2]	26,906	18.9	35,840	25.3	33.2	42,404	9.6

Note: (1) Metropolitan Statistical Area - see Appendix A for areas included; (2) people of Hispanic origin can be of any race
Source: 1980/1990 Census of Housing and Population, Summary Tape File 3C

Ancestry

Area	German	Irish	English	Italian	U.S.	French	Polish	Dutch
City	4.8	8.8	4.0	12.7	2.0	2.1	4.7	0.4
MSA[1]	11.6	17.7	11.0	19.7	2.1	4.0	9.7	0.9
U.S.	23.3	15.6	13.1	5.9	5.3	4.2	3.8	2.5

Note: Figures are percentages and include persons that reported multiple ancestry (eg. if a person reported being Irish and Italian, they were included in both columns); (1) Metropolitan Statistical Area - see Appendix A for areas included
Source: 1990 Census of Population and Housing, Summary Tape File 3C

Age

Area	Median Age (Years)	Age Distribution (%)						
		Under 5	Under 18	18-24	25-44	45-64	65+	80+
City	30.8	8.1	26.1	11.1	32.8	16.4	13.6	3.1
MSA[1]	34.6	7.0	23.3	9.8	32.2	20.0	14.7	3.1
U.S.	32.9	7.3	25.6	10.5	32.6	18.7	12.5	2.8

Note: (1) Metropolitan Statistical Area - see Appendix A for areas included
Source: 1990 Census of Population and Housing, Summary Tape File 3C

Male/Female Ratio

Area	Number of males per 100 females (all ages)	Number of males per 100 females (18 years old+)
City	90.1	85.8
MSA[1]	92.6	88.9
U.S.	95.0	91.9

Note: (1) Metropolitan Statistical Area - see Appendix A for areas included
Source: 1990 Census of Population, General Population Characteristics

INCOME

Per Capita/Median/Average Income

Area	Per Capita ($)	Median Household ($)	Average Household ($)
City	13,156	28,704	34,679
MSA[1]	18,611	40,874	50,037
U.S.	14,420	30,056	38,453

Note: all figures are for 1989; (1) Metropolitan Statistical Area - see Appendix A for areas included
Source: 1990 Census of Population and Housing, Summary Tape File 3C

Household Income Distribution by Race

Income ($)	City (%)					U.S. (%)				
	Total	White	Black	Other	Hisp.[1]	Total	White	Black	Other	Hisp.[1]
Less than 5,000	6.6	5.1	8.8	10.6	10.3	6.2	4.8	15.2	8.6	8.8
5,000 - 9,999	11.7	11.9	10.6	13.1	15.9	9.3	8.6	14.2	9.9	11.1
10,000 - 14,999	8.6	8.5	8.5	9.1	8.8	8.8	8.5	11.0	9.8	11.0
15,000 - 24,999	16.5	15.6	18.7	17.0	17.3	17.5	17.3	18.9	18.5	20.5
25,000 - 34,999	16.3	15.9	16.9	17.2	15.1	15.8	16.1	14.2	15.4	16.4
35,000 - 49,999	16.9	17.1	16.4	17.3	16.4	17.9	18.6	13.3	16.1	16.0
50,000 - 74,999	15.9	17.4	13.7	11.5	12.7	15.0	15.8	9.3	13.4	11.1
75,000 - 99,999	4.8	5.2	4.7	3.0	2.7	5.1	5.5	2.6	4.7	3.1
100,000+	2.7	3.3	1.7	1.1	0.9	4.4	4.8	1.3	3.7	1.9

Note: all figures are for 1989; (1) people of Hispanic origin can be of any race
Source: 1990 Census of Population and Housing, Summary Tape File 3C

Effective Buying Income

Area	Per Capita ($)	Median Household ($)	Average Household ($)
City	15,455	34,340	41,599
MSA[1]	24,668	50,028	65,683
U.S.	15,444	33,201	41,849

Note: data as of 1/1/97; (1) Metropolitan Statistical Area - see Appendix A for areas included
Source: Standard Rate & Data Service, Newspaper Advertising Source, 2/98

Effective Household Buying Income Distribution

Area	% of Households Earning						
	$10,000 -$19,999	$20,000 -$34,999	$35,000 -$49,999	$50,000 -$74,999	$75,000 -$99,000	$100,000 -$124,999	$125,000 and up
City	15.9	21.3	17.3	19.5	8.0	2.6	1.7
MSA[1]	10.1	16.1	15.8	22.8	12.4	6.0	8.9
U.S.	16.5	23.4	18.3	18.2	6.4	2.1	2.4

Note: data as of 1/1/97; (1) Metropolitan Statistical Area - see Appendix A for areas included
Source: Standard Rate & Data Service, Newspaper Advertising Source, 2/98

Poverty Rates by Race and Age

Area	Total (%)	By Race (%)				By Age (%)		
		White	Black	Other	Hisp.[2]	Under 5 years old	Under 18 years old	65 years and over
City	17.1	12.7	20.7	27.7	30.7	30.9	29.1	11.2
MSA[1]	7.8	5.4	18.8	23.6	26.9	14.9	13.2	7.3
U.S.	13.1	9.8	29.5	23.1	25.3	20.1	18.3	12.8

Note: figures show the percent of people living below the poverty line in 1989. The average poverty threshold was $12,674 for a family of four in 1989; (1) Metropolitan Statistical Area - see Appendix A for areas included; (2) people of Hispanic origin can be of any race
Source: 1990 Census of Population and Housing, Summary Tape File 3C

EMPLOYMENT

Labor Force and Employment

Area	Civilian Labor Force			Workers Employed		
	Dec. '95	Dec. '96	% Chg.	Dec. '95	Dec. '96	% Chg.
City	60,479	59,183	-2.1	54,281	54,624	0.6
MSA[1]	218,542	216,238	-1.1	204,217	205,510	0.6
U.S.	134,583,000	136,742,000	1.6	127,903,000	130,785,000	2.3

Note: Data is not seasonally adjusted and covers workers 16 years of age and older; (1) Metropolitan Statistical Area - see Appendix A for areas included
Source: Bureau of Labor Statistics, http://stats.bls.gov

Unemployment Rate

Area	1997											
	Jan.	Feb.	Mar.	Apr.	May	Jun.	Jul.	Aug.	Sep.	Oct.	Nov.	Dec.
City	10.6	10.2	9.4	9.3	8.6	9.3	8.8	7.9	7.0	7.2	7.6	7.7
MSA[1]	6.9	6.5	5.9	5.7	5.8	6.4	6.3	5.6	4.8	5.0	5.1	5.0
U.S.	5.9	5.7	5.5	4.8	4.7	5.2	5.0	4.8	4.7	4.4	4.3	4.4

Note: Data is not seasonally adjusted and covers workers 16 years of age and older; All figures are percentages; (1) Metropolitan Statistical Area - see Appendix A for areas included
Source: Bureau of Labor Statistics, http://stats.bls.gov

Employment by Industry

Sector	MSA[1]		U.S.
	Number of Employees	Percent of Total	Percent of Total
Services	58,600	31.4	29.0
Retail Trade	32,800	17.6	18.5
Government	21,100	11.3	16.1
Manufacturing	40,000	21.4	15.0
Finance/Insurance/Real Estate	10,400	5.6	5.7
Wholesale Trade	9,900	5.3	5.4
Transportation/Public Utilities	7,200	3.9	5.3
Construction	6,500	3.5	4.5
Mining	0	0.0	0.5

Note: Figures cover non-farm employment as of 12/97 and are not seasonally adjusted; (1) Metropolitan Statistical Area - see Appendix A for areas included
Source: Bureau of Labor Statistics, http://stats.bls.gov

Employment by Occupation

Occupation Category	City (%)	MSA[1] (%)	U.S. (%)
White Collar	49.6	62.5	58.1
Executive/Admin./Management	8.7	14.3	12.3
Professional	10.3	15.0	14.1
Technical & Related Support	3.0	3.7	3.7
Sales	8.7	11.5	11.8
Administrative Support/Clerical	18.8	18.1	16.3
Blue Collar	32.0	24.8	26.2
Precision Production/Craft/Repair	11.9	12.0	11.3
Machine Operators/Assem./Insp.	11.7	6.9	6.8
Transportation/Material Movers	4.0	3.0	4.1
Cleaners/Helpers/Laborers	4.5	3.0	3.9
Services	17.5	11.8	13.2
Farming/Forestry/Fishing	0.9	0.8	2.5

Note: figures cover employed persons 16 years old and over; (1) Metropolitan Statistical Area - see Appendix A for areas included
Source: 1990 Census of Population and Housing, Summary Tape File 3C

Occupational Employment Projections: 1994 - 2005

Occupations Expected to have the Largest Job Growth (ranked by numerical growth)	Fast-Growing Occupations (ranked by percent growth)
1. Salespersons, retail	1. Electronic pagination systems workers
2. Waiters & waitresses	2. Computer engineers
3. Registered nurses	3. Amusement and recreation attendants
4. General managers & top executives	4. Patternmakers and layout workers
5. Systems analysts	5. Physical therapy assistants and aides
6. Cashiers	6. Computer scientists
7. Janitors/cleaners/maids, ex. priv. hshld.	7. Securities, financial services sales
8. Marketing & sales, supervisors	8. Systems analysts
9. Nursing aides/orderlies/attendants	9. Occupational therapy assistants
10. Clerical supervisors	10. Human services workers

Projections cover Connecticut.
Source: U.S. Department of Labor, Employment and Training Administration, America's Labor Market Information System (ALMIS)

Average Wages

Occupation	Wage	Occupation	Wage
Professional/Technical/Clerical	$/Week	**Health/Protective Services**	$/Week
Accountants III	-	Corrections Officers	-
Attorneys III	-	Firefighters	-
Budget Analysts III	-	Nurses, Licensed Practical II	-
Buyers/Contracting Specialists II	-	Nurses, Registered II	-
Clerks, Accounting III	-	Nursing Assistants II	-
Clerks, General III	-	Police Officers I	-
Computer Operators II	-	**Hourly Workers**	$/Hour
Computer Programmers II	-	Forklift Operators	-
Drafters II	-	General Maintenance Workers	-
Engineering Technicians III	-	Guards I	-
Engineering Technicians, Civil III	-	Janitors	-
Engineers III	-	Maintenance Electricians	-
Key Entry Operators I	-	Maintenance Electronics Techs II	-
Personnel Assistants III	-	Maintenance Machinists	-
Personnel Specialists III	-	Maintenance Mechanics, Machinery	-
Secretaries III	-	Material Handling Laborers	-
Switchboard Operator-Receptionist	-	Motor Vehicle Mechanics	-
Systems Analysts II	-	Shipping/Receiving Clerks	-
Systems Analysts Supervisor/Mgr II	-	Tool and Die Makers	-
Tax Collectors II	-	Truckdrivers, Tractor Trailer	-
Word Processors II	-	Warehouse Specialists	-

Note: Wage data includes full-time workers only for 0/ 0 and cover the Metropolitan Statistical Area (see Appendix A for areas included). Dashes indicate that data was not available.
Source: Bureau of Labor Statistics, Occupational Compensation Survey

TAXES

Major State and Local Tax Rates

State Corp. Income (%)	State Personal Income (%)	Residential Property (effective rate per $100)	Sales & Use State (%)	Sales & Use Local (%)	State Gasoline (cents/ gallon)	State Cigarette (cents/ 20-pack)
10.5	3.0 - 4.5	3.96	6.0	None	36	50

Note: Personal/corporate income tax rates as of 1/97. Sales, gasoline and cigarette tax rates as of 1/98.
Source: Federation of Tax Administrators, www.taxadmin.org; Washington D.C. Department of Finance and Revenue, Tax Rates and Tax Burdens in the District of Columbia: A Nationwide Comparison, June 1997; Chamber of Commerce

Total Taxes Per Capita and as a Percent of Income

Area	Per Capita Income ($)	Per Capita Taxes ($)			Taxes as Pct. of Income (%)		
		Total	Federal	State/ Local	Total	Federal	State/ Local
Connecticut	35,341	13,709	9,091	4,618	38.8	25.7	13.1
U.S.	26,187	9,205	6,127	3,078	35.2	23.4	11.8

Note: Figures are for 1997
Source: Tax Foundation, Web Site, www.taxfoundation.org

COMMERCIAL REAL ESTATE

Office Market

Class/ Location	Total Space (sq. ft.)	Vacant Space (sq. ft.)	Vac. Rate (%)	Under Constr. (sq. ft.)	Net Absorp. (sq. ft.)	Rental Rates ($/sq.ft./yr.)
Class A						
CBD	992,508	2,759	0.3	0	41	15.50-15.50
Outside CBD	4,195,715	372,176	8.9	123,956	-76,545	11.50-26.50
Class B						
CBD	1,433,423	469,216	32.7	0	40,623	6.50-21.50
Outside CBD	698,224	125,516	18.0	0	52,042	11.50-23.50

Note: Data as of 10/97 and covers Greater Bridgeport; CBD = Central Business District; n/a not available;
Source: Society of Industrial and Office Realtors, 1998 Comparative Statistics of Industrial and Office Real Estate Markets

"The economy in the greater Bridgeport area is expected to continue to expand at a modest pace during 1998. The state of Connecticut offers several business incentive plans for firms interested in expanding or locating in the City of Bridgeport, are all coordinated by the City's Office of Planning and Economic Development. Our SIOR reporters expect to see both absorption and rental rates increase at a moderate pace during 1998, accompanied by a substantial increase in construction activity. 'A' space outside of the CBD, landlord concessions during 1998 will not be as generous as in the recent past." *Society of Industrial and Office Realtors, 1998 Comparative Statistics of Industrial and Office Real Estate Markets*

Industrial Market

Location	Total Space (sq. ft.)	Vacant Space (sq. ft.)	Vac. Rate (%)	Under Constr. (sq. ft.)	Net Absorp. (sq. ft.)	Net Lease ($/sq.ft./yr.)
Central City	20,000,000	484,000	2.4	50,000	197,000	4.00-5.00
Suburban	5,345,000	475,000	8.9	40,000	372,000	5.75-7.00

Note: Data as of 10/97 and covers Bridgeport; n/a not available
Source: Society of Industrial and Office Realtors, 1998 Comparative Statistics of Industrial and Office Real Estate Markets

"Due to the proximity to the markets of New York City and Fairfield County, CT, the outlook for the warehousing/distribution and High-Tech/R&D markets in Bridgeport during 1998 is good. The outlook for the manufacturing sector is less optimistic due to the shrinking industrial base. Some potential market constraints are congested highways and a shortage of sites available for development. Our SIOR reporter expects High-Tech/R&D space to account for the biggest share of absorption during 1998 followed by warehousing/distribution and manufacturing. Demand for High-Tech/R&D space was practically nonexistent as recently as 1995. More than 200,000 sq. ft. of additional space has been proposed for 1998; two large projects are proceeding on a speculative basis. An increase in overall absorption during 1998 will lead to increases in lease and sales prices in the one to five percent range before the new construction comes on line." *Society of Industrial and Office Realtors, 1998 Comparative Statistics of Industrial and Office Real Estate Markets*

COMMERCIAL UTILITIES

Typical Monthly Electric Bills

Area	Commercial Service ($/month)		Industrial Service ($/month)	
	12 kW demand 1,500 kWh	100 kW demand 30,000 kWh	1,000 kW demand 400,000 kWh	20,000 kW demand 10,000,000 kWh
City	n/a	n/a	n/a	n/a
U.S.	162	2,360	25,590	545,677

Note: Based on rates in effect July 1, 1997; n/a not available
Source: Edison Electric Institute, Typical Residential, Commercial and Industrial Bills, Summer 1997

TRANSPORTATION

Transportation Statistics

Avg. travel time to work (min.)	19.6
Interstate highways	I-95
Bus lines	
In-city	Greater Bridgeport Transit District, 72 vehicles
Inter-city	12
Passenger air service	
Airport	Igor Sikorsky Memorial
Airlines	1
Aircraft departures	n/a
Enplaned passengers	n/a
Rail service	Amtrak
Motor freight carriers	166 (includes Fairfield County)
Major waterways/ports	Long Island Sound; Port of Bridgeport

Source: OAG, Business Travel Planner, Summer 1997; Editor & Publisher Market Guide, 1998; FAA Airport Activity Statistics, 1996; Amtrak National Time Table, Northeast Timetable, Fall/Winter 1997-98; 1990 Census of Population and Housing, STF 3C; Chamber of Commerce/Economic Development 1997; Jane's Urban Transport Systems 1997-98; Transit Fact Book 1997

Means of Transportation to Work

Area	Car/Truck/Van		Public Transportation			Bicycle	Walked	Other Means	Worked at Home
	Drove Alone	Car-pooled	Bus	Subway	Railroad				
City	69.4	16.6	5.2	0.0	1.0	0.1	5.1	1.2	1.3
MSA[1]	79.3	11.4	1.8	0.0	1.8	0.1	2.7	0.7	2.1
U.S.	73.2	13.4	3.0	1.5	0.5	0.4	3.9	1.2	3.0

Note: figures shown are percentages and only include workers 16 years old and over; (1) Metropolitan Statistical Area - see Appendix A for areas included
Source: 1990 Census of Population and Housing, Summary Tape File 3C

BUSINESSES

Major Business Headquarters

Company Name	1997 Rankings	
	Fortune 500	Forbes 500
No companies listed.		

Note: Companies listed are located in the city; Dashes indicate no ranking
Fortune 500: companies that produce a 10-K are ranked 1 - 500 based on 1996 revenue
Forbes 500: private companies are ranked 1 - 500 based on 1996 revenue
Source: Forbes 12/1/97; Fortune 4/28/97

Minority Business Opportunity

One of the 500 largest Hispanic-owned companies in the U.S. are located in Bridgeport.
Hispanic Business, June 1997

HOTELS & MOTELS

Hotels/Motels

Area	Hotels/ Motels	Rooms	Luxury-Level Hotels/Motels		Average Minimum Rates ($)		
			♦♦♦♦	♦♦♦♦♦	♦♦	♦♦♦	♦♦♦♦
City	1	235	0	0	n/a	n/a	n/a
Airport	2	238	0	0	n/a	n/a	n/a
Total	3	473	0	0	n/a	n/a	n/a

Note: n/a not available; Classifications range from one diamond (budget properties with basic amenities) to five diamond (luxury properties with the finest service, rooms and facilities).
Source: OAG, Business Travel Planner, Summer 1997

CONVENTION CENTERS

Major Convention Centers

Center Name	Meeting Rooms	Exhibit Space (sf)
None listed in city		

Source: Trade Shows Worldwide 1997

Living Environment

COST OF LIVING

Cost of Living Index

Composite Index	Housing	Utilities	Groceries	Health Care	Trans-portation	Misc. Goods/ Services
n/a	n/a	n/a	n/a	n/a	n/a	n/a

Note: U.S. = 100; n/a not available
Source: ACCRA, Cost of Living Index, 3rd Quarter 1997

HOUSING

Median Home Prices and Housing Affordability

Area	Median Price[2] 3rd Qtr. 1997 ($)	HOI[3] 3rd Qtr. 1997	Afford-ability Rank[4]
MSA[1]	n/a	n/a	n/a
U.S.	127,000	63.7	-

Note: (1) Metropolitan Statistical Area - see Appendix A for areas included; (2) U.S. figures calculated from the sales of 625,000 new and existing homes in 195 markets; (3) Housing Opportunity Index - percent of homes sold that were within the reach of the median income household at the prevailing mortgage interest rate; (4) Rank is from 1-195 with 1 being most affordable; n/a not available
Source: National Association of Home Builders, Housing Opportunity Index, 3rd Quarter 1997

Average New Home Price

Area	Price ($)
City	n/a
U.S.	135,710

Note: n/a not available
Source: ACCRA, Cost of Living Index, 3rd Quarter 1997

Average Apartment Rent

Area	Rent ($/mth)
City	n/a
U.S.	569

Note: n/a not available
Source: ACCRA, Cost of Living Index, 3rd Quarter 1997

RESIDENTIAL UTILITIES

Average Residential Utility Costs

Area	All Electric ($/mth)	Part Electric ($/mth)	Other Energy ($/mth)	Phone ($/mth)
City	n/a	n/a	n/a	n/a
U.S.	109.40	55.25	43.64	19.48

Note: n/a not available
Source: ACCRA, Cost of Living Index, 3rd Quarter 1997

HEALTH CARE

Average Health Care Costs

Area	Hospital ($/day)	Doctor ($/visit)	Dentist ($/visit)
City	n/a	n/a	n/a
U.S.	392.91	48.76	60.84

Note: n/a not available
Source: ACCRA, Cost of Living Index, 3rd Quarter 1997

Distribution of Office-Based Physicians

Area	Family/Gen. Practitioners	Specialists		
		Medical	Surgical	Other
Metro Area[1]	122	848	542	476

Note: Data as of December 31, 1996; (1) Fairfield County
Source: American Medical Assn., Physician Characteristics & Distribution in the U.S., 1997-1998

Hospitals

Bridgeport has 2 general medical and surgical hospitals, 1 psychiatric. *AHA Guide to the Healthcare Field 1997-98*

EDUCATION

Public School District Statistics

District Name	Num. Sch.	Enroll.	Classroom Teachers[1]	Pupils per Teacher	Minority Pupils (%)	Current Exp.[2] ($/pupil)
Bridgeport School District	40	21,519	1,355	15.9	88.4	7,708

Note: Data covers the 1995-1996 school year unless otherwise noted; (1) Excludes teachers reported as working in school district offices rather than in schools; (2) Based on 1993-94 enrollment collected by the Census Bureau, not the enrollment figure shown in column 3; SD = School District; ISD = Independent School District; n/a not available
Source: National Center for Education Statistics, Common Core of Data Survey; Bureau of the Census

Educational Quality

School District	Education Quotient[1]	Graduate Outcome[2]	Community Index[3]	Resource Index[4]
Bridgeport	104.0	51.0	145.0	117.0

Note: Nearly 1,000 secondary school districts were rated in terms of educational quality. The scores range from a low of 50 to a high of 150; (1) Average of the Graduate Outcome, Community and Resource indexes; (2) Based on graduation rates and college board scores (SAT/ACT); (3) Based on the surrounding community's average level of education and the area's average income level; (4) Based on teacher salaries, per-pupil expenditures and student-teacher ratios.
Source: Expansion Management, Ratings Issue 1997

Educational Attainment by Race

Area	High School Graduate (%)					Bachelor's Degree (%)				
	Total	White	Black	Other	Hisp.[2]	Total	White	Black	Other	Hisp.[2]
City	61.1	63.5	63.0	43.2	42.0	12.3	15.0	7.0	7.5	5.3
MSA[1]	75.8	78.0	65.1	51.9	47.5	23.0	24.7	9.2	16.0	8.0
U.S.	75.2	77.9	63.1	60.4	49.8	20.3	21.5	11.4	19.4	9.2

Note: figures shown cover persons 25 years old and over; (1) Metropolitan Statistical Area - see Appendix A for areas included; (2) people of Hispanic origin can be of any race
Source: 1990 Census of Population and Housing, Summary Tape File 3C

School Enrollment by Type

Area	Preprimary				Elementary/High School			
	Public		Private		Public		Private	
	Enrollment	%	Enrollment	%	Enrollment	%	Enrollment	%
City	1,453	70.8	600	29.2	20,451	81.7	4,577	18.3
MSA[1]	5,196	54.6	4,326	45.4	57,944	84.6	10,541	15.4
U.S.	2,679,029	59.5	1,824,256	40.5	38,379,689	90.2	4,187,099	9.8

Note: figures shown cover persons 3 years old and over;
(1) Metropolitan Statistical Area - see Appendix A for areas included
Source: 1990 Census of Population and Housing, Summary Tape File 3C

School Enrollment by Race

Area	Preprimary (%)				Elementary/High School (%)			
	White	Black	Other	Hisp.[1]	White	Black	Other	Hisp.[1]
City	44.7	38.7	16.7	32.7	43.7	34.5	21.8	37.6
MSA[2]	83.4	11.1	5.5	9.4	75.6	15.1	9.3	15.8
U.S.	80.4	12.5	7.1	7.8	74.1	15.6	10.3	12.5

Note: figures shown cover persons 3 years old and over; (1) people of Hispanic origin can be of any race; (2) Metropolitan Statistical Area - see Appendix A for areas included
Source: 1990 Census of Population and Housing, Summary Tape File 3C

SAT/ACT Scores

Area/District	1997 SAT				1997 ACT	
	Percent of Graduates Tested (%)	Average Math Score	Average Verbal Score	Average Combined Score	Percent of Graduates Tested (%)	Average Composite Score
Bridgeport	n/a	n/a	n/a	n/a	n/a	n/a
State	79	507	509	1,016	3	21.7
U.S.	42	511	505	1,016	36	21.0

Note: Math and verbal SAT scores are out of a possible 800; ACT scores are out of a possible 36
Caution: Comparing or ranking states/cities on the basis of SAT/ACT scores alone is invalid and strongly discouraged by the The College Board and The American College Testing Program as students who take the tests are self-selected and do not represent the entire student population.
Source: American College Testing Program, 1997; College Board, 1997

Classroom Teacher Salaries in Public Schools

District	B.A. Degree		M.A. Degree		Ph.D. Degree	
	Min. ($)	Max ($)	Min. ($)	Max. ($)	Min. ($)	Max. ($)
Bridgeport	30,000	45,670	31,000	54,090	32,750	60,750
Average[1]	26,120	39,270	28,175	44,667	31,643	49,825

Note: Salaries are for 1996-1997; (1) Based on all school districts covered
Source: American Federation of Teachers (unpublished data)

Higher Education

Two-Year Colleges		Four-Year Colleges		Medical Schools	Law Schools	Voc/ Tech
Public	Private	Public	Private			
1	0	0	1	0	0	5

Source: College Blue Book, Occupational Education 1997; Medical School Admission Requirements, 1998-99; Peterson's Guide to Two-Year Colleges, 1997; Peterson's Guide to Four-Year Colleges, 1997; Barron's Guide to Law Schools 1997

MAJOR EMPLOYERS

Major Employers

Bridgeport Hospital
People's Bank
Bridgeport Health Care Center
Southern Connecticut Gas Co.
Casco Products Corp. (auto electrical equip.)
St. Vincent's Medical Center
Remington Products (electric housewares)
Bridgeport Jai Alai
Country Home Bakery

Note: companies listed are located in the city
Source: Dun's Business Rankings 1997; Ward's Business Directory, 1997

PUBLIC SAFETY

Crime Rate

Area	All Crimes	Violent Crimes				Property Crimes		
		Murder	Forcible Rape	Robbery	Aggrav. Assault	Burglary	Larceny -Theft	Motor Vehicle Theft
City	8,300.6	33.1	45.9	712.7	792.4	1,863.7	3,065.1	1,787.8
Suburbs[1]	3,260.1	1.6	18.8	53.8	80.7	678.6	2,067.1	359.6
MSA[2]	4,740.9	10.8	26.7	247.4	289.8	1,026.8	2,360.3	779.2
U.S.	5,078.9	7.4	36.1	202.4	388.2	943.0	2,975.9	525.9

Note: Crime rate is the number of crimes per 100,000 pop.; (1) defined as all areas within the MSA but located outside the central city; (2) Metropolitan Statistical Area - see Appendix A for areas incl.
Source: FBI Uniform Crime Reports 1996

RECREATION

Culture and Recreation

Museums	Symphony Orchestras	Opera Companies	Dance Companies	Professional Theatres	Zoos	Pro Sports Teams
3	1	0	0	1	1	0

Source: International Directory of the Performing Arts, 1996; Official Museum Directory, 1998; Chamber of Commerce/Economic Development 1997

Library System

The Bridgeport Public Library has four branches, holdings of 469,745 volumes and a budget of $3,226,824 (1995-1996). *American Library Directory, 1997-1998*

MEDIA

Newspapers

Name	Type	Freq.	Distribution	Circulation
The Connecticut Post	General	7x/wk	Area	70,000

Note: Includes newspapers with circulations of 500 or more located in the city; Source: Burrelle's Media Directory, 1998 Edition

AM Radio Stations

Call Letters	Freq. (kHz)	Target Audience	Station Format	Music Format
WICC	600	General	M/N/S	Adult Contemporary
WLAD	800	General	M/N/S/T	Adult Contemporary
WREF	850	General	M/N/S	Big Band/MOR/Oldies
WINE	940	General	N/T	n/a
WMMM	1260	General	M/N/S/T	Big Band/Christian/Oldies/Spanish
WNLK	1350	General	M/N/S	Adult Contemporary
WSTC	1400	General	M/N/S/T	Adult Standards/Jazz
WCUM	1450	Hispanic	M/N/S	Spanish
WGCH	1490	n/a	M/T	Adult Contemporary/Classical/Spanish

Note: Stations included broadcast in the Bridgeport metro area; n/a not available
Station Format: E = Educational; M = Music; N = News; S = Sports; T = Talk
Music Format: AOR = Album Oriented Rock; MOR = Middle-of-the-Road
Source: Burrelle's Media Directory, 1998 Edition

FM Radio Stations

Call Letters	Freq. (mHz)	Target Audience	Station Format	Music Format
WMNR	88.1	General	M	Big Band/Classical/Jazz
WVOF	88.5	n/a	E/M/N/S/T	n/a
WEDW	88.5	General	M/N	Classical
WPKN	89.5	n/a	M	n/a
WRXC	90.1	General	M	Big Band/Classical
WWPT	90.3	General	E/M/N/S/T	AOR
WSHU	91.1	General	M/N/S	Classical
WGRS	91.5	General	M	Big Band/Classical/Jazz
WXCI	91.7	n/a	M	Alternative
WSLX	91.9	General	M	Classical
WFAR	93.3	General	M/N/S	n/a
WRKI	95.1	n/a	M	AOR/Classic Rock
WEFX	95.9	General	M/N/S	Classic Rock
WKHL	96.7	General	M	Oldies
WDAQ	98.3	n/a	M	Adult Contemporary
WEZN	99.9	n/a	M	Adult Contemporary
WAXB	105.5	General	M/N/S	Oldies
WEBE	107.9	n/a	M	Adult Contemporary

Note: Stations included broadcast in the Bridgeport metro area; n/a not available
Station Format: E = Educational; M = Music; N = News; S = Sports; T = Talk
Music Format: AOR = Album Oriented Rock; MOR = Middle-of-the-Road
Source: Burrelle's Media Directory, 1998 Edition

Television Stations

Name	Ch.	Affiliation	Type	Owner
No stations listed.				

Note: Stations included broadcast in the Bridgeport metro area
Source: Burrelle's Media Directory, 1998 Edition

CLIMATE

Average and Extreme Temperatures

Temperature	Jan	Feb	Mar	Apr	May	Jun	Jul	Aug	Sep	Oct	Nov	Dec	Ann
Extreme High (°F)	65	67	84	91	92	96	103	100	99	85	78	65	103
Average High (°F)	37	38	46	57	67	76	82	81	74	64	53	41	60
Average Temp. (°F)	30	32	39	49	59	68	74	73	66	56	46	35	52
Average Low (°F)	23	24	31	40	50	59	65	65	57	47	38	27	44
Extreme Low (°F)	-7	-5	4	18	31	41	49	44	36	26	16	-4	-7

Note: Figures cover the years 1948-1992
Source: National Climatic Data Center, International Station Meteorological Climate Summary, 3/95

Average Precipitation/Snowfall/Humidity

Precip./Humidity	Jan	Feb	Mar	Apr	May	Jun	Jul	Aug	Sep	Oct	Nov	Dec	Ann
Avg. Precip. (in.)	3.2	2.9	3.7	3.7	3.7	3.1	3.7	3.8	3.0	3.2	3.8	3.5	41.4
Avg. Snowfall (in.)	7	7	5	1	Tr	0	0	0	0	Tr	1	5	25
Avg. Rel. Hum. 7am (%)	73	72	72	72	76	77	79	80	81	79	77	74	76
Avg. Rel. Hum. 4pm (%)	61	59	56	55	59	60	60	61	61	60	62	63	60

Note: Figures cover the years 1948-1992; Tr = Trace amounts (<0.05 in. of rain; <0.5 in. of snow)
Source: National Climatic Data Center, International Station Meteorological Climate Summary, 3/95

Weather Conditions

Temperature			Daytime Sky			Precipitation		
32°F & below	45°F & below	90°F & above	Clear	Partly cloudy	Cloudy	0.01 inch or more precip.	0.1 inch or more snow/ice	Thunder-storms
100	193	7	80	146	139	118	17	22

Note: Figures are average number of days per year and covers the years 1948-1992
Source: National Climatic Data Center, International Station Meteorological Climate Summary, 3/95

AIR & WATER QUALITY

Maximum Pollutant Concentrations

	Particulate Matter (ug/m3)	Carbon Monoxide (ppm)	Sulfur Dioxide (ppm)	Nitrogen Dioxide (ppm)	Ozone (ppm)	Lead (ug/m3)
MSA[1] Level	63	3	0.023	0.024	0.13	0.02
NAAQS[2]	150	9	0.140	0.053	0.12	1.50
Met NAAQS?	Yes	Yes	Yes	Yes	No	Yes

Note: (1) Metropolitan Statistical Area - see Appendix A for areas included; (2) National Ambient Air Quality Standards; ppm = parts per million; ug/m3 = micrograms per cubic meter; n/a not available
Source: EPA, National Air Quality and Emissions Trends Report, 1996

Pollutant Standards Index

Data not available. *EPA, National Air Quality and Emissions Trends Report, 1996*

Drinking Water

Water System Name	Pop. Served	Primary Water Source Type	Number of Violations in Fiscal Year 1997	Type of Violation/ Contaminants
BHC Main System	324,859	Surface	1	Failure to filter

Note: Data as of January 16, 1998
Source: EPA, Office of Ground Water and Drinking Water, Safe Drinking Water Information System

Bridgeport tap water is alkaline, very soft and fluoridated.
Editor & Publisher Market Guide, 1998

Charlotte, North Carolina

Background

Charlotte's relationship with England began amiably enough. Settled by Scotch-Irish and German migrants from Pennsylvania, New Jersey, and Virginia in 1750, the area was named in honor of Charlotte Sophia of Mecklenburg-Strelitz, Queen to England's King George III. The county in which Charlotte lies was named for Queen Charlotte Sophia's Duchy of Mecklenburg.

However, proverbial thunderstorms roared, and lightning streaked across the sky on this friendship in 1775 when the citizens of Charlotte signed the Mecklenburg Resolves, a document invalidating the power of the King and the English Parliament over their lives. The British General, Lord Cornwallis found subduing these treasoners so difficult, that he called Charlotte a "Hornet's Nest of Rebellion".

Today, a better behaved Charlotte is the largest metropolitan area in the Carolinas. Its over one million residents make their living from a variety of jobs in retailing, distribution, manufacturing, and finance. The city, the center of a booming banking industry, is now the financial capital of the South and the third largest banking center in the United States. Its role as the nucleus of the Carolinas crescent, an industrial arc extending from Raleigh, North Carolina to Greenville, South Carolina adds to its prosperity as well.

Charlotte is one of North Carolina's economic "hot spots" with growth predicted at 19 percent by the year 2005. The city and the metro area had more than $1 billion in investments by new and expanding firms and created more than 13,000 new jobs. Charlotte has also become a major call center operator, with 15 centers employing more than 3,000 people. Bell South, EDS, Vanguard and First Data all plan to either expand or open call center operations in the Charlotte area. *Site Selection July/July 1997*

Charlotte is located in the Piedmont of the Carolinas, a transitional area of rolling country between the mountains to the west and the Coastal Plain to the east.

The city enjoys a moderate climate, characterized by cool winters and quite warm summers. Winter weather is changeable, with occasional cold periods, but extreme cold is rare. Snow is infrequent. Summers are long and warm with afternoon temperatures in the low 90s. Rainfall is generally evenly distributed throughout the year. Hurricanes which do strike the Carolina coast can produce heavy rain but seldom cause dangerous winds.

General Rankings and Evaluative Comments

- Charlotte was ranked #113 out of 300 cities by *Money's* 1997 "Survey of the Best Places to Live." Criteria used: health services, crime, economy, housing, education, transportation, weather, leisure and the arts. The city was ranked #84 in 1996 and #206 in 1995. *Money, July 1997; Money, September 1996; Money, September 1995*

- *Ladies Home Journal* ranked America's 200 largest cities based on the qualities women care about most. Charlotte ranked 48 out of 200. Criteria: low crime rate, good public schools, well-paying jobs, quality health and child care, the presence of women in government, proportion of women-owned businesses, size of the wage gap with men, local economy, divorce rates, the ratio of single men to single women, whether there are laws that require at least the same number of public toilets for women as men, and the probability of good hair days. *Ladies Home Journal, November 1997*

- Charlotte was ranked #105 out of 219 cities in terms of children's health, safety, and economic well-being. Criteria: total population, percent population change, birth rate, child immunization rate, infant mortality rate, percent low birth weight infants, percent of births to teens, physician-to-population ratio, student-to-teacher ratio, dropout rate, unemployment rate, median family income, percent of children in poverty, violent and property crime rates, number of juvenile arrests for violent crimes as a percent of the total crime index, number of days with pollution standard index (PSI) over 100, pounds toxic releases per 1,000 people and number of superfund sites. *Zero Population Growth, Children's Environmental Index 1997*

- *Yahoo! Internet Life* selected "America's 100 Most Wired Cities & Towns". 50 cities were large and 50 cities were small. Charlotte ranked 41 out of 50 large cities. Criteria: Internet users per capita, number of networked computers, number of registered domain names, Internet backbone traffic, and the per-capita number of Web sites devoted to each city. *Yahoo! Internet Life, March 1998*

- Nationsbank Corp., headquartered in Charlotte, is among the "100 Best Companies for Working Mothers." Criteria: pay compared with competition, opportunities for women to advance, support for child care, flexible work schedules and family-friendly benefits. *Working Mother, October 1997*

- According to *Working Mother,* "No state has more action or more enthusiasm for improving child care than North Carolina. And no governor deserves more credit for fighting for child care than Jim Hunt. His 'Smart Start' program has as its goal affordable, quality early childhood education for every child who needs it. In the past four years, the state has created more than 30,000 new slots for child care and improved care for more than 150,000 kids.

  The program ran up against some resistance in the state legislature in the past, but now a solid majority embrace the core tenets of Smart Start. This year, for example, state lawmakers decided to award permanent funding for the state's caregiver training program, Teacher Education and Compensation Helps (T.E.A.C.H.)—more than $1 million a year in recurring funds. That means child care advocates won't have to come back every year to fight for money for early education. The T.E.A.C.H. program is now being copied by other states, including Illinois.

  With all this progress, it's a shame that North Carolina's key standards aren't better. One adult is still allowed to care for up to five babies, and caregivers are not required to have any education or training before they start work (a bill now before the legislature may change this). This state could do better on these critical aspects of child care." *Working Mother, July/August 1997*

Business Environment

STATE ECONOMY

State Economic Profile

"North Carolina's strength is its development of technologically advanced industries, ranging from computer software development in biotechnology. North Carolina's weakness is its ailing textile and apparel industries....

North Carolina's population continues to expand at a robust 1.7% year-over-year rate, nearly twice the national average. In 1996 net domestic migration contributed 1.1 percentage points to North Carolina's population growth rate, compared to just 0.4 for the southern region, making the state's economic expansion particularly dependent on migration....

Apart from job losses in the apparel and textile industries, North Carolina's economy remains healthy, and employment growth is outpacing the nation. The long-term outlook for North Carolina is positive. Its emergency as a center for high-tech employment continues to attract relocations and expansions to metro areas such as Raleigh and Charlotte. A downside risk to the economy is strong growth in government sector employment, which may leave the state susceptible to government spending cuts in the future...." *National Association of Realtors, Economic Profiles: The Fifty States, July 1997*

IMPORTS/EXPORTS

Total Export Sales

Area	1993 ($000)	1994 ($000)	1995 ($000)	1996 ($000)	% Chg. 1993-96	% Chg. 1995-96
MSA[1]	1,563,725	1,782,827	2,087,970	2,291,296	46.5	9.7
U.S.	464,858,354	512,415,609	583,030,524	622,827,063	34.0	6.8

Note: (1) Metropolitan Statistical Area - see Appendix A for areas included
Source: U.S. Department of Commerce, International Trade Association, Metropolitan Area Exports: An Export Performance Report on Over 250 U.S. Cities, October 1997

Imports/Exports by Port

Type	Cargo Value			Share of U.S. Total	
	1995 (US$mil.)	1996 (US$mil.)	% Change 1995-1996	1995 (%)	1996 (%)
Imports	0	0	0	0	0
Exports	0	0	0	0	0

Source: Global Trade Information Services, WaterBorne Trade Atlas 1997

CITY FINANCES

City Government Finances

Component	FY92 ($000)	FY92 (per capita $)
Revenue	472,749	1,115.22
Expenditure	566,347	1,336.02
Debt Outstanding	999,281	2,357.32
Cash & Securities	677,473	1,598.17

Source: U.S. Bureau of the Census, City Government Finances: 1991-92

City Government Revenue by Source

Source	FY92 ($000)	FY92 (per capita $)	FY92 (%)
From Federal Government	21,692	51.17	4.6
From State Governments	49,503	116.78	10.5
From Local Governments	39,337	92.80	8.3
Property Taxes	140,111	330.52	29.6
General Sales Taxes	0	0.00	0.0
Selective Sales Taxes	12,172	28.71	2.6
Income Taxes	0	0.00	0.0
Current Charges	103,874	245.04	22.0
Utility/Liquor Store	34,061	80.35	7.2
Employee Retirement[1]	11,111	26.21	2.4
Other	60,888	143.64	12.9

Note: (1) Excludes "city contributions," classified as "nonrevenue," intragovernmental transfers.
Source: U.S. Bureau of the Census, City Government Finances: 1991-92

City Government Expenditures by Function

Function	FY92 ($000)	FY92 (per capita $)	FY92 (%)
Educational Services	0	0.00	0.0
Employee Retirement[1]	5,137	12.12	0.9
Environment/Housing	174,711	412.15	30.8
Government Administration	19,778	46.66	3.5
Interest on General Debt	59,676	140.78	10.5
Public Safety	77,006	181.66	13.6
Social Services	3,513	8.29	0.6
Transportation	97,761	230.62	17.3
Utility/Liquor Store	61,140	144.23	10.8
Other	67,625	159.53	11.9

Note: (1) Payments to beneficiaries including withdrawal of contributions.
Source: U.S. Bureau of the Census, City Government Finances: 1991-92

Municipal Bond Ratings

Area	Moody's	S & P
Charlotte	Aaa	AAA

Note: n/a not available; n/r not rated
Source: Moody's Bond Record, 2/98; Statistical Abstract of the U.S., 1997; Governing Magazine, 9/97, 3/98

POPULATION

Population Growth

Area	1980	1990	% Chg. 1980-90	July 1996 Estimate	% Chg. 1990-96
City	314,447	396,003	25.9	441,297	11.4
MSA[1]	971,391	1,162,093	19.6	1,321,068	13.7
U.S.	226,545,805	248,765,170	9.8	265,179,411	6.6

Note: (1) Metropolitan Statistical Area - see Appendix A for areas included
Source: 1980/1990 Census of Housing and Population, Summary Tape File 3C; Census Bureau Population Estimates

Population Characteristics

Race	City 1980 Population	City 1980 %	City 1990 Population	City 1990 %	% Chg. 1980-90	MSA[1] 1990 Population	MSA[1] 1990 %
White	212,293	67.5	259,710	65.6	22.3	911,871	78.5
Black	97,896	31.1	126,128	31.9	28.8	231,450	19.9
Amer Indian/Esk/Aleut	1,162	0.4	1,529	0.4	31.6	4,692	0.4
Asian/Pacific Islander	2,393	0.8	6,686	1.7	179.4	10,762	0.9
Other	703	0.2	1,950	0.5	177.4	3,318	0.3
Hispanic Origin[2]	3,418	1.1	5,261	1.3	53.9	9,817	0.8

Note: (1) Metropolitan Statistical Area - see Appendix A for areas included; (2) people of Hispanic origin can be of any race
Source: 1980/1990 Census of Housing and Population, Summary Tape File 3C

Ancestry

Area	German	Irish	English	Italian	U.S.	French	Polish	Dutch
City	17.0	11.8	14.3	2.4	5.7	2.6	1.4	2.0
MSA[1]	22.1	14.0	12.8	1.9	9.4	2.2	1.1	2.7
U.S.	23.3	15.6	13.1	5.9	5.3	4.2	3.8	2.5

Note: Figures are percentages and include persons that reported multiple ancestry (eg. if a person reported being Irish and Italian, they were included in both columns); (1) Metropolitan Statistical Area - see Appendix A for areas included
Source: 1990 Census of Population and Housing, Summary Tape File 3C

Age

Area	Median Age (Years)	Age Distribution (%) Under 5	Under 18	18-24	25-44	45-64	65+	80+
City	32.0	7.5	24.3	10.6	37.3	18.0	9.8	2.0
MSA[1]	32.7	7.2	24.8	10.9	34.2	19.3	10.9	2.2
U.S.	32.9	7.3	25.6	10.5	32.6	18.7	12.5	2.8

Note: (1) Metropolitan Statistical Area - see Appendix A for areas included
Source: 1990 Census of Population and Housing, Summary Tape File 3C

Male/Female Ratio

Area	Number of males per 100 females (all ages)	Number of males per 100 females (18 years old+)
City	90.2	86.7
MSA[1]	93.0	89.8
U.S.	95.0	91.9

Note: (1) Metropolitan Statistical Area - see Appendix A for areas included
Source: 1990 Census of Population, General Population Characteristics

INCOME

Per Capita/Median/Average Income

Area	Per Capita ($)	Median Household ($)	Average Household ($)
City	16,793	31,873	41,578
MSA[1]	14,611	31,125	38,214
U.S.	14,420	30,056	38,453

Note: all figures are for 1989; (1) Metropolitan Statistical Area - see Appendix A for areas included
Source: 1990 Census of Population and Housing, Summary Tape File 3C

Household Income Distribution by Race

Income ($)	City (%)					U.S. (%)				
	Total	White	Black	Other	Hisp.[1]	Total	White	Black	Other	Hisp.[1]
Less than 5,000	5.5	2.8	12.3	4.3	5.1	6.2	4.8	15.2	8.6	8.8
5,000 - 9,999	6.7	5.3	10.3	4.9	2.9	9.3	8.6	14.2	9.9	11.1
10,000 - 14,999	7.5	6.0	11.2	7.4	7.0	8.8	8.5	11.0	9.8	11.0
15,000 - 24,999	18.0	16.3	22.2	21.9	25.0	17.5	17.3	18.9	18.5	20.5
25,000 - 34,999	17.2	17.0	17.5	19.2	21.7	15.8	16.1	14.2	15.4	16.4
35,000 - 49,999	18.8	20.1	15.4	20.1	18.6	17.9	18.6	13.3	16.1	16.0
50,000 - 74,999	15.7	18.6	8.6	16.2	14.2	15.0	15.8	9.3	13.4	11.1
75,000 - 99,999	5.6	7.2	1.7	4.0	2.7	5.1	5.5	2.6	4.7	3.1
100,000+	5.1	6.8	0.9	2.1	2.8	4.4	4.8	1.3	3.7	1.9

Note: all figures are for 1989; (1) people of Hispanic origin can be of any race
Source: 1990 Census of Population and Housing, Summary Tape File 3C

Effective Buying Income

Area	Per Capita ($)	Median Household ($)	Average Household ($)
City	18,589	36,642	46,138
MSA[1]	16,599	35,921	43,456
U.S.	15,444	33,201	41,849

Note: data as of 1/1/97; (1) Metropolitan Statistical Area - see Appendix A for areas included
Source: Standard Rate & Data Service, Newspaper Advertising Source, 2/98

Effective Household Buying Income Distribution

Area	% of Households Earning						
	$10,000 -$19,999	$20,000 -$34,999	$35,000 -$49,999	$50,000 -$74,999	$75,000 -$99,000	$100,000 -$124,999	$125,000 and up
City	13.6	24.2	19.2	19.8	7.6	2.7	3.1
MSA[1]	14.6	23.7	19.6	20.2	7.1	2.3	2.2
U.S.	16.5	23.4	18.3	18.2	6.4	2.1	2.4

Note: data as of 1/1/97; (1) Metropolitan Statistical Area - see Appendix A for areas included
Source: Standard Rate & Data Service, Newspaper Advertising Source, 2/98

Poverty Rates by Race and Age

Area	Total (%)	By Race (%)				By Age (%)		
		White	Black	Other	Hisp.[2]	Under 5 years old	Under 18 years old	65 years and over
City	10.8	5.1	22.5	12.2	9.9	18.4	16.0	13.8
MSA[1]	9.6	6.2	22.9	11.6	11.1	14.3	12.9	15.2
U.S.	13.1	9.8	29.5	23.1	25.3	20.1	18.3	12.8

Note: figures show the percent of people living below the poverty line in 1989. The average poverty threshold was $12,674 for a family of four in 1989; (1) Metropolitan Statistical Area - see Appendix A for areas included; (2) people of Hispanic origin can be of any race
Source: 1990 Census of Population and Housing, Summary Tape File 3C

EMPLOYMENT

Labor Force and Employment

Area	Civilian Labor Force			Workers Employed		
	Dec. '95	Dec. '96	% Chg.	Dec. '95	Dec. '96	% Chg.
City	267,762	263,588	-1.6	260,166	257,530	-1.0
MSA[1]	745,185	735,222	-1.3	720,854	717,807	-0.4
U.S.	134,583,000	136,742,000	1.6	127,903,000	130,785,000	2.3

Note: Data is not seasonally adjusted and covers workers 16 years of age and older;
(1) Metropolitan Statistical Area - see Appendix A for areas included
Source: Bureau of Labor Statistics, http://stats.bls.gov

Charlotte was listed among the top 20 metro areas (out of 114 major areas) in terms of projected job growth from 1997 to 2002 with an annual percent change of 2.1%.
Standard & Poor's DRI, July 23, 1997

Unemployment Rate

Area	1997											
	Jan.	Feb.	Mar.	Apr.	May	Jun.	Jul.	Aug.	Sep.	Oct.	Nov.	Dec.
City	3.2	3.0	2.7	2.4	3.0	3.5	3.2	3.3	2.9	2.6	2.6	2.3
MSA[1]	3.5	3.3	2.9	2.6	3.0	3.6	3.5	3.3	3.0	2.8	2.6	2.4
U.S.	5.9	5.7	5.5	4.8	4.7	5.2	5.0	4.8	4.7	4.4	4.3	4.4

Note: Data is not seasonally adjusted and covers workers 16 years of age and older; All figures are percentages; (1) Metropolitan Statistical Area - see Appendix A for areas included
Source: Bureau of Labor Statistics, http://stats.bls.gov

Employment by Industry

Sector	MSA[1]		U.S.
	Number of Employees	Percent of Total	Percent of Total
Services	188,200	24.5	29.0
Retail Trade	132,700	17.3	18.5
Government	92,800	12.1	16.1
Manufacturing	145,200	18.9	15.0
Finance/Insurance/Real Estate	54,000	7.0	5.7
Wholesale Trade	54,700	7.1	5.4
Transportation/Public Utilities	53,200	6.9	5.3
Construction/Mining	47,400	6.2	5.0

Note: Figures cover non-farm employment as of 12/97 and are not seasonally adjusted; (1) Metropolitan Statistical Area - see Appendix A for areas included
Source: Bureau of Labor Statistics, http://stats.bls.gov

Employment by Occupation

Occupation Category	City (%)	MSA[1] (%)	U.S. (%)
White Collar	65.3	55.6	58.1
Executive/Admin./Management	15.0	12.1	12.3
Professional	13.7	11.4	14.1
Technical & Related Support	3.7	3.4	3.7
Sales	15.0	12.8	11.8
Administrative Support/Clerical	17.8	15.9	16.3
Blue Collar	22.0	32.4	26.2
Precision Production/Craft/Repair	8.8	12.7	11.3
Machine Operators/Assem./Insp.	5.6	11.0	6.8
Transportation/Material Movers	3.6	4.0	4.1
Cleaners/Helpers/Laborers	4.0	4.6	3.9
Services	11.9	10.7	13.2
Farming/Forestry/Fishing	0.9	1.3	2.5

Note: figures cover employed persons 16 years old and over; (1) Metropolitan Statistical Area - see Appendix A for areas included
Source: 1990 Census of Population and Housing, Summary Tape File 3C

Occupational Employment Projections: 1992 - 2000

Occupations Expected to have the Largest Job Growth (ranked by numerical growth)	Fast-Growing Occupations[1] (ranked by percent growth)
1. Salespersons, retail	1. Taxi drivers & chauffeurs
2. Cashiers	2. Computer engineers
3. General office clerks	3. Systems analysts
4. Registered nurses	4. Human services workers
5. Waiters & waitresses	5. Teachers, special education
6. General managers & top executives	6. Physical therapy assistants and aides
7. First line supervisor, sales & related	7. Corrections officers & jailers
8. Nursing aides/orderlies/attendants	8. Personal and home care aides
9. Janitors/cleaners/maids, ex. priv. hshld.	9. Paralegals
10. Guards	10. Travel agents

Projections cover Cabarrus, Gaston, Lincoln, Mecklenburg, Rowan and Union Counties.
Note: (1) Excludes occupations with total job growth less than 100
Source: Employment Security Commission of North Carolina, Occupational Trends: 1992 to 2000

Average Wages

Occupation	Wage	Occupation	Wage
Professional/Technical/Clerical	$/Week	**Health/Protective Services**	$/Week
Accountants III	778	Corrections Officers	404
Attorneys III	-	Firefighters	569
Budget Analysts III	-	Nurses, Licensed Practical II	-
Buyers/Contracting Specialists II	658	Nurses, Registered II	-
Clerks, Accounting III	448	Nursing Assistants II	-
Clerks, General III	397	Police Officers I	557
Computer Operators II	467	**Hourly Workers**	$/Hour
Computer Programmers II	605	Forklift Operators	10.58
Drafters II	453	General Maintenance Workers	9.44
Engineering Technicians III	-	Guards I	6.39
Engineering Technicians, Civil III	-	Janitors	6.54
Engineers III	910	Maintenance Electricians	14.54
Key Entry Operators I	334	Maintenance Electronics Techs II	15.82
Personnel Assistants III	481	Maintenance Machinists	14.85
Personnel Specialists III	830	Maintenance Mechanics, Machinery	13.78
Secretaries III	526	Material Handling Laborers	7.25
Switchboard Operator-Receptionist	352	Motor Vehicle Mechanics	14.69
Systems Analysts II	870	Shipping/Receiving Clerks	9.54
Systems Analysts Supervisor/Mgr II	-	Tool and Die Makers	14.35
Tax Collectors II	-	Truckdrivers, Tractor Trailer	12.91
Word Processors II	488	Warehouse Specialists	-

Note: Wage data includes full-time workers only for 10/95 and cover the Metropolitan Statistical Area (see Appendix A for areas included). Dashes indicate that data was not available.
Source: Bureau of Labor Statistics, Occupational Compensation Survey, 5/96

TAXES

Major State and Local Tax Rates

State Corp. Income (%)	State Personal Income (%)	Residential Property (effective rate per $100)	Sales & Use State (%)	Sales & Use Local (%)	State Gasoline (cents/ gallon)	State Cigarette (cents/ 20-pack)
7.5	6.0 - 7.75	1.12	4.0	2.0	22.6	5

Note: Personal/corporate income tax rates as of 1/97. Sales, gasoline and cigarette tax rates as of 1/98.
Source: Federation of Tax Administrators, www.taxadmin.org; Washington D.C. Department of Finance and Revenue, Tax Rates and Tax Burdens in the District of Columbia: A Nationwide Comparison, June 1997; Chamber of Commerce

Total Taxes Per Capita and as a Percent of Income

Area	Per Capita Income ($)	Per Capita Taxes ($)			Taxes as Pct. of Income (%)		
		Total	Federal	State/ Local	Total	Federal	State/ Local
North Carolina	24,648	8,158	5,419	2,739	33.1	22.0	11.1
U.S.	26,187	9,205	6,127	3,078	35.2	23.4	11.8

Note: Figures are for 1997
Source: Tax Foundation, Web Site, www.taxfoundation.org

Estimated Tax Burden

Area	State Income	Local Income	Property	Sales	Total
Charlotte	2,994	0	2,700	822	6,516

Note: The numbers are estimates of taxes paid by a married couple with two kids and annual earnings of $65,000. Sales tax estimates assume they spend average amounts on food, clothing, household goods and gasoline. Property tax estimates assume they live in a $225,000 home.
Source: Kiplinger's Personal Finance Magazine, June 1997

COMMERCIAL REAL ESTATE

Office Market

Class/ Location	Total Space (sq. ft.)	Vacant Space (sq. ft.)	Vac. Rate (%)	Under Constr. (sq. ft.)	Net Absorp. (sq. ft.)	Rental Rates ($/sq.ft./yr.)
Class A						
CBD	6,024,530	140,835	2.3	1,085,500	428,467	22.00-28.00
Outside CBD	8,223,477	500,500	6.1	1,059,200	941,082	16.00-24.00
Class B						
CBD	3,666,076	420,000	11.5	0	157,372	15.00-19.00
Outside CBD	4,704,255	371,539	7.9	50,000	242,946	12.00-18.00

Note: Data as of 10/97 and covers Charlotte; CBD = Central Business District; n/a not available;
Source: Society of Industrial and Office Realtors, 1998 Comparative Statistics of Industrial and Office Real Estate Markets

"The Charlotte metropolitan area boasts a low cost of doing business, a low cost of living, and solid track record of job creation which has led to strong in-migration. Financial services continue to be the primary driver of the local economy and a major component in the demand for office space. Our SIOR reporter anticipates a moderate acceleration in both absorption and construction during 1998 leading to an increase in vacancy rates. In addition, free rent and more allowances in suburban buildings started to appear during the later part of 1997. With more vacant space on the market, some of the upward pressure on rental rates will be removed. Landlord concessions should become more common during 1998." *Society of Industrial and Office Realtors, 1998 Comparative Statistics of Industrial and Office Real Estate Markets*

Industrial Market

Location	Total Space (sq. ft.)	Vacant Space (sq. ft.)	Vac. Rate (%)	Under Constr. (sq. ft.)	Net Absorp. (sq. ft.)	Lease ($/sq.ft./yr.)
Central City	3,507,861	571,781	16.3	n/a	-24,555	n/a
Suburban	122,492,139	17,393,883	14.2	1,190,200	2,412,122	3.00-5.00

Note: Data as of 10/97 and covers Charlotte; n/a not available
Source: Society of Industrial and Office Realtors, 1998 Comparative Statistics of Industrial and Office Real Estate Markets

"Approximately 850,000 sq. ft. of warehouse space and 340,000 sq. ft. of 'flex' space were being speculatively developed during the latter part of 1997. This space is contained within new suburban business parks. Prospects for growth are improving as Charlotte's beltway becomes completed in many areas. New development, could be restricted by lack of utilities in out-reach areas. Employment growth is expected to slow somewhat when compared to the past five years. Projections call for annual growth of 1.6 percent per year through 2001, versus the 3.5 percent annual growth measured since 1992. Our local SIOR reporter positively points out that availability in the Charlotte market will grab the attention of potential corporate relocations." *Society of Industrial and Office Realtors, 1998 Comparative Statistics of Industrial and Office Real Estate Markets*

Retail Market

Shopping Center Inventory (sq. ft.)	Shopping Center Construction (sq. ft.)	Construction as a Percent of Inventory (%)	Torto Wheaton Rent Index[1] ($/sq. ft.)
27,498,000	782,000	2.8	10.61

Note: Data as of 1997 and covers the Metropolitan Statistical Area - see Appendix A for areas included; (1) Index is based on a model that predicts what the average rent should be for leases with certain characteristics, in certain locations during certain years.
Source: National Association of Realtors, 1997-1998 Market Conditions Report

"The retail rent index in Charlotte has leveled off at around $10.50 as demand has caught up with some very ambitious building in recent years. The Charlotte economy has been outperforming the nation in nearly every category. Employment and population growth have been among the strongest in the nation, and average annual wages have grown over 5.0% per year compared to 3.7% nationally. However, developers realize that Charlotte's growth won't continue forever. New construction is expected to diminish over the next few years." National Association of Realtors, 1997-1998 Market Conditions Report

COMMERCIAL UTILITIES

Typical Monthly Electric Bills

Area	Commercial Service ($/month)		Industrial Service ($/month)	
	12 kW demand 1,500 kWh	100 kW demand 30,000 kWh	1,000 kW demand 400,000 kWh	20,000 kW demand 10,000,000 kWh
City	151	1,832	21,037	458,608
U.S.	162	2,360	25,590	545,677

Note: Based on rates in effect July 1, 1997
Source: Edison Electric Institute, Typical Residential, Commercial and Industrial Bills, Summer 1997

TRANSPORTATION

Transportation Statistics

Avg. travel time to work (min.)	21.5
Interstate highways	I-77; I-85
Bus lines	
In-city	Charlotte Transit, 152 vehicles
Inter-city	2
Passenger air service	
Airport	Charlotte-Douglas International
Airlines	14
Aircraft departures	136,774 (1995)
Enplaned passengers	9,588,900 (1995)
Rail service	Amtrak
Motor freight carriers	294
Major waterways/ports	None

Source: OAG, Business Travel Planner, Summer 1997; Editor & Publisher Market Guide, 1998; FAA Airport Activity Statistics, 1996; Amtrak National Time Table, Northeast Timetable, Fall/Winter 1997-98; 1990 Census of Population and Housing, STF 3C; Chamber of Commerce/Economic Development 1997; Jane's Urban Transport Systems 1997-98; Transit Fact Book 1997

A survey of 90,000 airline passengers during the first half of 1997 ranked most of the largest airports in the U.S. Charlotte-Douglas International ranked number 3 out of 36. Criteria: cleanliness, quality of restaurants, attractiveness, speed of baggage delivery, ease of reaching gates, available ground transportation, ease of following signs and closeness of parking. *Plog Research Inc., First Half 1997*

Means of Transportation to Work

Area	Car/Truck/Van		Public Transportation			Bicycle	Walked	Other Means	Worked at Home
	Drove Alone	Car-pooled	Bus	Subway	Railroad				
City	77.2	12.9	4.3	0.0	0.0	0.2	2.2	1.0	2.2
MSA[1]	78.8	14.5	1.7	0.0	0.0	0.1	2.1	1.0	1.9
U.S.	73.2	13.4	3.0	1.5	0.5	0.4	3.9	1.2	3.0

Note: figures shown are percentages and only include workers 16 years old and over; (1) Metropolitan Statistical Area - see Appendix A for areas included
Source: 1990 Census of Population and Housing, Summary Tape File 3C

BUSINESSES

Major Business Headquarters

Company Name	1997 Rankings	
	Fortune 500	Forbes 500
Baker & Taylor	-	249
Belk Stores Services	-	74
Duke Power	300	-
First Union	114	-
GS Industries	-	212
Hendrick Automotive Group	-	53
Nationsbank	62	-
Nucor	371	-

Note: Companies listed are located in the city; Dashes indicate no ranking
Fortune 500: companies that produce a 10-K are ranked 1 - 500 based on 1996 revenue
Forbes 500: private companies are ranked 1 - 500 based on 1996 revenue
Source: Forbes 12/1/97; Fortune 4/28/97

Women-Owned Businesses: Number, Employment, Sales and Share

Area	Women-Owned Businesses in 1996				Share of Women-Owned Businesses in 1996	
	Number	Employment	Sales ($000)	Rank[2]	Percent (%)	Rank[3]
MSA[1]	36,000	87,000	11,069,300	40	34.2	44

Note: (1) Metropolitan Statistical Area - see Appendix A for areas included; (2) Calculated on an averaging of number of businesses, employment and sales and ranges from 1 to 50 where 1 is best; (3) Ranges from 1 to 50 where 1 is best
Source: The National Foundation for Women Business Owners, 1996 Facts on Women-Owned Businesses: Trends in the Top 50 Metropolitan Areas, March 26, 1997

Women-Owned Businesses: Growth

Area	Growth in Women-Owned Businesses (% change from 1987 to 1996)				Relative Growth in the Number of Women-Owned and All Businesses (% change from 1987 to 1996)			
	Num.	Empl.	Sales	Rank[2]	Women-Owned	All Firms	Absolute Difference	Relative Difference
MSA[1]	104.8	241.4	303.4	11	104.8	73.6	31.2	1.4:1

Note: (1) Metropolitan Statistical Area - see Appendix A for areas included; (2) Calculated on an averaging of the percent growth of number of businesses, employment and sales and ranges from 1 to 50 where 1 is best
Source: The National Foundation for Women Business Owners, 1996 Facts on Women-Owned Businesses: Trends in the Top 50 Metropolitan Areas, March 26, 1997

Minority Business Opportunity

Charlotte is home to two companies which are on the Black Enterprise Auto Dealer 100 list (largest based on gross sales): S & J Enterprises (Ford/Subaru); Hubbard Investments (GM/Isuzu/Chrysler/Kia). Criteria: 1) operational in previous calendar year; 2) at least 51% black-owned. *Black Enterprise, June 1997*

Charlotte is home to one company which is on the Hispanic Business Fastest-Growing 100 list (greatest sales growth from 1992 to 1996): Zapata Engineering (engineering and construction svcs.) *Hispanic Business, July/August 1997*

Small Business Opportunity

Charlotte was included among *Entrepreneur* magazines listing of the "20 Best Cities for Small Business." It was ranked #5 among large metro areas. Criteria: risk of failure, business performance, economic growth, affordability and state attitude towards business. *Entrepreneur, 10/97*

HOTELS & MOTELS

Hotels/Motels

Area	Hotels/ Motels	Rooms	Luxury-Level Hotels/Motels		Average Minimum Rates ($)		
			♦♦♦♦	♦♦♦♦♦	♦♦	♦♦♦	♦♦♦♦
City	55	8,446	1	0	71	100	200
Airport	15	2,275	0	0	n/a	n/a	n/a
Suburbs	18	2,175	0	0	n/a	n/a	n/a
Total	88	12,896	1	0	n/a	n/a	n/a

Note: n/a not available; Classifications range from one diamond (budget properties with basic amenities) to five diamond (luxury properties with the finest service, rooms and facilities).
Source: OAG, Business Travel Planner, Summer 1997

CONVENTION CENTERS

Major Convention Centers

Center Name	Meeting Rooms	Exhibit Space (sf)
Charlotte Convention Center	46	412,500
New Charlotte Convention Center	46	412,500
Adam's Mark Hotel-Charlotte	31	52,000
Charlotte Merchandise Mart	1	224,000

Source: Trade Shows Worldwide 1997

Living Environment

COST OF LIVING

Cost of Living Index

Composite Index	Housing	Utilities	Groceries	Health Care	Trans-portation	Misc. Goods/ Services
100.5	99.9	104.3	100.6	100.6	97.2	101.0

Note: U.S. = 100
Source: ACCRA, Cost of Living Index, 3rd Quarter 1997

HOUSING

Median Home Prices and Housing Affordability

Area	Median Price[2] 3rd Qtr. 1997 ($)	HOI[3] 3rd Qtr. 1997	Afford-ability Rank[4]
MSA[1]	134,000	57.9	157
U.S.	127,000	63.7	-

Note: (1) Metropolitan Statistical Area - see Appendix A for areas included; (2) U.S. figures calculated from the sales of 625,000 new and existing homes in 195 markets; (3) Housing Opportunity Index - percent of homes sold that were within the reach of the median income household at the prevailing mortgage interest rate; (4) Rank is from 1-195 with 1 being most affordable
Source: National Association of Home Builders, Housing Opportunity Index, 3rd Quarter 1997

It is projected that the median price of existing single-family homes in the metro area will increase by 5.5% in 1998. Nationwide, home prices are projected to increase 6.6%. *Kiplinger's Personal Finance Magazine, January 1998*

Average New Home Price

Area	Price ($)
City	138,400
U.S.	135,710

Note: Figures are based on a new home with 1,800 sq. ft. of living area on an 8,000 sq. ft. lot.
Source: ACCRA, Cost of Living Index, 3rd Quarter 1997

Average Apartment Rent

Area	Rent ($/mth)
City	543
U.S.	569

Note: Figures are based on an unfurnished two bedroom, 1-1/2 or 2 bath apartment, approximately 950 sq. ft. in size, excluding all utilities except water
Source: ACCRA, Cost of Living Index, 3rd Quarter 1997

RESIDENTIAL UTILITIES

Average Residential Utility Costs

Area	All Electric ($/mth)	Part Electric ($/mth)	Other Energy ($/mth)	Phone ($/mth)
City	109.12	-	-	17.51
U.S.	109.40	55.25	43.64	19.48

Source: ACCRA, Cost of Living Index, 3rd Quarter 1997

HEALTH CARE

Average Health Care Costs

Area	Hospital ($/day)	Doctor ($/visit)	Dentist ($/visit)
City	367.00	52.80	58.60
U.S.	392.91	48.76	60.84

Note: Hospital - based on a semi-private room. Doctor - based on a general practitioner's routine exam of an established patient. Dentist - based on adult teeth cleaning and periodic oral exam.
Source: ACCRA, Cost of Living Index, 3rd Quarter 1997

Distribution of Office-Based Physicians

Area	Family/Gen. Practitioners	Specialists		
		Medical	Surgical	Other
MSA[1]	279	667	622	514

Note: Data as of 12/31/96; (1) Metropolitan Statistical Area - see Appendix A for areas included
Source: American Medical Assn., Physician Characteristics & Distribution in the U.S., 1997-1998

Hospitals

Charlotte has 4 general medical and surgical hospitals, 1 eye, ear, nose and throat, 1 rehabilitation, 1 orthopedic, 1 alcoholism and other chemical dependency. *AHA Guide to the Healthcare Field 1997-98*

EDUCATION

Public School District Statistics

District Name	Num. Sch.	Enroll.	Classroom Teachers[1]	Pupils per Teacher	Minority Pupils (%)	Current Exp.[2] ($/pupil)
Charlotte-Mecklenburg Schools	126	89,544	5,248	17.1	46.6	4,951

Note: Data covers the 1995-1996 school year unless otherwise noted; (1) Excludes teachers reported as working in school district offices rather than in schools; (2) Based on 1993-94 enrollment collected by the Census Bureau, not the enrollment figure shown in column 3; SD = School District; ISD = Independent School District; n/a not available
Source: National Center for Education Statistics, Common Core of Data Survey; Bureau of the Census

Educational Quality

School District	Education Quotient[1]	Graduate Outcome[2]	Community Index[3]	Resource Index[4]
Charlotte-Mecklenburg	94.0	84.0	131.0	68.0

Note: Nearly 1,000 secondary school districts were rated in terms of educational quality. The scores range from a low of 50 to a high of 150; (1) Average of the Graduate Outcome, Community and Resource indexes; (2) Based on graduation rates and college board scores (SAT/ACT); (3) Based on the surrounding community's average level of education and the area's average income level; (4) Based on teacher salaries, per-pupil expenditures and student-teacher ratios.
Source: Expansion Management, Ratings Issue 1997

Educational Attainment by Race

Area	High School Graduate (%)					Bachelor's Degree (%)				
	Total	White	Black	Other	Hisp.[2]	Total	White	Black	Other	Hisp.[2]
City	81.0	86.9	66.5	71.9	73.2	28.4	34.5	12.5	27.7	21.9
MSA[1]	72.5	74.8	61.7	68.7	69.5	19.6	21.4	10.5	24.5	19.9
U.S.	75.2	77.9	63.1	60.4	49.8	20.3	21.5	11.4	19.4	9.2

Note: figures shown cover persons 25 years old and over; (1) Metropolitan Statistical Area - see Appendix A for areas included; (2) people of Hispanic origin can be of any race
Source: 1990 Census of Population and Housing, Summary Tape File 3C

School Enrollment by Type

Area	Preprimary				Elementary/High School			
	Public		Private		Public		Private	
	Enrollment	%	Enrollment	%	Enrollment	%	Enrollment	%
City	4,071	53.5	3,540	46.5	55,638	89.3	6,640	10.7
MSA[1]	10,978	56.1	8,605	43.9	176,791	92.7	13,957	7.3
U.S.	2,679,029	59.5	1,824,256	40.5	38,379,689	90.2	4,187,099	9.8

Note: figures shown cover persons 3 years old and over;
(1) Metropolitan Statistical Area - see Appendix A for areas included
Source: 1990 Census of Population and Housing, Summary Tape File 3C

School Enrollment by Race

Area	Preprimary (%)				Elementary/High School (%)			
	White	Black	Other	Hisp.[1]	White	Black	Other	Hisp.[1]
City	67.5	30.4	2.0	1.3	53.0	43.8	3.2	1.4
MSA[2]	78.5	19.9	1.6	0.8	71.2	26.7	2.0	1.0
U.S.	80.4	12.5	7.1	7.8	74.1	15.6	10.3	12.5

Note: figures shown cover persons 3 years old and over; (1) people of Hispanic origin can be of any race; (2) Metropolitan Statistical Area - see Appendix A for areas included
Source: 1990 Census of Population and Housing, Summary Tape File 3C

SAT/ACT Scores

Area/District	1997 SAT				1997 ACT	
	Percent of Graduates Tested (%)	Average Math Score	Average Verbal Score	Average Combined Score	Percent of Graduates Tested (%)	Average Composite Score
Charlotte-Mecklenburg	69	497	494	991	9	19.6
State	59	488	490	978	11	19.3
U.S.	42	511	505	1,016	36	21.0

Note: Math and verbal SAT scores are out of a possible 800; ACT scores are out of a possible 36
Caution: Comparing or ranking states/cities on the basis of SAT/ACT scores alone is invalid and strongly discouraged by the The College Board and The American College Testing Program as students who take the tests are self-selected and do not represent the entire student population.
Source: Charlotte-Mecklenburg Schools, Research, Assessment & Planning, 1997; American College Testing Program, 1997; College Board, 1997

Classroom Teacher Salaries in Public Schools

District	B.A. Degree		M.A. Degree		Ph.D. Degree	
	Min. ($)	Max ($)	Min. ($)	Max. ($)	Min. ($)	Max. ($)
Charlotte	23,599	43,765	25,504	46,930	28,034	49,460
Average[1]	26,120	39,270	28,175	44,667	31,643	49,825

Note: Salaries are for 1996-1997; (1) Based on all school districts covered; n/a not available
Source: American Federation of Teachers (unpublished data)

Higher Education

Two-Year Colleges		Four-Year Colleges		Medical Schools	Law Schools	Voc/ Tech
Public	Private	Public	Private			
1	0	1	3	0	0	15

Source: College Blue Book, Occupational Education 1997; Medical School Admission Requirements, 1998-99; Peterson's Guide to Two-Year Colleges, 1997; Peterson's Guide to Four-Year Colleges, 1997; Barron's Guide to Law Schools 1997

MAJOR EMPLOYERS

Major Employers

Cato Corp. (women's clothing stores)	Charlotte Mecklenburg Hospital Authority
Duke Power	Radiator Specialty Co.
First Union Corp.	First Union National Bank
Highland Mills	Knight Publishing
Lance Inc. (cookies & crackers)	Mercy Hospital
NB Holdings Corp. (banking)	Presbyterian Hospital
NationsBank Corp.	Coca-Cola Bottling Co.
Presbyterian-Orthopedic Hospital	Sea-Land Service

Note: companies listed are located in the city
Source: Dun's Business Rankings 1997; Ward's Business Directory, 1997

PUBLIC SAFETY

Crime Rate

Area	All Crimes	Violent Crimes				Property Crimes		
		Murder	Forcible Rape	Robbery	Aggrav. Assault	Burglary	Larceny -Theft	Motor Vehicle Theft
City	9,659.1	12.8	55.2	468.2	1,072.8	1,845.8	5,450.4	753.9
Suburbs[1]	4,753.3	6.0	31.6	113.4	361.7	1,044.4	2,971.6	224.8
MSA[2]	6,841.0	8.9	41.6	264.4	664.3	1,385.4	4,026.4	449.9
U.S.	5,078.9	7.4	36.1	202.4	388.2	943.0	2,975.9	525.9

Note: Crime rate is the number of crimes per 100,000 pop.; (1) defined as all areas within the MSA but located outside the central city; (2) Metropolitan Statistical Area - see Appendix A for areas incl.
Source: FBI Uniform Crime Reports 1996

RECREATION

Culture and Recreation

Museums	Symphony Orchestras	Opera Companies	Dance Companies	Professional Theatres	Zoos	Pro Sports Teams
4	2	1	1	1	0	2

Source: International Directory of the Performing Arts, 1996; Official Museum Directory, 1998; Chamber of Commerce/Economic Development 1997

Library System

The Public Library of Charlotte & Mecklenburg County has 21 branches, holdings of 1,309,612 volumes and a budget of $15,753,616 (1995-1996). *American Library Directory, 1997-1998*

MEDIA

Newspapers

Name	Type	Freq.	Distribution	Circulation
The Catholic News Herald	Religious	1x/wk	Local	35,000
The Charlotte Observer	n/a	7x/wk	Area	236,579
Charlotte Post	Black	1x/wk	Area	11,847
The Mecklenburg Times	General	2x/wk	Local	1,000
Star of Zion	Black	2x/mo	Local	8,000

Note: Includes newspapers with circulations of 1,000 or more located in the city; n/a not available
Source: Burrelle's Media Directory, 1998 Edition

AM Radio Stations

Call Letters	Freq. (kHz)	Target Audience	Station Format	Music Format
WFNZ	610	General	S	n/a
WNOW	1030	Religious	T	n/a
WBT	1110	n/a	N/S/T	n/a
WHVN	1240	General	M/N/T	Christian
WGAS	1420	General	M	Christian
WNMX	1480	General	M/N	n/a
WOGR	1540	Religious	M/N	Adult Contemporary/Christian

Note: Stations included broadcast in the Charlotte metro area; n/a not available
Station Format: E = Educational; M = Music; N = News; S = Sports; T = Talk
Source: Burrelle's Media Directory, 1998 Edition

FM Radio Stations

Call Letters	Freq. (mHz)	Target Audience	Station Format	Music Format
WDAV	89.9	General	M	Classical
WFAE	90.7	General	E/M/N/T	Jazz
WXRC	95.7	General	M/N/S	AOR
WWMG	96.1	General	M/N	Oldies
WTDR	96.9	General	M/N/S	Country
WPEG	97.9	General	M	Urban Contemporary
WRFX	99.7	General	M/N/S	AOR/Adult Standards/Classic Rock
WBAV	101.9	General	M	Adult Contemporary
WSOC	103.7	General	M/N/S	Country
WSSS	104.7	n/a	M	Oldies
WEND	106.5	General	M	Alternative
WLNK	107.9	General	M	Adult Contemporary

Note: Stations included broadcast in the Charlotte metro area; n/a not available
Station Format: E = Educational; M = Music; N = News; S = Sports; T = Talk
Music Format: AOR = Album Oriented Rock; MOR = Middle-of-the-Road
Source: Burrelle's Media Directory, 1998 Edition

Television Stations

Name	Ch.	Affiliation	Type	Owner
WBTV	3	CBS	Commercial	Jefferson-Pilot Communications Company
WSOC	9	ABC	Commercial	Cox Enterprises Inc.
WCCB	18	Fox	Commercial	Bahakel Communications
WCNC	36	NBC	Commercial	Journal Broadcasting of Charlotte Inc.
WTVI	42	PBS	Public	Charlotte-Mecklenburg Public Broadcasting Authority
WJZY	46	UPN	Commercial	Capitol Broadcasting
WFVT	55	WB	Commercial	Family Fifty Five Inc.

Note: Stations included broadcast in the Charlotte metro area
Source: Burrelle's Media Directory, 1998 Edition

CLIMATE

Average and Extreme Temperatures

Temperature	Jan	Feb	Mar	Apr	May	Jun	Jul	Aug	Sep	Oct	Nov	Dec	Ann
Extreme High (°F)	78	81	86	93	97	103	103	103	104	98	85	77	104
Average High (°F)	51	54	62	72	80	86	89	88	82	72	62	53	71
Average Temp. (°F)	41	44	51	61	69	76	79	78	72	61	51	43	61
Average Low (°F)	31	33	40	48	57	65	69	68	62	50	40	33	50
Extreme Low (°F)	-5	5	4	25	32	45	53	53	39	24	11	2	-5

Note: Figures cover the years 1948-1990
Source: National Climatic Data Center, International Station Meteorological Climate Summary, 3/95

Average Precipitation/Snowfall/Humidity

Precip./Humidity	Jan	Feb	Mar	Apr	May	Jun	Jul	Aug	Sep	Oct	Nov	Dec	Ann
Avg. Precip. (in.)	3.6	3.8	4.5	3.0	3.7	3.4	3.9	3.9	3.4	3.2	3.1	3.4	42.8
Avg. Snowfall (in.)	2	2	1	Tr	0	0	0	0	0	0	Tr	1	6
Avg. Rel. Hum. 7am (%)	78	77	78	78	82	83	86	89	89	87	83	79	82
Avg. Rel. Hum. 4pm (%)	53	49	46	43	49	51	54	55	54	50	50	54	51

Note: Figures cover the years 1948-1990; Tr = Trace amounts (<0.05 in. of rain; <0.5 in. of snow)
Source: National Climatic Data Center, International Station Meteorological Climate Summary, 3/95

Weather Conditions

Temperature			Daytime Sky			Precipitation		
10°F & below	32°F & below	90°F & above	Clear	Partly cloudy	Cloudy	0.01 inch or more precip.	0.1 inch or more snow/ice	Thunder-storms
1	65	44	98	142	125	113	3	41

Note: Figures are average number of days per year and covers the years 1948-1990
Source: National Climatic Data Center, International Station Meteorological Climate Summary, 3/95

AIR & WATER QUALITY

Maximum Pollutant Concentrations

	Particulate Matter (ug/m3)	Carbon Monoxide (ppm)	Sulfur Dioxide (ppm)	Nitrogen Dioxide (ppm)	Ozone (ppm)	Lead (ug/m3)
MSA[1] Level	53	5	0.015	0.016	0.13	0.01
NAAQS[2]	150	9	0.140	0.053	0.12	1.50
Met NAAQS?	Yes	Yes	Yes	Yes	No	Yes

Note: (1) Metropolitan Statistical Area - see Appendix A for areas included; (2) National Ambient Air Quality Standards; ppm = parts per million; ug/m3 = micrograms per cubic meter; n/a not available
Source: EPA, National Air Quality and Emissions Trends Report, 1996

Pollutant Standards Index

In the Charlotte MSA (see Appendix A for areas included), the Pollutant Standards Index (PSI) exceeded 100 on 6 days in 1996. A PSI value greater than 100 indicates that air quality would be in the unhealthful range on that day. *EPA, National Air Quality and Emissions Trends Report, 1996*

Drinking Water

Water System Name	Pop. Served	Primary Water Source Type	Number of Violations in Fiscal Year 1997	Type of Violation/ Contaminants
Charlotte-Mecklenburg Utility	413,500	Surface	None	None

Note: Data as of January 16, 1998
Source: EPA, Office of Ground Water and Drinking Water, Safe Drinking Water Information System

Charlotte tap water is alkaline, very soft and fluoridated.
Editor & Publisher Market Guide, 1998

Cincinnati, Ohio

Background

The fashion in which Cincinnati derived its name runs like a group of gallant gentlemen paying excessive praise to long ago elders. After the American Revolution, former Continental Army soldiers formed a fraternal organization called the Society of Cincinnati, alluding to the Roman General Lucius Quinctius Cincinnatus. In 1790 General Arthur St. Clair, a member of that society, and the first governor of the Northwest Territory, felt that this lovely city overlooking the Ohio River could only be called Cincinnati. As if that were not enough, he had to pay homage to fellow fraternal member, Alexander Hamilton. St. Clair named the county, in which Cincinnati lies, after him.

Since its incorporation as a city in 1819, the Miami and Erie Canals have played great roles in Cincinnati's economic growth. Because of these waterways, farmers had the transportation necessary to sell their produce in town. From there, businesses would process the farmers' wares such as corn, pigs, and wheat into products such as whiskey, pork and flour. Incidentally, the South which was Cincinnati's greatest market for pork, made the city's loyalties difficult to declare during the Civil War. However, Cincinnati finally decided upon where its sympathies lay, when its political climate made it a major station of the underground railroad; as well as the haven where Harriet Beecher Stowe could write her classic, "Uncle Tom's Cabin".

In a move to attract overseas tourist dollars, Cincinnati has joined forces with Louisville (KY) and Indianapolis (IN) to market the three city triangle area as a package to foreign tourists, from Britain, France, Germany and later Japan. Cincinnati itself gets at least 200,000 foreign tourists a year and nearly 4 million total tourists annually, with the visitors spending over $2 billion in 1996. What makes this three city experiment unique is that it is the first three-city, three-state partnership aimed solely at European tourists. *New York Times 7/4/97*

Today, the city with its centralized location is not only home to the University of Cincinnati and Xavier University but also has attracted numerous Fortune 500 corporate headquarters.

Cincinnati experiences a rather wide range of temperatures from winter to summer. Summers are warm and quite humid, with the temperature reaching 100 degrees or more in one year out of three. Winters are moderately cold with numerous periods of extensive cloudiness.

General Rankings and Evaluative Comments

- Cincinnati was ranked #194 out of 300 cities by *Money's* 1997 "Survey of the Best Places to Live." Criteria used: health services, crime, economy, housing, education, transportation, weather, leisure and the arts. The city was ranked #257 in 1996 and #145 in 1995. *Money, July 1997; Money, September 1996; Money, September 1995*

- *Ladies Home Journal* ranked America's 200 largest cities based on the qualities women care about most. Cincinnati ranked 19 out of 200. Criteria: low crime rate, good public schools, well-paying jobs, quality health and child care, the presence of women in government, proportion of women-owned businesses, size of the wage gap with men, local economy, divorce rates, the ratio of single men to single women, whether there are laws that require at least the same number of public toilets for women as men, and the probability of good hair days. *Ladies Home Journal, November 1997*

- Cincinnati was ranked #172 out of 219 cities in terms of children's health, safety, and economic well-being. Criteria: total population, percent population change, birth rate, child immunization rate, infant mortality rate, percent low birth weight infants, percent of births to teens, physician-to-population ratio, student-to-teacher ratio, dropout rate, unemployment rate, median family income, percent of children in poverty, violent and property crime rates, number of juvenile arrests for violent crimes as a percent of the total crime index, number of days with pollution standard index (PSI) over 100, pounds toxic releases per 1,000 people and number of superfund sites. *Zero Population Growth, Children's Environmental Index 1997*

- *Yahoo! Internet Life* selected "America's 100 Most Wired Cities & Towns". 50 cities were large and 50 cities were small. Cincinnati ranked 25 out of 50 large cities. Criteria: Internet users per capita, number of networked computers, number of registered domain names, Internet backbone traffic, and the per-capita number of Web sites devoted to each city. *Yahoo! Internet Life, March 1998*

- Procter & Gamble and Ohio National Financial (life insurance), headquartered in Cincinnati, are among the "100 Best Companies to Work for in America." Criteria: trust in management, pride in work/company, camaraderie, company responses to the Hewitt People Practices Inventory, and employee responses to their Great Place to Work survey. The companies also had to be at least 10 years old and have a minimum of 500 employees. *Fortune, January 12, 1998*

- Proctor & Gamble, headquartered in Cincinnati, is among the "100 Best Companies for Working Mothers." Criteria: pay compared with competition, opportunities for women to advance, support for child care, flexible work schedules and family-friendly benefits. *Working Mother, October 1997*

- According to *Working Mother,* "Ohio has been working hard to create child care for its residents and has put serious money into the effort. As we went to press, the governor and state lawmakers appeared ready to boost funding significantly, so that 80,000 kids would receive care by 1998, an increase of 20,000 in two years. That's real progress. Ohio also expanded its pre-K programs.

  The state now helps to fund an innovative program called RISE (Resources and Instruction for Staff Excellence) to train child care teachers to build closer relationships with parents. The $1.25 million grant is being used to create parent-teacher sessions on child development. Such sessions not only cement relationships between teachers and parents, but also help answer parents' questions about discipline and development." *Working Mother, July/August 1997*

Business Environment

STATE ECONOMY

State Economic Profile

"A relatively strong economy has allowed Ohio's legislators to cut personal income taxes over the past several years. Last year, Ohio implemented the second largest tax cut of any state. In addition to personal tax cuts, Ohio is extending large investment tax credits to manufacturers and restructuring the corporate franchise tax. Other tax incentives are also offered to businesses that are expanding or locating in the state.

A number of business considerations are prompting manufacturers to shrink their Ohio operations. These include improvements in efficiency; the desire to shift to non-unionized production facilities, mainly in the low-cost South; cheaper Mexican labor costs; and finally operational consolidations.

Population growth of under 0.4% during 1996 was the weakest in the Great Lakes region; however, net out-migration declined last year compared to the previous two years. Ohio lost about 15,000 residents in 1996. In addition, Ohio does not draw a sufficient number of international migrants to offset the losses.

Ohio's economy will experience slower growth in the near term as manufacturers attempt to avoid inventory build-ups. Longer term, the state's traditional heavy industries will remain vulnerable to cyclical downturns. Diversification into high-tech industries in northern Ohio and the expansion of auto-related manufacturing in the southern part of the state will help dampen the decline. Ohio will continue to develop as a center of financial services and distribution activity. Poor population trends, however, will limit the growth of various population-based industries in the state...." *National Association of Realtors, Economic Profiles: The Fifty States, July 1997*

IMPORTS/EXPORTS

Total Export Sales

Area	1993 ($000)	1994 ($000)	1995 ($000)	1996 ($000)	% Chg. 1993-96	% Chg. 1995-96
MSA[1]	3,898,151	4,056,506	4,256,653	4,784,140	22.7	12.4
U.S.	464,858,354	512,415,609	583,030,524	622,827,063	34.0	6.8

Note: (1) Metropolitan Statistical Area - see Appendix A for areas included
Source: U.S. Department of Commerce, International Trade Association, Metropolitan Area Exports: An Export Performance Report on Over 250 U.S. Cities, October 1997

Imports/Exports by Port

Type	Cargo Value			Share of U.S. Total	
	1995 (US$mil.)	1996 (US$mil.)	% Change 1995-1996	1995 (%)	1996 (%)
Imports	0	0	0	0	0
Exports	0	0	0	0	0

Source: Global Trade Information Services, WaterBorne Trade Atlas 1997

CITY FINANCES

City Government Finances

Component	FY92 ($000)	FY92 (per capita $)
Revenue	675,058	1,873.15
Expenditure	659,385	1,829.66
Debt Outstanding	259,517	720.11
Cash & Securities	1,358,049	3,768.32

Source: U.S. Bureau of the Census, City Government Finances: 1991-92

City Government Revenue by Source

Source	FY92 ($000)	FY92 (per capita $)	FY92 (%)
From Federal Government	26,948	74.78	4.0
From State Governments	50,132	139.11	7.4
From Local Governments	18,636	51.71	2.8
Property Taxes	43,195	119.86	6.4
General Sales Taxes	0	0.00	0.0
Selective Sales Taxes	4,040	11.21	0.6
Income Taxes	175,002	485.60	25.9
Current Charges	116,948	324.51	17.3
Utility/Liquor Store	64,154	178.01	9.5
Employee Retirement[1]	87,809	243.65	13.0
Other	88,194	244.72	13.1

Note: (1) Excludes "city contributions," classified as "nonrevenue," intragovernmental transfers.
Source: U.S. Bureau of the Census, City Government Finances: 1991-92

City Government Expenditures by Function

Function	FY92 ($000)	FY92 (per capita $)	FY92 (%)
Educational Services	0	0.00	0.0
Employee Retirement[1]	53,156	147.50	8.1
Environment/Housing	211,662	587.32	32.1
Government Administration	32,066	88.98	4.9
Interest on General Debt	12,526	34.76	1.9
Public Safety	121,152	336.17	18.4
Social Services	32,368	89.81	4.9
Transportation	74,925	207.90	11.4
Utility/Liquor Store	80,747	224.06	12.2
Other	40,783	113.16	6.2

Note: (1) Payments to beneficiaries including withdrawal of contributions.
Source: U.S. Bureau of the Census, City Government Finances: 1991-92

Municipal Bond Ratings

Area	Moody's	S & P
Cincinnati	Aa2	AA+

Note: n/a not available; n/r not rated
Source: Moody's Bond Record, 2/98; Statistical Abstract of the U.S., 1997; Governing Magazine, 9/97, 3/98

POPULATION

Population Growth

Area	1980	1990	% Chg. 1980-90	July 1996 Estimate	% Chg. 1990-96
City	385,457	364,040	-5.6	345,818	-5.0
MSA[1]	1,401,491	1,452,645	3.6	1,597,352	10.0
U.S.	226,545,805	248,765,170	9.8	265,179,411	6.6

Note: (1) Metropolitan Statistical Area - see Appendix A for areas included
Source: 1980/1990 Census of Housing and Population, Summary Tape File 3C; Census Bureau Population Estimates

Population Characteristics

Race	City 1980 Population	City 1980 %	City 1990 Population	City 1990 %	% Chg. 1980-90	MSA[1] 1990 Population	MSA[1] 1990 %
White	251,332	65.2	220,207	60.5	-12.4	1,246,669	85.8
Black	130,490	33.9	138,110	37.9	5.8	190,029	13.1
Amer Indian/Esk/Aleut	567	0.1	592	0.2	4.4	2,258	0.2
Asian/Pacific Islander	2,332	0.6	4,184	1.1	79.4	11,362	0.8
Other	736	0.2	947	0.3	28.7	2,327	0.2
Hispanic Origin[2]	2,988	0.8	2,319	0.6	-22.4	7,579	0.5

Note: (1) Metropolitan Statistical Area - see Appendix A for areas included; (2) people of Hispanic origin can be of any race
Source: 1980/1990 Census of Housing and Population, Summary Tape File 3C

Ancestry

Area	German	Irish	English	Italian	U.S.	French	Polish	Dutch
City	30.7	14.7	8.5	3.3	3.3	2.3	1.2	1.4
MSA[1]	44.2	20.3	13.8	3.7	4.7	3.3	1.3	2.3
U.S.	23.3	15.6	13.1	5.9	5.3	4.2	3.8	2.5

Note: Figures are percentages and include persons that reported multiple ancestry (eg. if a person reported being Irish and Italian, they were included in both columns); (1) Metropolitan Statistical Area - see Appendix A for areas included
Source: 1990 Census of Population and Housing, Summary Tape File 3C

Age

Area	Median Age (Years)	Age Distribution (%) Under 5	Under 18	18-24	25-44	45-64	65+	80+
City	30.8	8.4	25.0	12.8	32.6	15.7	13.9	3.7
MSA[1]	32.4	7.9	26.8	10.1	32.6	18.4	12.0	2.8
U.S.	32.9	7.3	25.6	10.5	32.6	18.7	12.5	2.8

Note: (1) Metropolitan Statistical Area - see Appendix A for areas included
Source: 1990 Census of Population and Housing, Summary Tape File 3C

Male/Female Ratio

Area	Number of males per 100 females (all ages)	Number of males per 100 females (18 years old+)
City	87.2	81.7
MSA[1]	92.1	87.8
U.S.	95.0	91.9

Note: (1) Metropolitan Statistical Area - see Appendix A for areas included
Source: 1990 Census of Population, General Population Characteristics

INCOME

Per Capita/Median/Average Income

Area	Per Capita ($)	Median Household ($)	Average Household ($)
City	12,547	21,006	29,010
MSA[1]	14,610	30,691	38,344
U.S.	14,420	30,056	38,453

Note: all figures are for 1989; (1) Metropolitan Statistical Area - see Appendix A for areas included
Source: 1990 Census of Population and Housing, Summary Tape File 3C

Household Income Distribution by Race

Income ($)	City (%)					U.S. (%)				
	Total	White	Black	Other	Hisp.[1]	Total	White	Black	Other	Hisp.[1]
Less than 5,000	13.5	7.2	25.0	14.3	19.1	6.2	4.8	15.2	8.6	8.8
5,000 - 9,999	13.6	11.3	17.6	14.5	14.1	9.3	8.6	14.2	9.9	11.1
10,000 - 14,999	10.7	10.3	11.3	15.9	10.0	8.8	8.5	11.0	9.8	11.0
15,000 - 24,999	19.3	20.1	18.1	16.5	14.4	17.5	17.3	18.9	18.5	20.5
25,000 - 34,999	14.7	16.2	12.0	13.0	20.4	15.8	16.1	14.2	15.4	16.4
35,000 - 49,999	14.1	16.6	9.5	11.8	11.2	17.9	18.6	13.3	16.1	16.0
50,000 - 74,999	8.8	11.0	5.0	7.6	7.5	15.0	15.8	9.3	13.4	11.1
75,000 - 99,999	2.7	3.5	1.1	2.7	2.0	5.1	5.5	2.6	4.7	3.1
100,000+	2.6	3.8	0.4	3.6	1.3	4.4	4.8	1.3	3.7	1.9

Note: all figures are for 1989; (1) people of Hispanic origin can be of any race
Source: 1990 Census of Population and Housing, Summary Tape File 3C

Effective Buying Income

Area	Per Capita ($)	Median Household ($)	Average Household ($)
City	14,779	25,127	34,610
MSA[1]	17,065	36,783	45,073
U.S.	15,444	33,201	41,849

Note: data as of 1/1/97; (1) Metropolitan Statistical Area - see Appendix A for areas included
Source: Standard Rate & Data Service, Newspaper Advertising Source, 2/98

Effective Household Buying Income Distribution

Area	% of Households Earning						
	$10,000 -$19,999	$20,000 -$34,999	$35,000 -$49,999	$50,000 -$74,999	$75,000 -$99,000	$100,000 -$124,999	$125,000 and up
City	19.5	23.1	15.2	12.9	4.4	1.4	1.9
MSA[1]	14.3	21.8	18.6	20.4	7.9	2.6	2.8
U.S.	16.5	23.4	18.3	18.2	6.4	2.1	2.4

Note: data as of 1/1/97; (1) Metropolitan Statistical Area - see Appendix A for areas included
Source: Standard Rate & Data Service, Newspaper Advertising Source, 2/98

Poverty Rates by Race and Age

Area	Total (%)	By Race (%)				By Age (%)		
		White	Black	Other	Hisp.[2]	Under 5 years old	Under 18 years old	65 years and over
City	24.3	14.7	39.4	24.8	29.7	42.0	37.4	17.3
MSA[1]	11.4	8.0	34.0	14.1	18.3	19.4	16.4	11.0
U.S.	13.1	9.8	29.5	23.1	25.3	20.1	18.3	12.8

Note: figures show the percent of people living below the poverty line in 1989. The average poverty threshold was $12,674 for a family of four in 1989; (1) Metropolitan Statistical Area - see Appendix A for areas included; (2) people of Hispanic origin can be of any race
Source: 1990 Census of Population and Housing, Summary Tape File 3C

EMPLOYMENT

Labor Force and Employment

Area	Civilian Labor Force			Workers Employed		
	Dec. '95	Dec. '96	% Chg.	Dec. '95	Dec. '96	% Chg.
City	174,911	178,407	2.0	165,942	170,114	2.5
MSA[1]	820,118	840,782	2.5	789,609	812,683	2.9
U.S.	134,583,000	136,742,000	1.6	127,903,000	130,785,000	2.3

Note: Data is not seasonally adjusted and covers workers 16 years of age and older; (1) Metropolitan Statistical Area - see Appendix A for areas included
Source: Bureau of Labor Statistics, http://stats.bls.gov

Unemployment Rate

Area	1997											
	Jan.	Feb.	Mar.	Apr.	May	Jun.	Jul.	Aug.	Sep.	Oct.	Nov.	Dec.
City	6.1	6.0	5.2	4.8	4.9	5.1	4.5	4.6	5.1	5.0	5.0	4.6
MSA[1]	4.7	4.8	4.0	3.7	3.5	3.6	3.3	3.3	3.5	3.6	3.4	3.3
U.S.	5.9	5.7	5.5	4.8	4.7	5.2	5.0	4.8	4.7	4.4	4.3	4.4

Note: Data is not seasonally adjusted and covers workers 16 years of age and older; All figures are percentages; (1) Metropolitan Statistical Area - see Appendix A for areas included
Source: Bureau of Labor Statistics, http://stats.bls.gov

Employment by Industry

Sector	MSA[1]		U.S.
	Number of Employees	Percent of Total	Percent of Total
Services	253,500	29.4	29.0
Retail Trade	170,200	19.7	18.5
Government	103,000	11.9	16.1
Manufacturing	141,400	16.4	15.0
Finance/Insurance/Real Estate	53,800	6.2	5.7
Wholesale Trade	56,500	6.5	5.4
Transportation/Public Utilities	44,700	5.2	5.3
Construction	39,600	4.6	4.5
Mining	700	0.1	0.5

Note: Figures cover non-farm employment as of 12/97 and are not seasonally adjusted; (1) Metropolitan Statistical Area - see Appendix A for areas included
Source: Bureau of Labor Statistics, http://stats.bls.gov

Employment by Occupation

Occupation Category	City (%)	MSA[1] (%)	U.S. (%)
White Collar	61.7	61.4	58.1
Executive/Admin./Management	11.7	13.2	12.3
Professional	17.6	14.5	14.1
Technical & Related Support	4.3	4.1	3.7
Sales	10.5	12.1	11.8
Administrative Support/Clerical	17.7	17.5	16.3
Blue Collar	20.9	25.1	26.2
Precision Production/Craft/Repair	7.8	10.6	11.3
Machine Operators/Assem./Insp.	6.2	6.7	6.8
Transportation/Material Movers	3.0	3.7	4.1
Cleaners/Helpers/Laborers	3.9	4.0	3.9
Services	16.6	12.6	13.2
Farming/Forestry/Fishing	0.7	1.0	2.5

Note: figures cover employed persons 16 years old and over; (1) Metropolitan Statistical Area - see Appendix A for areas included
Source: 1990 Census of Population and Housing, Summary Tape File 3C

Occupational Employment Projections: 1994 - 2005

Occupations Expected to have the Largest Job Growth (ranked by numerical growth)	Fast-Growing Occupations (ranked by percent growth)
1. Waiters & waitresses	1. All other computer scientists
2. Salespersons, retail	2. Personal and home care aides
3. General managers & top executives	3. Computer engineers
4. Computer systems analysts	4. Home health aides
5. Registered nurses	5. Computer systems analysts
6. Hand packers & packagers	6. Computer support specialists
7. Nursing aides/orderlies/attendants	7. Medical assistants
8. Guards	8. Speech-language pathologists/audiologists
9. Receptionists and information clerks	9. Physical therapists
10. Janitors/cleaners/maids, ex. priv. hshld.	10. Human services workers

Projections cover Cincinnati-Hamilton County (SDA 7/8).
Source: Ohio Bureau of Employment Services, SDA 7/8, Job Outlook: 1994-2005

Average Wages

Occupation	Wage	Occupation	Wage
Professional/Technical/Clerical	$/Week	**Health/Protective Services**	$/Week
Accountants III	755	Corrections Officers	465
Attorneys III	-	Firefighters	719
Budget Analysts III	-	Nurses, Licensed Practical II	-
Buyers/Contracting Specialists II	662	Nurses, Registered II	-
Clerks, Accounting III	445	Nursing Assistants II	-
Clerks, General III	414	Police Officers I	682
Computer Operators II	488	**Hourly Workers**	$/Hour
Computer Programmers II	658	Forklift Operators	-
Drafters II	477	General Maintenance Workers	10.63
Engineering Technicians III	584	Guards I	7.04
Engineering Technicians, Civil III	639	Janitors	7.59
Engineers III	980	Maintenance Electricians	19.19
Key Entry Operators I	330	Maintenance Electronics Techs II	-
Personnel Assistants III	452	Maintenance Machinists	14.82
Personnel Specialists III	831	Maintenance Mechanics, Machinery	18.12
Secretaries III	545	Material Handling Laborers	10.41
Switchboard Operator-Receptionist	337	Motor Vehicle Mechanics	16.14
Systems Analysts II	1,014	Shipping/Receiving Clerks	10.86
Systems Analysts Supervisor/Mgr II	1,328	Tool and Die Makers	17.03
Tax Collectors II	-	Truckdrivers, Tractor Trailer	-
Word Processors II	456	Warehouse Specialists	11.99

Note: Wage data includes full-time workers only for 5/96 and cover the Metropolitan Statistical Area (see Appendix A for areas included). Dashes indicate that data was not available.
Source: Bureau of Labor Statistics, Occupational Compensation Survey, 9/96

TAXES

Major State and Local Tax Rates

State Corp. Income (%)	State Personal Income (%)	Residential Property (effective rate per $100)	Sales & Use State (%)	Sales & Use Local (%)	State Gasoline (cents/ gallon)	State Cigarette (cents/ 20-pack)
5.1 - 8.9[a]	0.693 - 7.004	n/a	5.0	1.0	22	24

Note: Personal/corporate income tax rates as of 1/97. Sales, gasoline and cigarette tax rates as of 1/98; (a) Or 5.82 mils times the value of the taxpayer's issued and outstanding share of stock. Minimum tax $50
Source: Federation of Tax Administrators, www.taxadmin.org; Washington D.C. Department of Finance and Revenue, Tax Rates and Tax Burdens in the District of Columbia: A Nationwide Comparison, June 1997; Chamber of Commerce

Total Taxes Per Capita and as a Percent of Income

Area	Per Capita Income ($)	Per Capita Taxes ($)			Taxes as Pct. of Income (%)		
		Total	Federal	State/ Local	Total	Federal	State/ Local
Ohio	25,222	8,829	5,818	3,010	35.0	23.1	11.9
U.S.	26,187	9,205	6,127	3,078	35.2	23.4	11.8

Note: Figures are for 1997
Source: Tax Foundation, Web Site, www.taxfoundation.org

COMMERCIAL REAL ESTATE

Office Market

Class/ Location	Total Space (sq. ft.)	Vacant Space (sq. ft.)	Vac. Rate (%)	Under Constr. (sq. ft.)	Net Absorp. (sq. ft.)	Rental Rates ($/sq.ft./yr.)
Class A						
CBD	6,785,950	453,065	6.7	0	203,209	16.75-23.75
Outside CBD	26,194,880	243,725	0.9	600,000	-243,725	10.00-16.50
Class B						
CBD	5,797,478	948,110	16.4	0	259,209	11.20-18.85
Outside CBD	31,858,350	863,250	2.7	0	117,353	n/a

Note: Data as of 10/97 and covers Cincinnati including Northern Kentucky; CBD = Central Business District; n/a not available;
Source: Society of Industrial and Office Realtors, 1998 Comparative Statistics of Industrial and Office Real Estate Markets

"Continued expansion in services will serve as the main growth engine affecting the office market. The MSA is gaining a reputation as an excellent location for back-office and call-center operations. Frugal office-users will focus on Northern Kentucky's lower cost of doing business as a rationale for relocation to that state. The overall economy is expected to remain strong for the short-term and has already begun to cause some tightness in local labor markets. This phenomena is likely to continue during 1998 despite improving population trends. Three office buildings are being planned for suburban markets along the I-75 and I-71 corridors, totaling 600,000 sq. ft. Although discussions have occurred, no construction is currently planned for the CBD." *Society of Industrial and Office Realtors, 1998 Comparative Statistics of Industrial and Office Real Estate Markets*

Industrial Market

Location	Total Space (sq. ft.)	Vacant Space (sq. ft.)	Vac. Rate (%)	Under Constr. (sq. ft.)	Net Absorp. (sq. ft.)	Net Lease ($/sq.ft./yr.)
Central City	78,700,000	850,000	1.1	0	-400,000	3.15-5.15
Suburban	116,100,000	6,600,000	5.7	1,550,000	2,300,000	2.90-4.90

Note: Data as of 10/97 and covers Cincinnati; n/a not available
Source: Society of Industrial and Office Realtors, 1998 Comparative Statistics of Industrial and Office Real Estate Markets

"This MSA benefits from its proximity to both the southern states and the major midwestern metros of Cleveland, Akron, Detroit, and Chicago to the north. Its well diversified industrial base and strong employers, including P&G and GE Aircraft, provide additional economic stability to this 195 million sq. ft. industrial market. Tax incentives in Cincinnati and generally lower business costs in Northern Kentucky place this MSA in position for stable growth through the end of the decade. Recent spec development has been limited to Northern Kentucky. However, SIOR's reporters expect the next growth spurt to occur on the north side of Cincinnati along I-75. Cyclical changes in the national economy and labor shortages will likely result in slower local growth than in recent years. Nonetheless, this industrial market can be expected to be one of the top performers in the Midwest during 1998." *Society of Industrial and Office Realtors, 1998 Comparative Statistics of Industrial and Office Real Estate Markets*

Retail Market

Shopping Center Inventory (sq. ft.)	Shopping Center Construction (sq. ft.)	Construction as a Percent of Inventory (%)	Torto Wheaton Rent Index[1] ($/sq. ft.)
28,415,000	560,000	2.0	12.40

Note: Data as of 1997 and covers the Metropolitan Statistical Area - see Appendix A for areas included; (1) Index is based on a model that predicts what the average rent should be for leases with certain characteristics, in certain locations during certain years.
Source: National Association of Realtors, 1997-1998 Market Conditions Report

"After declining for three consecutive years, Cincinnati's retail rent index rebounded in 1995, and has inched higher over the past two years. Retail rents currently stand slightly below the Midwest average of $12.27. Sluggish population growth and mild personal income gains have restrained the retail sector. Nonetheless, unprecedented levels of planning and development by city officials and business leaders have aided the area's economy. The city recently attempted to lure Nordstrom to the downtown area, and the Fountain Place development managed to keep Lazarus and Saks from moving to the suburbs. Solid levels of absorption should push retail rents higher over the next few years." *National Association of Realtors, 1997-1998 Market Conditions Report*

COMMERCIAL UTILITIES

Typical Monthly Electric Bills

Area	Commercial Service ($/month)		Industrial Service ($/month)	
	12 kW demand 1,500 kWh	100 kW demand 30,000 kWh	1,000 kW demand 400,000 kWh	20,000 kW demand 10,000,000 kWh
City	179	2,169	23,462	438,748
U.S.	162	2,360	25,590	545,677

Note: Based on rates in effect July 1, 1997
Source: Edison Electric Institute, Typical Residential, Commercial and Industrial Bills, Summer 1997

TRANSPORTATION

Transportation Statistics

Avg. travel time to work (min.)	21.1
Interstate highways	I-71; I-74; I-75
Bus lines	
In-city	SW Ohio Regional TA, 378 vehicles
Inter-city	3
Passenger air service	
Airport	Cincinnati-Northern Kentucky International Airport
Airlines	8
Aircraft departures	89,767 (1995)
Enplaned passengers	5,964,637 (1995)
Rail service	Amtrak
Motor freight carriers	85
Major waterways/ports	Ohio River; Port of Cincinnati

Source: OAG, Business Travel Planner, Summer 1997; Editor & Publisher Market Guide, 1998; FAA Airport Activity Statistics, 1996; Amtrak National Time Table, Northeast Timetable, Fall/Winter 1997-98; 1990 Census of Population and Housing, STF 3C; Chamber of Commerce/Economic Development 1997; Jane's Urban Transport Systems 1997-98; Transit Fact Book 1997

Means of Transportation to Work

Area	Car/Truck/Van		Public Transportation			Bicycle	Walked	Other Means	Worked at Home
	Drove Alone	Car-pooled	Bus	Subway	Railroad				
City	67.4	12.6	10.9	0.0	0.0	0.2	5.9	0.9	2.0
MSA[1]	78.6	11.6	4.1	0.0	0.0	0.1	2.8	0.7	2.1
U.S.	73.2	13.4	3.0	1.5	0.5	0.4	3.9	1.2	3.0

Note: figures shown are percentages and only include workers 16 years old and over; (1) Metropolitan Statistical Area - see Appendix A for areas included
Source: 1990 Census of Population and Housing, Summary Tape File 3C

BUSINESSES

Major Business Headquarters

Company Name	1997 Rankings: Fortune 500	1997 Rankings: Forbes 500
American Financial Group	331	-
Cinergy	415	-
Eagle-Picher Industries	-	230
Federated Dept. Stores	75	-
Kroger	28	-
Procter & Gamble	18	-

Note: Companies listed are located in the city; Dashes indicate no ranking
Fortune 500: companies that produce a 10-K are ranked 1 - 500 based on 1996 revenue
Forbes 500: private companies are ranked 1 - 500 based on 1996 revenue
Source: Forbes 12/1/97; Fortune 4/28/97

Fast-Growing Businesses

Cincinnati was ranked #10 out of 24 (#1 is best) in terms of the best-performing local stocks in 1996 according to the Money/Norby Cities Index. The index measures stocks of companies that have headquarters in 24 metro areas. *Money, 2/7/97*

Women-Owned Businesses: Number, Employment, Sales and Share

Area	Women-Owned Businesses in 1996				Share of Women-Owned Businesses in 1996	
	Number	Employment	Sales ($000)	Rank[2]	Percent (%)	Rank[3]
MSA[1]	44,300	96,500	11,999,400	36	35.4	37

Note: (1) Metropolitan Statistical Area - see Appendix A for areas included; (2) Calculated on an averaging of number of businesses, employment and sales and ranges from 1 to 50 where 1 is best; (3) Ranges from 1 to 50 where 1 is best
Source: The National Foundation for Women Business Owners, 1996 Facts on Women-Owned Businesses: Trends in the Top 50 Metropolitan Areas, March 26, 1997

Women-Owned Businesses: Growth

Area	Growth in Women-Owned Businesses (% change from 1987 to 1996)				Relative Growth in the Number of Women-Owned and All Businesses (% change from 1987 to 1996)			
	Num.	Empl.	Sales	Rank[2]	Women-Owned	All Firms	Absolute Difference	Relative Difference
MSA[1]	85.2	116.9	248.7	33	85.2	56.5	28.7	1.5:1

Note: (1) Metropolitan Statistical Area - see Appendix A for areas included; (2) Calculated on an averaging of the percent growth of number of businesses, employment and sales and ranges from 1 to 50 where 1 is best
Source: The National Foundation for Women Business Owners, 1996 Facts on Women-Owned Businesses: Trends in the Top 50 Metropolitan Areas, March 26, 1997

Minority Business Opportunity

Cincinnati is home to one company which is on the Black Enterprise Auto Dealer 100 list (largest based on gross sales): Kemper Dodge Inc. (Chrysler). Criteria: 1) operational in previous calendar year; 2) at least 51% black-owned. *Black Enterprise, June 1997*

Small Business Opportunity

According to *Forbes*, Cincinnati is home to one of America's 200 best small companies: Meridian Diagnostics. Criteria: companies must be publicly traded, U.S.-based corporations with latest 12-month sales of between $5 and $350 million. Earnings must be at least $1 million for the 12-month period. Limited partnerships, REITs and closed-end mutual funds were not considered. Banks, S&Ls and electric utilities were not included. *Forbes, November 3, 1997*

HOTELS & MOTELS

Hotels/Motels

Area	Hotels/ Motels	Rooms	Luxury-Level Hotels/Motels		Average Minimum Rates ($)		
			♦♦♦♦	♦♦♦♦♦	♦♦	♦♦♦	♦♦♦♦
City	31	6,591	2	0	60	105	170
Airport	15	2,385	0	0	n/a	n/a	n/a
Suburbs	48	6,857	0	0	n/a	n/a	n/a
Total	94	15,833	2	0	n/a	n/a	n/a

Note: n/a not available; Classifications range from one diamond (budget properties with basic amenities) to five diamond (luxury properties with the finest service, rooms and facilities).
Source: OAG, Business Travel Planner, Summer 1997

CONVENTION CENTERS

Major Convention Centers

Center Name	Meeting Rooms	Exhibit Space (sf)
Cincinnati Gardens Arena and Exhibition Center	n/a	53,000
Cincinnati Convention-Exposition Center	41	162,000

Note: n/a not available
Source: Trade Shows Worldwide 1997

Living Environment

COST OF LIVING

Cost of Living Index

Composite Index	Housing	Utilities	Groceries	Health Care	Trans-portation	Misc. Goods/ Services
98.9	96.1	99.2	101.2	95.7	99.3	100.5

Note: U.S. = 100
Source: ACCRA, Cost of Living Index, 3rd Quarter 1997

HOUSING

Median Home Prices and Housing Affordability

Area	Median Price[2] 3rd Qtr. 1997 ($)	HOI[3] 3rd Qtr. 1997	Afford-ability Rank[4]
MSA[1]	106,000	72.6	71
U.S.	127,000	63.7	-

Note: (1) Metropolitan Statistical Area - see Appendix A for areas included; (2) U.S. figures calculated from the sales of 625,000 new and existing homes in 195 markets; (3) Housing Opportunity Index - percent of homes sold that were within the reach of the median income household at the prevailing mortgage interest rate; (4) Rank is from 1-195 with 1 being most affordable
Source: National Association of Home Builders, Housing Opportunity Index, 3rd Quarter 1997

It is projected that the median price of existing single-family homes in the metro area will increase by 11.8% in 1998. Nationwide, home prices are projected to increase 6.6%.
Kiplinger's Personal Finance Magazine, January 1998

Average New Home Price

Area	Price ($)
City	130,868
U.S.	135,710

Note: Figures are based on a new home with 1,800 sq. ft. of living area on an 8,000 sq. ft. lot.
Source: ACCRA, Cost of Living Index, 3rd Quarter 1997

Average Apartment Rent

Area	Rent ($/mth)
City	581
U.S.	569

Note: Figures are based on an unfurnished two bedroom, 1-1/2 or 2 bath apartment, approximately 950 sq. ft. in size, excluding all utilities except water
Source: ACCRA, Cost of Living Index, 3rd Quarter 1997

RESIDENTIAL UTILITIES

Average Residential Utility Costs

Area	All Electric ($/mth)	Part Electric ($/mth)	Other Energy ($/mth)	Phone ($/mth)
City	-	61.45	38.72	21.15
U.S.	109.40	55.25	43.64	19.48

Source: ACCRA, Cost of Living Index, 3rd Quarter 1997

HEALTH CARE

Average Health Care Costs

Area	Hospital ($/day)	Doctor ($/visit)	Dentist ($/visit)
City	390.40	46.60	56.70
U.S.	392.91	48.76	60.84

Note: Hospital - based on a semi-private room. Doctor - based on a general practitioner's routine exam of an established patient. Dentist - based on adult teeth cleaning and periodic oral exam.
Source: ACCRA, Cost of Living Index, 3rd Quarter 1997

Distribution of Office-Based Physicians

Area	Family/Gen. Practitioners	Specialists		
		Medical	Surgical	Other
MSA[1]	370	1,000	772	806

Note: Data as of 12/31/96; (1) Metropolitan Statistical Area - see Appendix A for areas included
Source: American Medical Assn., Physician Characteristics & Distribution in the U.S., 1997-1998

Hospitals

Cincinnati has 12 general medical and surgical hospitals, 1 psychiatric, 1 rehabilitation, 1 alcoholism and other chemical dependency, 1 children's general, 1 children's other specialty. *AHA Guide to the Healthcare Field 1997-98*

According to *U.S. News and World Report,* Cincinnati has 3 of the best hospitals in the U.S.: **University of Cincinnati Hospital**, noted for AIDS, cancer, cardiology, endocrinology, gastroenterology, geriatrics, gynecology, neurology, otolaryngology, pulmonology; **Children's Hospital Medical Center**, noted for pediatrics; **Jewish Hospital of Cincinnati,** noted for geriatrics; *U.S. News and World Report, "America's Best Hospitals", 7/28/97*

EDUCATION

Public School District Statistics

District Name	Num. Sch.	Enroll.	Classroom Teachers[1]	Pupils per Teacher	Minority Pupils (%)	Current Exp.[2] ($/pupil)
Cincinnati City SD	82	52,172	3,050	17.1	68.9	6,438
Deer Park Community City SD	4	1,577	83	19.0	n/a	n/a
Finneytown Local SD	5	1,885	101	18.7	n/a	n/a
Forest Hills Local SD	8	8,174	399	20.5	n/a	n/a
Indian Hill Ex Vill SD	4	1,927	128	15.1	n/a	n/a
Lockland City SD	3	929	49	19.0	n/a	n/a
Madeira City SD	3	1,369	84	16.3	n/a	n/a
Mariemont City SD	4	1,652	97	17.0	n/a	n/a
Mount Healthy City SD	10	4,027	231	17.4	n/a	n/a
North College Hill City SD	4	1,509	72	21.0	n/a	n/a
Northwest Local SD	14	10,720	546	19.6	n/a	n/a
Oak Hills Local SD	8	8,357	389	21.5	n/a	n/a
Princeton City SD	11	6,917	519	13.3	n/a	n/a
Sycamore Community City SD	8	6,161	381	16.2	n/a	n/a
West Clermont Local SD	14	9,160	477	19.2	n/a	n/a
Winton Woods City SD	8	4,527	278	16.3	n/a	n/a

Note: Data covers the 1995-1996 school year unless otherwise noted; (1) Excludes teachers reported as working in school district offices rather than in schools; (2) Based on 1993-94 enrollment collected by the Census Bureau, not the enrollment figure shown in column 3; SD = School District; ISD = Independent School District; n/a not available
Source: National Center for Education Statistics, Common Core of Data Survey; Bureau of the Census

Educational Quality

School District	Education Quotient[1]	Graduate Outcome[2]	Community Index[3]	Resource Index[4]
Cincinnati City	90.0	64.0	100.0	105.0

Note: Nearly 1,000 secondary school districts were rated in terms of educational quality. The scores range from a low of 50 to a high of 150; (1) Average of the Graduate Outcome, Community and Resource indexes; (2) Based on graduation rates and college board scores (SAT/ACT); (3) Based on the surrounding community's average level of education and the area's average income level; (4) Based on teacher salaries, per-pupil expenditures and student-teacher ratios.
Source: Expansion Management, Ratings Issue 1997

Educational Attainment by Race

Area	High School Graduate (%)					Bachelor's Degree (%)				
	Total	White	Black	Other	Hisp.[2]	Total	White	Black	Other	Hisp.[2]
City	69.6	74.7	59.4	83.5	76.4	22.2	28.9	7.9	56.6	42.0
MSA[1]	74.9	76.5	62.7	82.7	79.2	20.5	21.6	9.8	46.8	34.9
U.S.	75.2	77.9	63.1	60.4	49.8	20.3	21.5	11.4	19.4	9.2

Note: figures shown cover persons 25 years old and over; (1) Metropolitan Statistical Area - see Appendix A for areas included; (2) people of Hispanic origin can be of any race
Source: 1990 Census of Population and Housing, Summary Tape File 3C

School Enrollment by Type

Area	Preprimary				Elementary/High School			
	Public		Private		Public		Private	
	Enrollment	%	Enrollment	%	Enrollment	%	Enrollment	%
City	3,651	56.7	2,789	43.3	45,797	81.3	10,524	18.7
MSA[1]	15,601	53.0	13,831	47.0	206,692	81.4	47,137	18.6
U.S.	2,679,029	59.5	1,824,256	40.5	38,379,689	90.2	4,187,099	9.8

Note: figures shown cover persons 3 years old and over;
(1) Metropolitan Statistical Area - see Appendix A for areas included
Source: 1990 Census of Population and Housing, Summary Tape File 3C

School Enrollment by Race

Area	Preprimary (%)				Elementary/High School (%)			
	White	Black	Other	Hisp.[1]	White	Black	Other	Hisp.[1]
City	58.4	39.9	1.7	0.9	45.6	53.0	1.4	0.6
MSA[2]	86.4	12.5	1.0	0.7	82.4	16.3	1.3	0.7
U.S.	80.4	12.5	7.1	7.8	74.1	15.6	10.3	12.5

Note: figures shown cover persons 3 years old and over; (1) people of Hispanic origin can be of any race; (2) Metropolitan Statistical Area - see Appendix A for areas included
Source: 1990 Census of Population and Housing, Summary Tape File 3C

SAT/ACT Scores

Area/District	1996 SAT				1996 ACT	
	Percent of Graduates Tested (%)	Average Math Score	Average Verbal Score	Average Combined Score	Percent of Graduates Tested (%)	Average Composite Score
Cincinnati PS	n/a	509	513	1,022	n/a	19.5
State	24	535	536	1,071	58	21.3
U.S.	41	508	505	1,013	35	20.9

Note: Math and verbal SAT scores are out of a possible 800; ACT scores are out of a possible 36
Caution: Comparing or ranking states/cities on the basis of SAT/ACT scores alone is invalid and strongly discouraged by the The College Board and The American College Testing Program as students who take the tests are self-selected and do not represent the entire student population. 1996 SAT scores cannot be compared to previous years due to recentering.
Source: Cincinnati Public Schools, Assessment & Accountability Services, 1996; American College Testing Program, 1996; College Board, 1996

Classroom Teacher Salaries in Public Schools

District	B.A. Degree		M.A. Degree		Ph.D. Degree	
	Min. ($)	Max ($)	Min. ($)	Max. ($)	Min. ($)	Max. ($)
Cincinnati	26,399	43,431	29,048	47,518	33,268	51,738
Average[1]	26,120	39,270	28,175	44,667	31,643	49,825

Note: Salaries are for 1996-1997; (1) Based on all school districts covered; n/a not available
Source: American Federation of Teachers (unpublished data)

Higher Education

Two-Year Colleges		Four-Year Colleges		Medical Schools	Law Schools	Voc/ Tech
Public	Private	Public	Private			
2	2	1	7	1	1	28

Source: College Blue Book, Occupational Education 1997; Medical School Admission Requirements, 1998-99; Peterson's Guide to Two-Year Colleges, 1997; Peterson's Guide to Four-Year Colleges, 1997; Barron's Guide to Law Schools 1997

MAJOR EMPLOYERS

Major Employers

Belcan Corp. (engineering)	Bethesda Hospital
Children's Hospital Medical Center	Chiquita Brands International
Cincinnati Bell Information Systems	Cincinnati Gas & Electric
Cinergy Corp.	Fifth Third Bank
Gibson Greetings	Good Samaritan Hospital
Jewish Hospital of Cincinnati	Prime Motor Inns Ltd.
Procter & Gamble	Senco Products (power-driven hand tools)
StarBank	Cincinnati Milacron (machinery)
Deaconess Hospital of Cincinnati	Western & Southern Life Insurance

Note: companies listed are located in the city
Source: Dun's Business Rankings 1997; Ward's Business Directory, 1997

PUBLIC SAFETY

Crime Rate

Area	All Crimes	Violent Crimes				Property Crimes		
		Murder	Forcible Rape	Robbery	Aggrav. Assault	Burglary	Larceny -Theft	Motor Vehicle Theft
City	7,616.7	8.9	87.4	492.2	499.4	1,577.7	4,445.7	505.5
Suburbs[1]	n/a	n/a	n/a	n/a	n/a	n/a	n/a	n/a
MSA[2]	n/a	n/a	n/a	n/a	n/a	n/a	n/a	n/a
U.S.	5,078.9	7.4	36.1	202.4	388.2	943.0	2,975.9	525.9

Note: Crime rate is the number of crimes per 100,000 pop.; (1) defined as all areas within the MSA but located outside the central city; (2) Metropolitan Statistical Area - see Appendix A for areas incl.
Source: FBI Uniform Crime Reports 1996

RECREATION

Culture and Recreation

Museums	Symphony Orchestras	Opera Companies	Dance Companies	Professional Theatres	Zoos	Pro Sports Teams
7	1	1	1	3	1	2

Source: International Directory of the Performing Arts, 1996; Official Museum Directory, 1998; Chamber of Commerce/Economic Development 1997

Library System

The Public Library of Cincinnati & Hamilton County has 41 branches, holdings of 4,655,058 volumes and a budget of $43,327,698 (1994). *American Library Directory, 1997-1998*

MEDIA

Newspapers

Name	Type	Freq.	Distribution	Circulation
The American Israelite	Religious	1x/wk	Local	7,000
Catholic Telegraph	Religious	1x/wk	Local	25,000
Christian Standard	Religious	1x/wk	Local	59,000
Cincinnati Carscope	General	1x/wk	Local	24,000
Cincinnati Court Index	n/a	5x/wk	Area	1,500
The Cincinnati Enquirer	General	7x/wk	Area	204,388
Cincinnati Herald	Black	1x/wk	Area	10,000
The Cincinnati Post	n/a	6x/wk	Area	84,919
Cincinnati Valley Courier	General	1x/wk	Local	5,400
Delhi Press	General	1x/wk	Local	10,393
Hilltop Press	General	1x/wk	Local	17,927
Northwest Press	General	1x/wk	Local	16,984
Price Hill Press	General	1x/wk	Local	8,784
Suburban Press and West Chester Press	General	1x/wk	Local	4,800
Tri-County Press	General	1x/wk	Local	7,880
Western Hills Press	General	1x/wk	Local	20,315

Note: Includes newspapers with circulations of 1,000 or more located in the city; n/a not available
Source: Burrelle's Media Directory, 1998 Edition

AM Radio Stations

Call Letters	Freq. (kHz)	Target Audience	Station Format	Music Format
WKRC	550	General	N/S/T	n/a
WLW	700	General	T	n/a
WNOP	740	General	M	Jazz
WTSJ	1050	General	E/M/S/T	Christian
WUBE	1230	General	M	Adult Standards
WAOZ	1360	General	N/T	n/a
WMOH	1450	General	N/S/T	n/a
WCIN	1480	n/a	M	Oldies

Note: Stations included broadcast in the Cincinnati metro area; n/a not available
Station Format: E = Educational; M = Music; N = News; S = Sports; T = Talk
Source: Burrelle's Media Directory, 1998 Edition

FM Radio Stations

Call Letters	Freq. (mHz)	Target Audience	Station Format	Music Format
WAIF	88.3	General	M/N/S	n/a
WJVS	88.3	General	M/N/S	Adult Contemporary/Contemporary Top 40
WOBO	88.7	General	E/M	Adult Contemporary/Country/Easy Listening/Jazz
WGUC	90.9	General	M/N	Classical
WVXU	91.7	General	E/M/N/S	Big Band/Jazz
WOFX	92.5	General	M/N/S	Classic Rock
WAKW	93.3	General	M	Christian
WVMX	94.1	General	M	Adult Contemporary
WVAE	94.9	General	M	Jazz
WYGY	96.5	General	M/N/S	Country
WRRM	98.5	General	M/N	Adult Contemporary
WIZF	100.9	Black	M	Urban Contemporary
WKRQ	101.9	General	M	Adult Contemporary
WEBN	102.7	General	M/N	AOR
WUBE	105.1	General	M/N/S	Country
WAQZ	107.1	General	M	Contemporary Top 40

Note: Stations included broadcast in the Cincinnati metro area; n/a not available
Station Format: E = Educational; M = Music; N = News; S = Sports; T = Talk
Music Format: AOR = Album Oriented Rock; MOR = Middle-of-the-Road
Source: Burrelle's Media Directory, 1998 Edition

Television Stations

Name	Ch.	Affiliation	Type	Owner
WLWT	5	NBC	Commercial	Argyle Television Inc.
WCPO	9	ABC	Commercial	Scripps Howard Broadcasting
WKRC	12	CBS	Commercial	Jacor Communications
WXIX	19	Fox	Commercial	Malrite Communications Group Inc.
WCET	48	PBS	Public	Greater Cincinnati TV Education Foundation
WSTR	64	UPN	Commercial	Sinclair Broadcasting Group

Note: Stations included broadcast in the Cincinnati metro area
Source: Burrelle's Media Directory, 1998 Edition

CLIMATE

Average and Extreme Temperatures

Temperature	Jan	Feb	Mar	Apr	May	Jun	Jul	Aug	Sep	Oct	Nov	Dec	Ann
Extreme High (°F)	74	72	84	89	93	102	103	102	102	89	81	75	103
Average High (°F)	38	42	52	64	74	82	86	85	78	67	53	42	64
Average Temp. (°F)	30	33	43	54	63	72	76	74	68	56	44	34	54
Average Low (°F)	21	24	33	43	52	61	65	63	56	45	35	26	44
Extreme Low (°F)	-25	-15	-11	17	27	39	47	43	33	16	0	-20	-25

Note: Figures cover the years 1948-1990
Source: National Climatic Data Center, International Station Meteorological Climate Summary, 3/95

Average Precipitation/Snowfall/Humidity

Precip./Humidity	Jan	Feb	Mar	Apr	May	Jun	Jul	Aug	Sep	Oct	Nov	Dec	Ann
Avg. Precip. (in.)	3.2	2.9	3.9	3.5	4.0	3.9	4.2	3.1	2.8	2.8	3.4	3.1	40.9
Avg. Snowfall (in.)	7	5	4	1	Tr	0	0	0	0	Tr	2	4	23
Avg. Rel. Hum. 7am (%)	79	78	77	76	79	82	85	87	87	83	79	79	81
Avg. Rel. Hum. 4pm (%)	65	60	55	50	51	53	54	52	52	51	58	65	55

Note: Figures cover the years 1948-1990; Tr = Trace amounts (<0.05 in. of rain; <0.5 in. of snow)
Source: National Climatic Data Center, International Station Meteorological Climate Summary, 3/95

Weather Conditions

Temperature			Daytime Sky			Precipitation		
10°F & below	32°F & below	90°F & above	Clear	Partly cloudy	Cloudy	0.01 inch or more precip.	0.1 inch or more snow/ice	Thunder-storms
14	107	23	80	126	159	127	25	39

Note: Figures are average number of days per year and covers the years 1948-1990
Source: National Climatic Data Center, International Station Meteorological Climate Summary, 3/95

AIR & WATER QUALITY

Maximum Pollutant Concentrations

	Particulate Matter (ug/m³)	Carbon Monoxide (ppm)	Sulfur Dioxide (ppm)	Nitrogen Dioxide (ppm)	Ozone (ppm)	Lead (ug/m³)
MSA[1] Level	72	3	0.045	0.029	0.12	0.22
NAAQS[2]	150	9	0.140	0.053	0.12	1.50
Met NAAQS?	Yes	Yes	Yes	Yes	Yes	Yes

Note: (1) Metropolitan Statistical Area - see Appendix A for areas included; (2) National Ambient Air Quality Standards; ppm = parts per million; ug/m³ = micrograms per cubic meter; n/a not available
Source: EPA, National Air Quality and Emissions Trends Report, 1996

Pollutant Standards Index

In the Cincinnati MSA (see Appendix A for areas included), the Pollutant Standards Index (PSI) exceeded 100 on 2 days in 1996. A PSI value greater than 100 indicates that air quality would be in the unhealthful range on that day. *EPA, National Air Quality and Emissions Trends Report, 1996*

Drinking Water

Water System Name	Pop. Served	Primary Water Source Type	Number of Violations in Fiscal Year 1997	Type of Violation/ Contaminants
City of Cincinnati-Miller	681,120	Surface	None	None

Note: Data as of January 16, 1998
Source: EPA, Office of Ground Water and Drinking Water, Safe Drinking Water Information System

Cincinnati tap water is alkaline, hard and fluoridated.
Editor & Publisher Market Guide, 1998

Cleveland, Ohio

Background

Founded in 1796 by General Moses Cleveland, on what was known as the Western Reserve of Connecticut, Cleveland began with very modest resources. Of all the people that General Cleveland led on his expedition, only three remained in the area. However, the completion of the Erie and Ohio Canals brought badly needed people and industry. By the 1840's, the population had grown by 500% from the decade before. While neighborhoods fell along racial and ethnic lines, the children of these immigrants intermarried, and surpassed their parents on socio-economic levels. Cleveland was a place where the American dream could be realized.

During World War I, a new wave of job seekers flooded Cleveland. These were largely blacks from Southern rural areas, and poor whites from the states of Kentucky, Tennessee, and West Virginia filling in for a shortage of workers in war goods production.

The next wave of job seekers did not have the same opportunities as their predecessors. There were fewer jobs to be had and the men were unskilled, thus making job competition difficult. These collapsing economic conditions set the stage for the urban unrest in the 1960's in the Hough neighborhood.

Cleveland has been undergoing an economic renaissance over the past five years with few projects representing more than $9 billion in capital investment. A public-private partnership has been responsible for the downtown sports complex, the Rock & Roll Hall of Fame and a vibrant new entertainment district. In addition construction is underway on a new football stadium for the Cleveland Browns and "40 percent of home buyers in the city of Cleveland are coming back from the suburbs," a reversal of national trends. The Port of Cleveland is the largest for overseas general cargo on Lake Erie serving over 50 nations. Cleveland is also moving in the direction of becoming a major biotechnology center with its renowned Cleveland Clinic supporting 500 ongoing research projects and being one of only four facilities in the U.S. receiving government funding for research on and development of an artificial heart. *Site Selection Aug/Sept 1997*

The construction of the 360 million Gateway Project in downtown Cleveland, a combination open-air stadium and indoor arena, home to the Cleveland Indians and the Cavaliers basketball team was recently completed.

Cleveland is on the south shore of Lake Erie in northeast Ohio. The metro area has a frontage of 31 miles. The Cuyahoga River runs through the city bisecting it.

Summers are moderately warm and humid with occasional days when temperatures rise above 90 degrees. Winters are relatively cold and cloudy with weather changes occurring every few days due to passing cold fronts.

Precipitation varies widely from year to year, but is generally abundant throughout the year. Snowfalls fluctuate widely. Tornadoes occasionally occur in Cuyahoga County.

General Rankings and Evaluative Comments

- Cleveland was ranked #163 out of 300 cities by *Money's* 1997 "Survey of the Best Places to Live." Criteria used: health services, crime, economy, housing, education, transportation, weather, leisure and the arts. The city was ranked #146 in 1996 and #205 in 1995. *Money, July 1997; Money, September 1996; Money, September 1995*

- Cleveland appeared on *Fortune's* list of "North America's Most Improved Cities" Rank: 6 out of 10. The selected cities satisfied basic business-location needs and also demonstrated improvement over a five- to ten-year period in a number of business and quality-of-life measures.

  "...Indeed, while all the cities included in FORTUNE's list this year have improved, Cleveland, once the butt of many a joke, may have come the furthest.

  During the past decade, Cleveland has become fun, inexpensive, and more prosperous than ever....

  The city's relatively low cost of doing business has attracted the nation's eighth-highest concentration of FORTUNE 500 companies to the Greater Cleveland area....And talk about culture—after you've gawked at the Hall of Fame's collection of 1,000 signed drumsticks, there's the universally acclaimed Cleveland Orchestra....

  Looking toward the future, Clevelanders are confident that their city is going to keep getting better...." *Fortune, 11/24/97*

- *Ladies Home Journal* ranked America's 200 largest cities based on the qualities women care about most. Cleveland ranked 178 out of 200. Criteria: low crime rate, good public schools, well-paying jobs, quality health and child care, the presence of women in government, proportion of women-owned businesses, size of the wage gap with men, local economy, divorce rates, the ratio of single men to single women, whether there are laws that require at least the same number of public toilets for women as men, and the probability of good hair days. *Ladies Home Journal, November 1997*

- Cleveland is among "The Best Places to Raise a Family". Rank: 41 out of 301 metro areas. Criteria: low crime rate, low drug and alcohol abuse, good public schools, high-quality health care, a clean environment, affordable cost of living and strong economic growth. *Reader's Digest, April 1997*

- Cleveland was ranked #208 out of 219 cities in terms of children's health, safety, and economic well-being. Criteria: total population, percent population change, birth rate, child immunization rate, infant mortality rate, percent low birth weight infants, percent of births to teens, physician-to-population ratio, student-to-teacher ratio, dropout rate, unemployment rate, median family income, percent of children in poverty, violent and property crime rates, number of juvenile arrests for violent crimes as a percent of the total crime index, number of days with pollution standard index (PSI) over 100, pounds toxic releases per 1,000 people and number of superfund sites. *Zero Population Growth, Children's Environmental Index 1997*

- *Yahoo! Internet Life* selected "America's 100 Most Wired Cities & Towns". 50 cities were large and 50 cities were small. Cleveland ranked 34 out of 50 large cities. Criteria: Internet users per capita, number of networked computers, number of registered domain names, Internet backbone traffic, and the per-capita number of Web sites devoted to each city. *Yahoo! Internet Life, March 1998*

- TRW Inc., headquartered in Cleveland, is among the "100 Best Companies for Working Mothers." Criteria: pay compared with competition, opportunities for women to advance, support for child care, flexible work schedules and family-friendly benefits. *Working Mother, October 1997*

- According to *Working Mother,* "Ohio has been working hard to create child care for its residents and has put serious money into the effort. As we went to press, the governor and state lawmakers appeared ready to boost funding significantly, so that 80,000 kids would receive care by 1998, an increase of 20,000 in two years. That's real progress. Ohio also expanded its pre-K programs.

The state now helps to fund an innovative program called RISE (Resources and Instruction for Staff Excellence) to train child care teachers to build closer relationships with parents. The $1.25 million grant is being used to create parent-teacher sessions on child development. Such sessions not only cement relationships between teachers and parents, but also help answer parents' questions about discipline and development." *Working Mother, July/August 1997*

Business Environment

STATE ECONOMY

State Economic Profile

"A relatively strong economy has allowed Ohio's legislators to cut personal income taxes over the past several years. Last year, Ohio implemented the second largest tax cut of any state. In addition to personal tax cuts, Ohio is extending large investment tax credits to manufacturers and restructuring the corporate franchise tax. Other tax incentives are also offered to businesses that are expanding or locating in the state.

A number of business considerations are prompting manufacturers to shrink their Ohio operations. These include improvements in efficiency; the desire to shift to non-unionized production facilities, mainly in the low-cost South; cheaper Mexican labor costs; and finally operational consolidations.

Population growth of under 0.4% during 1996 was the weakest in the Great Lakes region; however, net out-migration declined last year compared to the previous two years. Ohio lost about 15,000 residents in 1996. In addition, Ohio does not draw a sufficient number of international migrants to offset the losses.

Ohio's economy will experience slower growth in the near term as manufacturers attempt to avoid inventory build-ups. Longer term, the state's traditional heavy industries will remain vulnerable to cyclical downturns. Diversification into high-tech industries in northern Ohio and the expansion of auto-related manufacturing in the southern part of the state will help dampen the decline. Ohio will continue to develop as a center of financial services and distribution activity. Poor population trends, however, will limit the growth of various population-based industries in the state...." *National Association of Realtors, Economic Profiles: The Fifty States, July 1997*

IMPORTS/EXPORTS

Total Export Sales

Area	1993 ($000)	1994 ($000)	1995 ($000)	1996 ($000)	% Chg. 1993-96	% Chg. 1995-96
MSA[1]	3,582,759	4,093,323	4,706,991	5,075,165	41.7	7.8
U.S.	464,858,354	512,415,609	583,030,524	622,827,063	34.0	6.8

Note: (1) Metropolitan Statistical Area - see Appendix A for areas included
Source: U.S. Department of Commerce, International Trade Association, Metropolitan Area Exports: An Export Performance Report on Over 250 U.S. Cities, October 1997

Imports/Exports by Port

Type	Cargo Value			Share of U.S. Total	
	1995 (US$mil.)	1996 (US$mil.)	% Change 1995-1996	1995 (%)	1996 (%)
Imports	328	423	29.05	0.08	0.11
Exports	37	10	-74.45	0.02	0.00

Source: Global Trade Information Services, WaterBorne Trade Atlas 1997

CITY FINANCES

City Government Finances

Component	FY94 ($000)	FY94 (per capita $)
Revenue	796,925	1,584.56
Expenditure	950,156	1,889.24
Debt Outstanding	1,100,492	2,188.16
Cash & Securities	589,505	1,172.14

Source: U.S. Bureau of the Census, City Government Finances: 1993-94

City Government Revenue by Source

Source	FY94 ($000)	FY94 (per capita $)	FY94 (%)
From Federal Government	72,685	144.52	9.1
From State Governments	73,792	146.72	9.3
From Local Governments	1,307	2.60	0.2
Property Taxes	50,977	101.36	6.4
General Sales Taxes	0	0.00	0.0
Selective Sales Taxes	5,491	10.92	0.7
Income Taxes	218,574	434.60	27.4
Current Charges	99,232	197.31	12.5
Utility/Liquor Store	204,358	406.33	25.6
Employee Retirement[1]	0	0.00	0.0
Other	70,509	140.20	8.8

Note: (1) Excludes "city contributions," classified as "nonrevenue," intragovernmental transfers.
Source: U.S. Bureau of the Census, City Government Finances: 1993-94

City Government Expenditures by Function

Function	FY94 ($000)	FY94 (per capita $)	FY94 (%)
Educational Services	0	0.00	0.0
Employee Retirement[1]	0	0.00	0.0
Environment/Housing	157,034	312.24	16.5
Government Administration	45,516	90.50	4.8
Interest on General Debt	22,809	45.35	2.4
Public Safety	213,869	425.25	22.5
Social Services	23,251	46.23	2.4
Transportation	142,497	283.33	15.0
Utility/Liquor Store	307,088	610.60	32.3
Other	38,092	75.74	4.0

Note: (1) Payments to beneficiaries including withdrawal of contributions.
Source: U.S. Bureau of the Census, City Government Finances: 1993-94

Municipal Bond Ratings

Area	Moody's	S & P
Cleveland	A2	A

Note: n/a not available; n/r not rated
Source: Moody's Bond Record, 2/98; Statistical Abstract of the U.S., 1997; Governing Magazine, 9/97, 3/98

POPULATION

Population Growth

Area	1980	1990	% Chg. 1980-90	July 1996 Estimate	% Chg. 1990-96
City	573,822	505,616	-11.9	498,246	-1.5
MSA[1]	1,898,825	1,831,122	-3.6	2,233,288	22.0
U.S.	226,545,805	248,765,170	9.8	265,179,411	6.6

Note: (1) Metropolitan Statistical Area - see Appendix A for areas included
Source: 1980/1990 Census of Housing and Population, Summary Tape File 3C; Census Bureau Population Estimates

Population Characteristics

Race	City					MSA[1]	
	1980		1990		% Chg. 1980-90	1990	
	Population	%	Population	%		Population	%
White	309,299	53.9	250,727	49.6	-18.9	1,435,694	78.4
Black	251,084	43.8	235,053	46.5	-6.4	355,237	19.4
Amer Indian/Esk/Aleut	1,282	0.2	1,531	0.3	19.4	3,396	0.2
Asian/Pacific Islander	3,372	0.6	4,885	1.0	44.9	20,376	1.1
Other	8,785	1.5	13,420	2.7	52.8	16,419	0.9
Hispanic Origin[2]	17,772	3.1	22,330	4.4	25.6	32,765	1.8

Note: (1) Metropolitan Statistical Area - see Appendix A for areas included; (2) people of Hispanic origin can be of any race
Source: 1980/1990 Census of Housing and Population, Summary Tape File 3C

Ancestry

Area	German	Irish	English	Italian	U.S.	French	Polish	Dutch
City	14.2	11.1	4.1	5.3	2.9	1.2	6.4	1.0
MSA[1]	25.2	15.1	9.9	9.8	2.7	2.0	9.3	1.5
U.S.	23.3	15.6	13.1	5.9	5.3	4.2	3.8	2.5

Note: Figures are percentages and include persons that reported multiple ancestry (eg. if a person reported being Irish and Italian, they were included in both columns); (1) Metropolitan Statistical Area - see Appendix A for areas included
Source: 1990 Census of Population and Housing, Summary Tape File 3C

Age

Area	Median Age (Years)	Age Distribution (%)						
		Under 5	Under 18	18-24	25-44	45-64	65+	80+
City	31.8	8.7	27.0	10.4	30.7	18.0	13.9	3.0
MSA[1]	34.7	7.1	24.6	9.0	31.7	20.1	14.6	3.0
U.S.	32.9	7.3	25.6	10.5	32.6	18.7	12.5	2.8

Note: (1) Metropolitan Statistical Area - see Appendix A for areas included
Source: 1990 Census of Population and Housing, Summary Tape File 3C

Male/Female Ratio

Area	Number of males per 100 females (all ages)	Number of males per 100 females (18 years old+)
City	88.2	83.4
MSA[1]	90.1	85.9
U.S.	95.0	91.9

Note: (1) Metropolitan Statistical Area - see Appendix A for areas included
Source: 1990 Census of Population, General Population Characteristics

INCOME

Per Capita/Median/Average Income

Area	Per Capita ($)	Median Household ($)	Average Household ($)
City	9,258	17,822	22,921
MSA[1]	15,092	30,560	38,413
U.S.	14,420	30,056	38,453

Note: all figures are for 1989; (1) Metropolitan Statistical Area - see Appendix A for areas included
Source: 1990 Census of Population and Housing, Summary Tape File 3C

Household Income Distribution by Race

Income ($)	City (%)					U.S. (%)				
	Total	White	Black	Other	Hisp.[1]	Total	White	Black	Other	Hisp.[1]
Less than 5,000	16.7	10.1	24.8	19.3	22.3	6.2	4.8	15.2	8.6	8.8
5,000 - 9,999	15.5	14.1	17.4	15.1	14.7	9.3	8.6	14.2	9.9	11.1
10,000 - 14,999	11.5	12.0	10.8	11.0	11.6	8.8	8.5	11.0	9.8	11.0
15,000 - 24,999	19.5	20.9	17.6	20.5	18.6	17.5	17.3	18.9	18.5	20.5
25,000 - 34,999	14.8	17.2	11.9	15.6	15.1	15.8	16.1	14.2	15.4	16.4
35,000 - 49,999	13.0	15.5	9.9	11.3	11.5	17.9	18.6	13.3	16.1	16.0
50,000 - 74,999	7.0	8.0	5.9	5.9	5.5	15.0	15.8	9.3	13.4	11.1
75,000 - 99,999	1.3	1.4	1.2	1.1	0.5	5.1	5.5	2.6	4.7	3.1
100,000+	0.7	0.9	0.4	0.1	0.3	4.4	4.8	1.3	3.7	1.9

Note: all figures are for 1989; (1) people of Hispanic origin can be of any race
Source: 1990 Census of Population and Housing, Summary Tape File 3C

Effective Buying Income

Area	Per Capita ($)	Median Household ($)	Average Household ($)
City	10,685	20,931	26,848
MSA[1]	16,708	35,395	43,214
U.S.	15,444	33,201	41,849

Note: data as of 1/1/97; (1) Metropolitan Statistical Area - see Appendix A for areas included
Source: Standard Rate & Data Service, Newspaper Advertising Source, 2/98

Effective Household Buying Income Distribution

Area	% of Households Earning						
	$10,000 -$19,999	$20,000 -$34,999	$35,000 -$49,999	$50,000 -$74,999	$75,000 -$99,000	$100,000 -$124,999	$125,000 and up
City	21.5	23.3	15.0	10.3	2.3	0.5	0.4
MSA[1]	15.0	22.1	18.9	19.6	7.3	2.3	2.5
U.S.	16.5	23.4	18.3	18.2	6.4	2.1	2.4

Note: data as of 1/1/97; (1) Metropolitan Statistical Area - see Appendix A for areas included
Source: Standard Rate & Data Service, Newspaper Advertising Source, 2/98

Poverty Rates by Race and Age

Area	Total (%)	By Race (%)				By Age (%)		
		White	Black	Other	Hisp.[2]	Under 5 years old	Under 18 years old	65 years and over
City	28.7	18.2	39.1	37.4	40.0	46.2	43.0	19.2
MSA[1]	11.8	6.8	31.0	22.0	30.6	20.5	18.1	9.5
U.S.	13.1	9.8	29.5	23.1	25.3	20.1	18.3	12.8

Note: figures show the percent of people living below the poverty line in 1989. The average poverty threshold was $12,674 for a family of four in 1989; (1) Metropolitan Statistical Area - see Appendix A for areas included; (2) people of Hispanic origin can be of any race
Source: 1990 Census of Population and Housing, Summary Tape File 3C

EMPLOYMENT

Labor Force and Employment

Area	Civilian Labor Force			Workers Employed		
	Dec. '95	Dec. '96	% Chg.	Dec. '95	Dec. '96	% Chg.
City	207,197	210,598	1.6	187,200	192,680	2.9
MSA[1]	1,111,117	1,132,800	2.0	1,051,656	1,082,447	2.9
U.S.	134,583,000	136,742,000	1.6	127,903,000	130,785,000	2.3

Note: Data is not seasonally adjusted and covers workers 16 years of age and older; (1) Metropolitan Statistical Area - see Appendix A for areas included
Source: Bureau of Labor Statistics, http://stats.bls.gov

Unemployment Rate

Area	1997											
	Jan.	Feb.	Mar.	Apr.	May	Jun.	Jul.	Aug.	Sep.	Oct.	Nov.	Dec.
City	11.1	11.0	10.1	9.4	9.0	8.6	7.8	8.0	8.8	8.5	8.7	8.5
MSA[1]	6.1	6.4	5.5	5.0	4.4	4.3	4.1	3.9	4.4	4.2	4.6	4.4
U.S.	5.9	5.7	5.5	4.8	4.7	5.2	5.0	4.8	4.7	4.4	4.3	4.4

Note: Data is not seasonally adjusted and covers workers 16 years of age and older; All figures are percentages; (1) Metropolitan Statistical Area - see Appendix A for areas included
Source: Bureau of Labor Statistics, http://stats.bls.gov

Employment by Industry

Sector	MSA[1]		U.S.
	Number of Employees	Percent of Total	Percent of Total
Services	339,800	29.3	29.0
Retail Trade	208,300	18.0	18.5
Government	147,400	12.7	16.1
Manufacturing	225,300	19.4	15.0
Finance/Insurance/Real Estate	74,100	6.4	5.7
Wholesale Trade	73,400	6.3	5.4
Transportation/Public Utilities	46,200	4.0	5.3
Construction	44,800	3.9	4.5
Mining	900	0.1	0.5

Note: Figures cover non-farm employment as of 12/97 and are not seasonally adjusted; (1) Metropolitan Statistical Area - see Appendix A for areas included
Source: Bureau of Labor Statistics, http://stats.bls.gov

Employment by Occupation

Occupation Category	City (%)	MSA[1] (%)	U.S. (%)
White Collar	47.7	61.5	58.1
Executive/Admin./Management	7.6	13.0	12.3
Professional	8.8	14.6	14.1
Technical & Related Support	3.9	4.0	3.7
Sales	8.4	12.1	11.8
Administrative Support/Clerical	19.1	17.8	16.3
Blue Collar	33.3	25.3	26.2
Precision Production/Craft/Repair	10.7	10.7	11.3
Machine Operators/Assem./Insp.	11.8	7.4	6.8
Transportation/Material Movers	5.2	3.6	4.1
Cleaners/Helpers/Laborers	5.6	3.6	3.9
Services	18.3	12.3	13.2
Farming/Forestry/Fishing	0.7	0.8	2.5

Note: figures cover employed persons 16 years old and over; (1) Metropolitan Statistical Area - see Appendix A for areas included
Source: 1990 Census of Population and Housing, Summary Tape File 3C

Occupational Employment Projections: 1994 - 2005

Occupations Expected to have the Largest Job Growth (ranked by numerical growth)	Fast-Growing Occupations (ranked by percent growth)
1. Salespersons, retail	1. All other computer scientists
2. Computer systems analysts	2. Personal and home care aides
3. Cashiers	3. Home health aides
4. General managers & top executives	4. Computer systems analysts
5. Guards	5. Computer engineers
6. Home health aides	6. Occupational therapists
7. Nursing aides/orderlies/attendants	7. Amusement and recreation attendants
8. Waiters & waitresses	8. Physical therapists
9. Registered nurses	9. Medical assistants
10. All other profess., paraprofess., tech.	10. Operations research analysts

Projections cover Cleveland-Cuyahoga County (SDA 20/21).
Source: Ohio Bureau of Employment Services, SDA 20/21, Job Outlook: 1994-2005

Average Wages

Occupation	Wage	Occupation	Wage
Professional/Technical/Clerical	$/Week	**Health/Protective Services**	$/Week
Accountants III	787	Corrections Officers	428
Attorneys III	1,293	Firefighters	738
Budget Analysts III	-	Nurses, Licensed Practical II	-
Buyers/Contracting Specialists II	647	Nurses, Registered II	-
Clerks, Accounting III	457	Nursing Assistants II	-
Clerks, General III	410	Police Officers I	704
Computer Operators II	-	**Hourly Workers**	$/Hour
Computer Programmers II	613	Forklift Operators	12.68
Drafters II	482	General Maintenance Workers	10.72
Engineering Technicians III	607	Guards I	6.69
Engineering Technicians, Civil III	603	Janitors	7.25
Engineers III	931	Maintenance Electricians	19.59
Key Entry Operators I	300	Maintenance Electronics Techs II	16.45
Personnel Assistants III	-	Maintenance Machinists	18.40
Personnel Specialists III	832	Maintenance Mechanics, Machinery	18.53
Secretaries III	569	Material Handling Laborers	-
Switchboard Operator-Receptionist	364	Motor Vehicle Mechanics	16.71
Systems Analysts II	899	Shipping/Receiving Clerks	11.29
Systems Analysts Supervisor/Mgr II	1,306	Tool and Die Makers	17.16
Tax Collectors II	581	Truckdrivers, Tractor Trailer	14.93
Word Processors II	496	Warehouse Specialists	11.72

Note: Wage data includes full-time workers only for 7/96 and cover the Metropolitan Statistical Area (see Appendix A for areas included). Dashes indicate that data was not available.
Source: Bureau of Labor Statistics, Occupational Compensation Survey, 1/97

TAXES

Major State and Local Tax Rates

State Corp. Income (%)	State Personal Income (%)	Residential Property (effective rate per $100)	Sales & Use State (%)	Sales & Use Local (%)	State Gasoline (cents/ gallon)	State Cigarette (cents/ 20-pack)
5.1 - 8.9[a]	0.693 - 7.004	n/a	5.0	2.0	22	24

Note: Personal/corporate income tax rates as of 1/97. Sales, gasoline and cigarette tax rates as of 1/98; (a) Or 5.82 mils times the value of the taxpayer's issued and outstanding share of stock. Minimum tax $50
Source: Federation of Tax Administrators, www.taxadmin.org; Washington D.C. Department of Finance and Revenue, Tax Rates and Tax Burdens in the District of Columbia: A Nationwide Comparison, June 1997; Chamber of Commerce

Total Taxes Per Capita and as a Percent of Income

Area	Per Capita Income ($)	Per Capita Taxes ($)			Taxes as Pct. of Income (%)		
		Total	Federal	State/ Local	Total	Federal	State/ Local
Ohio	25,222	8,829	5,818	3,010	35.0	23.1	11.9
U.S.	26,187	9,205	6,127	3,078	35.2	23.4	11.8

Note: Figures are for 1997
Source: Tax Foundation, Web Site, www.taxfoundation.org

Estimated Tax Burden

Area	State Income	Local Income	Property	Sales	Total
Cleveland	2,391	1,300	3,600	595	7,886

Note: The numbers are estimates of taxes paid by a married couple with two kids and annual earnings of $65,000. Sales tax estimates assume they spend average amounts on food, clothing, household goods and gasoline. Property tax estimates assume they live in a $225,000 home.
Source: Kiplinger's Personal Finance Magazine, June 1997

COMMERCIAL REAL ESTATE

Office Market

Class/ Location	Total Space (sq. ft.)	Vacant Space (sq. ft.)	Vac. Rate (%)	Under Constr. (sq. ft.)	Net Absorp. (sq. ft.)	Rental Rates ($/sq.ft./yr.)
Class A						
CBD	10,746,116	1,010,135	9.4	0	257,907	17.00-30.00
Outside CBD	3,482,962	438,853	12.6	194,000	353,070	16.00-23.00
Class B						
CBD	11,307,749	1,911,010	16.9	0	463,617	13.50-17.50
Outside CBD	10,594,014	1,356,034	12.8	0	-243,663	13.00-17.00

Note: Data as of 10/97 and covers Cleveland; CBD = Central Business District; n/a not available;
Source: Society of Industrial and Office Realtors, 1998 Comparative Statistics of Industrial and Office Real Estate Markets

"Economic growth is expected to be moderate but steady over the forecast period. The cost of land for office buildings requires high-quality developments with rental rates in the high-teens to low 20-dollar range. Mergers and acquisitions provide a stimulus for change in the Cleveland MSA. While some relocations to the area are expected, demand for space will probably be moderate. Increased absorption of one to five percent will result primarily from the expansion of local start-up companies. The SIOR reporters expect that new suburban construction will most likely stimulate absorption of Class 'A' space. In addition, several developers are positioned to start construction upon signature of a significant lead tenant, especially in the eastern and southern suburbs." *Society of Industrial and Office Realtors, 1998 Comparative Statistics of Industrial and Office Real Estate Markets*

Industrial Market

Location	Total Space (sq. ft.)	Vacant Space (sq. ft.)	Vac. Rate (%)	Under Constr. (sq. ft.)	Net Absorp. (sq. ft.)	Gross Lease ($/sq.ft./yr.)
Central City	92,340,000	9,443,000	10.2	350,000	1,853,000	2.00-4.25
Suburban	214,286,000	8,267,000	3.9	2,900,000	5,149,000	2.70-6.40

Note: Data as of 10/97 and covers ; n/a not available
Source: Society of Industrial and Office Realtors, 1998 Comparative Statistics of Industrial and Office Real Estate Markets

"Strong and solid demand for warehouse and manufacturing space continues throughout the Greater Cleveland area. There has been no let-up since 1994 and this trend is expected to continue into the foreseeable future—certainly through 1998. Speculative development is on the rise. REITs and well-known area developers are vying for their share. More than 1,150,000 sq. ft. of spec development has been announced for 1998. Progressive Brownfield legislation bodes well for Cleveland. Significant employer shortages have been reported in a number of sub-markets. The lack of developable land limits the potential for future industrial growth and development. Expect changes in the national and world economy to also have an effect on future expansion." *Society of Industrial and Office Realtors, 1998 Comparative Statistics of Industrial and Office Real Estate Markets*

Retail Market

Shopping Center Inventory (sq. ft.)	Shopping Center Construction (sq. ft.)	Construction as a Percent of Inventory (%)	Torto Wheaton Rent Index[1] ($/sq. ft.)
36,832,000	0	0.0	9.72

Note: Data as of 1997 and covers the Metropolitan Statistical Area - see Appendix A for areas included; (1) Index is based on a model that predicts what the average rent should be for leases with certain characteristics, in certain locations during certain years.
Source: National Association of Realtors, 1997-1998 Market Conditions Report

"Beginning in 1994, a boom in business investment and strong consumer spending sparked activity in Cleveland's retail market. Large scale projects, such as Jacob's Field and Tower City Mall, added to the area's growing tourism industry.During the period, the retail rent index rose 17%. The boom, however, has cooled off, and many industry experts are watching closely to see if Cleveland can support new retail activity over the long haul. Indeed, the area's lackluster population growth, expected to be only 0.1% annually over the next five years, will be a major deterrent to economic growth." *National Association of Realtors, 1997-1998 Market Conditions Report*

COMMERCIAL UTILITIES

Typical Monthly Electric Bills

Area	Commercial Service ($/month)		Industrial Service ($/month)	
	12 kW demand 1,500 kWh	100 kW demand 30,000 kWh	1,000 kW demand 400,000 kWh	20,000 kW demand 10,000,000 kWh
City	200	3,504	35,515	713,523
U.S.	162	2,360	25,590	545,677

Note: Based on rates in effect July 1, 1997
Source: Edison Electric Institute, Typical Residential, Commercial and Industrial Bills, Summer 1997

TRANSPORTATION

Transportation Statistics

Avg. travel time to work (min.)	22.5
Interstate highways	I-71; I-77; I-80; I-90
Bus lines	
In-city	Greater Cleveland Regional TA, 785 vehicles
Inter-city	6
Passenger air service	
Airport	Cleveland-Hopkins International
Airlines	9
Aircraft departures	97,382 (1995)
Enplaned passengers	5,108,514 (1995)
Rail service	Amtrak; Light Rail
Motor freight carriers	99
Major waterways/ports	Lake Erie; Port of Cleveland

Source: OAG, Business Travel Planner, Summer 1997; Editor & Publisher Market Guide, 1998; FAA Airport Activity Statistics, 1996; Amtrak National Time Table, Northeast Timetable, Fall/Winter 1997-98; 1990 Census of Population and Housing, STF 3C; Chamber of Commerce/Economic Development 1997; Jane's Urban Transport Systems 1997-98; Transit Fact Book 1997

Means of Transportation to Work

Area	Car/Truck/Van: Drove Alone	Car/Truck/Van: Car-pooled	Public Transportation: Bus	Public Transportation: Subway	Public Transportation: Railroad	Bicycle	Walked	Other Means	Worked at Home
City	64.8	14.0	13.0	0.6	0.1	0.1	5.0	1.2	1.2
MSA[1]	77.7	10.5	5.5	0.4	0.1	0.1	2.9	0.8	2.0
U.S.	73.2	13.4	3.0	1.5	0.5	0.4	3.9	1.2	3.0

Note: figures shown are percentages and only include workers 16 years old and over;
(1) Metropolitan Statistical Area - see Appendix A for areas included
Source: 1990 Census of Population and Housing, Summary Tape File 3C

BUSINESSES

Major Business Headquarters

Company Name	1997 Rankings: Fortune 500	1997 Rankings: Forbes 500
Eaton	207	-
IMG	-	179
Jones Day Reavis & Pogue	-	481
Keycorp	241	-
LTV	329	-
MTD Products	-	324
National City Corp.	290	-
Parker Hannifin	378	-
Reltec	-	310
Sealy	-	305
Sherwin-Williams	330	-
TRW	135	-

Note: Companies listed are located in the city; Dashes indicate no ranking
Fortune 500: companies that produce a 10-K are ranked 1 - 500 based on 1996 revenue
Forbes 500: private companies are ranked 1 - 500 based on 1996 revenue
Source: Forbes 12/1/97; Fortune 4/28/97

Fast-Growing Businesses

Cleveland was ranked #12 out of 24 (#1 is best) in terms of the best-performing local stocks in 1996 according to the Money/Norby Cities Index. The index measures stocks of companies that have headquarters in 24 metro areas. *Money, 2/7/97*

Women-Owned Businesses: Number, Employment, Sales and Share

Area	Women-Owned Businesses in 1996: Number	Employment	Sales ($000)	Rank[2]	Share of Women-Owned Businesses in 1996: Percent (%)	Rank[3]
MSA[1]	59,800	190,600	18,427,000	24	34.9	41

Note: (1) Metropolitan Statistical Area - see Appendix A for areas included; (2) Calculated on an averaging of number of businesses, employment and sales and ranges from 1 to 50 where 1 is best; (3) Ranges from 1 to 50 where 1 is best
Source: The National Foundation for Women Business Owners, 1996 Facts on Women-Owned Businesses: Trends in the Top 50 Metropolitan Areas, March 26, 1997

Women-Owned Businesses: Growth

Area	Growth in Women-Owned Businesses (% change from 1987 to 1996): Num.	Empl.	Sales	Rank[2]	Relative Growth in the Number of Women-Owned and All Businesses (% change from 1987 to 1996): Women-Owned	All Firms	Absolute Difference	Relative Difference
MSA[1]	82.4	277.9	290.3	15	82.4	53.0	29.4	1.6:1

Note: (1) Metropolitan Statistical Area - see Appendix A for areas included; (2) Calculated on an averaging of the percent growth of number of businesses, employment and sales and ranges from 1 to 50 where 1 is best
Source: The National Foundation for Women Business Owners, 1996 Facts on Women-Owned Businesses: Trends in the Top 50 Metropolitan Areas, March 26, 1997

Minority Business Opportunity

Cleveland is home to one company which is on the Black Enterprise Industrial/Service 100 list (largest based on gross sales): Ozanne Construction Co. Inc. (general construction and construction mgmt.). Criteria: 1) operational in previous calendar year; 2) at least 51% black-owned; 3) manufactures/owns the product it sells or provides industrial or consumer services. Brokerages, real estate firms and firms that provide professional services are not eligible. *Black Enterprise, July 1997*

HOTELS & MOTELS

Hotels/Motels

Area	Hotels/ Motels	Rooms	Luxury-Level Hotels/Motels		Average Minimum Rates ($)		
			♦♦♦♦	♦♦♦♦♦	♦♦	♦♦♦	♦♦♦♦
City	11	3,451	2	0	n/a	n/a	n/a
Airport	17	2,773	0	0	n/a	n/a	n/a
Suburbs	52	5,811	0	0	n/a	n/a	n/a
Total	80	12,035	2	0	n/a	n/a	n/a

Note: n/a not available; Classifications range from one diamond (budget properties with basic amenities) to five diamond (luxury properties with the finest service, rooms and facilities).
Source: OAG, Business Travel Planner, Summer 1997

CONVENTION CENTERS

Major Convention Centers

Center Name	Meeting Rooms	Exhibit Space (sf)
Cleveland Convention Center	37	375,000
The Forum Conference & Education Center	12	22,000
International Expo Center	20	1,500,000
Sheraton Cleveland City Centre Hotel	1	n/a
Cleveland State University Convocation Center	n/a	300,000

Note: n/a not available
Source: Trade Shows Worldwide 1997

Living Environment

COST OF LIVING

Cost of Living Index

Composite Index	Housing	Utilities	Groceries	Health Care	Trans-portation	Misc. Goods/ Services
104.5	104.9	124.6	104.0	109.0	102.3	99.4

Note: U.S. = 100
Source: ACCRA, Cost of Living Index, 3rd Quarter 1997

HOUSING

Median Home Prices and Housing Affordability

Area	Median Price[2] 3rd Qtr. 1997 ($)	HOI[3] 3rd Qtr. 1997	Afford-ability Rank[4]
MSA[1]	106,000	71.0	89
U.S.	127,000	63.7	–

Note: (1) Metropolitan Statistical Area - see Appendix A for areas included; (2) U.S. figures calculated from the sales of 625,000 new and existing homes in 195 markets; (3) Housing Opportunity Index - percent of homes sold that were within the reach of the median income household at the prevailing mortgage interest rate; (4) Rank is from 1-195 with 1 being most affordable
Source: National Association of Home Builders, Housing Opportunity Index, 3rd Quarter 1997

It is projected that the median price of existing single-family homes in the metro area will increase by 9.1% in 1998. Nationwide, home prices are projected to increase 6.6%. *Kiplinger's Personal Finance Magazine, January 1998*

Average New Home Price

Area	Price ($)
City	137,683
U.S.	135,710

Note: Figures are based on a new home with 1,800 sq. ft. of living area on an 8,000 sq. ft. lot.
Source: ACCRA, Cost of Living Index, 3rd Quarter 1997

Average Apartment Rent

Area	Rent ($/mth)
City	690
U.S.	569

Note: Figures are based on an unfurnished two bedroom, 1-1/2 or 2 bath apartment, approximately 950 sq. ft. in size, excluding all utilities except water
Source: ACCRA, Cost of Living Index, 3rd Quarter 1997

RESIDENTIAL UTILITIES

Average Residential Utility Costs

Area	All Electric ($/mth)	Part Electric ($/mth)	Other Energy ($/mth)	Phone ($/mth)
City	–	78.62	50.53	22.37
U.S.	109.40	55.25	43.64	19.48

Source: ACCRA, Cost of Living Index, 3rd Quarter 1997

HEALTH CARE

Average Health Care Costs

Area	Hospital ($/day)	Doctor ($/visit)	Dentist ($/visit)
City	666.40	43.87	59.50
U.S.	392.91	48.76	60.84

Note: Hospital - based on a semi-private room. Doctor - based on a general practitioner's routine exam of an established patient. Dentist - based on adult teeth cleaning and periodic oral exam.
Source: ACCRA, Cost of Living Index, 3rd Quarter 1997

Distribution of Office-Based Physicians

Area	Family/Gen. Practitioners	Specialists		
		Medical	Surgical	Other
MSA[1]	341	1,748	1,212	1,364

Note: Data as of 12/31/96; (1) Metropolitan Statistical Area - see Appendix A for areas included
Source: American Medical Assn., Physician Characteristics & Distribution in the U.S., 1997-1998

Hospitals

Cleveland has 15 general medical and surgical hospitals, 1 psychiatric, 1 alcoholism and other chemical dependency, 1 children's other specialty. *AHA Guide to the Healthcare Field 1997-98*

According to *U.S. News and World Report,* Cleveland has 4 of the best hospitals in the U.S.: **Cleveland Clinic**, noted for AIDS, cancer, cardiology, endocrinology, gastroenterology, geriatrics, gynecology, neurology, orthopedics, otolaryngology, psychiatry, pulmonology, rehabilitation, rheumatology, urology; **University Hospitals**, noted for cancer, cardiology, geriatrics, neurology, otolaryngology, rheumatology; **University Hospitals of Cleveland (Rainbow Babies)**, noted for pediatrics; **Mount Sinai Medical Center**, noted for geriatrics; *U.S. News and World Report, "America's Best Hospitals", 7/28/97*

Cleveland Clinic Foundation is among the 100 best-run hospitals in the U.S.
Modern Healthcare, January 5, 1998

EDUCATION

Public School District Statistics

District Name	Num. Sch.	Enroll.	Classroom Teachers[1]	Pupils per Teacher	Minority Pupils (%)	Current Exp.[2] ($/pupil)
Cleveland City SD	131	74,380	4,326	17.2	79.3	6,280
Orange City SD	5	2,322	190	12.2	n/a	n/a

Note: Data covers the 1995-1996 school year unless otherwise noted; (1) Excludes teachers reported as working in school district offices rather than in schools; (2) Based on 1993-94 enrollment collected by the Census Bureau, not the enrollment figure shown in column 3; SD = School District; ISD = Independent School District; n/a not available
Source: National Center for Education Statistics, Common Core of Data Survey; Bureau of the Census

Educational Quality

School District	Education Quotient[1]	Graduate Outcome[2]	Community Index[3]	Resource Index[4]
Cleveland City	85.0	51.0	84.0	119.0

Note: Nearly 1,000 secondary school districts were rated in terms of educational quality. The scores range from a low of 50 to a high of 150; (1) Average of the Graduate Outcome, Community and Resource indexes; (2) Based on graduation rates and college board scores (SAT/ACT); (3) Based on the surrounding community's average level of education and the area's average income level; (4) Based on teacher salaries, per-pupil expenditures and student-teacher ratios.
Source: Expansion Management, Ratings Issue 1997

Educational Attainment by Race

Area	High School Graduate (%)					Bachelor's Degree (%)				
	Total	White	Black	Other	Hisp.[2]	Total	White	Black	Other	Hisp.[2]
City	58.8	61.9	55.6	49.3	44.7	8.1	10.2	5.0	13.9	6.2
MSA[1]	75.7	78.7	62.4	69.6	56.6	19.9	22.0	8.5	35.4	13.8
U.S.	75.2	77.9	63.1	60.4	49.8	20.3	21.5	11.4	19.4	9.2

Note: figures shown cover persons 25 years old and over; (1) Metropolitan Statistical Area - see Appendix A for areas included; (2) people of Hispanic origin can be of any race
Source: 1990 Census of Population and Housing, Summary Tape File 3C

School Enrollment by Type

Area	Preprimary				Elementary/High School			
	Public		Private		Public		Private	
	Enrollment	%	Enrollment	%	Enrollment	%	Enrollment	%
City	4,923	62.6	2,939	37.4	69,894	78.7	18,875	21.3
MSA[1]	19,818	55.4	15,951	44.6	241,493	80.6	58,046	19.4
U.S.	2,679,029	59.5	1,824,256	40.5	38,379,689	90.2	4,187,099	9.8

Note: figures shown cover persons 3 years old and over;
(1) Metropolitan Statistical Area - see Appendix A for areas included
Source: 1990 Census of Population and Housing, Summary Tape File 3C

School Enrollment by Race

Area	Preprimary (%)				Elementary/High School (%)			
	White	Black	Other	Hisp.[1]	White	Black	Other	Hisp.[1]
City	43.5	53.1	3.4	5.4	37.6	57.0	5.4	6.5
MSA[2]	80.4	17.1	2.4	2.0	71.5	25.4	3.1	2.7
U.S.	80.4	12.5	7.1	7.8	74.1	15.6	10.3	12.5

Note: figures shown cover persons 3 years old and over; (1) people of Hispanic origin can be of any race; (2) Metropolitan Statistical Area - see Appendix A for areas included
Source: 1990 Census of Population and Housing, Summary Tape File 3C

SAT/ACT Scores

Area/District	1997 SAT				1997 ACT	
	Percent of Graduates Tested (%)	Average Math Score	Average Verbal Score	Average Combined Score	Percent of Graduates Tested (%)	Average Composite Score
Cleveland PS	23	412	422	834	9	21.7
State	25	536	535	1,071	60	21.3
U.S.	42	511	505	1,016	36	21.0

Note: Math and verbal SAT scores are out of a possible 800; ACT scores are out of a possible 36
Caution: Comparing or ranking states/cities on the basis of SAT/ACT scores alone is invalid and strongly discouraged by the The College Board and The American College Testing Program as students who take the tests are self-selected and do not represent the entire student population.
Source: Cleveland Public Schools, Assessment & Accountability Services, 1997; American College Testing Program, 1997; College Board, 1997

Classroom Teacher Salaries in Public Schools

District	B.A. Degree		M.A. Degree		Ph.D. Degree	
	Min. ($)	Max ($)	Min. ($)	Max. ($)	Min. ($)	Max. ($)
Cleveland	26,765	44,119	28,163	51,506	n/a	n/a
Average[1]	26,120	39,270	28,175	44,667	31,643	49,825

Note: Salaries are for 1996-1997; (1) Based on all school districts covered; n/a not available
Source: American Federation of Teachers (unpublished data)

Higher Education

Two-Year Colleges		Four-Year Colleges		Medical Schools	Law Schools	Voc/ Tech
Public	Private	Public	Private			
1	3	1	5	1	2	16

Source: College Blue Book, Occupational Education 1997; Medical School Admission Requirements, 1998-99; Peterson's Guide to Two-Year Colleges, 1997; Peterson's Guide to Four-Year Colleges, 1997; Barron's Guide to Law Schools 1997

MAJOR EMPLOYERS

Major Employers

American Greetings Corp.	BP America (petroleum)
Cleveland Clinic	CTF Hotel Management
Fairview General Hospital	KeyCorp
Lincoln Electric Co.	Metro Health System
Mt. Sinai Medical Center	Nestle's Frozen Food
Picker International (x-ray apparatus)	Plain Dealer Publishing
Progressive Corp. (insurance)	University Hospitals of Cleveland
Opinionation (research)	Cleveland Electric Illuminating Co.
Blue Cross & Blue Shield of NE Ohio	Southwest Community Health Systems

Note: companies listed are located in the city
Source: Dun's Business Rankings 1997; Ward's Business Directory, 1997

PUBLIC SAFETY

Crime Rate

Area	All Crimes	Violent Crimes				Property Crimes		
		Murder	Forcible Rape	Robbery	Aggrav. Assault	Burglary	Larceny -Theft	Motor Vehicle Theft
City	7,541.4	20.8	129.6	818.9	569.1	1,553.9	2,709.6	1,739.5
Suburbs[1]	n/a	n/a	n/a	n/a	n/a	n/a	n/a	n/a
MSA[2]	n/a	n/a	n/a	n/a	n/a	n/a	n/a	n/a
U.S.	5,078.9	7.4	36.1	202.4	388.2	943.0	2,975.9	525.9

Note: Crime rate is the number of crimes per 100,000 pop.; (1) defined as all areas within the MSA but located outside the central city; (2) Metropolitan Statistical Area - see Appendix A for areas incl.
Source: FBI Uniform Crime Reports 1996

RECREATION

Culture and Recreation

Museums	Symphony Orchestras	Opera Companies	Dance Companies	Professional Theatres	Zoos	Pro Sports Teams
13	1	1	2	2	1	2

Source: International Directory of the Performing Arts, 1996; Official Museum Directory, 1998; Chamber of Commerce/Economic Development 1997

Library System

The Cleveland Public Library has 27 branches, holdings of 2,638,584 volumes and a budget of $40,554,080 (1996). *American Library Directory, 1997-1998*

MEDIA

Newspapers

Name	Type	Freq.	Distribution	Circulation
Amerikanski Slovenec-Glasilo KSKJ	Religious	20x/yr	National	10,700
Chagrin Herald Sun	General	1x/wk	Local	18,127
Cincinnati Call and Post	General	1x/wk	Local	12,000
Cleveland Call and Post	Black	1x/wk	Local	20,000
Cleveland Free Times	n/a	1x/wk	Area	50,000
Cleveland Jewish News	Religious	1x/wk	Local	15,500
Euclid Sun Journal	General	1x/wk	Local	12,227
Garfield-Maple Sun	General	1x/wk	Local	11,079
Lakewood Sun Post	General	1x/wk	Local	12,135
The Medina Sun	General	1x/wk	Local	11,851
The News Sun	n/a	1x/wk	Local	17,274
The Plain Dealer	n/a	7x/wk	Area	400,593
Solon Herald Sun	General	1x/wk	Local	18,127
State Edition Call and Post	General	1x/wk	State	10,000
The Sun Herald	General	1x/wk	Local	17,864
Sun Messenger	n/a	1x/wk	Local	15,033
Sun Press	General	1x/wk	Local	20,754
The Sun Star	General	1x/wk	Local	12,088
West Side Sun News	n/a	1x/wk	Local	17,565

Note: Includes newspapers with circulations of 10,000 or more located in the city; n/a not available
Source: Burrelle's Media Directory, 1998 Edition

AM Radio Stations

Call Letters	Freq. (kHz)	Target Audience	Station Format	Music Format
WRMR	850	General	M	Adult Standards/Big Band
WCCD	1000	General	M/N/T	Christian
WTAM	1100	General	N/S/T	n/a
WKNR	1220	General	S	n/a
WERE	1300	n/a	T	n/a
WHK	1420	General	T	n/a
WJMO	1490	General	M	Oldies/R&B
WABQ	1540	General	M/N/S/T	Christian

Note: Stations included broadcast in the Cleveland metro area; n/a not available
Station Format: E = Educational; M = Music; N = News; S = Sports; T = Talk
Source: Burrelle's Media Directory, 1998 Edition

FM Radio Stations

Call Letters	Freq. (mHz)	Target Audience	Station Format	Music Format
WBWC	88.3	General	M/N/S	n/a
WUJC	88.7	General	M/N/S	n/a
WCSB	89.3	General	E/M/T	n/a
WCPN	90.3	General	M/N/S	Classical/Jazz/R&B
WRUW	91.1	General	M	n/a
WKHR	91.5	n/a	E/M	Adult Standards/Big Band
WZJM	92.3	General	M/N/S	Contemporary Top 40
WZAK	93.1	Black	M/N/S	n/a
WCLV	95.5	General	M/N/S	Classical
WNCX	98.5	n/a	M	Classic Rock
WGAR	99.5	General	M	Country
WMMS	100.7	General	M/N/S	Alternative
WDOK	102.1	General	M/N	Adult Contemporary
WCRF	103.3	Religious	M/N/S	Christian
WQAL	104.1	General	M/N/S	Adult Contemporary/Contemporary Top 40
WMJI	105.7	General	M/N/S	Oldies
WLTF	106.5	General	M/N/S	Adult Contemporary
WENZ	107.9	General	M	Alternative

Note: Stations included broadcast in the Cleveland metro area; n/a not available
Station Format: E = Educational; M = Music; N = News; S = Sports; T = Talk
Source: Burrelle's Media Directory, 1998 Edition

Television Stations

Name	Ch.	Affiliation	Type	Owner
WKYC	3	NBC	Commercial	Multimedia
WEWS	5	ABC	Commercial	Scripps Howard Broadcasting
WJW	8	Fox	Commercial	Fox Television Stations Inc.
WOIO	19	CBS	Commercial	Malrite Communications Group Inc.
WVIZ	25	PBS	Public	Educational TV Association of Metropolitan Cleveland
WUAB	43	n/a	Commercial	Malrite Communications Group Inc.
WBNX	55	Fox/WB	Commercial	Winston Broadcasting Network Inc.
WQHS	61	HSN	Commercial	HSN Inc.
WOAC	67	n/a	Commercial	Whitehead Media

Note: Stations included broadcast in the Cleveland metro area
Source: Burrelle's Media Directory, 1998 Edition

CLIMATE

Average and Extreme Temperatures

Temperature	Jan	Feb	Mar	Apr	May	Jun	Jul	Aug	Sep	Oct	Nov	Dec	Ann
Extreme High (°F)	73	69	82	88	92	104	100	102	101	89	82	77	104
Average High (°F)	33	36	46	58	69	79	83	81	74	63	50	38	59
Average Temp. (°F)	26	28	37	49	59	68	73	71	64	54	43	31	50
Average Low (°F)	19	20	28	38	48	58	62	61	54	44	35	24	41
Extreme Low (°F)	-19	-15	-5	10	25	31	41	38	34	19	3	-15	-19

Note: Figures cover the years 1948-1990
Source: National Climatic Data Center, International Station Meteorological Climate Summary, 3/95

Average Precipitation/Snowfall/Humidity

Precip./Humidity	Jan	Feb	Mar	Apr	May	Jun	Jul	Aug	Sep	Oct	Nov	Dec	Ann
Avg. Precip. (in.)	2.4	2.3	3.1	3.4	3.5	3.5	3.5	3.4	3.2	2.6	3.2	2.9	37.1
Avg. Snowfall (in.)	13	12	10	2	Tr	0	0	0	0	1	5	12	55
Avg. Rel. Hum. 7am (%)	79	79	78	76	77	78	81	85	84	81	78	78	79
Avg. Rel. Hum. 4pm (%)	70	67	62	56	54	55	55	58	58	58	65	70	61

Note: Figures cover the years 1948-1990; Tr = Trace amounts (<0.05 in. of rain; <0.5 in. of snow)
Source: National Climatic Data Center, International Station Meteorological Climate Summary, 3/95

Weather Conditions

Temperature			Daytime Sky			Precipitation		
5°F & below	32°F & below	90°F & above	Clear	Partly cloudy	Cloudy	0.01 inch or more precip.	0.1 inch or more snow/ice	Thunder-storms
11	123	12	63	127	175	157	48	34

Note: Figures are average number of days per year and covers the years 1948-1990
Source: National Climatic Data Center, International Station Meteorological Climate Summary, 3/95

AIR & WATER QUALITY

Maximum Pollutant Concentrations

	Particulate Matter (ug/m^3)	Carbon Monoxide (ppm)	Sulfur Dioxide (ppm)	Nitrogen Dioxide (ppm)	Ozone (ppm)	Lead (ug/m^3)
MSA[1] Level	123	9	0.049	0.026	0.12	0.04
NAAQS[2]	150	9	0.140	0.053	0.12	1.50
Met NAAQS?	Yes	Yes	Yes	Yes	Yes	Yes

Note: (1) Metropolitan Statistical Area - see Appendix A for areas included; (2) National Ambient Air Quality Standards; ppm = parts per million; ug/m³ = micrograms per cubic meter; n/a not available
Source: EPA, National Air Quality and Emissions Trends Report, 1996

Pollutant Standards Index

In the Cleveland MSA (see Appendix A for areas included), the Pollutant Standards Index (PSI) exceeded 100 on 5 days in 1996. A PSI value greater than 100 indicates that air quality would be in the unhealthful range on that day. *EPA, National Air Quality and Emissions Trends Report, 1996*

Drinking Water

Water System Name	Pop. Served	Primary Water Source Type	Number of Violations in Fiscal Year 1997	Type of Violation/ Contaminants
City of Cleveland-Baldwin Point	424,027	Surface	None	None
City of Cleveland-Crown Plant	198,665	Surface	None	None
City of Cleveland-Morgan Plant	352,888	Surface	None	None
City of Cleveland-Nottingham Pl.	326,846	Surface	2	Too much fluoride

Note: Data as of January 16, 1998
Source: EPA, Office of Ground Water and Drinking Water, Safe Drinking Water Information System

Cleveland tap water is alkaline, hard and fluoridated.
Editor & Publisher Market Guide, 1998

Durham, North Carolina

Background

Durham, situated in northcentral North Carolina the greatest tobacco-growing area in the world, produces about 20% of the cigarettes made in the United States. Despite its long identity as a "tobacco town," Durham is gaining more prominence in the area of medicine and research. It is part of the Research Triangle Park region, a center for industrial and governmental research.

The area was first settled by Scotch-Irish and English in 1750 and its growth is connected with the coming of the railroad. Prior to the Civil War the discovery that the soil could produce a fine bright tobacco stimulated the industrial development. Early tobacco factories were operated by John Green and William T. Blackwell whose product was called "Bull Durham". They were the first to mechanize the industry and began to manufacture cigarettes as the American Tobacco Company.

The Duke family whose early fortunes were made in the tobacco industry, is credited with making Durham the important medical and educational center that it is today.

The city also manufactures a number of products including hosiery and cotton textiles, machinery, containers, proprietary medicines, chemicals, furniture, lumber products, building materials, flour, and food for livestock.

Centrally located between the mountains on the west and the coast to the south and east, the Durham area enjoys a pleasant climate. The mountains form a partial barrier to cold air masses moving from the west. As a result, there are few days in the midst of winter when the temperature falls below 20 degrees. In the summer tropical air is present over the eastern and central sections of North Carolina bringing warm temperatures and rather high humidity to the area. Durham is situated far enough from the coast so that the bad weather effects of coastal storms are reduced. While snow and sleet usually occur each year, excessive accumulations of snow are rare.

General Rankings and Evaluative Comments

- Durham was ranked #16 out of 300 cities by *Money's* 1997 "Survey of the Best Places to Live." Criteria used: health services, crime, economy, housing, education, transportation, weather, leisure and the arts. The city was ranked #24 in 1996 and #8 in 1995. *Money, July 1997; Money, September 1996; Money, September 1995*

- Durham appeared on *Fortune's* list of "North America's Most Improved Cities" Rank: 5 out of 10. The selected cities satisfied basic business-location needs and also demonstrated improvement over a five- to ten-year period in a number of business and quality-of-life measures.

  "In North Carolina, good things come in threes. The cities of Raleigh, Durham, and Chapel Hill are all within a 20-mile radius. A trio of universities—Duke, the University of North Carolina at Chapel Hill, and North Carolina State University—mark the three corners of the area's famed Research Triangle Park. Inside the Triangle, dozens of companies...constantly swap brainpower with the local universities....

  If the area is a major draw for companies, it's having the same effect on people as well...The influx of new talent has also given salaries a big boost....

  Still, Raleigh-Durham's real appeal is its quality of life. A number of Broadway plays have come to Duke University's Bryan Center to do their dry run as part of the university's Broadway Preview Series. College football and basketball are a religion in these parts....

  It also helps to have companies that value quality of life just as much as their employees do. With their ponds, softball diamonds, and jogging trails, most of the Triangle's sprawling corporate facilities look more like summer camp than cutting-edge companies....

  ...it's hard to find a better city for raising kids. An innovative countywide school program gives every Raleigh family the option of sending their children to school on a year-round basis. And next year two new museums—one devoted to international culture, the other to natural science—will open...." *Fortune, 11/24/97*

- *Ladies Home Journal* ranked America's 200 largest cities based on the qualities women care about most. Durham ranked 2 out of 200. Criteria: low crime rate, good public schools, well-paying jobs, quality health and child care, the presence of women in government, proportion of women-owned businesses, size of the wage gap with men, local economy, divorce rates, the ratio of single men to single women, whether there are laws that require at least the same number of public toilets for women as men, and the probability of good hair days. *Ladies Home Journal, November 1997*

- Durham is among the 10 healthiest cities for women. Rank: 2 out of 10. Criteria: 1) number of doctors, psychologists and dietitians; 2) quality of hospital gynecology departments; 3) number of working mothers; 4) rate of violent crimes; 5) cleanliness of air and water; 6) number of fitness opportunities; 7) quality of public schools. *American Health, January/February 1997*

- Durham was ranked #87 out of 219 cities in terms of children's health, safety, and economic well-being. Criteria: total population, percent population change, birth rate, child immunization rate, infant mortality rate, percent low birth weight infants, percent of births to teens, physician-to-population ratio, student-to-teacher ratio, dropout rate, unemployment rate, median family income, percent of children in poverty, violent and property crime rates, number of juvenile arrests for violent crimes as a percent of the total crime index, number of days with pollution standard index (PSI) over 100, pounds toxic releases per 1,000 people and number of superfund sites. *Zero Population Growth, Children's Environmental Index 1997*

- Durham appeared on the *Utne Reader's* list of "America's 10 Most Enlightened Towns". Criteria: access to alternative health care, lively media, sense of local culture, diverse spiritual opportunities, good urban design, progressive local politics, commitment to racial equality, tolerance for gays and lesbians, and decent conditions for working-class citizens. *Utne Reader, May/June 1997*

- Durham appeared on *Sales & Marketing Management's* list of the 20 hottest domestic markets to do business in. Rank: 9 out of 20. America's 320 Metropolitan Statistical Areas were ranked based on the market's potential to buy products in certain industries like high-tech, manufacturing, office equipment and business services, as well as population and household income growth. The study had nine criteria in all.

  "The future home of the National Hockey League's Carolina Hurricanes, this Atlantic Coast market has become popular during the past five years. Of our top 20 markets, Raleigh/Durham is the highest ranked in population growth. And with four major universities in the area, the market's educational purchasing power is among the highest in the country." *Sales & Marketing Management, January 1998*

- According to *Working Mother,* "No state has more action or more enthusiasm for improving child care than North Carolina. And no governor deserves more credit for fighting for child care than Jim Hunt. His 'Smart Start' program has as its goal affordable, quality early childhood education for every child who needs it. In the past four years, the state has created more than 30,000 new slots for child care and improved care for more than 150,000 kids.

  The program ran up against some resistance in the state legislature in the past, but now a solid majority embrace the core tenets of Smart Start. This year, for example, state lawmakers decided to award permanent funding for the state's caregiver training program, Teacher Education and Compensation Helps (T.E.A.C.H.)—more than $1 million a year in recurring funds. That means child care advocates won't have to come back every year to fight for money for early education. The T.E.A.C.H. program is now being copied by other states, including Illinois.

  With all this progress, it's a shame that North Carolina's key standards aren't better. One adult is still allowed to care for up to five babies, and caregivers are not required to have any education or training before they start work (a bill now before the legislature may change this). This state could do better on these critical aspects of child care." *Working Mother, July/August 1997*

Business Environment

STATE ECONOMY

State Economic Profile

"North Carolina's strength is its development of technologically advanced industries, ranging from computer software development in biotechnology. North Carolina's weakness is its ailing textile and apparel industries....

North Carolina's population continues to expand at a robust 1.7% year-over-year rate, nearly twice the national average. In 1996 net domestic migration contributed 1.1 percentage points to North Carolina's population growth rate, compared to just 0.4 for the southern region, making the state's economic expansion particularly dependent on migration....

Apart from job losses in the apparel and textile industries, North Carolina's economy remains healthy, and employment growth is outpacing the nation. The long-term outlook for North Carolina is positive. Its emergency as a center for high-tech employment continues to attract relocations and expansions to metro areas such as Raleigh and Charlotte. A downside risk to the economy is strong growth in government sector employment, which may leave the state susceptible to government spending cuts in the future...." *National Association of Realtors, Economic Profiles: The Fifty States, July 1997*

IMPORTS/EXPORTS

Total Export Sales

Area	1993 ($000)	1994 ($000)	1995 ($000)	1996 ($000)	% Chg. 1993-96	% Chg. 1995-96
MSA[1]	n/a	n/a	n/a	n/a	n/a	n/a
U.S.	464,858,354	512,415,609	583,030,524	622,827,063	34.0	6.8

Note: (1) Metropolitan Statistical Area - see Appendix A for areas included
Source: U.S. Department of Commerce, International Trade Association, Metropolitan Area Exports: An Export Performance Report on Over 250 U.S. Cities, October 1997

Imports/Exports by Port

Type	Cargo Value			Share of U.S. Total	
	1995 (US$mil.)	1996 (US$mil.)	% Change 1995-1996	1995 (%)	1996 (%)
Imports	0	0	0	0	0
Exports	0	0	0	0	0

Source: Global Trade Information Services, WaterBorne Trade Atlas 1997

CITY FINANCES

City Government Finances

Component	FY92 ($000)	FY92 (per capita $)
Revenue	128,992	900.62
Expenditure	122,160	852.92
Debt Outstanding	139,364	973.04
Cash & Securities	69,323	484.01

Source: U.S. Bureau of the Census, City Government Finances: 1991-92

City Government Revenue by Source

Source	FY92 ($000)	FY92 (per capita $)	FY92 (%)
From Federal Government	3,664	25.58	2.8
From State Governments	13,132	91.69	10.2
From Local Governments	13,743	95.95	10.7
Property Taxes	37,635	262.77	29.2
General Sales Taxes	0	0.00	0.0
Selective Sales Taxes	565	3.94	0.4
Income Taxes	0	0.00	0.0
Current Charges	29,401	205.28	22.8
Utility/Liquor Store	17,590	122.81	13.6
Employee Retirement[1]	0	0.00	0.0
Other	13,262	92.59	10.3

Note: (1) Excludes "city contributions," classified as "nonrevenue," intragovernmental transfers.
Source: U.S. Bureau of the Census, City Government Finances: 1991-92

City Government Expenditures by Function

Function	FY92 ($000)	FY92 (per capita $)	FY92 (%)
Educational Services	0	0.00	0.0
Employee Retirement[1]	0	0.00	0.0
Environment/Housing	35,479	247.71	29.0
Government Administration	8,264	57.70	6.8
Interest on General Debt	5,804	40.52	4.8
Public Safety	33,158	231.51	27.1
Social Services	0	0.00	0.0
Transportation	12,423	86.74	10.2
Utility/Liquor Store	16,899	117.99	13.8
Other	10,133	70.75	8.3

Note: (1) Payments to beneficiaries including withdrawal of contributions.
Source: U.S. Bureau of the Census, City Government Finances: 1991-92

Municipal Bond Ratings

Area	Moody's	S & P
Durham	Aa1	n/a

Note: n/a not available; n/r not rated
Source: Moody's Bond Record, 2/98; Statistical Abstract of the U.S., 1997; Governing Magazine, 9/97, 3/98

POPULATION

Population Growth

Area	1980	1990	% Chg. 1980-90	July 1996 Estimate	% Chg. 1990-96
City	100,847	136,594	35.4	149,799	9.7
MSA[1]	561,222	735,480	31.0	n/a	n/a
U.S.	226,545,805	248,765,170	9.8	265,179,411	6.6

Note: (1) Metropolitan Statistical Area - see Appendix A for areas included
Source: 1980/1990 Census of Housing and Population, Summary Tape File 3C; Census Bureau Population Estimates

Population Characteristics

Race	City					MSA[1]	
	1980		1990		% Chg. 1980-90	1990	
	Population	%	Population	%		Population	%
White	52,308	51.9	70,513	51.6	34.8	533,421	72.5
Black	47,489	47.1	62,393	45.7	31.4	183,225	24.9
Amer Indian/Esk/Aleut	230	0.2	358	0.3	55.7	2,017	0.3
Asian/Pacific Islander	709	0.7	2,676	2.0	277.4	13,940	1.9
Other	111	0.1	654	0.5	489.2	2,877	0.4
Hispanic Origin[2]	970	1.0	1,713	1.3	76.6	8,386	1.1

Note: (1) Metropolitan Statistical Area - see Appendix A for areas included; (2) people of Hispanic origin can be of any race
Source: 1980/1990 Census of Housing and Population, Summary Tape File 3C

Ancestry

Area	German	Irish	English	Italian	U.S.	French	Polish	Dutch
City	11.5	9.1	13.3	2.0	4.7	1.9	1.7	1.2
MSA[1]	16.3	12.4	19.0	2.6	7.5	2.8	1.7	1.5
U.S.	23.3	15.6	13.1	5.9	5.3	4.2	3.8	2.5

Note: Figures are percentages and include persons that reported multiple ancestry (eg. if a person reported being Irish and Italian, they were included in both columns); (1) Metropolitan Statistical Area - see Appendix A for areas included
Source: 1990 Census of Population and Housing, Summary Tape File 3C

Age

Area	Median Age (Years)	Age Distribution (%)						
		Under 5	Under 18	18-24	25-44	45-64	65+	80+
City	30.6	7.3	22.1	14.9	37.0	14.8	11.2	2.8
MSA[1]	31.2	6.8	22.5	14.0	37.6	16.9	8.9	2.0
U.S.	32.9	7.3	25.6	10.5	32.6	18.7	12.5	2.8

Note: (1) Metropolitan Statistical Area - see Appendix A for areas included
Source: 1990 Census of Population and Housing, Summary Tape File 3C

Male/Female Ratio

Area	Number of males per 100 females (all ages)	Number of males per 100 females (18 years old+)
City	86.4	83.0
MSA[1]	92.9	90.5
U.S.	95.0	91.9

Note: (1) Metropolitan Statistical Area - see Appendix A for areas included
Source: 1990 Census of Population, General Population Characteristics

INCOME

Per Capita/Median/Average Income

Area	Per Capita ($)	Median Household ($)	Average Household ($)
City	14,498	27,256	34,524
MSA[1]	16,170	33,290	40,686
U.S.	14,420	30,056	38,453

Note: all figures are for 1989; (1) Metropolitan Statistical Area - see Appendix A for areas included
Source: 1990 Census of Population and Housing, Summary Tape File 3C

Household Income Distribution by Race

Income ($)	City (%)					U.S. (%)				
	Total	White	Black	Other	Hisp.[1]	Total	White	Black	Other	Hisp.[1]
Less than 5,000	8.1	4.7	12.8	8.1	4.6	6.2	4.8	15.2	8.6	8.8
5,000 - 9,999	8.7	6.4	11.7	8.8	6.4	9.3	8.6	14.2	9.9	11.1
10,000 - 14,999	9.4	7.6	11.7	12.3	17.7	8.8	8.5	11.0	9.8	11.0
15,000 - 24,999	18.9	17.0	21.3	20.9	23.1	17.5	17.3	18.9	18.5	20.5
25,000 - 34,999	17.2	17.1	17.2	20.1	14.5	15.8	16.1	14.2	15.4	16.4
35,000 - 49,999	16.4	18.4	13.9	14.2	23.7	17.9	18.6	13.3	16.1	16.0
50,000 - 74,999	13.9	18.0	8.6	12.6	8.0	15.0	15.8	9.3	13.4	11.1
75,000 - 99,999	4.1	5.9	1.8	2.3	1.2	5.1	5.5	2.6	4.7	3.1
100,000+	3.2	5.0	1.0	0.9	1.0	4.4	4.8	1.3	3.7	1.9

Note: all figures are for 1989; (1) people of Hispanic origin can be of any race
Source: 1990 Census of Population and Housing, Summary Tape File 3C

Effective Buying Income

Area	Per Capita ($)	Median Household ($)	Average Household ($)
City	16,255	31,409	39,243
MSA[1]	17,867	37,519	45,056
U.S.	15,444	33,201	41,849

Note: data as of 1/1/97; (1) Metropolitan Statistical Area - see Appendix A for areas included
Source: Standard Rate & Data Service, Newspaper Advertising Source, 2/98

Effective Household Buying Income Distribution

Area	% of Households Earning						
	$10,000 -$19,999	$20,000 -$34,999	$35,000 -$49,999	$50,000 -$74,999	$75,000 -$99,000	$100,000 -$124,999	$125,000 and up
City	16.5	25.3	17.8	17.2	5.7	1.8	1.9
MSA[1]	13.9	22.3	18.9	21.4	8.0	2.6	2.5
U.S.	16.5	23.4	18.3	18.2	6.4	2.1	2.4

Note: data as of 1/1/97; (1) Metropolitan Statistical Area - see Appendix A for areas included
Source: Standard Rate & Data Service, Newspaper Advertising Source, 2/98

Poverty Rates by Race and Age

Area	Total (%)	By Race (%)				By Age (%)		
		White	Black	Other	Hisp.[2]	Under 5 years old	Under 18 years old	65 years and over
City	14.9	7.6	22.7	18.6	19.4	23.2	20.5	16.7
MSA[1]	10.2	6.5	20.5	18.2	15.9	13.3	11.5	15.3
U.S.	13.1	9.8	29.5	23.1	25.3	20.1	18.3	12.8

Note: figures show the percent of people living below the poverty line in 1989. The average poverty threshold was $12,674 for a family of four in 1989; (1) Metropolitan Statistical Area - see Appendix A for areas included; (2) people of Hispanic origin can be of any race
Source: 1990 Census of Population and Housing, Summary Tape File 3C

EMPLOYMENT

Labor Force and Employment

Area	Civilian Labor Force			Workers Employed		
	Dec. '95	Dec. '96	% Chg.	Dec. '95	Dec. '96	% Chg.
City	83,269	83,620	0.4	80,992	81,953	1.2
MSA[1]	587,379	591,986	0.8	575,408	582,236	1.2
U.S.	134,583,000	136,742,000	1.6	127,903,000	130,785,000	2.3

Note: Data is not seasonally adjusted and covers workers 16 years of age and older; (1) Metropolitan Statistical Area - see Appendix A for areas included
Source: Bureau of Labor Statistics, http://stats.bls.gov

Durham was listed among the top 20 metro areas (out of 114 major areas) in terms of projected job growth from 1997 to 2002 with an annual percent change of 2.7%. *Standard & Poor's DRI, July 23, 1997*

Unemployment Rate

Area	1997											
	Jan.	Feb.	Mar.	Apr.	May	Jun.	Jul.	Aug.	Sep.	Oct.	Nov.	Dec.
City	3.0	3.2	2.7	2.2	2.4	3.1	2.9	3.0	2.6	2.5	2.3	2.0
MSA[1]	2.3	2.1	1.9	1.6	1.9	2.3	2.1	2.2	1.9	1.8	1.8	1.6
U.S.	5.9	5.7	5.5	4.8	4.7	5.2	5.0	4.8	4.7	4.4	4.3	4.4

Note: Data is not seasonally adjusted and covers workers 16 years of age and older; All figures are percentages; (1) Metropolitan Statistical Area - see Appendix A for areas included
Source: Bureau of Labor Statistics, http://stats.bls.gov

Employment by Industry

Sector	MSA[1]		U.S.
	Number of Employees	Percent of Total	Percent of Total
Services	194,500	30.9	29.0
Retail Trade	103,500	16.4	18.5
Government	123,400	19.6	16.1
Manufacturing	84,900	13.5	15.0
Finance/Insurance/Real Estate	30,100	4.8	5.7
Wholesale Trade	30,000	4.8	5.4
Transportation/Public Utilities	27,600	4.4	5.3
Construction/Mining	35,400	5.6	5.0

Note: Figures cover non-farm employment as of 12/97 and are not seasonally adjusted; (1) Metropolitan Statistical Area - see Appendix A for areas included
Source: Bureau of Labor Statistics, http://stats.bls.gov

Employment by Occupation

Occupation Category	City (%)	MSA[1] (%)	U.S. (%)
White Collar	67.8	68.9	58.1
Executive/Admin./Management	12.1	14.3	12.3
Professional	22.0	19.3	14.1
Technical & Related Support	7.0	6.5	3.7
Sales	9.8	11.8	11.8
Administrative Support/Clerical	17.0	16.9	16.3
Blue Collar	17.0	18.5	26.2
Precision Production/Craft/Repair	7.5	9.1	11.3
Machine Operators/Assem./Insp.	4.4	4.3	6.8
Transportation/Material Movers	2.5	2.5	4.1
Cleaners/Helpers/Laborers	2.6	2.6	3.9
Services	14.3	11.1	13.2
Farming/Forestry/Fishing	0.8	1.4	2.5

Note: figures cover employed persons 16 years old and over; (1) Metropolitan Statistical Area - see Appendix A for areas included
Source: 1990 Census of Population and Housing, Summary Tape File 3C

Occupational Employment Projections: 1992 - 2000

Occupations Expected to have the Largest Job Growth (ranked by numerical growth)	Fast-Growing Occupations[1] (ranked by percent growth)
1. Salespersons, retail	1. Computer engineers
2. Janitors/cleaners/maids, ex. priv. hshld.	2. Systems analysts
3. Cashiers	3. Physical therapy assistants and aides
4. Registered nurses	4. Dental hygienists
5. Waiters & waitresses	5. Dental assistants
6. Teachers, secondary school	6. Paralegals
7. General office clerks	7. Physical therapists
8. Teachers, elementary school	8. Teachers, special education
9. General managers & top executives	9. Medical assistants
10. Systems analysts	10. Radiologic technicians

Projections cover Chatham, Durham, Franklin, Johnston, Orange and Wake Counties.
Note: (1) Excludes occupations with total job growth less than 100
Source: Employment Security Commission of North Carolina, Occupational Trends: 1992 to 2000

Average Wages

Occupation	Wage	Occupation	Wage
Professional/Technical/Clerical	$/Week	**Health/Protective Services**	$/Week
Accountants III	-	Corrections Officers	-
Attorneys III	-	Firefighters	-
Budget Analysts III	-	Nurses, Licensed Practical II	-
Buyers/Contracting Specialists II	-	Nurses, Registered II	-
Clerks, Accounting III	443	Nursing Assistants II	-
Clerks, General III	-	Police Officers I	-
Computer Operators II	383	**Hourly Workers**	$/Hour
Computer Programmers II	-	Forklift Operators	10.39
Drafters II	547	General Maintenance Workers	8.84
Engineering Technicians III	-	Guards I	-
Engineering Technicians, Civil III	-	Janitors	5.58
Engineers III	-	Maintenance Electricians	17.51
Key Entry Operators I	289	Maintenance Electronics Techs II	17.26
Personnel Assistants III	-	Maintenance Machinists	-
Personnel Specialists III	-	Maintenance Mechanics, Machinery	14.84
Secretaries III	492	Material Handling Laborers	-
Switchboard Operator-Receptionist	359	Motor Vehicle Mechanics	15.05
Systems Analysts II	904	Shipping/Receiving Clerks	9.22
Systems Analysts Supervisor/Mgr II	-	Tool and Die Makers	-
Tax Collectors II	-	Truckdrivers, Tractor Trailer	13.89
Word Processors II	411	Warehouse Specialists	10.43

Note: Wage data includes full-time workers only for 5/95 and cover the Metropolitan Statistical Area (see Appendix A for areas included). Dashes indicate that data was not available.
Source: Bureau of Labor Statistics, Occupational Compensation Survey

TAXES

Major State and Local Tax Rates

State Corp. Income (%)	State Personal Income (%)	Residential Property (effective rate per $100)	Sales & Use State (%)	Sales & Use Local (%)	State Gasoline (cents/ gallon)	State Cigarette (cents/ 20-pack)
7.5	6.0 - 7.75	n/a	4.0	2.0	22.6	5

Note: Personal/corporate income tax rates as of 1/97. Sales, gasoline and cigarette tax rates as of 1/98.
Source: Federation of Tax Administrators, www.taxadmin.org; Washington D.C. Department of Finance and Revenue, Tax Rates and Tax Burdens in the District of Columbia: A Nationwide Comparison, June 1997; Chamber of Commerce

Total Taxes Per Capita and as a Percent of Income

Area	Per Capita Income ($)	Per Capita Taxes ($)			Taxes as Pct. of Income (%)		
		Total	Federal	State/ Local	Total	Federal	State/ Local
North Carolina	24,648	8,158	5,419	2,739	33.1	22.0	11.1
U.S.	26,187	9,205	6,127	3,078	35.2	23.4	11.8

Note: Figures are for 1997
Source: Tax Foundation, Web Site, www.taxfoundation.org

Estimated Tax Burden

Area	State Income	Local Income	Property	Sales	Total
Durham	2,994	0	2,475	822	6,291

Note: The numbers are estimates of taxes paid by a married couple with two kids and annual earnings of $65,000. Sales tax estimates assume they spend average amounts on food, clothing, household goods and gasoline. Property tax estimates assume they live in a $225,000 home.
Source: Kiplinger's Personal Finance Magazine, June 1997

COMMERCIAL REAL ESTATE

Office Market

Class/ Location	Total Space (sq. ft.)	Vacant Space (sq. ft.)	Vac. Rate (%)	Under Constr. (sq. ft.)	Net Absorp. (sq. ft.)	Rental Rates ($/sq.ft./yr.)
Class A						
CBD	2,435,277	331,414	13.6	0	-33,667	15.00-19.00
Outside CBD	11,101,460	689,288	6.2	1,139,267	692,078	16.50-22.00
Class B						
CBD	1,288,169	163,055	12.7	0	-28,399	11.00-14.50
Outside CBD	6,726,107	359,598	5.3	0	-13,759	14.00-16.50

Note: Data as of 10/97 and covers Raleigh, Cary, Chapel Hill, Durham, and Research Triangle Park; CBD = Central Business District; n/a not available;
Source: Society of Industrial and Office Realtors, 1998 Comparative Statistics of Industrial and Office Real Estate Markets

"Lenders' conservative requirements and developers' caution should continue to prevent overbuilding. New construction is significantly pre-leased. All building is concentrated in the suburbs and is driven by the activity of two REITs. Several large corporations have announced property purchases in the Research Triangle Park area and have plans to build additions to existing facilities. Employment growth is expected to slow when compared to the earlier nineties, but will still post above-average gains. The area's high proportion of government and university employment plus its growing high-tech industry should reduce cyclical volatility. Low business costs and high quality of life will prompt further in-migration of population and corporations. Even so, workforce availability will remain extremely tight, estimated at less than three percent for the balance of the decade." *Society of Industrial and Office Realtors, 1998 Comparative Statistics of Industrial and Office Real Estate Markets*

Industrial Market

Location	Total Space (sq. ft.)	Vacant Space (sq. ft.)	Vac. Rate (%)	Under Constr. (sq. ft.)	Net Absorp. (sq. ft.)	Net Lease ($/sq.ft./yr.)
Central City	n/a	n/a	n/a	n/a	n/a	n/a
Suburban	20,400,000	760,000	3.7	360,000	90,000	3.25-4.75

Note: Data as of 10/97 and covers Raleigh/Durham; n/a not available
Source: Society of Industrial and Office Realtors, 1998 Comparative Statistics of Industrial and Office Real Estate Markets

"New speculative development will be concentrated along the I-40/Airport Corridor. Late in 1997, more than 350,000 sq. ft. of space was under construction. Developers have not been put off by significant increases in construction costs marketwide, which soared by more than 33 percent, or as much as $20 per sq. ft. Raleigh/Durham will still rate as one of the top locations to live and work. There will continue to be an influx of high-tech companies that want or need to be near Research Triangle Park. The area's strong job growth and high quality of life will continue to entice workers. Low costs of doing business, a concentration of some of the country's foremost research institutes, and the pool of skilled workers will also work to attract and retain private enterprise." *Society of Industrial and Office Realtors, 1998 Comparative Statistics of Industrial and Office Real Estate Markets*

COMMERCIAL UTILITIES

Typical Monthly Electric Bills

Area	Commercial Service ($/month)		Industrial Service ($/month)	
	12 kW demand 1,500 kWh	100 kW demand 30,000 kWh	1,000 kW demand 400,000 kWh	20,000 kW demand 10,000,000 kWh
City	128	1,933	24,842	552,800
U.S.	162	2,360	25,590	545,677

Note: Based on rates in effect July 1, 1997
Source: Edison Electric Institute, Typical Residential, Commercial and Industrial Bills, Summer 1997

TRANSPORTATION

Transportation Statistics

Avg. travel time to work (min.)	17.4
Interstate highways	I-40; I-85
Bus lines	
In-city	Capital Area Transit
Inter-city	3
Passenger air service	
Airport	Raleigh-Durham International
Airlines	16
Aircraft departures	45,884 (1995)
Enplaned passengers	2,791,046 (1995)
Rail service	Amtrak
Motor freight carriers	19
Major waterways/ports	None

Source: OAG, Business Travel Planner, Summer 1997; Editor & Publisher Market Guide, 1998; FAA Airport Activity Statistics, 1996; Amtrak National Time Table, Northeast Timetable, Fall/Winter 1997-98; 1990 Census of Population and Housing, STF 3C; Chamber of Commerce/Economic Development 1997; Jane's Urban Transport Systems 1997-98; Transit Fact Book 1997

A survey of 90,000 airline passengers during the first half of 1997 ranked most of the largest airports in the U.S. Raleigh-Durham International ranked number 18 out of 36. Criteria: cleanliness, quality of restaurants, attractiveness, speed of baggage delivery, ease of reaching gates, available ground transportation, ease of following signs and closeness of parking. *Plog Research Inc., First Half 1997*

Means of Transportation to Work

Area	Car/Truck/Van		Public Transportation			Bicycle	Walked	Other Means	Worked at Home
	Drove Alone	Car-pooled	Bus	Subway	Railroad				
City	73.4	15.5	2.9	0.0	0.0	0.5	4.5	1.2	1.9
MSA[1]	78.0	13.3	1.8	0.0	0.0	0.4	3.1	1.0	2.3
U.S.	73.2	13.4	3.0	1.5	0.5	0.4	3.9	1.2	3.0

Note: figures shown are percentages and only include workers 16 years old and over;
(1) Metropolitan Statistical Area - see Appendix A for areas included
Source: 1990 Census of Population and Housing, Summary Tape File 3C

BUSINESSES

Major Business Headquarters

Company Name	1997 Rankings	
	Fortune 500	Forbes 500
No companies listed.		

Note: Companies listed are located in the city; Dashes indicate no ranking
Fortune 500: companies that produce a 10-K are ranked 1 - 500 based on 1996 revenue
Forbes 500: private companies are ranked 1 - 500 based on 1996 revenue
Source: Forbes 12/1/97; Fortune 4/28/97

Fast-Growing Businesses

According to Deloitte & Touche LLP, Durham is home to one of America's 100 fastest-growing high-technology companies: Intrex Inc. Companies are ranked by percentage growth in revenue over a five-year period. Criteria for inclusion: must be a U.S. company developing and/or providing technology products or services; company must have been in business for five years with 1992 revenues of at least $50,000. *Deloitte & Touche LLP, January 7, 1998*

Small Business Opportunity

Durham was included among *Entrepreneur* magazines listing of the "20 Best Cities for Small Business." It was ranked #3 among mid-size metro areas. Criteria: risk of failure, business performance, economic growth, affordability and state attitude towards business. *Entrepreneur, 10/97*

HOTELS & MOTELS

Hotels/Motels

Area	Hotels/ Motels	Rooms	Luxury-Level Hotels/Motels		Average Minimum Rates ($)		
			♦♦♦♦	♦♦♦♦♦	♦♦	♦♦♦	♦♦♦♦
City	24	3,358	1	0	66	104	160
Suburbs	7	824	0	0	n/a	n/a	n/a
Total	31	4,182	1	0	n/a	n/a	n/a

Note: n/a not available; Classifications range from one diamond (budget properties with basic amenities) to five diamond (luxury properties with the finest service, rooms and facilities).
Source: OAG, Business Travel Planner, Summer 1997

CONVENTION CENTERS

Major Convention Centers

Center Name	Meeting Rooms	Exhibit Space (sf)
Duke University	n/a	n/a
Durham Civic Center Complex	39	18,120

Note: n/a not available
Source: Trade Shows Worldwide 1997

Living Environment

COST OF LIVING

Cost of Living Index

Composite Index	Housing	Utilities	Groceries	Health Care	Trans-portation	Misc. Goods/ Services
104.1	113.0	99.1	101.3	104.1	97.3	101.0

Note: U.S. = 100; Figures are for Raleigh-Durham
Source: ACCRA, Cost of Living Index, 3rd Quarter 1997

HOUSING

Median Home Prices and Housing Affordability

Area	Median Price[2] 3rd Qtr. 1997 ($)	HOI[3] 3rd Qtr. 1997	Afford-ability Rank[4]
MSA[1]	143,000	61.3	138
U.S.	127,000	63.7	-

Note: (1) Metropolitan Statistical Area - see Appendix A for areas included; (2) U.S. figures calculated from the sales of 625,000 new and existing homes in 195 markets; (3) Housing Opportunity Index - percent of homes sold that were within the reach of the median income household at the prevailing mortgage interest rate; (4) Rank is from 1-195 with 1 being most affordable
Source: National Association of Home Builders, Housing Opportunity Index, 3rd Quarter 1997

It is projected that the median price of existing single-family homes in the metro area will increase by 4.0% in 1998. Nationwide, home prices are projected to increase 6.6%. *Kiplinger's Personal Finance Magazine, January 1998*

Average New Home Price

Area	Price ($)
City[1]	154,621
U.S.	135,710

Note: Figures are based on a new home with 1,800 sq. ft. of living area on an 8,000 sq. ft. lot; (1) Raleigh-Durham
Source: ACCRA, Cost of Living Index, 3rd Quarter 1997

Average Apartment Rent

Area	Rent ($/mth)
City[1]	697
U.S.	569

Note: Figures are based on an unfurnished two bedroom, 1-1/2 or 2 bath apartment, approximately 950 sq. ft. in size, excluding all utilities except water; (1) Raleigh-Durham
Source: ACCRA, Cost of Living Index, 3rd Quarter 1997

RESIDENTIAL UTILITIES

Average Residential Utility Costs

Area	All Electric ($/mth)	Part Electric ($/mth)	Other Energy ($/mth)	Phone ($/mth)
City[1]	102.74	-	-	17.86
U.S.	109.40	55.25	43.64	19.48

Note: (1) Raleigh-Durham
Source: ACCRA, Cost of Living Index, 3rd Quarter 1997

HEALTH CARE

Average Health Care Costs

Area	Hospital ($/day)	Doctor ($/visit)	Dentist ($/visit)
City[1]	316.00	56.50	64.62
U.S.	392.91	48.76	60.84

Note: Hospital - based on a semi-private room. Doctor - based on a general practitioner's routine exam of an established patient. Dentist - based on adult teeth cleaning and periodic oral exam; (1) (1) Raleigh-Durham
Source: ACCRA, Cost of Living Index, 3rd Quarter 1997

Distribution of Office-Based Physicians

Area	Family/Gen. Practitioners	Specialists		
		Medical	Surgical	Other
MSA[1]	280	895	620	850

Note: Data as of 12/31/96; (1) Metropolitan Statistical Area - see Appendix A for areas included
Source: American Medical Assn., Physician Characteristics & Distribution in the U.S., 1997-1998

Hospitals

Durham has 3 general medical and surgical hospitals, 1 eye, ear, nose and throat. *AHA Guide to the Healthcare Field 1997-98*

According to *U.S. News and World Report,* Durham has 1 of the best hospitals in the U.S.: **Duke University Medical Center**, noted for AIDS, cancer, cardiology, endocrinology, gastroenterology, geriatrics, gynecology, neurology, ophthalmology, orthopedics, otolaryngology, pediatrics, psychiatry, pulmonology, rheumatology, urology; *U.S. News and World Report, "America's Best Hospitals", 7/28/97*

EDUCATION

Public School District Statistics

District Name	Num. Sch.	Enroll.	Classroom Teachers[1]	Pupils per Teacher	Minority Pupils (%)	Current Exp.[2] ($/pupil)
Durham Public Schools	45	28,472	2,005	14.2	60.3	5,231
NC School of Science And Math	1	548	55	10.0	n/a	n/a

Note: Data covers the 1995-1996 school year unless otherwise noted; (1) Excludes teachers reported as working in school district offices rather than in schools; (2) Based on 1993-94 enrollment collected by the Census Bureau, not the enrollment figure shown in column 3; SD = School District; ISD = Independent School District; n/a not available
Source: National Center for Education Statistics, Common Core of Data Survey; Bureau of the Census

Educational Quality

School District	Education Quotient[1]	Graduate Outcome[2]	Community Index[3]	Resource Index[4]
Durham Public	86.0	73.0	126.0	58.0

Note: Nearly 1,000 secondary school districts were rated in terms of educational quality. The scores range from a low of 50 to a high of 150; (1) Average of the Graduate Outcome, Community and Resource indexes; (2) Based on graduation rates and college board scores (SAT/ACT); (3) Based on the surrounding community's average level of education and the area's average income level; (4) Based on teacher salaries, per-pupil expenditures and student-teacher ratios.
Source: Expansion Management, Ratings Issue 1997

Educational Attainment by Race

Area	High School Graduate (%)					Bachelor's Degree (%)				
	Total	White	Black	Other	Hisp.[2]	Total	White	Black	Other	Hisp.[2]
City	78.5	85.6	68.1	89.7	75.0	35.4	45.1	20.8	60.9	40.9
MSA[1]	82.4	87.2	66.0	86.3	77.2	34.8	39.2	17.8	55.6	36.6
U.S.	75.2	77.9	63.1	60.4	49.8	20.3	21.5	11.4	19.4	9.2

Note: figures shown cover persons 25 years old and over; (1) Metropolitan Statistical Area - see Appendix A for areas included; (2) people of Hispanic origin can be of any race
Source: 1990 Census of Population and Housing, Summary Tape File 3C

School Enrollment by Type

Area	Preprimary				Elementary/High School			
	Public		Private		Public		Private	
	Enrollment	%	Enrollment	%	Enrollment	%	Enrollment	%
City	1,182	45.1	1,438	54.9	17,680	92.1	1,516	7.9
MSA[1]	6,751	46.9	7,652	53.1	99,864	92.8	7,735	7.2
U.S.	2,679,029	59.5	1,824,256	40.5	38,379,689	90.2	4,187,099	9.8

Note: figures shown cover persons 3 years old and over;
(1) Metropolitan Statistical Area - see Appendix A for areas included
Source: 1990 Census of Population and Housing, Summary Tape File 3C

School Enrollment by Race

Area	Preprimary (%)				Elementary/High School (%)			
	White	Black	Other	Hisp.[1]	White	Black	Other	Hisp.[1]
City	53.8	43.1	3.1	0.6	35.5	62.1	2.4	1.2
MSA[2]	78.1	19.4	2.6	1.2	65.4	31.9	2.7	1.2
U.S.	80.4	12.5	7.1	7.8	74.1	15.6	10.3	12.5

Note: figures shown cover persons 3 years old and over; (1) people of Hispanic origin can be of any race; (2) Metropolitan Statistical Area - see Appendix A for areas included
Source: 1990 Census of Population and Housing, Summary Tape File 3C

SAT/ACT Scores

Area/District	1997 SAT				1997 ACT	
	Percent of Graduates Tested (%)	Average Math Score	Average Verbal Score	Average Combined Score	Percent of Graduates Tested (%)	Average Composite Score
Durham PS	78	492	492	984	n/a	n/a
State	59	488	490	978	11	19.3
U.S.	42	511	505	1,016	36	21.0

Note: Math and verbal SAT scores are out of a possible 800; ACT scores are out of a possible 36
Caution: Comparing or ranking states/cities on the basis of SAT/ACT scores alone is invalid and strongly discouraged by the The College Board and The American College Testing Program as students who take the tests are self-selected and do not represent the entire student population.
Source: Durham Public Schools, 1997; College Board, 1997; American College Testing Program, 1997

Classroom Teacher Salaries in Public Schools

District	B.A. Degree		M.A. Degree		Ph.D. Degree	
	Min. ($)	Max ($)	Min. ($)	Max. ($)	Min. ($)	Max. ($)
Durham	23,463	42,449	24,926	45,100	27,709	47,883
Average[1]	26,120	39,270	28,175	44,667	31,643	49,825

Note: Salaries are for 1996-1997; (1) Based on all school districts covered
Source: American Federation of Teachers (unpublished data)

Higher Education

Two-Year Colleges		Four-Year Colleges		Medical Schools	Law Schools	Voc/ Tech
Public	Private	Public	Private			
1	0	1	1	1	2	3

Source: College Blue Book, Occupational Education 1997; Medical School Admission Requirements, 1998-99; Peterson's Guide to Two-Year Colleges, 1997; Peterson's Guide to Four-Year Colleges, 1997; Barron's Guide to Law Schools 1997

MAJOR EMPLOYERS

Major Employers

Blue Cross & Blue Shield of NC	Durham County Hospital Corp.
PBM Graphics	Liggett Group
Broadband Technologies (fiber optics)	Midway Airlines
Organon Teknika Corp. (laboratory instruments)	Pilling Weck Inc. (medical instruments)
Private Diagnostic Clinic	Reichold Chemicals
Advanced Technology Applications (computer hardware)	Durham Herald

Note: companies listed are located in the city
Source: Dun's Business Rankings 1997; Ward's Business Directory, 1997

PUBLIC SAFETY

Crime Rate

Area	All Crimes	Violent Crimes				Property Crimes		
		Murder	Forcible Rape	Robbery	Aggrav. Assault	Burglary	Larceny -Theft	Motor Vehicle Theft
City	11,333.3	27.6	56.5	545.2	507.5	2,844.4	6,326.9	1,025.1
Suburbs[1]	5,158.1	6.8	22.1	141.1	302.0	1,041.7	3,311.2	333.1
MSA[2]	6,076.4	9.9	27.2	201.2	332.5	1,309.8	3,759.7	436.0
U.S.	5,078.9	7.4	36.1	202.4	388.2	943.0	2,975.9	525.9

Note: Crime rate is the number of crimes per 100,000 pop.; (1) defined as all areas within the MSA but located outside the central city; (2) Metropolitan Statistical Area - see Appendix A for areas incl.
Source: FBI Uniform Crime Reports 1996

RECREATION

Culture and Recreation

Museums	Symphony Orchestras	Opera Companies	Dance Companies	Professional Theatres	Zoos	Pro Sports Teams
5	2	1	1	1	0	0

Source: International Directory of the Performing Arts, 1996; Official Museum Directory, 1998; Chamber of Commerce/Economic Development 1997

Library System

The Durham County Library has seven branches, holdings of 423,183 volumes and a budget of $4,475,255 (1995-1996). *American Library Directory, 1997-1998*

MEDIA

Newspapers

Name	Type	Freq.	Distribution	Circulation
The Carolina Times	Black	1x/wk	Area	5,823
The Chronicle	n/a	5x/wk	Campus	community & alumni
Herald-Sun	General	7x/wk	Area	55,000
The Independent	General	1x/wk	Area	50,000

Note: Includes newspapers with circulations of 500 or more located in the city; n/a not available
Source: Burrelle's Media Directory, 1998 Edition

AM Radio Stations

Call Letters	Freq. (kHz)	Target Audience	Station Format	Music Format
WDNC	620	General	M/N/S/T	Oldies
WSRC	1410	Religious	M	Christian
WRTP	1530	Religious	M/N/S	Adult Contemporary/Christian

Note: Stations included broadcast in the Durham metro area
Station Format: E = Educational; M = Music; N = News; S = Sports; T = Talk
Source: Burrelle's Media Directory, 1998 Edition

FM Radio Stations

Call Letters	Freq. (mHz)	Target Audience	Station Format	Music Format
WXDU	88.7	n/a	M/N/S	n/a
WFXC	107.1	General	M	Urban Contemporary

Note: Stations included broadcast in the Durham metro area; n/a not available
Station Format: E = Educational; M = Music; N = News; S = Sports; T = Talk
Source: Burrelle's Media Directory, 1998 Edition

Television Stations

Name	Ch.	Affiliation	Type	Owner
WUNC	4	PBS	Public	University of N. Carolina Board of Governors
WTVD	11	ABC	Commercial	ABC Inc.
WUND	12	PBS	Public	University of N. Carolina Board of Governors
WUNE	17	PBS	Public	University of N. Carolina Board of Governors
WUNM	19	PBS	Public	University of N. Carolina Board of Governors
WUNK	25	PBS	Public	University of N. Carolina Board of Governors
WUNL	26	PBS	Public	University of N. Carolina Board of Governors
WUNU	31	PBS	Public	University of N. Carolina Board of Governors
WUNF	33	PBS	Public	University of N. Carolina Board of Governors
WUNP	36	PBS	Public	University of N. Carolina Board of Governors
WUNJ	39	PBS	Public	University of N. Carolina Board of Governors
WUNG	58	PBS	Public	University of N. Carolina Board of Governors

Note: Stations included broadcast in the Durham metro area
Source: Burrelle's Media Directory, 1998 Edition

CLIMATE

Average and Extreme Temperatures

Temperature	Jan	Feb	Mar	Apr	May	Jun	Jul	Aug	Sep	Oct	Nov	Dec	Ann
Extreme High (°F)	79	84	90	95	97	104	105	105	104	98	88	79	105
Average High (°F)	50	53	61	72	79	86	89	87	81	72	62	53	71
Average Temp. (°F)	40	43	50	59	67	75	78	77	71	60	51	42	60
Average Low (°F)	29	31	38	46	55	63	68	67	60	48	39	32	48
Extreme Low (°F)	-9	5	11	23	29	38	48	46	37	19	11	4	-9

Note: Figures cover the years 1948-1990
Source: National Climatic Data Center, International Station Meteorological Climate Summary, 3/95

Average Precipitation/Snowfall/Humidity

Precip./Humidity	Jan	Feb	Mar	Apr	May	Jun	Jul	Aug	Sep	Oct	Nov	Dec	Ann
Avg. Precip. (in.)	3.4	3.6	3.6	2.9	3.9	3.6	4.4	4.4	3.2	2.9	3.0	3.1	42.0
Avg. Snowfall (in.)	2	3	1	Tr	0	0	0	0	0	0	Tr	1	8
Avg. Rel. Hum. 7am (%)	79	79	79	80	84	86	88	91	91	90	84	81	84
Avg. Rel. Hum. 4pm (%)	53	49	46	43	51	54	57	59	57	53	51	53	52

Note: Figures cover the years 1948-1990; Tr = Trace amounts (<0.05 in. of rain; <0.5 in. of snow)
Source: National Climatic Data Center, International Station Meteorological Climate Summary, 3/95

Weather Conditions

Temperature			Daytime Sky			Precipitation		
32°F & below	45°F & below	90°F & above	Clear	Partly cloudy	Cloudy	0.01 inch or more precip.	0.1 inch or more snow/ice	Thunder-storms
77	160	39	98	143	124	110	3	42

Note: Figures are average number of days per year and covers the years 1948-1990
Source: National Climatic Data Center, International Station Meteorological Climate Summary, 3/95

AIR & WATER QUALITY

Maximum Pollutant Concentrations

	Particulate Matter (ug/m^3)	Carbon Monoxide (ppm)	Sulfur Dioxide (ppm)	Nitrogen Dioxide (ppm)	Ozone (ppm)	Lead (ug/m^3)
MSA[1] Level	49	6	0.010	n/a	0.11	n/a
NAAQS[2]	150	9	0.140	0.053	0.12	1.50
Met NAAQS?	Yes	Yes	Yes	n/a	Yes	n/a

Note: (1) Metropolitan Statistical Area - see Appendix A for areas included; (2) National Ambient Air Quality Standards; ppm = parts per million; ug/m^3 = micrograms per cubic meter; n/a not available
Source: EPA, National Air Quality and Emissions Trends Report, 1996

Pollutant Standards Index

In the Durham MSA (see Appendix A for areas included), the Pollutant Standards Index (PSI) exceeded 100 on 0 days in 1996. A PSI value greater than 100 indicates that air quality would be in the unhealthful range on that day. *EPA, National Air Quality and Emissions Trends Report, 1996*

Drinking Water

Water System Name	Pop. Served	Primary Water Source Type	Number of Violations in Fiscal Year 1997	Type of Violation/ Contaminants
City of Durham	150,000	Surface	None	None

Note: Data as of January 16, 1998
Source: EPA, Office of Ground Water and Drinking Water, Safe Drinking Water Information System

Durham tap water is alkaline, soft and fluoridated.
Editor & Publisher Market Guide, 1998

Greensboro, North Carolina

Background

Greensboro is a quiet community in northern North Carolina. Along with Winston-Salem and High Point, the three cities form an urban triangle.

The city was the site of the Battle of Guilford Courthouse during the American Revolution on March 15, 1781; as well as the birthplace of notable Americans such as Dolly Madison, wife of the fourth President of the United States, James Madison; and William Sydney Porter, otherwise known as the author, O. Henry.

During the mid to late 19th century, the economy of the city was largely based upon textile production. While that still remains a vital role in Greensboro, petroleum, pharmaceutical products, furniture, tobacco, and electronic equipment have come into prominence as well. These industries give Greensboro about 500 manufacturing plants in its surrounding area.

Greensboro is one of the anchors of the newly emerging center for business opportunities in North Carolina, the Piedmont Triad. Along with Winston-Salem and High Point, it has become a major metro area for attracting new plants and facilities. The city in Guilford County, saw over 2,000 new jobs created in 1996 by new and expanding companies. *Site Selection June/July 1997*

Greensboro is the largest city in the Piedmont Triad region. Both winter temperatures and rainfall are modified by the Blue Ridge Mountain barrier on the northwest. The summer temperatures vary with cloudiness and shower activity, but are generally mild. Northwesterly winds rarely bring heavy or prolonged winter rain or snow.

Damaging storms are infrequent and the occurrence of tornadoes is rare. Hurricanes have produced heavy rainfall, but no winds of destructive force.

General Rankings and Evaluative Comments

- Greensboro was ranked #79 out of 300 cities by *Money's* 1997 "Survey of the Best Places to Live." Criteria used: health services, crime, economy, housing, education, transportation, weather, leisure and the arts. The city was ranked #161 in 1996 and #90 in 1995. *Money, July 1997; Money, September 1996; Money, September 1995*

- *Ladies Home Journal* ranked America's 200 largest cities based on the qualities women care about most. Greensboro ranked 49 out of 200. Criteria: low crime rate, good public schools, well-paying jobs, quality health and child care, the presence of women in government, proportion of women-owned businesses, size of the wage gap with men, local economy, divorce rates, the ratio of single men to single women, whether there are laws that require at least the same number of public toilets for women as men, and the probability of good hair days. *Ladies Home Journal, November 1997*

- Greensboro was ranked #72 out of 219 cities in terms of children's health, safety, and economic well-being. Criteria: total population, percent population change, birth rate, child immunization rate, infant mortality rate, percent low birth weight infants, percent of births to teens, physician-to-population ratio, student-to-teacher ratio, dropout rate, unemployment rate, median family income, percent of children in poverty, violent and property crime rates, number of juvenile arrests for violent crimes as a percent of the total crime index, number of days with pollution standard index (PSI) over 100, pounds toxic releases per 1,000 people and number of superfund sites. *Zero Population Growth, Children's Environmental Index 1997*

- According to *Working Mother,* "No state has more action or more enthusiasm for improving child care than North Carolina. And no governor deserves more credit for fighting for child care than Jim Hunt. His 'Smart Start' program has as its goal affordable, quality early childhood education for every child who needs it. In the past four years, the state has created more than 30,000 new slots for child care and improved care for more than 150,000 kids.

  The program ran up against some resistance in the state legislature in the past, but now a solid majority embrace the core tenets of Smart Start. This year, for example, state lawmakers decided to award permanent funding for the state's caregiver training program, Teacher Education and Compensation Helps (T.E.A.C.H.)—more than $1 million a year in recurring funds. That means child care advocates won't have to come back every year to fight for money for early education. The T.E.A.C.H. program is now being copied by other states, including Illinois.

  With all this progress, it's a shame that North Carolina's key standards aren't better. One adult is still allowed to care for up to five babies, and caregivers are not required to have any education or training before they start work (a bill now before the legislature may change this). This state could do better on these critical aspects of child care." *Working Mother, July/August 1997*

Business Environment

STATE ECONOMY

State Economic Profile

"North Carolina's strength is its development of technologically advanced industries, ranging from computer software development in biotechnology. North Carolina's weakness is its ailing textile and apparel industries....

North Carolina's population continues to expand at a robust 1.7% year-over-year rate, nearly twice the national average. In 1996 net domestic migration contributed 1.1 percentage points to North Carolina's population growth rate, compared to just 0.4 for the southern region, making the state's economic expansion particularly dependent on migration....

Apart from job losses in the apparel and textile industries, North Carolina's economy remains healthy, and employment growth is outpacing the nation. The long-term outlook for North Carolina is positive. Its emergency as a center for high-tech employment continues to attract relocations and expansions to metro areas such as Raleigh and Charlotte. A downside risk to the economy is strong growth in government sector employment, which may leave the state susceptible to government spending cuts in the future...." *National Association of Realtors, Economic Profiles: The Fifty States, July 1997*

IMPORTS/EXPORTS

Total Export Sales

Area	1993 ($000)	1994 ($000)	1995 ($000)	1996 ($000)	% Chg. 1993-96	% Chg. 1995-96
MSA[1]	2,453,096	2,773,310	3,356,262	3,495,639	42.5	4.2
U.S.	464,858,354	512,415,609	583,030,524	622,827,063	34.0	6.8

Note: (1) Metropolitan Statistical Area - see Appendix A for areas included
Source: U.S. Department of Commerce, International Trade Association, Metropolitan Area Exports: An Export Performance Report on Over 250 U.S. Cities, October 1997

Imports/Exports by Port

Type	Cargo Value			Share of U.S. Total	
	1995 (US$mil.)	1996 (US$mil.)	% Change 1995-1996	1995 (%)	1996 (%)
Imports	0	0	0	0	0
Exports	0	0	0	0	0

Source: Global Trade Information Services, WaterBorne Trade Atlas 1997

CITY FINANCES

City Government Finances

Component	FY92 ($000)	FY92 (per capita $)
Revenue	176,995	938.64
Expenditure	187,686	995.34
Debt Outstanding	178,095	944.48
Cash & Securities	148,371	786.84

Source: U.S. Bureau of the Census, City Government Finances: 1991-92

City Government Revenue by Source

Source	FY92 ($000)	FY92 (per capita $)	FY92 (%)
From Federal Government	4,058	21.52	2.3
From State Governments	21,387	113.42	12.1
From Local Governments	17,967	95.28	10.2
Property Taxes	59,998	318.18	33.9
General Sales Taxes	0	0.00	0.0
Selective Sales Taxes	1,624	8.61	0.9
Income Taxes	0	0.00	0.0
Current Charges	26,089	138.36	14.7
Utility/Liquor Store	25,651	136.03	14.5
Employee Retirement[1]	0	0.00	0.0
Other	20,221	107.24	11.4

Note: (1) Excludes "city contributions," classified as "nonrevenue," intragovernmental transfers.
Source: U.S. Bureau of the Census, City Government Finances: 1991-92

City Government Expenditures by Function

Function	FY92 ($000)	FY92 (per capita $)	FY92 (%)
Educational Services	4,568	24.23	2.4
Employee Retirement[1]	0	0.00	0.0
Environment/Housing	57,606	305.50	30.7
Government Administration	12,096	64.15	6.4
Interest on General Debt	5,333	28.28	2.8
Public Safety	42,240	224.01	22.5
Social Services	357	1.89	0.2
Transportation	27,323	144.90	14.6
Utility/Liquor Store	28,392	150.57	15.1
Other	9,771	51.82	5.2

Note: (1) Payments to beneficiaries including withdrawal of contributions.
Source: U.S. Bureau of the Census, City Government Finances: 1991-92

Municipal Bond Ratings

Area	Moody's	S & P
Greensboro	Aa1	n/a

Note: n/a not available; n/r not rated
Source: Moody's Bond Record, 2/98; Statistical Abstract of the U.S., 1997; Governing Magazine, 9/97, 3/98

POPULATION

Population Growth

Area	1980	1990	% Chg. 1980-90	July 1996 Estimate	% Chg. 1990-96
City	155,684	183,521	17.9	195,426	6.5
MSA[1]	851,444	942,091	10.6	1,141,238	21.1
U.S.	226,545,805	248,765,170	9.8	265,179,411	6.6

Note: (1) Metropolitan Statistical Area - see Appendix A for areas included
Source: 1980/1990 Census of Housing and Population, Summary Tape File 3C; Census Bureau Population Estimates

Population Characteristics

Race	City 1980 Population	City 1980 %	City 1990 Population	City 1990 %	% Chg. 1980-90	MSA[1] 1990 Population	MSA[1] 1990 %
White	102,771	66.0	117,349	63.9	14.2	748,794	79.5
Black	51,207	32.9	62,356	34.0	21.8	181,869	19.3
Amer Indian/Esk/Aleut	659	0.4	779	0.4	18.2	3,186	0.3
Asian/Pacific Islander	748	0.5	2,573	1.4	244.0	6,373	0.7
Other	299	0.2	464	0.3	55.2	1,869	0.2
Hispanic Origin[2]	1,201	0.8	1,389	0.8	15.7	6,122	0.6

Note: (1) Metropolitan Statistical Area - see Appendix A for areas included; (2) people of Hispanic origin can be of any race
Source: 1980/1990 Census of Housing and Population, Summary Tape File 3C

Ancestry

Area	German	Irish	English	Italian	U.S.	French	Polish	Dutch
City	15.7	11.7	15.4	2.1	7.2	2.1	1.2	2.0
MSA[1]	20.5	12.6	15.4	1.6	12.5	2.0	0.8	2.9
U.S.	23.3	15.6	13.1	5.9	5.3	4.2	3.8	2.5

Note: Figures are percentages and include persons that reported multiple ancestry (eg. if a person reported being Irish and Italian, they were included in both columns); (1) Metropolitan Statistical Area - see Appendix A for areas included
Source: 1990 Census of Population and Housing, Summary Tape File 3C

Age

Area	Median Age (Years)	Age Distribution (%) Under 5	Under 18	18-24	25-44	45-64	65+	80+
City	32.2	6.4	21.6	14.8	33.8	18.0	11.8	2.5
MSA[1]	34.0	6.6	23.1	11.1	33.3	20.4	12.1	2.6
U.S.	32.9	7.3	25.6	10.5	32.6	18.7	12.5	2.8

Note: (1) Metropolitan Statistical Area - see Appendix A for areas included
Source: 1990 Census of Population and Housing, Summary Tape File 3C

Male/Female Ratio

Area	Number of males per 100 females (all ages)	Number of males per 100 females (18 years old+)
City	86.9	82.6
MSA[1]	91.7	87.9
U.S.	95.0	91.9

Note: (1) Metropolitan Statistical Area - see Appendix A for areas included
Source: 1990 Census of Population, General Population Characteristics

INCOME

Per Capita/Median/Average Income

Area	Per Capita ($)	Median Household ($)	Average Household ($)
City	15,644	29,184	37,886
MSA[1]	14,588	29,254	36,588
U.S.	14,420	30,056	38,453

Note: all figures are for 1989; (1) Metropolitan Statistical Area - see Appendix A for areas included
Source: 1990 Census of Population and Housing, Summary Tape File 3C

Household Income Distribution by Race

Income ($)	City (%)					U.S. (%)				
	Total	White	Black	Other	Hisp.[1]	Total	White	Black	Other	Hisp.[1]
Less than 5,000	5.9	3.8	10.5	9.5	4.9	6.2	4.8	15.2	8.6	8.8
5,000 - 9,999	8.4	7.2	11.1	6.9	10.0	9.3	8.6	14.2	9.9	11.1
10,000 - 14,999	9.2	7.7	12.8	6.3	13.5	8.8	8.5	11.0	9.8	11.0
15,000 - 24,999	19.2	17.5	22.9	23.9	28.1	17.5	17.3	18.9	18.5	20.5
25,000 - 34,999	16.9	16.8	17.1	18.4	11.2	15.8	16.1	14.2	15.4	16.4
35,000 - 49,999	18.1	19.3	15.3	14.2	12.6	17.9	18.6	13.3	16.1	16.0
50,000 - 74,999	13.8	16.4	7.9	15.0	12.3	15.0	15.8	9.3	13.4	11.1
75,000 - 99,999	4.2	5.1	2.0	4.4	4.2	5.1	5.5	2.6	4.7	3.1
100,000+	4.4	6.2	0.4	1.4	3.3	4.4	4.8	1.3	3.7	1.9

Note: all figures are for 1989; (1) people of Hispanic origin can be of any race
Source: 1990 Census of Population and Housing, Summary Tape File 3C

Effective Buying Income

Area	Per Capita ($)	Median Household ($)	Average Household ($)
City	16,710	32,101	40,890
MSA[1]	15,870	32,494	39,841
U.S.	15,444	33,201	41,849

Note: data as of 1/1/97; (1) Metropolitan Statistical Area - see Appendix A for areas included
Source: Standard Rate & Data Service, Newspaper Advertising Source, 2/98

Effective Household Buying Income Distribution

Area	% of Households Earning						
	$10,000 -$19,999	$20,000 -$34,999	$35,000 -$49,999	$50,000 -$74,999	$75,000 -$99,000	$100,000 -$124,999	$125,000 and up
City	17.1	25.4	18.6	17.2	5.3	1.9	2.5
MSA[1]	16.8	25.4	19.5	17.8	5.2	1.7	2.0
U.S.	16.5	23.4	18.3	18.2	6.4	2.1	2.4

Note: data as of 1/1/97; (1) Metropolitan Statistical Area - see Appendix A for areas included
Source: Standard Rate & Data Service, Newspaper Advertising Source, 2/98

Poverty Rates by Race and Age

Area	Total (%)	By Race (%)				By Age (%)		
		White	Black	Other	Hisp.[2]	Under 5 years old	Under 18 years old	65 years and over
City	11.6	6.8	20.7	17.0	15.0	18.6	15.6	12.1
MSA[1]	10.0	7.1	21.8	19.5	19.9	15.3	13.3	16.0
U.S.	13.1	9.8	29.5	23.1	25.3	20.1	18.3	12.8

Note: figures show the percent of people living below the poverty line in 1989. The average poverty threshold was $12,674 for a family of four in 1989; (1) Metropolitan Statistical Area - see Appendix A for areas included; (2) people of Hispanic origin can be of any race
Source: 1990 Census of Population and Housing, Summary Tape File 3C

EMPLOYMENT

Labor Force and Employment

Area	Civilian Labor Force			Workers Employed		
	Dec. '95	Dec. '96	% Chg.	Dec. '95	Dec. '96	% Chg.
City	115,862	113,053	-2.4	112,322	110,208	-1.9
MSA[1]	640,560	626,638	-2.2	622,882	611,157	-1.9
U.S.	134,583,000	136,742,000	1.6	127,903,000	130,785,000	2.3

Note: Data is not seasonally adjusted and covers workers 16 years of age and older;
(1) Metropolitan Statistical Area - see Appendix A for areas included
Source: Bureau of Labor Statistics, http://stats.bls.gov

Unemployment Rate

Area	1997											
	Jan.	Feb.	Mar.	Apr.	May	Jun.	Jul.	Aug.	Sep.	Oct.	Nov.	Dec.
City	3.5	4.0	3.6	2.3	2.9	3.3	3.6	3.4	3.1	2.9	2.8	2.5
MSA[1]	3.2	3.2	2.9	2.3	2.7	3.1	3.2	3.1	2.7	2.6	2.7	2.5
U.S.	5.9	5.7	5.5	4.8	4.7	5.2	5.0	4.8	4.7	4.4	4.3	4.4

Note: Data is not seasonally adjusted and covers workers 16 years of age and older; All figures are percentages; (1) Metropolitan Statistical Area - see Appendix A for areas included
Source: Bureau of Labor Statistics, http://stats.bls.gov

Employment by Industry

Sector	MSA[1]		U.S.
	Number of Employees	Percent of Total	Percent of Total
Services	165,500	25.8	29.0
Retail Trade	108,700	17.0	18.5
Government	70,200	10.9	16.1
Manufacturing	165,600	25.8	15.0
Finance/Insurance/Real Estate	33,100	5.2	5.7
Wholesale Trade	34,500	5.4	5.4
Transportation/Public Utilities	31,900	5.0	5.3
Construction/Mining	31,700	4.9	5.0

Note: Figures cover non-farm employment as of 12/97 and are not seasonally adjusted; (1) Metropolitan Statistical Area - see Appendix A for areas included
Source: Bureau of Labor Statistics, http://stats.bls.gov

Employment by Occupation

Occupation Category	City (%)	MSA[1] (%)	U.S. (%)
White Collar	63.9	53.4	58.1
Executive/Admin./Management	13.5	11.1	12.3
Professional	14.7	12.0	14.1
Technical & Related Support	3.5	3.3	3.7
Sales	14.4	11.3	11.8
Administrative Support/Clerical	17.8	15.6	16.3
Blue Collar	22.7	34.3	26.2
Precision Production/Craft/Repair	8.2	12.9	11.3
Machine Operators/Assem./Insp.	7.4	12.8	6.8
Transportation/Material Movers	3.3	4.3	4.1
Cleaners/Helpers/Laborers	3.7	4.3	3.9
Services	12.5	10.8	13.2
Farming/Forestry/Fishing	0.8	1.5	2.5

Note: figures cover employed persons 16 years old and over; (1) Metropolitan Statistical Area - see Appendix A for areas included
Source: 1990 Census of Population and Housing, Summary Tape File 3C

Occupational Employment Projections: 1992 - 2000

Occupations Expected to have the Largest Job Growth (ranked by numerical growth)	Fast-Growing Occupations[1] (ranked by percent growth)
1. Salespersons, retail	1. Paralegals
2. Janitors/cleaners/maids, ex. priv. hshld.	2. Computer engineers
3. Cashiers	3. Systems analysts
4. Waiters & waitresses	4. Pest controllers & assistants
5. General office clerks	5. Secretaries, legal
6. Registered nurses	6. Physical therapy assistants and aides
7. General managers & top executives	7. Hotel desk clerks
8. First line supervisor, sales & related	8. Child care workers, private household
9. Maids/housekeepers	9. Home health aides
10. Food preparation workers	10. Lawyers

Projections cover Alamance, Davidson, Davie, Forsyth, Guilford, Randolf, Stokes and Yadkin Counties.
Note: (1) Excludes occupations with total job growth less than 100
Source: Employment Security Commission of North Carolina, Occupational Trends: 1992 to 2000

Average Wages

Occupation	Wage	Occupation	Wage
Professional/Technical/Clerical	$/Week	**Health/Protective Services**	$/Week
Accountants III	-	Corrections Officers	-
Attorneys III	-	Firefighters	-
Budget Analysts III	-	Nurses, Licensed Practical II	-
Buyers/Contracting Specialists II	-	Nurses, Registered II	-
Clerks, Accounting III	430	Nursing Assistants II	-
Clerks, General III	452	Police Officers I	-
Computer Operators II	430	**Hourly Workers**	$/Hour
Computer Programmers II	619	Forklift Operators	11.18
Drafters II	515	General Maintenance Workers	10.27
Engineering Technicians III	-	Guards I	6.30
Engineering Technicians, Civil III	-	Janitors	5.43
Engineers III	-	Maintenance Electricians	14.98
Key Entry Operators I	331	Maintenance Electronics Techs II	15.38
Personnel Assistants III	-	Maintenance Machinists	17.40
Personnel Specialists III	-	Maintenance Mechanics, Machinery	14.69
Secretaries III	506	Material Handling Laborers	8.25
Switchboard Operator-Receptionist	343	Motor Vehicle Mechanics	14.58
Systems Analysts II	963	Shipping/Receiving Clerks	9.65
Systems Analysts Supervisor/Mgr II	-	Tool and Die Makers	16.14
Tax Collectors II	-	Truckdrivers, Tractor Trailer	13.76
Word Processors II	-	Warehouse Specialists	-

Note: Wage data includes full-time workers only for 7/96 and cover the Metropolitan Statistical Area (see Appendix A for areas included). Dashes indicate that data was not available.
Source: Bureau of Labor Statistics, Occupational Compensation Survey, 12/96

TAXES

Major State and Local Tax Rates

State Corp. Income (%)	State Personal Income (%)	Residential Property (effective rate per $100)	Sales & Use State (%)	Sales & Use Local (%)	State Gasoline (cents/ gallon)	State Cigarette (cents/ 20-pack)
7.5	6.0 - 7.75	n/a	4.0	2.0	22.6	5

Note: Personal/corporate income tax rates as of 1/97. Sales, gasoline and cigarette tax rates as of 1/98.
Source: Federation of Tax Administrators, www.taxadmin.org; Washington D.C. Department of Finance and Revenue, Tax Rates and Tax Burdens in the District of Columbia: A Nationwide Comparison, June 1997; Chamber of Commerce

Total Taxes Per Capita and as a Percent of Income

Area	Per Capita Income ($)	Per Capita Taxes ($)			Taxes as Pct. of Income (%)		
		Total	Federal	State/ Local	Total	Federal	State/ Local
North Carolina	24,648	8,158	5,419	2,739	33.1	22.0	11.1
U.S.	26,187	9,205	6,127	3,078	35.2	23.4	11.8

Note: Figures are for 1997
Source: Tax Foundation, Web Site, www.taxfoundation.org

COMMERCIAL REAL ESTATE

Office Market

Class/ Location	Total Space (sq. ft.)	Vacant Space (sq. ft.)	Vac. Rate (%)	Under Constr. (sq. ft.)	Net Absorp. (sq. ft.)	Rental Rates ($/sq.ft./yr.)
Class A						
CBD	2,415,289	52,702	2.2	0	24,655	16.00-20.00
Outside CBD	3,068,615	104,610	3.4	185,177	503,679	15.50-19.53
Class B						
CBD	2,095,990	398,533	19.0	0	28,720	12.00-14.25
Outside CBD	5,827,980	899,248	15.4	315,500	53,194	11.00-16.00

Note: Data as of 10/97 and covers Greensboro; CBD = Central Business District; n/a not available;
Source: Society of Industrial and Office Realtors, 1998 Comparative Statistics of Industrial and Office Real Estate Markets

"Speculative development is underway in the Piedmont Triad Airport area where two new buildings will add 142,000 sq. ft. Another 108,000 sq. ft. property is being built on spec in Greensboro's Northwest sub-market. The finance, medical and banking sectors are leading demand generators. Even though the financial industry accounts for a small portion of jobs, 5.3 percent, it has accounted for one-quarter of all new jobs in the twelve months ended July 1997 thanks to expansion of financial service firms such as Wachovia Bank and Trust. Most major industries, particularly the office-based, are expected to expand this year. One constraint could be the limited availability of labor. Unemployment is anticipated to remain below three percent." *Society of Industrial and Office Realtors, 1998 Comparative Statistics of Industrial and Office Real Estate Markets*

Industrial Market

Location	Total Space (sq. ft.)	Vacant Space (sq. ft.)	Vac. Rate (%)	Under Constr. (sq. ft.)	Net Absorp. (sq. ft.)	Gross Lease ($/sq.ft./yr.)
Central City	n/a	n/a	n/a	n/a	n/a	n/a
Suburban	29,300,000	2,720,200	9.3	750,000	-69,030	3.75-6.20

Note: Data as of 10/97 and covers the Triad Area (Greensboro/High Point/Winston-Salem); n/a not available
Source: Society of Industrial and Office Realtors, 1998 Comparative Statistics of Industrial and Office Real Estate Markets

"SIOR's observer expects speculative construction driven by REITs to continue in the coming year. At least 750,000 sq. ft. of high-cube and flex space is underway, mostly in the airport area. Liberty Property Trust has 329,600 sq. ft. under development; Childress Klein is constructing 118,000 sq. ft.; Highwoods Forsyth has 109,800 sq. ft. under construction; and Samet is developing 80,000 sq. ft. Greensboro's low cost of doing business should attract industrial relocations and spur local expansions, fostering a return of positive net absorption. Vacancy levels are expected to remain above nine percent, however, due to speculative development. Most, market indicators are projected to remain unchanged during 1998 except for a modest increase in the sales prices of warehouse/distribution and manufacturing facilities." *Society of Industrial and Office Realtors, 1998 Comparative Statistics of Industrial and Office Real Estate Markets*

COMMERCIAL UTILITIES

Typical Monthly Electric Bills

Area	Commercial Service ($/month)		Industrial Service ($/month)	
	12 kW demand 1,500 kWh	100 kW demand 30,000 kWh	1,000 kW demand 400,000 kWh	20,000 kW demand 10,000,000 kWh
City	151	1,832	21,037	458,608
U.S.	162	2,360	25,590	545,677

Note: Based on rates in effect July 1, 1997
Source: Edison Electric Institute, Typical Residential, Commercial and Industrial Bills, Summer 1997

TRANSPORTATION

Transportation Statistics

Avg. travel time to work (min.)	16.7
Interstate highways	I-40; I-85
Bus lines	
In-city	Greensboro TA
Inter-city	2
Passenger air service	
Airport	Piedmont Triad International
Airlines	8
Aircraft departures	38,745 (1995)
Enplaned passengers	1,615,987 (1995)
Rail service	Amtrak
Motor freight carriers	n/a
Major waterways/ports	None

Source: OAG, Business Travel Planner, Summer 1997; Editor & Publisher Market Guide, 1998; FAA Airport Activity Statistics, 1996; Amtrak National Time Table, Northeast Timetable, Fall/Winter 1997-98; 1990 Census of Population and Housing, STF 3C; Chamber of Commerce/Economic Development 1997; Jane's Urban Transport Systems 1997-98; Transit Fact Book 1997

Means of Transportation to Work

Area	Car/Truck/Van		Public Transportation			Bicycle	Walked	Other Means	Worked at Home
	Drove Alone	Car-pooled	Bus	Subway	Railroad				
City	79.1	12.5	1.5	0.0	0.0	0.3	3.6	1.2	1.8
MSA[1]	79.1	14.5	1.0	0.0	0.0	0.1	2.3	0.8	2.1
U.S.	73.2	13.4	3.0	1.5	0.5	0.4	3.9	1.2	3.0

Note: figures shown are percentages and only include workers 16 years old and over;
(1) Metropolitan Statistical Area - see Appendix A for areas included
Source: 1990 Census of Population and Housing, Summary Tape File 3C

BUSINESSES

Major Business Headquarters

Company Name	1997 Rankings	
	Fortune 500	Forbes 500
No companies listed.		

Note: Companies listed are located in the city; Dashes indicate no ranking
Fortune 500: companies that produce a 10-K are ranked 1 - 500 based on 1996 revenue
Forbes 500: private companies are ranked 1 - 500 based on 1996 revenue
Source: Forbes 12/1/97; Fortune 4/28/97

Fast-Growing Businesses

According to Deloitte & Touche LLP, Greensboro is home to one of America's 100 fastest-growing high-technology companies: RF MicroDevices Inc. Companies are ranked by percentage growth in revenue over a five-year period. Criteria for inclusion: must be a U.S. company developing and/or providing technology products or services; company must have been in business for five years with 1992 revenues of at least $50,000. *Deloitte & Touche LLP, January 7, 1998*

Women-Owned Businesses: Number, Employment, Sales and Share

Area	Women-Owned Businesses in 1996				Share of Women-Owned Businesses in 1996	
	Number	Employment	Sales ($000)	Rank[2]	Percent (%)	Rank[3]
MSA[1]	34,100	84,900	9,772,400	48	33.9	45

Note: (1) Metropolitan Statistical Area - see Appendix A for areas included; (2) Calculated on an averaging of number of businesses, employment and sales and ranges from 1 to 50 where 1 is best; (3) Ranges from 1 to 50 where 1 is best
Source: The National Foundation for Women Business Owners, 1996 Facts on Women-Owned Businesses: Trends in the Top 50 Metropolitan Areas, March 26, 1997

Women-Owned Businesses: Growth

Area	Growth in Women-Owned Businesses (% change from 1987 to 1996)				Relative Growth in the Number of Women-Owned and All Businesses (% change from 1987 to 1996)			
	Num.	Empl.	Sales	Rank[2]	Women-Owned	All Firms	Absolute Difference	Relative Difference
MSA[1]	87.4	166.2	208.7	30	87.4	61.8	25.6	1.4:1

Note: (1) Metropolitan Statistical Area - see Appendix A for areas included; (2) Calculated on an averaging of the percent growth of number of businesses, employment and sales and ranges from 1 to 50 where 1 is best
Source: The National Foundation for Women Business Owners, 1996 Facts on Women-Owned Businesses: Trends in the Top 50 Metropolitan Areas, March 26, 1997

Small Business Opportunity

Greensboro was included among *Entrepreneur* magazines listing of the "20 Best Cities for Small Business." It was ranked #4 among large metro areas. Criteria: risk of failure, business performance, economic growth, affordability and state attitude towards business. *Entrepreneur, 10/97*

HOTELS & MOTELS

Hotels/Motels

Area	Hotels/ Motels	Rooms	Luxury-Level Hotels/Motels		Average Minimum Rates ($)		
			♦♦♦♦	♦♦♦♦♦	♦♦	♦♦♦	♦♦♦♦
City	22	3,403	0	0	52	106	n/a
Airport	7	1,310	0	0	n/a	n/a	n/a
Suburbs	7	748	0	0	n/a	n/a	n/a
Total	36	5,461	0	0	n/a	n/a	n/a

Note: n/a not available; Classifications range from one diamond (budget properties with basic amenities) to five diamond (luxury properties with the finest service, rooms and facilities).
Source: OAG, Business Travel Planner, Summer 1997

CONVENTION CENTERS

Major Convention Centers

Center Name	Meeting Rooms	Exhibit Space (sf)
Greensboro Coliseum Complex	2	140,000
Joseph S. Koury Convention Center	78	100,000

Source: Trade Shows Worldwide 1997

Living Environment

COST OF LIVING

Cost of Living Index

Composite Index	Housing	Utilities	Groceries	Health Care	Trans-portation	Misc. Goods/ Services
94.9	93.1	104.7	94.4	79.4	98.6	96.2

Note: U.S. = 100
Source: ACCRA, Cost of Living Index, 2nd Quarter 1996

HOUSING

Median Home Prices and Housing Affordability

Area	Median Price[2] 3rd Qtr. 1997 ($)	HOI[3] 3rd Qtr. 1997	Afford-ability Rank[4]
MSA[1]	118,000	61.4	137
U.S.	127,000	63.7	-

Note: (1) Metropolitan Statistical Area - see Appendix A for areas included; (2) U.S. figures calculated from the sales of 625,000 new and existing homes in 195 markets; (3) Housing Opportunity Index - percent of homes sold that were within the reach of the median income household at the prevailing mortgage interest rate; (4) Rank is from 1-195 with 1 being most affordable
Source: National Association of Home Builders, Housing Opportunity Index, 3rd Quarter 1997

Average New Home Price

Area	Price ($)
City	126,400
U.S.	132,005

Note: Figures are based on a new home with 1,800 sq. ft. of living area on an 8,000 sq. ft. lot.
Source: ACCRA, Cost of Living Index, 2nd Quarter 1996

Average Apartment Rent

Area	Rent ($/mth)
City	505
U.S.	553

Note: Figures are based on an unfurnished two bedroom, 1-1/2 or 2 bath apartment, approximately 950 sq. ft. in size, excluding all utilities except water
Source: ACCRA, Cost of Living Index, 2nd Quarter 1996

RESIDENTIAL UTILITIES

Average Residential Utility Costs

Area	All Electric ($/mth)	Part Electric ($/mth)	Other Energy ($/mth)	Phone ($/mth)
City	111.18	-	-	17.56
U.S.	112.48	57.49	42.55	19.50

Source: ACCRA, Cost of Living Index, 2nd Quarter 1996

HEALTH CARE

Average Health Care Costs

Area	Hospital ($/day)	Doctor ($/visit)	Dentist ($/visit)
City	210.00	40.80	41.80
U.S.	378.47	45.86	57.32

Note: Hospital - based on a semi-private room. Doctor - based on a general practitioner's routine exam of an established patient. Dentist - based on adult teeth cleaning and periodic oral exam.
Source: ACCRA, Cost of Living Index, 2nd Quarter 1996

Distribution of Office-Based Physicians

Area	Family/Gen. Practitioners	Specialists		
		Medical	Surgical	Other
MSA[1]	249	651	556	499

Note: Data as of 12/31/96; (1) Metropolitan Statistical Area - see Appendix A for areas included
Source: American Medical Assn., Physician Characteristics & Distribution in the U.S., 1997-1998

Hospitals

Greensboro has 3 general medical and surgical hospitals, 1 psychiatric, 1 children's psychiatric. *AHA Guide to the Healthcare Field 1997-98*

EDUCATION

Public School District Statistics

District Name	Num. Sch.	Enroll.	Classroom Teachers[1]	Pupils per Teacher	Minority Pupils (%)	Current Exp.[2] ($/pupil)
Guilford County Schools	93	57,211	3,585	16.0	42.8	5,223

Note: Data covers the 1995-1996 school year unless otherwise noted; (1) Excludes teachers reported as working in school district offices rather than in schools; (2) Based on 1993-94 enrollment collected by the Census Bureau, not the enrollment figure shown in column 3; SD = School District; ISD = Independent School District; n/a not available
Source: National Center for Education Statistics, Common Core of Data Survey; Bureau of the Census

Educational Quality

School District	Education Quotient[1]	Graduate Outcome[2]	Community Index[3]	Resource Index[4]
Guilford	85.0	79.0	115.0	60.0

Note: Nearly 1,000 secondary school districts were rated in terms of educational quality. The scores range from a low of 50 to a high of 150; (1) Average of the Graduate Outcome, Community and Resource indexes; (2) Based on graduation rates and college board scores (SAT/ACT); (3) Based on the surrounding community's average level of education and the area's average income level; (4) Based on teacher salaries, per-pupil expenditures and student-teacher ratios.
Source: Expansion Management, Ratings Issue 1997

Educational Attainment by Race

Area	High School Graduate (%)					Bachelor's Degree (%)				
	Total	White	Black	Other	Hisp.[2]	Total	White	Black	Other	Hisp.[2]
City	79.2	83.3	70.6	63.6	75.0	29.9	35.0	17.7	35.1	29.3
MSA[1]	72.0	73.3	66.1	63.1	70.0	19.2	20.2	14.0	27.5	21.4
U.S.	75.2	77.9	63.1	60.4	49.8	20.3	21.5	11.4	19.4	9.2

Note: figures shown cover persons 25 years old and over; (1) Metropolitan Statistical Area - see Appendix A for areas included; (2) people of Hispanic origin can be of any race
Source: 1990 Census of Population and Housing, Summary Tape File 3C

School Enrollment by Type

Area	Preprimary				Elementary/High School			
	Public		Private		Public		Private	
	Enrollment	%	Enrollment	%	Enrollment	%	Enrollment	%
City	1,840	54.1	1,564	45.9	23,934	92.5	1,927	7.5
MSA[1]	8,849	58.2	6,354	41.8	136,757	93.7	9,199	6.3
U.S.	2,679,029	59.5	1,824,256	40.5	38,379,689	90.2	4,187,099	9.8

Note: figures shown cover persons 3 years old and over;
(1) Metropolitan Statistical Area - see Appendix A for areas included
Source: 1990 Census of Population and Housing, Summary Tape File 3C

School Enrollment by Race

Area	Preprimary (%)				Elementary/High School (%)			
	White	Black	Other	Hisp.[1]	White	Black	Other	Hisp.[1]
City	66.1	30.7	3.2	0.2	54.1	43.1	2.9	1.0
MSA[2]	78.2	20.4	1.4	1.0	74.1	24.2	1.7	0.8
U.S.	80.4	12.5	7.1	7.8	74.1	15.6	10.3	12.5

Note: figures shown cover persons 3 years old and over; (1) people of Hispanic origin can be of any race; (2) Metropolitan Statistical Area - see Appendix A for areas included
Source: 1990 Census of Population and Housing, Summary Tape File 3C

SAT/ACT Scores

Area/District	1997 SAT				1997 ACT	
	Percent of Graduates Tested (%)	Average Math Score	Average Verbal Score	Average Combined Score	Percent of Graduates Tested (%)	Average Composite Score
Guilford County	73	490	493	983	n/a	n/a
State	59	488	490	978	11	19.3
U.S.	42	511	505	1,016	36	21.0

Note: Math and verbal SAT scores are out of a possible 800; ACT scores are out of a possible 36
Caution: Comparing or ranking states/cities on the basis of SAT/ACT scores alone is invalid and strongly discouraged by the The College Board and The American College Testing Program as students who take the tests are self-selected and do not represent the entire student population.
Source: Guilford County Schools, Office of Administration, 1997; American College Testing Program, 1997; College Board, 1997

Classroom Teacher Salaries in Public Schools

District	B.A. Degree		M.A. Degree		Ph.D. Degree	
	Min. ($)	Max ($)	Min. ($)	Max. ($)	Min. ($)	Max. ($)
Greensboro	23,490	42,740	25,040	45,410	27,750	48,290
Average[1]	26,120	39,270	28,175	44,667	31,643	49,825

Note: Salaries are for 1996-1997; (1) Based on all school districts covered; n/a not available
Source: American Federation of Teachers (unpublished data)

Higher Education

Two-Year Colleges		Four-Year Colleges		Medical Schools	Law Schools	Voc/ Tech
Public	Private	Public	Private			
0	0	2	3	0	0	5

Source: College Blue Book, Occupational Education 1997; Medical School Admission Requirements, 1998-99; Peterson's Guide to Two-Year Colleges, 1997; Peterson's Guide to Four-Year Colleges, 1997; Barron's Guide to Law Schools 1997

MAJOR EMPLOYERS

Major Employers

Legwear Holdings Corp.
Crown Automotive Co.
Guilford Mills
Moses Cone Health System
Volvo GM Heavy Truck Corp.
Wesley Long Community Hospital
Burlington Industries
Greensboro News & Record
Jefferson-Pilot Corp. (life insurance)
Triad International Maintenance Corp.
Wendover Funding
Wrangler Inc.

Note: companies listed are located in the city
Source: Dun's Business Rankings 1997; Ward's Business Directory, 1997

PUBLIC SAFETY

Crime Rate

Area	All Crimes	Violent Crimes				Property Crimes		
		Murder	Forcible Rape	Robbery	Aggrav. Assault	Burglary	Larceny -Theft	Motor Vehicle Theft
City	8,068.0	11.3	46.8	349.4	540.9	1,588.7	5,015.1	515.8
Suburbs[1]	5,746.3	6.7	33.9	170.8	385.6	1,325.2	3,443.9	380.3
MSA[2]	6,157.5	7.5	36.2	202.4	413.1	1,371.9	3,722.2	404.3
U.S.	5,078.9	7.4	36.1	202.4	388.2	943.0	2,975.9	525.9

Note: Crime rate is the number of crimes per 100,000 pop.; (1) defined as all areas within the MSA but located outside the central city; (2) Metropolitan Statistical Area - see Appendix A for areas incl.
Source: FBI Uniform Crime Reports 1996

RECREATION

Culture and Recreation

Museums	Symphony Orchestras	Opera Companies	Dance Companies	Professional Theatres	Zoos	Pro Sports Teams
5	1	1	1	1	1	0

Source: International Directory of the Performing Arts, 1996; Official Museum Directory, 1998; Chamber of Commerce/Economic Development 1997

Library System

The Greensboro Public Library has eight branches, holdings of 759,831 volumes and a budget of $5,728,877 (1995-1996). *American Library Directory, 1997-1998*

MEDIA

Newspapers

Name	Type	Freq.	Distribution	Circulation
Carolina Peacemaker	Black	1x/wk	Local	6,200
Greensboro News & Record	General	7x/wk	Area	95,348
North Carolina Christian Advocate	Religious	2x/mo	Area	12,500
Triad Business News	General	1x/wk	Local	16,000

Note: Includes newspapers with circulations of 1,000 or more located in the city; Source: Burrelle's Media Directory, 1998 Edition

AM Radio Stations

Call Letters	Freq. (kHz)	Target Audience	Station Format	Music Format
WXII	830	General	N	n/a
WPET	950	General	M	Christian
WMFR	1230	General	N/T	n/a
WTCK	1320	General	S/T	n/a
WKEW	1400	General	S/T	n/a
WQMG	1510	Religious	M	Christian

Note: Stations included broadcast in the Greensboro metro area; n/a not available
Station Format: E = Educational; M = Music; N = News; S = Sports; T = Talk
Source: Burrelle's Media Directory, 1998 Edition

FM Radio Stations

Call Letters	Freq. (mHz)	Target Audience	Station Format	Music Format
WNAA	90.1	Black	M/T	Urban Contemporary
WWIH	90.3	General	M	n/a
WKRR	92.3	General	M	Classic Rock
WHPE	95.5	Religious	M	Christian
WQMG	97.1	n/a	M	n/a
WIST	98.3	General	M/N/S	Adult Contemporary
WKSI	98.7	General	M/N	Country
WMAG	99.5	General	M	Adult Contemporary
WHSL	100.3	General	M	Country/Oldies
WJMH	102.1	General	M/N	Urban Contemporary
WKZL	107.5	General	M	Adult Contemporary

Note: Stations included broadcast in the Greensboro metro area; n/a not available
Station Format: E = Educational; M = Music; N = News; S = Sports; T = Talk
Source: Burrelle's Media Directory, 1998 Edition

Television Stations

Name	Ch.	Affiliation	Type	Owner
WFMY	2	CBS	Commercial	Gannett Broadcasting Company Inc.
WGHP	8	Fox	Commercial	WGHP Trust
WAAP	16	n/a	Commercial	Paxson Communications Corporation
WBFX	20	WB/Fox Kids Worldwide	Commercial	Pappas Telecasting of Lexington LP
WUPN	48	Fox	Commercial	Guilford Telecasters, Inc.
WLXI	61	TBN	Non-Commercial	Tri-State Christian Broadcasting Inc.

Note: Stations included broadcast in the Greensboro metro area
Source: Burrelle's Media Directory, 1998 Edition

CLIMATE

Average and Extreme Temperatures

Temperature	Jan	Feb	Mar	Apr	May	Jun	Jul	Aug	Sep	Oct	Nov	Dec	Ann
Extreme High (°F)	78	81	89	91	96	102	102	103	100	95	85	78	103
Average High (°F)	48	51	60	70	78	84	87	86	80	70	60	50	69
Average Temp. (°F)	38	41	49	58	67	74	78	76	70	59	49	40	58
Average Low (°F)	28	30	37	46	55	63	67	66	59	47	37	30	47
Extreme Low (°F)	-8	-1	5	23	32	42	49	45	37	20	10	0	-8

Note: Figures cover the years 1948-1990
Source: National Climatic Data Center, International Station Meteorological Climate Summary, 3/95

Average Precipitation/Snowfall/Humidity

Precip./Humidity	Jan	Feb	Mar	Apr	May	Jun	Jul	Aug	Sep	Oct	Nov	Dec	Ann
Avg. Precip. (in.)	3.2	3.4	3.7	3.1	3.7	3.8	4.5	4.2	3.4	3.4	2.9	3.3	42.5
Avg. Snowfall (in.)	4	3	2	Tr	0	0	0	0	0	0	Tr	1	10
Avg. Rel. Hum. 7am (%)	80	78	78	77	82	84	87	90	90	88	83	80	83
Avg. Rel. Hum. 4pm (%)	53	50	47	44	51	54	57	58	56	51	51	54	52

Note: Figures cover the years 1948-1990; Tr = Trace amounts (<0.05 in. of rain; <0.5 in. of snow)
Source: National Climatic Data Center, International Station Meteorological Climate Summary, 3/95

Weather Conditions

Temperature			Daytime Sky			Precipitation		
10°F & below	32°F & below	90°F & above	Clear	Partly cloudy	Cloudy	0.01 inch or more precip.	0.1 inch or more snow/ice	Thunderstorms
3	85	32	94	143	128	113	5	43

Note: Figures are average number of days per year and covers the years 1948-1990
Source: National Climatic Data Center, International Station Meteorological Climate Summary, 3/95

AIR & WATER QUALITY

Maximum Pollutant Concentrations

	Particulate Matter (ug/m^3)	Carbon Monoxide (ppm)	Sulfur Dioxide (ppm)	Nitrogen Dioxide (ppm)	Ozone (ppm)	Lead (ug/m^3)
MSA[1] Level	58	4	0.026	0.016	0.12	n/a
NAAQS[2]	150	9	0.140	0.053	0.12	1.50
Met NAAQS?	Yes	Yes	Yes	Yes	Yes	n/a

Note: (1) Metropolitan Statistical Area - see Appendix A for areas included; (2) National Ambient Air Quality Standards; ppm = parts per million; ug/m^3 = micrograms per cubic meter; n/a not available
Source: EPA, National Air Quality and Emissions Trends Report, 1996

Pollutant Standards Index

In the Greensboro MSA (see Appendix A for areas included), the Pollutant Standards Index (PSI) exceeded 100 on 2 days in 1996. A PSI value greater than 100 indicates that air quality would be in the unhealthful range on that day. *EPA, National Air Quality and Emissions Trends Report, 1996*

Drinking Water

Water System Name	Pop. Served	Primary Water Source Type	Number of Violations in Fiscal Year 1997	Type of Violation/ Contaminants
City of Greensboro	215,000	Surface	None	None

Note: Data as of January 16, 1998
Source: EPA, Office of Ground Water and Drinking Water, Safe Drinking Water Information System

Greensboro tap water is alkaline, soft.
Editor & Publisher Market Guide, 1998

Lexington, Kentucky

Background

Lexington has managed to combine the frenzied pace of a major city with the slow tempo of a small town without losing the traditions and gentility of its southern heritage.

Since its settlement in 1775, Lexington has grown to become Kentucky's second largest city and the commercial center of the Bluegrass region. The town was founded in 1779 and incorporated in 1832.

It is noted for its training of thoroughbred horses and marketing of burley tobacco. Hemp was Lexington's major antebellum crop until the rope from which it was made was no longer used for ship rigging. After the Civil War the farmers in the area switched to tobacco as their primary crop.

The city is also the chief producer of bluegrass seed and white barley in the United States. Manufactures include paper products, air-conditioning and heating equipment, electric typewriters, metal products, and bourbon whiskey.

Surrounded by horse farms and rolling Bluegrass meadows, Lexington was once known as the "Athens of the West" when a large number of early American artists, poets, musicians and architects settled here. They all left their imprint on the city.

Lexington has a definite continental climate with a rather large daily temperature range. The climate is temperate and well suited to a varied plant and animal life. The area is subject to rather sudden and sweeping changes in temperature with the spells generally of short duration. Temperatures above 100 degrees and below zero degrees are relatively rare.

General Rankings and Evaluative Comments

- Lexington was ranked #165 out of 300 cities by *Money's* 1997 "Survey of the Best Places to Live." Criteria used: health services, crime, economy, housing, education, transportation, weather, leisure and the arts. The city was ranked #143 in 1996 and #125 in 1995. *Money, July 1997; Money, September 1996; Money, September 1995*

- *Ladies Home Journal* ranked America's 200 largest cities based on the qualities women care about most. Lexington ranked 13 out of 200. Criteria: low crime rate, good public schools, well-paying jobs, quality health and child care, the presence of women in government, proportion of women-owned businesses, size of the wage gap with men, local economy, divorce rates, the ratio of single men to single women, whether there are laws that require at least the same number of public toilets for women as men, and the probability of good hair days. *Ladies Home Journal, November 1997*

- Lexington was ranked #34 out of 219 cities in terms of children's health, safety, and economic well-being. Criteria: total population, percent population change, birth rate, child immunization rate, infant mortality rate, percent low birth weight infants, percent of births to teens, physician-to-population ratio, student-to-teacher ratio, dropout rate, unemployment rate, median family income, percent of children in poverty, violent and property crime rates, number of juvenile arrests for violent crimes as a percent of the total crime index, number of days with pollution standard index (PSI) over 100, pounds toxic releases per 1,000 people and number of superfund sites. *Zero Population Growth, Children's Environmental Index 1997*

- According to *Working Mother,* "State legislators agreed to spend an additional $1 million on prekindergarten programs, bringing total funding to more than $38 million. This boosted the number of children served in pre-K to about 21,000—about 1,000 more than last year. The lawmakers are also earmarking any surplus in the state education budget for pre-K—a wonderful innovation.

  At the same time, however, they voted to lower overall child care spending by $6 million over the next two years and to raise fees for families that use state-sponsored child care. This will impose a hardship on many families who depended on such subsidized child care.

  Still, children who do find a space in child care will be safer from disease. Within 30 days of enrolling in a child care program, every child must now have a shot to prevent meningitis. By this time next year children will be required to have a hepatitis shot as well." *Working Mother, July/August 1997*

Business Environment

STATE ECONOMY

State Economic Profile

"Kentucky is posting steady, albeit slightly below-average, economic growth....

...Kentucky's wage income is expanding faster than the national rate. Importantly, these wage gains are allowing households to work down high debt burdens. Thus, Kentucky's consumer delinquency rates are slightly below rates found in West Virginia, Ohio, and Tennessee.

Kentucky's manufacturing industries will experience slow growth due to cuts in apparel industries and stalled job expansions at most durable goods makers. Overall, state apparel manufacturers are contracting at a 10% twelve-month rate and account for half of the manufacturing industry's losses. The apparel industry losses will cancel any gains made by automobile-related companies well into 1998.

With apparel, coal mining, and tobacco manufacturers playing a less prominent role in the state's economy longer term, Kentucky's economic performance will increasingly rely on higher value-added durable goods manufacturers and office-intensive business services firms. Although Kentucky's average wages are slightly lower than in Illinois, Indiana, and Ohio, the state's extremely affordable housing offsets its lower per capita income.

Although Kentucky is ranked as an above-average performer over the next five years, projections of economic growth are constrained by the high percentage of high school dropouts, and the lack of college-educated residents. Although the state has low business costs, the shortage of highly skilled labor distorts this inherent cost advantage by retarding the expansion of more high-tech industries as is ongoing in the West. Overall, Kentucky will be one of the stronger southern economies over the long run." *National Association of Realtors, Economic Profiles: The Fifty States, July 1997*

IMPORTS/EXPORTS

Total Export Sales

Area	1993 ($000)	1994 ($000)	1995 ($000)	1996 ($000)	% Chg. 1993-96	% Chg. 1995-96
MSA[1]	624,190	1,078,566	1,235,009	1,499,919	140.3	21.5
U.S.	464,858,354	512,415,609	583,030,524	622,827,063	34.0	6.8

Note: (1) Metropolitan Statistical Area - see Appendix A for areas included
Source: U.S. Department of Commerce, International Trade Association, Metropolitan Area Exports: An Export Performance Report on Over 250 U.S. Cities, October 1997

Imports/Exports by Port

Type	Cargo Value			Share of U.S. Total	
	1995 (US$mil.)	1996 (US$mil.)	% Change 1995-1996	1995 (%)	1996 (%)
Imports	0	0	0	0	0
Exports	0	0	0	0	0

Source: Global Trade Information Services, WaterBorne Trade Atlas 1997

CITY FINANCES

City Government Finances

Component	FY92 ($000)	FY92 (per capita $)
Revenue	221,415	953.51
Expenditure	203,486	876.30
Debt Outstanding	413,906	1,782.46
Cash & Securities	430,175	1,852.53

Source: U.S. Bureau of the Census, City Government Finances: 1991-92

City Government Revenue by Source

Source	FY92 ($000)	FY92 (per capita $)	FY92 (%)
From Federal Government	10,538	45.38	4.8
From State Governments	5,661	24.38	2.6
From Local Governments	141	0.61	0.1
Property Taxes	24,060	103.61	10.9
General Sales Taxes	0	0.00	0.0
Selective Sales Taxes	6,072	26.15	2.7
Income Taxes	59,819	257.61	27.0
Current Charges	59,224	255.05	26.7
Utility/Liquor Store	1,344	5.79	0.6
Employee Retirement[1]	23,369	100.64	10.6
Other	31,187	134.31	14.1

Note: (1) Excludes "city contributions," classified as "nonrevenue," intragovernmental transfers.
Source: U.S. Bureau of the Census, City Government Finances: 1991-92

City Government Expenditures by Function

Function	FY92 ($000)	FY92 (per capita $)	FY92 (%)
Educational Services	7,683	33.09	3.8
Employee Retirement[1]	8,728	37.59	4.3
Environment/Housing	48,352	208.23	23.8
Government Administration	14,131	60.85	6.9
Interest on General Debt	27,660	119.12	13.6
Public Safety	46,715	201.18	23.0
Social Services	17,762	76.49	8.7
Transportation	13,681	58.92	6.7
Utility/Liquor Store	4,890	21.06	2.4
Other	13,884	59.79	6.8

Note: (1) Payments to beneficiaries including withdrawal of contributions.
Source: U.S. Bureau of the Census, City Government Finances: 1991-92

Municipal Bond Ratings

Area	Moody's	S & P
Lexington	n/r	AAA

Note: n/a not available; n/r not rated
Source: Moody's Bond Record, 2/98; Statistical Abstract of the U.S., 1997; Governing Magazine, 9/97, 3/98

POPULATION

Population Growth

Area	1980	1990	% Chg. 1980-90	July 1996 Estimate	% Chg. 1990-96
City	204,165	225,366	10.4	n/a	n/a
MSA[1]	317,629	348,428	9.7	441,073	26.6
U.S.	226,545,805	248,765,170	9.8	265,179,411	6.6

Note: (1) Metropolitan Statistical Area - see Appendix A for areas included
Source: 1980/1990 Census of Housing and Population, Summary Tape File 3C; Census Bureau Population Estimates

Population Characteristics

Race	City					MSA[1]	
	1980		1990		% Chg. 1980-90	1990	
	Population	%	Population	%		Population	%
White	174,934	85.7	190,795	84.7	9.1	305,969	87.8
Black	26,979	13.2	30,172	13.4	11.8	37,234	10.7
Amer Indian/Esk/Aleut	271	0.1	432	0.2	59.4	689	0.2
Asian/Pacific Islander	1,580	0.8	3,345	1.5	111.7	3,744	1.1
Other	401	0.2	622	0.3	55.1	792	0.2
Hispanic Origin[2]	1,279	0.6	2,358	1.0	84.4	2,994	0.9

Note: (1) Metropolitan Statistical Area - see Appendix A for areas included; (2) people of Hispanic origin can be of any race
Source: 1980/1990 Census of Housing and Population, Summary Tape File 3C

Ancestry

Area	German	Irish	English	Italian	U.S.	French	Polish	Dutch
City	22.1	18.1	19.5	2.3	8.5	3.2	1.1	2.3
MSA[1]	21.2	17.9	18.8	1.9	10.9	3.0	1.0	2.3
U.S.	23.3	15.6	13.1	5.9	5.3	4.2	3.8	2.5

Note: Figures are percentages and include persons that reported multiple ancestry (eg. if a person reported being Irish and Italian, they were included in both columns); (1) Metropolitan Statistical Area - see Appendix A for areas included
Source: 1990 Census of Population and Housing, Summary Tape File 3C

Age

Area	Median Age (Years)	Age Distribution (%)						
		Under 5	Under 18	18-24	25-44	45-64	65+	80+
City	31.2	6.7	22.4	14.5	36.4	16.8	9.9	2.0
MSA[1]	31.7	6.8	23.9	13.1	35.1	17.6	10.3	2.2
U.S.	32.9	7.3	25.6	10.5	32.6	18.7	12.5	2.8

Note: (1) Metropolitan Statistical Area - see Appendix A for areas included
Source: 1990 Census of Population and Housing, Summary Tape File 3C

Male/Female Ratio

Area	Number of males per 100 females (all ages)	Number of males per 100 females (18 years old+)
City	91.7	88.2
MSA[1]	92.3	88.7
U.S.	95.0	91.9

Note: (1) Metropolitan Statistical Area - see Appendix A for areas included
Source: 1990 Census of Population, General Population Characteristics

INCOME

Per Capita/Median/Average Income

Area	Per Capita ($)	Median Household ($)	Average Household ($)
City	14,962	28,056	36,979
MSA[1]	13,945	27,558	35,698
U.S.	14,420	30,056	38,453

Note: all figures are for 1989; (1) Metropolitan Statistical Area - see Appendix A for areas included
Source: 1990 Census of Population and Housing, Summary Tape File 3C

Household Income Distribution by Race

Income ($)	City (%)					U.S. (%)				
	Total	White	Black	Other	Hisp.[1]	Total	White	Black	Other	Hisp.[1]
Less than 5,000	7.7	5.8	20.5	9.1	8.3	6.2	4.8	15.2	8.6	8.8
5,000 - 9,999	9.1	8.1	15.8	14.1	11.5	9.3	8.6	14.2	9.9	11.1
10,000 - 14,999	9.4	8.8	13.3	13.3	8.7	8.8	8.5	11.0	9.8	11.0
15,000 - 24,999	18.1	18.0	18.8	18.6	21.6	17.5	17.3	18.9	18.5	20.5
25,000 - 34,999	16.1	16.8	11.8	9.7	7.0	15.8	16.1	14.2	15.4	16.4
35,000 - 49,999	17.1	18.0	10.8	12.8	16.1	17.9	18.6	13.3	16.1	16.0
50,000 - 74,999	13.9	14.9	7.1	10.1	19.3	15.0	15.8	9.3	13.4	11.1
75,000 - 99,999	4.5	4.9	1.4	5.1	4.3	5.1	5.5	2.6	4.7	3.1
100,000+	4.2	4.7	0.7	7.2	3.2	4.4	4.8	1.3	3.7	1.9

Note: all figures are for 1989; (1) people of Hispanic origin can be of any race
Source: 1990 Census of Population and Housing, Summary Tape File 3C

Effective Buying Income

Area	Per Capita ($)	Median Household ($)	Average Household ($)
City	17,053	32,781	42,491
MSA[1]	15,830	32,322	41,331
U.S.	15,444	33,201	41,849

Note: data as of 1/1/97; (1) Metropolitan Statistical Area - see Appendix A for areas included
Source: Standard Rate & Data Service, Newspaper Advertising Source, 2/98

Effective Household Buying Income Distribution

Area	% of Households Earning						
	$10,000 -$19,999	$20,000 -$34,999	$35,000 -$49,999	$50,000 -$74,999	$75,000 -$99,000	$100,000 -$124,999	$125,000 and up
City	16.4	23.5	17.4	17.6	6.6	2.3	2.8
MSA[1]	16.9	23.1	17.5	17.7	6.5	2.0	2.4
U.S.	16.5	23.4	18.3	18.2	6.4	2.1	2.4

Note: data as of 1/1/97; (1) Metropolitan Statistical Area - see Appendix A for areas included
Source: Standard Rate & Data Service, Newspaper Advertising Source, 2/98

Poverty Rates by Race and Age

Area	Total (%)	By Race (%)				By Age (%)		
		White	Black	Other	Hisp.[2]	Under 5 years old	Under 18 years old	65 years and over
City	14.1	10.9	34.0	22.1	26.4	19.9	18.8	13.2
MSA[1]	14.2	11.9	32.7	20.9	24.3	21.1	18.9	16.3
U.S.	13.1	9.8	29.5	23.1	25.3	20.1	18.3	12.8

Note: figures show the percent of people living below the poverty line in 1989. The average poverty threshold was $12,674 for a family of four in 1989; (1) Metropolitan Statistical Area - see Appendix A for areas included; (2) people of Hispanic origin can be of any race
Source: 1990 Census of Population and Housing, Summary Tape File 3C

EMPLOYMENT

Labor Force and Employment

Area	Civilian Labor Force			Workers Employed		
	Dec. '95	Dec. '96	% Chg.	Dec. '95	Dec. '96	% Chg.
City	138,982	146,439	5.4	135,791	143,495	5.7
MSA[1]	244,981	258,071	5.3	238,883	252,437	5.7
U.S.	134,583,000	136,742,000	1.6	127,903,000	130,785,000	2.3

Note: Data is not seasonally adjusted and covers workers 16 years of age and older; (1) Metropolitan Statistical Area - see Appendix A for areas included
Source: Bureau of Labor Statistics, http://stats.bls.gov

Unemployment Rate

Area	1997											
	Jan.	Feb.	Mar.	Apr.	May	Jun.	Jul.	Aug.	Sep.	Oct.	Nov.	Dec.
City	2.5	2.5	2.2	2.2	2.2	2.5	2.3	2.6	2.9	2.3	2.0	2.0
MSA[1]	2.9	2.9	2.5	2.5	2.4	2.7	2.5	2.7	2.9	2.4	2.1	2.2
U.S.	5.9	5.7	5.5	4.8	4.7	5.2	5.0	4.8	4.7	4.4	4.3	4.4

Note: Data is not seasonally adjusted and covers workers 16 years of age and older; All figures are percentages; (1) Metropolitan Statistical Area - see Appendix A for areas included
Source: Bureau of Labor Statistics, http://stats.bls.gov

Employment by Industry

Sector	MSA[1]		U.S.
	Number of Employees	Percent of Total	Percent of Total
Services	73,600	26.5	29.0
Retail Trade	51,500	18.6	18.5
Government	57,000	20.5	16.1
Manufacturing	47,900	17.3	15.0
Finance/Insurance/Real Estate	10,400	3.7	5.7
Wholesale Trade	12,700	4.6	5.4
Transportation/Public Utilities	11,000	4.0	5.3
Construction	13,200	4.8	4.5
Mining	300	0.1	0.5

Note: Figures cover non-farm employment as of 12/97 and are not seasonally adjusted; (1) Metropolitan Statistical Area - see Appendix A for areas included
Source: Bureau of Labor Statistics, http://stats.bls.gov

Employment by Occupation

Occupation Category	City (%)	MSA[1] (%)	U.S. (%)
White Collar	66.3	61.0	58.1
Executive/Admin./Management	13.6	12.3	12.3
Professional	18.8	16.3	14.1
Technical & Related Support	4.8	4.3	3.7
Sales	13.4	12.3	11.8
Administrative Support/Clerical	15.7	15.8	16.3
Blue Collar	17.3	21.4	26.2
Precision Production/Craft/Repair	7.8	9.3	11.3
Machine Operators/Assem./Insp.	4.0	5.6	6.8
Transportation/Material Movers	3.0	3.4	4.1
Cleaners/Helpers/Laborers	2.6	3.1	3.9
Services	13.9	13.4	13.2
Farming/Forestry/Fishing	2.5	4.2	2.5

Note: figures cover employed persons 16 years old and over; (1) Metropolitan Statistical Area - see Appendix A for areas included
Source: 1990 Census of Population and Housing, Summary Tape File 3C

Occupational Employment Projections: 1994 - 2005

Occupations Expected to have the Largest Job Growth (ranked by numerical growth)	Fast-Growing Occupations (ranked by percent growth)
1. Cashiers	1. Personal and home care aides
2. Salespersons, retail	2. Electronic pagination systems workers
3. General managers & top executives	3. Amusement and recreation attendants
4. Janitors/cleaners/maids, ex. priv. hshld.	4. Metal molding machine operators
5. Food service workers	5. Occupational therapy assistants
6. Registered nurses	6. Physical therapy assistants and aides
7. Nursing aides/orderlies/attendants	7. Systems analysts
8. Receptionists and information clerks	8. Computer engineers
9. Secretaries, except legal & medical	9. Occupational therapists
10. Marketing & sales, supervisors	10. Physical therapists

Projections cover Fayette, Franklin, Scott, Harrison, Nicholas, Bourbon, Anderson, Woodford, Mercer, Boyle, Lincoln, Garrard, Jessamine, Clark, Madison, Powell and Estill Counties.
Source: Cabinet for Workforce Development, Department for Employment Services, Bluegrass Area Occupational Outlook to 2005

Average Wages

Occupation	Wage	Occupation	Wage
Professional/Technical/Clerical	$/Week	**Health/Protective Services**	$/Week
Accountants III	-	Corrections Officers	-
Attorneys III	-	Firefighters	-
Budget Analysts III	-	Nurses, Licensed Practical II	-
Buyers/Contracting Specialists II	-	Nurses, Registered II	-
Clerks, Accounting III	407	Nursing Assistants II	-
Clerks, General III	-	Police Officers I	-
Computer Operators II	409	**Hourly Workers**	$/Hour
Computer Programmers II	-	Forklift Operators	11.07
Drafters II	439	General Maintenance Workers	7.79
Engineering Technicians III	536	Guards I	6.90
Engineering Technicians, Civil III	-	Janitors	6.03
Engineers III	-	Maintenance Electricians	16.31
Key Entry Operators I	339	Maintenance Electronics Techs II	17.37
Personnel Assistants III	-	Maintenance Machinists	-
Personnel Specialists III	-	Maintenance Mechanics, Machinery	16.36
Secretaries III	517	Material Handling Laborers	12.13
Switchboard Operator-Receptionist	333	Motor Vehicle Mechanics	14.67
Systems Analysts II	882	Shipping/Receiving Clerks	9.08
Systems Analysts Supervisor/Mgr II	-	Tool and Die Makers	18.49
Tax Collectors II	-	Truckdrivers, Tractor Trailer	16.32
Word Processors II	-	Warehouse Specialists	-

Note: Wage data includes full-time workers only for 8/96 and cover the Metropolitan Statistical Area (see Appendix A for areas included). Dashes indicate that data was not available.
Source: Bureau of Labor Statistics, Occupational Compensation Survey, 1/97

TAXES

Major State and Local Tax Rates

State Corp. Income (%)	State Personal Income (%)	Residential Property (effective rate per $100)	Sales & Use		State Gasoline (cents/ gallon)	State Cigarette (cents/ 20-pack)
			State (%)	Local (%)		
4.0 - 8.25	2.0 - 6.0	n/a	6.0	None	16.4[a]	3

Note: Personal/corporate income tax rates as of 1/97. Sales, gasoline and cigarette tax rates as of 1/98; (a) Rate is comprised of 15 cents excise and 1.4 cents motor carrier tax.
Source: Federation of Tax Administrators, www.taxadmin.org; Washington D.C. Department of Finance and Revenue, Tax Rates and Tax Burdens in the District of Columbia: A Nationwide Comparison, June 1997; Chamber of Commerce

Total Taxes Per Capita and as a Percent of Income

Area	Per Capita Income ($)	Per Capita Taxes ($)			Taxes as Pct. of Income (%)		
		Total	Federal	State/ Local	Total	Federal	State/ Local
Kentucky	21,415	7,324	4,757	2,568	34.2	22.2	12.0
U.S.	26,187	9,205	6,127	3,078	35.2	23.4	11.8

Note: Figures are for 1997
Source: Tax Foundation, Web Site, www.taxfoundation.org

COMMERCIAL REAL ESTATE

Data not available at time of publication.

COMMERCIAL UTILITIES

Typical Monthly Electric Bills

Area	Commercial Service ($/month)		Industrial Service ($/month)	
	12 kW demand 1,500 kWh	100 kW demand 30,000 kWh	1,000 kW demand 400,000 kWh	20,000 kW demand 10,000,000 kWh
City	91	1,272	14,661	313,282
U.S.	162	2,360	25,590	545,677

Note: Based on rates in effect July 1, 1997
Source: Edison Electric Institute, Typical Residential, Commercial and Industrial Bills, Summer 1997

TRANSPORTATION

Transportation Statistics

Avg. travel time to work (min.)	17.5
Interstate highways	I-64; I-75
Bus lines	
In-city	Lexington TA
Inter-city	1
Passenger air service	
Airport	Blue Grass Airport
Airlines	9
Aircraft departures	9,367 (1995)
Enplaned passengers	342,913 (1995)
Rail service	No Amtrak service
Motor freight carriers	56
Major waterways/ports	None

Source: OAG, Business Travel Planner, Summer 1997; Editor & Publisher Market Guide, 1998; FAA Airport Activity Statistics, 1996; Amtrak National Time Table, Northeast Timetable, Fall/Winter 1997-98; 1990 Census of Population and Housing, STF 3C; Chamber of Commerce/Economic Development 1997; Jane's Urban Transport Systems 1997-98; Transit Fact Book 1997

Means of Transportation to Work

Area	Car/Truck/Van		Public Transportation			Bicycle	Walked	Other Means	Worked at Home
	Drove Alone	Car-pooled	Bus	Subway	Railroad				
City	78.4	11.6	1.5	0.0	0.0	0.3	5.1	0.6	2.4
MSA[1]	77.9	12.7	1.0	0.0	0.0	0.2	4.7	0.6	2.8
U.S.	73.2	13.4	3.0	1.5	0.5	0.4	3.9	1.2	3.0

Note: figures shown are percentages and only include workers 16 years old and over;
(1) Metropolitan Statistical Area - see Appendix A for areas included
Source: 1990 Census of Population and Housing, Summary Tape File 3C

BUSINESSES

Major Business Headquarters

Company Name	1997 Rankings	
	Fortune 500	Forbes 500
Clark Material Handling	-	478
Long John Silver's	-	366
Mason & Hanger	-	476

Note: Companies listed are located in the city; Dashes indicate no ranking
Fortune 500: companies that produce a 10-K are ranked 1 - 500 based on 1996 revenue
Forbes 500: private companies are ranked 1 - 500 based on 1996 revenue
Source: Forbes 12/1/97; Fortune 4/28/97

Fast-Growing Businesses

According to *Inc.*, Lexington is home to one of America's 100 fastest-growing private companies: Wyncom. Criteria for inclusion: must be an independent, privately-held, U.S. corporation, proprietorship or partnership; sales of at least $200,000 in 1993; five-year operating/sales history; increase in 1997 sales over 1996 sales; holding companies, regulated banks, and utilities were excluded. *Inc. 500, 1997*

HOTELS & MOTELS

Hotels/Motels

Area	Hotels/ Motels	Rooms	Luxury-Level Hotels/Motels		Average Minimum Rates ($)		
			♦♦♦♦	♦♦♦♦♦	♦♦	♦♦♦	♦♦♦♦
City	25	4,153	0	0	49	94	n/a
Airport	2	131	0	0	n/a	n/a	n/a
Suburbs	8	912	0	0	n/a	n/a	n/a
Total	35	5,196	0	0	n/a	n/a	n/a

Note: n/a not available; Classifications range from one diamond (budget properties with basic amenities) to five diamond (luxury properties with the finest service, rooms and facilities).
Source: OAG, Business Travel Planner, Summer 1997

CONVENTION CENTERS

Major Convention Centers

Center Name	Meeting Rooms	Exhibit Space (sf)
Lexington Convention Center	10	66,000

Source: Trade Shows Worldwide 1997

Living Environment

COST OF LIVING

Cost of Living Index

Composite Index	Housing	Utilities	Groceries	Health Care	Trans-portation	Misc. Goods/ Services
97.3	95.4	80.5	99.2	100.9	97.8	101.3

Note: U.S. = 100; Figures are for the Metropolitan Statistical Area - see Appendix A for areas included
Source: ACCRA, Cost of Living Index, 3rd Quarter 1997

HOUSING

Median Home Prices and Housing Affordability

Area	Median Price[2] 3rd Qtr. 1997 ($)	HOI[3] 3rd Qtr. 1997	Afford-ability Rank[4]
MSA[1]	100,000	72.8	70
U.S.	127,000	63.7	–

Note: (1) Metropolitan Statistical Area - see Appendix A for areas included; (2) U.S. figures calculated from the sales of 625,000 new and existing homes in 195 markets; (3) Housing Opportunity Index - percent of homes sold that were within the reach of the median income household at the prevailing mortgage interest rate; (4) Rank is from 1-195 with 1 being most affordable
Source: National Association of Home Builders, Housing Opportunity Index, 3rd Quarter 1997

Average New Home Price

Area	Price ($)
MSA[1]	123,280
U.S.	135,710

Note: Figures are based on a new home with 1,800 sq. ft. of living area on an 8,000 sq. ft. lot; (1) Metropolitan Statistical Area - see Appendix A for areas included
Source: ACCRA, Cost of Living Index, 3rd Quarter 1997

Average Apartment Rent

Area	Rent ($/mth)
MSA[1]	666
U.S.	569

Note: Figures are based on an unfurnished two bedroom, 1-1/2 or 2 bath apartment, approximately 950 sq. ft. in size, excluding all utilities except water; (1) Metropolitan Statistical Area - see Appendix A for areas included
Source: ACCRA, Cost of Living Index, 3rd Quarter 1997

RESIDENTIAL UTILITIES

Average Residential Utility Costs

Area	All Electric ($/mth)	Part Electric ($/mth)	Other Energy ($/mth)	Phone ($/mth)
MSA[1]	–	31.70	41.84	26.61
U.S.	109.40	55.25	43.64	19.48

Note: (1) (1) Metropolitan Statistical Area - see Appendix A for areas included
Source: ACCRA, Cost of Living Index, 3rd Quarter 1997

HEALTH CARE

Average Health Care Costs

Area	Hospital ($/day)	Doctor ($/visit)	Dentist ($/visit)
MSA[1]	365.00	55.20	55.80
U.S.	392.91	48.76	60.84

Note: Hospital - based on a semi-private room. Doctor - based on a general practitioner's routine exam of an established patient. Dentist - based on adult teeth cleaning and periodic oral exam; (1) Metropolitan Statistical Area - see Appendix A for areas included
Source: ACCRA, Cost of Living Index, 3rd Quarter 1997

Distribution of Office-Based Physicians

Area	Family/Gen. Practitioners	Specialists		
		Medical	Surgical	Other
MSA[1]	135	370	284	363

Note: Data as of 12/31/96; (1) Metropolitan Statistical Area - see Appendix A for areas included
Source: American Medical Assn., Physician Characteristics & Distribution in the U.S., 1997-1998

Hospitals

Lexington has 6 general medical and surgical hospitals, 3 psychiatric, 1 rehabilitation, 1 children's other specialty. *AHA Guide to the Healthcare Field 1997-98*

EDUCATION

Public School District Statistics

District Name	Num. Sch.	Enroll.	Classroom Teachers[1]	Pupils per Teacher	Minority Pupils (%)	Current Exp.[2] ($/pupil)
Fayette Co	57	32,880	2,116	15.5	26.2	4,847

Note: Data covers the 1995-1996 school year unless otherwise noted; (1) Excludes teachers reported as working in school district offices rather than in schools; (2) Based on 1993-94 enrollment collected by the Census Bureau, not the enrollment figure shown in column 3; SD = School District; ISD = Independent School District; n/a not available
Source: National Center for Education Statistics, Common Core of Data Survey; Bureau of the Census

Educational Quality

School District	Education Quotient[1]	Graduate Outcome[2]	Community Index[3]	Resource Index[4]
Fayette County	112.0	115.0	119.0	103.0

Note: Nearly 1,000 secondary school districts were rated in terms of educational quality. The scores range from a low of 50 to a high of 150; (1) Average of the Graduate Outcome, Community and Resource indexes; (2) Based on graduation rates and college board scores (SAT/ACT); (3) Based on the surrounding community's average level of education and the area's average income level; (4) Based on teacher salaries, per-pupil expenditures and student-teacher ratios.
Source: Expansion Management, Ratings Issue 1997

Educational Attainment by Race

Area	High School Graduate (%)					Bachelor's Degree (%)				
	Total	White	Black	Other	Hisp.[2]	Total	White	Black	Other	Hisp.[2]
City	80.2	82.5	63.1	86.6	72.4	30.6	32.8	10.3	59.5	24.4
MSA[1]	75.9	77.3	61.8	84.6	72.5	25.3	26.7	9.2	55.8	22.9
U.S.	75.2	77.9	63.1	60.4	49.8	20.3	21.5	11.4	19.4	9.2

Note: figures shown cover persons 25 years old and over; (1) Metropolitan Statistical Area - see Appendix A for areas included; (2) people of Hispanic origin can be of any race
Source: 1990 Census of Population and Housing, Summary Tape File 3C

School Enrollment by Type

Area	Preprimary				Elementary/High School			
	Public		Private		Public		Private	
	Enrollment	%	Enrollment	%	Enrollment	%	Enrollment	%
City	1,718	45.0	2,100	55.0	29,574	90.0	3,284	10.0
MSA[1]	2,832	50.7	2,759	49.3	50,759	91.9	4,490	8.1
U.S.	2,679,029	59.5	1,824,256	40.5	38,379,689	90.2	4,187,099	9.8

Note: figures shown cover persons 3 years old and over;
(1) Metropolitan Statistical Area - see Appendix A for areas included
Source: 1990 Census of Population and Housing, Summary Tape File 3C

School Enrollment by Race

Area	Preprimary (%)				Elementary/High School (%)			
	White	Black	Other	Hisp.[1]	White	Black	Other	Hisp.[1]
City	83.6	13.3	3.1	0.7	77.4	20.3	2.3	1.1
MSA[2]	86.2	11.1	2.7	0.7	83.7	14.7	1.7	0.9
U.S.	80.4	12.5	7.1	7.8	74.1	15.6	10.3	12.5

Note: figures shown cover persons 3 years old and over; (1) people of Hispanic origin can be of any race; (2) Metropolitan Statistical Area - see Appendix A for areas included
Source: 1990 Census of Population and Housing, Summary Tape File 3C

SAT/ACT Scores

Area/District	1997 SAT				1997 ACT	
	Percent of Graduates Tested (%)	Average Math Score	Average Verbal Score	Average Combined Score	Percent of Graduates Tested (%)	Average Composite Score
Fayette County	42	570	558	1,128	78	22.0
State	12	546	548	1,094	65	20.1
U.S.	42	511	505	1,016	36	21.0

Note: Math and verbal SAT scores are out of a possible 800; ACT scores are out of a possible 36
Caution: Comparing or ranking states/cities on the basis of SAT/ACT scores alone is invalid and strongly discouraged by the The College Board and The American College Testing Program as students who take the tests are self-selected and do not represent the entire student population.
Source: Fayette Country Public Schools, Office of Research & Evaluation, 1997; American College Testing Program, 1997; College Board, 1997

Classroom Teacher Salaries in Public Schools

District	B.A. Degree		M.A. Degree		Ph.D. Degree	
	Min. ($)	Max ($)	Min. ($)	Max. ($)	Min. ($)	Max. ($)
Lexington	23,630	36,732	25,940	40,802	29,672	47,344
Average[1]	26,120	39,270	28,175	44,667	31,643	49,825

Note: Salaries are for 1996-1997; (1) Based on all school districts covered; n/a not available
Source: American Federation of Teachers (unpublished data)

Higher Education

Two-Year Colleges		Four-Year Colleges		Medical Schools	Law Schools	Voc/ Tech
Public	Private	Public	Private			
1	2	1	2	1	1	6

Source: College Blue Book, Occupational Education 1997; Medical School Admission Requirements, 1998-99; Peterson's Guide to Two-Year Colleges, 1997; Peterson's Guide to Four-Year Colleges, 1997; Barron's Guide to Law Schools 1997

MAJOR EMPLOYERS

Major Employers

BankOne Lexington
Central Kentucky Life Insurance
Interim Personnel of Central Kentucky
Kentucky Utilities
Long John Silver's Restaurant
University of Kentucky Hospital
Professional Service Management
CHCK Inc. (management services)
Clark Material Handling Co.
Kentucky Central Life Insurance
Lexington Herald-Leader Co.
Link-Belt Construction Equip.
Lexmark International Group (computers)
Accordia of Lexington (business consulting)

Note: companies listed are located in the city
Source: Dun's Business Rankings 1997; Ward's Business Directory, 1997

PUBLIC SAFETY

Crime Rate

Area	All Crimes	Violent Crimes				Property Crimes		
		Murder	Forcible Rape	Robbery	Aggrav. Assault	Burglary	Larceny -Theft	Motor Vehicle Theft
City	6,356.2	5.8	50.6	240.1	532.0	1,199.7	3,948.6	379.4
Suburbs[1]	n/a	n/a	n/a	n/a	n/a	n/a	n/a	n/a
MSA[2]	n/a	n/a	n/a	n/a	n/a	n/a	n/a	n/a
U.S.	5,078.9	7.4	36.1	202.4	388.2	943.0	2,975.9	525.9

Note: Crime rate is the number of crimes per 100,000 pop.; (1) defined as all areas within the MSA but located outside the central city; (2) Metropolitan Statistical Area - see Appendix A for areas incl.
Source: FBI Uniform Crime Reports 1996

RECREATION

Culture and Recreation

Museums	Symphony Orchestras	Opera Companies	Dance Companies	Professional Theatres	Zoos	Pro Sports Teams
7	1	0	1	2	0	0

Source: International Directory of the Performing Arts, 1996; Official Museum Directory, 1998; Chamber of Commerce/Economic Development 1997

Library System

The Lexington Public Library has four branches, holdings of 625,252 volumes and a budget of $7,472,328 (1995-1996). *American Library Directory, 1997-1998*

MEDIA

Newspapers

Name	Type	Freq.	Distribution	Circulation
The Kentucky Kernel	n/a	5x/wk	Campus & community	17,000
Lexington Herald-Leader	n/a	7x/wk	Area	119,317

Note: Includes newspapers with circulations of 1,000 or more located in the city; n/a not available
Source: Burrelle's Media Directory, 1998 Edition

AM Radio Stations

Call Letters	Freq. (kHz)	Target Audience	Station Format	Music Format
WVLK	590	General	M/N/S/T	Adult Contemporary
WLAP	630	n/a	N/T	n/a
WCGW	770	General	M/N/S/T	Christian
WNVL	1250	General	M	Christian/Urban Contemporary
WLXG	1300	General	N/S/T	n/a
WTKT	1580	General	M	Big Band/MOR/R&B

Note: Stations included broadcast in the Lexington metro area; n/a not available
Station Format: E = Educational; M = Music; N = News; S = Sports; T = Talk
Music Format: AOR = Album Oriented Rock; MOR = Middle-of-the-Road
Source: Burrelle's Media Directory, 1998 Edition

FM Radio Stations

Call Letters	Freq. (mHz)	Target Audience	Station Format	Music Format
WRFL	88.1	General	M	Alternative
WUKY	91.3	General	M/N/S	Jazz
WVLK	92.9	General	M/N/S	Country
WMXL	94.5	General	M	Adult Contemporary
WGKS	96.9	General	M	Adult Contemporary
WKQQ	98.1	General	M/N/S	AOR/Classic Rock/Jazz/Oldies
WLRO	101.5	n/a	M/N/S	Classic Rock/Oldies
WLTO	102.5	General	n/a	n/a
WJMM	106.3	Religious	M/N/S/T	Christian

Note: Stations included broadcast in the Lexington metro area; n/a not available
Station Format: E = Educational; M = Music; N = News; S = Sports; T = Talk
Music Format: AOR = Album Oriented Rock; MOR = Middle-of-the-Road
Source: Burrelle's Media Directory, 1998 Edition

Television Stations

Name	Ch.	Affiliation	Type	Owner
WKPC	15	PBS	Public	Kentucky Authority for Educational TV
WLEX	18	NBC	Commercial	WLEX Inc.
WKMU	21	PBS	Public	Kentucky Authority for Educational TV
WKPI	22	PBS	Public	Kentucky Authority for Educational TV
WKZT	23	PBS	Public	Kentucky Authority for Educational TV
WKAS	25	PBS	Public	Kentucky Authority for Educational TV
WKYT	27	CBS	Commercial	Gray Kentucky Television, Inc.
WKPD	29	PBS	Public	Kentucky Authority for Educational TV
WKSO	29	PBS	Public	Kentucky Authority for Educational TV
WKON	31	PBS	Public	Kentucky Authority for Educational TV
WKHA	35	PBS	Public	Kentucky Authority for Educational TV
WKMA	35	PBS	Public	Kentucky Authority for Educational TV
WTVQ	36	ABC	Commercial	Media General Inc.
WKMR	38	PBS	Public	Kentucky Authority for Educational TV
WKLE	46	PBS	Public	Kentucky Authority for Educational TV
WKOH	52	PBS	Public	Kentucky Authority for Educational TV
WKGB	53	PBS	Public	Kentucky Authority for Educational TV
WCVN	54	PBS	Public	Kentucky Authority for Educational TV
WDKY	56	Fox	Commercial	Superior Communications Group Inc.
WKMJ	68	PBS	Public	Kentucky Authority for Educational TV

Note: Stations included broadcast in the Lexington metro area
Source: Burrelle's Media Directory, 1998 Edition

CLIMATE

Average and Extreme Temperatures

Temperature	Jan	Feb	Mar	Apr	May	Jun	Jul	Aug	Sep	Oct	Nov	Dec	Ann
Extreme High (°F)	76	75	82	88	92	101	103	103	103	91	83	75	103
Average High (°F)	40	44	54	66	75	83	86	85	79	68	55	44	65
Average Temp. (°F)	32	36	45	55	64	73	76	75	69	57	46	36	55
Average Low (°F)	24	26	34	44	54	62	66	65	58	46	36	28	45
Extreme Low (°F)	-21	-15	-2	18	26	39	47	42	35	20	-3	-19	-21

Note: Figures cover the years 1948-1990
Source: National Climatic Data Center, International Station Meteorological Climate Summary, 3/95

Average Precipitation/Snowfall/Humidity

Precip./Humidity	Jan	Feb	Mar	Apr	May	Jun	Jul	Aug	Sep	Oct	Nov	Dec	Ann
Avg. Precip. (in.)	3.6	3.4	4.4	3.9	4.3	4.0	4.8	3.7	3.0	2.4	3.5	3.9	45.1
Avg. Snowfall (in.)	6	5	3	Tr	Tr	0	0	0	0	Tr	1	3	17
Avg. Rel. Hum. 7am (%)	81	80	77	75	78	80	83	85	85	83	81	81	81
Avg. Rel. Hum. 4pm (%)	67	61	55	51	54	54	56	55	54	53	60	66	57

Note: Figures cover the years 1948-1990; Tr = Trace amounts (<0.05 in. of rain; <0.5 in. of snow)
Source: National Climatic Data Center, International Station Meteorological Climate Summary, 3/95

Weather Conditions

Temperature			Daytime Sky			Precipitation		
10°F & below	32°F & below	90°F & above	Clear	Partly cloudy	Cloudy	0.01 inch or more precip.	0.1 inch or more snow/ice	Thunder-storms
11	96	22	86	136	143	129	17	44

Note: Figures are average number of days per year and covers the years 1948-1990
Source: National Climatic Data Center, International Station Meteorological Climate Summary, 3/95

AIR & WATER QUALITY

Maximum Pollutant Concentrations

	Particulate Matter (ug/m³)	Carbon Monoxide (ppm)	Sulfur Dioxide (ppm)	Nitrogen Dioxide (ppm)	Ozone (ppm)	Lead (ug/m³)
MSA[1] Level	60	3	0.020	0.014	0.10	0.04
NAAQS[2]	150	9	0.140	0.053	0.12	1.50
Met NAAQS?	Yes	Yes	Yes	Yes	Yes	Yes

Note: (1) Metropolitan Statistical Area - see Appendix A for areas included; (2) National Ambient Air Quality Standards; ppm = parts per million; ug/m³ = micrograms per cubic meter; n/a not available
Source: EPA, National Air Quality and Emissions Trends Report, 1996

Pollutant Standards Index

Data not available. *EPA, National Air Quality and Emissions Trends Report, 1996*

Drinking Water

Water System Name	Pop. Served	Primary Water Source Type	Number of Violations in Fiscal Year 1997	Type of Violation/ Contaminants
Kentucky-American Water Co.	281,094	Surface	1	(1)

Note: Data as of January 16, 1998; (1) System failed to conduct initial or repeat sampling, or to accurately report an analytical result for a specific contaminant (TTHM).
Source: EPA, Office of Ground Water and Drinking Water, Safe Drinking Water Information System

Lexington tap water is alkaline, medium and fluoridated.
Editor & Publisher Market Guide, 1998

New York, New York

Background

There are few cities in the world that can compare with New York's frenetic excitement. New York is snappy, quick, loaded with attitude, and beautiful as with its famous skyline and the world's best known bridge, the Brooklyn Bridge.

The largest city in New York State is located on the southernmost extension of the state, at the mouth of the Hudson River. The area was first explored by Giovanni De Verrazano in 1524, and then by Henry Hudson in 1609. The first Dutch settlers came in 1624, and by 1625, the area had become the permanent settlement of New Amsterdam. A year later, as we have all learned from our history books, the island of Manhattan was bought for a mere $24 by Peter Minuit from the local tribes.

After New York was no longer the temporary capitals of both New York State and the United States, the city continued to grow in importance and in stature. It became the city, where, according to Frank Sinatra, "If you can make it there, you'll make it anywhere." After all, with the very best in the arts such as the Metropolitan Museum of Art, The Museum of Modern Art, and the Guggenheim Museum; education such as New York University, Columbia University, and a host of excellent primary and secondary schools; finance such as the New York and the American Stock Exchanges; fashion; theatres; restaurants; political activism; and so forth challenging your senses, how can one not rise to the occasion and measure oneself against such excellence. Yes, New York is competitive, and even stressful sometimes, but it's still home to over 7 million people.

1996 saw ground broken for a 48-story office tower at 42nd Street and Broadway. In addition the Disney Corporation is renovating the New Amsterdam Theater, Madame Tussaud's Wax Museum is planning a major new attraction and AMC is building the city's largest movie house, with 25 screens. The 42nd Street project, according to John S. Dyson, deputy mayor for finance and economic development will create 2,800 jobs and more than $330 million in economic activity. *Site Selection, October 1996*

Another major project will be Harlem USA, a $56 million, retail-entertainment complex that will house a Disney store, multi-screen movie theater, indoor ice-skating rink, health center and a 53,000-square-foot supermarket. Scheduled opening is set for 1998. *USA Today, 9/16/96*

Though New York City ranks low in job growth compared with other large metropolitan areas like Atlanta and Dallas and its unemployment rate is above the national rate, the city still continues to dominate such high-paying industries ranging from advertising to broadcasting. It is still the world's undisputed financial capital and home to over 1,000 small companies in the software business. Being a center of cultural life gives the city a long-lasting allure. The overall crime rate is down to its lowest level in 30 years and The National Civic League names New York City as one of the country's 10 all-American cities in 1997. According to a 1997 Harris Poll, New York was ranked the city that most people wanted to live in or near.

The New York metro area is close to the path of most storm and frontal systems which move across the continent. The city can experience higher temperatures in summer and lower ones in winter although it is on the coast. The passage of many weather systems helps to reduce the duration of both cold and warm spells and serves to circulate the air, reducing stagnation.

General Rankings and Evaluative Comments

- New York was ranked #151 out of 300 cities by *Money's* 1997 "Survey of the Best Places to Live." Criteria used: health services, crime, economy, housing, education, transportation, weather, leisure and the arts. The city was ranked #231 in 1996 and #141 in 1995. *Money, July 1997; Money, September 1996; Money, September 1995*

- New York appeared on *Fortune's* list of "North America's Most Improved Cities" Rank: 1 out of 10. The selected cities satisfied basic business-location needs and also demonstrated improvement over a five- to ten-year period in a number of business and quality-of-life measures.

  "In the past few years...gritty, in-your-face New York has done an astonishing 180. Residents wax poetic when they discuss the city's transformation....

  The most glowing reports focused on the dramatic decline in the city's crime rate. Since 1993 the rate of serious crimes has plummeted 44%, and total crime is at its lowest in 18 years....

  A better quality of life is, of course, very good for business. After years of watching FORTUNE 500 companies abandon the city for the 'burbs', New York has secured commitments from 34 major companies...to stay at least 15 years.

  New York has applied this aggressive approach to retaining small businesses as well....

  By retaining and recruiting companies, New York has finally reversed a decade of job loss in the city. Since 1993 the private sector has created 173,600 jobs....

  New York's comeback is no secret, thanks to impressive growth in film and television production—an industry that had been largely driven from New York by high costs and bureaucratic red tape.

  But many people aren't content to see New York on TV: Tourism reached an all-time high in 1996 with 31 million visitors, a 21% increase over 1990...

  In part, tourists are responding to the cleanup—of certain old haunts: Times Square....has become as family-friendly as Disneyland....

  New Yorkers once again believe in their city...." *Fortune, 11/24/97*

- *Ladies Home Journal* ranked America's 200 largest cities based on the qualities women care about most. New York ranked 155 out of 200. Criteria: low crime rate, good public schools, well-paying jobs, quality health and child care, the presence of women in government, proportion of women-owned businesses, size of the wage gap with men, local economy, divorce rates, the ratio of single men to single women, whether there are laws that require at least the same number of public toilets for women as men, and the probability of good hair days. *Ladies Home Journal, November 1997*

- New York was ranked #139 out of 219 cities in terms of children's health, safety, and economic well-being. Criteria: total population, percent population change, birth rate, child immunization rate, infant mortality rate, percent low birth weight infants, percent of births to teens, physician-to-population ratio, student-to-teacher ratio, dropout rate, unemployment rate, median family income, percent of children in poverty, violent and property crime rates, number of juvenile arrests for violent crimes as a percent of the total crime index, number of days with pollution standard index (PSI) over 100, pounds toxic releases per 1,000 people and number of superfund sites. *Zero Population Growth, Children's Environmental Index 1997*

- Heritage Hills of Westchester, located 29 miles north of New York City, is among America's best retirement communities. Criteria: communities must have state-of-the-art facilities, newly built homes for sale, and give you the most value for your money in every price range. Communities must also welcome newcomers of all races and religions. *New Choices, July/August 1997*

- New York appeared on *Ebony's* list of the best cities for African-Americans. Rank: 4 out of 4. The cities were selected based on a survey of the 100 Most Influential Black Americans. They were asked which city offered the best overall experience for African-Americans, and which dream city they would select if they could live anywhere they wanted to. *Ebony* also asked opinion-makers which cities offered the best cultural experiences, the best schools and the most diversity.

"New York City—with Broadway, Harlem, and a unique mix of Blacks from all over the world—was overwhelmingly chosen the city with the best social life. And with a large-Afro-Caribbean population, which includes Jamaicans, Haitians and Trinidadians, New York ranked as the top city for Black culture." *Ebony, 9/97*

- New York is among the 20 most livable cities for gay men and lesbians. The list was divided between 10 cities you might expect and 10 surprises. New York was on the cities you would expect list. Rank: 2 out of 10. Criteria: legal protection from antigay discrimination, an annual gay pride celebration, a community center, gay bookstores and publications, and an array of organizations, religious groups, and health care facilities that cater to the needs of the local gay community. *The Advocate, June 1997*

- New York was selected by *Swing* magazine as being one of "The 10 Best Places to Live" in the U.S. It was also named the "Best Place for Cultural Experience".
The cities were selected based on census data, cost of living, economic growth, and entertainment options. Swing also read local papers, talked to industry insiders, and interviewed young people. *Swing, July/August 1997*

- New York appeared on *Travel & Leisure's* list of the world's best cities.
Rank: 21 out of 25. Criteria: activities/attractions, culture/arts, people, restaurants/food, and value. *Travel & Leisure, September 1997*

- *Conde Nast Traveler* polled 37,000 readers in terms of travel satisfaction. Cities were ranked based on the following criteria: people/friendliness, environment/ambiance, cultural enrichment, restaurants and fun/energy. New York appeared in the top thirty, ranking number 10, with an overall rating of 68.7 out of 100 based on all the criteria. The cities were also ranked in each category separately. New York appeared in the top 10 based on cultural enrichment, ranking number 3 with a rating of 86.9 out of 100. New York appeared in the top 10 based on restaurants, ranking number 4 with a rating of 87.5 out of 100. New York appeared in the top 10 based on fun/energy, ranking number 5 with a rating of 81.5 out of 100. *Conde Nast Traveler, Readers' Choice Poll 1997*

- *Yahoo! Internet Life* selected "America's 100 Most Wired Cities & Towns". 50 cities were large and 50 cities were small. New York ranked 8 out of 50 large cities. Criteria: Internet users per capita, number of networked computers, number of registered domain names, Internet backbone traffic, and the per-capita number of Web sites devoted to each city. Yahoo! Internet Life, March 1998

- *Reader's Digest* non-scientifically ranked the 12 largest U.S. metropolitan areas in terms of having the worst drivers. The New York metro area ranked number 1. The areas were selected by asking approximately 1,200 readers on the *Reader's Digest* Web site and 200 interstate bus drivers and long-haul truckers which metro areas have the worst drivers. Their responses were factored in with fatality, insurance and rental-car rates to create the rankings. *Reader's Digest, March 1998*

- Goldman Sachs, J.P. Morgan and Merrill Lynch, headquartered in New York, are among the "100 Best Companies to Work for in America." Criteria: trust in management, pride in work/company, camaraderie, company responses to the Hewitt People Practices Inventory, and employee responses to their Great Place to Work survey. The companies also had to be at least 10 years old and have a minimum of 500 employees. *Fortune, January 12, 1998*

- AT&T, Avon Products, Bankers Trust New York, Chase Manhattan Bank, Citicorp/Citibank, Coopers & Lybrand LLP, Merrill Lynch & Co., J.P. Morgan, and Price Waterhouse, headquartered in New York, are among the "100 Best Companies for Working Mothers." Criteria: pay compared with competition, opportunities for women to advance, support for child care, flexible work schedules and family-friendly benefits. *Working Mother, October 1997*

- According to *Working Mother,* "Governor Pataki recommended that child care aid be available only to parents with kids under the age of six. This proposal would obviously save New York State money—but it would be a blow to many working moms, and a big loss to school-age programs across the state.—State lawmakers did provide some minimal help for many families. In 1996, the legislature expanded the state child care tax credit by allowing it to be added to parents' tax refunds. That will provide many families with a refund as high as $432.

  Over all, child care in New York seems to be in a holding pattern. Nearly a million kids in the state will need state-subsidized child care in 1997; so far, only 100,000 receive it." *Working Mother, July/August 1997*

Business Environment

STATE ECONOMY

State Economic Profile

"New York's economy is enjoying a stable, albeit modest expansion....

Governor Pataki's fiscal year 1998 budget proposal calls for $6.1 billion in tax cuts to businesses and consumers, continuing his program of tax relief put in place two years ago. The proposed spending cuts include about one billion dollars in cuts to Medicaid, which will hurt New York's hospitals which are already contending with price deregulation and cost pressures from insurers.

Residential construction is climbing downstate, while it is dropping precipitously in the northern portion of the state. Last year, residential permits fell to a 14-year low in the major upstate metropolitan areas. As labor market conditions continue to stagnate in the region, the residential market will show little improvement over the forecast horizon.

Continued job losses in state government and at hospitals keep New York's near-term economic outlook poor. Moreover, the state is still absorbing the thousands of government and banking jobs eliminated in recent years. Longer term, New York's outlook is not much better. The impact of restructuring in these industries will be felt for the next few years. The restructuring, combined with the state's high costs of doing business, declining manufacturing industry, and aging infrastructure, will keep New York in the spotlight as one of the weakest performers in the nation." *National Association of Realtors, Economic Profiles: The Fifty States, July 1997*

IMPORTS/EXPORTS

Total Export Sales

Area	1993 ($000)	1994 ($000)	1995 ($000)	1996 ($000)	% Chg. 1993-96	% Chg. 1995-96
MSA[1]	28,192,822	23,543,749	27,131,084	27,970,507	-0.8	3.1
U.S.	464,858,354	512,415,609	583,030,524	622,827,063	34.0	6.8

Note: (1) Metropolitan Statistical Area - see Appendix A for areas included
Source: U.S. Department of Commerce, International Trade Association, Metropolitan Area Exports: An Export Performance Report on Over 250 U.S. Cities, October 1997

Imports/Exports by Port

Type	Cargo Value			Share of U.S. Total	
	1995 (US$mil.)	1996 (US$mil.)	% Change 1995-1996	1995 (%)	1996 (%)
Imports	46,100	45,413	-1.49	11.77	11.84
Exports	21,221	22,221	4.71	9.27	9.38

Source: Global Trade Information Services, WaterBorne Trade Atlas 1997

CITY FINANCES

City Government Finances

Component	FY94 ($000)	FY94 (per capita $)
Revenue	44,930,293	6,101.76
Expenditure	49,002,330	6,654.76
Debt Outstanding	40,295,356	5,472.31
Cash & Securities	61,986,313	8,418.05

Source: U.S. Bureau of the Census, City Government Finances: 1993-94

City Government Revenue by Source

Source	FY94 ($000)	FY94 (per capita $)	FY94 (%)
From Federal Government	1,476,961	200.58	3.3
From State Governments	14,193,538	1,927.55	31.6
From Local Governments	141,530	19.22	0.3
Property Taxes	7,870,393	1,068.84	17.5
General Sales Taxes	2,503,646	340.01	5.6
Selective Sales Taxes	1,143,078	155.24	2.5
Income Taxes	6,069,153	824.22	13.5
Current Charges	4,252,073	577.45	9.5
Utility/Liquor Store	2,165,917	294.14	4.8
Employee Retirement[1]	3,267,783	443.78	7.3
Other	1,846,221	250.73	4.1

Note: (1) Excludes "city contributions," classified as "nonrevenue," intragovernmental transfers.
Source: U.S. Bureau of the Census, City Government Finances: 1993-94

City Government Expenditures by Function

Function	FY94 ($000)	FY94 (per capita $)	FY94 (%)
Educational Services	9,308,163	1,264.09	19.0
Employee Retirement[1]	3,731,065	506.70	7.6
Environment/Housing	4,526,245	614.69	9.2
Government Administration	1,250,636	169.84	2.6
Interest on General Debt	1,786,406	242.60	3.6
Public Safety	4,071,222	552.89	8.3
Social Services	11,807,299	1,603.49	24.1
Transportation	1,066,127	144.79	2.2
Utility/Liquor Store	4,420,933	600.38	9.0
Other	7,034,234	955.28	14.4

Note: (1) Payments to beneficiaries including withdrawal of contributions.
Source: U.S. Bureau of the Census, City Government Finances: 1993-94

Municipal Bond Ratings

Area	Moody's	S & P
New York	Baa1	BBB+

Note: n/a not available; n/r not rated
Source: Moody's Bond Record, 2/98; Statistical Abstract of the U.S., 1997; Governing Magazine, 9/97, 3/98

POPULATION

Population Growth

Area	1980	1990	% Chg. 1980-90	July 1996 Estimate	% Chg. 1990-96
City	7,071,639	7,322,564	3.5	7,380,906	0.8
MSA[1]	8,274,961	8,546,846	3.3	8,643,437	1.1
U.S.	226,545,805	248,765,170	9.8	265,179,411	6.6

Note: (1) Metropolitan Statistical Area - see Appendix A for areas included
Source: 1980/1990 Census of Housing and Population, Summary Tape File 3C; Census Bureau Population Estimates

Population Characteristics

Race	City 1980 Population	City 1980 %	City 1990 Population	City 1990 %	% Chg. 1980-90	MSA[1] 1990 Population	MSA[1] 1990 %
White	4,348,605	61.5	3,831,907	52.3	-11.9	4,832,376	56.5
Black	1,788,377	25.3	2,107,137	28.8	17.8	2,254,576	26.4
Amer Indian/Esk/Aleut	13,400	0.2	22,718	0.3	69.5	24,822	0.3
Asian/Pacific Islander	245,759	3.5	510,549	7.0	107.7	553,987	6.5
Other	675,498	9.6	850,253	11.6	25.9	881,085	10.3
Hispanic Origin[2]	1,406,024	19.9	1,737,927	23.7	23.6	1,842,127	21.6

Note: (1) Metropolitan Statistical Area - see Appendix A for areas included; (2) people of Hispanic origin can be of any race
Source: 1980/1990 Census of Housing and Population, Summary Tape File 3C

Ancestry

Area	German	Irish	English	Italian	U.S.	French	Polish	Dutch
City	5.4	7.3	2.4	11.5	2.1	0.9	4.1	0.3
MSA[1]	6.4	8.9	3.0	13.2	2.3	1.0	4.3	0.4
U.S.	23.3	15.6	13.1	5.9	5.3	4.2	3.8	2.5

Note: Figures are percentages and include persons that reported multiple ancestry (eg. if a person reported being Irish and Italian, they were included in both columns); (1) Metropolitan Statistical Area - see Appendix A for areas included
Source: 1990 Census of Population and Housing, Summary Tape File 3C

Age

Area	Median Age (Years)	Under 5	Under 18	18-24	25-44	45-64	65+	80+
City	33.6	6.9	23.0	10.3	33.9	19.8	13.0	3.1
MSA[1]	33.9	6.8	23.0	10.2	33.7	20.1	13.0	3.1
U.S.	32.9	7.3	25.6	10.5	32.6	18.7	12.5	2.8

Age Distribution (%) applies to columns Under 5 through 80+.

Note: (1) Metropolitan Statistical Area - see Appendix A for areas included
Source: 1990 Census of Population and Housing, Summary Tape File 3C

Male/Female Ratio

Area	Number of males per 100 females (all ages)	Number of males per 100 females (18 years old+)
City	88.1	84.5
MSA[1]	88.6	85.0
U.S.	95.0	91.9

Note: (1) Metropolitan Statistical Area - see Appendix A for areas included
Source: 1990 Census of Population, General Population Characteristics

INCOME

Per Capita/Median/Average Income

Area	Per Capita ($)	Median Household ($)	Average Household ($)
City	16,281	29,823	41,741
MSA[1]	17,397	31,659	45,159
U.S.	14,420	30,056	38,453

Note: all figures are for 1989; (1) Metropolitan Statistical Area - see Appendix A for areas included
Source: 1990 Census of Population and Housing, Summary Tape File 3C

Household Income Distribution by Race

Income ($)	City (%)					U.S. (%)				
	Total	White	Black	Other	Hisp.[1]	Total	White	Black	Other	Hisp.[1]
Less than 5,000	8.9	6.1	13.4	12.9	14.4	6.2	4.8	15.2	8.6	8.8
5,000 - 9,999	11.3	10.1	12.6	13.5	16.3	9.3	8.6	14.2	9.9	11.1
10,000 - 14,999	7.5	7.1	7.8	9.0	9.4	8.8	8.5	11.0	9.8	11.0
15,000 - 24,999	15.2	13.5	17.9	17.7	18.1	17.5	17.3	18.9	18.5	20.5
25,000 - 34,999	14.1	13.7	14.7	14.5	14.5	15.8	16.1	14.2	15.4	16.4
35,000 - 49,999	15.9	16.7	14.9	14.5	13.7	17.9	18.6	13.3	16.1	16.0
50,000 - 74,999	14.6	16.4	12.3	11.5	9.5	15.0	15.8	9.3	13.4	11.1
75,000 - 99,999	6.0	7.5	4.1	3.6	2.7	5.1	5.5	2.6	4.7	3.1
100,000+	6.4	9.0	2.2	2.7	1.4	4.4	4.8	1.3	3.7	1.9

Note: all figures are for 1989; (1) people of Hispanic origin can be of any race
Source: 1990 Census of Population and Housing, Summary Tape File 3C

Effective Buying Income

Area	Per Capita ($)	Median Household ($)	Average Household ($)
City	16,875	32,417	44,604
MSA[1]	17,841	35,520	48,736
U.S.	15,444	33,201	41,849

Note: data as of 1/1/97; (1) Metropolitan Statistical Area - see Appendix A for areas included
Source: Standard Rate & Data Service, Newspaper Advertising Source, 2/98

Effective Household Buying Income Distribution

Area	% of Households Earning						
	$10,000 -$19,999	$20,000 -$34,999	$35,000 -$49,999	$50,000 -$74,999	$75,000 -$99,000	$100,000 -$124,999	$125,000 and up
City	15.5	21.1	16.2	17.0	7.0	2.7	3.7
MSA[1]	14.4	19.9	16.1	18.2	8.2	3.4	4.7
U.S.	16.5	23.4	18.3	18.2	6.4	2.1	2.4

Note: data as of 1/1/97; (1) Metropolitan Statistical Area - see Appendix A for areas included
Source: Standard Rate & Data Service, Newspaper Advertising Source, 2/98

Poverty Rates by Race and Age

Area	Total (%)	By Race (%)				By Age (%)		
		White	Black	Other	Hisp.[2]	Under 5 years old	Under 18 years old	65 years and over
City	19.3	12.3	25.3	29.4	33.2	30.5	30.1	16.5
MSA[1]	17.5	10.8	24.8	28.4	32.3	27.5	27.1	15.3
U.S.	13.1	9.8	29.5	23.1	25.3	20.1	18.3	12.8

Note: figures show the percent of people living below the poverty line in 1989. The average poverty threshold was $12,674 for a family of four in 1989; (1) Metropolitan Statistical Area - see Appendix A for areas included; (2) people of Hispanic origin can be of any race
Source: 1990 Census of Population and Housing, Summary Tape File 3C

EMPLOYMENT

Labor Force and Employment

Area	Civilian Labor Force			Workers Employed		
	Dec. '95	Dec. '96	% Chg.	Dec. '95	Dec. '96	% Chg.
City	8,711,639	8,747,089	0.4	8,185,010	8,248,488	0.8
MSA[1]	3,969,059	3,988,748	0.5	3,654,143	3,701,557	1.3
U.S.	134,583,000	136,742,000	1.6	127,903,000	130,785,000	2.3

Note: Data is not seasonally adjusted and covers workers 16 years of age and older; (1) Metropolitan Statistical Area - see Appendix A for areas included
Source: Bureau of Labor Statistics, http://stats.bls.gov

Unemployment Rate

Area	1997											
	Jan.	Feb.	Mar.	Apr.	May	Jun.	Jul.	Aug.	Sep.	Oct.	Nov.	Dec.
City	7.1	7.1	7.0	6.4	6.3	6.3	6.6	6.2	6.1	6.1	5.9	5.7
MSA[1]	8.9	8.9	9.0	8.6	8.4	8.8	8.9	8.5	8.1	8.2	7.7	7.2
U.S.	5.9	5.7	5.5	4.8	4.7	5.2	5.0	4.8	4.7	4.4	4.3	4.4

Note: Data is not seasonally adjusted and covers workers 16 years of age and older; All figures are percentages; (1) Metropolitan Statistical Area - see Appendix A for areas included
Source: Bureau of Labor Statistics, http://stats.bls.gov

Employment by Industry

Sector	MSA[1]		U.S.
	Number of Employees	Percent of Total	Percent of Total
Services	1,489,500	37.2	29.0
Retail Trade	501,100	12.5	18.5
Government	608,800	15.2	16.1
Manufacturing	316,000	7.9	15.0
Finance/Insurance/Real Estate	508,300	12.7	5.7
Wholesale Trade	224,400	5.6	5.4
Transportation/Public Utilities	236,500	5.9	5.3
Construction/Mining	121,900	3.0	5.0

Note: Figures cover non-farm employment as of 12/97 and are not seasonally adjusted; (1) Metropolitan Statistical Area - see Appendix A for areas included
Source: Bureau of Labor Statistics, http://stats.bls.gov

Employment by Occupation

Occupation Category	City (%)	MSA[1] (%)	U.S. (%)
White Collar	64.6	65.5	58.1
Executive/Admin./Management	13.5	14.2	12.3
Professional	17.0	17.5	14.1
Technical & Related Support	3.1	3.1	3.7
Sales	10.3	10.6	11.8
Administrative Support/Clerical	20.6	20.0	16.3
Blue Collar	19.2	18.7	26.2
Precision Production/Craft/Repair	7.5	7.7	11.3
Machine Operators/Assem./Insp.	4.9	4.5	6.8
Transportation/Material Movers	3.7	3.6	4.1
Cleaners/Helpers/Laborers	3.1	2.9	3.9
Services	16.0	15.4	13.2
Farming/Forestry/Fishing	0.3	0.4	2.5

Note: figures cover employed persons 16 years old and over; (1) Metropolitan Statistical Area - see Appendix A for areas included
Source: 1990 Census of Population and Housing, Summary Tape File 3C

Occupational Employment Projections: 1995 - 1998

Occupations Expected to have the Largest Job Growth (ranked by numerical growth)	Fast-Growing Occupations[1] (ranked by percent growth)
1. Securities, financial services sales	1. Computer engineers
2. Guards	2. Ushers/lobby attendants/ticket takers
3. Salespersons, retail	3. Systems analysts
4. Janitors/cleaners/maids, ex. priv. hshld.	4. Computer scientists
5. Home health aides	5. Producers/directors/actors/entertainers
6. Systems analysts	6. Musicians
7. Producers/directors/actors/entertainers	7. Counter & rental clerks
8. Cashiers	8. Amusement and recreation attendants
9. Waiters & waitresses	9. Medical assistants
10. Maintenance repairers, general utility	10. Personal and home care aides

Projections cover New York City.
Note: (1) Based on minimum absolute job change of 500 jobs
Source: New York State Department of Labor, Occupational Outlook, New York City

Average Wages

Occupation	Wage	Occupation	Wage
Professional/Technical/Clerical	$/Week	**Health/Protective Services**	$/Week
Accountants III	831	Corrections Officers	748
Attorneys III	1,289	Firefighters	809
Budget Analysts III	895	Nurses, Licensed Practical II	575
Buyers/Contracting Specialists II	731	Nurses, Registered II	980
Clerks, Accounting III	511	Nursing Assistants II	410
Clerks, General III	440	Police Officers I	752
Computer Operators II	498	**Hourly Workers**	$/Hour
Computer Programmers II	675	Forklift Operators	13.54
Drafters II	692	General Maintenance Workers	14.65
Engineering Technicians III	-	Guards I	8.09
Engineering Technicians, Civil III	622	Janitors	12.32
Engineers III	972	Maintenance Electricians	22.55
Key Entry Operators I	418	Maintenance Electronics Techs II	-
Personnel Assistants III	536	Maintenance Machinists	20.94
Personnel Specialists III	813	Maintenance Mechanics, Machinery	16.15
Secretaries III	619	Material Handling Laborers	-
Switchboard Operator-Receptionist	428	Motor Vehicle Mechanics	19.99
Systems Analysts II	991	Shipping/Receiving Clerks	11.41
Systems Analysts Supervisor/Mgr II	1,569	Tool and Die Makers	-
Tax Collectors II	639	Truckdrivers, Tractor Trailer	17.90
Word Processors II	532	Warehouse Specialists	12.47

Note: Wage data includes full-time workers only for 5/95 and cover the Metropolitan Statistical Area (see Appendix A for areas included). Dashes indicate that data was not available.
Source: Bureau of Labor Statistics, Occupational Compensation Survey, 10/95

TAXES

Major State and Local Tax Rates

State Corp. Income (%)	State Personal Income (%)	Residential Property (effective rate per $100)	Sales & Use		State Gasoline (cents/ gallon)	State Cigarette (cents/ 20-pack)
			State (%)	Local (%)		
9.0	4.0 - 6.85	0.86	4.0	4.25	8	56

Note: Personal/corporate income tax rates as of 1/97. Sales, gasoline and cigarette tax rates as of 1/98.
Source: Federation of Tax Administrators, www.taxadmin.org; Washington D.C. Department of Finance and Revenue, Tax Rates and Tax Burdens in the District of Columbia: A Nationwide Comparison, June 1997; Chamber of Commerce

Total Taxes Per Capita and as a Percent of Income

Area	Per Capita Income ($)	Per Capita Taxes ($)			Taxes as Pct. of Income (%)		
		Total	Federal	State/ Local	Total	Federal	State/ Local
New York	30,461	11,859	7,188	4,671	38.9	23.6	15.3
U.S.	26,187	9,205	6,127	3,078	35.2	23.4	11.8

Note: Figures are for 1997
Source: Tax Foundation, Web Site, www.taxfoundation.org

Estimated Tax Burden

Area	State Income	Local Income	Property	Sales	Total
New York	3,225	2,600	2,925	701	9,451

Note: The numbers are estimates of taxes paid by a married couple with two kids and annual earnings of $65,000. Sales tax estimates assume they spend average amounts on food, clothing, household goods and gasoline. Property tax estimates assume they live in a $225,000 home.
Source: Kiplinger's Personal Finance Magazine, June 1997

COMMERCIAL REAL ESTATE

Office Market

Class/ Location	Total Space (sq. ft.)	Vacant Space (sq. ft.)	Vac. Rate (%)	Under Constr. (sq. ft.)	Net Absorp. (sq. ft.)	Rental Rates ($/sq.ft./yr.)
Class A						
CBD	178,342,000	15,529,000	8.7	1,600,000	3,389,000	20.00-65.00
Outside CBD	55,643,000	5,536,000	9.9	n/a	4,732,000	15.00-47.00
Class B						
CBD	66,370,000	7,861,000	11.8	n/a	2,118,000	18.00-40.00
Outside CBD	35,047,000	6,484,000	18.5	n/a	-942,000	12.00-28.00

Note: Data as of 10/97 and covers Manhattan; CBD=Midtown; Outside CBD=Downtown; CBD = Central Business District; n/a not available;
Source: Society of Industrial and Office Realtors, 1998 Comparative Statistics of Industrial and Office Real Estate Markets

"At the end of 1997 1.6 million sq. ft. of office space was under construction in Midtown. Two new owner/user buildings are currently in the planning stages. Reuters has indicated it would like to move its North American headquarters into a new 850,000 sq. ft. building on Times Square, taking 600,000 sq. ft. of the space for itself. Bear Stearns has plans to put up a new building on Madison Avenue for sole occupancy. Absorption during 1998 is expected to increase from the strong 1997 pace, leading to additional increases in rental rates as vacancy rates fall even further. Sales prices are expected to increase again during 1988." *Society of Industrial and Office Realtors, 1998 Comparative Statistics of Industrial and Office Real Estate Markets*

Industrial Market

Location	Total Space (sq. ft.)	Vacant Space (sq. ft.)	Vac. Rate (%)	Under Constr. (sq. ft.)	Net Absorp. (sq. ft.)	Gross Lease ($/sq.ft./yr.)
Central City	213,838,448	25,205,434	11.8	n/a	9,538,325	n/a
Suburban	n/a	n/a	n/a	n/a	n/a	n/a

Note: Data as of 10/97 and covers Brooklyn/Queens; n/a not available
Source: Society of Industrial and Office Realtors, 1998 Comparative Statistics of Industrial and Office Real Estate Markets

"There was little speculative development in Brooklyn and Queens during 1997. The lack of competitively priced land will likely prevent speculative development from taking place during 1998. Strong investor activity led to sharp increases in sales prices during 1997. It is anticipated that sales prices will increase again during 1998 but the rate of increase should slow somewhat. Our SIOR reporter expects retail development will absorb more industrial properties, while city agencies fuel the demand for warehouse/distribution space. A large block of manufacturing space will be vacated during 1998 when the Swingline Stapler Corporation vacates its facilities in Long Island City. Manufacturing firms located in the New York area have a very difficult time competing in the world market. Losing another manufacturer is hard to accept but it is just one more firm in a long line as the structure of the local economy changes." *Society of Industrial and Office Realtors, 1998 Comparative Statistics of Industrial and Office Real Estate Markets*

COMMERCIAL UTILITIES

Typical Monthly Electric Bills

Area	Commercial Service ($/month)		Industrial Service ($/month)	
	12 kW demand 1,500 kWh	100 kW demand 30,000 kWh	1,000 kW demand 400,000 kWh	20,000 kW demand 10,000,000 kWh
City	416	4,647	47,727	1,186,989
U.S.	162	2,360	25,590	545,677

Note: Based on rates in effect July 1, 1997
Source: Edison Electric Institute, Typical Residential, Commercial and Industrial Bills, Summer 1997

TRANSPORTATION

Transportation Statistics

Avg. travel time to work (min.)	36.5
Interstate highways	I-78; I-87; I-95
Bus lines	
In-city	Metropolitan Transportation Authority (NYC Transit), 3,554 vehicles
Inter-city	26+
Passenger air service	
Airport	J.F.K. International; LaGuardia; Newark International
Airlines	93
Aircraft departures	394,740 (1995)
Enplaned passengers	30,865,118 (1995)
Rail service	Amtrak; Metro-North; LIRR; Metro (city subway); Staten Island Rapid Transit
Motor freight carriers	369
Major waterways/ports	Port of New York/New Jersey

Source: OAG, Business Travel Planner, Summer 1997; Editor & Publisher Market Guide, 1998; FAA Airport Activity Statistics, 1996; Amtrak National Time Table, Northeast Timetable, Fall/Winter 1997-98; 1990 Census of Population and Housing, STF 3C; Chamber of Commerce/Economic Development 1997; Jane's Urban Transport Systems 1997-98; Transit Fact Book 1997

A survey of 90,000 airline passengers during the first half of 1997 ranked most of the largest airports in the U.S. Newark International ranked #27, LaGuardia #33, and John F. Kennedy International #35 out of 36. Criteria: cleanliness, quality of restaurants, attractiveness, speed of baggage delivery, ease of reaching gates, available ground transportation, ease of following signs and closeness of parking. *Plog Research Inc., First Half 1997*

Means of Transportation to Work

Area	Car/Truck/Van		Public Transportation			Bicycle	Walked	Other Means	Worked at Home
	Drove Alone	Car-pooled	Bus	Subway	Railroad				
City	24.0	8.5	12.7	36.7	1.7	0.3	10.7	2.9	2.4
MSA[1]	30.7	8.9	11.4	30.9	3.0	0.3	9.7	2.6	2.5
U.S.	73.2	13.4	3.0	1.5	0.5	0.4	3.9	1.2	3.0

Note: figures shown are percentages and only include workers 16 years old and over;
(1) Metropolitan Statistical Area - see Appendix A for areas included
Source: 1990 Census of Population and Housing, Summary Tape File 3C

BUSINESSES

Major Business Headquarters

Company Name	1997 Rankings	
	Fortune 500	Forbes 500
AT&T	7	-
Amerada Hess	164	-
American Express	64	-
American Intl. Group	23	-
Andersen Worldwide	-	7
Asarco	485	-
Avon Products	293	-
Bank of New York	251	-
Bankers Trust N.Y.	155	-
Bear Stearns	288	-
Bloomberg Financial Markets	-	184
Bristol-Myers Squibb	76	-
Chase Manhattan Corp.	25	-
Citicorp	20	-
Colgate-Palmolive	167	-
College Retirement Equities Fund	86	-
Consolidated Edison	208	-
Continental Grain	-	5
Coopers & Lybrand	-	13
Dean Witter Discover	162	-
Dover	334	-
Ernst & Young	-	10
Este Lauder	422	-
Gilman Investment	-	371
Goldman Sachs Group	-	4
GoodTimes Entertainment	-	461
Gould Paper	-	240
Guardian Life Ins. Co. of America	210	-
Harris Chemical Group	-	299
Hartz Group	-	346
Hearst	-	47
Helmsley Enterprises	-	79
Horsehead Industries	-	323
ICC Industries	-	207
ITT	218	-
J Crew	-	257
J.P. Morgan	73	-
KPMG Peat Marwick	-	9
Lehman Brothers	80	-
Loew's	46	-
M Fabrikant & Sons	-	283
MacAndrews & Forbes Holdings	-	20
Marsh & Mclennan	327	-
McCrory	-	488
McGraw-Hill	441	-
McKinsey & Co	-	76
Merrill Lynch	30	-
Metropolitan Life Insurance	35	-
Morgan Stanley Group	96	-
New York Life Insurance	63	-
New York Times	494	-
Nynex	91	-
Omnicom Group	492	-
Painewebber Group	252	-
Parsons Brinckerhoff	-	344
Perry H Koplik & Sons	-	421

continued next page

Major Business Headquarters (continued)

Company Name	1997 Rankings	
	Fortune 500	Forbes 500
Pfizer	118	-
Philip Morris	10	-
Price Waterhouse	-	25
RJR Nabisco Holdings	66	-
Red Apple Group	-	67
Reliance Group Holdings	439	-
Renco Group	-	51
Republic New York	410	-
Salomon	163	-
Skadden Arps Slate Meagher & Flom	-	297
TLC Beatrice Intl. Holdings	-	62
Teachers Insurance & Annuity	88	-
Time Warner	141	-
Tishman Realty & Construction	-	325
Towers Perrin	-	182
Transammonia	-	54
Travelers Group	40	-
Turner Corp.	405	-
Viacom	112	-
Warren Equities	-	225
Westvaco	442	-
Woolworth	184	-
Young & Rubicam	-	124

Note: Companies listed are located in the city; Dashes indicate no ranking
Fortune 500: companies that produce a 10-K are ranked 1 - 500 based on 1996 revenue
Forbes 500: private companies are ranked 1 - 500 based on 1996 revenue
Source: Forbes 12/1/97; Fortune 4/28/97

Fast-Growing Businesses

According to *Inc.*, New York is home to three of America's 100 fastest-growing private companies: Duke & Company, Transaction Information Systems and PC Ware. Criteria for inclusion: must be an independent, privately-held, U.S. corporation, proprietorship or partnership; sales of at least $200,000 in 1993; five-year operating/sales history; increase in 1997 sales over 1996 sales; holding companies, regulated banks, and utilities were excluded. *Inc. 500, 1997*

New York is home to three of *Business Week's* "hot growth" companies: Complete Management, Belco Oil & Gas and Ovid Technologies. Criteria: sales and earnings, return on capital and stock price. *Business Week, 5/26/97*

According to *Fortune*, New York is home to one of America's 100 fastest-growing companies: York Research. Companies were ranked based on three years' earnings-per-share growth using least squares analysis to smooth out distortions. Criteria for inclusion: public companies with sales of least $50 million. Companies that lost money in the most recent quarter, or ended in the red for the past four quarters as a whole, were not eligible. Limited partnerships and REITs were also not considered. *Fortune, 9/29/97*

New York was ranked #2 out of 24 (#1 is best) in terms of the best-performing local stocks in 1996 according to the Money/Norby Cities Index. The index measures stocks of companies that have headquarters in 24 metro areas. *Money, 2/7/97*

Women-Owned Businesses: Number, Employment, Sales and Share

Area	Women-Owned Businesses in 1996				Share of Women-Owned Businesses in 1996	
	Number	Employment	Sales ($000)	Rank[2]	Percent (%)	Rank[3]
MSA[1]	248,700	754,000	127,203,300	1	36.7	25

Note: (1) Metropolitan Statistical Area - see Appendix A for areas included; (2) Calculated on an averaging of number of businesses, employment and sales and ranges from 1 to 50 where 1 is best; (3) Ranges from 1 to 50 where 1 is best
Source: The National Foundation for Women Business Owners, 1996 Facts on Women-Owned Businesses: Trends in the Top 50 Metropolitan Areas, March 26, 1997

Women-Owned Businesses: Growth

Area	Growth in Women-Owned Businesses (% change from 1987 to 1996)				Relative Growth in the Number of Women-Owned and All Businesses (% change from 1987 to 1996)			
	Num.	Empl.	Sales	Rank[2]	Women-Owned	All Firms	Absolute Difference	Relative Difference
MSA[1]	67.8	158.5	199.9	43	67.8	47.5	20.3	1.4:1

Note: (1) Metropolitan Statistical Area - see Appendix A for areas included; (2) Calculated on an averaging of the percent growth of number of businesses, employment and sales and ranges from 1 to 50 where 1 is best
Source: The National Foundation for Women Business Owners, 1996 Facts on Women-Owned Businesses: Trends in the Top 50 Metropolitan Areas, March 26, 1997

Minority Business Opportunity

New York is home to companies which are on the Black Enterprise Industrial/Service 100 list (largest based on gross sales): TLC Beatrice International Holdings Inc. (international food processor/distributor); Uniworld Group Inc. (advertising, promotion, event marketing, direct response); Granite Broadcasting Corp. (network TV affiliates); Essence Communications Inc. (magazine publishing, catalog sales, entertainment); The Chisholm-Mingo Group Inc. (advertising, public relations and promotions); Rush Communications & Affiliated Companies (music publishing, TV, film, radio production, music and fashion); Restoration Supermarket Corp. (supermarket and drugstore retail sales); Earl G. Graves Ltd. (magazine publishing); Inner City Broadcasting Corp. (radio, TV, cable TV franchise); Consolidated Beverage Corp. (beverage wholesaler, exporter and importer); American Urban Radio Networks (radio broadcasting); Advanced Technological Solutions Inc. (computer and electronic services). Criteria: 1) operational in previous calendar year; 2) at least 51% black-owned; 3) manufactures/owns the product it sells or provides industrial or consumer services. Brokerages, real estate firms and firms that provide professional services are not eligible. *Black Enterprise, July 1997*

New York is home to one company which is on the Black Enterprise Auto Dealer 100 list (largest based on gross sales): Dick Gidron Ford Inc. (Ford). Criteria: 1) operational in previous calendar year; 2) at least 51% black-owned. *Black Enterprise, June 1997*

Eight of the 500 largest Hispanic-owned companies in the U.S. are located in New York. *Hispanic Business, June 1997*

New York is home to three companies which are on the Hispanic Business Fastest-Growing 100 list (greatest sales growth from 1992 to 1996): D.A.O.R. Security Inc. (security svcs.), Integral Construction Corp. (construction mgmt. & general contracting), and ExtraNet Telecommunications Inc. (telecom. svcs.) *Hispanic Business, July/August 1997*

New York was listed among the top 25 metropolitan areas in terms of the number of Hispanic-owned companies. The city was ranked number 3 with 69,936 companies. *Hispanic Business, May 1997*

Small Business Opportunity

According to *Forbes*, New York is home to one of America's 200 best small companies: Ovid Technologies. Criteria: companies must be publicly traded, U.S.-based corporations with latest 12-month sales of between $5 and $350 million. Earnings must be at least $1 million for the 12-month period. Limited partnerships, REITs and closed-end mutual funds were not considered. Banks, S&Ls and electric utilities were not included. *Forbes, November 3, 1997*

HOTELS & MOTELS

Hotels/Motels

Area	Hotels/ Motels	Rooms	Luxury-Level Hotels/Motels		Average Minimum Rates ($)		
			♦♦♦♦	♦♦♦♦♦	♦♦	♦♦♦	♦♦♦♦
City	151	50,664	17	3	147	216	294
Airport	15	3,395	0	0	n/a	n/a	n/a
Suburbs	19	3,214	0	0	n/a	n/a	n/a
Total	185	57,273	17	3	n/a	n/a	n/a

Note: n/a not available; Classifications range from one diamond (budget properties with basic amenities) to five diamond (luxury properties with the finest service, rooms and facilities).
Source: OAG, Business Travel Planner, Summer 1997

New York is home to two of the top 100 hotels in the world according to *Travel & Leisure*: Ritz-Carlton and Four Seasons. Criteria: value, rooms/ambience, location, facilities/activities and service. *Travel & Leisure, September 1997*

CONVENTION CENTERS

Major Convention Centers

Center Name	Meeting Rooms	Exhibit Space (sf)
Chase MetroTech Conference Center (Brooklyn)	14	n/a
International Design Center/New York	11	88,000
Chase Development Center	55	n/a
The Coleman Center	9	n/a
Downtown Executive Conference Center	10	n/a
Grand Hyatt New York	49	18,500
Hotel Macklowe and Macklowe Conference Center	33	17,000
Jacob K. Javits Convention Center	100	900,000
Marriott-Frenchmen's Reef Beach Resort	13	n/a
New York Design Center	n/a	n/a
New York Hilton and Towers at Rockefeller Center	47	81,500
New York Merchandise Mart	n/a	n/a
The Show Piers New York Passenger Ship Terminal	n/a	12,000
Smith Barney Conference Center	25	n/a
Viacom Conference & Training Center	8	3,200
World Trade Institute	11	8,682
Lombardi-Center-Fordham University	6	45,000
Madison Square Garden/Paramount Theater	4	36,000
Manhattan Center	1	10,000

Note: n/a not available
Source: Trade Shows Worldwide 1997

Living Environment

COST OF LIVING

Cost of Living Index

Composite Index	Housing	Utilities	Groceries	Health Care	Trans-portation	Misc. Goods/ Services
226.9	445.3	179.4	137.8	191.2	122.3	131.3

Note: U.S. = 100; Figures are for Manhattan
Source: ACCRA, Cost of Living Index, 3rd Quarter 1997

HOUSING

Median Home Prices and Housing Affordability

Area	Median Price[2] 3rd Qtr. 1997 ($)	HOI[3] 3rd Qtr. 1997	Afford-ability Rank[4]
MSA[1]	158,000	47.3	177
U.S.	127,000	63.7	-

Note: (1) Metropolitan Statistical Area - see Appendix A for areas included; (2) U.S. figures calculated from the sales of 625,000 new and existing homes in 195 markets; (3) Housing Opportunity Index - percent of homes sold that were within the reach of the median income household at the prevailing mortgage interest rate; (4) Rank is from 1-195 with 1 being most affordable
Source: National Association of Home Builders, Housing Opportunity Index, 3rd Quarter 1997

It is projected that the median price of existing single-family homes in the metro area will increase by 3.8% in 1998. Nationwide, home prices are projected to increase 6.6%.
Kiplinger's Personal Finance Magazine, January 1998

Average New Home Price

Area	Price ($)
City[1]	584,333
U.S.	135,710

Note: Figures are based on a new home with 1,800 sq. ft. of living area on an 8,000 sq. ft. lot; (1) Manhattan
Source: ACCRA, Cost of Living Index, 3rd Quarter 1997

Average Apartment Rent

Area	Rent ($/mth)
City[1]	2,920
U.S.	569

Note: Figures are based on an unfurnished two bedroom, 1-1/2 or 2 bath apartment, approximately 950 sq. ft. in size, excluding all utilities except water; (1) Manhattan
Source: ACCRA, Cost of Living Index, 3rd Quarter 1997

RESIDENTIAL UTILITIES

Average Residential Utility Costs

Area	All Electric ($/mth)	Part Electric ($/mth)	Other Energy ($/mth)	Phone ($/mth)
City[1]	-	97.51	95.16	24.06
U.S.	109.40	55.25	43.64	19.48

Note: (1) Manhattan
Source: ACCRA, Cost of Living Index, 3rd Quarter 1997

HEALTH CARE

Average Health Care Costs

Area	Hospital ($/day)	Doctor ($/visit)	Dentist ($/visit)
City[1]	1,359.00	87.00	92.00
U.S.	392.91	48.76	60.84

Note: Hospital - based on a semi-private room. Doctor - based on a general practitioner's routine exam of an established patient. Dentist - based on adult teeth cleaning and periodic oral exam; (1) (1) Manhattan
Source: ACCRA, Cost of Living Index, 3rd Quarter 1997

Distribution of Office-Based Physicians

Area	Family/Gen. Practitioners	Specialists		
		Medical	Surgical	Other
MSA[1]	895	9,050	4,634	5,705

Note: Data as of 12/31/96; (1) Metropolitan Statistical Area - see Appendix A for areas included
Source: American Medical Assn., Physician Characteristics & Distribution in the U.S., 1997-1998

Hospitals

New York has 60 general medical and surgical hospitals, 8 psychiatric, 2 eye, ear, nose and throat, 1 orthopedic, 2 chronic disease, 1 alcoholism and other chemical dependency, 4 other specialty, 2 children's psychiatric. *AHA Guide to the Healthcare Field 1997-98*

According to *U.S. News and World Report,* New York has 11 of the best hospitals in the U.S.: **New York University Medical Center**, noted for AIDS, gastroenterology, geriatrics, orthopedics, otolaryngology, psychiatry, rheumatology, urology; **New York Hospital-Cornell Medical Center**, noted for psychiatry; **Mount Sinai Medical Center**, noted for AIDS, cancer, cardiology, gastroenterology, geriatrics, gynecology, neurology, otolaryngology, rehabilitation, rheumatology, urology; **Columbia-Presbyterian Medical Center**, noted for AIDS, cardiology, endocrinology, geriatrics, gynecology, neurology, orthopedics, otolaryngology, pediatrics, psychiatry, pulmonology, rheumatology, urology; **Beth Israel Medical Center**, noted for rheumatology; **Memorial Sloan-Kettering Cancer Center**, noted for AIDS, cancer, gastroenterology, gynecology, otolaryngology, rheumatology, urology; **Hospital for Special Surgery**, noted for orthopedics, rheumatology; **Hospital for Joint Diseases-Orthopedic Institute**, noted for orthopedics, rheumatology; **Manhattan Eye, Ear and Throat Hospital**, noted for ophthalmology; **New York Eye & Ear Infirmary**, noted for ophthalmology; **New York University Medical Center (Rush Institute)**, noted for rehabilitation; *U.S. News and World Report, "America's Best Hospitals", 7/28/97*

Staten Island Hospital is among the 100 best-run hospitals in the U.S.
Modern Healthcare, January 5, 1998

EDUCATION

Public School District Statistics

District Name	Num. Sch.	Enroll.	Classroom Teachers[1]	Pupils per Teacher	Minority Pupils (%)	Current Exp.[2] ($/pupil)
New York City	1,108	1,049,039	54,591	19.2	83.5	7,504

Note: Data covers the 1995-1996 school year unless otherwise noted; (1) Excludes teachers reported as working in school district offices rather than in schools; (2) Based on 1993-94 enrollment collected by the Census Bureau, not the enrollment figure shown in column 3; SD = School District; ISD = Independent School District; n/a not available
Source: National Center for Education Statistics, Common Core of Data Survey; Bureau of the Census

Educational Quality

School District	Education Quotient[1]	Graduate Outcome[2]	Community Index[3]	Resource Index[4]
New York	n/a	n/a	n/a	n/a

Note: Nearly 1,000 secondary school districts were rated in terms of educational quality. The scores range from a low of 50 to a high of 150; (1) Average of the Graduate Outcome, Community and Resource indexes; (2) Based on graduation rates and college board scores (SAT/ACT); (3) Based on the surrounding community's average level of education and the area's average income level; (4) Based on teacher salaries, per-pupil expenditures and student-teacher ratios.
Source: Expansion Management, Ratings Issue 1997

Educational Attainment by Race

Area	High School Graduate (%)					Bachelor's Degree (%)				
	Total	White	Black	Other	Hisp.[2]	Total	White	Black	Other	Hisp.[2]
City	68.3	74.2	64.1	54.6	47.9	23.0	29.2	12.4	17.7	8.2
MSA[1]	70.3	76.1	64.4	55.7	48.6	24.6	30.6	12.7	18.9	8.6
U.S.	75.2	77.9	63.1	60.4	49.8	20.3	21.5	11.4	19.4	9.2

Note: figures shown cover persons 25 years old and over; (1) Metropolitan Statistical Area - see Appendix A for areas included; (2) people of Hispanic origin can be of any race
Source: 1990 Census of Population and Housing, Summary Tape File 3C

School Enrollment by Type

Area	Preprimary				Elementary/High School			
	Public		Private		Public		Private	
	Enrollment	%	Enrollment	%	Enrollment	%	Enrollment	%
City	54,891	55.5	43,933	44.5	934,140	79.1	246,344	20.9
MSA[1]	66,531	53.1	58,729	46.9	1,086,038	79.3	283,106	20.7
U.S.	2,679,029	59.5	1,824,256	40.5	38,379,689	90.2	4,187,099	9.8

Note: figures shown cover persons 3 years old and over;
(1) Metropolitan Statistical Area - see Appendix A for areas included
Source: 1990 Census of Population and Housing, Summary Tape File 3C

School Enrollment by Race

Area	Preprimary (%)				Elementary/High School (%)			
	White	Black	Other	Hisp.[1]	White	Black	Other	Hisp.[1]
City	47.4	35.6	17.1	21.2	38.6	36.8	24.6	32.6
MSA[2]	55.0	30.1	14.9	18.2	43.6	34.0	22.5	29.7
U.S.	80.4	12.5	7.1	7.8	74.1	15.6	10.3	12.5

Note: figures shown cover persons 3 years old and over; (1) people of Hispanic origin can be of any race; (2) Metropolitan Statistical Area - see Appendix A for areas included
Source: 1990 Census of Population and Housing, Summary Tape File 3C

SAT/ACT Scores

Area/District	1996 SAT				1996 ACT	
	Percent of Graduates Tested (%)	Average Math Score	Average Verbal Score	Average Combined Score	Percent of Graduates Tested (%)	Average Composite Score
New York City PS	n/a	465	448	913	n/a	n/a
State	73	499	497	996	16	21.7
U.S.	41	508	505	1,013	35	20.9

Note: Math and verbal SAT scores are out of a possible 800; ACT scores are out of a possible 36
Caution: Comparing or ranking states/cities on the basis of SAT/ACT scores alone is invalid and strongly discouraged by the The College Board and The American College Testing Program as students who take the tests are self-selected and do not represent the entire student population. 1996 SAT scores cannot be compared to previous years due to recentering.
Source: New York City Board of Education, Division of High Schools, 1996; College Board, 1996; American College Testing Program, 1996

Classroom Teacher Salaries in Public Schools

District	B.A. Degree		M.A. Degree		Ph.D. Degree	
	Min. ($)	Max ($)	Min. ($)	Max. ($)	Min. ($)	Max. ($)
New York	28,749	39,656	32,474	43,381	36,199	47,106
Average[1]	26,120	39,270	28,175	44,667	31,643	49,825

Note: Salaries are for 1996-1997; (1) Based on all school districts covered
Source: American Federation of Teachers (unpublished data)

Higher Education

Two-Year Colleges		Four-Year Colleges		Medical Schools	Law Schools	Voc/ Tech
Public	Private	Public	Private			
7	11	13	33	6	8	75

Source: College Blue Book, Occupational Education 1997; Medical School Admission Requirements, 1998-99; Peterson's Guide to Two-Year Colleges, 1997; Peterson's Guide to Four-Year Colleges, 1997; Barron's Guide to Law Schools 1997

MAJOR EMPLOYERS

Major Employers

American Express	Bear Stearns
Beth Israel Medical Center	Chase Manhattan Corp.
Citicorp Credit Services	Equitable Companies
Goldman Sachs	Helmsley Enterprises
JP Morgan & Co.	Merrill Lynch & Co.
Metro North Commuter RR Co.	Montefiore Medical Center
Morgan Stanley	New York Life Insurance
New York Telephone	Prudential Securities
Renco Holdings (steel)	Mount Sinai Hospital
Society of the New York Hospital	Time
Port Authority of NY/NJ	Teachers Insurance & Annunity Assoc.

Note: companies listed are located in the city
Source: Dun's Business Rankings 1997; Ward's Business Directory, 1997

PUBLIC SAFETY

Crime Rate

Area	All Crimes	Violent Crimes				Property Crimes		
		Murder	Forcible Rape	Robbery	Aggrav. Assault	Burglary	Larceny -Theft	Motor Vehicle Theft
City	5,212.2	13.4	31.8	676.7	622.3	834.8	2,210.6	822.7
Suburbs[1]	3,085.6	3.7	10.6	139.2	164.5	482.6	1,936.0	349.1
MSA[2]	4,896.6	12.0	28.6	597.0	554.4	782.5	2,169.8	752.4
U.S.	5,078.9	7.4	36.1	202.4	388.2	943.0	2,975.9	525.9

Note: Crime rate is the number of crimes per 100,000 pop.; (1) defined as all areas within the MSA but located outside the central city; (2) Metropolitan Statistical Area - see Appendix A for areas incl.
Source: FBI Uniform Crime Reports 1996

RECREATION

Culture and Recreation

Museums	Symphony Orchestras	Opera Companies	Dance Companies	Professional Theatres	Zoos	Pro Sports Teams
99	25	25	15	30	3	5

Source: International Directory of the Performing Arts, 1996; Official Museum Directory, 1998; Chamber of Commerce/Economic Development 1997

Library System

The Brooklyn Public Library has 59 branches, holdings of 5,947,870 volumes and a budget of $58,867,153 (1995-1996). The New York Public Library (research libraries) has 78 branches, holdings of 5,465,081 volumes and a budget of $n/a. Note: n/a means not available.
American Library Directory, 1997-1998

MEDIA

Newspapers

Name	Type	Freq.	Distribution	Circulation
Bay News	n/a	1x/wk	Local	176,000
Brooklyn Graphic	n/a	1x/wk	Local	111,000
Caribbean Life-Bronx Edition	n/a	1x/wk	Local	187,000
Catholic New York	Religious	1x/wk	Area	131,273
The Jewish Herald	Religious	2x/mo	Local	288,000
The Jewish Press	Religious	1x/wk	Local	100,000
Kings Courier	n/a	1x/wk	Local	118,000
The Marketeer Islander	General	1x/wk	Local	479,000
National Black Monitor	Black	1x/mo	United States	1,150,000
The New York Daily News	n/a	7x/wk	Area	800,000
New York Jewish Week	Religious	1x/wk	Local	110,000
New York Post	n/a	7x/wk	Area	418,255
New York Press	General	1x/wk	Local	103,000
The New York Times	General	7x/wk	International	1,149,700
Our Town	General	1x/wk	Local	119,000
Parade	General	1x/wk	United States	37,800,000
Park Slope Courier	n/a	1x/wk	Local	138,000
React	General	1x/wk	n/a	4,000,000
The Village Voice	General	1x/wk	Local	235,000
The Wall Street Journal	n/a	5x/wk	International	1,841,188

Note: Includes newspapers with circulations of 100,000 or more located in the city; n/a not available
Source: Burrelle's Media Directory, 1998 Edition

AM Radio Stations

Call Letters	Freq. (kHz)	Target Audience	Station Format	Music Format
WLGC	590	General	M	Contemporary Top 40
WSKQ	620	Hispanic	M	Oldies
WCCR	640	General	M/N/S	n/a
WFAN	660	General	S	n/a
WOR	710	General	T	n/a
WABC	770	General	N/T	n/a
WNYC	820	General	N/T	n/a
WCBS	880	General	N	n/a
WRKL	910	General	M/N/S	Adult Contemporary
WINS	1010	General	N	n/a
WEVD	1050	General	N/T	n/a
WBBR	1130	General	N	n/a
WLIB	1190	General	T	n/a
WFAS	1230	General	N/S/T	n/a
WADO	1280	Hispanic	M/N/T	Spanish
WLIR	1300	General	M	Adult Standards/Big Band/Oldies
WVIP	1310	General	M/N	Adult Standards/Big Band/Jazz
WKDM	1380	Hispanic	M/T	Spanish
WLNA	1420	General	N/S/T	n/a
WVOX	1460	General	M/N/S	n/a
WZRC	1480	Asian	M/N/T	n/a
WPUT	1510	General	M/N/S	Country
WQEW	1560	General	M	Adult Standards/Big Band/Oldies
WWRL	1600	n/a	M/T	Christian/R&B/Urban Contemporary

Note: Stations included broadcast in the New York metro area; n/a not available
Station Format: E = Educational; M = Music; N = News; S = Sports; T = Talk
Source: Burrelle's Media Directory, 1998 Edition

FM Radio Stations

Call Letters	Freq. (mHz)	Target Audience	Station Format	Music Format
WARY	88.1	n/a	M	AOR
WNYK	88.7	Religious	M	Adult Contemporary/Alternative/Christian/Classic Rock/Jazz/R&B/Spanish/Urban Contemporary
WSIA	88.9	General	M/N/S	Alternative/Jazz
WNYU	89.1	General	E/M/N/S	n/a
WKCR	89.9	General	E/M/N/S/T	Classical/Jazz/Spanish
WHCR	90.3	General	M/N/S/T	Urban Contemporary
WFUV	90.7	General	M/N/S/T	AOR/Adult Contemporary/Alternative
WKRB	90.9	General	M	Contemporary Top 40
WOSS	91.1	General	M/N/S	n/a
WNYE	91.5	General	E/M/S	n/a
WXRK	92.3	General	M	Alternative
WPAT	93.1	Hispanic	M/N	Adult Contemporary/Contemporary Top 40/Spanish
WRTN	93.5	General	M	Big Band/Jazz
WNYC	93.9	General	M/N/S	Classical
WPLJ	95.5	General	M	Adult Contemporary
WQXR	96.3	General	M/N/S	Classical
WQHT	97.1	General	M	Contemporary Top 40
WSKQ	97.9	Hispanic	M	Spanish
WRKS	98.7	General	M	Urban Contemporary
WBAI	99.5	n/a	E/M/N/T	Alternative/Jazz
WHUD	100.7	n/a	M/N/S	Adult Contemporary
WCBS	101.1	General	M/N/S	Oldies
WQCD	101.9	General	M	Jazz
WNEW	102.7	General	M	Classic Rock
WFAS	103.9	General	M	Adult Contemporary
WAXQ	104.3	General	M	Classic Rock
WDBZ	105.1	General	M/N	Adult Contemporary
WNWK	105.9	General	M	n/a
WZZN	106.3	General	M	Adult Contemporary
WLTW	106.7	General	M/N/S	Adult Contemporary
WWXY	107.1	General	M	Country
WBLS	107.5	General	M	Urban Contemporary

Note: Stations included broadcast in the New York metro area; n/a not available
Station Format: E = Educational; M = Music; N = News; S = Sports; T = Talk
Music Format: AOR = Album Oriented Rock; MOR = Middle-of-the-Road
Source: Burrelle's Media Directory, 1998 Edition

Television Stations

Name	Ch.	Affiliation	Type	Owner
WCBS	2	CBS	Commercial	Westinghouse Broadcasting Company
WNBC	4	NBC	Commercial	General Electric Company
WNYW	5	Fox	Commercial	Fox Television Stations Inc.
WABC	7	ABC	Commercial	ABC Inc.
WPIX	11	n/a	Commercial	Tribune Broadcasting Co.
WNET	13	PBS	Public	Educational Broadcasting Corporation
WNYE	25	PBS	Public	New York City Board of Education
WPXN	31	n/a	Commercial	Paxson Communications Corporation
WHAI	43	n/a	Commercial	Paxon Communications

Note: Stations included broadcast in the New York metro area
Source: Burrelle's Media Directory, 1998 Edition

CLIMATE

Average and Extreme Temperatures

Temperature	Jan	Feb	Mar	Apr	May	Jun	Jul	Aug	Sep	Oct	Nov	Dec	Ann
Extreme High (°F)	68	75	85	96	97	101	104	99	99	88	81	72	104
Average High (°F)	38	41	50	61	72	80	85	84	76	65	54	43	62
Average Temp. (°F)	32	34	43	53	63	72	77	76	68	58	48	37	55
Average Low (°F)	26	27	35	44	54	63	68	67	60	49	41	31	47
Extreme Low (°F)	-2	-2	8	21	36	46	53	50	40	29	17	-1	-2

Note: Figures cover the years 1962-1992
Source: National Climatic Data Center, International Station Meteorological Climate Summary, 3/95

Average Precipitation/Snowfall/Humidity

Precip./Humidity	Jan	Feb	Mar	Apr	May	Jun	Jul	Aug	Sep	Oct	Nov	Dec	Ann
Avg. Precip. (in.)	3.5	3.1	4.0	3.9	4.5	3.8	4.5	4.1	4.1	3.3	4.5	3.8	47.0
Avg. Snowfall (in.)	7	8	4	Tr	Tr	0	0	0	0	Tr	Tr	3	23
Avg. Rel. Hum. 7am (%)	67	67	66	64	72	74	74	76	78	75	72	69	71
Avg. Rel. Hum. 4pm (%)	55	53	50	45	52	55	53	54	56	55	57	58	53

Note: Figures cover the years 1962-1992; Tr = Trace amounts (<0.05 in. of rain; <0.5 in. of snow)
Source: National Climatic Data Center, International Station Meteorological Climate Summary, 3/95

Weather Conditions

Temperature			Daytime Sky			Precipitation		
32°F & below	45°F & below	90°F & above	Clear	Partly cloudy	Cloudy	0.01 inch or more precip.	0.1 inch or more snow/ice	Thunder-storms
75	170	18	85	166	114	120	11	20

Note: Figures are average number of days per year and covers the years 1962-1992
Source: National Climatic Data Center, International Station Meteorological Climate Summary, 3/95

AIR & WATER QUALITY

Maximum Pollutant Concentrations

	Particulate Matter (ug/m³)	Carbon Monoxide (ppm)	Sulfur Dioxide (ppm)	Nitrogen Dioxide (ppm)	Ozone (ppm)	Lead (ug/m³)
MSA[1] Level	87	6	0.055	0.042	0.12	0.16
NAAQS[2]	150	9	0.140	0.053	0.12	1.50
Met NAAQS?	Yes	Yes	Yes	Yes	Yes	Yes

Note: (1) Metropolitan Statistical Area - see Appendix A for areas included; (2) National Ambient Air Quality Standards; ppm = parts per million; ug/m³ = micrograms per cubic meter; n/a not available
Source: EPA, National Air Quality and Emissions Trends Report, 1996

Pollutant Standards Index

In the New York MSA (see Appendix A for areas included), the Pollutant Standards Index (PSI) exceeded 100 on 7 days in 1996. A PSI value greater than 100 indicates that air quality would be in the unhealthful range on that day. *EPA, National Air Quality and Emissions Trends Report, 1996*

Drinking Water

Water System Name	Pop. Served	Primary Water Source Type	Number of Violations in Fiscal Year 1997	Type of Violation/ Contaminants
Jamaica Water Supply Co. (Bronx)	518,000	Ground	None	None
New York City-Aqueduct System	6,552,718	Surface	1	Failure to filter

Note: Data as of January 16, 1998
Source: EPA, Office of Ground Water and Drinking Water, Safe Drinking Water Information System

New York City tap water has three major sources: the Catskills & Delaware subsystems (neutral, soft, average pH 7.0) and Croton subsystem (alkaline, moderately hard, average pH 7.1). All three supplies are fluoridated and chlorinated.
Editor & Publisher Market Guide, 1998

Norfolk, Virginia

Background

Because Norfolk, Virginia possesses one of the finest harbors in the world, it is only natural that the city should center its economy and culture around the Navy and maritime trade.

Located 205 miles southeast of Washington, D.C., Norfolk is home to the largest naval installation in the world. Outside of San Diego, Norfolk has more naval officers, retired or otherwise, than any other city. Its 45-foot deep channel can accommodate the largest of ships, from nuclear supercarriers, to merchant ships carrying cargo of tobacco, coal, or petroleum.

The city was founded in 1682, when English settlers bought the land for 10,000 pounds of tobacco. The 18th century saw Norfolk enjoy a prosperous trade with the West Indies. However, British troops bombarded the city on January 1, 1771. To prevent further razing by the British, the Virginia Militia destroyed what was left of the city themselves.

Norfolk was once again the scene of fighting during the Civil War. The most famous battle during this period occurred in Hampton Roads, the natural channel through which the James River and its tributaries flow into the Chesapeake Bay, between the CSS Virginia, or Merrimac, and the USS Monitor.

In addition to the Navy providing for most of the payroll of Norfolk, the city has a diversified economy in food and beverage processing and the production of candy, peanuts, insecticides, flags, paint, furniture, and women's clothing.

The geographic location of the city allows for generally mild winters, beautiful spring and autumn days and nights, and summers which are warm and long but tempered by cool periods.

General Rankings and Evaluative Comments

- Norfolk was ranked #115 out of 300 cities by *Money's* 1997 "Survey of the Best Places to Live." Criteria used: health services, crime, economy, housing, education, transportation, weather, leisure and the arts. The city was ranked #117 in 1996 and #283 in 1995. *Money, July 1997; Money, September 1996; Money, September 1995*

- *Ladies Home Journal* ranked America's 200 largest cities based on the qualities women care about most. Norfolk ranked 68 out of 200. Criteria: low crime rate, good public schools, well-paying jobs, quality health and child care, the presence of women in government, proportion of women-owned businesses, size of the wage gap with men, local economy, divorce rates, the ratio of single men to single women, whether there are laws that require at least the same number of public toilets for women as men, and the probability of good hair days. *Ladies Home Journal, November 1997*

- Norfolk was ranked #149 out of 219 cities in terms of children's health, safety, and economic well-being. Criteria: total population, percent population change, birth rate, child immunization rate, infant mortality rate, percent low birth weight infants, percent of births to teens, physician-to-population ratio, student-to-teacher ratio, dropout rate, unemployment rate, median family income, percent of children in poverty, violent and property crime rates, number of juvenile arrests for violent crimes as a percent of the total crime index, number of days with pollution standard index (PSI) over 100, pounds toxic releases per 1,000 people and number of superfund sites. *Zero Population Growth, Children's Environmental Index 1997*

- According to *Working Mother,* "Child care advocates and Governor George Allen remained at odds all year, fighting over standards for child care. At one point, members of a child care council that Allen had appointed proposed lowering standards for caregiver training and reducing some adult-to child ratios for preschool children. Fortunately, the proposals were beaten back in the state legislature.

  On the positive side, the state did finally put up matching funds to secure its full share of federal child care funds (although there is concern among advocates over how these funds will be distributed). Virginia also set aside some modest funds for caregiver training." *Working Mother, July/August 1997*

Business Environment

STATE ECONOMY

State Economic Profile

"Although Virginia's exposure to manufacturing is somewhat less than the national average, the state still has a high exposure to secularly shrinking industries such as shipbuilding, apparel and textile. While these three industries constitute less than 25% of Virginia's manufacturing base, they more than account for the loss of manufacturing 4,400 jobs last year.

Since the 1990s began, house price appreciation in Virginia has been running well under the national rate. For example, house prices statewide rose only 3.0% last year, versus a 4.6% gain nationally. Over the last three years, new housing permits issued have averaged 45,000 per year, far above household formation rates, which have been running at 30,000 yearly. While Virginia's household formation rate will pick up as its economy firms, new housing activity must moderate from current levels to avoid an oversupplied market.

The impact of manufacturing and defense-related layoffs is increasingly being offset by strong private-sector employment growth. Low business costs and agglomeration economies will continue to attract not only lower-wage, back-office operations, but, increasingly, high-tech manufacturing and research facilities that pay higher-than-average wages. Strong population growth and in-migration will insure steady demand for retail goods and housing. Virginia is ranked well above average for long-term growth." *National Association of Realtors, Economic Profiles: The Fifty States, July 1997*

IMPORTS/EXPORTS

Total Export Sales

Area	1993 ($000)	1994 ($000)	1995 ($000)	1996 ($000)	% Chg. 1993-96	% Chg. 1995-96
MSA[1]	677,160	807,674	1,005,516	1,256,850	85.6	25.0
U.S.	464,858,354	512,415,609	583,030,524	622,827,063	34.0	6.8

Note: (1) Metropolitan Statistical Area - see Appendix A for areas included
Source: U.S. Department of Commerce, International Trade Association, Metropolitan Area Exports: An Export Performance Report on Over 250 U.S. Cities, October 1997

Imports/Exports by Port

Type	Cargo Value			Share of U.S. Total	
	1995 (US$mil.)	1996 (US$mil.)	% Change 1995-1996	1995 (%)	1996 (%)
Imports	10,415	11,042	6.02	2.66	2.88
Exports	13,245	13,707	3.49	5.79	5.79

Source: Global Trade Information Services, WaterBorne Trade Atlas 1997

CITY FINANCES

City Government Finances

Component	FY92 ($000)	FY92 (per capita $)
Revenue	633,413	2,497.27
Expenditure	645,970	2,546.78
Debt Outstanding	1,022,535	4,031.41
Cash & Securities	1,151,712	4,540.70

Source: U.S. Bureau of the Census, City Government Finances: 1991-92

City Government Revenue by Source

Source	FY92 ($000)	FY92 (per capita $)	FY92 (%)
From Federal Government	47,795	188.43	7.5
From State Governments	151,719	598.16	24.0
From Local Governments	11,379	44.86	1.8
Property Taxes	126,735	499.66	20.0
General Sales Taxes	19,068	75.18	3.0
Selective Sales Taxes	49,800	196.34	7.9
Income Taxes	0	0.00	0.0
Current Charges	93,327	367.95	14.7
Utility/Liquor Store	33,117	130.57	5.2
Employee Retirement[1]	34,162	134.69	5.4
Other	66,311	261.44	10.5

Note: (1) Excludes "city contributions," classified as "nonrevenue," intragovernmental transfers.
Source: U.S. Bureau of the Census, City Government Finances: 1991-92

City Government Expenditures by Function

Function	FY92 ($000)	FY92 (per capita $)	FY92 (%)
Educational Services	201,132	792.98	31.1
Employee Retirement[1]	15,304	60.34	2.4
Environment/Housing	111,589	439.95	17.3
Government Administration	35,498	139.95	5.5
Interest on General Debt	51,880	204.54	8.0
Public Safety	69,126	272.53	10.7
Social Services	61,425	242.17	9.5
Transportation	47,852	188.66	7.4
Utility/Liquor Store	44,376	174.96	6.9
Other	7,788	30.70	1.2

Note: (1) Payments to beneficiaries including withdrawal of contributions.
Source: U.S. Bureau of the Census, City Government Finances: 1991-92

Municipal Bond Ratings

Area	Moody's	S & P
Norfolk	A1	A1

Note: n/a not available; n/r not rated
Source: Moody's Bond Record, 2/98; Statistical Abstract of the U.S., 1997; Governing Magazine, 9/97, 3/98

POPULATION

Population Growth

Area	1980	1990	% Chg. 1980-90	July 1996 Estimate	% Chg. 1990-96
City	266,979	261,229	-2.2	233,430	-10.6
MSA[1]	1,160,311	1,396,107	20.3	1,540,252	10.3
U.S.	226,545,805	248,765,170	9.8	265,179,411	6.6

Note: (1) Metropolitan Statistical Area - see Appendix A for areas included
Source: 1980/1990 Census of Housing and Population, Summary Tape File 3C; Census Bureau Population Estimates

Population Characteristics

Race	City 1980 Population	%	City 1990 Population	%	% Chg. 1980-90	MSA[1] 1990 Population	%
White	163,052	61.1	148,132	56.7	-9.2	947,500	67.9
Black	93,977	35.2	102,135	39.1	8.7	398,011	28.5
Amer Indian/Esk/Aleut	822	0.3	1,397	0.5	70.0	5,315	0.4
Asian/Pacific Islander	7,075	2.7	6,680	2.6	-5.6	34,897	2.5
Other	2,053	0.8	2,885	1.1	40.5	10,384	0.7
Hispanic Origin[2]	5,792	2.2	7,240	2.8	25.0	31,310	2.2

Note: (1) Metropolitan Statistical Area - see Appendix A for areas included; (2) people of Hispanic origin can be of any race
Source: 1980/1990 Census of Housing and Population, Summary Tape File 3C

Ancestry

Area	German	Irish	English	Italian	U.S.	French	Polish	Dutch
City	14.6	11.9	11.0	3.5	5.9	2.9	1.8	1.6
MSA[1]	17.4	13.4	15.5	3.9	7.7	3.3	2.1	1.7
U.S.	23.3	15.6	13.1	5.9	5.3	4.2	3.8	2.5

Note: Figures are percentages and include persons that reported multiple ancestry (eg. if a person reported being Irish and Italian, they were included in both columns); (1) Metropolitan Statistical Area - see Appendix A for areas included
Source: 1990 Census of Population and Housing, Summary Tape File 3C

Age

Area	Median Age (Years)	Age Distribution (%) Under 5	Under 18	18-24	25-44	45-64	65+	80+
City	27.2	8.3	23.0	21.6	31.8	13.1	10.5	2.1
MSA[1]	29.7	8.3	26.4	13.6	34.8	16.2	9.0	1.6
U.S.	32.9	7.3	25.6	10.5	32.6	18.7	12.5	2.8

Note: (1) Metropolitan Statistical Area - see Appendix A for areas included
Source: 1990 Census of Population and Housing, Summary Tape File 3C

Male/Female Ratio

Area	Number of males per 100 females (all ages)	Number of males per 100 females (18 years old+)
City	114.0	117.8
MSA[1]	100.4	99.4
U.S.	95.0	91.9

Note: (1) Metropolitan Statistical Area - see Appendix A for areas included
Source: 1990 Census of Population, General Population Characteristics

INCOME

Per Capita/Median/Average Income

Area	Per Capita ($)	Median Household ($)	Average Household ($)
City	11,643	23,563	29,947
MSA[1]	13,495	30,841	36,794
U.S.	14,420	30,056	38,453

Note: all figures are for 1989; (1) Metropolitan Statistical Area - see Appendix A for areas included
Source: 1990 Census of Population and Housing, Summary Tape File 3C

Household Income Distribution by Race

Income ($)	City (%)					U.S. (%)				
	Total	White	Black	Other	Hisp.[1]	Total	White	Black	Other	Hisp.[1]
Less than 5,000	9.3	4.3	17.8	7.5	4.7	6.2	4.8	15.2	8.6	8.8
5,000 - 9,999	9.7	7.1	14.4	6.4	5.8	9.3	8.6	14.2	9.9	11.1
10,000 - 14,999	10.7	9.2	12.9	13.8	16.7	8.8	8.5	11.0	9.8	11.0
15,000 - 24,999	23.2	23.0	23.4	24.3	27.0	17.5	17.3	18.9	18.5	20.5
25,000 - 34,999	17.5	19.1	14.8	18.4	20.3	15.8	16.1	14.2	15.4	16.4
35,000 - 49,999	15.4	18.5	10.0	17.7	12.9	17.9	18.6	13.3	16.1	16.0
50,000 - 74,999	9.3	11.9	5.2	8.7	8.5	15.0	15.8	9.3	13.4	11.1
75,000 - 99,999	2.7	3.7	0.9	2.1	1.9	5.1	5.5	2.6	4.7	3.1
100,000+	2.2	3.3	0.6	1.0	2.2	4.4	4.8	1.3	3.7	1.9

Note: all figures are for 1989; (1) people of Hispanic origin can be of any race
Source: 1990 Census of Population and Housing, Summary Tape File 3C

Effective Buying Income

Area	Per Capita ($)	Median Household ($)	Average Household ($)
City	12,710	25,356	36,375
MSA[1]	14,280	32,844	39,678
U.S.	15,444	33,201	41,849

Note: data as of 1/1/97; (1) Metropolitan Statistical Area - see Appendix A for areas included
Source: Standard Rate & Data Service, Newspaper Advertising Source, 2/98

Effective Household Buying Income Distribution

Area	% of Households Earning						
	$10,000 -$19,999	$20,000 -$34,999	$35,000 -$49,999	$50,000 -$74,999	$75,000 -$99,000	$100,000 -$124,999	$125,000 and up
City	21.2	28.4	16.8	11.5	3.2	1.0	1.2
MSA[1]	15.7	26.9	20.7	18.2	4.9	1.3	1.3
U.S.	16.5	23.4	18.3	18.2	6.4	2.1	2.4

Note: data as of 1/1/97; (1) Metropolitan Statistical Area - see Appendix A for areas included
Source: Standard Rate & Data Service, Newspaper Advertising Source, 2/98

Poverty Rates by Race and Age

Area	Total (%)	By Race (%)				By Age (%)		
		White	Black	Other	Hisp.[2]	Under 5 years old	Under 18 years old	65 years and over
City	19.3	10.1	32.7	15.1	15.0	29.2	28.6	15.3
MSA[1]	11.5	5.9	25.1	9.5	10.5	17.8	16.4	12.5
U.S.	13.1	9.8	29.5	23.1	25.3	20.1	18.3	12.8

Note: figures show the percent of people living below the poverty line in 1989. The average poverty threshold was $12,674 for a family of four in 1989; (1) Metropolitan Statistical Area - see Appendix A for areas included; (2) people of Hispanic origin can be of any race
Source: 1990 Census of Population and Housing, Summary Tape File 3C

EMPLOYMENT

Labor Force and Employment

Area	Civilian Labor Force			Workers Employed		
	Dec. '95	Dec. '96	% Chg.	Dec. '95	Dec. '96	% Chg.
City	86,563	88,536	2.3	81,147	84,285	3.9
MSA[1]	709,006	728,929	2.8	676,602	702,316	3.8
U.S.	134,583,000	136,742,000	1.6	127,903,000	130,785,000	2.3

Note: Data is not seasonally adjusted and covers workers 16 years of age and older; (1) Metropolitan Statistical Area - see Appendix A for areas included
Source: Bureau of Labor Statistics, http://stats.bls.gov

Unemployment Rate

Area	1997											
	Jan.	Feb.	Mar.	Apr.	May	Jun.	Jul.	Aug.	Sep.	Oct.	Nov.	Dec.
City	6.5	6.6	6.7	6.9	7.5	8.6	7.5	7.4	7.3	6.0	5.5	4.8
MSA[1]	5.0	4.9	4.6	4.7	5.3	6.1	5.4	5.3	5.2	4.3	4.1	3.7
U.S.	5.9	5.7	5.5	4.8	4.7	5.2	5.0	4.8	4.7	4.4	4.3	4.4

Note: Data is not seasonally adjusted and covers workers 16 years of age and older; All figures are percentages; (1) Metropolitan Statistical Area - see Appendix A for areas included
Source: Bureau of Labor Statistics, http://stats.bls.gov

Employment by Industry

Sector	MSA[1]		U.S.
	Number of Employees	Percent of Total	Percent of Total
Services	193,500	28.7	29.0
Retail Trade	136,600	20.3	18.5
Government	145,600	21.6	16.1
Manufacturing	69,000	10.2	15.0
Finance/Insurance/Real Estate	31,500	4.7	5.7
Wholesale Trade	24,300	3.6	5.4
Transportation/Public Utilities	32,400	4.8	5.3
Construction/Mining	40,300	6.0	5.0

Note: Figures cover non-farm employment as of 12/97 and are not seasonally adjusted; (1) Metropolitan Statistical Area - see Appendix A for areas included
Source: Bureau of Labor Statistics, http://stats.bls.gov

Employment by Occupation

Occupation Category	City (%)	MSA[1] (%)	U.S. (%)
White Collar	54.8	59.3	58.1
Executive/Admin./Management	10.1	12.4	12.3
Professional	13.1	14.7	14.1
Technical & Related Support	3.9	4.3	3.7
Sales	11.5	12.3	11.8
Administrative Support/Clerical	16.2	15.6	16.3
Blue Collar	26.5	25.3	26.2
Precision Production/Craft/Repair	12.4	13.5	11.3
Machine Operators/Assem./Insp.	4.4	4.2	6.8
Transportation/Material Movers	5.2	3.9	4.1
Cleaners/Helpers/Laborers	4.4	3.7	3.9
Services	17.5	14.2	13.2
Farming/Forestry/Fishing	1.2	1.2	2.5

Note: figures cover employed persons 16 years old and over; (1) Metropolitan Statistical Area - see Appendix A for areas included
Source: 1990 Census of Population and Housing, Summary Tape File 3C

Occupational Employment Projections: 1990 - 2005

Occupations Expected to have the Largest Job Growth (ranked by numerical growth)	Fast-Growing Occupations[1] (ranked by percent growth)
1. Salespersons, retail	1. Computer engineers
2. Cashiers	2. Physical therapists
3. General managers & top executives	3. Travel agents
4. Registered nurses	4. Medical assistants
5. Secretaries, except legal & medical	5. Computer programmers
6. Food preparation workers	6. Human services workers
7. General office clerks	7. Paralegals
8. Waiters & waitresses	8. Corrections officers & jailers
9. Janitors/cleaners/maids, ex. priv. hshld.	9. Travel agents
10. Nursing aides/orderlies/attendants	10. Radiologic technicians

Projections cover the Norfolk-Virginia Beach-Newport News MSA (Virginia portion only) - see Appendix A for areas included.
Note: (1) Includes occupations with total job growth of at least 100
Source: Virginia Employment Commission, Industry and Occupational Employment Projections: 1990-2005

Average Wages

Occupation	Wage	Occupation	Wage
Professional/Technical/Clerical	$/Week	**Health/Protective Services**	$/Week
Accountants III	-	Corrections Officers	-
Attorneys III	-	Firefighters	-
Budget Analysts III	-	Nurses, Licensed Practical II	-
Buyers/Contracting Specialists II	-	Nurses, Registered II	-
Clerks, Accounting III	424	Nursing Assistants II	-
Clerks, General III	420	Police Officers I	-
Computer Operators II	425	**Hourly Workers**	$/Hour
Computer Programmers II	605	Forklift Operators	8.27
Drafters II	474	General Maintenance Workers	8.71
Engineering Technicians III	-	Guards I	5.58
Engineering Technicians, Civil III	-	Janitors	5.81
Engineers III	-	Maintenance Electricians	17.60
Key Entry Operators I	-	Maintenance Electronics Techs II	13.03
Personnel Assistants III	-	Maintenance Machinists	-
Personnel Specialists III	-	Maintenance Mechanics, Machinery	16.18
Secretaries III	492	Material Handling Laborers	7.49
Switchboard Operator-Receptionist	294	Motor Vehicle Mechanics	13.53
Systems Analysts II	812	Shipping/Receiving Clerks	7.94
Systems Analysts Supervisor/Mgr II	-	Tool and Die Makers	-
Tax Collectors II	-	Truckdrivers, Tractor Trailer	10.04
Word Processors II	-	Warehouse Specialists	-

Note: Wage data includes full-time workers only for 4/96 and cover the Metropolitan Statistical Area (see Appendix A for areas included). Dashes indicate that data was not available.
Source: Bureau of Labor Statistics, Occupational Compensation Survey, 9/96

TAXES

Major State and Local Tax Rates

State Corp. Income (%)	State Personal Income (%)	Residential Property (effective rate per $100)	Sales & Use		State Gasoline (cents/ gallon)	State Cigarette (cents/ 20-pack)
			State (%)	Local (%)		
6.0	2.0 - 5.75	n/a	3.5	1.0	17.5[a]	2.5[b]

Note: Personal/corporate income tax rates as of 1/97. Sales, gasoline and cigarette tax rates as of 1/98; (a) Does not include a 2% local option tax; (b) Counties and cities may impose an additional tax of 2 - 15 cents per pack
Source: Federation of Tax Administrators, www.taxadmin.org; Washington D.C. Department of Finance and Revenue, Tax Rates and Tax Burdens in the District of Columbia: A Nationwide Comparison, June 1997; Chamber of Commerce

Total Taxes Per Capita and as a Percent of Income

Area	Per Capita Income ($)	Per Capita Taxes ($)			Taxes as Pct. of Income (%)		
		Total	Federal	State/ Local	Total	Federal	State/ Local
Virginia	26,908	9,421	6,365	3,056	35.0	23.7	11.4
U.S.	26,187	9,205	6,127	3,078	35.2	23.4	11.8

Note: Figures are for 1997
Source: Tax Foundation, Web Site, www.taxfoundation.org

COMMERCIAL REAL ESTATE

Office Market

Class/ Location	Total Space (sq. ft.)	Vacant Space (sq. ft.)	Vac. Rate (%)	Under Constr. (sq. ft.)	Net Absorp. (sq. ft.)	Rental Rates ($/sq.ft./yr.)
Class A						
CBD	1,679,724	149,718	8.9	0	63,151	13.00-17.00
Outside CBD	3,571,180	208,957	5.9	0	202,275	14.50-19.00
Class B						
CBD	1,233,635	259,135	21.0	0	19,386	9.00-14.50
Outside CBD	8,912,538	797,993	9.0	0	339,146	11.00-15.00

Note: Data as of 10/97 and covers Norfolk, Virginia Beach, Newport News and the Hampton Roads area; CBD = Central Business District; n/a not available;
Source: Society of Industrial and Office Realtors, 1998 Comparative Statistics of Industrial and Office Real Estate Markets

"The Norfolk economy continues to transform itself successfully from a military and shipbuilding center to a more diversified high-technology manufacturing area. Economic growth is robust, at three percent per year, outpacing the nation and the South. In June 1997, the first speculative office building in seven years was completed. By late September this building was 60 percent leased. Development centers on the Oyster Point areas of Newport News and in the Hampton Roads Center of Hampton. Plans for another bridge-tunnel linking the south side with the Virginia Peninsula were approved during 1997 to make the port of Hampton Roads more accessible. Absorption is expected to pick up six to 10 percent during 1998, setting the stage for an increase in new construction." *Society of Industrial and Office Realtors, 1998 Comparative Statistics of Industrial and Office Real Estate Markets*

Industrial Market

Location	Total Space (sq. ft.)	Vacant Space (sq. ft.)	Vac. Rate (%)	Under Constr. (sq. ft.)	Net Absorp. (sq. ft.)	Net Lease ($/sq.ft./yr.)
Central City	3,444,368	236,187	6.9	n/a	n/a	2.75-4.00
Suburban	64,721,556	5,880,300	9.1	650,000	n/a	3.00-5.50

Note: Data as of 10/97 and covers Hampton Roads (Newport News, Norfolk and Virginia Beach); n/a not available
Source: Society of Industrial and Office Realtors, 1998 Comparative Statistics of Industrial and Office Real Estate Markets

"Layoffs in the region's primary shipbuilding industry should be temporary as the region weans itself from military spending. Cargo shipping is booming. At the same time Norfolk is transforming itself into a high technology manufacturing center. Some speculative building is already present even though sales prices have not matched new construction costs. Speculative activity is present in smaller, multi-tenant facilities with a high percentage of finished office space. Some speculative high-bay and shell buildings will also come on-line in 1998. Shortages of warehouse/distribution product in the 5,000 to 20,000 sq. ft. size range and for structures more than 250,000 sq. ft. could push up sales prices. High Tech/R&D space is also in short supply. Marketing of some obsolete urban real estate facilities for reuse as industrial parks will be an attempt to capture some of the larger region's robust economic growth in its urban centers." *Society of Industrial and Office Realtors, 1998 Comparative Statistics of Industrial and Office Real Estate Markets*

COMMERCIAL UTILITIES

Typical Monthly Electric Bills

Area	Commercial Service ($/month) 12 kW demand 1,500 kWh	Commercial Service ($/month) 100 kW demand 30,000 kWh	Industrial Service ($/month) 1,000 kW demand 400,000 kWh	Industrial Service ($/month) 20,000 kW demand 10,000,000 kWh
City	133	2,204	21,806	428,249
U.S.	162	2,360	25,590	545,677

Note: Based on rates in effect July 1, 1997
Source: Edison Electric Institute, Typical Residential, Commercial and Industrial Bills, Summer 1997

TRANSPORTATION

Transportation Statistics

Avg. travel time to work (min.)	20.6
Interstate highways	I-64
Bus lines	
In-city	Tidewater Regional Transit
Inter-city	1
Passenger air service	
Airport	Norfolk International Airport
Airlines	12
Aircraft departures	19,986 (1995)
Enplaned passengers	1,179,815 (1995)
Rail service	No Amtrak Service
Motor freight carriers	135
Major waterways/ports	Chesapeake Bay; Hampton Roads

Source: OAG, Business Travel Planner, Summer 1997; Editor & Publisher Market Guide, 1998; FAA Airport Activity Statistics, 1996; Amtrak National Time Table, Northeast Timetable, Fall/Winter 1997-98; 1990 Census of Population and Housing, STF 3C; Chamber of Commerce/Economic Development 1997; Jane's Urban Transport Systems 1997-98; Transit Fact Book 1997

Means of Transportation to Work

Area	Car/Truck/Van		Public Transportation			Bicycle	Walked	Other Means	Worked at Home
	Drove Alone	Car-pooled	Bus	Subway	Railroad				
City	56.0	13.9	4.4	0.0	0.0	0.8	4.8	1.9	18.2
MSA[1]	72.7	14.1	2.0	0.0	0.0	0.5	3.7	1.6	5.3
U.S.	73.2	13.4	3.0	1.5	0.5	0.4	3.9	1.2	3.0

Note: figures shown are percentages and only include workers 16 years old and over;
(1) Metropolitan Statistical Area - see Appendix A for areas included
Source: 1990 Census of Population and Housing, Summary Tape File 3C

BUSINESSES

Major Business Headquarters

Company Name	1997 Rankings Fortune 500	1997 Rankings Forbes 500
Farm Fresh	-	274
Landmark Communications	-	412
Norfolk Southern	298	-

Note: Companies listed are located in the city; Dashes indicate no ranking
Fortune 500: companies that produce a 10-K are ranked 1 - 500 based on 1996 revenue
Forbes 500: private companies are ranked 1 - 500 based on 1996 revenue
Source: Forbes 12/1/97; Fortune 4/28/97

Women-Owned Businesses: Number, Employment, Sales and Share

Area	Women-Owned Businesses in 1996				Share of Women-Owned Businesses in 1996	
	Number	Employment	Sales ($000)	Rank[2]	Percent (%)	Rank[3]
MSA[1]	35,900	70,500	10,248,300	44	39.1	8

Note: (1) Metropolitan Statistical Area - see Appendix A for areas included; (2) Calculated on an averaging of number of businesses, employment and sales and ranges from 1 to 50 where 1 is best; (3) Ranges from 1 to 50 where 1 is best
Source: The National Foundation for Women Business Owners, 1996 Facts on Women-Owned Businesses: Trends in the Top 50 Metropolitan Areas, March 26, 1997

Women-Owned Businesses: Growth

Area	Growth in Women-Owned Businesses (% change from 1987 to 1996)				Relative Growth in the Number of Women-Owned and All Businesses (% change from 1987 to 1996)			
	Num.	Empl.	Sales	Rank[2]	Women-Owned	All Firms	Absolute Difference	Relative Difference
MSA[1]	82.0	92.5	252.3	35	82.0	52.1	29.9	1.6:1

Note: (1) Metropolitan Statistical Area - see Appendix A for areas included; (2) Calculated on an averaging of the percent growth of number of businesses, employment and sales and ranges from 1 to 50 where 1 is best
Source: The National Foundation for Women Business Owners, 1996 Facts on Women-Owned Businesses: Trends in the Top 50 Metropolitan Areas, March 26, 1997

HOTELS & MOTELS

Hotels/Motels

Area	Hotels/ Motels	Rooms	Luxury-Level Hotels/Motels		Average Minimum Rates ($)		
			♦♦♦♦	♦♦♦♦♦	♦♦	♦♦♦	♦♦♦♦
City	20	2,916	0	0	53	84	n/a
Airport	12	2,097	0	0	n/a	n/a	n/a
Suburbs	79	8,507	0	0	n/a	n/a	n/a
Total	111	13,520	0	0	n/a	n/a	n/a

Note: n/a not available; Classifications range from one diamond (budget properties with basic amenities) to five diamond (luxury properties with the finest service, rooms and facilities).
Source: OAG, Business Travel Planner, Summer 1997

CONVENTION CENTERS

Major Convention Centers

Center Name	Meeting Rooms	Exhibit Space (sf)
Norfolk SCOPE	6	85,000
Norfolk Waterside Convention	19	14,400
Old Dominion University Exhibition Hall	n/a	80,000
Omni Norfolk	15	18,440
Quality Inn Lake Wright Resort/Convention Center	12	21,812

Note: n/a not available
Source: Trade Shows Worldwide 1997

Living Environment

COST OF LIVING

Cost of Living Index

Composite Index	Housing	Utilities	Groceries	Health Care	Trans-portation	Misc. Goods/ Services
n/a	n/a	n/a	n/a	n/a	n/a	n/a

Note: U.S. = 100; n/a not available
Source: ACCRA, Cost of Living Index, 3rd Quarter 1997

HOUSING

Median Home Prices and Housing Affordability

Area	Median Price[2] 3rd Qtr. 1997 ($)	HOI[3] 3rd Qtr. 1997	Afford-ability Rank[4]
MSA[1]	104,000	70.5	91
U.S.	127,000	63.7	–

Note: (1) Metropolitan Statistical Area - see Appendix A for areas included; (2) U.S. figures calculated from the sales of 625,000 new and existing homes in 195 markets; (3) Housing Opportunity Index - percent of homes sold that were within the reach of the median income household at the prevailing mortgage interest rate; (4) Rank is from 1-195 with 1 being most affordable
Source: National Association of Home Builders, Housing Opportunity Index, 3rd Quarter 1997

It is projected that the median price of existing single-family homes in the metro area will increase by 6.8% in 1998. Nationwide, home prices are projected to increase 6.6%.
Kiplinger's Personal Finance Magazine, January 1998

Average New Home Price

Area	Price ($)
City	n/a
U.S.	135,710

Note: n/a not available
Source: ACCRA, Cost of Living Index, 3rd Quarter 1997

Average Apartment Rent

Area	Rent ($/mth)
City	n/a
U.S.	569

Note: n/a not available
Source: ACCRA, Cost of Living Index, 3rd Quarter 1997

RESIDENTIAL UTILITIES

Average Residential Utility Costs

Area	All Electric ($/mth)	Part Electric ($/mth)	Other Energy ($/mth)	Phone ($/mth)
City	n/a	n/a	n/a	n/a
U.S.	109.40	55.25	43.64	19.48

Note: n/a not available
Source: ACCRA, Cost of Living Index, 3rd Quarter 1997

HEALTH CARE

Average Health Care Costs

Area	Hospital ($/day)	Doctor ($/visit)	Dentist ($/visit)
City	n/a	n/a	n/a
U.S.	392.91	48.76	60.84

Note: n/a not available
Source: ACCRA, Cost of Living Index, 3rd Quarter 1997

Distribution of Office-Based Physicians

Area	Family/Gen. Practitioners	Specialists		
		Medical	Surgical	Other
MSA[1]	397	724	680	624

Note: Data as of 12/31/96; (1) Metropolitan Statistical Area - see Appendix A for areas included
Source: American Medical Assn., Physician Characteristics & Distribution in the U.S., 1997-1998

Hospitals

Norfolk has 4 general medical and surgical hospitals, 1 psychiatric, 1 chronic disease, 1 children's general. *AHA Guide to the Healthcare Field 1997-98*

EDUCATION

Public School District Statistics

District Name	Num. Sch.	Enroll.	Classroom Teachers[1]	Pupils per Teacher	Minority Pupils (%)	Current Exp.[2] ($/pupil)
Norfolk City Public Schls	58	36,771	n/a	n/a	68.0	5,225

Note: Data covers the 1995-1996 school year unless otherwise noted; (1) Excludes teachers reported as working in school district offices rather than in schools; (2) Based on 1993-94 enrollment collected by the Census Bureau, not the enrollment figure shown in column 3; SD = School District; ISD = Independent School District; n/a not available
Source: National Center for Education Statistics, Common Core of Data Survey; Bureau of the Census

Educational Quality

School District	Education Quotient[1]	Graduate Outcome[2]	Community Index[3]	Resource Index[4]
Norfolk City	81.0	55.0	65.0	122.0

Note: Nearly 1,000 secondary school districts were rated in terms of educational quality. The scores range from a low of 50 to a high of 150; (1) Average of the Graduate Outcome, Community and Resource indexes; (2) Based on graduation rates and college board scores (SAT/ACT); (3) Based on the surrounding community's average level of education and the area's average income level; (4) Based on teacher salaries, per-pupil expenditures and student-teacher ratios.
Source: Expansion Management, Ratings Issue 1997

Educational Attainment by Race

Area	High School Graduate (%)					Bachelor's Degree (%)				
	Total	White	Black	Other	Hisp.[2]	Total	White	Black	Other	Hisp.[2]
City	72.7	80.7	58.8	77.8	84.2	16.8	21.8	7.9	23.5	16.0
MSA[1]	79.1	84.2	64.9	80.0	85.6	20.1	23.3	11.3	22.3	16.1
U.S.	75.2	77.9	63.1	60.4	49.8	20.3	21.5	11.4	19.4	9.2

Note: figures shown cover persons 25 years old and over; (1) Metropolitan Statistical Area - see Appendix A for areas included; (2) people of Hispanic origin can be of any race
Source: 1990 Census of Population and Housing, Summary Tape File 3C

School Enrollment by Type

Area	Preprimary				Elementary/High School			
	Public		Private		Public		Private	
	Enrollment	%	Enrollment	%	Enrollment	%	Enrollment	%
City	2,322	59.2	1,600	40.8	33,000	91.0	3,245	9.0
MSA[1]	14,319	54.5	11,942	45.5	218,089	92.8	16,852	7.2
U.S.	2,679,029	59.5	1,824,256	40.5	38,379,689	90.2	4,187,099	9.8

Note: figures shown cover persons 3 years old and over;
(1) Metropolitan Statistical Area - see Appendix A for areas included
Source: 1990 Census of Population and Housing, Summary Tape File 3C

School Enrollment by Race

Area	Preprimary (%)				Elementary/High School (%)			
	White	Black	Other	Hisp.[1]	White	Black	Other	Hisp.[1]
City	60.5	35.6	3.9	3.4	41.5	54.4	4.1	2.5
MSA[2]	71.3	25.7	2.9	2.7	60.2	35.5	4.3	2.3
U.S.	80.4	12.5	7.1	7.8	74.1	15.6	10.3	12.5

Note: figures shown cover persons 3 years old and over; (1) people of Hispanic origin can be of any race; (2) Metropolitan Statistical Area - see Appendix A for areas included
Source: 1990 Census of Population and Housing, Summary Tape File 3C

SAT/ACT Scores

Area/District	1997 SAT				1997 ACT	
	Percent of Graduates Tested (%)	Average Math Score	Average Verbal Score	Average Combined Score	Percent of Graduates Tested (%)	Average Composite Score
Norfolk	n/a	441	448	889	n/a	n/a
State	69	497	506	1,003	6	20.7
U.S.	42	511	505	1,016	36	21.0

Note: Math and verbal SAT scores are out of a possible 800; ACT scores are out of a possible 36
Caution: Comparing or ranking states/cities on the basis of SAT/ACT scores alone is invalid and strongly discouraged by the The College Board and The American College Testing Program as students who take the tests are self-selected and do not represent the entire student population.
Source: Norfolk Public Schools, Department of Research, Testing & Statistics, 1997; College Board, 1997; American College Testing Program, 1997

Classroom Teacher Salaries in Public Schools

District	B.A. Degree		M.A. Degree		Ph.D. Degree	
	Min. ($)	Max ($)	Min. ($)	Max. ($)	Min. ($)	Max. ($)
Norfolk	26,500	42,300	28,640	44,440	31,340	47,140
Average[1]	26,120	39,270	28,175	44,667	31,643	49,825

Note: Salaries are for 1996-1997; (1) Based on all school districts covered; n/a not available
Source: American Federation of Teachers (unpublished data)

Higher Education

Two-Year Colleges		Four-Year Colleges		Medical Schools	Law Schools	Voc/ Tech
Public	Private	Public	Private			
0	2	2	1	1	0	8

Source: College Blue Book, Occupational Education 1997; Medical School Admission Requirements, 1998-99; Peterson's Guide to Two-Year Colleges, 1997; Peterson's Guide to Four-Year Colleges, 1997; Barron's Guide to Law Schools 1997

MAJOR EMPLOYERS

Major Employers

Children's Hospital of the Kings Daughters
Dollar Tree Stores
First Hospital Corp.
Landmark Communications
Norfolk Shipbuilding & Drydock Corp.
Tidewater Construction Corp.
DePaul Medical Center
Farm Fresh Inc.
General Foam Plastics Corp.
Metro Machine Corp.
Norfolk Southern Corp.

Note: companies listed are located in the city
Source: Dun's Business Rankings 1997; Ward's Business Directory, 1997

PUBLIC SAFETY

Crime Rate

Area	All Crimes	Violent Crimes				Property Crimes		
		Murder	Forcible Rape	Robbery	Aggrav. Assault	Burglary	Larceny -Theft	Motor Vehicle Theft
City	7,665.6	24.8	57.7	438.7	426.9	1,124.6	4,900.5	692.4
Suburbs[1]	4,902.5	7.8	35.8	163.4	217.6	741.0	3,432.8	304.0
MSA[2]	5,338.2	10.5	39.2	206.8	250.6	801.5	3,664.2	365.3
U.S.	5,078.9	7.4	36.1	202.4	388.2	943.0	2,975.9	525.9

Note: Crime rate is the number of crimes per 100,000 pop.; (1) defined as all areas within the MSA but located outside the central city; (2) Metropolitan Statistical Area - see Appendix A for areas incl.
Source: FBI Uniform Crime Reports 1996

RECREATION

Culture and Recreation

Museums	Symphony Orchestras	Opera Companies	Dance Companies	Professional Theatres	Zoos	Pro Sports Teams
5	1	1	2	4	1	0

Source: International Directory of the Performing Arts, 1996; Official Museum Directory, 1998; Chamber of Commerce/Economic Development 1997

Library System

The Norfolk Public Library has 11 branches, holdings of 909,565 volumes and a budget of $4,484,950 (1995-1996). *American Library Directory, 1997-1998*

MEDIA

Newspapers

Name	Type	Freq.	Distribution	Circulation
The Booster	General	1x/mo	Local	10,000
Casemate	n/a	2x/mo	Local	5,000
The Compass	General	1x/wk	Local	15,000
El Eco de Virginia	Hispanic	2x/mo	Regional	30,000
The Flag Ship	n/a	1x/wk	Area	40,000
The Flyer	n/a	1x/wk	Local	13,500
Hampton Roads Metro Weekender	Black	1x/wk	Local	40,000
Jet Observer	n/a	2x/mo	Local	8,000
New Journal & Guide	Black	1x/wk	National	30,000
Traveller	n/a	1x/wk	Local	10,000
The Virginian-Pilot	General	7x/wk	Area	201,236
The Wheel	n/a	1x/wk	Local	10,000

Note: Includes newspapers with circulations of 1,000 or more located in the city; n/a not available
Source: Burrelle's Media Directory, 1998 Edition

AM Radio Stations

Call Letters	Freq. (kHz)	Target Audience	Station Format	Music Format
WTAR	790	General	N/S/T	n/a
WNIS	850	General	N/T	n/a
WPCE	1400	General	M/N/S	Christian

Note: Stations included broadcast in the Norfolk metro area; n/a not available
Station Format: E = Educational; M = Music; N = News; S = Sports; T = Talk
Source: Burrelle's Media Directory, 1998 Edition

FM Radio Stations

Call Letters	Freq. (mHz)	Target Audience	Station Format	Music Format
WHRV	89.5	General	M/N	Alternative/Jazz
WHRO	90.3	General	M	Classical
WMYK	92.1	General	M/N/S	Contemporary Top 40
WFOG	92.9	General	M/N/S	Adult Contemporary
WPTE	94.9	n/a	M/N	Adult Contemporary
WLTY	95.7	General	M/N/S	Country
WROX	96.1	General	M	AOR
WOWI	102.9	n/a	M/N/S	Urban Contemporary
WJCD	105.3	n/a	M/N/S	Adult Contemporary/Jazz

Note: Stations included broadcast in the Norfolk metro area; n/a not available
Station Format: E = Educational; M = Music; N = News; S = Sports; T = Talk
Music Format: AOR = Album Oriented Rock; MOR = Middle-of-the-Road
Source: Burrelle's Media Directory, 1998 Edition

Television Stations

Name	Ch.	Affiliation	Type	Owner
WTKR	3	CBS	Commercial	New York Times Company
WVEC	13	ABC	Commercial	A.H. Belo Corporation
WHRO	15	PBS	Public	Hampton Roads Educational Telecommunications Association
WTVZ	33	Fox	Commercial	Sinclair Broadcast Group

Note: Stations included broadcast in the Norfolk metro area
Source: Burrelle's Media Directory, 1998 Edition

CLIMATE

Average and Extreme Temperatures

Temperature	Jan	Feb	Mar	Apr	May	Jun	Jul	Aug	Sep	Oct	Nov	Dec	Ann
Extreme High (°F)	78	81	88	97	97	101	103	104	99	95	86	80	104
Average High (°F)	48	50	58	68	76	84	87	86	80	70	61	52	68
Average Temp. (°F)	40	42	49	58	67	75	79	78	72	62	53	44	60
Average Low (°F)	32	33	40	48	57	66	70	70	64	53	43	35	51
Extreme Low (°F)	-3	8	18	28	36	45	54	49	45	27	20	7	-3

Note: Figures cover the years 1948-1990
Source: National Climatic Data Center, International Station Meteorological Climate Summary, 3/95

Average Precipitation/Snowfall/Humidity

Precip./Humidity	Jan	Feb	Mar	Apr	May	Jun	Jul	Aug	Sep	Oct	Nov	Dec	Ann
Avg. Precip. (in.)	3.6	3.4	3.7	3.1	3.8	3.6	5.1	5.4	4.0	3.3	3.0	3.2	45.0
Avg. Snowfall (in.)	3	3	1	Tr	0	0	0	0	0	0	Tr	1	8
Avg. Rel. Hum. 7am (%)	74	74	74	73	77	79	82	84	83	82	79	75	78
Avg. Rel. Hum. 4pm (%)	59	57	54	51	56	57	60	63	62	61	58	59	58

Note: Figures cover the years 1948-1990; Tr = Trace amounts (<0.05 in. of rain; <0.5 in. of snow)
Source: National Climatic Data Center, International Station Meteorological Climate Summary, 3/95

Weather Conditions

Temperature			Daytime Sky			Precipitation		
10°F & below	32°F & below	90°F & above	Clear	Partly cloudy	Cloudy	0.01 inch or more precip.	0.1 inch or more snow/ice	Thunder-storms
< 1	54	32	89	149	127	115	6	37

Note: Figures are average number of days per year and covers the years 1948-1990
Source: National Climatic Data Center, International Station Meteorological Climate Summary, 3/95

AIR & WATER QUALITY

Maximum Pollutant Concentrations

	Particulate Matter (ug/m³)	Carbon Monoxide (ppm)	Sulfur Dioxide (ppm)	Nitrogen Dioxide (ppm)	Ozone (ppm)	Lead (ug/m³)
MSA[1] Level	50	6	0.025	0.018	0.10	0.03
NAAQS[2]	150	9	0.140	0.053	0.12	1.50
Met NAAQS?	Yes	Yes	Yes	Yes	Yes	Yes

Note: (1) Metropolitan Statistical Area - see Appendix A for areas included; (2) National Ambient Air Quality Standards; ppm = parts per million; ug/m³ = micrograms per cubic meter; n/a not available
Source: EPA, National Air Quality and Emissions Trends Report, 1996

Pollutant Standards Index

In the Norfolk MSA (see Appendix A for areas included), the Pollutant Standards Index (PSI) exceeded 100 on 0 days in 1996. A PSI value greater than 100 indicates that air quality would be in the unhealthful range on that day. *EPA, National Air Quality and Emissions Trends Report, 1996*

Drinking Water

Water System Name	Pop. Served	Primary Water Source Type	Number of Violations in Fiscal Year 1997	Type of Violation/ Contaminants
Norfolk City Moores Bridges	295,000	Surface	None	None

Note: Data as of January 16, 1998
Source: EPA, Office of Ground Water and Drinking Water, Safe Drinking Water Information System

Norfolk tap water is slightly soft, fluoridated and has low alkalinity.
Editor & Publisher Market Guide, 1998

Philadelphia, Pennsylvania

Background

Philadelphia, "The City of Brotherly Love", might shock some to know that its history was not founded upon brotherly love at all. The largest city in Pennsylvania, on the southeast corner of the state was settled by Swedes and Finns in 1638, in a settlement known as New Sweden. The settlement was seized in 1655 by Peter Stuyvesant, Director General of New Amsterdam for the Dutch Crown. In turn, King Charles II of England conferred land between the Connecticut and Delaware Rivers, upon his brother, the Duke of York inconsiderate of any previous claims by the Dutch. Naturally, the two countries went to war. However, thanks to a generous loan by Admiral Sir William Penn, the land fell permanently into English hands. To repay the loan, the King gave Sir William's son, also named William, sole proprietorship of the state of present day Pennsylvania. At the same time, he was probably glad to be rid of a subject heavily influenced by a dissenting religious sect known as the Society of Friends, or Quakers.

Pennsylvania's landlord had the vision and the financial means with which to carry out a simple but radical experiment for the times: a city built upon religious tolerance. Amazingly enough, the place of religious outcasts prospered. Thanks to forests abundant in natural resources, and ports busy with international trade, Philadelphia was a bustling, ideal American city.

While the region's manufacturing activities have been declining for the last few years, the service sector has emerged as the predominant economic force driving current and future growth in the city. Greater Philadelphia has the second largest health care industry in the nation. It has become a major materials development and processing center. More than 100,000 individuals are involved in the manufacture of chemicals, advanced materials, glass, plastics, industrial gases, metals, composites and textiles.

According to the Association of University Related Research Parks, the University City Science Center located in Philadelphia is ranked #3 out of the top 10 research parks in the U.S. with 140 companies. *World Trade 4/97*

The city claimed firsts in many cultural, educational, and political arenas. The Pennsylvania Academy of Fine Arts is the oldest museum and fine arts school in the country; the University of Pennsylvania, which Benjamin Franklin helped found, is the oldest university in the country; and of course, on July 4, 1776, the United States had been born, when "longhaired radicals" such as Thomas Jefferson, George Washington, and John Hancock signed The Declaration of Independence, breaking away from the mother country forever.

The Appalachian Mountains to the west and the Atlantic Ocean to the east have a moderating effect on the city's climate. Temperatures below zero or above 100 degrees are a rarity.

General Rankings and Evaluative Comments

- Philadelphia was ranked #187 out of 300 cities by *Money's* 1997 "Survey of the Best Places to Live." Criteria used: health services, crime, economy, housing, education, transportation, weather, leisure and the arts. The city was ranked #233 in 1996 and #269 in 1995. *Money, July 1997; Money, September 1996; Money, September 1995*

- *Ladies Home Journal* ranked America's 200 largest cities based on the qualities women care about most. Philadelphia ranked 169 out of 200. Criteria: low crime rate, good public schools, well-paying jobs, quality health and child care, the presence of women in government, proportion of women-owned businesses, size of the wage gap with men, local economy, divorce rates, the ratio of single men to single women, whether there are laws that require at least the same number of public toilets for women as men, and the probability of good hair days. *Ladies Home Journal, November 1997*

- Philadelphia was ranked #198 out of 219 cities in terms of children's health, safety, and economic well-being. Criteria: total population, percent population change, birth rate, child immunization rate, infant mortality rate, percent low birth weight infants, percent of births to teens, physician-to-population ratio, student-to-teacher ratio, dropout rate, unemployment rate, median family income, percent of children in poverty, violent and property crime rates, number of juvenile arrests for violent crimes as a percent of the total crime index, number of days with pollution standard index (PSI) over 100, pounds toxic releases per 1,000 people and number of superfund sites. *Zero Population Growth, Children's Environmental Index 1997*

- *Yahoo! Internet Life* selected "America's 100 Most Wired Cities & Towns". 50 cities were large and 50 cities were small. Philadelphia ranked 19 out of 50 large cities. Criteria: Internet users per capita, number of networked computers, number of registered domain names, Internet backbone traffic, and the per-capita number of Web sites devoted to each city. *Yahoo! Internet Life, March 1998*

- *Reader's Digest* non-scientifically ranked the 12 largest U.S. metropolitan areas in terms of having the worst drivers. The Philadelphia metro area ranked number 8. The areas were selected by asking approximately 1,200 readers on the *Reader's Digest* Web site and 200 interstate bus drivers and long-haul truckers which metro areas have the worst drivers. Their responses were factored in with fatality, insurance and rental-car rates to create the rankings. *Reader's Digest, March 1998*

- Rosenbluth International (corporate travel agent), headquartered in Philadelphia, is among the "100 Best Companies to Work for in America." Criteria: trust in management, pride in work/company, camaraderie, company responses to the Hewitt People Practices Inventory, and employee responses to their Great Place to Work survey. The companies also had to be at least 10 years old and have a minimum of 500 employees. *Fortune, January 12, 1998*

- Cigna Corp., headquartered in Philadelphia, is among the "100 Best Companies for Working Mothers." Criteria: pay compared with competition, opportunities for women to advance, support for child care, flexible work schedules and family-friendly benefits. *Working Mother, October 1997*

- According to *Working Mother,* "The situation in this state is a mixed bag: Ratios and training requirements are quite good, but child care centers and family child care homes rarely get surprise inspection visits, and there's no statewide resource & referral (R&R) system to help parents find care. But change is in the works. The state is using some of its federal money to create an R&R network this year, and legislation is pending to require unannounced inspections. Both would be welcome developments.

  As we went to press, parents and child advocates here were responding to Governor Tom Ridge's latest budget proposal. He says he's made the largest-ever increase in child care funds—$68 million. But nearly all of that is federal money, the governor allotted only $1 million in new state funds for child care aid to parents in low-income jobs. Meanwhile, 11,700 children needing subsidized care are on a waiting list, and the state has a budget surplus of nearly $500 million!" *Working Mother, July/August 1997*

Business Environment

STATE ECONOMY

State Economic Profile

"Pennsylvania's economy is steadily improving....The revival is broad-based, with Pennsylvania's largest industries—services, retail trade, and manufacturing, all improving....

Last year, Pennsylvania lowered its business costs by enacting several business tax cuts and reforming the workers compensation system. This year, a healthy fiscal situation in Pennsylvania has led to a state budget that includes a 3.7% increase in state spending during fiscal 1998 and another $167 million in tax cuts.

Philadelphia's convention center has created an estimated 6,200 jobs and significantly boosted the hotel and retail markets in the metro area since it opened in 1993. For Philadelphia's hotels, the convention center has meant more business, with the occupancy rate increasing to 70% from 64% prior to the convention center's opening. Because of strong demand, at least four more hotel projects are planned for downtown Philadelphia. A one-half percent sales tax increase will be used to partially finance the expansion of Pittsburgh's convention center. If approved, the $300 million project will significantly expand the center's exhibit, meeting and parking space, while also adding over 50 hotel rooms.

A relatively high rate of consumer spending (retail sales grew by 9% in Pennsylvania and by only 5% in the U.S. last year), in combination with below average income growth, is leading to surging personal bankruptcy filings in pennsylvania. Personal bankruptcy filings increased by 44% in the state last year, compared to 29% at the national level.

With a high cost of doing business, poor demographic trends, and strong union activity, Pennsylvania will have difficulty attracting new and growing industries to replace its aging manufacturers. Pennsylvania will underperform the nation in both the near and long term." *National Association of Realtors, Economic Profiles: The Fifty States, July 1997*

IMPORTS/EXPORTS

Total Export Sales

Area	1993 ($000)	1994 ($000)	1995 ($000)	1996 ($000)	% Chg. 1993-96	% Chg. 1995-96
MSA[1]	5,869,148	6,545,836	7,896,893	7,727,940	31.7	-2.1
U.S.	464,858,354	512,415,609	583,030,524	622,827,063	34.0	6.8

Note: (1) Metropolitan Statistical Area - see Appendix A for areas included
Source: U.S. Department of Commerce, International Trade Association, Metropolitan Area Exports: An Export Performance Report on Over 250 U.S. Cities, October 1997

Imports/Exports by Port

Type	Cargo Value			Share of U.S. Total	
	1995 (US$mil.)	1996 (US$mil.)	% Change 1995-1996	1995 (%)	1996 (%)
Imports	5,676	6,716	18.33	1.45	1.75
Exports	1,516	3,321	119.09	0.66	1.40

Source: Global Trade Information Services, WaterBorne Trade Atlas 1997

CITY FINANCES

City Government Finances

Component	FY94 ($000)	FY94 (per capita $)
Revenue	3,979,708	2,614.14
Expenditure	3,998,386	2,626.40
Debt Outstanding	3,673,489	2,412.99
Cash & Securities	3,362,497	2,208.71

Source: U.S. Bureau of the Census, City Government Finances: 1993-94

City Government Revenue by Source

Source	FY94 ($000)	FY94 (per capita $)	FY94 (%)
From Federal Government	214,513	140.91	5.4
From State Governments	772,904	507.69	19.4
From Local Governments	84,002	55.18	2.1
Property Taxes	343,202	225.44	8.6
General Sales Taxes	83,690	54.97	2.1
Selective Sales Taxes	47,270	31.05	1.2
Income Taxes	821,701	539.75	20.6
Current Charges	420,978	276.53	10.6
Utility/Liquor Store	675,216	443.53	17.0
Employee Retirement[1]	158,189	103.91	4.0
Other	358,043	235.19	9.0

Note: (1) Excludes "city contributions," classified as "nonrevenue," intragovernmental transfers.
Source: U.S. Bureau of the Census, City Government Finances: 1993-94

City Government Expenditures by Function

Function	FY94 ($000)	FY94 (per capita $)	FY94 (%)
Educational Services	53,039	34.84	1.3
Employee Retirement[1]	330,636	217.18	8.3
Environment/Housing	424,265	278.69	10.6
Government Administration	398,688	261.88	10.0
Interest on General Debt	92,596	60.82	2.3
Public Safety	663,376	435.75	16.6
Social Services	628,790	413.03	15.7
Transportation	173,895	114.23	4.3
Utility/Liquor Store	711,727	467.51	17.8
Other	521,374	342.47	13.0

Note: (1) Payments to beneficiaries including withdrawal of contributions.
Source: U.S. Bureau of the Census, City Government Finances: 1993-94

Municipal Bond Ratings

Area	Moody's	S & P
Philadelphia	Baa	BBB

Note: n/a not available; n/r not rated
Source: Moody's Bond Record, 2/98; Statistical Abstract of the U.S., 1997; Governing Magazine, 9/97, 3/98

POPULATION

Population Growth

Area	1980	1990	% Chg. 1980-90	July 1996 Estimate	% Chg. 1990-96
City	1,688,210	1,585,577	-6.1	1,478,002	-6.8
MSA[1]	4,716,818	4,856,881	3.0	4,952,929	2.0
U.S.	226,545,805	248,765,170	9.8	265,179,411	6.6

Note: (1) Metropolitan Statistical Area - see Appendix A for areas included
Source: 1980/1990 Census of Housing and Population, Summary Tape File 3C; Census Bureau Population Estimates

Population Characteristics

Race	City 1980 Population	City 1980 %	City 1990 Population	City 1990 %	% Chg. 1980-90	MSA[1] 1990 Population	MSA[1] 1990 %
White	988,337	58.5	848,894	53.5	-14.1	3,718,464	76.6
Black	638,788	37.8	632,430	39.9	-1.0	930,017	19.1
Amer Indian/Esk/Aleut	2,799	0.2	3,325	0.2	18.8	8,851	0.2
Asian/Pacific Islander	19,950	1.2	43,174	2.7	116.4	103,234	2.1
Other	38,336	2.3	57,754	3.6	50.7	96,315	2.0
Hispanic Origin[2]	63,570	3.8	84,186	5.3	32.4	164,601	3.4

Note: (1) Metropolitan Statistical Area - see Appendix A for areas included; (2) people of Hispanic origin can be of any race
Source: 1980/1990 Census of Housing and Population, Summary Tape File 3C

Ancestry

Area	German	Irish	English	Italian	U.S.	French	Polish	Dutch
City	13.0	16.9	4.7	11.2	1.7	1.0	5.8	0.5
MSA[1]	23.6	22.8	11.3	14.4	2.1	2.1	6.5	1.5
U.S.	23.3	15.6	13.1	5.9	5.3	4.2	3.8	2.5

Note: Figures are percentages and include persons that reported multiple ancestry (eg. if a person reported being Irish and Italian, they were included in both columns); (1) Metropolitan Statistical Area - see Appendix A for areas included
Source: 1990 Census of Population and Housing, Summary Tape File 3C

Age

Area	Median Age (Years)	Age Distribution (%) Under 5	Under 18	18-24	25-44	45-64	65+	80+
City	33.1	7.3	23.9	11.4	30.8	18.6	15.2	3.4
MSA[1]	33.7	7.3	24.4	10.3	32.4	19.5	13.5	2.9
U.S.	32.9	7.3	25.6	10.5	32.6	18.7	12.5	2.8

Note: (1) Metropolitan Statistical Area - see Appendix A for areas included
Source: 1990 Census of Population and Housing, Summary Tape File 3C

Male/Female Ratio

Area	Number of males per 100 females (all ages)	Number of males per 100 females (18 years old+)
City	86.8	82.6
MSA[1]	91.8	88.0
U.S.	95.0	91.9

Note: (1) Metropolitan Statistical Area - see Appendix A for areas included
Source: 1990 Census of Population, General Population Characteristics

INCOME

Per Capita/Median/Average Income

Area	Per Capita ($)	Median Household ($)	Average Household ($)
City	12,091	24,603	31,208
MSA[1]	16,386	35,437	44,191
U.S.	14,420	30,056	38,453

Note: all figures are for 1989; (1) Metropolitan Statistical Area - see Appendix A for areas included
Source: 1990 Census of Population and Housing, Summary Tape File 3C

Household Income Distribution by Race

Income ($)	City (%)					U.S. (%)				
	Total	White	Black	Other	Hisp.[1]	Total	White	Black	Other	Hisp.[1]
Less than 5,000	10.0	6.4	14.6	18.6	19.1	6.2	4.8	15.2	8.6	8.8
5,000 - 9,999	12.7	11.2	14.9	15.3	18.0	9.3	8.6	14.2	9.9	11.1
10,000 - 14,999	9.9	9.3	10.4	12.5	12.4	8.8	8.5	11.0	9.8	11.0
15,000 - 24,999	18.0	17.3	19.0	19.6	19.4	17.5	17.3	18.9	18.5	20.5
25,000 - 34,999	15.2	15.8	14.5	13.5	12.9	15.8	16.1	14.2	15.4	16.4
35,000 - 49,999	16.4	18.0	14.5	11.2	10.4	17.9	18.6	13.3	16.1	16.0
50,000 - 74,999	12.2	14.6	9.2	6.5	6.1	15.0	15.8	9.3	13.4	11.1
75,000 - 99,999	3.3	4.3	2.0	1.5	1.1	5.1	5.5	2.6	4.7	3.1
100,000+	2.2	3.0	0.9	1.2	0.6	4.4	4.8	1.3	3.7	1.9

Note: all figures are for 1989; (1) people of Hispanic origin can be of any race
Source: 1990 Census of Population and Housing, Summary Tape File 3C

Effective Buying Income

Area	Per Capita ($)	Median Household ($)	Average Household ($)
City	13,878	28,551	36,435
MSA[1]	19,160	42,422	52,092
U.S.	15,444	33,201	41,849

Note: data as of 1/1/97; (1) Metropolitan Statistical Area - see Appendix A for areas included
Source: Standard Rate & Data Service, Newspaper Advertising Source, 2/98

Effective Household Buying Income Distribution

Area	% of Households Earning						
	$10,000 -$19,999	$20,000 -$34,999	$35,000 -$49,999	$50,000 -$74,999	$75,000 -$99,000	$100,000 -$124,999	$125,000 and up
City	18.3	22.3	16.8	16.1	5.3	1.5	1.4
MSA[1]	12.3	19.0	17.8	22.6	10.3	4.0	4.4
U.S.	16.5	23.4	18.3	18.2	6.4	2.1	2.4

Note: data as of 1/1/97; (1) Metropolitan Statistical Area - see Appendix A for areas included
Source: Standard Rate & Data Service, Newspaper Advertising Source, 2/98

Poverty Rates by Race and Age

Area	Total (%)	By Race (%)				By Age (%)		
		White	Black	Other	Hisp.[2]	Under 5 years old	Under 18 years old	65 years and over
City	20.3	11.1	29.0	41.6	45.3	31.9	30.3	16.3
MSA[1]	10.4	5.6	25.5	30.1	35.2	15.9	15.0	10.4
U.S.	13.1	9.8	29.5	23.1	25.3	20.1	18.3	12.8

Note: figures show the percent of people living below the poverty line in 1989. The average poverty threshold was $12,674 for a family of four in 1989; (1) Metropolitan Statistical Area - see Appendix A for areas included; (2) people of Hispanic origin can be of any race
Source: 1990 Census of Population and Housing, Summary Tape File 3C

EMPLOYMENT

Labor Force and Employment

Area	Civilian Labor Force			Workers Employed		
	Dec. '95	Dec. '96	% Chg.	Dec. '95	Dec. '96	% Chg.
City	654,379	665,513	1.7	617,097	629,699	2.0
MSA[1]	2,479,691	2,508,190	1.1	2,370,799	2,410,923	1.7
U.S.	134,583,000	136,742,000	1.6	127,903,000	130,785,000	2.3

Note: Data is not seasonally adjusted and covers workers 16 years of age and older; (1) Metropolitan Statistical Area - see Appendix A for areas included
Source: Bureau of Labor Statistics, http://stats.bls.gov

Unemployment Rate

Area	1997											
	Jan.	Feb.	Mar.	Apr.	May	Jun.	Jul.	Aug.	Sep.	Oct.	Nov.	Dec.
City	6.2	6.2	6.3	6.6	7.0	6.8	7.0	6.9	7.5	6.7	6.4	5.4
MSA[1]	5.0	4.9	4.9	4.8	5.0	5.0	5.3	5.0	5.1	4.5	4.4	3.9
U.S.	5.9	5.7	5.5	4.8	4.7	5.2	5.0	4.8	4.7	4.4	4.3	4.4

Note: Data is not seasonally adjusted and covers workers 16 years of age and older; All figures are percentages; (1) Metropolitan Statistical Area - see Appendix A for areas included
Source: Bureau of Labor Statistics, http://stats.bls.gov

Employment by Industry

Sector	MSA[1]		U.S.
	Number of Employees	Percent of Total	Percent of Total
Services	819,900	35.6	29.0
Retail Trade	390,800	17.0	18.5
Government	300,000	13.0	16.1
Manufacturing	306,600	13.3	15.0
Finance/Insurance/Real Estate	158,800	6.9	5.7
Wholesale Trade	127,700	5.5	5.4
Transportation/Public Utilities	109,400	4.8	5.3
Construction/Mining	89,900	3.9	5.0

Note: Figures cover non-farm employment as of 12/97 and are not seasonally adjusted; (1) Metropolitan Statistical Area - see Appendix A for areas included
Source: Bureau of Labor Statistics, http://stats.bls.gov

Employment by Occupation

Occupation Category	City (%)	MSA[1] (%)	U.S. (%)
White Collar	60.0	64.5	58.1
Executive/Admin./Management	10.3	13.6	12.3
Professional	14.5	15.9	14.1
Technical & Related Support	3.8	4.1	3.7
Sales	9.7	12.0	11.8
Administrative Support/Clerical	21.8	18.9	16.3
Blue Collar	23.2	22.6	26.2
Precision Production/Craft/Repair	9.0	10.3	11.3
Machine Operators/Assem./Insp.	6.2	5.2	6.8
Transportation/Material Movers	3.9	3.6	4.1
Cleaners/Helpers/Laborers	4.0	3.5	3.9
Services	16.3	11.9	13.2
Farming/Forestry/Fishing	0.5	1.0	2.5

Note: figures cover employed persons 16 years old and over; (1) Metropolitan Statistical Area - see Appendix A for areas included
Source: 1990 Census of Population and Housing, Summary Tape File 3C

Occupational Employment Projections: 1994 - 2005

Occupations Expected to have the Largest Job Growth (ranked by numerical growth)	Fast-Growing Occupations (ranked by percent growth)
1. Registered nurses	1. Electronic pagination systems workers
2. Systems analysts	2. Personal and home care aides
3. Waiters & waitresses	3. Systems analysts
4. Cashiers	4. Computer engineers
5. Salespersons, retail	5. Home health aides
6. Nursing aides/orderlies/attendants	6. Human services workers
7. Teachers aides, clerical & paraprofess.	7. Computer scientists
8. General managers & top executives	8. Manicurists
9. Home health aides	9. Physical therapists
10. Child care workers, private household	10. Residential counselors

Projections cover Pennsylvania.
Source: U.S. Department of Labor, Employment and Training Administration, America's Labor Market Information System (ALMIS)

Average Wages

Occupation	Wage	Occupation	Wage
Professional/Technical/Clerical	$/Week	**Health/Protective Services**	$/Week
Accountants III	835	Corrections Officers	653
Attorneys III	1,088	Firefighters	701
Budget Analysts III	839	Nurses, Licensed Practical II	-
Buyers/Contracting Specialists II	639	Nurses, Registered II	-
Clerks, Accounting III	459	Nursing Assistants II	-
Clerks, General III	402	Police Officers I	729
Computer Operators II	445	**Hourly Workers**	$/Hour
Computer Programmers II	636	Forklift Operators	12.29
Drafters II	575	General Maintenance Workers	11.19
Engineering Technicians III	778	Guards I	7.53
Engineering Technicians, Civil III	596	Janitors	11.84
Engineers III	960	Maintenance Electricians	17.67
Key Entry Operators I	366	Maintenance Electronics Techs II	18.95
Personnel Assistants III	600	Maintenance Machinists	18.67
Personnel Specialists III	810	Maintenance Mechanics, Machinery	16.59
Secretaries III	538	Material Handling Laborers	9.98
Switchboard Operator-Receptionist	370	Motor Vehicle Mechanics	15.44
Systems Analysts II	988	Shipping/Receiving Clerks	12.49
Systems Analysts Supervisor/Mgr II	1,397	Tool and Die Makers	17.72
Tax Collectors II	571	Truckdrivers, Tractor Trailer	13.29
Word Processors II	473	Warehouse Specialists	17.18

Note: Wage data includes full-time workers only for 11/96 and cover the Metropolitan Statistical Area (see Appendix A for areas included). Dashes indicate that data was not available.
Source: Bureau of Labor Statistics, Occupational Compensation Survey, 4/97

TAXES

Major State and Local Tax Rates

State Corp. Income (%)	State Personal Income (%)	Residential Property (effective rate per $100)	Sales & Use State (%)	Sales & Use Local (%)	State Gasoline (cents/ gallon)	State Cigarette (cents/ 20-pack)
9.99	2.8	2.64	6.0	1.0	25.9[a]	31

Note: Personal/corporate income tax rates as of 1/97. Sales, gasoline and cigarette tax rates as of 1/98; (a) Rate is comprised of 12 cents excise and 13.9 cent motor carrier tax
Source: Federation of Tax Administrators, www.taxadmin.org; Washington D.C. Department of Finance and Revenue, Tax Rates and Tax Burdens in the District of Columbia: A Nationwide Comparison, June 1997; Chamber of Commerce

Total Taxes Per Capita and as a Percent of Income

Area	Per Capita Income ($)	Per Capita Taxes ($)			Taxes as Pct. of Income (%)		
		Total	Federal	State/ Local	Total	Federal	State/ Local
Pennsylvania	26,194	9,229	6,216	3,013	35.2	23.7	11.5
U.S.	26,187	9,205	6,127	3,078	35.2	23.4	11.8

Note: Figures are for 1997
Source: Tax Foundation, Web Site, www.taxfoundation.org

Estimated Tax Burden

Area	State Income	Local Income	Property	Sales	Total
Philadelphia	1,820	3,224	4,050	595	9,689

Note: The numbers are estimates of taxes paid by a married couple with two kids and annual earnings of $65,000. Sales tax estimates assume they spend average amounts on food, clothing, household goods and gasoline. Property tax estimates assume they live in a $225,000 home.
Source: Kiplinger's Personal Finance Magazine, June 1997

COMMERCIAL REAL ESTATE

Office Market

Class/ Location	Total Space (sq. ft.)	Vacant Space (sq. ft.)	Vac. Rate (%)	Under Constr. (sq. ft.)	Net Absorp. (sq. ft.)	Rental Rates ($/sq.ft./yr.)
Class A						
CBD	25,347,774	2,342,181	9.2	0	446,074	18.50-24.50
Outside CBD	21,999,408	1,362,024	6.2	1,107,300	1,696,008	19.00-26.00
Class B						
CBD	15,307,212	2,950,731	19.3	0	876,072	12.50-15.00
Outside CBD	21,790,138	2,614,816	12.0	0	395,184	15.00-18.50

Note: Data as of 10/97 and covers Philadelphia; CBD = Central Business District; n/a not available;
Source: Society of Industrial and Office Realtors, 1998 Comparative Statistics of Industrial and Office Real Estate Markets

"The near term outlook for Philadelphia real estate is reassuring. As a result of a state level program to retain existing jobs and attract new firms two notable expansions have been announced. SAP America, a software firm, announced plans to build a new $100,000,000 facility and add 2400 jobs over the next several years. Smith Kline Beecham, one of the area's top employers, will build a new facility and create 500 new jobs. These new positions are important for the Philadelphia market because they are export oriented. Rather than selling into the Philadelphia market these firms target a national market and attract income to the Philadelphia market. Expansion the export-oriented firms serves as a catalyst for growth in the local economy as a whole." *Society of Industrial and Office Realtors, 1998 Comparative Statistics of Industrial and Office Real Estate Markets*

Industrial Market

Location	Total Space (sq. ft.)	Vacant Space (sq. ft.)	Vac. Rate (%)	Under Constr. (sq. ft.)	Net Absorp. (sq. ft.)	Net Lease ($/sq.ft./yr.)
Central City	101,125,000	13,900,275	13.7	72,000	-724,500	2.00-4.00
Suburban	150,025,000	15,876,460	10.6	1,222,079	537,540	3.00-6.00

Note: Data as of 10/97 and covers Philadelphia; n/a not available
Source: Society of Industrial and Office Realtors, 1998 Comparative Statistics of Industrial and Office Real Estate Markets

"The outlook for the Philadelphia market during 1998 is upbeat. The return of shipbuilding to the Philadelphia area is the best thing that has happened to its economy and the industrial real estate market in years. Philadelphia has a guarantee of at least three ships for this facility and local officials are hoping to build several more. The 1,000 direct jobs created will lead to additional jobs in the local economy as well. As an added benefit, an entire industrial facility that is not well-suited to other uses is fully leased. More than one million sq. ft. of industrial space was under construction at the end of 1997. The outlook for 1998 is for additional new construction, both speculative and build-to-suit. With a diverse corporate base supporting the economy, sales and lease prices are expected to increase 6-10 percent during 1998." *Society of Industrial and Office Realtors, 1998 Comparative Statistics of Industrial and Office Real Estate Markets*

Retail Market

Shopping Center Inventory (sq. ft.)	Shopping Center Construction (sq. ft.)	Construction as a Percent of Inventory (%)	Torto Wheaton Rent Index[1] ($/sq. ft.)
73,675,000	410,000	0.6	15.09

Note: Data as of 1997 and covers the Metropolitan Statistical Area - see Appendix A for areas included; (1) Index is based on a model that predicts what the average rent should be for leases with certain characteristics, in certain locations during certain years.
Source: National Association of Realtors, 1997-1998 Market Conditions Report

"Philadelphia's retail market is fairing poorly. Philadelphia's rents have remained relatively flat over the past five years, but are still among the highest rents in the nation. Construction has fallen dramatically during the last two years, and is the lowest of the Northeast metros as a percent of inventory. This has occurred due to the double-edged sword of an outflow of residents and slow income growth. Combined with tepid employment growth due to cutbacks in the healthcare and telecommunications industries and severe job losses at the Naval Shipyard the last few years, this should restrict retail activity in the near-term." *National Association of Realtors, 1997-1998 Market Conditions Report*

COMMERCIAL UTILITIES

Typical Monthly Electric Bills

Area	Commercial Service ($/month)		Industrial Service ($/month)	
	12 kW demand 1,500 kWh	100 kW demand 30,000 kWh	1,000 kW demand 400,000 kWh	20,000 kW demand 10,000,000 kWh
City	291	3,853	38,346	918,316
U.S.	162	2,360	25,590	545,677

Note: Based on rates in effect July 1, 1997
Source: Edison Electric Institute, Typical Residential, Commercial and Industrial Bills, Summer 1997

TRANSPORTATION

Transportation Statistics

Avg. travel time to work (min.)	27.4
Interstate highways	I-76; I-95
Bus lines	
In-city	Southeastern PATA, 1,434 vehicles
Inter-city	2
Passenger air service	
Airport	Philadelphia International
Airlines	17
Aircraft departures	126,198 (1995)
Enplaned passengers	8,019,756 (1995)
Rail service	Amtrak; Light Rail; Metro
Motor freight carriers	100
Major waterways/ports	Port of Philadelphia

Source: OAG, Business Travel Planner, Summer 1997; Editor & Publisher Market Guide, 1998; FAA Airport Activity Statistics, 1996; Amtrak National Time Table, Northeast Timetable, Fall/Winter 1997-98; 1990 Census of Population and Housing, STF 3C; Chamber of Commerce/Economic Development 1997; Jane's Urban Transport Systems 1997-98; Transit Fact Book 1997

A survey of 90,000 airline passengers during the first half of 1997 ranked most of the largest airports in the U.S. Philadelphia International ranked number 31 out of 36. Criteria: cleanliness, quality of restaurants, attractiveness, speed of baggage delivery, ease of reaching gates, available ground transportation, ease of following signs and closeness of parking. *Plog Research Inc., First Half 1997*

Means of Transportation to Work

Area	Car/Truck/Van		Public Transportation			Bicycle	Walked	Other Means	Worked at Home
	Drove Alone	Car-pooled	Bus	Subway	Railroad				
City	44.7	13.2	18.5	7.0	1.8	0.6	10.4	2.1	1.8
MSA[1]	67.8	11.9	6.3	2.7	2.1	0.3	5.4	1.2	2.3
U.S.	73.2	13.4	3.0	1.5	0.5	0.4	3.9	1.2	3.0

Note: figures shown are percentages and only include workers 16 years old and over; (1) Metropolitan Statistical Area - see Appendix A for areas included
Source: 1990 Census of Population and Housing, Summary Tape File 3C

BUSINESSES

Major Business Headquarters

Company Name	1997 Rankings	
	Fortune 500	Forbes 500
Aramark	235	19
Bell Atlantic	99	-
Berwind	-	198
Cigna	54	-
Comcast	339	-
Conrail	366	-
Corestates Financial Corp.	323	-
Crown Cork & Seal	179	-
Day & Zimmermann	-	194
Pacifico Organization	-	429
Peco Energy	318	-
Rohm & Haas	345	-
Sun	148	-

Note: Companies listed are located in the city; Dashes indicate no ranking
Fortune 500: companies that produce a 10-K are ranked 1 - 500 based on 1996 revenue
Forbes 500: private companies are ranked 1 - 500 based on 1996 revenue
Source: Forbes 12/1/97; Fortune 4/28/97

Fast-Growing Businesses

According to Deloitte & Touche LLP, Philadelphia is home to one of America's 100 fastest-growing high-technology companies: Brunson Communications Inc. Companies are ranked by percentage growth in revenue over a five-year period. Criteria for inclusion: must be a U.S. company developing and/or providing technology products or services; company must have been in business for five years with 1992 revenues of at least $50,000. *Deloitte & Touche LLP, January 7, 1998*

Philadelphia was ranked #11 out of 24 (#1 is best) in terms of the best-performing local stocks in 1996 according to the Money/Norby Cities Index. The index measures stocks of companies that have headquarters in 24 metro areas. *Money, 2/7/97*

Women-Owned Businesses: Number, Employment, Sales and Share

Area	Women-Owned Businesses in 1996				Share of Women-Owned Businesses in 1996	
	Number	Employment	Sales ($000)	Rank[2]	Percent (%)	Rank[3]
MSA[1]	127,100	448,500	56,281,800	4	33.4	47

Note: (1) Metropolitan Statistical Area - see Appendix A for areas included; (2) Calculated on an averaging of number of businesses, employment and sales and ranges from 1 to 50 where 1 is best; (3) Ranges from 1 to 50 where 1 is best
Source: The National Foundation for Women Business Owners, 1996 Facts on Women-Owned Businesses: Trends in the Top 50 Metropolitan Areas, March 26, 1997

Women-Owned Businesses: Growth

Area	Growth in Women-Owned Businesses (% change from 1987 to 1996)				Relative Growth in the Number of Women-Owned and All Businesses (% change from 1987 to 1996)			
	Num.	Empl.	Sales	Rank[2]	Women-Owned	All Firms	Absolute Difference	Relative Difference
MSA[1]	70.2	213.9	238.6	32	70.2	47.4	22.8	1.5:1

Note: (1) Metropolitan Statistical Area - see Appendix A for areas included; (2) Calculated on an averaging of the percent growth of number of businesses, employment and sales and ranges from 1 to 50 where 1 is best
Source: The National Foundation for Women Business Owners, 1996 Facts on Women-Owned Businesses: Trends in the Top 50 Metropolitan Areas, March 26, 1997

Minority Business Opportunity

Philadelphia is home to one company which is on the Black Enterprise Industrial/Service 100 list (largest based on gross sales): Philadelphia Coca-Cola Bottling Co. Inc. (soft drink bottling). Criteria: 1) operational in previous calendar year; 2) at least 51% black-owned; 3) manufactures/owns the product it sells or provides industrial or consumer services. Brokerages, real estate firms and firms that provide professional services are not eligible. *Black Enterprise, July 1997*

Small Business Opportunity

According to *Forbes*, Philadelphia is home to one of America's 200 best small companies: CMAC Investments. Criteria: companies must be publicly traded, U.S.-based corporations with latest 12-month sales of between $5 and $350 million. Earnings must be at least $1 million for the 12-month period. Limited partnerships, REITs and closed-end mutual funds were not considered. Banks, S&Ls and electric utilities were not included. *Forbes, November 3, 1997*

HOTELS & MOTELS

Hotels/Motels

Area	Hotels/ Motels	Rooms	Luxury-Level Hotels/Motels		Average Minimum Rates ($)		
			♦♦♦♦	♦♦♦♦♦	♦♦	♦♦♦	♦♦♦♦
City	32	8,116	4	0	90	135	242
Airport	14	3,460	0	0	n/a	n/a	n/a
Suburbs	60	8,745	0	0	n/a	n/a	n/a
Total	106	20,321	4	0	n/a	n/a	n/a

Note: n/a not available; Classifications range from one diamond (budget properties with basic amenities) to five diamond (luxury properties with the finest service, rooms and facilities).
Source: OAG, Business Travel Planner, Summer 1997

CONVENTION CENTERS

Major Convention Centers

Center Name	Meeting Rooms	Exhibit Space (sf)
Marketplace Design Center	4	20,000
Pennsylvania Convention Center	n/a	495,000
Philadelphia Civic Center	n/a	382,000
Sugarloaf-Albert M. Greenfield Conference Center	20	n/a
Wyndham Franklin Plaza	28	60,000

Note: n/a not available
Source: Trade Shows Worldwide 1997

Living Environment

COST OF LIVING

Cost of Living Index

Composite Index	Housing	Utilities	Groceries	Health Care	Trans- portation	Misc. Goods/ Services
122.5	140.0	169.8	109.0	102.8	119.2	107.1

Note: U.S. = 100
Source: ACCRA, Cost of Living Index, 3rd Quarter 1997

HOUSING

Median Home Prices and Housing Affordability

Area	Median Price[2] 3rd Qtr. 1997 ($)	HOI[3] 3rd Qtr. 1997	Afford- ability Rank[4]
MSA[1]	143,000	55.2	166
U.S.	127,000	63.7	–

Note: (1) Metropolitan Statistical Area - see Appendix A for areas included; (2) U.S. figures calculated from the sales of 625,000 new and existing homes in 195 markets; (3) Housing Opportunity Index - percent of homes sold that were within the reach of the median income household at the prevailing mortgage interest rate; (4) Rank is from 1-195 with 1 being most affordable
Source: National Association of Home Builders, Housing Opportunity Index, 3rd Quarter 1997

It is projected that the median price of existing single-family homes in the metro area will increase by 3.0% in 1998. Nationwide, home prices are projected to increase 6.6%. *Kiplinger's Personal Finance Magazine, January 1998*

Average New Home Price

Area	Price ($)
City	193,138
U.S.	135,710

Note: Figures are based on a new home with 1,800 sq. ft. of living area on an 8,000 sq. ft. lot.
Source: ACCRA, Cost of Living Index, 3rd Quarter 1997

Average Apartment Rent

Area	Rent ($/mth)
City	726
U.S.	569

Note: Figures are based on an unfurnished two bedroom, 1-1/2 or 2 bath apartment, approximately 950 sq. ft. in size, excluding all utilities except water
Source: ACCRA, Cost of Living Index, 3rd Quarter 1997

RESIDENTIAL UTILITIES

Average Residential Utility Costs

Area	All Electric ($/mth)	Part Electric ($/mth)	Other Energy ($/mth)	Phone ($/mth)
City	187.42	–	–	16.51
U.S.	109.40	55.25	43.64	19.48

Source: ACCRA, Cost of Living Index, 3rd Quarter 1997

HEALTH CARE

Average Health Care Costs

Area	Hospital ($/day)	Doctor ($/visit)	Dentist ($/visit)
City	447.00	47.50	61.25
U.S.	392.91	48.76	60.84

Note: Hospital - based on a semi-private room. Doctor - based on a general practitioner's routine exam of an established patient. Dentist - based on adult teeth cleaning and periodic oral exam.
Source: ACCRA, Cost of Living Index, 3rd Quarter 1997

Distribution of Office-Based Physicians

Area	Family/Gen. Practitioners	Specialists		
		Medical	Surgical	Other
MSA[1]	903	3,861	2,571	3,202

Note: Data as of 12/31/96; (1) Metropolitan Statistical Area - see Appendix A for areas included
Source: American Medical Assn., Physician Characteristics & Distribution in the U.S., 1997-1998

Hospitals

Philadelphia has 27 general medical and surgical hospitals, 3 psychiatric, 1 rehabilitation, 3 other specialty, 2 children's general, 3 children's other specialty. *AHA Guide to the Healthcare Field 1997-98*

According to *U.S. News and World Report,* Philadelphia has 7 of the best hospitals in the U.S.: **Hospital of the University of Pennsylvania**, noted for AIDS, cancer, cardiology, endocrinology, gastroenterology, geriatrics, gynecology, neurology, orthopedics, otolaryngology, pulmonology, rheumatology, urology; **Thomas Jefferson University Hospital**, noted for gynecology, orthopedics, rehabilitation; **Fox Chase Cancer Center**, noted for cancer; **Temple University Hospital**, noted for cardiology, endocrinology, neurology, otolaryngology, pulmonology, rheumatology; **Wills Eye Hospital**, noted for ophthalmology; **Children's Hospital of Philadelphia**, noted for pediatrics; **Albert Einstein Medical Center (Moss Rehab Hospital)**, noted for rehabilitation; *U.S. News and World Report, "America's Best Hospitals", 7/28/97*

Thomas Jefferson University Hospitals is among the 100 best-run hospitals in the U.S. *Modern Healthcare, January 5, 1998*

EDUCATION

Public School District Statistics

District Name	Num. Sch.	Enroll.	Classroom Teachers[1]	Pupils per Teacher	Minority Pupils (%)	Current Exp.[2] ($/pupil)
Philadelphia City SD	258	210,503	10,973	19.2	79.6	5,456

Note: Data covers the 1995-1996 school year unless otherwise noted; (1) Excludes teachers reported as working in school district offices rather than in schools; (2) Based on 1993-94 enrollment collected by the Census Bureau, not the enrollment figure shown in column 3; SD = School District; ISD = Independent School District; n/a not available
Source: National Center for Education Statistics, Common Core of Data Survey; Bureau of the Census

Educational Quality

School District	Education Quotient[1]	Graduate Outcome[2]	Community Index[3]	Resource Index[4]
Philadelphia City	64.0	52.0	54.0	87.0

Note: Nearly 1,000 secondary school districts were rated in terms of educational quality. The scores range from a low of 50 to a high of 150; (1) Average of the Graduate Outcome, Community and Resource indexes; (2) Based on graduation rates and college board scores (SAT/ACT); (3) Based on the surrounding community's average level of education and the area's average income level; (4) Based on teacher salaries, per-pupil expenditures and student-teacher ratios.
Source: Expansion Management, Ratings Issue 1997

Educational Attainment by Race

Area	High School Graduate (%)					Bachelor's Degree (%)				
	Total	White	Black	Other	Hisp.[2]	Total	White	Black	Other	Hisp.[2]
City	64.3	68.1	60.2	51.4	44.7	15.2	19.0	9.1	17.3	8.2
MSA[1]	75.9	79.2	63.8	62.6	51.8	22.8	25.2	10.9	26.5	11.7
U.S.	75.2	77.9	63.1	60.4	49.8	20.3	21.5	11.4	19.4	9.2

Note: figures shown cover persons 25 years old and over; (1) Metropolitan Statistical Area - see Appendix A for areas included; (2) people of Hispanic origin can be of any race
Source: 1990 Census of Population and Housing, Summary Tape File 3C

School Enrollment by Type

Area	Preprimary				Elementary/High School			
	Public		Private		Public		Private	
	Enrollment	%	Enrollment	%	Enrollment	%	Enrollment	%
City	13,314	55.4	10,702	44.6	179,728	70.8	74,032	29.2
MSA[1]	48,214	48.5	51,171	51.5	595,382	76.8	179,754	23.2
U.S.	2,679,029	59.5	1,824,256	40.5	38,379,689	90.2	4,187,099	9.8

Note: figures shown cover persons 3 years old and over;
(1) Metropolitan Statistical Area - see Appendix A for areas included
Source: 1990 Census of Population and Housing, Summary Tape File 3C

School Enrollment by Race

Area	Preprimary (%)				Elementary/High School (%)			
	White	Black	Other	Hisp.[1]	White	Black	Other	Hisp.[1]
City	49.3	44.6	6.0	4.7	41.6	48.6	9.8	8.4
MSA[2]	79.3	16.9	3.8	3.0	69.7	23.9	6.4	5.3
U.S.	80.4	12.5	7.1	7.8	74.1	15.6	10.3	12.5

Note: figures shown cover persons 3 years old and over; (1) people of Hispanic origin can be of any race; (2) Metropolitan Statistical Area - see Appendix A for areas included
Source: 1990 Census of Population and Housing, Summary Tape File 3C

SAT/ACT Scores

Area/District	1997 SAT				1997 ACT	
	Percent of Graduates Tested (%)	Average Math Score	Average Verbal Score	Average Combined Score	Percent of Graduates Tested (%)	Average Composite Score
Philadelphia	n/a	425	425	850	n/a	n/a
State	72	495	498	993	8	21.0
U.S.	42	511	505	1,016	36	21.0

Note: Math and verbal SAT scores are out of a possible 800; ACT scores are out of a possible 36
Caution: Comparing or ranking states/cities on the basis of SAT/ACT scores alone is invalid and strongly discouraged by the The College Board and The American College Testing Program as students who take the tests are self-selected and do not represent the entire student population.
Source: School District of Philadelphia, Office of Assessment & Accountability, 1997; College Board, 1997; American College Testing Program, 1997

Classroom Teacher Salaries in Public Schools

District	B.A. Degree		M.A. Degree		Ph.D. Degree	
	Min. ($)	Max ($)	Min. ($)	Max. ($)	Min. ($)	Max. ($)
Philadelphia	28,135	43,934	28,676	49,616	29,759	56,270
Average[1]	26,120	39,270	28,175	44,667	31,643	49,825

Note: Salaries are for 1996-1997; (1) Based on all school districts covered
Source: American Federation of Teachers (unpublished data)

Higher Education

Two-Year Colleges		Four-Year Colleges		Medical Schools	Law Schools	Voc/ Tech
Public	Private	Public	Private			
1	7	1	14	5	2	48

Source: College Blue Book, Occupational Education 1997; Medical School Admission Requirements, 1998-99; Peterson's Guide to Two-Year Colleges, 1997; Peterson's Guide to Four-Year Colleges, 1997; Barron's Guide to Law Schools 1997

MAJOR EMPLOYERS

Major Employers

Albert Einstein Medical Center	Children's Hospital of Philadelphia
Cigna Corp.	Episcopal Hospital
Graduate Hospital	Independence Blue Cross
Jeanes Hospital	Peco Energy Co.
Philadelphia Newspapers	Presbyterian Medical Center Foundation
Food Distribution Center	Southeastern Pennsylvania Transportation Authority
Crown Beverage Packaging	Reliance Insurance
Finishing Co. (demolition)	Questpoint (computer processing)
Federal Reserve Bank of Philadelphia	Aramark Corp. (eating places)
Tasty Baking Co.	

Note: companies listed are located in the city
Source: Dun's Business Rankings 1997; Ward's Business Directory, 1997

PUBLIC SAFETY

Crime Rate

Area	All Crimes	Violent Crimes				Property Crimes		
		Murder	Forcible Rape	Robbery	Aggrav. Assault	Burglary	Larceny -Theft	Motor Vehicle Theft
City	6,920.0	27.1	46.1	1,013.1	442.6	1,060.2	2,817.6	1,513.4
Suburbs[1]	3,613.2	2.7	21.1	130.0	225.8	586.1	2,223.5	423.9
MSA[2]	4,630.8	10.2	28.8	401.8	292.5	732.0	2,406.3	759.2
U.S.	5,078.9	7.4	36.1	202.4	388.2	943.0	2,975.9	525.9

Note: Crime rate is the number of crimes per 100,000 pop.; (1) defined as all areas within the MSA but located outside the central city; (2) Metropolitan Statistical Area - see Appendix A for areas incl.
Source: FBI Uniform Crime Reports 1996

RECREATION

Culture and Recreation

Museums	Symphony Orchestras	Opera Companies	Dance Companies	Professional Theatres	Zoos	Pro Sports Teams
40	2	3	3	8	1	4

Source: International Directory of the Performing Arts, 1996; Official Museum Directory, 1998; Chamber of Commerce/Economic Development 1997

Library System

The Free Library of Philadelphia has 49 branches, holdings of 6,687,777 volumes and a budget of $52,978,845 (1995-1996). *American Library Directory, 1997-1998*

MEDIA

Newspapers

Name	Type	Freq.	Distribution	Circulation
Al Dia	Hispanic	1x/wk	Local	29,000
Catholic Standard & Times	Religious	1x/wk	Area	71,962
Jewish Exponent	Religious	1x/wk	Local	65,000
The Leader	n/a	1x/wk	Local	29,000
Olney Times	General	1x/wk	Area	25,000
Philadelphia City Paper	n/a	1x/wk	Regional	109,000
Philadelphia Daily News	General	6x/wk	Area	180,000
Philadelphia Inquirer	General	7x/wk	Area	457,932
Philadelphia New Observer Newspaper	Black	1x/wk	Local	80,000
Philadelphia Tribune	Black	3x/wk	Area	126,000
Philadelphia Weekly	n/a	1x/wk	Area	114,200
Scoop U.S.A.	Black	1x/wk	Local	30,000
South Philadelphia Review-Chronicle	n/a	1x/wk	Local	76,300

Note: Includes newspapers with circulations of 25,000 or more located in the city; n/a not available
Source: Burrelle's Media Directory, 1998 Edition

AM Radio Stations

Call Letters	Freq. (kHz)	Target Audience	Station Format	Music Format
WFIL	560	General	E/M/N/S/T	Adult Contemporary/Christian/Easy Listening
WIP	610	General	S/T	n/a
WPHE	690	Hispanic	M/T	Spanish
WTEL	860	Hispanic	M	Adult Contemporary/Spanish
WZZD	990	Religious	M	Adult Contemporary/Christian
KYW	1060	General	N	n/a
WPHT	1210	General	T	n/a
WHAT	1340	Black/Relig	E/M/S/T	Christian
WDAS	1480	Black	M/N/S	n/a
WNWR	1540	General	E/M/T	Christian/Classical/Spanish

Note: Stations included broadcast in the Philadelphia metro area; n/a not available
Station Format: E = Educational; M = Music; N = News; S = Sports; T = Talk
Source: Burrelle's Media Directory, 1998 Edition

FM Radio Stations

Call Letters	Freq. (mHz)	Target Audience	Station Format	Music Format
WPEB	88.1	General	E/M/T	n/a
WXPN	88.5	General	M	Adult Contemporary
WRTI	90.1	General	E/M/N/S	Classical/Jazz
WHYY	90.9	General	N	n/a
WRTY	91.1	Black	E/M/N/S	Jazz
WRTX	91.7	General	E/M/N/S	Jazz
WKDU	91.7	General	M	n/a
WXTU	92.5	General	M/N/S	Country
WMMR	93.3	General	M/N/S	AOR/Classic Rock
WYSP	94.1	Men	M/S/T	AOR
WCHR	94.5	Religious	E/M/N/T	Christian
WRSD	94.9	n/a	M	Adult Contemporary
WXXM	95.7	General	M	Adult Contemporary
WOGL	98.1	General	M	Oldies
WUSL	98.9	Black	M	Urban Contemporary
WBEB	101.1	General	M	Adult Contemporary
WPHI	103.9	General	M	Urban Contemporary
WDAS	105.3	Black	E/M/N/S	Urban Contemporary

Note: Stations included broadcast in the Philadelphia metro area; n/a not available
Station Format: E = Educational; M = Music; N = News; S = Sports; T = Talk
Music Format: AOR = Album Oriented Rock; MOR = Middle-of-the-Road
Source: Burrelle's Media Directory, 1998 Edition

Television Stations

Name	Ch.	Affiliation	Type	Owner
KYW	3	CBS	Commercial	Westinghouse Broadcasting Company
WPVI	6	ABC	Commercial	ABC Inc.
WCAU	10	NBC	Commercial	General Electric Company
WHYY	12	PBS	Public	n/a
WPHL	17	WB	Commercial	Chicago Tribune
WTXF	29	Fox	Commercial	Fox Television Stations Inc.
WYBE	35	PBS	Public	Independence Public Media of Philadelphia Inc.
WGTW	48	n/a	Commercial	Brunson Communications
WPSG	57	UPN	Commercial	Paramount Stations Group
WTGI	61	n/a	Commercial	Paxson Communications Corporation

Note: Stations included broadcast in the Philadelphia metro area
Source: Burrelle's Media Directory, 1998 Edition

CLIMATE

Average and Extreme Temperatures

Temperature	Jan	Feb	Mar	Apr	May	Jun	Jul	Aug	Sep	Oct	Nov	Dec	Ann
Extreme High (°F)	74	74	85	94	96	100	104	101	100	89	84	72	104
Average High (°F)	39	42	51	63	73	82	86	85	78	67	55	43	64
Average Temp. (°F)	32	34	42	53	63	72	77	76	68	57	47	36	55
Average Low (°F)	24	26	33	43	53	62	67	66	59	47	38	28	45
Extreme Low (°F)	-7	-4	7	19	28	44	51	44	35	25	15	1	-7

Note: Figures cover the years 1948-1990
Source: National Climatic Data Center, International Station Meteorological Climate Summary, 3/95

Average Precipitation/Snowfall/Humidity

Precip./Humidity	Jan	Feb	Mar	Apr	May	Jun	Jul	Aug	Sep	Oct	Nov	Dec	Ann
Avg. Precip. (in.)	3.2	2.8	3.7	3.5	3.7	3.6	4.1	4.0	3.3	2.7	3.4	3.3	41.4
Avg. Snowfall (in.)	7	7	4	Tr	Tr	0	0	0	0	Tr	1	4	22
Avg. Rel. Hum. 7am (%)	74	73	73	72	75	77	80	82	84	83	79	75	77
Avg. Rel. Hum. 4pm (%)	60	55	51	48	51	52	54	55	55	54	57	60	54

Note: Figures cover the years 1948-1990; Tr = Trace amounts (<0.05 in. of rain; <0.5 in. of snow)
Source: National Climatic Data Center, International Station Meteorological Climate Summary, 3/95

Weather Conditions

Temperature			Daytime Sky			Precipitation		
10°F & below	32°F & below	90°F & above	Clear	Partly cloudy	Cloudy	0.01 inch or more precip.	0.1 inch or more snow/ice	Thunder-storms
5	94	23	81	146	138	117	14	27

Note: Figures are average number of days per year and covers the years 1948-1990
Source: National Climatic Data Center, International Station Meteorological Climate Summary, 3/95

AIR & WATER QUALITY

Maximum Pollutant Concentrations

	Particulate Matter (ug/m³)	Carbon Monoxide (ppm)	Sulfur Dioxide (ppm)	Nitrogen Dioxide (ppm)	Ozone (ppm)	Lead (ug/m³)
MSA[1] Level	356	6	0.063	0.034	0.13	0.76
NAAQS[2]	150	9	0.140	0.053	0.12	1.50
Met NAAQS?	No	Yes	Yes	Yes	No	Yes

Note: (1) Metropolitan Statistical Area - see Appendix A for areas included; (2) National Ambient Air Quality Standards; ppm = parts per million; ug/m³ = micrograms per cubic meter; n/a not available
Source: EPA, National Air Quality and Emissions Trends Report, 1996

Pollutant Standards Index

In the Philadelphia MSA (see Appendix A for areas included), the Pollutant Standards Index (PSI) exceeded 100 on 22 days in 1996. A PSI value greater than 100 indicates that air quality would be in the unhealthful range on that day. *EPA, National Air Quality and Emissions Trends Report, 1996*

Drinking Water

Water System Name	Pop. Served	Primary Water Source Type	Number of Violations in Fiscal Year 1997	Type of Violation/ Contaminants
Philadelphia Water Dept.	1,755,000	Surface	None	None

Note: Data as of January 16, 1998
Source: EPA, Office of Ground Water and Drinking Water, Safe Drinking Water Information System

Philadelphia tap water is slightly acid, moderately hard (Schuykill River), moderately soft (Delaware River); fluoridated.
Editor & Publisher Market Guide, 1998

Pittsburgh, Pennsylvania

Background

Pittsburgh was once the creaking, croaking, belching giant of heavy industry. Thanks to a plentiful supply of bituminous coal beds and limestone deposits nearby, the city had forged a prosperous economy based upon steel, glass, rubber, petroleum, and machinery. However, unregulated spews of soot into the air by these factories earned Pittsburgh the title of ''Smoky City''. To rid their city of such an objectionable name, concerned citizens and politicians passed smoke-control laws. Today, Pittsburgh's renaissance is a result of these people's unflagging faith in their city.

In the 18th century, the area in and around the Ohio Valley and the Allegheny River, where present day Pittsburgh lies, was claimed by both British and French flags. After being lobbed back and forth between the two, the land finally fell into British hands. The city was named Pittsborough, for the British Prime Minister at the time, William Pitt.

Almost immediately, the city showed signs of what it was to become. In 1792, the first blast furnace was built by George Anschulz. In 1797, the first glass factory was opened; and in 1804, the first cotton factory was opened. Irish, Scottish, and a smattering of English immigrants provided the labor pool for these factories. During the Civil War, this labor pool was augmented by a wave of German immigrants. Finally, during the late 19th century, Poles, Czechs, Slovaks, Italians, Russians, and Hungarians completed the picture in the colorful quilt of Pittsburgh's workforce. The last wave particularly contributed their sweat and toil to the fortunes of captains of industry such as Andrew Carnegie, Henry Clay Frick, and Charles M. Schwab.

Fortunately for the city, these industrialists gave back to the city in the form of their cultural and educational patronage. The Carnegie Institute is renowned for the Museum of Art and the Museum of Natural History. The Frick Art Museum is a noted private collection featuring such artists as Rubens, Tintoretto, Fragonard, and Boucher.

1997 found Pittsburgh at a crossroads of progress. High technology, health care services and high-tech health-care products manufacturers and financial institutions have become dominant forces behind a steadily diversifying economy. New Internet software and computer software companies have set up operations in or near Pittsburgh. In all 3,600 high-tech companies have created 100,000 jobs in the past 10 years. Real estate costs and crime rates are among the lowest of any large city in the country and the city is moving ahead with the expansion of the Convention Center and the construction of two downtown stadiums for the Pirates (baseball) and the Steelers (football). *New York Times 9/21/97*

The city is a little over 100 miles southeast of Lake Erie. Its nearness to the Great Lakes and to the Atlantic Seaboard helps to modify its humid continental type of climate. Winter is influenced primarily by Canadian air masses which are infrequently tempered by air from the Gulf of Mexico. During the summer Gulf air brings warm humid weather.

Once every four years the Monongahela and Ohio Rivers, which meet in Pittsburgh, combine to cause the Ohio River to reach the 25 foot flood stage. The 30-foot level which is more serious is reached much less often.

General Rankings and Evaluative Comments

- Pittsburgh was ranked #164 out of 300 cities by *Money's* 1997 "Survey of the Best Places to Live." Criteria used: health services, crime, economy, housing, education, transportation, weather, leisure and the arts. The city was ranked #149 in 1996 and #97 in 1995. *Money, July 1997; Money, September 1996; Money, September 1995*

- *Ladies Home Journal* ranked America's 200 largest cities based on the qualities women care about most. Pittsburgh ranked 7 out of 200. Criteria: low crime rate, good public schools, well-paying jobs, quality health and child care, the presence of women in government, proportion of women-owned businesses, size of the wage gap with men, local economy, divorce rates, the ratio of single men to single women, whether there are laws that require at least the same number of public toilets for women as men, and the probability of good hair days. *Ladies Home Journal, November 1997*

- Pittsburgh is among "The Best Places to Raise a Family". Rank: 5 out of 301 metro areas. Criteria: low crime rate, low drug and alcohol abuse, good public schools, high-quality health care, a clean environment, affordable cost of living and strong economic growth.

  "This is the city that got its face dirty helping build the rest of the country, then cleaned itself up in a spectacular renaissance 30 years ago. Today, skyscrapers soar above three rivers flowing amid green hills.

  Among our top ten places to raise a family, the Pittsburgh area had the lowest property- and violent-crime rate...." Pittsburgh's medical facilities, museums, sports attractions and schools are considered quite good. *Reader's Digest, April 1997*

- Pittsburgh was ranked #142 out of 219 cities in terms of children's health, safety, and economic well-being. Criteria: total population, percent population change, birth rate, child immunization rate, infant mortality rate, percent low birth weight infants, percent of births to teens, physician-to-population ratio, student-to-teacher ratio, dropout rate, unemployment rate, median family income, percent of children in poverty, violent and property crime rates, number of juvenile arrests for violent crimes as a percent of the total crime index, number of days with pollution standard index (PSI) over 100, pounds toxic releases per 1,000 people and number of superfund sites. *Zero Population Growth, Children's Environmental Index 1997*

- *Yahoo! Internet Life* selected "America's 100 Most Wired Cities & Towns". 50 cities were large and 50 cities were small. Pittsburgh ranked 14 out of 50 large cities. Criteria: Internet users per capita, number of networked computers, number of registered domain names, Internet backbone traffic, and the per-capita number of Web sites devoted to each city. *Yahoo! Internet Life, March 1998*

- University of Pittsburgh Medical Center, headquartered in Pittsburgh, is among the "100 Best Companies for Working Mothers." Criteria: pay compared with competition, opportunities for women to advance, support for child care, flexible work schedules and family-friendly benefits. *Working Mother, October 1997*

- According to *Working Mother,* "The situation in this state is a mixed bag: Ratios and training requirements are quite good, but child care centers and family child care homes rarely get surprise inspection visits, and there's no statewide resource & referral (R&R) system to help parents find care. But change is in the works. The state is using some of its federal money to create an R&R network this year, and legislation is pending to require unannounced inspections. Both would be welcome developments.

  As we went to press, parents and child advocates here were responding to Governor Tom Ridge's latest budget proposal. He says he's made the largest-ever increase in child care funds—$68 million. But nearly all of that is federal money, the governor allotted only $1 million in new state funds for child care aid to parents in low-income jobs. Meanwhile, 11,700 children needing subsidized care are on a waiting list, and the state has a budget surplus of nearly $500 million!" *Working Mother, July/August 1997*

Business Environment

STATE ECONOMY

State Economic Profile

"Pennsylvania's economy is steadily improving....The revival is broad-based, with Pennsylvania's largest industries—services, retail trade, and manufacturing, all improving....

Last year, Pennsylvania lowered its business costs by enacting several business tax cuts and reforming the workers compensation system. This year, a healthy fiscal situation in Pennsylvania has led to a state budget that includes a 3.7% increase in state spending during fiscal 1998 and another $167 million in tax cuts.

Philadelphia's convention center has created an estimated 6,200 jobs and significantly boosted the hotel and retail markets in the metro area since it opened in 1993. For Philadelphia's hotels, the convention center has meant more business, with the occupancy rate increasing to 70% from 64% prior to the convention center's opening. Because of strong demand, at least four more hotel projects are planned for downtown Philadelphia. A one-half percent sales tax increase will be used to partially finance the expansion of Pittsburgh's convention center. If approved, the $300 million project will significantly expand the center's exhibit, meeting and parking space, while also adding over 50 hotel rooms.

A relatively high rate of consumer spending (retail sales grew by 9% in Pennsylvania and by only 5% in the U.S. last year), in combination with below average income growth, is leading to surging personal bankruptcy filings in pennsylvania. Personal bankruptcy filings increased by 44% in the state last year, compared to 29% at the national level.

With a high cost of doing business, poor demographic trends, and strong union activity, Pennsylvania will have difficulty attracting new and growing industries to replace its aging manufacturers. Pennsylvania will underperform the nation in both the near and long term." *National Association of Realtors, Economic Profiles: The Fifty States, July 1997*

IMPORTS/EXPORTS

Total Export Sales

Area	1993 ($000)	1994 ($000)	1995 ($000)	1996 ($000)	% Chg. 1993-96	% Chg. 1995-96
MSA[1]	2,989,745	3,150,610	3,982,169	3,933,687	31.6	-1.2
U.S.	464,858,354	512,415,609	583,030,524	622,827,063	34.0	6.8

Note: (1) Metropolitan Statistical Area - see Appendix A for areas included
Source: U.S. Department of Commerce, International Trade Association, Metropolitan Area Exports: An Export Performance Report on Over 250 U.S. Cities, October 1997

Imports/Exports by Port

Type	Cargo Value			Share of U.S. Total	
	1995 (US$mil.)	1996 (US$mil.)	% Change 1995-1996	1995 (%)	1996 (%)
Imports	0	0	0	0	0
Exports	0	0	0	0	0

Source: Global Trade Information Services, WaterBorne Trade Atlas 1997

CITY FINANCES

City Government Finances

Component	FY92 ($000)	FY92 (per capita $)
Revenue	406,994	1,112.32
Expenditure	428,721	1,171.70
Debt Outstanding	660,819	1,806.03
Cash & Securities	399,269	1,091.21

Source: U.S. Bureau of the Census, City Government Finances: 1991-92

City Government Revenue by Source

Source	FY92 ($000)	FY92 (per capita $)	FY92 (%)
From Federal Government	20,818	56.90	5.1
From State Governments	21,444	58.61	5.3
From Local Governments	48,331	132.09	11.9
Property Taxes	121,850	333.02	29.9
General Sales Taxes	0	0.00	0.0
Selective Sales Taxes	29,155	79.68	7.2
Income Taxes	36,625	100.10	9.0
Current Charges	12,361	33.78	3.0
Utility/Liquor Store	0	0.00	0.0
Employee Retirement[1]	33,792	92.35	8.3
Other	82,618	225.80	20.3

Note: (1) Excludes "city contributions," classified as "nonrevenue," intragovernmental transfers.
Source: U.S. Bureau of the Census, City Government Finances: 1991-92

City Government Expenditures by Function

Function	FY92 ($000)	FY92 (per capita $)	FY92 (%)
Educational Services	5,708	15.60	1.3
Employee Retirement[1]	33,864	92.55	7.9
Environment/Housing	64,532	176.37	15.1
Government Administration	29,821	81.50	7.0
Interest on General Debt	44,618	121.94	10.4
Public Safety	102,810	280.98	24.0
Social Services	7,147	19.53	1.7
Transportation	21,694	59.29	5.1
Utility/Liquor Store	16,232	44.36	3.8
Other	102,295	279.57	23.9

Note: (1) Payments to beneficiaries including withdrawal of contributions.
Source: U.S. Bureau of the Census, City Government Finances: 1991-92

Municipal Bond Ratings

Area	Moody's	S & P
Pittsburgh	Baa1	BBB

Note: n/a not available; n/r not rated
Source: Moody's Bond Record, 2/98; Statistical Abstract of the U.S., 1997; Governing Magazine, 9/97, 3/98

POPULATION

Population Growth

Area	1980	1990	% Chg. 1980-90	July 1996 Estimate	% Chg. 1990-96
City	423,938	369,879	-12.8	350,363	-5.3
MSA[1]	2,218,870	2,056,705	-7.3	2,379,411	15.7
U.S.	226,545,805	248,765,170	9.8	265,179,411	6.6

Note: (1) Metropolitan Statistical Area - see Appendix A for areas included
Source: 1980/1990 Census of Housing and Population, Summary Tape File 3C; Census Bureau Population Estimates

Population Characteristics

Race	City					MSA[1]	
	1980		1990		% Chg. 1980-90	1990	
	Population	%	Population	%		Population	%
White	318,287	75.1	266,636	72.1	-16.2	1,867,837	90.8
Black	101,549	24.0	95,635	25.9	-5.8	168,568	8.2
Amer Indian/Esk/Aleut	584	0.1	662	0.2	13.4	2,161	0.1
Asian/Pacific Islander	2,818	0.7	5,780	1.6	105.1	14,766	0.7
Other	700	0.2	1,166	0.3	66.6	3,373	0.2
Hispanic Origin[2]	3,196	0.8	3,415	0.9	6.9	10,451	0.5

Note: (1) Metropolitan Statistical Area - see Appendix A for areas included; (2) people of Hispanic origin can be of any race
Source: 1980/1990 Census of Housing and Population, Summary Tape File 3C

Ancestry

Area	German	Irish	English	Italian	U.S.	French	Polish	Dutch
City	25.4	17.8	5.9	12.4	1.5	1.5	9.5	0.6
MSA[1]	33.6	20.0	11.1	15.4	1.8	2.2	10.0	1.8
U.S.	23.3	15.6	13.1	5.9	5.3	4.2	3.8	2.5

Note: Figures are percentages and include persons that reported multiple ancestry (eg. if a person reported being Irish and Italian, they were included in both columns); (1) Metropolitan Statistical Area - see Appendix A for areas included
Source: 1990 Census of Population and Housing, Summary Tape File 3C

Age

Area	Median Age (Years)	Age Distribution (%)						
		Under 5	Under 18	18-24	25-44	45-64	65+	80+
City	34.5	6.1	19.9	13.7	30.3	18.2	17.9	3.9
MSA[1]	36.9	6.2	21.7	9.2	30.6	21.0	17.4	3.5
U.S.	32.9	7.3	25.6	10.5	32.6	18.7	12.5	2.8

Note: (1) Metropolitan Statistical Area - see Appendix A for areas included
Source: 1990 Census of Population and Housing, Summary Tape File 3C

Male/Female Ratio

Area	Number of males per 100 females (all ages)	Number of males per 100 females (18 years old+)
City	86.8	82.9
MSA[1]	89.4	85.5
U.S.	95.0	91.9

Note: (1) Metropolitan Statistical Area - see Appendix A for areas included
Source: 1990 Census of Population, General Population Characteristics

INCOME

Per Capita/Median/Average Income

Area	Per Capita ($)	Median Household ($)	Average Household ($)
City	12,580	20,747	29,587
MSA[1]	14,052	26,700	34,902
U.S.	14,420	30,056	38,453

Note: all figures are for 1989; (1) Metropolitan Statistical Area - see Appendix A for areas included
Source: 1990 Census of Population and Housing, Summary Tape File 3C

Household Income Distribution by Race

Income ($)	City (%)					U.S. (%)				
	Total	White	Black	Other	Hisp.[1]	Total	White	Black	Other	Hisp.[1]
Less than 5,000	10.9	7.3	21.3	24.6	12.7	6.2	4.8	15.2	8.6	8.8
5,000 - 9,999	15.9	13.9	22.5	13.1	11.0	9.3	8.6	14.2	9.9	11.1
10,000 - 14,999	11.5	11.3	11.9	13.1	14.8	8.8	8.5	11.0	9.8	11.0
15,000 - 24,999	19.2	19.8	17.5	18.1	16.2	17.5	17.3	18.9	18.5	20.5
25,000 - 34,999	14.8	15.9	11.5	12.6	16.5	15.8	16.1	14.2	15.4	16.4
35,000 - 49,999	13.3	14.8	9.0	7.3	15.1	17.9	18.6	13.3	16.1	16.0
50,000 - 74,999	8.9	10.3	4.7	6.1	7.9	15.0	15.8	9.3	13.4	11.1
75,000 - 99,999	2.6	3.1	1.0	1.3	3.3	5.1	5.5	2.6	4.7	3.1
100,000+	2.9	3.6	0.7	3.7	2.5	4.4	4.8	1.3	3.7	1.9

Note: all figures are for 1989; (1) people of Hispanic origin can be of any race
Source: 1990 Census of Population and Housing, Summary Tape File 3C

Effective Buying Income

Area	Per Capita ($)	Median Household ($)	Average Household ($)
City	15,660	26,111	37,231
MSA[1]	17,668	34,352	43,998
U.S.	15,444	33,201	41,849

Note: data as of 1/1/97; (1) Metropolitan Statistical Area - see Appendix A for areas included
Source: Standard Rate & Data Service, Newspaper Advertising Source, 2/98

Effective Household Buying Income Distribution

Area	% of Households Earning						
	$10,000 -$19,999	$20,000 -$34,999	$35,000 -$49,999	$50,000 -$74,999	$75,000 -$99,000	$100,000 -$124,999	$125,000 and up
City	20.8	22.4	15.2	13.2	4.9	1.6	2.5
MSA[1]	16.8	22.3	17.7	18.5	7.6	2.6	2.8
U.S.	16.5	23.4	18.3	18.2	6.4	2.1	2.4

Note: data as of 1/1/97; (1) Metropolitan Statistical Area - see Appendix A for areas included
Source: Standard Rate & Data Service, Newspaper Advertising Source, 2/98

Poverty Rates by Race and Age

Area	Total (%)	By Race (%)				By Age (%)		
		White	Black	Other	Hisp.[2]	Under 5 years old	Under 18 years old	65 years and over
City	21.4	14.0	40.9	38.1	23.6	37.0	32.5	14.4
MSA[1]	12.2	10.0	35.9	23.2	19.4	20.4	17.9	10.5
U.S.	13.1	9.8	29.5	23.1	25.3	20.1	18.3	12.8

Note: figures show the percent of people living below the poverty line in 1989. The average poverty threshold was $12,674 for a family of four in 1989; (1) Metropolitan Statistical Area - see Appendix A for areas included; (2) people of Hispanic origin can be of any race
Source: 1990 Census of Population and Housing, Summary Tape File 3C

EMPLOYMENT

Labor Force and Employment

Area	Civilian Labor Force			Workers Employed		
	Dec. '95	Dec. '96	% Chg.	Dec. '95	Dec. '96	% Chg.
City	163,794	164,810	0.6	157,253	158,320	0.7
MSA[1]	1,151,704	1,159,657	0.7	1,104,770	1,112,270	0.7
U.S.	134,583,000	136,742,000	1.6	127,903,000	130,785,000	2.3

Note: Data is not seasonally adjusted and covers workers 16 years of age and older; (1) Metropolitan Statistical Area - see Appendix A for areas included
Source: Bureau of Labor Statistics, http://stats.bls.gov

Unemployment Rate

Area	1997											
	Jan.	Feb.	Mar.	Apr.	May	Jun.	Jul.	Aug.	Sep.	Oct.	Nov.	Dec.
City	4.8	4.9	4.9	5.1	5.4	5.2	5.4	5.1	5.1	4.5	4.3	3.9
MSA[1]	5.2	5.3	5.2	5.0	5.1	5.1	5.1	4.8	4.7	4.0	4.3	4.1
U.S.	5.9	5.7	5.5	4.8	4.7	5.2	5.0	4.8	4.7	4.4	4.3	4.4

Note: Data is not seasonally adjusted and covers workers 16 years of age and older; All figures are percentages; (1) Metropolitan Statistical Area - see Appendix A for areas included
Source: Bureau of Labor Statistics, http://stats.bls.gov

Employment by Industry

Sector	MSA[1]		U.S.
	Number of Employees	Percent of Total	Percent of Total
Services	370,200	34.1	29.0
Retail Trade	207,000	19.1	18.5
Government	128,900	11.9	16.1
Manufacturing	138,700	12.8	15.0
Finance/Insurance/Real Estate	62,400	5.8	5.7
Wholesale Trade	58,300	5.4	5.4
Transportation/Public Utilities	66,000	6.1	5.3
Construction	48,700	4.5	4.5
Mining	4,700	0.4	0.5

Note: Figures cover non-farm employment as of 12/97 and are not seasonally adjusted; (1) Metropolitan Statistical Area - see Appendix A for areas included
Source: Bureau of Labor Statistics, http://stats.bls.gov

Employment by Occupation

Occupation Category	City (%)	MSA[1] (%)	U.S. (%)
White Collar	63.3	61.9	58.1
Executive/Admin./Management	10.4	12.2	12.3
Professional	17.8	15.7	14.1
Technical & Related Support	4.9	4.3	3.7
Sales	10.6	12.6	11.8
Administrative Support/Clerical	19.7	17.1	16.3
Blue Collar	17.7	23.1	26.2
Precision Production/Craft/Repair	7.4	10.4	11.3
Machine Operators/Assem./Insp.	3.6	4.6	6.8
Transportation/Material Movers	3.3	4.0	4.1
Cleaners/Helpers/Laborers	3.5	4.0	3.9
Services	18.5	14.1	13.2
Farming/Forestry/Fishing	0.5	0.9	2.5

Note: figures cover employed persons 16 years old and over; (1) Metropolitan Statistical Area - see Appendix A for areas included
Source: 1990 Census of Population and Housing, Summary Tape File 3C

Occupational Employment Projections: 1994 - 2005

Occupations Expected to have the Largest Job Growth (ranked by numerical growth)	Fast-Growing Occupations (ranked by percent growth)
1. Registered nurses	1. Electronic pagination systems workers
2. Systems analysts	2. Personal and home care aides
3. Waiters & waitresses	3. Systems analysts
4. Cashiers	4. Computer engineers
5. Salespersons, retail	5. Home health aides
6. Nursing aides/orderlies/attendants	6. Human services workers
7. Teachers aides, clerical & paraprofess.	7. Computer scientists
8. General managers & top executives	8. Manicurists
9. Home health aides	9. Physical therapists
10. Child care workers, private household	10. Residential counselors

Projections cover Pennsylvania.
Source: U.S. Department of Labor, Employment and Training Administration, America's Labor Market Information System (ALMIS)

Average Wages

Occupation	Wage	Occupation	Wage
Professional/Technical/Clerical	$/Week	**Health/Protective Services**	$/Week
Accountants III	790	Corrections Officers	581
Attorneys III	1,194	Firefighters	741
Budget Analysts III	-	Nurses, Licensed Practical II	-
Buyers/Contracting Specialists II	650	Nurses, Registered II	-
Clerks, Accounting III	437	Nursing Assistants II	-
Clerks, General III	400	Police Officers I	710
Computer Operators II	403	**Hourly Workers**	$/Hour
Computer Programmers II	597	Forklift Operators	12.62
Drafters II	-	General Maintenance Workers	10.52
Engineering Technicians III	644	Guards I	6.02
Engineering Technicians, Civil III	-	Janitors	7.98
Engineers III	909	Maintenance Electricians	16.49
Key Entry Operators I	322	Maintenance Electronics Techs II	16.22
Personnel Assistants III	-	Maintenance Machinists	16.69
Personnel Specialists III	756	Maintenance Mechanics, Machinery	15.59
Secretaries III	530	Material Handling Laborers	12.19
Switchboard Operator-Receptionist	319	Motor Vehicle Mechanics	16.61
Systems Analysts II	894	Shipping/Receiving Clerks	-
Systems Analysts Supervisor/Mgr II	1,321	Tool and Die Makers	19.66
Tax Collectors II	555	Truckdrivers, Tractor Trailer	15.68
Word Processors II	-	Warehouse Specialists	10.55

Note: Wage data includes full-time workers only for 5/96 and cover the Metropolitan Statistical Area (see Appendix A for areas included). Dashes indicate that data was not available.
Source: Bureau of Labor Statistics, Occupational Compensation Survey, 10/96

TAXES

Major State and Local Tax Rates

State Corp. Income (%)	State Personal Income (%)	Residential Property (effective rate per $100)	Sales & Use State (%)	Sales & Use Local (%)	State Gasoline (cents/ gallon)	State Cigarette (cents/ 20-pack)
9.99	2.8	n/a	6.0	1.0	25.9[a]	31

Note: Personal/corporate income tax rates as of 1/97. Sales, gasoline and cigarette tax rates as of 1/98; (a) Rate is comprised of 12 cents excise and 13.9 cent motor carrier tax
Source: Federation of Tax Administrators, www.taxadmin.org; Washington D.C. Department of Finance and Revenue, Tax Rates and Tax Burdens in the District of Columbia: A Nationwide Comparison, June 1997; Chamber of Commerce

Total Taxes Per Capita and as a Percent of Income

Area	Per Capita Income ($)	Per Capita Taxes ($)			Taxes as Pct. of Income (%)		
		Total	Federal	State/ Local	Total	Federal	State/ Local
Pennsylvania	26,194	9,229	6,216	3,013	35.2	23.7	11.5
U.S.	26,187	9,205	6,127	3,078	35.2	23.4	11.8

Note: Figures are for 1997
Source: Tax Foundation, Web Site, www.taxfoundation.org

Estimated Tax Burden

Area	State Income	Local Income	Property	Sales	Total
Pittsburgh	1,820	1,869	5,400	595	9,684

Note: The numbers are estimates of taxes paid by a married couple with two kids and annual earnings of $65,000. Sales tax estimates assume they spend average amounts on food, clothing, household goods and gasoline. Property tax estimates assume they live in a $225,000 home.
Source: Kiplinger's Personal Finance Magazine, June 1997

COMMERCIAL REAL ESTATE

Office Market

Class/ Location	Total Space (sq. ft.)	Vacant Space (sq. ft.)	Vac. Rate (%)	Under Constr. (sq. ft.)	Net Absorp. (sq. ft.)	Rental Rates ($/sq.ft./yr.)
Class A						
CBD	14,149,919	1,150,583	8.1	n/a	236,987	14.00-35.00
Outside CBD	7,894,024	1,015,123	12.9	n/a	255,648	13.50-25.00
Class B						
CBD	2,472,927	377,614	15.3	n/a	-89,210	12.00-18.00
Outside CBD	7,312,817	982,336	13.4	n/a	51,417	7.00-17.00

Note: Data as of 10/97 and covers Pittsburgh; CBD = Central Business District; n/a not available;
Source: Society of Industrial and Office Realtors, 1998 Comparative Statistics of Industrial and Office Real Estate Markets

"The near term for the Pittsburgh market is for a continued slow and steady expansion. Overall employment growth in the market has lagged behind the national pace for the last four years. This will probably be the case during 1998 as well. Net absorption is anticipated to increase slightly during 1998, leading to a modest drop in vacancy rates. With Class 'A' vacancy rates in the single digit range inside the CBD, there will be some upward pressure on rental rates. Construction is expected to pick up during 1998, though not in the Golden Triangle downtown. The most likely areas for new office construction are along the I-79 Corridor to the north and south of the CBD." *Society of Industrial and Office Realtors, 1998 Comparative Statistics of Industrial and Office Real Estate Markets*

Industrial Market

Location	Total Space (sq. ft.)	Vacant Space (sq. ft.)	Vac. Rate (%)	Under Constr. (sq. ft.)	Net Absorp. (sq. ft.)	Gross Lease ($/sq.ft./yr.)
Central City	n/a	n/a	n/a	n/a	n/a	3.00-4.50
Suburban	33,550,000	4,970,000	14.8	700,000	2,587,000	3.25-4.25

Note: Data as of 10/97 and covers Pittsburgh; n/a not available
Source: Society of Industrial and Office Realtors, 1998 Comparative Statistics of Industrial and Office Real Estate Markets

"Due to the lack of supply, speculative development should increase in 1998, especially north and south of the city. The local economy is being led by high-tech and light manufacturing companies. The area's excellent access to large markets and extensive transportation network are some of its greatest assets to industrial users. Absorption is expected to retreat from the high levels observed in 1997. This will relieve some of the pressure in the market but lease prices will still increase slightly. Sales prices and site prices are both expected to increase between six and ten percent during 1998." *Society of Industrial and Office Realtors, 1998 Comparative Statistics of Industrial and Office Real Estate Markets*

COMMERCIAL UTILITIES

Typical Monthly Electric Bills

Area	Commercial Service ($/month)		Industrial Service ($/month)	
	12 kW demand 1,500 kWh	100 kW demand 30,000 kWh	1,000 kW demand 400,000 kWh	20,000 kW demand 10,000,000 kWh
City	314	2,905	29,029	567,605
U.S.	162	2,360	25,590	545,677

Note: Based on rates in effect July 1, 1997
Source: Edison Electric Institute, Typical Residential, Commercial and Industrial Bills, Summer 1997

TRANSPORTATION

Transportation Statistics

Avg. travel time to work (min.)	21.1
Interstate highways	I-70; I-76; I-79
Bus lines	
In-city	Port Authority of Allegheny County, 1,063 vehicles
Inter-city	11
Passenger air service	
Airport	Pittsburgh International Airport
Airlines	8
Aircraft departures	147,812 (1995)
Enplaned passengers	9,209,903 (1995)
Rail service	Amtrak; Tramway/Light Rail
Motor freight carriers	163
Major waterways/ports	Port of Pittsburgh

Source: OAG, Business Travel Planner, Summer 1997; Editor & Publisher Market Guide, 1998; FAA Airport Activity Statistics, 1996; Amtrak National Time Table, Northeast Timetable, Fall/Winter 1997-98; 1990 Census of Population and Housing, STF 3C; Chamber of Commerce/Economic Development 1997; Jane's Urban Transport Systems 1997-98; Transit Fact Book 1997

A survey of 90,000 airline passengers during the first half of 1997 ranked most of the largest airports in the U.S. Pittsburgh International ranked number 2 out of 36. Criteria: cleanliness, quality of restaurants, attractiveness, speed of baggage delivery, ease of reaching gates, available ground transportation, ease of following signs and closeness of parking. *Plog Research Inc., First Half 1997*

Means of Transportation to Work

Area	Car/Truck/Van		Public Transportation			Bicycle	Walked	Other Means	Worked at Home
	Drove Alone	Car-pooled	Bus	Subway	Railroad				
City	48.9	13.5	21.1	0.3	0.0	0.4	12.6	1.3	1.8
MSA[1]	70.7	12.9	7.7	0.2	0.0	0.1	5.1	1.1	2.1
U.S.	73.2	13.4	3.0	1.5	0.5	0.4	3.9	1.2	3.0

Note: figures shown are percentages and only include workers 16 years old and over;
(1) Metropolitan Statistical Area - see Appendix A for areas included
Source: 1990 Census of Population and Housing, Summary Tape File 3C

BUSINESSES

Major Business Headquarters

Company Name	1997 Rankings	
	Fortune 500	Forbes 500
Alcoa	97	-
Allegheny Teledyne	359	-
Consolidated Natural Gas	360	-
Dick Corp	-	390
Giant Eagle	-	36
H.J. Heinz	161	-
Mellon Bank	299	-
PNC Bank Corp.	228	-
PPG Industries	199	-
USX-Marathon Group	42	-
Wesco Distribution	-	57
Westinghouse Electric	156	-

Note: Companies listed are located in the city; Dashes indicate no ranking
Fortune 500: companies that produce a 10-K are ranked 1 - 500 based on 1996 revenue
Forbes 500: private companies are ranked 1 - 500 based on 1996 revenue
Source: Forbes 12/1/97; Fortune 4/28/97

Fast-Growing Businesses

Pittsburgh was ranked #19 out of 24 (#1 is best) in terms of the best-performing local stocks in 1996 according to the Money/Norby Cities Index. The index measures stocks of companies that have headquarters in 24 metro areas. *Money, 2/7/97*

Women-Owned Businesses: Number, Employment, Sales and Share

Area	Women-Owned Businesses in 1996				Share of Women-Owned Businesses in 1996	
	Number	Employment	Sales ($000)	Rank[2]	Percent (%)	Rank[3]
MSA[1]	54,800	141,800	17,619,900	29	31.7	50

Note: (1) Metropolitan Statistical Area - see Appendix A for areas included; (2) Calculated on an averaging of number of businesses, employment and sales and ranges from 1 to 50 where 1 is best; (3) Ranges from 1 to 50 where 1 is best
Source: The National Foundation for Women Business Owners, 1996 Facts on Women-Owned Businesses: Trends in the Top 50 Metropolitan Areas, March 26, 1997

Women-Owned Businesses: Growth

Area	Growth in Women-Owned Businesses (% change from 1987 to 1996)				Relative Growth in the Number of Women-Owned and All Businesses (% change from 1987 to 1996)			
	Num.	Empl.	Sales	Rank[2]	Women-Owned	All Firms	Absolute Difference	Relative Difference
MSA[1]	68.6	152.9	222.8	41	68.6	47.1	21.5	1.5:1

Note: (1) Metropolitan Statistical Area - see Appendix A for areas included; (2) Calculated on an averaging of the percent growth of number of businesses, employment and sales and ranges from 1 to 50 where 1 is best
Source: The National Foundation for Women Business Owners, 1996 Facts on Women-Owned Businesses: Trends in the Top 50 Metropolitan Areas, March 26, 1997

Small Business Opportunity

According to *Forbes*, Pittsburgh is home to one of America's 200 best small companies: Respironics. Criteria: companies must be publicly traded, U.S.-based corporations with latest 12-month sales of between $5 and $350 million. Earnings must be at least $1 million for the 12-month period. Limited partnerships, REITs and closed-end mutual funds were not considered. Banks, S&Ls and electric utilities were not included. *Forbes, November 3, 1997*

HOTELS & MOTELS

Hotels/Motels

Area	Hotels/ Motels	Rooms	Luxury-Level Hotels/Motels		Average Minimum Rates ($)		
			♦♦♦♦	♦♦♦♦♦	♦♦	♦♦♦	♦♦♦♦
City	25	6,048	2	0	81	116	157
Airport	9	1,436	0	0	n/a	n/a	n/a
Suburbs	19	2,281	0	0	n/a	n/a	n/a
Total	53	9,765	2	0	n/a	n/a	n/a

Note: n/a not available; Classifications range from one diamond (budget properties with basic amenities) to five diamond (luxury properties with the finest service, rooms and facilities).
Source: OAG, Business Travel Planner, Summer 1997

CONVENTION CENTERS

Major Convention Centers

Center Name	Meeting Rooms	Exhibit Space (sf)
David L. Lawrence Convention Center	25	131,000
Expomart Radisson	22	106,000
Pittsburgh Civic Arena	5	n/a

Note: n/a not available
Source: Trade Shows Worldwide 1997

Living Environment

COST OF LIVING

Cost of Living Index

Composite Index	Housing	Utilities	Groceries	Health Care	Trans-portation	Misc. Goods/ Services
108.4	111.0	132.5	102.6	98.8	112.6	103.8

Note: U.S. = 100
Source: ACCRA, Cost of Living Index, 1st Quarter 1997

HOUSING

Median Home Prices and Housing Affordability

Area	Median Price[2] 3rd Qtr. 1997 ($)	HOI[3] 3rd Qtr. 1997	Afford-ability Rank[4]
MSA[1]	92,000	60.3	145
U.S.	127,000	63.7	–

Note: (1) Metropolitan Statistical Area - see Appendix A for areas included; (2) U.S. figures calculated from the sales of 625,000 new and existing homes in 195 markets; (3) Housing Opportunity Index - percent of homes sold that were within the reach of the median income household at the prevailing mortgage interest rate; (4) Rank is from 1-195 with 1 being most affordable
Source: National Association of Home Builders, Housing Opportunity Index, 3rd Quarter 1997

It is projected that the median price of existing single-family homes in the metro area will increase by 5.6% in 1998. Nationwide, home prices are projected to increase 6.6%. *Kiplinger's Personal Finance Magazine, January 1998*

Average New Home Price

Area	Price ($)
City	151,450
U.S.	133,782

Note: Figures are based on a new home with 1,800 sq. ft. of living area on an 8,000 sq. ft. lot.
Source: ACCRA, Cost of Living Index, 1st Quarter 1997

Average Apartment Rent

Area	Rent ($/mth)
City	598
U.S.	563

Note: Figures are based on an unfurnished two bedroom, 1-1/2 or 2 bath apartment, approximately 950 sq. ft. in size, excluding all utilities except water
Source: ACCRA, Cost of Living Index, 1st Quarter 1997

RESIDENTIAL UTILITIES

Average Residential Utility Costs

Area	All Electric ($/mth)	Part Electric ($/mth)	Other Energy ($/mth)	Phone ($/mth)
City	–	80.62	62.61	20.13
U.S.	110.19	56.83	45.14	19.36

Source: ACCRA, Cost of Living Index, 1st Quarter 1997

HEALTH CARE

Average Health Care Costs

Area	Hospital ($/day)	Doctor ($/visit)	Dentist ($/visit)
City	518.33	36.60	60.60
U.S.	385.60	47.34	59.26

Note: Hospital - based on a semi-private room. Doctor - based on a general practitioner's routine exam of an established patient. Dentist - based on adult teeth cleaning and periodic oral exam.
Source: ACCRA, Cost of Living Index, 1st Quarter 1997

Distribution of Office-Based Physicians

Area	Family/Gen. Practitioners	Specialists		
		Medical	Surgical	Other
MSA[1]	577	1,721	1,265	1,403

Note: Data as of 12/31/96; (1) Metropolitan Statistical Area - see Appendix A for areas included
Source: American Medical Assn., Physician Characteristics & Distribution in the U.S., 1997-1998

Hospitals

Pittsburgh has 16 general medical and surgical hospitals, 1 psychiatric, 1 obstetrics and gynecology, 2 rehabilitation, 1 prison hospital, 2 other specialty, 1 children's general, 1 children's psychiatric, 1 children's other specialty. *AHA Guide to the Healthcare Field 1997-98*

According to *U.S. News and World Report,* Pittsburgh has 4 of the best hospitals in the U.S.: **University of Pittsburgh Medical Center**, noted for gastroenterology, neurology, orthopedics, otolaryngology, pulmonology, rheumatology; **Children's Hospital of Pittsburgh**, noted for pediatrics; **Allegheny General Hospital**, noted for cancer, gastroenterology, geriatrics, neurology, orthopedics, otolaryngology; **Magee-Womens Hospital**, noted for gynecology; *U.S. News and World Report, "America's Best Hospitals", 7/28/97*

EDUCATION

Public School District Statistics

District Name	Num. Sch.	Enroll.	Classroom Teachers[1]	Pupils per Teacher	Minority Pupils (%)	Current Exp.[2] ($/pupil)
Avonworth SD	2	1,286	63	20.4	n/a	n/a
Baldwin-Whitehall SD	5	4,742	263	18.0	n/a	n/a
Brentwood Borough SD	4	1,396	73	19.1	n/a	n/a
Chartiers Valley SD	9	2,876	177	16.2	n/a	n/a
Fox Chapel Area SD	6	4,231	300	14.1	n/a	n/a
Keystone Oaks SD	7	2,904	181	16.0	n/a	n/a
Mt Lebanon SD	9	5,411	334	16.2	n/a	n/a
North Allegheny SD	13	8,273	503	16.4	n/a	n/a
North Hills SD	9	4,977	294	16.9	n/a	n/a
Northgate SD	3	1,660	97	17.1	n/a	n/a
Penn Hills SD	8	5,837	346	16.9	n/a	n/a
Pittsburgh SD	86	39,761	2,477	16.1	57.1	8,386
Plum Borough SD	7	4,358	232	18.8	n/a	n/a
Upper Saint Clair SD	6	3,929	228	17.2	n/a	n/a
West Jefferson Hills SD	5	2,920	149	19.6	n/a	n/a
Woodland Hills SD	9	6,072	308	19.7	n/a	n/a

Note: Data covers the 1995-1996 school year unless otherwise noted; (1) Excludes teachers reported as working in school district offices rather than in schools; (2) Based on 1993-94 enrollment collected by the Census Bureau, not the enrollment figure shown in column 3; SD = School District; ISD = Independent School District; n/a not available
Source: National Center for Education Statistics, Common Core of Data Survey; Bureau of the Census

Educational Quality

School District	Education Quotient[1]	Graduate Outcome[2]	Community Index[3]	Resource Index[4]
Pittsburgh	n/a	n/a	n/a	n/a

Note: Nearly 1,000 secondary school districts were rated in terms of educational quality. The scores range from a low of 50 to a high of 150; (1) Average of the Graduate Outcome, Community and Resource indexes; (2) Based on graduation rates and college board scores (SAT/ACT); (3) Based on the surrounding community's average level of education and the area's average income level; (4) Based on teacher salaries, per-pupil expenditures and student-teacher ratios.
Source: Expansion Management, Ratings Issue 1997

Educational Attainment by Race

Area	High School Graduate (%)					Bachelor's Degree (%)				
	Total	White	Black	Other	Hisp.[2]	Total	White	Black	Other	Hisp.[2]
City	72.4	74.0	66.3	87.7	78.4	20.1	22.6	8.8	62.2	39.2
MSA[1]	77.4	78.0	68.6	86.1	80.6	19.5	19.9	10.1	56.1	30.0
U.S.	75.2	77.9	63.1	60.4	49.8	20.3	21.5	11.4	19.4	9.2

Note: figures shown cover persons 25 years old and over; (1) Metropolitan Statistical Area - see Appendix A for areas included; (2) people of Hispanic origin can be of any race
Source: 1990 Census of Population and Housing, Summary Tape File 3C

School Enrollment by Type

Area	Preprimary				Elementary/High School			
	Public		Private		Public		Private	
	Enrollment	%	Enrollment	%	Enrollment	%	Enrollment	%
City	3,400	58.5	2,412	41.5	36,244	75.8	11,549	24.2
MSA[1]	20,226	54.8	16,696	45.2	254,093	86.0	41,306	14.0
U.S.	2,679,029	59.5	1,824,256	40.5	38,379,689	90.2	4,187,099	9.8

Note: figures shown cover persons 3 years old and over;
(1) Metropolitan Statistical Area - see Appendix A for areas included
Source: 1990 Census of Population and Housing, Summary Tape File 3C

School Enrollment by Race

Area	Preprimary (%)				Elementary/High School (%)			
	White	Black	Other	Hisp.[1]	White	Black	Other	Hisp.[1]
City	66.4	31.4	2.2	1.4	59.1	38.9	2.1	1.1
MSA[2]	89.5	9.1	1.4	0.8	87.5	11.3	1.3	0.6
U.S.	80.4	12.5	7.1	7.8	74.1	15.6	10.3	12.5

Note: figures shown cover persons 3 years old and over; (1) people of Hispanic origin can be of any race; (2) Metropolitan Statistical Area - see Appendix A for areas included
Source: 1990 Census of Population and Housing, Summary Tape File 3C

SAT/ACT Scores

Area/District	1997 SAT				1997 ACT	
	Percent of Graduates Tested (%)	Average Math Score	Average Verbal Score	Average Combined Score	Percent of Graduates Tested (%)	Average Composite Score
Pittsburgh	n/a	460	464	924	n/a	n/a
State	72	495	498	993	8	21.0
U.S.	42	511	505	1,016	36	21.0

Note: Math and verbal SAT scores are out of a possible 800; ACT scores are out of a possible 36
Caution: Comparing or ranking states/cities on the basis of SAT/ACT scores alone is invalid and strongly discouraged by the The College Board and The American College Testing Program as students who take the tests are self-selected and do not represent the entire student population.
Source: Pittsburgh Public Schools, Student Information Management, 1997; College Board, 1997; American College Testing Program, 1997

Classroom Teacher Salaries in Public Schools

District	B.A. Degree		M.A. Degree		Ph.D. Degree	
	Min. ($)	Max ($)	Min. ($)	Max. ($)	Min. ($)	Max. ($)
Pittsburgh	32,300	57,400	33,800	60,600	35,400	62,200
Average[1]	26,120	39,270	28,175	44,667	31,643	49,825

Note: Salaries are for 1996-1997; (1) Based on all school districts covered; n/a not available
Source: American Federation of Teachers (unpublished data)

Higher Education

Two-Year Colleges		Four-Year Colleges		Medical Schools	Law Schools	Voc/ Tech
Public	Private	Public	Private			
2	10	1	6	1	2	22

Source: College Blue Book, Occupational Education 1997; Medical School Admission Requirements, 1998-99; Peterson's Guide to Two-Year Colleges, 1997; Peterson's Guide to Four-Year Colleges, 1997; Barron's Guide to Law Schools 1997

MAJOR EMPLOYERS

Major Employers

Allegheny General Hospital	Aluminum Co. of America
Associated Cleaning Consultants & Service	Children's Hospital of Pittsburgh
Island Creek Coal Inc.	Magee-Womens Hospital
Mellon Bank Corp.	Mercy Hospital of Pittsburgh
Presbyterian-University Hospital	PPG Industries
Shadyside Hospital	St. Francis Medical Center
USX Corp. (oil & gas)	PG Publishing
Veritus (nursing homes)	Federated Investors
St. Margaret Health System	

Note: companies listed are located in the city
Source: Dun's Business Rankings 1997; Ward's Business Directory, 1997

PUBLIC SAFETY

Crime Rate

Area	All Crimes	Violent Crimes				Property Crimes		
		Murder	Forcible Rape	Robbery	Aggrav. Assault	Burglary	Larceny -Theft	Motor Vehicle Theft
City	5,296.0	13.3	58.1	441.7	290.7	860.6	2,838.5	793.1
Suburbs[1]	2,211.6	1.8	16.9	51.0	147.2	372.7	1,411.4	210.5
MSA[2]	2,665.1	3.4	23.0	108.5	168.3	444.5	1,621.2	296.2
U.S.	5,078.9	7.4	36.1	202.4	388.2	943.0	2,975.9	525.9

Note: Crime rate is the number of crimes per 100,000 pop.; (1) defined as all areas within the MSA but located outside the central city; (2) Metropolitan Statistical Area - see Appendix A for areas incl.
Source: FBI Uniform Crime Reports 1996

RECREATION

Culture and Recreation

Museums	Symphony Orchestras	Opera Companies	Dance Companies	Professional Theatres	Zoos	Pro Sports Teams
9	2	2	2	3	1	3

Source: International Directory of the Performing Arts, 1996; Official Museum Directory, 1998; Chamber of Commerce/Economic Development 1997

Library System

The Carnegie Library of Pittsburgh has 17 branches, holdings of 1,987,799 volumes and a budget of $n/a (1995). The Upper Saint Clair Township Library has no branches, holdings of 82,000 volumes and a budget of $771,668 (1995). Note: n/a means not available. *American Library Directory, 1997-1998*

MEDIA

Newspapers

Name	Type	Freq.	Distribution	Circulation
Byzantine Catholic World	n/a	2x/mo	Area	7,000
Green Sheet Advertiser	n/a	1x/wk	Local	300,000
The Jewish Chronicle	Religious	1x/wk	Local	13,500
New Pittsburgh Courier	Black	2x/wk	Local	31,923
Northside Chronicle	Black	1x/mo	Local	10,000
Observer	General	n/a	Regional	110,000
The Pitt News	n/a	5x/wk	Campus & community	14,000
Pittsburgh Catholic	Religious	1x/wk	Local	109,500
Pittsburgh City Paper	Alternative	1x/wk	Local	80,500
Pittsburgh Legal Journal	n/a	5x/wk	Local	1,700
Pittsburgh Post-Gazette	General	7x/wk	Area	241,798
Pittsburgh South Reporter	General	1x/wk	Local	12,000
Pittsburgh Union	n/a	24x/yr	National	13,000
South Hills Record	General	1x/wk	Local	8,032

Note: Includes newspapers with circulations of 1,000 or more located in the city; n/a not available
Source: Burrelle's Media Directory, 1998 Edition

AM Radio Stations

Call Letters	Freq. (kHz)	Target Audience	Station Format	Music Format
WWCS	540	General	M/N	n/a
WPIT	730	General	M/T	Christian
WEDO	810	n/a	M/N/S/T	n/a
WYJZ	860	General	M/N/S	n/a
WWSW	970	General	M	Oldies
KDKA	1020	General	N/S/T	n/a
WTAE	1250	General	N/S/T	n/a
WJAS	1320	General	M	Big Band/Oldies
WIXZ	1360	General	S	n/a
KQV	1410	General	N	n/a
WMBA	1460	General	N/S/T	n/a
WXVX	1510	General	M/N/S	n/a
WCXJ	1550	General	M	Christian/Urban Contemporary
WPLW	1590	General	M	Adult Contemporary

Note: Stations included broadcast in the Pittsburgh metro area; n/a not available
Station Format: E = Educational; M = Music; N = News; S = Sports; T = Talk
Source: Burrelle's Media Directory, 1998 Edition

FM Radio Stations

Call Letters	Freq. (mHz)	Target Audience	Station Format	Music Format
WRCT	88.3	General	M/N/S	n/a
WQED	89.3	General	M	Classical
WDUQ	90.5	General	M/N	Big Band/Jazz
WYEP	91.3	General	M/N	Alternative
WPTS	92.1	General	M/N/S/T	n/a
WLTJ	92.9	General	M/N/S	Adult Contemporary
WBZZ	93.7	General	M	Contemporary Top 40
WWSW	94.5	General	M	Oldies
WVTY	96.1	General	M/N/S	Adult Contemporary
WRRK	96.9	General	M	Classic Rock
WSHH	99.7	General	M	Adult Contemporary
WZPT	100.7	General	M/N/S	Oldies
WORD	101.5	General	M/T	Christian
WDVE	102.5	General	M/S	AOR
WXDX	105.9	General	M/N/S	Alternative
WAMO	106.7	Black	M/N/S	n/a
WDSY	107.9	General	M	Country

Note: Stations included broadcast in the Pittsburgh metro area; n/a not available
Station Format: E = Educational; M = Music; N = News; S = Sports; T = Talk
Music Format: AOR = Album Oriented Rock; MOR = Middle-of-the-Road
Source: Burrelle's Media Directory, 1998 Edition

Television Stations

Name	Ch.	Affiliation	Type	Owner
KDKA	2	CBS	Commercial	Westinghouse Broadcast Division
WTAE	4	ABC	Commercial	Hearst-Arygle
WPXI	11	NBC	Commercial	Cox Enterprises Inc.
WQED	13	PBS	Public	WQED
WQEX	16	PBS	Public	WQED Pittsburgh
WPTT	22	UPN	Commercial	Eddie Edwards Sr.
WBPA	29	WB	Commercial	Venture Technology Group Inc.
WPCB	40	n/a	Commercial	Cornerstone Television Inc.
WPGH	53	Fox	Commercial	Sinclair Broadcast Group
WNEU	63	n/a	Commercial	Bon-Tele Network Inc.

Note: Stations included broadcast in the Pittsburgh metro area
Source: Burrelle's Media Directory, 1998 Edition

CLIMATE

Average and Extreme Temperatures

Temperature	Jan	Feb	Mar	Apr	May	Jun	Jul	Aug	Sep	Oct	Nov	Dec	Ann
Extreme High (°F)	75	69	83	89	91	98	103	100	97	89	82	74	103
Average High (°F)	35	38	48	61	71	79	83	81	75	63	50	39	60
Average Temp. (°F)	28	30	39	50	60	68	73	71	64	53	42	32	51
Average Low (°F)	20	22	29	39	49	57	62	61	54	43	34	25	41
Extreme Low (°F)	-18	-12	-1	14	26	34	42	39	31	16	-1	-12	-18

Note: Figures cover the years 1948-1990
Source: National Climatic Data Center, International Station Meteorological Climate Summary, 3/95

Average Precipitation/Snowfall/Humidity

Precip./Humidity	Jan	Feb	Mar	Apr	May	Jun	Jul	Aug	Sep	Oct	Nov	Dec	Ann
Avg. Precip. (in.)	2.8	2.4	3.4	3.3	3.6	3.9	3.8	3.2	2.8	2.4	2.7	2.8	37.1
Avg. Snowfall (in.)	11	9	8	2	Tr	0	0	0	0	Tr	4	8	43
Avg. Rel. Hum. 7am (%)	76	75	75	73	76	79	82	86	85	81	78	77	79
Avg. Rel. Hum. 4pm (%)	64	60	54	49	50	51	53	54	55	53	60	66	56

Note: Figures cover the years 1948-1990; Tr = Trace amounts (<0.05 in. of rain; <0.5 in. of snow)
Source: National Climatic Data Center, International Station Meteorological Climate Summary, 3/95

Weather Conditions

Temperature			Daytime Sky			Precipitation		
5°F & below	32°F & below	90°F & above	Clear	Partly cloudy	Cloudy	0.01 inch or more precip.	0.1 inch or more snow/ice	Thunder-storms
9	121	8	62	137	166	154	42	35

Note: Figures are average number of days per year and covers the years 1948-1990
Source: National Climatic Data Center, International Station Meteorological Climate Summary, 3/95

AIR & WATER QUALITY

Maximum Pollutant Concentrations

	Particulate Matter (ug/m³)	Carbon Monoxide (ppm)	Sulfur Dioxide (ppm)	Nitrogen Dioxide (ppm)	Ozone (ppm)	Lead (ug/m³)
MSA[1] Level	123	4	0.070	0.030	0.11	0.07
NAAQS[2]	150	9	0.140	0.053	0.12	1.50
Met NAAQS?	Yes	Yes	Yes	Yes	Yes	Yes

Note: (1) Metropolitan Statistical Area - see Appendix A for areas included; (2) National Ambient Air Quality Standards; ppm = parts per million; ug/m³ = micrograms per cubic meter; n/a not available
Source: EPA, National Air Quality and Emissions Trends Report, 1996

Pollutant Standards Index

In the Pittsburgh MSA (see Appendix A for areas included), the Pollutant Standards Index (PSI) exceeded 100 on 1 day in 1996. A PSI value greater than 100 indicates that air quality would be in the unhealthful range on that day. *EPA, National Air Quality and Emissions Trends Report, 1996*

Drinking Water

Water System Name	Pop. Served	Primary Water Source Type	Number of Violations in Fiscal Year 1997	Type of Violation/ Contaminants
PA American Water Co.-Pittsburgh	615,543	Surface	None	None
Pittsburgh Water & Sewer Auth.	370,000	Surface	None	None

Note: Data as of January 16, 1998
Source: EPA, Office of Ground Water and Drinking Water, Safe Drinking Water Information System

Pittsburgh tap water is alkaline, soft 9 months, hard 3 months (June, July, August); fluoridated. *Editor & Publisher Market Guide, 1998*

Raleigh, North Carolina

Background

Raleigh, North Carolina is named for Queen Elizabeth I's swashbuckling favorite, Sir Walter Raleigh. In her name, he plundered Spanish ships for gold in the New World, and founded the first English settlement along the North Carolina coast. Of course, his excessive piracy led to his execution in 1618.

Raleigh is the capital of North Carolina, and its cultural and educational center. Located 120 miles west of the Atlantic Ocean, Raleigh is the retail and wholesale locus of eastern North Carolina. Its number of federal, state, and local government offices provide jobs for the economy of the surrounding area. The construction of the Research Triangle Park—a complex of research laboratories between the cities of Raleigh, Durham, and Chapel Hill—has pumped money into the local economy as well.

Since 1992 the city has been home to high-tech businesses and first rate universities like North Carolina State, Duke, and the University of North Carolina. The region has a high business start up rate, a low unemployment rate and average wages above the state level. The Research Triangle Park is the largest university-affiliated research park in the world, with 99 companies employing over 36,000 workers. It is home to such companies as IBM, DuPont, Motorola, and Harris Microelectronics. *Site Selection June/July 1997*

The ''City of Oaks'', so named for its tree-lined streets, provides a picturesque backdrop for the city's unique ambience. On one end of the spectrum, one can take in the modern architecture of Edward Durrell Stone's North Carolina Museum of Art, the same architect who designed the John F. Kennedy Center in Washington, D.C. Or, one can stand in admiration of the antebellum structures, such as the Greek Revival Capitol Building, completed in 1840, after the first capitol building burned down in 1831; or any number of old homes used as government office buildings. The city's grid design streets makes exploration of this fine city a simple affair.

Because it is centrally located between the mountains on the west and the coast on the south and east, the Raleigh area enjoys a pleasant climate. The mountains form a partial barrier to cold air masses moving from the west. As a result, there are few days in the midst of winter when the temperature falls below 20 degrees. In the summer tropical air is present over the eastern and central sections of North Carolina bringing warm temperatures and rather high humidity to the area. Raleigh is situated far enough from the coast so that the bad weather effects of coastal storms are reduced. While snow and sleet usually occur each year, excessive accumulations of snow are rare.

General Rankings and Evaluative Comments

- Raleigh was ranked #16 out of 300 cities by *Money's* 1997 "Survey of the Best Places to Live." Criteria used: health services, crime, economy, housing, education, transportation, weather, leisure and the arts. The city was ranked #24 in 1996 and #8 in 1995. *Money, July 1997; Money, September 1996; Money, September 1995*

- Raleigh appeared on *Fortune's* list of "North America's Most Improved Cities" Rank: 5 out of 10. The selected cities satisfied basic business-location needs and also demonstrated improvement over a five- to ten-year period in a number of business and quality-of-life measures.

  Fortune, 11/24/97

- *Ladies Home Journal* ranked America's 200 largest cities based on the qualities women care about most. Raleigh ranked 6 out of 200. Criteria: low crime rate, good public schools, well-paying jobs, quality health and child care, the presence of women in government, proportion of women-owned businesses, size of the wage gap with men, local economy, divorce rates, the ratio of single men to single women, whether there are laws that require at least the same number of public toilets for women as men, and the probability of good hair days. *Ladies Home Journal, November 1997*

- Raleigh is among the 10 healthiest cities for women. Rank: 2 out of 10. Criteria: 1) number of doctors, psychologists and dietitians; 2) quality of hospital gynecology departments; 3) number of working mothers; 4) rate of violent crimes; 5) cleanliness of air and water; 6) number of fitness opportunities; 7) quality of public schools. *American Health, January/February 1997*

- Raleigh was ranked #42 out of 219 cities in terms of children's health, safety, and economic well-being. Criteria: total population, percent population change, birth rate, child immunization rate, infant mortality rate, percent low birth weight infants, percent of births to teens, physician-to-population ratio, student-to-teacher ratio, dropout rate, unemployment rate, median family income, percent of children in poverty, violent and property crime rates, number of juvenile arrests for violent crimes as a percent of the total crime index, number of days with pollution standard index (PSI) over 100, pounds toxic releases per 1,000 people and number of superfund sites. *Zero Population Growth, Children's Environmental Index 1997*

- Carolina Trace Country Club, located 38 miles south of Raleigh, is among America's best retirement communities. Criteria: communities must have state-of-the-art facilities, newly built homes for sale, and give you the most value for your money in every price range. Communities must also welcome newcomers of all races and religions. *New Choices, July/August 1997*

- Raleigh appeared on *New Mobility's* list of "10 Disability Friendly Cities". Rank: 5 out of 10. Criteria: affordable and accessible housing, transportation, quality medical care, personal assistance services and strong advocacy.

  "...Raleigh's Capitol Area Transit's mainline transportation is fully accessible, while Accessible Raleigh Transportation System operates a two-tiered paratransit service.

  Raleigh has no independent living center, but the State Vocational Rehabilitation Department dispenses independent living services through programs that assist with home and transportation modifications, skills training and limited PCA.

  ...Finding a place to live present the usual problems, but architect Ron Mace and his Center for Accessible Housing have made a significant difference in Raleigh.

  Look to Raleigh for leisure activities such as semi-professional theater, a symphony orchestra, the Hartford Whalers, the Durham Bulls and top college sports." *New Mobility, December 1997*

- Raleigh appeared on *Sales & Marketing Management's* list of the 20 hottest domestic markets to do business in. Rank: 9 out of 20. America's 320 Metropolitan Statistical Areas were ranked based on the market's potential to buy products in certain industries like high-tech, manufacturing, office equipment and business services, as well as population and household income growth. The study had nine criteria in all.

"The future home of the National Hockey League's Carolina Hurricanes, this Atlantic Coast market has become popular during the past five years. Of our top 20 markets, Raleigh/Durham is the highest ranked in population growth. And with four major universities in the area, the market's educational purchasing power is among the highest in the country." *Sales & Marketing Management, January 1998*

- Rex Healthcare Inc., headquartered in Raleigh, is among the "100 Best Companies for Working Mothers." Criteria: pay compared with competition, opportunities for women to advance, support for child care, flexible work schedules and family-friendly benefits. *Working Mother, October 1997*

- According to *Working Mother,* "No state has more action or more enthusiasm for improving child care than North Carolina. And no governor deserves more credit for fighting for child care than Jim Hunt. His 'Smart Start' program has as its goal affordable, quality early childhood education for every child who needs it. In the past four years, the state has created more than 30,000 new slots for child care and improved care for more than 150,000 kids.

  The program ran up against some resistance in the state legislature in the past, but now a solid majority embrace the core tenets of Smart Start. This year, for example, state lawmakers decided to award permanent funding for the state's caregiver training program, Teacher Education and Compensation Helps (T.E.A.C.H.)—more than $1 million a year in recurring funds. That means child care advocates won't have to come back every year to fight for money for early education. The T.E.A.C.H. program is now being copied by other states, including Illinois.

  With all this progress, it's a shame that North Carolina's key standards aren't better. One adult is still allowed to care for up to five babies, and caregivers are not required to have any education or training before they start work (a bill now before the legislature may change this). This state could do better on these critical aspects of child care." *Working Mother, July/August 1997*

Business Environment

STATE ECONOMY

State Economic Profile

"North Carolina's strength is its development of technologically advanced industries, ranging from computer software development in biotechnology. North Carolina's weakness is its ailing textile and apparel industries....

North Carolina's population continues to expand at a robust 1.7% year-over-year rate, nearly twice the national average. In 1996 net domestic migration contributed 1.1 percentage points to North Carolina's population growth rate, compared to just 0.4 for the southern region, making the state's economic expansion particularly dependent on migration....

Apart from job losses in the apparel and textile industries, North Carolina's economy remains healthy, and employment growth is outpacing the nation. The long-term outlook for North Carolina is positive. Its emergency as a center for high-tech employment continues to attract relocations and expansions to metro areas such as Raleigh and Charlotte. A downside risk to the economy is strong growth in government sector employment, which may leave the state susceptible to government spending cuts in the future...." *National Association of Realtors, Economic Profiles: The Fifty States, July 1997*

IMPORTS/EXPORTS

Total Export Sales

Area	1993 ($000)	1994 ($000)	1995 ($000)	1996 ($000)	% Chg. 1993-96	% Chg. 1995-96
MSA[1]	1,620,884	1,758,673	2,093,206	2,609,828	61.0	24.7
U.S.	464,858,354	512,415,609	583,030,524	622,827,063	34.0	6.8

Note: (1) Metropolitan Statistical Area - see Appendix A for areas included
Source: U.S. Department of Commerce, International Trade Association, Metropolitan Area Exports: An Export Performance Report on Over 250 U.S. Cities, October 1997

Imports/Exports by Port

Type	Cargo Value			Share of U.S. Total	
	1995 (US$mil.)	1996 (US$mil.)	% Change 1995-1996	1995 (%)	1996 (%)
Imports	0	0	0	0	0
Exports	0	0	0	0	0

Source: Global Trade Information Services, WaterBorne Trade Atlas 1997

CITY FINANCES

City Government Finances

Component	FY92 ($000)	FY92 (per capita $)
Revenue	187,923	840.65
Expenditure	196,961	881.08
Debt Outstanding	154,545	691.33
Cash & Securities	165,666	741.08

Source: U.S. Bureau of the Census, City Government Finances: 1991-92

City Government Revenue by Source

Source	FY92 ($000)	FY92 (per capita $)	FY92 (%)
From Federal Government	3,011	13.47	1.6
From State Governments	22,117	98.94	11.8
From Local Governments	21,945	98.17	11.7
Property Taxes	68,750	307.54	36.6
General Sales Taxes	0	0.00	0.0
Selective Sales Taxes	1,949	8.72	1.0
Income Taxes	0	0.00	0.0
Current Charges	27,908	124.84	14.9
Utility/Liquor Store	17,984	80.45	9.6
Employee Retirement[1]	0	0.00	0.0
Other	24,259	108.52	12.9

Note: (1) Excludes "city contributions," classified as "nonrevenue," intragovernmental transfers.
Source: U.S. Bureau of the Census, City Government Finances: 1991-92

City Government Expenditures by Function

Function	FY92 ($000)	FY92 (per capita $)	FY92 (%)
Educational Services	0	0.00	0.0
Employee Retirement[1]	0	0.00	0.0
Environment/Housing	57,812	258.61	29.4
Government Administration	9,473	42.38	4.8
Interest on General Debt	6,204	27.75	3.1
Public Safety	37,283	166.78	18.9
Social Services	993	4.44	0.5
Transportation	24,808	110.97	12.6
Utility/Liquor Store	33,200	148.52	16.9
Other	27,188	121.62	13.8

Note: (1) Payments to beneficiaries including withdrawal of contributions.
Source: U.S. Bureau of the Census, City Government Finances: 1991-92

Municipal Bond Ratings

Area	Moody's	S & P
Raleigh	Aaa	AAA

Note: n/a not available; n/r not rated
Source: Moody's Bond Record, 2/98; Statistical Abstract of the U.S., 1997; Governing Magazine, 9/97, 3/98

POPULATION

Population Growth

Area	1980	1990	% Chg. 1980-90	July 1996 Estimate	% Chg. 1990-96
City	150,255	207,951	38.4	243,835	17.3
MSA[1]	561,222	735,480	31.0	1,025,253	39.4
U.S.	226,545,805	248,765,170	9.8	265,179,411	6.6

Note: (1) Metropolitan Statistical Area - see Appendix A for areas included
Source: 1980/1990 Census of Housing and Population, Summary Tape File 3C; Census Bureau Population Estimates

Population Characteristics

Race	City					MSA[1]	
	1980		1990		% Chg. 1980-90	1990	
	Population	%	Population	%		Population	%
White	106,574	70.9	144,193	69.3	35.3	533,421	72.5
Black	41,241	27.4	57,236	27.5	38.8	183,225	24.9
Amer Indian/Esk/Aleut	209	0.1	604	0.3	189.0	2,017	0.3
Asian/Pacific Islander	1,556	1.0	5,131	2.5	229.8	13,940	1.9
Other	675	0.4	787	0.4	16.6	2,877	0.4
Hispanic Origin[2]	1,382	0.9	2,454	1.2	77.6	8,386	1.1

Note: (1) Metropolitan Statistical Area - see Appendix A for areas included; (2) people of Hispanic origin can be of any race
Source: 1980/1990 Census of Housing and Population, Summary Tape File 3C

Ancestry

Area	German	Irish	English	Italian	U.S.	French	Polish	Dutch
City	16.5	11.4	19.5	2.6	5.3	2.7	1.6	1.3
MSA[1]	16.3	12.4	19.0	2.6	7.5	2.8	1.7	1.5
U.S.	23.3	15.6	13.1	5.9	5.3	4.2	3.8	2.5

Note: Figures are percentages and include persons that reported multiple ancestry (eg. if a person reported being Irish and Italian, they were included in both columns); (1) Metropolitan Statistical Area - see Appendix A for areas included
Source: 1990 Census of Population and Housing, Summary Tape File 3C

Age

Area	Median Age (Years)	Age Distribution (%)						
		Under 5	Under 18	18-24	25-44	45-64	65+	80+
City	30.2	6.2	19.5	17.5	38.6	15.6	8.8	1.9
MSA[1]	31.2	6.8	22.5	14.0	37.6	16.9	8.9	2.0
U.S.	32.9	7.3	25.6	10.5	32.6	18.7	12.5	2.8

Note: (1) Metropolitan Statistical Area - see Appendix A for areas included
Source: 1990 Census of Population and Housing, Summary Tape File 3C

Male/Female Ratio

Area	Number of males per 100 females (all ages)	Number of males per 100 females (18 years old+)
City	93.6	92.8
MSA[1]	92.9	90.5
U.S.	95.0	91.9

Note: (1) Metropolitan Statistical Area - see Appendix A for areas included
Source: 1990 Census of Population, General Population Characteristics

INCOME

Per Capita/Median/Average Income

Area	Per Capita ($)	Median Household ($)	Average Household ($)
City	16,896	32,451	40,243
MSA[1]	16,170	33,290	40,686
U.S.	14,420	30,056	38,453

Note: all figures are for 1989; (1) Metropolitan Statistical Area - see Appendix A for areas included
Source: 1990 Census of Population and Housing, Summary Tape File 3C

Household Income Distribution by Race

Income ($)	City (%)					U.S. (%)				
	Total	White	Black	Other	Hisp.[1]	Total	White	Black	Other	Hisp.[1]
Less than 5,000	5.6	3.5	11.2	13.9	5.8	6.2	4.8	15.2	8.6	8.8
5,000 - 9,999	6.7	5.2	11.4	5.6	7.0	9.3	8.6	14.2	9.9	11.1
10,000 - 14,999	7.7	6.3	11.8	11.5	7.2	8.8	8.5	11.0	9.8	11.0
15,000 - 24,999	17.7	16.4	21.5	16.5	17.0	17.5	17.3	18.9	18.5	20.5
25,000 - 34,999	16.1	15.5	18.0	15.0	13.9	15.8	16.1	14.2	15.4	16.4
35,000 - 49,999	18.9	19.8	16.0	18.7	18.4	17.9	18.6	13.3	16.1	16.0
50,000 - 74,999	17.0	20.1	7.8	12.7	22.7	15.0	15.8	9.3	13.4	11.1
75,000 - 99,999	5.6	7.1	1.5	2.1	2.2	5.1	5.5	2.6	4.7	3.1
100,000+	4.7	6.1	0.8	4.0	5.8	4.4	4.8	1.3	3.7	1.9

Note: all figures are for 1989; (1) people of Hispanic origin can be of any race
Source: 1990 Census of Population and Housing, Summary Tape File 3C

Effective Buying Income

Area	Per Capita ($)	Median Household ($)	Average Household ($)
City	18,383	36,109	44,162
MSA[1]	17,867	37,519	45,056
U.S.	15,444	33,201	41,849

Note: data as of 1/1/97; (1) Metropolitan Statistical Area - see Appendix A for areas included
Source: Standard Rate & Data Service, Newspaper Advertising Source, 2/98

Effective Household Buying Income Distribution

Area	% of Households Earning						
	$10,000 -$19,999	$20,000 -$34,999	$35,000 -$49,999	$50,000 -$74,999	$75,000 -$99,999	$100,000 -$124,999	$125,000 and up
City	14.5	23.6	18.7	20.5	7.2	2.5	2.5
MSA[1]	13.9	22.3	18.9	21.4	8.0	2.6	2.5
U.S.	16.5	23.4	18.3	18.2	6.4	2.1	2.4

Note: data as of 1/1/97; (1) Metropolitan Statistical Area - see Appendix A for areas included
Source: Standard Rate & Data Service, Newspaper Advertising Source, 2/98

Poverty Rates by Race and Age

Area	Total (%)	By Race (%)				By Age (%)		
		White	Black	Other	Hisp.[2]	Under 5 years old	Under 18 years old	65 years and over
City	11.8	7.4	21.7	24.4	17.4	17.4	14.7	13.0
MSA[1]	10.2	6.5	20.5	18.2	15.9	13.3	11.5	15.3
U.S.	13.1	9.8	29.5	23.1	25.3	20.1	18.3	12.8

Note: figures show the percent of people living below the poverty line in 1989. The average poverty threshold was $12,674 for a family of four in 1989; (1) Metropolitan Statistical Area - see Appendix A for areas included; (2) people of Hispanic origin can be of any race
Source: 1990 Census of Population and Housing, Summary Tape File 3C

EMPLOYMENT

Labor Force and Employment

Area	Civilian Labor Force			Workers Employed		
	Dec. '95	Dec. '96	% Chg.	Dec. '95	Dec. '96	% Chg.
City	153,644	154,918	0.8	150,408	152,192	1.2
MSA[1]	587,379	591,986	0.8	575,408	582,236	1.2
U.S.	134,583,000	136,742,000	1.6	127,903,000	130,785,000	2.3

Note: Data is not seasonally adjusted and covers workers 16 years of age and older; (1) Metropolitan Statistical Area - see Appendix A for areas included
Source: Bureau of Labor Statistics, http://stats.bls.gov

Raleigh was listed among the top 20 metro areas (out of 114 major areas) in terms of projected job growth from 1997 to 2002 with an annual percent change of 2.7%.
Standard & Poor's DRI, July 23, 1997

Unemployment Rate

Area	1997											
	Jan.	Feb.	Mar.	Apr.	May	Jun.	Jul.	Aug.	Sep.	Oct.	Nov.	Dec.
City	2.2	2.0	1.8	1.6	2.0	2.4	2.3	2.4	2.1	2.0	2.0	1.8
MSA[1]	2.3	2.1	1.9	1.6	1.9	2.3	2.1	2.2	1.9	1.8	1.8	1.6
U.S.	5.9	5.7	5.5	4.8	4.7	5.2	5.0	4.8	4.7	4.4	4.3	4.4

Note: Data is not seasonally adjusted and covers workers 16 years of age and older; All figures are percentages; (1) Metropolitan Statistical Area - see Appendix A for areas included
Source: Bureau of Labor Statistics, http://stats.bls.gov

Employment by Industry

Sector	MSA[1]		U.S.
	Number of Employees	Percent of Total	Percent of Total
Services	194,500	30.9	29.0
Retail Trade	103,500	16.4	18.5
Government	123,400	19.6	16.1
Manufacturing	84,900	13.5	15.0
Finance/Insurance/Real Estate	30,100	4.8	5.7
Wholesale Trade	30,000	4.8	5.4
Transportation/Public Utilities	27,600	4.4	5.3
Construction/Mining	35,400	5.6	5.0

Note: Figures cover non-farm employment as of 12/97 and are not seasonally adjusted; (1) Metropolitan Statistical Area - see Appendix A for areas included
Source: Bureau of Labor Statistics, http://stats.bls.gov

Employment by Occupation

Occupation Category	City (%)	MSA[1] (%)	U.S. (%)
White Collar	73.4	68.9	58.1
Executive/Admin./Management	16.0	14.3	12.3
Professional	19.5	19.3	14.1
Technical & Related Support	6.6	6.5	3.7
Sales	14.2	11.8	11.8
Administrative Support/Clerical	17.2	16.9	16.3
Blue Collar	14.1	18.5	26.2
Precision Production/Craft/Repair	6.7	9.1	11.3
Machine Operators/Assem./Insp.	2.8	4.3	6.8
Transportation/Material Movers	2.3	2.5	4.1
Cleaners/Helpers/Laborers	2.5	2.6	3.9
Services	11.7	11.1	13.2
Farming/Forestry/Fishing	0.8	1.4	2.5

Note: figures cover employed persons 16 years old and over; (1) Metropolitan Statistical Area - see Appendix A for areas included
Source: 1990 Census of Population and Housing, Summary Tape File 3C

Occupational Employment Projections: 1992 - 2000

Occupations Expected to have the Largest Job Growth (ranked by numerical growth)	Fast-Growing Occupations[1] (ranked by percent growth)
1. Salespersons, retail	1. Computer engineers
2. Janitors/cleaners/maids, ex. priv. hshld.	2. Systems analysts
3. Cashiers	3. Physical therapy assistants and aides
4. Registered nurses	4. Dental hygienists
5. Waiters & waitresses	5. Dental assistants
6. Teachers, secondary school	6. Paralegals
7. General office clerks	7. Physical therapists
8. Teachers, elementary school	8. Teachers, special education
9. General managers & top executives	9. Medical assistants
10. Systems analysts	10. Radiologic technicians

Projections cover Chatham, Durham, Franklin, Johnston, Orange and Wake Counties.
Note: (1) Excludes occupations with total job growth less than 100
Source: Employment Security Commission of North Carolina, Occupational Trends: 1992 to 2000

Average Wages

Occupation	Wage	Occupation	Wage
Professional/Technical/Clerical	$/Week	**Health/Protective Services**	$/Week
Accountants III	-	Corrections Officers	-
Attorneys III	-	Firefighters	-
Budget Analysts III	-	Nurses, Licensed Practical II	-
Buyers/Contracting Specialists II	-	Nurses, Registered II	-
Clerks, Accounting III	443	Nursing Assistants II	-
Clerks, General III	-	Police Officers I	-
Computer Operators II	383	**Hourly Workers**	$/Hour
Computer Programmers II	-	Forklift Operators	10.39
Drafters II	547	General Maintenance Workers	8.84
Engineering Technicians III	-	Guards I	-
Engineering Technicians, Civil III	-	Janitors	5.58
Engineers III	-	Maintenance Electricians	17.51
Key Entry Operators I	289	Maintenance Electronics Techs II	17.26
Personnel Assistants III	-	Maintenance Machinists	-
Personnel Specialists III	-	Maintenance Mechanics, Machinery	14.84
Secretaries III	492	Material Handling Laborers	-
Switchboard Operator-Receptionist	359	Motor Vehicle Mechanics	15.05
Systems Analysts II	904	Shipping/Receiving Clerks	9.22
Systems Analysts Supervisor/Mgr II	-	Tool and Die Makers	-
Tax Collectors II	-	Truckdrivers, Tractor Trailer	13.89
Word Processors II	411	Warehouse Specialists	10.43

Note: Wage data includes full-time workers only for 5/95 and cover the Metropolitan Statistical Area (see Appendix A for areas included). Dashes indicate that data was not available.
Source: Bureau of Labor Statistics, Occupational Compensation Survey

TAXES

Major State and Local Tax Rates

State Corp. Income (%)	State Personal Income (%)	Residential Property (effective rate per $100)	Sales & Use		State Gasoline (cents/ gallon)	State Cigarette (cents/ 20-pack)
			State (%)	Local (%)		
7.5	6.0 - 7.75	n/a	4.0	2.0	22.6	5

Note: Personal/corporate income tax rates as of 1/97. Sales, gasoline and cigarette tax rates as of 1/98.
Source: Federation of Tax Administrators, www.taxadmin.org; Washington D.C. Department of Finance and Revenue, Tax Rates and Tax Burdens in the District of Columbia: A Nationwide Comparison, June 1997; Chamber of Commerce

Total Taxes Per Capita and as a Percent of Income

Area	Per Capita Income ($)	Per Capita Taxes ($)			Taxes as Pct. of Income (%)		
		Total	Federal	State/ Local	Total	Federal	State/ Local
North Carolina	24,648	8,158	5,419	2,739	33.1	22.0	11.1
U.S.	26,187	9,205	6,127	3,078	35.2	23.4	11.8

Note: Figures are for 1997
Source: Tax Foundation, Web Site, www.taxfoundation.org

Estimated Tax Burden

Area	State Income	Local Income	Property	Sales	Total
Raleigh	2,994	0	2,475	822	6,291

Note: The numbers are estimates of taxes paid by a married couple with two kids and annual earnings of $65,000. Sales tax estimates assume they spend average amounts on food, clothing, household goods and gasoline. Property tax estimates assume they live in a $225,000 home.
Source: Kiplinger's Personal Finance Magazine, June 1997

COMMERCIAL REAL ESTATE

Office Market

Class/ Location	Total Space (sq. ft.)	Vacant Space (sq. ft.)	Vac. Rate (%)	Under Constr. (sq. ft.)	Net Absorp. (sq. ft.)	Rental Rates ($/sq.ft./yr.)
Class A						
CBD	2,435,277	331,414	13.6	0	-33,667	15.00-19.00
Outside CBD	11,101,460	689,288	6.2	1,139,267	692,078	16.50-22.00
Class B						
CBD	1,288,169	163,055	12.7	0	-28,399	11.00-14.50
Outside CBD	6,726,107	359,598	5.3	0	-13,759	14.00-16.50

Note: Data as of 10/97 and covers Raleigh, Cary, Chapel Hill, Durham, and Research Triangle Park; CBD = Central Business District; n/a not available;
Source: Society of Industrial and Office Realtors, 1998 Comparative Statistics of Industrial and Office Real Estate Markets

"Lenders' conservative requirements and developers' caution should continue to prevent overbuilding. New construction is significantly pre-leased. All building is concentrated in the suburbs and is driven by the activity of two REITs. Several large corporations have announced property purchases in the Research Triangle Park area and have plans to build additions to existing facilities. Employment growth is expected to slow when compared to the earlier nineties, but will still post above-average gains. The area's high proportion of government and university employment plus its growing high-tech industry should reduce cyclical volatility. Low business costs and high quality of life will prompt further in-migration of population and corporations. Even so, workforce availability will remain extremely tight, estimated at less than three percent for the balance of the decade." *Society of Industrial and Office Realtors, 1998 Comparative Statistics of Industrial and Office Real Estate Markets*

Industrial Market

Location	Total Space (sq. ft.)	Vacant Space (sq. ft.)	Vac. Rate (%)	Under Constr. (sq. ft.)	Net Absorp. (sq. ft.)	Net Lease ($/sq.ft./yr.)
Central City	n/a	n/a	n/a	n/a	n/a	n/a
Suburban	20,400,000	760,000	3.7	360,000	90,000	3.25-4.75

Note: Data as of 10/97 and covers Raleigh/Durham; n/a not available
Source: Society of Industrial and Office Realtors, 1998 Comparative Statistics of Industrial and Office Real Estate Markets

"New speculative development will be concentrated along the I-40/Airport Corridor. Late in 1997, more than 350,000 sq. ft. of space was under construction. Developers have not been put off by significant increases in construction costs marketwide, which soared by more than 33 percent, or as much as $20 per sq. ft. Raleigh/Durham will still rate as one of the top locations to live and work. There will continue to be an influx of high-tech companies that want or need to be near Research Triangle Park. The area's strong job growth and high quality of life will continue to entice workers. Low costs of doing business, a concentration of some of the country's foremost research institutes, and the pool of skilled workers will also work to attract and retain private enterprise." *Society of Industrial and Office Realtors, 1998 Comparative Statistics of Industrial and Office Real Estate Markets*

COMMERCIAL UTILITIES

Typical Monthly Electric Bills

Area	Commercial Service ($/month)		Industrial Service ($/month)	
	12 kW demand 1,500 kWh	100 kW demand 30,000 kWh	1,000 kW demand 400,000 kWh	20,000 kW demand 10,000,000 kWh
City	128	1,933	24,842	552,800
U.S.	162	2,360	25,590	545,677

Note: Based on rates in effect July 1, 1997
Source: Edison Electric Institute, Typical Residential, Commercial and Industrial Bills, Summer 1997

TRANSPORTATION

Transportation Statistics

Avg. travel time to work (min.)	18.1
Interstate highways	I-40; I-85
Bus lines	
In-city	Capital Area Transit
Inter-city	3
Passenger air service	
Airport	Raleigh-Durham International
Airlines	13
Aircraft departures	45,884 (1995)
Enplaned passengers	2,791,046 (1995)
Rail service	Amtrak
Motor freight carriers	34
Major waterways/ports	None

Source: OAG, Business Travel Planner, Summer 1997; Editor & Publisher Market Guide, 1998; FAA Airport Activity Statistics, 1996; Amtrak National Time Table, Northeast Timetable, Fall/Winter 1997-98; 1990 Census of Population and Housing, STF 3C; Chamber of Commerce/Economic Development 1997; Jane's Urban Transport Systems 1997-98; Transit Fact Book 1997

A survey of 90,000 airline passengers during the first half of 1997 ranked most of the largest airports in the U.S. Raleigh-Durham International ranked number 18 out of 36. Criteria: cleanliness, quality of restaurants, attractiveness, speed of baggage delivery, ease of reaching gates, available ground transportation, ease of following signs and closeness of parking. *Plog Research Inc., First Half 1997*

Means of Transportation to Work

Area	Car/Truck/Van		Public Transportation			Bicycle	Walked	Other Means	Worked at Home
	Drove Alone	Car-pooled	Bus	Subway	Railroad				
City	79.0	11.3	2.7	0.0	0.0	0.4	3.5	1.1	2.0
MSA[1]	78.0	13.3	1.8	0.0	0.0	0.4	3.1	1.0	2.3
U.S.	73.2	13.4	3.0	1.5	0.5	0.4	3.9	1.2	3.0

Note: figures shown are percentages and only include workers 16 years old and over;
(1) Metropolitan Statistical Area - see Appendix A for areas included
Source: 1990 Census of Population and Housing, Summary Tape File 3C

BUSINESSES

Major Business Headquarters

Company Name	1997 Rankings	
	Fortune 500	Forbes 500
Carolina Power & Light	454	-
General Parts	-	251

Note: Companies listed are located in the city; Dashes indicate no ranking
Fortune 500: companies that produce a 10-K are ranked 1 - 500 based on 1996 revenue
Forbes 500: private companies are ranked 1 - 500 based on 1996 revenue
Source: Forbes 12/1/97; Fortune 4/28/97

Fast-Growing Businesses

According to Deloitte & Touche LLP, Raleigh is home to one of America's 100 fastest-growing high-technology companies: Indelible Blue Inc. Companies are ranked by percentage growth in revenue over a five-year period. Criteria for inclusion: must be a U.S. company developing and/or providing technology products or services; company must have been in business for five years with 1992 revenues of at least $50,000. *Deloitte & Touche LLP, January 7, 1998*

Small Business Opportunity

Raleigh was included among *Entrepreneur* magazines listing of the "20 Best Cities for Small Business." It was ranked #3 among mid-size metro areas. Criteria: risk of failure, business performance, economic growth, affordability and state attitude towards business. *Entrepreneur, 10/97*

According to *Forbes*, Raleigh is home to one of America's 200 best small companies: Medic Computer Systems. Criteria: companies must be publicly traded, U.S.-based corporations with latest 12-month sales of between $5 and $350 million. Earnings must be at least $1 million for the 12-month period. Limited partnerships, REITs and closed-end mutual funds were not considered. Banks, S&Ls and electric utilities were not included. *Forbes, November 3, 1997*

HOTELS & MOTELS

Hotels/Motels

Area	Hotels/ Motels	Rooms	Luxury-Level Hotels/Motels		Average Minimum Rates ($)		
			♦♦♦♦	♦♦♦♦♦	♦♦	♦♦♦	♦♦♦♦
City	33	5,103	0	0	66	86	n/a
Airport	14	1,898	0	0	n/a	n/a	n/a
Suburbs	3	224	0	0	n/a	n/a	n/a
Total	50	7,225	0	0	n/a	n/a	n/a

Note: n/a not available; Classifications range from one diamond (budget properties with basic amenities) to five diamond (luxury properties with the finest service, rooms and facilities).
Source: OAG, Business Travel Planner, Summer 1997

CONVENTION CENTERS

Major Convention Centers

Center Name	Meeting Rooms	Exhibit Space (sf)
Dorton Arena and Kerr Scott Building	n/a	25,000
North Carolina State Fairgrounds	n/a	136,500
McKimmon Conference Center/NC State University	14	11,800

Note: n/a not available
Source: Trade Shows Worldwide 1997

Living Environment

COST OF LIVING

Cost of Living Index

Composite Index	Housing	Utilities	Groceries	Health Care	Trans-portation	Misc. Goods/ Services
104.1	113.0	99.1	101.3	104.1	97.3	101.0

Note: U.S. = 100; Figures are for Raleigh-Durham
Source: ACCRA, Cost of Living Index, 3rd Quarter 1997

HOUSING

Median Home Prices and Housing Affordability

Area	Median Price[2] 3rd Qtr. 1997 ($)	HOI[3] 3rd Qtr. 1997	Afford-ability Rank[4]
MSA[1]	143,000	61.3	138
U.S.	127,000	63.7	–

Note: (1) Metropolitan Statistical Area - see Appendix A for areas included; (2) U.S. figures calculated from the sales of 625,000 new and existing homes in 195 markets; (3) Housing Opportunity Index - percent of homes sold that were within the reach of the median income household at the prevailing mortgage interest rate; (4) Rank is from 1-195 with 1 being most affordable
Source: National Association of Home Builders, Housing Opportunity Index, 3rd Quarter 1997

It is projected that the median price of existing single-family homes in the metro area will increase by 4.0% in 1998. Nationwide, home prices are projected to increase 6.6%. *Kiplinger's Personal Finance Magazine, January 1998*

Average New Home Price

Area	Price ($)
City[1]	154,621
U.S.	135,710

Note: Figures are based on a new home with 1,800 sq. ft. of living area on an 8,000 sq. ft. lot; (1) Raleigh-Durham
Source: ACCRA, Cost of Living Index, 3rd Quarter 1997

Average Apartment Rent

Area	Rent ($/mth)
City[1]	697
U.S.	569

Note: Figures are based on an unfurnished two bedroom, 1-1/2 or 2 bath apartment, approximately 950 sq. ft. in size, excluding all utilities except water; (1) Raleigh-Durham
Source: ACCRA, Cost of Living Index, 3rd Quarter 1997

RESIDENTIAL UTILITIES

Average Residential Utility Costs

Area	All Electric ($/mth)	Part Electric ($/mth)	Other Energy ($/mth)	Phone ($/mth)
City[1]	102.74	–	–	17.86
U.S.	109.40	55.25	43.64	19.48

Note: (1) Raleigh-Durham
Source: ACCRA, Cost of Living Index, 3rd Quarter 1997

HEALTH CARE

Average Health Care Costs

Area	Hospital ($/day)	Doctor ($/visit)	Dentist ($/visit)
City[1]	316.00	56.50	64.62
U.S.	392.91	48.76	60.84

Note: Hospital - based on a semi-private room. Doctor - based on a general practitioner's routine exam of an established patient. Dentist - based on adult teeth cleaning and periodic oral exam; (1) (1) Raleigh-Durham
Source: ACCRA, Cost of Living Index, 3rd Quarter 1997

Distribution of Office-Based Physicians

Area	Family/Gen. Practitioners	Specialists		
		Medical	Surgical	Other
MSA[1]	280	895	620	850

Note: Data as of 12/31/96; (1) Metropolitan Statistical Area - see Appendix A for areas included
Source: American Medical Assn., Physician Characteristics & Distribution in the U.S., 1997-1998

Hospitals

Raleigh has 3 general medical and surgical hospitals, 2 psychiatric, 1 alcoholism and other chemical dependency, 1 prison hospital. *AHA Guide to the Healthcare Field 1997-98*

EDUCATION

Public School District Statistics

District Name	Num. Sch.	Enroll.	Classroom Teachers[1]	Pupils per Teacher	Minority Pupils (%)	Current Exp.[2] ($/pupil)
NC Schools for the Deaf/Blind	4	942	234	4.0	n/a	n/a
Wake County Schools	98	81,438	5,166	15.8	31.5	4,527

Note: Data covers the 1995-1996 school year unless otherwise noted; (1) Excludes teachers reported as working in school district offices rather than in schools; (2) Based on 1993-94 enrollment collected by the Census Bureau, not the enrollment figure shown in column 3; SD = School District; ISD = Independent School District; n/a not available
Source: National Center for Education Statistics, Common Core of Data Survey; Bureau of the Census

Educational Quality

School District	Education Quotient[1]	Graduate Outcome[2]	Community Index[3]	Resource Index[4]
Wake County	119.0	106.0	143.0	108.0

Note: Nearly 1,000 secondary school districts were rated in terms of educational quality. The scores range from a low of 50 to a high of 150; (1) Average of the Graduate Outcome, Community and Resource indexes; (2) Based on graduation rates and college board scores (SAT/ACT); (3) Based on the surrounding community's average level of education and the area's average income level; (4) Based on teacher salaries, per-pupil expenditures and student-teacher ratios.
Source: Expansion Management, Ratings Issue 1997

Educational Attainment by Race

Area	High School Graduate (%)					Bachelor's Degree (%)				
	Total	White	Black	Other	Hisp.[2]	Total	White	Black	Other	Hisp.[2]
City	86.6	92.1	70.3	85.6	81.8	40.6	47.0	19.9	55.4	45.0
MSA[1]	82.4	87.2	66.0	86.3	77.2	34.8	39.2	17.8	55.6	36.6
U.S.	75.2	77.9	63.1	60.4	49.8	20.3	21.5	11.4	19.4	9.2

Note: figures shown cover persons 25 years old and over; (1) Metropolitan Statistical Area - see Appendix A for areas included; (2) people of Hispanic origin can be of any race
Source: 1990 Census of Population and Housing, Summary Tape File 3C

School Enrollment by Type

Area	Preprimary				Elementary/High School			
	Public		Private		Public		Private	
	Enrollment	%	Enrollment	%	Enrollment	%	Enrollment	%
City	1,680	44.8	2,074	55.2	24,478	93.2	1,782	6.8
MSA[1]	6,751	46.9	7,652	53.1	99,864	92.8	7,735	7.2
U.S.	2,679,029	59.5	1,824,256	40.5	38,379,689	90.2	4,187,099	9.8

Note: figures shown cover persons 3 years old and over;
(1) Metropolitan Statistical Area - see Appendix A for areas included
Source: 1990 Census of Population and Housing, Summary Tape File 3C

School Enrollment by Race

Area	Preprimary (%)				Elementary/High School (%)			
	White	Black	Other	Hisp.[1]	White	Black	Other	Hisp.[1]
City	75.4	21.2	3.4	1.9	59.1	37.3	3.6	1.2
MSA[2]	78.1	19.4	2.6	1.2	65.4	31.9	2.7	1.2
U.S.	80.4	12.5	7.1	7.8	74.1	15.6	10.3	12.5

Note: figures shown cover persons 3 years old and over; (1) people of Hispanic origin can be of any race; (2) Metropolitan Statistical Area - see Appendix A for areas included
Source: 1990 Census of Population and Housing, Summary Tape File 3C

SAT/ACT Scores

Area/District	1997 SAT				1997 ACT	
	Percent of Graduates Tested (%)	Average Math Score	Average Verbal Score	Average Combined Score	Percent of Graduates Tested (%)	Average Composite Score
Wake County	74	529	518	1,047	n/a	n/a
State	59	488	490	978	11	19.3
U.S.	42	511	505	1,016	36	21.0

Note: Math and verbal SAT scores are out of a possible 800; ACT scores are out of a possible 36
Caution: Comparing or ranking states/cities on the basis of SAT/ACT scores alone is invalid and strongly discouraged by the The College Board and The American College Testing Program as students who take the tests are self-selected and do not represent the entire student population.
Source: Wake County Public Schools, Evaluation & Research, 1997; American College Testing Program, 1997; College Board, 1997

Classroom Teacher Salaries in Public Schools

District	B.A. Degree		M.A. Degree		Ph.D. Degree	
	Min. ($)	Max ($)	Min. ($)	Max. ($)	Min. ($)	Max. ($)
Raleigh	23,463	43,510	24,926	46,228	27,709	49,080
Average[1]	26,120	39,270	28,175	44,667	31,643	49,825

Note: Salaries are for 1996-1997; (1) Based on all school districts covered; n/a not available
Source: American Federation of Teachers (unpublished data)

Higher Education

Two-Year Colleges		Four-Year Colleges		Medical Schools	Law Schools	Voc/ Tech
Public	Private	Public	Private			
0	2	1	4	0	0	6

Source: College Blue Book, Occupational Education 1997; Medical School Admission Requirements, 1998-99; Peterson's Guide to Two-Year Colleges, 1997; Peterson's Guide to Four-Year Colleges, 1997; Barron's Guide to Law Schools 1997

MAJOR EMPLOYERS

Major Employers

Carolina Power & Light
GE Capital Mortgage Corp.
Long Group (help supply services)
NC Farm Bureau Mutual Insurance
Penncorp Financial
Texfe Industries (fabric mills)
Waste Industries
RDS Corp. (building cleaning services)
Exide Electronics Corp.
HCA Raleigh Community Hospital
Medic Computer Systems
News & Observer Publishing
Rex Hospital
Wake County Hospital System
Pepcom Industries (beverages)

Note: companies listed are located in the city
Source: Dun's Business Rankings 1997; Ward's Business Directory, 1997

PUBLIC SAFETY

Crime Rate

Area	All Crimes	Violent Crimes				Property Crimes		
		Murder	Forcible Rape	Robbery	Aggrav. Assault	Burglary	Larceny -Theft	Motor Vehicle Theft
City	6,966.4	10.2	36.7	298.6	514.7	1,280.3	4,264.7	561.2
Suburbs[1]	5,787.0	9.8	24.1	169.5	273.3	1,319.4	3,595.5	395.3
MSA[2]	6,076.4	9.9	27.2	201.2	332.5	1,309.8	3,759.7	436.0
U.S.	5,078.9	7.4	36.1	202.4	388.2	943.0	2,975.9	525.9

Note: Crime rate is the number of crimes per 100,000 pop.; (1) defined as all areas within the MSA but located outside the central city; (2) Metropolitan Statistical Area - see Appendix A for areas incl.
Source: FBI Uniform Crime Reports 1996

RECREATION

Culture and Recreation

Museums	Symphony Orchestras	Opera Companies	Dance Companies	Professional Theatres	Zoos	Pro Sports Teams
4	1	1	4	3	0	0

Source: International Directory of the Performing Arts, 1996; Official Museum Directory, 1998; Chamber of Commerce/Economic Development 1997

Library System

The Wake County Public Library System has 17 branches, holdings of 1,072,645 volumes and a budget of $9,132,210 (1995-1996). *American Library Directory, 1997-1998*

MEDIA

Newspapers

Name	Type	Freq.	Distribution	Circulation
Baptist Informer	Black	1x/mo	Local	9,000
The Carolinian	Black	2x/wk	Area	17,700
The Citizen	General	1x/wk	Local	10,000
Dimensions	Black	2x/mo	Area	10,000
Middle American News	n/a	1x/mo	National	60,000
N C Catholic	Religious	2x/mo	Local	41,000
The News & Observer	n/a	7x/wk	Area	153,000

Note: Includes newspapers with circulations of 1,000 or more located in the city; n/a not available
Source: Burrelle's Media Directory, 1998 Edition

AM Radio Stations

Call Letters	Freq. (kHz)	Target Audience	Station Format	Music Format
WETC	540	General	M/N	Christian/Country/Spanish
WLLE	570	General	M/N/T	R&B
WPTF	680	n/a	T	n/a
WRBZ	850	General	N/S/T	n/a
WPJL	1240	Religious	M/N/S	Christian
WCRY	1460	General	M	Christian
WDUR	1490	General	M	R&B
WCLY	1550	Religious	M	Christian
WHPY	1590	n/a	M	Christian

Note: Stations included broadcast in the Raleigh metro area; n/a not available
Station Format: E = Educational; M = Music; N = News; S = Sports; T = Talk
Source: Burrelle's Media Directory, 1998 Edition

FM Radio Stations

Call Letters	Freq. (mHz)	Target Audience	Station Format	Music Format
WKNC	88.1	General	M/N/S	n/a
WXDU	88.7	n/a	M/N/S	n/a
WSHA	88.9	General	M	Christian/Jazz/R&B
WCPE	89.7	General	M/N	Classical
WRSN	93.9	n/a	M/N	Classic Rock
WQDR	94.7	General	M	Country
WKIX	96.1	General	M/N/S	Country
WQOK	97.5	General	M/N/S	Urban Contemporary
WTRG	100.7	General	M/N/S	Oldies
WRAL	101.5	General	M	Adult Contemporary
WZZU	103.9	General	M	Classic Rock
WFXK	104.3	General	M	Urban Contemporary
WDCG	105.1	General	M	Adult Contemporary
WRDU	106.1	General	M/N/S	AOR
WFXC	107.1	General	M	Urban Contemporary

Note: Stations included broadcast in the Raleigh metro area; n/a not available
Station Format: E = Educational; M = Music; N = News; S = Sports; T = Talk
Music Format: AOR = Album Oriented Rock; MOR = Middle-of-the-Road
Source: Burrelle's Media Directory, 1998 Edition

Television Stations

Name	Ch.	Affiliation	Type	Owner
WRAL	5	CBS	Commercial	Capitol Broadcasting Company, Inc.
WNCN	17	NBC	Commercial	General Electric Company
WLFL	22	Fox/UPN	Commercial	Sinclair Broadcast Group
WRDC	28	Fox/UPN	Commercial	Sinclair Broadcast Group
WRAY	30	n/a	n/a	Dan Beth Communications
WRMY	47	n/a	Commercial	Paxson Communications Corporation
WRAZ	50	WB	Commercial	Carolina Broadcasting Systems Inc.

Note: Stations included broadcast in the Raleigh metro area
Source: Burrelle's Media Directory, 1998 Edition

CLIMATE

Average and Extreme Temperatures

Temperature	Jan	Feb	Mar	Apr	May	Jun	Jul	Aug	Sep	Oct	Nov	Dec	Ann
Extreme High (°F)	79	84	90	95	97	104	105	105	104	98	88	79	105
Average High (°F)	50	53	61	72	79	86	89	87	81	72	62	53	71
Average Temp. (°F)	40	43	50	59	67	75	78	77	71	60	51	42	60
Average Low (°F)	29	31	38	46	55	63	68	67	60	48	39	32	48
Extreme Low (°F)	-9	5	11	23	29	38	48	46	37	19	11	4	-9

Note: Figures cover the years 1948-1990
Source: National Climatic Data Center, International Station Meteorological Climate Summary, 3/95

Average Precipitation/Snowfall/Humidity

Precip./Humidity	Jan	Feb	Mar	Apr	May	Jun	Jul	Aug	Sep	Oct	Nov	Dec	Ann
Avg. Precip. (in.)	3.4	3.6	3.6	2.9	3.9	3.6	4.4	4.4	3.2	2.9	3.0	3.1	42.0
Avg. Snowfall (in.)	2	3	1	Tr	0	0	0	0	0	0	Tr	1	8
Avg. Rel. Hum. 7am (%)	79	79	79	80	84	86	88	91	91	90	84	81	84
Avg. Rel. Hum. 4pm (%)	53	49	46	43	51	54	57	59	57	53	51	53	52

Note: Figures cover the years 1948-1990; Tr = Trace amounts (<0.05 in. of rain; <0.5 in. of snow)
Source: National Climatic Data Center, International Station Meteorological Climate Summary, 3/95

Weather Conditions

Temperature			Daytime Sky			Precipitation		
32°F & below	45°F & below	90°F & above	Clear	Partly cloudy	Cloudy	0.01 inch or more precip.	0.1 inch or more snow/ice	Thunder-storms
77	160	39	98	143	124	110	3	42

Note: Figures are average number of days per year and covers the years 1948-1990
Source: National Climatic Data Center, International Station Meteorological Climate Summary, 3/95

AIR & WATER QUALITY

Maximum Pollutant Concentrations

	Particulate Matter (ug/m³)	Carbon Monoxide (ppm)	Sulfur Dioxide (ppm)	Nitrogen Dioxide (ppm)	Ozone (ppm)	Lead (ug/m³)
MSA[1] Level	49	6	0.010	n/a	0.11	n/a
NAAQS[2]	150	9	0.140	0.053	0.12	1.50
Met NAAQS?	Yes	Yes	Yes	n/a	Yes	n/a

Note: (1) Metropolitan Statistical Area - see Appendix A for areas included; (2) National Ambient Air Quality Standards; ppm = parts per million; ug/m³ = micrograms per cubic meter; n/a not available
Source: EPA, National Air Quality and Emissions Trends Report, 1996

Pollutant Standards Index

In the Raleigh MSA (see Appendix A for areas included), the Pollutant Standards Index (PSI) exceeded 100 on 0 days in 1996. A PSI value greater than 100 indicates that air quality would be in the unhealthful range on that day. *EPA, National Air Quality and Emissions Trends Report, 1996*

Drinking Water

Water System Name	Pop. Served	Primary Water Source Type	Number of Violations in Fiscal Year 1997	Type of Violation/ Contaminants
City of Raleigh	225,000	Surface	None	None

Note: Data as of January 16, 1998
Source: EPA, Office of Ground Water and Drinking Water, Safe Drinking Water Information System

Raleigh tap water is neutral, soft and fluoridated.
Editor & Publisher Market Guide, 1998

Richmond, Virginia

Background

Richmond is the genteel and aristocratic capital of Virginia. Home to blueblooded old families such as the Byrds, Lees, and Davises, Richmond has played a vital role in both U.S. and Confederate histories.

Richmond was first claimed in 1607 as English territory by John Smith - of Pocahantas fame - and Christopher Newport. In 1679, the area was granted to William Byrd I, with the understanding that he establish a settlement. His son, William Byrd II continued his father's work, and along with William Mayo, surveyed lots for what was to be named Richmond.

During the Revolutionary War, Richmond played host to two Virginia Conventions. These Conventions, which held founding fathers, such as George Washington, Thomas Jefferson, Benjamin Harrison, and Patrick Henry in the same room, ratified the Constitution as the law of the land for the emerging nation.

No sooner, however, had the United States congealed as a nation when dissension split the nation in two, causing fragmentation once again. During this time, Richmond was called upon to serve as the Confederate States' Capital, although the city was one of the most reluctant to secede. From the Roman Temple inspired Capitol designed by Thomas Jefferson, Jefferson Davis ruled as President of the Confederacy.

Today, unsurprisingly, Richmond ranks high in its position as an authority on both Southern and Virginia history. The Virginia State Library, the Confederate Museum, The Virginia Historical Society, and its state capitol attest to this.

After its moments in the spotlight, Richmond wisely stepped down to a position of economic stability. Richmond witnessed low unemployment rates during both the depression and the late 1970's. With restoration of historic districts such as Jackson Ward — a neighborhood that saw its first Black-owned banks and insurance companies, Shockoe Slip — an old milling and tobacco center, and The Fan District — a neighborhood of 19th century townhouses and the Virginia Commonwealth University, whose streets fan out to the west, a new vitality has come to downtown Richmond.

Virginia has experienced recent economic growth because of its attraction to companies involved in high-technology. There was over $4 billion in economic development activity in 1995 with the northern part of the state being home to 300 high-tech companies. Richmond is the site of a $3 billion Motorola microprocessor facility, and the company along with Siemens will invest over another billion in the White Oak Semiconductor Plant, also in Richmond. One of the new research and development parks, the Virginia Biotechnology Research Park is also located in Richmond. *World Trade 4/97*

The climate of Richmond is classified as modified continental with its warm summer and humid, mild winters. If it snows the accumulation remains on the ground only for one or two days. Ice storms are not uncommon but are not usually severe enough to cause considerable damage.

Hurricanes and tropical storms, when they occur, are responsible for the flooding during the summer and early fall months. Tornadoes are infrequent but some notable occurrences have been observed in the Richmond area.

General Rankings and Evaluative Comments

- Richmond was ranked #160 out of 300 cities by *Money's* 1997 "Survey of the Best Places to Live." Criteria used: health services, crime, economy, housing, education, transportation, weather, leisure and the arts. The city was ranked #135 in 1996 and #276 in 1995. *Money, July 1997; Money, September 1996; Money, September 1995*

- Richmond appeared on *Fortune's* list of "North America's Most Improved Cities" Rank: 10 out of 10. The selected cities satisfied basic business-location needs and also demonstrated improvement over a five- to ten-year period in a number of business and quality-of-life measures.

  "Like a faded Southern belle waxing nostalgic for her moonlight-and-magnolia heyday, Richmond seemed doomed to find glory only in reliving its brief moment of power as the capital of the Confederacy; it has long since been eclipsed by the towns it once dwarfed—Atlanta and Charlotte. But enter the 1990s. With a rejuvenated statewide economic development program, coupled with an aggressive Richmond-focused industrial recruitment initiative begun in 1994, it has blossomed into a much more business-friendly town....

  Richmond has bolstered its image as a technology center thanks in large part to a corporate-led campaign to strengthen Virginia Commonwealth University, which now has an engineering school as well as a biotechnology research park adjacent to its medical school....

  Business and government have also joined forces to give the neglected James River waterfront a complete makeover. In additional to commercial and retail development along the river...there's been a dramatic increase in the area's wildlife population since the early 1990s...it is...the only city in the continental U.S. with a pair of breeding bald eagles living within the city limits.

  The natural beauty of the river, combined with the city's rich history, make it an easy place to attract workers...." *Fortune, 11/24/97*

- *Ladies Home Journal* ranked America's 200 largest cities based on the qualities women care about most. Richmond ranked 17 out of 200. Criteria: low crime rate, good public schools, well-paying jobs, quality health and child care, the presence of women in government, proportion of women-owned businesses, size of the wage gap with men, local economy, divorce rates, the ratio of single men to single women, whether there are laws that require at least the same number of public toilets for women as men, and the probability of good hair days. *Ladies Home Journal, November 1997*

- Richmond was ranked #176 out of 219 cities in terms of children's health, safety, and economic well-being. Criteria: total population, percent population change, birth rate, child immunization rate, infant mortality rate, percent low birth weight infants, percent of births to teens, physician-to-population ratio, student-to-teacher ratio, dropout rate, unemployment rate, median family income, percent of children in poverty, violent and property crime rates, number of juvenile arrests for violent crimes as a percent of the total crime index, number of days with pollution standard index (PSI) over 100, pounds toxic releases per 1,000 people and number of superfund sites. *Zero Population Growth, Children's Environmental Index 1997*

- According to *Working Mother,* "Child care advocates and Governor George Allen remained at odds all year, fighting over standards for child care. At one point, members of a child care council that Allen had appointed proposed lowering standards for caregiver training and reducing some adult-to child ratios for preschool children. Fortunately, the proposals were beaten back in the state legislature.

  On the positive side, the state did finally put up matching funds to secure its full share of federal child care funds (although there is concern among advocates over how these funds will be distributed). Virginia also set aside some modest funds for caregiver training." *Working Mother, July/August 1997*

Business Environment

STATE ECONOMY

State Economic Profile

"Although Virginia's exposure to manufacturing is somewhat less than the national average, the state still has a high exposure to secularly shrinking industries such as shipbuilding, apparel and textile. While these three industries constitute less than 25% of Virginia's manufacturing base, they more than account for the loss of manufacturing 4,400 jobs last year.

Since the 1990s began, house price appreciation in Virginia has been running well under the national rate. For example, house prices statewide rose only 3.0% last year, versus a 4.6% gain nationally. Over the last three years, new housing permits issued have averaged 45,000 per year, far above household formation rates, which have been running at 30,000 yearly. While Virginia's household formation rate will pick up as its economy firms, new housing activity must moderate from current levels to avoid an oversupplied market.

The impact of manufacturing and defense-related layoffs is increasingly being offset by strong private-sector employment growth. Low business costs and agglomeration economies will continue to attract not only lower-wage, back-office operations, but, increasingly, high-tech manufacturing and research facilities that pay higher-than-average wages. Strong population growth and in-migration will insure steady demand for retail goods and housing. Virginia is ranked well above average for long-term growth." *National Association of Realtors, Economic Profiles: The Fifty States, July 1997*

IMPORTS/EXPORTS

Total Export Sales

Area	1993 ($000)	1994 ($000)	1995 ($000)	1996 ($000)	% Chg. 1993-96	% Chg. 1995-96
MSA[1]	4,012,151	5,260,571	5,389,333	5,609,352	39.8	4.1
U.S.	464,858,354	512,415,609	583,030,524	622,827,063	34.0	6.8

Note: (1) Metropolitan Statistical Area - see Appendix A for areas included
Source: U.S. Department of Commerce, International Trade Association, Metropolitan Area Exports: An Export Performance Report on Over 250 U.S. Cities, October 1997

Imports/Exports by Port

Type	Cargo Value			Share of U.S. Total	
	1995 (US$mil.)	1996 (US$mil.)	% Change 1995-1996	1995 (%)	1996 (%)
Imports	492	570	15.88	0.13	0.15
Exports	1,284	1,501	16.90	0.56	0.63

Source: Global Trade Information Services, WaterBorne Trade Atlas 1997

CITY FINANCES

City Government Finances

Component	FY92 ($000)	FY92 (per capita $)
Revenue	715,137	3,571.27
Expenditure	739,700	3,693.94
Debt Outstanding	1,004,338	5,015.50
Cash & Securities	685,531	3,423.43

Source: U.S. Bureau of the Census, City Government Finances: 1991-92

City Government Revenue by Source

Source	FY92 ($000)	FY92 (per capita $)	FY92 (%)
From Federal Government	36,987	184.71	5.2
From State Governments	159,005	794.04	22.2
From Local Governments	1,948	9.73	0.3
Property Taxes	165,944	828.70	23.2
General Sales Taxes	20,321	101.48	2.8
Selective Sales Taxes	40,968	204.59	5.7
Income Taxes	0	0.00	0.0
Current Charges	89,623	447.56	12.5
Utility/Liquor Store	123,694	617.71	17.3
Employee Retirement[1]	19,169	95.73	2.7
Other	57,478	287.04	8.0

Note: (1) Excludes "city contributions," classified as "nonrevenue," intragovernmental transfers.
Source: U.S. Bureau of the Census, City Government Finances: 1991-92

City Government Expenditures by Function

Function	FY92 ($000)	FY92 (per capita $)	FY92 (%)
Educational Services	184,048	919.10	24.9
Employee Retirement[1]	22,315	111.44	3.0
Environment/Housing	135,238	675.36	18.3
Government Administration	31,063	155.12	4.2
Interest on General Debt	33,199	165.79	4.5
Public Safety	95,459	476.71	12.9
Social Services	56,666	282.98	7.7
Transportation	18,848	94.12	2.5
Utility/Liquor Store	142,172	709.98	19.2
Other	20,692	103.33	2.8

Note: (1) Payments to beneficiaries including withdrawal of contributions.
Source: U.S. Bureau of the Census, City Government Finances: 1991-92

Municipal Bond Ratings

Area	Moody's	S & P
Richmond	A1	AA

Note: n/a not available; n/r not rated
Source: Moody's Bond Record, 2/98; Statistical Abstract of the U.S., 1997; Governing Magazine, 9/97, 3/98

POPULATION

Population Growth

Area	1980	1990	% Chg. 1980-90	July 1996 Estimate	% Chg. 1990-96
City	219,214	203,056	-7.4	198,267	-2.4
MSA[1]	761,311	865,640	13.7	935,174	8.0
U.S.	226,545,805	248,765,170	9.8	265,179,411	6.6

Note: (1) Metropolitan Statistical Area - see Appendix A for areas included
Source: 1980/1990 Census of Housing and Population, Summary Tape File 3C; Census Bureau Population Estimates

Population Characteristics

Race	City					MSA[1]	
	1980		1990		% Chg. 1980-90	1990	
	Population	%	Population	%		Population	%
White	104,984	47.9	87,928	43.3	-16.2	595,909	68.8
Black	112,426	51.3	112,406	55.4	-0.0	252,376	29.2
Amer Indian/Esk/Aleut	330	0.2	441	0.2	33.6	2,610	0.3
Asian/Pacific Islander	1,110	0.5	1,664	0.8	49.9	11,768	1.4
Other	364	0.2	617	0.3	69.5	2,977	0.3
Hispanic Origin[2]	2,210	1.0	1,744	0.9	-21.1	8,788	1.0

Note: (1) Metropolitan Statistical Area - see Appendix A for areas included; (2) people of Hispanic origin can be of any race
Source: 1980/1990 Census of Housing and Population, Summary Tape File 3C

Ancestry

Area	German	Irish	English	Italian	U.S.	French	Polish	Dutch
City	9.3	7.4	13.2	1.8	4.2	1.8	1.0	0.9
MSA[1]	15.8	12.4	18.9	2.8	8.0	2.8	1.5	1.5
U.S.	23.3	15.6	13.1	5.9	5.3	4.2	3.8	2.5

Note: Figures are percentages and include persons that reported multiple ancestry (eg. if a person reported being Irish and Italian, they were included in both columns); (1) Metropolitan Statistical Area - see Appendix A for areas included
Source: 1990 Census of Population and Housing, Summary Tape File 3C

Age

Area	Median Age (Years)	Age Distribution (%)						
		Under 5	Under 18	18-24	25-44	45-64	65+	80+
City	33.1	6.9	20.8	12.9	33.9	17.1	15.3	3.7
MSA[1]	33.2	7.2	24.3	10.3	35.4	18.7	11.3	2.3
U.S.	32.9	7.3	25.6	10.5	32.6	18.7	12.5	2.8

Note: (1) Metropolitan Statistical Area - see Appendix A for areas included
Source: 1990 Census of Population and Housing, Summary Tape File 3C

Male/Female Ratio

Area	Number of males per 100 females (all ages)	Number of males per 100 females (18 years old+)
City	83.9	80.0
MSA[1]	90.7	87.1
U.S.	95.0	91.9

Note: (1) Metropolitan Statistical Area - see Appendix A for areas included
Source: 1990 Census of Population, General Population Characteristics

INCOME

Per Capita/Median/Average Income

Area	Per Capita ($)	Median Household ($)	Average Household ($)
City	13,993	23,551	32,497
MSA[1]	15,848	33,489	40,785
U.S.	14,420	30,056	38,453

Note: all figures are for 1989; (1) Metropolitan Statistical Area - see Appendix A for areas included
Source: 1990 Census of Population and Housing, Summary Tape File 3C

Household Income Distribution by Race

Income ($)	City (%)					U.S. (%)				
	Total	White	Black	Other	Hisp.[1]	Total	White	Black	Other	Hisp.[1]
Less than 5,000	10.6	5.0	16.4	12.1	3.6	6.2	4.8	15.2	8.6	8.8
5,000 - 9,999	11.1	9.5	13.1	4.7	8.5	9.3	8.6	14.2	9.9	11.1
10,000 - 14,999	10.9	8.9	12.9	10.3	12.5	8.8	8.5	11.0	9.8	11.0
15,000 - 24,999	19.8	18.8	20.6	27.9	30.4	17.5	17.3	18.9	18.5	20.5
25,000 - 34,999	15.5	16.1	14.9	16.9	19.6	15.8	16.1	14.2	15.4	16.4
35,000 - 49,999	15.1	17.3	12.9	15.1	8.2	17.9	18.6	13.3	16.1	16.0
50,000 - 74,999	10.1	12.9	7.3	8.3	10.2	15.0	15.8	9.3	13.4	11.1
75,000 - 99,999	3.4	5.3	1.5	2.5	3.0	5.1	5.5	2.6	4.7	3.1
100,000+	3.4	6.2	0.5	2.3	4.0	4.4	4.8	1.3	3.7	1.9

Note: all figures are for 1989; (1) people of Hispanic origin can be of any race
Source: 1990 Census of Population and Housing, Summary Tape File 3C

Effective Buying Income

Area	Per Capita ($)	Median Household ($)	Average Household ($)
City	14,164	24,224	33,076
MSA[1]	16,770	36,194	43,187
U.S.	15,444	33,201	41,849

Note: data as of 1/1/97; (1) Metropolitan Statistical Area - see Appendix A for areas included
Source: Standard Rate & Data Service, Newspaper Advertising Source, 2/98

Effective Household Buying Income Distribution

Area	% of Households Earning						
	$10,000 -$19,999	$20,000 -$34,999	$35,000 -$49,999	$50,000 -$74,999	$75,000 -$99,000	$100,000 -$124,999	$125,000 and up
City	21.5	25.4	15.3	11.1	3.4	1.2	1.7
MSA[1]	14.5	23.5	20.1	21.0	6.6	1.9	2.1
U.S.	16.5	23.4	18.3	18.2	6.4	2.1	2.4

Note: data as of 1/1/97; (1) Metropolitan Statistical Area - see Appendix A for areas included
Source: Standard Rate & Data Service, Newspaper Advertising Source, 2/98

Poverty Rates by Race and Age

Area	Total (%)	By Race (%)				By Age (%)		
		White	Black	Other	Hisp.[2]	Under 5 years old	Under 18 years old	65 years and over
City	20.9	10.3	28.9	19.0	17.1	37.6	35.8	16.5
MSA[1]	9.8	5.0	21.1	10.9	11.1	16.1	14.0	11.3
U.S.	13.1	9.8	29.5	23.1	25.3	20.1	18.3	12.8

Note: figures show the percent of people living below the poverty line in 1989. The average poverty threshold was $12,674 for a family of four in 1989; (1) Metropolitan Statistical Area - see Appendix A for areas included; (2) people of Hispanic origin can be of any race
Source: 1990 Census of Population and Housing, Summary Tape File 3C

EMPLOYMENT

Labor Force and Employment

Area	Civilian Labor Force			Workers Employed		
	Dec. '95	Dec. '96	% Chg.	Dec. '95	Dec. '96	% Chg.
City	96,150	101,755	5.8	91,480	97,910	7.0
MSA[1]	481,057	510,458	6.1	463,897	496,502	7.0
U.S.	134,583,000	136,742,000	1.6	127,903,000	130,785,000	2.3

Note: Data is not seasonally adjusted and covers workers 16 years of age and older;
(1) Metropolitan Statistical Area - see Appendix A for areas included
Source: Bureau of Labor Statistics, http://stats.bls.gov

Unemployment Rate

Area	1997											
	Jan.	Feb.	Mar.	Apr.	May	Jun.	Jul.	Aug.	Sep.	Oct.	Nov.	Dec.
City	5.1	5.0	4.6	4.6	5.1	5.9	5.3	5.4	5.5	4.5	4.2	3.8
MSA[1]	3.8	3.7	3.3	3.4	3.8	4.3	3.6	3.8	3.9	3.3	3.1	2.7
U.S.	5.9	5.7	5.5	4.8	4.7	5.2	5.0	4.8	4.7	4.4	4.3	4.4

Note: Data is not seasonally adjusted and covers workers 16 years of age and older; All figures are percentages; (1) Metropolitan Statistical Area - see Appendix A for areas included
Source: Bureau of Labor Statistics, http://stats.bls.gov

Employment by Industry

Sector	MSA[1]		U.S.
	Number of Employees	Percent of Total	Percent of Total
Services	140,000	26.1	29.0
Retail Trade	99,700	18.6	18.5
Government	97,300	18.2	16.1
Manufacturing	61,600	11.5	15.0
Finance/Insurance/Real Estate	44,300	8.3	5.7
Wholesale Trade	30,600	5.7	5.4
Transportation/Public Utilities	27,900	5.2	5.3
Construction	33,800	6.3	4.5
Mining	800	0.1	0.5

Note: Figures cover non-farm employment as of 12/97 and are not seasonally adjusted; (1) Metropolitan Statistical Area - see Appendix A for areas included
Source: Bureau of Labor Statistics, http://stats.bls.gov

Employment by Occupation

Occupation Category	City (%)	MSA[1] (%)	U.S. (%)
White Collar	59.9	63.1	58.1
Executive/Admin./Management	11.5	13.9	12.3
Professional	15.9	14.3	14.1
Technical & Related Support	3.7	4.1	3.7
Sales	11.0	12.3	11.8
Administrative Support/Clerical	17.9	18.5	16.3
Blue Collar	21.4	23.5	26.2
Precision Production/Craft/Repair	7.3	10.9	11.3
Machine Operators/Assem./Insp.	6.0	5.2	6.8
Transportation/Material Movers	4.0	3.8	4.1
Cleaners/Helpers/Laborers	4.0	3.6	3.9
Services	17.9	12.4	13.2
Farming/Forestry/Fishing	0.9	1.1	2.5

Note: figures cover employed persons 16 years old and over; (1) Metropolitan Statistical Area - see Appendix A for areas included
Source: 1990 Census of Population and Housing, Summary Tape File 3C

Occupational Employment Projections: 1990 - 2005

Occupations Expected to have the Largest Job Growth (ranked by numerical growth)	Fast-Growing Occupations[1] (ranked by percent growth)
1. Salespersons, retail	1. Paralegals
2. Cashiers	2. Physical therapists
3. Registered nurses	3. Personal and home care aides
4. General managers & top executives	4. Operations research analysts
5. General office clerks	5. Computer engineers
6. Secretaries, except legal & medical	6. Human services workers
7. Receptionists and information clerks	7. Radiologic technicians
8. Nursing aides/orderlies/attendants	8. Travel agents
9. Janitors/cleaners/maids, ex. priv. hshld.	9. Medical assistants
10. Truck drivers, light	10. Home health aides

Projections cover the Richmond-Petersburg MSA - see Appendix A for areas included.
Note: (1) Includes occupations with total job growth of at least 100
Source: Virginia Employment Commission, Industry and Occupational Employment Projections: 1990-2005

Average Wages

Occupation	Wage	Occupation	Wage
Professional/Technical/Clerical	$/Week	**Health/Protective Services**	$/Week
Accountants III	809	Corrections Officers	-
Attorneys III	1,048	Firefighters	-
Budget Analysts III	-	Nurses, Licensed Practical II	-
Buyers/Contracting Specialists II	700	Nurses, Registered II	-
Clerks, Accounting III	444	Nursing Assistants II	-
Clerks, General III	-	Police Officers I	643
Computer Operators II	-	**Hourly Workers**	$/Hour
Computer Programmers II	609	Forklift Operators	13.17
Drafters II	-	General Maintenance Workers	9.62
Engineering Technicians III	-	Guards I	-
Engineering Technicians, Civil III	488	Janitors	6.44
Engineers III	976	Maintenance Electricians	20.05
Key Entry Operators I	-	Maintenance Electronics Techs II	-
Personnel Assistants III	-	Maintenance Machinists	17.39
Personnel Specialists III	781	Maintenance Mechanics, Machinery	19.54
Secretaries III	570	Material Handling Laborers	10.59
Switchboard Operator-Receptionist	-	Motor Vehicle Mechanics	13.73
Systems Analysts II	911	Shipping/Receiving Clerks	10.60
Systems Analysts Supervisor/Mgr II	1,379	Tool and Die Makers	-
Tax Collectors II	-	Truckdrivers, Tractor Trailer	15.37
Word Processors II	445	Warehouse Specialists	11.57

Note: Wage data includes full-time workers only for 8/96 and cover the Metropolitan Statistical Area (see Appendix A for areas included). Dashes indicate that data was not available.
Source: Bureau of Labor Statistics, Occupational Compensation Survey, 1/97

TAXES

Major State and Local Tax Rates

State Corp. Income (%)	State Personal Income (%)	Residential Property (effective rate per $100)	Sales & Use State (%)	Sales & Use Local (%)	State Gasoline (cents/ gallon)	State Cigarette (cents/ 20-pack)
6.0	2.0 - 5.75	n/a	3.5	1.0	17.5[a]	2.5[b]

Note: Personal/corporate income tax rates as of 1/97. Sales, gasoline and cigarette tax rates as of 1/98; (a) Does not include a 2% local option tax; (b) Counties and cities may impose an additional tax of 2 - 15 cents per pack
Source: Federation of Tax Administrators, www.taxadmin.org; Washington D.C. Department of Finance and Revenue, Tax Rates and Tax Burdens in the District of Columbia: A Nationwide Comparison, June 1997; Chamber of Commerce

Total Taxes Per Capita and as a Percent of Income

Area	Per Capita Income ($)	Per Capita Taxes ($)			Taxes as Pct. of Income (%)		
		Total	Federal	State/ Local	Total	Federal	State/ Local
Virginia	26,908	9,421	6,365	3,056	35.0	23.7	11.4
U.S.	26,187	9,205	6,127	3,078	35.2	23.4	11.8

Note: Figures are for 1997
Source: Tax Foundation, Web Site, www.taxfoundation.org

Estimated Tax Burden

Area	State Income	Local Income	Property	Sales	Total
Richmond	2,698	0	2,025	617	5,340

Note: The numbers are estimates of taxes paid by a married couple with two kids and annual earnings of $65,000. Sales tax estimates assume they spend average amounts on food, clothing, household goods and gasoline. Property tax estimates assume they live in a $225,000 home.
Source: Kiplinger's Personal Finance Magazine, June 1997

COMMERCIAL REAL ESTATE

Office Market

Class/ Location	Total Space (sq. ft.)	Vacant Space (sq. ft.)	Vac. Rate (%)	Under Constr. (sq. ft.)	Net Absorp. (sq. ft.)	Rental Rates ($/sq.ft./yr.)
Class A						
CBD	4,736,302	170,000	3.6	n/a	208,677	15.50-24.00
Outside CBD	7,285,998	510,000	7.0	480,000	488,015	11.00-18.00
Class B						
CBD	2,803,599	562,431	20.1	n/a	53,046	10.00-11.00
Outside CBD	4,031,863	309,011	7.7	n/a	46,351	11.00-15.50

Note: Data as of 10/97 and covers Richmond; CBD = Central Business District; n/a not available;
Source: Society of Industrial and Office Realtors, 1998 Comparative Statistics of Industrial and Office Real Estate Markets

"The majority of new development is concentrated in and around the Insbrook area regarded as one of the premier office parks in the market. Most of this development has been fueled by REITs, specifically Highwoods and Liberty Property Trust. More than 500,000 sq. ft. of new speculative space will be delivered in 1998. In addition, several existing buildings will be offering large blocks of space. This new space will be as quickly absorbed as was the case in 1997. Due to acquisitions and consolidations of Richmond-based banks, such as Wachovia's purchase of Central Fidelity, demand is expected to be positive but modest in 1998. The demand gap is already being filled, however, by the more than 75 suppliers that have established offices in and around Richmond. These firms plan to support the new Motorola-Seimens White Oak Semiconductor plant, currently under construction." *Society of Industrial and Office Realtors, 1998 Comparative Statistics of Industrial and Office Real Estate Markets*

Industrial Market

Location	Total Space (sq. ft.)	Vacant Space (sq. ft.)	Vac. Rate (%)	Under Constr. (sq. ft.)	Net Absorp. (sq. ft.)	Gross Lease ($/sq.ft./yr.)
Central City	4,530,404	544,250	12.0	0	98,214	2.25-5.50
Suburban	16,540,748	1,725,442	10.4	758,800	993,155	3.00-6.00

Note: Data as of 10/97 and covers Richmond; n/a not available
Source: Society of Industrial and Office Realtors, 1998 Comparative Statistics of Industrial and Office Real Estate Markets

"Activity in the High Tech/R&D market should speed up as Richmond's economy diversifies from a heavy manufacturing center to a magnet for the technology industry. High-Tech/R&D construction is predicted to grow by six to ten percent. Lease prices and the absorption pace should accelerate by one to five percent for that segment. The Motorola/Seimens $1.5 billion semiconductor plant under construction in Eastern Henrico County is scheduled to open in the second half of 1998 and provides the basis to support the above predictions. Marketwide, approximately 412,200 sq. ft. of speculative construction is planned to come on-line in 1998. About 60 percent was already underway by the third quarter 1997. Flexible facilities, or 'office/service' space, are being developed on a speculative basis in all four quadrants of the suburbs, with 231,600 sq. ft. in progress." *Society of Industrial and Office Realtors, 1998 Comparative Statistics of Industrial and Office Real Estate Markets*

COMMERCIAL UTILITIES

Typical Monthly Electric Bills

Area	Commercial Service ($/month)		Industrial Service ($/month)	
	12 kW demand 1,500 kWh	100 kW demand 30,000 kWh	1,000 kW demand 400,000 kWh	20,000 kW demand 10,000,000 kWh
City	133	2,204	21,806	428,249
U.S.	162	2,360	25,590	545,677

Note: Based on rates in effect July 1, 1997
Source: Edison Electric Institute, Typical Residential, Commercial and Industrial Bills, Summer 1997

TRANSPORTATION

Transportation Statistics

Avg. travel time to work (min.)	20.1
Interstate highways	I-64; I-85; I-95
Bus lines	
In-city	Greater Richmond Transit Co.
Inter-city	4
Passenger air service	
Airport	Richmond International
Airlines	11
Aircraft departures	22,171 (1995)
Enplaned passengers	998,742 (1995)
Rail service	Amtrak
Motor freight carriers	80
Major waterways/ports	Port of Richmond

Source: OAG, Business Travel Planner, Summer 1997; Editor & Publisher Market Guide, 1998; FAA Airport Activity Statistics, 1996; Amtrak National Time Table, Northeast Timetable, Fall/Winter 1997-98; 1990 Census of Population and Housing, STF 3C; Chamber of Commerce/Economic Development 1997; Jane's Urban Transport Systems 1997-98; Transit Fact Book 1997

Means of Transportation to Work

Area	Car/Truck/Van		Public Transportation			Bicycle	Walked	Other Means	Worked at Home
	Drove Alone	Car-pooled	Bus	Subway	Railroad				
City	64.5	13.8	12.5	0.0	0.0	1.0	5.4	1.1	1.7
MSA[1]	77.2	13.4	3.5	0.0	0.0	0.3	2.5	0.9	2.1
U.S.	73.2	13.4	3.0	1.5	0.5	0.4	3.9	1.2	3.0

Note: figures shown are percentages and only include workers 16 years old and over;
(1) Metropolitan Statistical Area - see Appendix A for areas included
Source: 1990 Census of Population and Housing, Summary Tape File 3C

BUSINESSES

Major Business Headquarters

Company Name	1997 Rankings	
	Fortune 500	Forbes 500
CSX	130	-
Carpenter	-	253
Circuit City Group	204	-
Dominion Resources	292	-
James River	253	-
Reynolds Metals	205	-
Ukrop's Super Markets	-	438
Universal	379	-

Note: Companies listed are located in the city; Dashes indicate no ranking
Fortune 500: companies that produce a 10-K are ranked 1 - 500 based on 1996 revenue
Forbes 500: private companies are ranked 1 - 500 based on 1996 revenue
Source: Forbes 12/1/97; Fortune 4/28/97

Minority Business Opportunity

Richmond is home to one company which is on the Black Enterprise Industrial/Service 100 list (largest based on gross sales): Community Pride Food Stores (supermarket). Criteria: 1) operational in previous calendar year; 2) at least 51% black-owned; 3) manufactures/owns the product it sells or provides industrial or consumer services. Brokerages, real estate firms and firms that provide professional services are not eligible. *Black Enterprise, July 1997*

Small Business Opportunity

Richmond was included among *Entrepreneur* magazines listing of the "20 Best Cities for Small Business." It was ranked #1 among mid-size metro areas. Criteria: risk of failure, business performance, economic growth, affordability and state attitude towards business. *Entrepreneur, 10/97*

HOTELS & MOTELS

Hotels/Motels

Area	Hotels/ Motels	Rooms	Luxury-Level Hotels/Motels		Average Minimum Rates ($)		
			♦♦♦♦	♦♦♦♦♦	♦♦	♦♦♦	♦♦♦♦
City	40	5,730	1	0	60	98	150
Airport	7	861	0	0	n/a	n/a	n/a
Suburbs	24	3,024	0	0	n/a	n/a	n/a
Total	71	9,615	1	0	n/a	n/a	n/a

Note: n/a not available; Classifications range from one diamond (budget properties with basic amenities) to five diamond (luxury properties with the finest service, rooms and facilities).
Source: OAG, Business Travel Planner, Summer 1997

CONVENTION CENTERS

Major Convention Centers

Center Name	Meeting Rooms	Exhibit Space (sf)
Hyatt Richmond	19	15,837
Richmond Centre for Conventions and Exhibitions	9	62,216
Richmond Coliseum	12	36,000
Richmond Marriott	26	22,773
Virginia State Fairgrounds at Strawberry Hill	n/a	200,000
Richmond Mosque	4	18,000

Note: n/a not available
Source: Trade Shows Worldwide 1997

Living Environment

COST OF LIVING

Cost of Living Index

Composite Index	Housing	Utilities	Groceries	Health Care	Trans-portation	Misc. Goods/ Services
104.8	103.8	124.4	99.2	106.1	106.5	102.9

Note: U.S. = 100
Source: ACCRA, Cost of Living Index, 3rd Quarter 1997

HOUSING

Median Home Prices and Housing Affordability

Area	Median Price[2] 3rd Qtr. 1997 ($)	HOI[3] 3rd Qtr. 1997	Afford-ability Rank[4]
MSA[1]	118,000	71.9	80
U.S.	127,000	63.7	–

Note: (1) Metropolitan Statistical Area - see Appendix A for areas included; (2) U.S. figures calculated from the sales of 625,000 new and existing homes in 195 markets; (3) Housing Opportunity Index - percent of homes sold that were within the reach of the median income household at the prevailing mortgage interest rate; (4) Rank is from 1-195 with 1 being most affordable
Source: National Association of Home Builders, Housing Opportunity Index, 3rd Quarter 1997

It is projected that the median price of existing single-family homes in the metro area will increase by 12.5% in 1998. Nationwide, home prices are projected to increase 6.6%. *Kiplinger's Personal Finance Magazine, January 1998*

Average New Home Price

Area	Price ($)
City	135,500
U.S.	135,710

Note: Figures are based on a new home with 1,800 sq. ft. of living area on an 8,000 sq. ft. lot.
Source: ACCRA, Cost of Living Index, 3rd Quarter 1997

Average Apartment Rent

Area	Rent ($/mth)
City	749
U.S.	569

Note: Figures are based on an unfurnished two bedroom, 1-1/2 or 2 bath apartment, approximately 950 sq. ft. in size, excluding all utilities except water
Source: ACCRA, Cost of Living Index, 3rd Quarter 1997

RESIDENTIAL UTILITIES

Average Residential Utility Costs

Area	All Electric ($/mth)	Part Electric ($/mth)	Other Energy ($/mth)	Phone ($/mth)
City	130.48	–	–	20.52
U.S.	109.40	55.25	43.64	19.48

Source: ACCRA, Cost of Living Index, 3rd Quarter 1997

HEALTH CARE

Average Health Care Costs

Area	Hospital ($/day)	Doctor ($/visit)	Dentist ($/visit)
City	428.80	51.14	64.50
U.S.	392.91	48.76	60.84

Note: Hospital - based on a semi-private room. Doctor - based on a general practitioner's routine exam of an established patient. Dentist - based on adult teeth cleaning and periodic oral exam.
Source: ACCRA, Cost of Living Index, 3rd Quarter 1997

Distribution of Office-Based Physicians

Area	Family/Gen. Practitioners	Specialists		
		Medical	Surgical	Other
MSA[1]	264	646	480	491

Note: Data as of 12/31/96; (1) Metropolitan Statistical Area - see Appendix A for areas included
Source: American Medical Assn., Physician Characteristics & Distribution in the U.S., 1997-1998

Hospitals

Richmond has 11 general medical and surgical hospitals, 2 psychiatric, 1 eye, ear, nose and throat, 1 rehabilitation, 1 orthopedic. *AHA Guide to the Healthcare Field 1997-98*

Medical College of Virginia Hospitals is among the 100 best-run hospitals in the U.S. *Modern Healthcare, January 5, 1998*

EDUCATION

Public School District Statistics

District Name	Num. Sch.	Enroll.	Classroom Teachers[1]	Pupils per Teacher	Minority Pupils (%)	Current Exp.[2] ($/pupil)
Henrico Cnty Public Schls	57	37,112	n/a	n/a	35.3	4,909
Richmond City Public Schls	61	27,708	n/a	n/a	91.6	6,856

Note: Data covers the 1995-1996 school year unless otherwise noted; (1) Excludes teachers reported as working in school district offices rather than in schools; (2) Based on 1993-94 enrollment collected by the Census Bureau, not the enrollment figure shown in column 3; SD = School District; ISD = Independent School District; n/a not available
Source: National Center for Education Statistics, Common Core of Data Survey; Bureau of the Census

Educational Quality

School District	Education Quotient[1]	Graduate Outcome[2]	Community Index[3]	Resource Index[4]
Richmond City	85.0	63.0	65.0	128.0

Note: Nearly 1,000 secondary school districts were rated in terms of educational quality. The scores range from a low of 50 to a high of 150; (1) Average of the Graduate Outcome, Community and Resource indexes; (2) Based on graduation rates and college board scores (SAT/ACT); (3) Based on the surrounding community's average level of education and the area's average income level; (4) Based on teacher salaries, per-pupil expenditures and student-teacher ratios.
Source: Expansion Management, Ratings Issue 1997

Educational Attainment by Race

Area	High School Graduate (%)					Bachelor's Degree (%)				
	Total	White	Black	Other	Hisp.[2]	Total	White	Black	Other	Hisp.[2]
City	68.1	80.1	56.3	76.2	75.1	24.2	39.4	9.5	33.2	26.9
MSA[1]	75.8	81.1	61.5	75.3	79.5	23.8	28.1	11.9	32.4	27.9
U.S.	75.2	77.9	63.1	60.4	49.8	20.3	21.5	11.4	19.4	9.2

Note: figures shown cover persons 25 years old and over; (1) Metropolitan Statistical Area - see Appendix A for areas included; (2) people of Hispanic origin can be of any race
Source: 1990 Census of Population and Housing, Summary Tape File 3C

School Enrollment by Type

Area	Preprimary				Elementary/High School			
	Public		Private		Public		Private	
	Enrollment	%	Enrollment	%	Enrollment	%	Enrollment	%
City	1,849	62.6	1,105	37.4	24,399	89.2	2,946	10.8
MSA[1]	9,730	59.5	6,628	40.5	130,034	93.0	9,840	7.0
U.S.	2,679,029	59.5	1,824,256	40.5	38,379,689	90.2	4,187,099	9.8

Note: figures shown cover persons 3 years old and over;
(1) Metropolitan Statistical Area - see Appendix A for areas included
Source: 1990 Census of Population and Housing, Summary Tape File 3C

School Enrollment by Race

Area	Preprimary (%)				Elementary/High School (%)			
	White	Black	Other	Hisp.[1]	White	Black	Other	Hisp.[1]
City	34.4	63.4	2.2	0.7	20.0	79.0	1.0	1.0
MSA[2]	72.2	26.1	1.7	1.2	61.8	35.5	2.7	1.2
U.S.	80.4	12.5	7.1	7.8	74.1	15.6	10.3	12.5

Note: figures shown cover persons 3 years old and over; (1) people of Hispanic origin can be of any race; (2) Metropolitan Statistical Area - see Appendix A for areas included
Source: 1990 Census of Population and Housing, Summary Tape File 3C

SAT/ACT Scores

Area/District	1997 SAT				1997 ACT	
	Percent of Graduates Tested (%)	Average Math Score	Average Verbal Score	Average Combined Score	Percent of Graduates Tested (%)	Average Composite Score
Richmond	51	451	464	915	7	18.2
State	69	497	506	1,003	6	20.7
U.S.	42	511	505	1,016	36	21.0

Note: Math and verbal SAT scores are out of a possible 800; ACT scores are out of a possible 36
Caution: Comparing or ranking states/cities on the basis of SAT/ACT scores alone is invalid and strongly discouraged by the The College Board and The American College Testing Program as students who take the tests are self-selected and do not represent the entire student population.
Source: Richmond Public Schools, Department of Instruction & Accountability, 1997; College Board, 1997; American College Testing Program, 1997

Classroom Teacher Salaries in Public Schools

District	B.A. Degree		M.A. Degree		Ph.D. Degree	
	Min. ($)	Max ($)	Min. ($)	Max. ($)	Min. ($)	Max. ($)
Richmond	25,572	41,395	26,851	43,464	29,129	46,534
Average[1]	26,120	39,270	28,175	44,667	31,643	49,825

Note: Salaries are for 1996-1997; (1) Based on all school districts covered; n/a not available
Source: American Federation of Teachers (unpublished data)

Higher Education

Two-Year Colleges		Four-Year Colleges		Medical Schools	Law Schools	Voc/ Tech
Public	Private	Public	Private			
1	2	1	2	1	1	15

Source: College Blue Book, Occupational Education 1997; Medical School Admission Requirements, 1998-99; Peterson's Guide to Two-Year Colleges, 1997; Peterson's Guide to Four-Year Colleges, 1997; Barron's Guide to Law Schools 1997

MAJOR EMPLOYERS

Major Employers

Blue Cross & Blue Shield of VA
Circuit City Stores
Federal Reserve Bank of Richmond
Health Corp of VA
William Byrd Press
Reynolds Metals
American Critical Care Services
Virginia Electric Power
Southern States Cooperative
Central Fidelity National Bank
Crestar Bank
HCA Health Services of VA
Johnston-Willis Ltd (hospitals)
Overnite Transportation Co.
Richmond Memorial Hospital
St. Mary's Hospital of Richmond
Sterile Concepts (medical supplies)

Note: companies listed are located in the city
Source: Dun's Business Rankings 1997; Ward's Business Directory, 1997

PUBLIC SAFETY

Crime Rate

Area	All Crimes	Violent Crimes				Property Crimes		
		Murder	Forcible Rape	Robbery	Aggrav. Assault	Burglary	Larceny -Theft	Motor Vehicle Theft
City	9,650.0	54.7	69.8	754.1	772.6	1,963.1	5,045.9	989.8
Suburbs[1]	4,276.2	5.1	21.9	101.8	171.3	634.3	3,120.1	221.7
MSA[2]	5,455.2	16.0	32.4	244.9	303.3	925.8	3,542.6	390.2
U.S.	5,078.9	7.4	36.1	202.4	388.2	943.0	2,975.9	525.9

Note: Crime rate is the number of crimes per 100,000 pop.; (1) defined as all areas within the MSA but located outside the central city; (2) Metropolitan Statistical Area - see Appendix A for areas incl.
Source: FBI Uniform Crime Reports 1996

RECREATION

Culture and Recreation

Museums	Symphony Orchestras	Opera Companies	Dance Companies	Professional Theatres	Zoos	Pro Sports Teams
15	2	1	1	2	0	0

Source: International Directory of the Performing Arts, 1996; Official Museum Directory, 1998; Chamber of Commerce/Economic Development 1997

Library System

The County of Henrico Public Library has 12 branches, holdings of 641,428 volumes and a budget of $6,231,093 (1995-1996). The Richmond Public Library has eight branches, holdings of 866,536 volumes and a budget of $3,594,372 (1995-1996). *American Library Directory, 1997-1998*

MEDIA

Newspapers

Name	Type	Freq.	Distribution	Circulation
Catholic Virginian	Religious	26x/yr	State	60,000
Religious Herald	Religious	1x/wk	National	25,000
Richmond Free Press	Black	1x/wk	Local	25,000
Richmond Times-Dispatch	General	7x/wk	Area	211,598

Note: Includes newspapers with circulations of 1,000 or more located in the city; Source: Burrelle's Media Directory, 1998 Edition

AM Radio Stations

Call Letters	Freq. (kHz)	Target Audience	Station Format	Music Format
WGGM	820	n/a	M/N/S	Christian/Country
WRVH	910	n/a	N/S	n/a
WXGI	950	General	M/N/S	Country
WRVA	1140	General	N/T	n/a
WTVR	1380	General	M/N/S	Adult Standards/Big Band/MOR
WFTH	1590	General	M	Christian

Note: Stations included broadcast in the Richmond metro area; n/a not available
Station Format: E = Educational; M = Music; N = News; S = Sports; T = Talk
Music Format: AOR = Album Oriented Rock; MOR = Middle-of-the-Road
Source: Burrelle's Media Directory, 1998 Edition

FM Radio Stations

Call Letters	Freq. (mHz)	Target Audience	Station Format	Music Format
WCVE	88.9	General	E/M/N	Classical/Jazz
WDCE	90.1	General	E/M/N/S/T	Alternative/Classical/Jazz/Urban Contemporary
WCDX	92.7	General	M	Urban Contemporary
WRVQ	94.5	General	M/N/S	Contemporary Top 40
WKHK	95.3	General	M	Country
WKLR	96.5	General	M	Classic Rock
WTVR	98.1	General	M/N	Adult Contemporary
WPLZ	99.3	General	M	Urban Contemporary
WRXL	102.1	General	M/N/S	AOR/Alternative/Classic Rock
WMXB	103.7	General	M/N/S	Adult Contemporary
WVGO	104.7	n/a	M/N/S	Alternative
WDYL	105.7	General	M	Christian
WBZU	106.5	General	M	Alternative

Note: Stations included broadcast in the Richmond metro area; n/a not available
Station Format: E = Educational; M = Music; N = News; S = Sports; T = Talk
Music Format: AOR = Album Oriented Rock; MOR = Middle-of-the-Road
Source: Burrelle's Media Directory, 1998 Edition

Television Stations

Name	Ch.	Affiliation	Type	Owner
WTVR	6	CBS	Commercial	Roy Park Broadcasting
WRIC	8	ABC	Commercial	Young Broadcasting Inc.
WWBT	12	NBC	Commercial	Jefferson Pilot Communications Company
WCVE	23	PBS	Public	Central Virginia Educational Telecommunications Corp.
WRLH	35	Fox	Commercial	Sullivan Broadcasting
WHTJ	41	PBS	Public	Central Virginia Educational Telecommunications Corp.
WCVW	57	PBS	Public	Central Virginia Educational Telecommunications Corp.
WUPV	65	UPN	Commercial	Lockwood Broadcasting

Note: Stations included broadcast in the Richmond metro area
Source: Burrelle's Media Directory, 1998 Edition

CLIMATE

Average and Extreme Temperatures

Temperature	Jan	Feb	Mar	Apr	May	Jun	Jul	Aug	Sep	Oct	Nov	Dec	Ann
Extreme High (°F)	80	82	91	96	98	104	105	103	103	99	86	80	105
Average High (°F)	47	50	59	69	78	85	88	86	81	71	60	50	69
Average Temp. (°F)	38	40	48	58	66	75	78	77	71	60	50	41	58
Average Low (°F)	28	30	37	45	55	63	68	67	60	48	38	31	48
Extreme Low (°F)	-6	-8	11	19	31	40	51	47	35	21	14	1	-8

Note: Figures cover the years 1921-1990
Source: National Climatic Data Center, International Station Meteorological Climate Summary, 3/95

Average Precipitation/Snowfall/Humidity

Precip./Humidity	Jan	Feb	Mar	Apr	May	Jun	Jul	Aug	Sep	Oct	Nov	Dec	Ann
Avg. Precip. (in.)	3.3	3.0	3.5	3.1	3.7	3.7	5.2	4.9	3.3	3.1	2.9	3.1	43.0
Avg. Snowfall (in.)	5	4	2	Tr	0	0	0	0	0	Tr	1	2	13
Avg. Rel. Hum. 7am (%)	79	79	78	76	81	82	85	89	90	89	84	80	83
Avg. Rel. Hum. 4pm (%)	54	51	46	43	51	53	56	58	57	53	51	55	52

Note: Figures cover the years 1921-1990; Tr = Trace amounts (<0.05 in. of rain; <0.5 in. of snow)
Source: National Climatic Data Center, International Station Meteorological Climate Summary, 3/95

Weather Conditions

Temperature			Daytime Sky			Precipitation		
10°F & below	32°F & below	90°F & above	Clear	Partly cloudy	Cloudy	0.01 inch or more precip.	0.1 inch or more snow/ice	Thunder-storms
3	79	41	90	147	128	115	7	43

Note: Figures are average number of days per year and covers the years 1921-1990
Source: National Climatic Data Center, International Station Meteorological Climate Summary, 3/95

AIR & WATER QUALITY

Maximum Pollutant Concentrations

	Particulate Matter (ug/m³)	Carbon Monoxide (ppm)	Sulfur Dioxide (ppm)	Nitrogen Dioxide (ppm)	Ozone (ppm)	Lead (ug/m³)
MSA[1] Level	69	3	0.027	0.022	0.11	0.01
NAAQS[2]	150	9	0.140	0.053	0.12	1.50
Met NAAQS?	Yes	Yes	Yes	Yes	Yes	Yes

Note: (1) Metropolitan Statistical Area - see Appendix A for areas included; (2) National Ambient Air Quality Standards; ppm = parts per million; ug/m³ = micrograms per cubic meter; n/a not available
Source: EPA, National Air Quality and Emissions Trends Report, 1996

Pollutant Standards Index

In the Richmond MSA (see Appendix A for areas included), the Pollutant Standards Index (PSI) exceeded 100 on 0 days in 1996. A PSI value greater than 100 indicates that air quality would be in the unhealthful range on that day. *EPA, National Air Quality and Emissions Trends Report, 1996*

Drinking Water

Water System Name	Pop. Served	Primary Water Source Type	Number of Violations in Fiscal Year 1997	Type of Violation/ Contaminants
City of Richmond WTP	209,000	Surface	None	None

Note: Data as of January 16, 1998
Source: EPA, Office of Ground Water and Drinking Water, Safe Drinking Water Information System

Richmond tap water is alkaline, soft and fluoridated.
Editor & Publisher Market Guide, 1998

Stamford, Connecticut

Background

In 1640 Nathaniel Turner, an agent for the New Haven Colony purchased the land now called Stamford from the Siwanoys tribe. It was settled in 1841 and remained a farming community until the middle of the 19th century. Industrial growth began after the railroad was built in the 1840's. The city still retains its New England charm despite its growth as a research and manufacturing center.

Located on Long Island Sound in southwestern Connecticut in Fairfield County, many of its residents commute to New York City which is about 36 miles away.

The city is noted for the laboratories that carry on industrial research in the optics, electronics, chemicals and pharmaceuticals. Industrial products include chemicals, postage meters, electronics, electric shavers, dies, cosmetics, and rubber.

Fairfield County is experiencing a boom in jobs along with a low unemployment rate. In Stamford, skilled programmer and clerical workers with computer experience are typical of the jobs that are in high demand. The city of Stamford is also looking into recruiting foreign technical workers under a public-private partnership with local employers. In addition, the University of Connecticut has developed a program at its Stamford Campus aimed at training technical workers. *New York Times 1/2/97*

Stamford was incorporated as a borough in 1830 and as a city in 1893.

The weather is influenced primarily by land and sea breezes. Temperatures are a bit lower than nearby inland locations in the summer months, while fall and winter months are more moderate. Snowfall is generally around 10 inches less than areas a few miles inland, due to the proximity to Long Island Sound. One of the hazards along the coastal areas is the flooding which may occur with the arrival of slow-moving deepening low pressure systems. This may result in tides three to five fee higher than normal.

General Rankings and Evaluative Comments

- Stamford was ranked #34 out of 300 cities by *Money's* 1997 "Survey of the Best Places to Live." Criteria used: health services, crime, economy, housing, education, transportation, weather, leisure and the arts. The city was ranked #112 in 1996 and #65 in 1995. *Money, July 1997; Money, September 1996; Money, September 1995*

- *Ladies Home Journal* ranked America's 200 largest cities based on the qualities women care about most. Stamford ranked 71 out of 200. Criteria: low crime rate, good public schools, well-paying jobs, quality health and child care, the presence of women in government, proportion of women-owned businesses, size of the wage gap with men, local economy, divorce rates, the ratio of single men to single women, whether there are laws that require at least the same number of public toilets for women as men, and the probability of good hair days. *Ladies Home Journal, November 1997*

- Stamford was ranked #13 out of 219 cities in terms of children's health, safety, and economic well-being. Criteria: total population, percent population change, birth rate, child immunization rate, infant mortality rate, percent low birth weight infants, percent of births to teens, physician-to-population ratio, student-to-teacher ratio, dropout rate, unemployment rate, median family income, percent of children in poverty, violent and property crime rates, number of juvenile arrests for violent crimes as a percent of the total crime index, number of days with pollution standard index (PSI) over 100, pounds toxic releases per 1,000 people and number of superfund sites. *Zero Population Growth, Children's Environmental Index 1997*

- Stamford appeared on *Sales & Marketing Management's* list of the 20 hottest domestic markets to do business in. Rank: 7 out of 20. America's 320 Metropolitan Statistical Areas were ranked based on the market's potential to buy products in certain industries like high-tech, manufacturing, office equipment and business services, as well as population and household income growth. The study had nine criteria in all. *Sales & Marketing Management, January 1998*

- Xerox, headquartered in Stamford, is among the "100 Best Companies to Work for in America." Criteria: trust in management, pride in work/company, camaraderie, company responses to the Hewitt People Practices Inventory, and employee responses to their Great Place to Work survey. The companies also had to be at least 10 years old and have a minimum of 500 employees. *Fortune, January 12, 1998*

- Xerox, headquartered in Stamford, is among the "100 Best Companies for Working Mothers." Criteria: pay compared with competition, opportunities for women to advance, support for child care, flexible work schedules and family-friendly benefits. *Working Mother, October 1997*

- According to *Working Mother,* "Connecticut remains a leader among the states on the child care front. Even with a tight state budget the governor and state lawmakers have pledged $10 million in new funds for early education. This means as many as 2,500 children will now have access to prekindergarten programs in four school districts.

  The governor is also committed to establishing many more child care programs across the state by the year 2000. Caregiver training and more pre-K programs are high on the agenda, according to advocate Jude Carroll of the Connecticut Association for Human Services. As we went to press, state lawmakers had just passed a bill to pay a higher rate to caregivers who meet NAEYC training requirements—giving them incentive to meet these higher standards.

  Despite these impressive strides, however, the state has taken a step back, drastically cutting funds for inspecting child care facilities. As a result, centers will merely be required to 'register' with the state, rather than meet stricter licensing standards, and child care facilities will no longer be inspected on a regular basis, unless they receive a complaint. (Connecticut is among the 10 best states for child care.)" *Working Mother, July/August 1997*

Business Environment

STATE ECONOMY

State Economic Profile

"Consistent positive signs are appearing in Connecticut's economy for the first time in a decade. Connecticut's growth is buoyed by the strong national economy, the vibrant expansion in neighboring Massachusetts, and by the strong performance of the state's major growth industry, gaming. Another important factor in the state's expansion is the lessening drag from Connecticut's former growth industries, primarily defense, aircraft, and insurance....

...Fairfield County is profiting from Wall Street's boom times and should benefit from the pending cut in capital gains tax....

Financial services has been one of the state's weakest industries since the decade began, but the outlook is brightening. Even as it continues to shrink in Hartford, financial services, particularly money management, is a promising growth industry for Fairfield. Several large money management boutiques, made up of expatriates from large New York City investment banks, have set up shop in Fairfield County.

Stronger employment growth, rising state tax revenues, the prospect of tax cuts, lower out-migration, and the emergence of new growth industries all bode well for the state's long-term outlook. Nonetheless, the hurdles to faster growth in Connecticut are still considerable. These include the state's very high cost of doing business and still-high defense exposure. Connecticut's economy will remain one of the slowest growing over the forecast horizon." *National Association of Realtors, Economic Profiles: The Fifty States, July 1997*

IMPORTS/EXPORTS

Total Export Sales

Area	1993 ($000)	1994 ($000)	1995 ($000)	1996 ($000)	% Chg. 1993-96	% Chg. 1995-96
MSA[1]	3,366,569	3,452,702	4,937,571	4,424,293	31.4	-10.4
U.S.	464,858,354	512,415,609	583,030,524	622,827,063	34.0	6.8

Note: (1) Metropolitan Statistical Area - see Appendix A for areas included
Source: U.S. Department of Commerce, International Trade Association, Metropolitan Area Exports: An Export Performance Report on Over 250 U.S. Cities, October 1997

Imports/Exports by Port

Type	Cargo Value			Share of U.S. Total	
	1995 (US$mil.)	1996 (US$mil.)	% Change 1995-1996	1995 (%)	1996 (%)
Imports	0	0	0	0	0
Exports	0	0	0	0	0

Source: Global Trade Information Services, WaterBorne Trade Atlas 1997

CITY FINANCES

City Government Finances

Component	FY92 ($000)	FY92 (per capita $)
Revenue	303,469	2,798.68
Expenditure	285,206	2,630.25
Debt Outstanding	143,413	1,322.60
Cash & Securities	239,752	2,211.06

Source: U.S. Bureau of the Census, City Government Finances: 1991-92

City Government Revenue by Source

Source	FY92 ($000)	FY92 (per capita $)	FY92 (%)
From Federal Government	0	0.00	0.0
From State Governments	30,964	285.56	10.2
From Local Governments	409	3.77	0.1
Property Taxes	220,574	2,034.20	72.7
General Sales Taxes	0	0.00	0.0
Selective Sales Taxes	0	0.00	0.0
Income Taxes	0	0.00	0.0
Current Charges	17,338	159.90	5.7
Utility/Liquor Store	0	0.00	0.0
Employee Retirement[1]	27,239	251.21	9.0
Other	6,945	64.05	2.3

Note: (1) Excludes "city contributions," classified as "nonrevenue," intragovernmental transfers.
Source: U.S. Bureau of the Census, City Government Finances: 1991-92

City Government Expenditures by Function

Function	FY92 ($000)	FY92 (per capita $)	FY92 (%)
Educational Services	125,671	1,158.97	44.1
Employee Retirement[1]	10,622	97.96	3.7
Environment/Housing	23,387	215.68	8.2
Government Administration	10,336	95.32	3.6
Interest on General Debt	9,331	86.05	3.3
Public Safety	36,944	340.71	13.0
Social Services	19,298	177.97	6.8
Transportation	11,921	109.94	4.2
Utility/Liquor Store	0	0.00	0.0
Other	37,696	347.64	13.2

Note: (1) Payments to beneficiaries including withdrawal of contributions.
Source: U.S. Bureau of the Census, City Government Finances: 1991-92

Municipal Bond Ratings

Area	Moody's	S & P
Stamford	Aaa	n/a

Note: n/a not available; n/r not rated
Source: Moody's Bond Record, 2/98; Statistical Abstract of the U.S., 1997; Governing Magazine, 9/97, 3/98

POPULATION

Population Growth

Area	1980	1990	% Chg. 1980-90	July 1996 Estimate	% Chg. 1990-96
City	102,453	108,056	5.5	110,056	1.9
MSA[1]	198,854	202,557	1.9	331,767	63.8
U.S.	226,545,805	248,765,170	9.8	265,179,411	6.6

Note: (1) Metropolitan Statistical Area - see Appendix A for areas included
Source: 1980/1990 Census of Housing and Population, Summary Tape File 3C; Census Bureau Population Estimates

Population Characteristics

Race	City 1980 Population	%	City 1990 Population	%	% Chg. 1980-90	MSA[1] 1990 Population	%
White	84,122	82.1	82,667	76.5	-1.7	172,380	85.1
Black	15,552	15.2	19,385	17.9	24.6	20,855	10.3
Amer Indian/Esk/Aleut	101	0.1	59	0.1	-41.6	117	0.1
Asian/Pacific Islander	1,282	1.3	2,310	2.1	80.2	5,086	2.5
Other	1,396	1.4	3,635	3.4	160.4	4,119	2.0
Hispanic Origin[2]	6,004	5.9	9,845	9.1	64.0	12,906	6.4

Note: (1) Metropolitan Statistical Area - see Appendix A for areas included; (2) people of Hispanic origin can be of any race
Source: 1980/1990 Census of Housing and Population, Summary Tape File 3C

Ancestry

Area	German	Irish	English	Italian	U.S.	French	Polish	Dutch
City	10.6	14.2	8.3	21.1	2.3	2.1	7.5	1.1
MSA[1]	14.2	17.3	15.2	18.8	2.3	3.0	6.3	1.6
U.S.	23.3	15.6	13.1	5.9	5.3	4.2	3.8	2.5

Note: Figures are percentages and include persons that reported multiple ancestry (eg. if a person reported being Irish and Italian, they were included in both columns); (1) Metropolitan Statistical Area - see Appendix A for areas included
Source: 1990 Census of Population and Housing, Summary Tape File 3C

Age

Area	Median Age (Years)	Age Distribution (%) Under 5	Under 18	18-24	25-44	45-64	65+	80+
City	34.9	6.8	20.4	9.0	36.2	21.3	13.2	3.1
MSA[1]	36.9	6.5	21.0	8.1	33.2	23.7	14.0	3.2
U.S.	32.9	7.3	25.6	10.5	32.6	18.7	12.5	2.8

Note: (1) Metropolitan Statistical Area - see Appendix A for areas included
Source: 1990 Census of Population and Housing, Summary Tape File 3C

Male/Female Ratio

Area	Number of males per 100 females (all ages)	Number of males per 100 females (18 years old+)
City	91.2	88.7
MSA[1]	90.9	87.7
U.S.	95.0	91.9

Note: (1) Metropolitan Statistical Area - see Appendix A for areas included
Source: 1990 Census of Population, General Population Characteristics

INCOME

Per Capita/Median/Average Income

Area	Per Capita ($)	Median Household ($)	Average Household ($)
City	27,092	49,787	69,312
MSA[1]	37,044	57,876	96,804
U.S.	14,420	30,056	38,453

Note: all figures are for 1989; (1) Metropolitan Statistical Area - see Appendix A for areas included
Source: 1990 Census of Population and Housing, Summary Tape File 3C

Household Income Distribution by Race

Income ($)	City (%)					U.S. (%)				
	Total	White	Black	Other	Hisp.[1]	Total	White	Black	Other	Hisp.[1]
Less than 5,000	2.9	2.1	6.9	4.3	3.4	6.2	4.8	15.2	8.6	8.8
5,000 - 9,999	5.3	5.0	7.7	3.0	7.4	9.3	8.6	14.2	9.9	11.1
10,000 - 14,999	4.2	4.0	5.7	3.5	5.6	8.8	8.5	11.0	9.8	11.0
15,000 - 24,999	10.2	8.6	17.5	14.8	17.0	17.5	17.3	18.9	18.5	20.5
25,000 - 34,999	11.5	10.5	17.6	10.5	14.5	15.8	16.1	14.2	15.4	16.4
35,000 - 49,999	16.0	16.0	15.8	16.8	22.8	17.9	18.6	13.3	16.1	16.0
50,000 - 74,999	21.0	21.7	16.7	23.0	16.8	15.0	15.8	9.3	13.4	11.1
75,000 - 99,999	11.8	12.6	7.5	13.0	6.3	5.1	5.5	2.6	4.7	3.1
100,000+	16.9	19.5	4.6	11.3	6.2	4.4	4.8	1.3	3.7	1.9

Note: all figures are for 1989; (1) people of Hispanic origin can be of any race
Source: 1990 Census of Population and Housing, Summary Tape File 3C

Effective Buying Income

Area	Per Capita ($)	Median Household ($)	Average Household ($)
City	29,991	57,929	77,345
MSA[1]	24,668	50,028	65,683
U.S.	15,444	33,201	41,849

Note: data as of 1/1/97; (1) Metropolitan Statistical Area - see Appendix A for areas included
Source: Standard Rate & Data Service, Newspaper Advertising Source, 2/98

Effective Household Buying Income Distribution

Area	% of Households Earning						
	$10,000 -$19,999	$20,000 -$34,999	$35,000 -$49,999	$50,000 -$74,999	$75,000 -$99,000	$100,000 -$124,999	$125,000 and up
City	8.0	14.1	14.1	22.1	14.6	7.7	13.2
MSA[1]	10.1	16.1	15.8	22.8	12.4	6.0	8.9
U.S.	16.5	23.4	18.3	18.2	6.4	2.1	2.4

Note: data as of 1/1/97; (1) Metropolitan Statistical Area - see Appendix A for areas included
Source: Standard Rate & Data Service, Newspaper Advertising Source, 2/98

Poverty Rates by Race and Age

Area	Total (%)	By Race (%)				By Age (%)		
		White	Black	Other	Hisp.[2]	Under 5 years old	Under 18 years old	65 years and over
City	6.3	3.9	15.2	9.9	12.3	10.4	10.3	7.5
MSA[1]	4.6	3.2	14.6	8.4	11.3	6.9	6.5	5.7
U.S.	13.1	9.8	29.5	23.1	25.3	20.1	18.3	12.8

Note: figures show the percent of people living below the poverty line in 1989. The average poverty threshold was $12,674 for a family of four in 1989; (1) Metropolitan Statistical Area - see Appendix A for areas included; (2) people of Hispanic origin can be of any race
Source: 1990 Census of Population and Housing, Summary Tape File 3C

EMPLOYMENT

Labor Force and Employment

Area	Civilian Labor Force			Workers Employed		
	Dec. '95	Dec. '96	% Chg.	Dec. '95	Dec. '96	% Chg.
City	63,912	63,940	0.0	61,111	61,790	1.1
MSA[1]	191,622	192,158	0.3	184,898	186,952	1.1
U.S.	134,583,000	136,742,000	1.6	127,903,000	130,785,000	2.3

Note: Data is not seasonally adjusted and covers workers 16 years of age and older;
(1) Metropolitan Statistical Area - see Appendix A for areas included
Source: Bureau of Labor Statistics, http://stats.bls.gov

Unemployment Rate

Area	1997											
	Jan.	Feb.	Mar.	Apr.	May	Jun.	Jul.	Aug.	Sep.	Oct.	Nov.	Dec.
City	4.7	4.6	4.0	3.7	3.9	4.2	4.3	3.9	3.2	3.4	3.6	3.4
MSA[1]	3.6	3.5	3.2	2.9	3.1	3.4	3.3	3.0	2.7	2.8	2.9	2.7
U.S.	5.9	5.7	5.5	4.8	4.7	5.2	5.0	4.8	4.7	4.4	4.3	4.4

Note: Data is not seasonally adjusted and covers workers 16 years of age and older; All figures are percentages; (1) Metropolitan Statistical Area - see Appendix A for areas included
Source: Bureau of Labor Statistics, http://stats.bls.gov

Employment by Industry

Sector	MSA[1]		U.S.
	Number of Employees	Percent of Total	Percent of Total
Services	74,700	35.5	29.0
Retail Trade	35,800	17.0	18.5
Government	18,300	8.7	16.1
Manufacturing	27,400	13.0	15.0
Finance/Insurance/Real Estate	25,400	12.1	5.7
Wholesale Trade	12,500	5.9	5.4
Transportation/Public Utilities	10,100	4.8	5.3
Construction/Mining	6,000	2.9	5.0

Note: Figures cover non-farm employment as of 12/97 and are not seasonally adjusted; (1) Metropolitan Statistical Area - see Appendix A for areas included
Source: Bureau of Labor Statistics, http://stats.bls.gov

Employment by Occupation

Occupation Category	City (%)	MSA[1] (%)	U.S. (%)
White Collar	70.8	75.1	58.1
Executive/Admin./Management	21.7	24.2	12.3
Professional	15.5	17.8	14.1
Technical & Related Support	2.7	2.6	3.7
Sales	12.8	14.7	11.8
Administrative Support/Clerical	18.1	15.8	16.3
Blue Collar	16.2	13.1	26.2
Precision Production/Craft/Repair	8.2	7.0	11.3
Machine Operators/Assem./Insp.	3.8	2.7	6.8
Transportation/Material Movers	2.1	1.7	4.1
Cleaners/Helpers/Laborers	2.1	1.8	3.9
Services	11.6	10.3	13.2
Farming/Forestry/Fishing	1.3	1.5	2.5

Note: figures cover employed persons 16 years old and over; (1) Metropolitan Statistical Area - see Appendix A for areas included
Source: 1990 Census of Population and Housing, Summary Tape File 3C

Occupational Employment Projections: 1994 - 2005

Occupations Expected to have the Largest Job Growth (ranked by numerical growth)	Fast-Growing Occupations (ranked by percent growth)
1. Salespersons, retail	1. Electronic pagination systems workers
2. Waiters & waitresses	2. Computer engineers
3. Registered nurses	3. Amusement and recreation attendants
4. General managers & top executives	4. Patternmakers and layout workers
5. Systems analysts	5. Physical therapy assistants and aides
6. Cashiers	6. Computer scientists
7. Janitors/cleaners/maids, ex. priv. hshld.	7. Securities, financial services sales
8. Marketing & sales, supervisors	8. Systems analysts
9. Nursing aides/orderlies/attendants	9. Occupational therapy assistants
10. Clerical supervisors	10. Human services workers

Projections cover Connecticut.
Source: U.S. Department of Labor, Employment and Training Administration, America's Labor Market Information System (ALMIS)

Average Wages

Occupation	Wage	Occupation	Wage
Professional/Technical/Clerical	$/Week	**Health/Protective Services**	$/Week
Accountants III	-	Corrections Officers	-
Attorneys III	-	Firefighters	-
Budget Analysts III	-	Nurses, Licensed Practical II	-
Buyers/Contracting Specialists II	-	Nurses, Registered II	-
Clerks, Accounting III	452	Nursing Assistants II	-
Clerks, General III	387	Police Officers I	-
Computer Operators II	419	**Hourly Workers**	$/Hour
Computer Programmers II	604	Forklift Operators	13.19
Drafters II	506	General Maintenance Workers	11.43
Engineering Technicians III	625	Guards I	7.00
Engineering Technicians, Civil III	-	Janitors	6.49
Engineers III	-	Maintenance Electricians	17.47
Key Entry Operators I	345	Maintenance Electronics Techs II	-
Personnel Assistants III	-	Maintenance Machinists	16.06
Personnel Specialists III	-	Maintenance Mechanics, Machinery	18.02
Secretaries III	536	Material Handling Laborers	10.54
Switchboard Operator-Receptionist	379	Motor Vehicle Mechanics	16.07
Systems Analysts II	862	Shipping/Receiving Clerks	10.78
Systems Analysts Supervisor/Mgr II	-	Tool and Die Makers	17.00
Tax Collectors II	-	Truckdrivers, Tractor Trailer	14.73
Word Processors II	457	Warehouse Specialists	12.27

Note: Wage data includes full-time workers only for 1/94 and cover Connecticut. Dashes indicate that data was not available.
Source: Bureau of Labor Statistics, Occupational Compensation Survey

TAXES

Major State and Local Tax Rates

State Corp. Income (%)	State Personal Income (%)	Residential Property (effective rate per $100)	Sales & Use		State Gasoline (cents/ gallon)	State Cigarette (cents/ 20-pack)
			State (%)	Local (%)		
10.5	3.0 - 4.5	n/a	6.0	None	36	50

Note: Personal/corporate income tax rates as of 1/97. Sales, gasoline and cigarette tax rates as of 1/98.
Source: Federation of Tax Administrators, www.taxadmin.org; Washington D.C. Department of Finance and Revenue, Tax Rates and Tax Burdens in the District of Columbia: A Nationwide Comparison, June 1997; Chamber of Commerce

Total Taxes Per Capita and as a Percent of Income

Area	Per Capita Income ($)	Per Capita Taxes ($)			Taxes as Pct. of Income (%)		
		Total	Federal	State/ Local	Total	Federal	State/ Local
Connecticut	35,341	13,709	9,091	4,618	38.8	25.7	13.1
U.S.	26,187	9,205	6,127	3,078	35.2	23.4	11.8

Note: Figures are for 1997
Source: Tax Foundation, Web Site, www.taxfoundation.org

COMMERCIAL REAL ESTATE

Office Market

Class/ Location	Total Space (sq. ft.)	Vacant Space (sq. ft.)	Vac. Rate (%)	Under Constr. (sq. ft.)	Net Absorp. (sq. ft.)	Rental Rates ($/sq.ft./yr.)
Class A						
CBD	13,611,952	1,152,362	8.5	790,000	411,229	22.50-44.00
Outside CBD	7,144,149	584,298	8.2	0	584,442	19.25-32.00
Class B						
CBD	3,530,193	506,304	14.3	0	25,000	19.00-21.00
Outside CBD	1,530,159	460,497	30.1	0	-452	17.50-19.50

Note: Data as of 10/97 and covers Western Fairfield County; CBD = Central Business District; n/a not available;
Source: Society of Industrial and Office Realtors, 1998 Comparative Statistics of Industrial and Office Real Estate Markets

"There were two projects underway at the end of 1997. A building with 120,000 sq. ft. of space was being renovated and a new building with 790,000 sq. ft. of space that has been under construction for more than a year will come on-line during 1998. Absorption is expected to increase 6-10 percent during 1998. Since there is very little vacant space outside of the CBD, a very sharp increase in absorption inside the CBD could occur during the year. With absorption concentrated inside the CBD, it may turn out that the additional construction will have very little impact on vacancy rates." *Society of Industrial and Office Realtors, 1998 Comparative Statistics of Industrial and Office Real Estate Markets*

Industrial Market

Location	Total Space (sq. ft.)	Vacant Space (sq. ft.)	Vac. Rate (%)	Under Constr. (sq. ft.)	Net Absorp. (sq. ft.)	Lease ($/sq.ft./yr.)
Central City	17,328,235	1,156,190	6.7	20,000	-142,360	3.00-7.00
Suburban	n/a	n/a	n/a	n/a	n/a	n/a

Note: Data as of 10/97 and covers Stamford/Norwalk; n/a not available
Source: Society of Industrial and Office Realtors, 1998 Comparative Statistics of Industrial and Office Real Estate Markets

"One of the constraints faced by the industrial real estate market in the Stamford area is a lack of the right product and the land to build new product. Older structures without high ceilings are not appealing to the mix of highly technical, high value-added firms which are interested in locating in the area. As a result, many functionally obsolete industrial buildings have been replaced by retailers. In Norwalk, 600,000 sq. ft. of the former Norden Systems complex was sold to a development group during 1997. Plans for this space are for renovation and subdivisions as High-Tech/R&D space. Half of the existing inventory in the market is older manufacturing facilities while half of the absorption tends to be warehouse/distribution. This mismatch is expected to lead to significant increases in sales and lease prices of warehouse/distribution space during 1998." *Society of Industrial and Office Realtors, 1998 Comparative Statistics of Industrial and Office Real Estate Markets*

Retail Market

Shopping Center Inventory (sq. ft.)	Shopping Center Construction (sq. ft.)	Construction as a Percent of Inventory (%)	Torto Wheaton Rent Index[1] ($/sq. ft.)
28,558,000	167,000	0.6	14.50

Note: Data as of 1997 and covers the Metropolitan Statistical Area - see Appendix A for areas included; (1) Index is based on a model that predicts what the average rent should be for leases with certain characteristics, in certain locations during certain years.
Source: National Association of Realtors, 1997-1998 Market Conditions Report

"Thanks to a healthy job market, the retail sector is in good shape, and it should continue to perform well. Rents have increased over 40% since 1992. Several large money management boutiques, made up of expatriates from large New York City investment banks, have set up shop in Fairfield County. While the number of new money management jobs created in Fairfield is fairly small, the multiplier effects on the local economy are disproportionately large, because of the huge salaries and bonuses paid in the industry. Employment in the financial services sector will swell when the Swiss Bank relocates to Fairfield County from Manhattan and brings 1,500 employees later this year, and up to 2,000 by the year 2000. In another major corporate move from New York, Zurich Reinsurance recently announced that it would move 400 jobs to Stamford." *National Association of Realtors, 1997-1998 Market Conditions Report*

COMMERCIAL UTILITIES

Typical Monthly Electric Bills

Area	Commercial Service ($/month)		Industrial Service ($/month)	
	12 kW demand 1,500 kWh	100 kW demand 30,000 kWh	1,000 kW demand 400,000 kWh	20,000 kW demand 10,000,000 kWh
City	n/a	n/a	n/a	n/a
U.S.	162	2,360	25,590	545,677

Note: Based on rates in effect July 1, 1997; n/a not available
Source: Edison Electric Institute, Typical Residential, Commercial and Industrial Bills, Summer 1997

TRANSPORTATION

Transportation Statistics

Avg. travel time to work (min.)	21.8
Interstate highways	I-95
Bus lines	
In-city	Connecticut Transit
Inter-city	2
Passenger air service	
Airport	Westchester County Airport (20 minutes away)
Airlines	n/a
Aircraft departures	9,692 (1995)
Enplaned passengers	339,270 (1995)
Rail service	Amtrak; Metro North
Motor freight carriers	5
Major waterways/ports	None

Source: OAG, Business Travel Planner, Summer 1997; Editor & Publisher Market Guide, 1998; FAA Airport Activity Statistics, 1996; Amtrak National Time Table, Northeast Timetable, Fall/Winter 1997-98; 1990 Census of Population and Housing, STF 3C; Chamber of Commerce/Economic Development 1997; Jane's Urban Transport Systems 1997-98; Transit Fact Book 1997

Means of Transportation to Work

Area	Car/Truck/Van: Drove Alone	Car/Truck/Van: Car-pooled	Public Transportation: Bus	Public Transportation: Subway	Public Transportation: Railroad	Bicycle	Walked	Other Means	Worked at Home
City	70.2	10.0	3.4	0.2	7.3	0.2	4.6	1.0	3.2
MSA[1]	68.0	8.5	2.0	0.2	11.0	0.1	4.2	1.2	4.7
U.S.	73.2	13.4	3.0	1.5	0.5	0.4	3.9	1.2	3.0

Note: figures shown are percentages and only include workers 16 years old and over; (1) Metropolitan Statistical Area - see Appendix A for areas included
Source: 1990 Census of Population and Housing, Summary Tape File 3C

BUSINESSES

Major Business Headquarters

Company Name	1997 Rankings: Fortune 500	1997 Rankings: Forbes 500
Champion International	243	-
GTE	41	-
General RE	180	-
Pitney Bowes	353	-
Tosco	146	-
Xerox	51	-

Note: Companies listed are located in the city; Dashes indicate no ranking
Fortune 500: companies that produce a 10-K are ranked 1 - 500 based on 1996 revenue
Forbes 500: private companies are ranked 1 - 500 based on 1996 revenue
Source: Forbes 12/1/97; Fortune 4/28/97

Fast-Growing Businesses

Stamford is home to one of *Business Week's* "hot growth" companies: International Telecommunications Data Systems. Criteria: sales and earnings, return on capital and stock price. *Business Week, 5/26/97*

According to *Fortune*, Stamford is home to one of America's 100 fastest-growing companies: Warrantech. Companies were ranked based on three years' earnings-per-share growth using least squares analysis to smooth out distortions. Criteria for inclusion: public companies with sales of least $50 million. Companies that lost money in the most recent quarter, or ended in the red for the past four quarters as a whole, were not eligible. Limited partnerships and REITs were also not considered. *Fortune, 9/29/97*

Small Business Opportunity

According to *Forbes*, Stamford is home to one of America's 200 best small companies: Hyperion Software. Criteria: companies must be publicly traded, U.S.-based corporations with latest 12-month sales of between $5 and $350 million. Earnings must be at least $1 million for the 12-month period. Limited partnerships, REITs and closed-end mutual funds were not considered. Banks, S&Ls and electric utilities were not included. *Forbes, November 3, 1997*

HOTELS & MOTELS

Hotels/Motels

Area	Hotels/ Motels	Rooms	Luxury-Level Hotels/Motels: ♦♦♦♦	Luxury-Level Hotels/Motels: ♦♦♦♦♦	Average Minimum Rates ($): ♦♦	Average Minimum Rates ($): ♦♦♦	Average Minimum Rates ($): ♦♦♦♦
City	6	1,597	0	0	n/a	n/a	n/a
Airport	1	157	0	0	n/a	n/a	n/a
Suburbs	1	322	0	0	n/a	n/a	n/a
Total	8	2,076	0	0	n/a	n/a	n/a

Note: n/a not available; Classifications range from one diamond (budget properties with basic amenities) to five diamond (luxury properties with the finest service, rooms and facilities).
Source: OAG, Business Travel Planner, Summer 1997

CONVENTION CENTERS

Major Convention Centers

Center Name	Meeting Rooms	Exhibit Space (sf)
None listed in city		

Source: Trade Shows Worldwide 1997

Living Environment

COST OF LIVING

Cost of Living Index

Composite Index	Housing	Utilities	Groceries	Health Care	Trans-portation	Misc. Goods/ Services
n/a	n/a	n/a	n/a	n/a	n/a	n/a

Note: U.S. = 100; n/a not available
Source: ACCRA, Cost of Living Index, 3rd Quarter 1997

HOUSING

Median Home Prices and Housing Affordability

Area	Median Price[2] 3rd Qtr. 1997 ($)	HOI[3] 3rd Qtr. 1997	Afford-ability Rank[4]
MSA[1]	n/a	n/a	n/a
U.S.	127,000	63.7	-

Note: (1) Metropolitan Statistical Area - see Appendix A for areas included; (2) U.S. figures calculated from the sales of 625,000 new and existing homes in 195 markets; (3) Housing Opportunity Index - percent of homes sold that were within the reach of the median income household at the prevailing mortgage interest rate; (4) Rank is from 1-195 with 1 being most affordable; n/a not available
Source: National Association of Home Builders, Housing Opportunity Index, 3rd Quarter 1997

Average New Home Price

Area	Price ($)
City	n/a
U.S.	135,710

Note: n/a not available
Source: ACCRA, Cost of Living Index, 3rd Quarter 1997

Average Apartment Rent

Area	Rent ($/mth)
City	n/a
U.S.	569

Note: n/a not available
Source: ACCRA, Cost of Living Index, 3rd Quarter 1997

RESIDENTIAL UTILITIES

Average Residential Utility Costs

Area	All Electric ($/mth)	Part Electric ($/mth)	Other Energy ($/mth)	Phone ($/mth)
City	n/a	n/a	n/a	n/a
U.S.	109.40	55.25	43.64	19.48

Note: n/a not available
Source: ACCRA, Cost of Living Index, 3rd Quarter 1997

HEALTH CARE

Average Health Care Costs

Area	Hospital ($/day)	Doctor ($/visit)	Dentist ($/visit)
City	n/a	n/a	n/a
U.S.	392.91	48.76	60.84

Note: n/a not available
Source: ACCRA, Cost of Living Index, 3rd Quarter 1997

Distribution of Office-Based Physicians

Area	Family/Gen. Practitioners	Specialists		
		Medical	Surgical	Other
Metro Area[1]	122	848	542	476

Note: Data as of December 31, 1996; (1) Fairfield County
Source: American Medical Assn., Physician Characteristics & Distribution in the U.S., 1997-1998

Hospitals

Stamford has 2 general medical and surgical hospitals. *AHA Guide to the Healthcare Field 1997-98*

EDUCATION

Public School District Statistics

District Name	Num. Sch.	Enroll.	Classroom Teachers[1]	Pupils per Teacher	Minority Pupils (%)	Current Exp.[2] ($/pupil)
Stamford School District	21	13,932	985	14.1	n/a	n/a

Note: Data covers the 1995-1996 school year unless otherwise noted; (1) Excludes teachers reported as working in school district offices rather than in schools; (2) Based on 1993-94 enrollment collected by the Census Bureau, not the enrollment figure shown in column 3; SD = School District; ISD = Independent School District; n/a not available
Source: National Center for Education Statistics, Common Core of Data Survey; Bureau of the Census

Educational Quality

School District	Education Quotient[1]	Graduate Outcome[2]	Community Index[3]	Resource Index[4]
Stamford	113.0	74.0	144.0	121.0

Note: Nearly 1,000 secondary school districts were rated in terms of educational quality. The scores range from a low of 50 to a high of 150; (1) Average of the Graduate Outcome, Community and Resource indexes; (2) Based on graduation rates and college board scores (SAT/ACT); (3) Based on the surrounding community's average level of education and the area's average income level; (4) Based on teacher salaries, per-pupil expenditures and student-teacher ratios.
Source: Expansion Management, Ratings Issue 1997

Educational Attainment by Race

Area	High School Graduate (%)					Bachelor's Degree (%)				
	Total	White	Black	Other	Hisp.[2]	Total	White	Black	Other	Hisp.[2]
City	81.2	84.0	69.7	67.7	59.6	35.1	39.1	14.4	29.8	12.5
MSA[1]	85.7	87.7	69.6	76.2	63.8	43.7	46.6	14.3	42.0	16.6
U.S.	75.2	77.9	63.1	60.4	49.8	20.3	21.5	11.4	19.4	9.2

Note: figures shown cover persons 25 years old and over; (1) Metropolitan Statistical Area - see Appendix A for areas included; (2) people of Hispanic origin can be of any race
Source: 1990 Census of Population and Housing, Summary Tape File 3C

School Enrollment by Type

Area	Preprimary				Elementary/High School			
	Public		Private		Public		Private	
	Enrollment	%	Enrollment	%	Enrollment	%	Enrollment	%
City	1,053	47.9	1,147	52.1	12,000	84.1	2,270	15.9
MSA[1]	2,043	43.1	2,692	56.9	22,828	81.6	5,132	18.4
U.S.	2,679,029	59.5	1,824,256	40.5	38,379,689	90.2	4,187,099	9.8

Note: figures shown cover persons 3 years old and over;
(1) Metropolitan Statistical Area - see Appendix A for areas included
Source: 1990 Census of Population and Housing, Summary Tape File 3C

School Enrollment by Race

Area	Preprimary (%)				Elementary/High School (%)			
	White	Black	Other	Hisp.[1]	White	Black	Other	Hisp.[1]
City	72.5	20.8	6.7	8.8	63.3	29.1	7.6	12.5
MSA[2]	84.8	10.1	5.1	5.1	77.1	15.9	7.0	8.5
U.S.	80.4	12.5	7.1	7.8	74.1	15.6	10.3	12.5

Note: figures shown cover persons 3 years old and over; (1) people of Hispanic origin can be of any race; (2) Metropolitan Statistical Area - see Appendix A for areas included
Source: 1990 Census of Population and Housing, Summary Tape File 3C

SAT/ACT Scores

Area/District	1997 SAT				1997 ACT	
	Percent of Graduates Tested (%)	Average Math Score	Average Verbal Score	Average Combined Score	Percent of Graduates Tested (%)	Average Composite Score
Stamford	74	480	470	950	n/a	n/a
State	79	507	509	1,016	3	21.7
U.S.	42	511	505	1,016	36	21.0

Note: Math and verbal SAT scores are out of a possible 800; ACT scores are out of a possible 36
Caution: Comparing or ranking states/cities on the basis of SAT/ACT scores alone is invalid and strongly discouraged by the The College Board and The American College Testing Program as students who take the tests are self-selected and do not represent the entire student population.
Source: Stamford Board of Education, Research Office, 1997; College Board, 1997; American College Testing Program, 1997

Classroom Teacher Salaries in Public Schools

District	B.A. Degree		M.A. Degree		Ph.D. Degree	
	Min. ($)	Max ($)	Min. ($)	Max. ($)	Min. ($)	Max. ($)
Stamford	32,273	48,250	35,510	57,661	39,858	67,218
Average[1]	26,120	39,270	28,175	44,667	31,643	49,825

Note: Salaries are for 1996-1997; (1) Based on all school districts covered
Source: American Federation of Teachers (unpublished data)

Higher Education

Two-Year Colleges		Four-Year Colleges		Medical Schools	Law Schools	Voc/ Tech
Public	Private	Public	Private			
0	0	1	1	0	0	8

Source: College Blue Book, Occupational Education 1997; Medical School Admission Requirements, 1998-99; Peterson's Guide to Two-Year Colleges, 1997; Peterson's Guide to Four-Year Colleges, 1997; Barron's Guide to Law Schools 1997

MAJOR EMPLOYERS

Major Employers

Hargro Enterprises (packaging paper)	Champion International Corp. (paper)
GTE Hospital	General Electric Capital Corp.
General RE Corp.	Citizens Telecom Services
Donnelley Marketing Holdings	Pitney Bowes
Sikorsky Aircraft Corp.	Stamford Hospital
St. Joseph's Medical Center	Xerox Corp.
Shamrock Building Services	Stamford Marketing Field Research
Cadbury Beverages	

Note: companies listed are located in the city
Source: Dun's Business Rankings 1997; Ward's Business Directory, 1997

PUBLIC SAFETY

Crime Rate

Area	All Crimes	Violent Crimes				Property Crimes		
		Murder	Forcible Rape	Robbery	Aggrav. Assault	Burglary	Larceny -Theft	Motor Vehicle Theft
City	4,623.7	5.6	16.8	197.8	191.3	656.9	3,109.2	446.0
Suburbs[1]	3,302.8	3.1	12.5	90.9	64.2	623.1	2,272.7	236.2
MSA[2]	3,729.8	3.9	13.9	125.5	105.3	634.0	2,543.1	304.1
U.S.	5,078.9	7.4	36.1	202.4	388.2	943.0	2,975.9	525.9

Note: Crime rate is the number of crimes per 100,000 pop.; (1) defined as all areas within the MSA but located outside the central city; (2) Metropolitan Statistical Area - see Appendix A for areas incl.
Source: FBI Uniform Crime Reports 1996

RECREATION

Culture and Recreation

Museums	Symphony Orchestras	Opera Companies	Dance Companies	Professional Theatres	Zoos	Pro Sports Teams
4	1	1	2	2	0	0

Source: International Directory of the Performing Arts, 1996; Official Museum Directory, 1998; Chamber of Commerce/Economic Development 1997

Library System

The Stamford Public Library has three branches, holdings of 358,902 volumes and a budget of $5,177,620 (1994-1995). *American Library Directory, 1997-1998*

MEDIA

Newspapers

Name	Type	Freq.	Distribution	Circulation
Fairfield County Weekly	n/a	1x/wk	Local	50,000
The Guide	General	1x/wk	Local	86,100
The Stamford Advocate	General	7x/wk	Local	28,151
Westchester County Weekly	n/a	1x/wk	Local	50,000

Note: Includes newspapers with circulations of 500 or more located in the city; n/a not available
Source: Burrelle's Media Directory, 1998 Edition

AM Radio Stations

Call Letters	Freq. (kHz)	Target Audience	Station Format	Music Format
WICC	600	General	M/N/S	Adult Contemporary
WLAD	800	General	M/N/S/T	Adult Contemporary
WREF	850	General	M/N/S	Big Band/MOR/Oldies
WINE	940	General	N/T	n/a
WMMM	1260	General	M/N/S/T	Big Band/Christian/Oldies/Spanish
WNLK	1350	General	M/N/S	Adult Contemporary
WSTC	1400	General	M/N/S/T	Adult Standards/Jazz
WCUM	1450	Hispanic	M/N/S	Spanish
WGCH	1490	n/a	M/T	Adult Contemporary/Classical/Spanish

Note: Stations included broadcast in the Stamford metro area; n/a not available
Station Format: E = Educational; M = Music; N = News; S = Sports; T = Talk
Music Format: AOR = Album Oriented Rock; MOR = Middle-of-the-Road
Source: Burrelle's Media Directory, 1998 Edition

FM Radio Stations

Call Letters	Freq. (mHz)	Target Audience	Station Format	Music Format
WMNR	88.1	General	M	Big Band/Classical/Jazz
WVOF	88.5	n/a	E/M/N/S/T	n/a
WEDW	88.5	General	M/N	Classical
WPKN	89.5	n/a	M	n/a
WRXC	90.1	General	M	Big Band/Classical
WWPT	90.3	General	E/M/N/S/T	AOR
WSHU	91.1	General	M/N/S	Classical
WGRS	91.5	General	M	Big Band/Classical/Jazz
WXCI	91.7	n/a	M	Alternative
WSLX	91.9	General	M	Classical
WFAR	93.3	General	M/N/S	n/a
WRKI	95.1	n/a	M	AOR/Classic Rock
WEFX	95.9	General	M/N/S	Classic Rock
WKHL	96.7	General	M	Oldies
WDAQ	98.3	n/a	M	Adult Contemporary
WEZN	99.9	n/a	M	Adult Contemporary
WAXB	105.5	General	M/N/S	Oldies
WEBE	107.9	n/a	M	Adult Contemporary

Note: Stations included broadcast in the Stamford metro area; n/a not available
Station Format: E = Educational; M = Music; N = News; S = Sports; T = Talk
Music Format: AOR = Album Oriented Rock; MOR = Middle-of-the-Road
Source: Burrelle's Media Directory, 1998 Edition

Television Stations

Name	Ch.	Affiliation	Type	Owner
No stations listed.				

Note: Stations included broadcast in the Stamford metro area
Source: Burrelle's Media Directory, 1998 Edition

CLIMATE

Average and Extreme Temperatures

Temperature	Jan	Feb	Mar	Apr	May	Jun	Jul	Aug	Sep	Oct	Nov	Dec	Ann
Extreme High (°F)	65	67	84	91	92	96	103	100	99	85	78	65	103
Average High (°F)	37	38	46	57	67	76	82	81	74	64	53	41	60
Average Temp. (°F)	30	32	39	49	59	68	74	73	66	56	46	35	52
Average Low (°F)	23	24	31	40	50	59	65	65	57	47	38	27	44
Extreme Low (°F)	-7	-5	4	18	31	41	49	44	36	26	16	-4	-7

Note: Figures cover the years 1948-1992
Source: National Climatic Data Center, International Station Meteorological Climate Summary, 3/95

Average Precipitation/Snowfall/Humidity

Precip./Humidity	Jan	Feb	Mar	Apr	May	Jun	Jul	Aug	Sep	Oct	Nov	Dec	Ann
Avg. Precip. (in.)	3.2	2.9	3.7	3.7	3.7	3.1	3.7	3.8	3.0	3.2	3.8	3.5	41.4
Avg. Snowfall (in.)	7	7	5	1	Tr	0	0	0	0	Tr	1	5	25
Avg. Rel. Hum. 7am (%)	73	72	72	72	76	77	79	80	81	79	77	74	76
Avg. Rel. Hum. 4pm (%)	61	59	56	55	59	60	60	61	61	60	62	63	60

Note: Figures cover the years 1948-1992; Tr = Trace amounts (<0.05 in. of rain; <0.5 in. of snow)
Source: National Climatic Data Center, International Station Meteorological Climate Summary, 3/95

Weather Conditions

Temperature			Daytime Sky			Precipitation		
32°F & below	45°F & below	90°F & above	Clear	Partly cloudy	Cloudy	0.01 inch or more precip.	0.1 inch or more snow/ice	Thunder-storms
100	193	7	80	146	139	118	17	22

Note: Figures are average number of days per year and covers the years 1948-1992
Source: National Climatic Data Center, International Station Meteorological Climate Summary, 3/95

AIR & WATER QUALITY

Maximum Pollutant Concentrations

	Particulate Matter (ug/m³)	Carbon Monoxide (ppm)	Sulfur Dioxide (ppm)	Nitrogen Dioxide (ppm)	Ozone (ppm)	Lead (ug/m³)
MSA[1] Level	65	4	0.026	n/a	0.12	n/a
NAAQS[2]	150	9	0.140	0.053	0.12	1.50
Met NAAQS?	Yes	Yes	Yes	n/a	Yes	n/a

Note: (1) Metropolitan Statistical Area - see Appendix A for areas included; (2) National Ambient Air Quality Standards; ppm = parts per million; ug/m³ = micrograms per cubic meter; n/a not available
Source: EPA, National Air Quality and Emissions Trends Report, 1996

Pollutant Standards Index

Data not available. *EPA, National Air Quality and Emissions Trends Report, 1996*

Drinking Water

Water System Name	Pop. Served	Primary Water Source Type	Number of Violations in Fiscal Year 1997	Type of Violation/ Contaminants
Stamford Water Company	85,000	Surface	None	None

Note: Data as of January 16, 1998
Source: EPA, Office of Ground Water and Drinking Water, Safe Drinking Water Information System

Stamford tap water is slightly acid, moderately soft and fluoridated.
Editor & Publisher Market Guide, 1998

Washington, D.C.

Background

The city and federal district of Washington, D.C. with it foreign Embassies and Consulates, is definitely cosmopolitan. However, underlying this international worldliness, is a decidedly patrician and Yankee air. So you had better watch your manners!

The small sliver of land designated as our country's capital grew out of a section of land carved from the state of Maryland, after many years of arguing. The Father of our country, George Washington, silenced bickering voices, and chose the present site we know today as Washington, D.C. In 1793, the first cornerstone of the White House was laid. In 1800, the north wing had been completed, and a drifting Congress found its home. President John Adams was the first President to reside at The White House. The building was burned down by the British during the War of 1812, and its final reconstruction was not completed until 1891!

The young Capital, which grows more confident and worldly every year, is a breathtaking collection of architectural styles: Greek Revival, Federal-Style, Victorian, and Baroque. All this blends in with the monuments and other sites that we know so well: the Washington Monument, the Lincoln Memorial, The White House, and the Jefferson Memorial.

As the political machine of the country, the main industry is, of course, government. This economic sector employs roughly 2.8 million people. With 20 million visitors a year, tourism has become Washington's second largest income producer. Economic activity not withstanding, Washington is also the home of four major universities: American, Georgetown, George Washington and Howard.

The District of Columbia is operating under a Congressional legislation that created a financial control board in 1995 to oversea the District's budget. The new 1998 budget bill has expanded the powers of the board in exchange for nearly $1 billion in federal aid over the next five years.

The authority of the Mayor and City Council to run major city agencies is now in the hands of the Board and this shift in power has already accelerated some new economic development. The District has experienced an increase of jobs in the private sector of nearly 9,000; new retail development; an increase in revenue due to aggressive tax collection; a positive "credit watch" status from Standard & Poor; an opera house, plans for a new convention center downtown; and construction of a new $100 million downtown sports arena. (The MCI Center) which opened in December of 1997. New York Times 8/8/97, 12/3/97; USA Today 11/18/97

Summertime in Washington is warm and humid and winter is cold, but not severe.

General Rankings and Evaluative Comments

- Washington was ranked #162 out of 300 cities by *Money's* 1997 "Survey of the Best Places to Live." Criteria used: health services, crime, economy, housing, education, transportation, weather, leisure and the arts. The city was ranked #128 in 1996 and #140 in 1995. *Money, July 1997; Money, September 1996; Money, September 1995*

- *Ladies Home Journal* ranked America's 200 largest cities based on the qualities women care about most. Washington ranked 21 out of 200. Criteria: low crime rate, good public schools, well-paying jobs, quality health and child care, the presence of women in government, proportion of women-owned businesses, size of the wage gap with men, local economy, divorce rates, the ratio of single men to single women, whether there are laws that require at least the same number of public toilets for women as men, and the probability of good hair days. *Ladies Home Journal, November 1997*

- Washington was ranked #207 out of 219 cities in terms of children's health, safety, and economic well-being. Criteria: total population, percent population change, birth rate, child immunization rate, infant mortality rate, percent low birth weight infants, percent of births to teens, physician-to-population ratio, student-to-teacher ratio, dropout rate, unemployment rate, median family income, percent of children in poverty, violent and property crime rates, number of juvenile arrests for violent crimes as a percent of the total crime index, number of days with pollution standard index (PSI) over 100, pounds toxic releases per 1,000 people and number of superfund sites. *Zero Population Growth, Children's Environmental Index 1997*

- Washington appeared on *Ebony's* list of the best cities for African-Americans. Rank: 2 out of 4. The cities were selected based on a survey of the 100 Most Influential Black Americans. They were asked which city offered the best overall experience for African-Americans, and which dream city they would select if they could live anywhere they wanted to. *Ebony* also asked opinion-makers which cities offered the best cultural experiences, the best schools and the most diversity. *Ebony, 9/97*

- Washington is among the 20 most livable cities for gay men and lesbians. The list was divided between 10 cities you might expect and 10 surprises. Washington was on the cities you would expect list. Rank: 9 out of 10. Criteria: legal protection from antigay discrimination, an annual gay pride celebration, a community center, gay bookstores and publications, and an array of organizations, religious groups, and health care facilities that cater to the needs of the local gay community. *The Advocate, June 1997*

- *Conde Nast Traveler* polled 37,000 readers in terms of travel satisfaction. Cities were ranked based on the following criteria: people/friendliness, environment/ambiance, cultural enrichment, restaurants and fun/energy. Washington appeared in the top thirty, ranking number 19, with an overall rating of 62.9 out of 100 based on all the criteria. The cities were also ranked in each category separately. Washington appeared in the top 10 based on cultural enrichment, ranking number 1 with a rating of 89.2 out of 100. Washington appeared in the top 10 based on restaurants, ranking number 10 with a rating of 69.7 out of 100. *Conde Nast Traveler, Readers' Choice Poll 1997*

- *Yahoo! Internet Life* selected "America's 100 Most Wired Cities & Towns". 50 cities were large and 50 cities were small. Washington ranked 3 out of 50 large cities. Criteria: Internet users per capita, number of networked computers, number of registered domain names, Internet backbone traffic, and the per-capita number of Web sites devoted to each city.Washington was highlighted as having the most backbone bandwidth. *Yahoo! Internet Life, March 1998*

- *Reader's Digest* non-scientifically ranked the 12 largest U.S. metropolitan areas in terms of having the worst drivers. The Washington metro area ranked number 3. The areas were selected by asking approximately 1,200 readers on the *Reader's Digest* Web site and 200 interstate bus drivers and long-haul truckers which metro areas have the worst drivers. Their responses were factored in with fatality, insurance and rental-car rates to create the rankings. *Reader's Digest, March 1998*

- Bureau of National Affairs (publishing) and Fannie Mae (mortgages), headquartered in Washington, are among the "100 Best Companies to Work for in America." Criteria: trust in management, pride in work/company, camaraderie, company responses to the Hewitt People Practices Inventory, and employee responses to their Great Place to Work survey. The companies also had to be at least 10 years old and have a minimum of 500 employees. *Fortune, January 12, 1998*

- Arnold & Porter, The Bureau of National Affairs, and Marriott International, headquartered in Washington, are among the "100 Best Companies for Working Mothers." Criteria: pay compared with competition, opportunities for women to advance, support for child care, flexible work schedules and family-friendly benefits. *Working Mother, October 1997*

- According to *Working Mother,* "Washington, D.C., has good health, safety and staffing standards in place. But 830 fewer kids under the age of six had access to child care this year because of a $4 million budget cut over the last two years.

  Even with its money problems, Washington, D.C., did manage to give 10 grants last year for school-age care, creating slots for 200 kids in 1996. That, at least, was a help for both working parents and their children. And the District promises that previously cut funding will be restored next year." *Working Mother, July/August 1997*

Business Environment

STATE ECONOMY

State Economic Profile

"The fortunes of the District of Columbia continue to decline. With its main industry—government—still in decline, the District is unable to capture the benefits of the strong national economy....Residential construction activity is completely absent; 1997's first quarter marked five consecutive quarters with no permit activity. The district's downtown office vacancy rate, above 10%, is bucking the national trend and is increasing. Faced with high taxes, declining infrastructure and job losses, population is in a freefall.

The District's only consolation from current federal cutbacks is that they soon will abate. Unfortunately, the recent budget compromise raises the threat of additional retrenchment by its largest industry. The budget compromise puts strict limits on nominal discretionary spending that result in about a 10% decline in real spending by 2002.

The Clinton Administration has proposed establishing a Federally-funded development agency and the federal takeover of several city functions—running prisons, paying the bulk of Medicaid costs, and assuming responsibility of the city's pension plan shortfalls. Republican Congressional leaders, however, support caps on federal income tax and capital tax rates for District residents.

Tourism remains an important part of its economy, accounting for an estimated 5% of the entire Washington metro gross product, according to the Washington, D.C. Convention and Visitors Bureau. Convention business has slumped in the city, mainly due to the small size of the Washington Convention Center.

The District of Columbia faces a bleak future. Beset by high tax rates and a crumbling infrastructure, it will have problems attracting private employers to fill the void left by government. There is some hope, however. If Congress acts on one of the revitalization plans, the District may reverse its long decline in employment and population." *National Association of Realtors, Economic Profiles: The Fifty States, July 1997*

IMPORTS/EXPORTS

Total Export Sales

Area	1993 ($000)	1994 ($000)	1995 ($000)	1996 ($000)	% Chg. 1993-96	% Chg. 1995-96
MSA[1]	7,250,600	7,969,303	8,350,435	8,083,517	11.5	-3.2
U.S.	464,858,354	512,415,609	583,030,524	622,827,063	34.0	6.8

Note: (1) Metropolitan Statistical Area - see Appendix A for areas included
Source: U.S. Department of Commerce, International Trade Association, Metropolitan Area Exports: An Export Performance Report on Over 250 U.S. Cities, October 1997

Imports/Exports by Port

Type	Cargo Value			Share of U.S. Total	
	1995 (US$mil.)	1996 (US$mil.)	% Change 1995-1996	1995 (%)	1996 (%)
Imports	0	0	n/c	0.00	0.00
Exports	5	0	0.00	0.00	0.00

Source: Global Trade Information Services, WaterBorne Trade Atlas 1997

CITY FINANCES

City Government Finances

Component	FY94 ($000)	FY94 (per capita $)
Revenue	4,991,420	8,787.37
Expenditure	5,285,531	9,305.15
Debt Outstanding	4,110,029	7,235.69
Cash & Securities	3,323,561	5,851.11

Source: U.S. Bureau of the Census, City Government Finances: 1993-94

City Government Revenue by Source

Source	FY94 ($000)	FY94 (per capita $)	FY94 (%)
From Federal Government	1,623,802	2,858.70	32.5
From State Governments	0	0.00	0.0
From Local Governments	72,642	127.89	1.5
Property Taxes	811,009	1,427.78	16.2
General Sales Taxes	472,540	831.90	9.5
Selective Sales Taxes	307,461	541.28	6.2
Income Taxes	798,725	1,406.15	16.0
Current Charges	271,473	477.93	5.4
Utility/Liquor Store	53,086	93.46	1.1
Employee Retirement[1]	231,923	408.30	4.6
Other	348,759	613.99	7.0

Note: (1) Excludes "city contributions," classified as "nonrevenue," intragovernmental transfers.
Source: U.S. Bureau of the Census, City Government Finances: 1993-94

City Government Expenditures by Function

Function	FY94 ($000)	FY94 (per capita $)	FY94 (%)
Educational Services	763,471	1,344.09	14.4
Employee Retirement[1]	279,576	492.19	5.3
Environment/Housing	458,065	806.42	8.7
Government Administration	294,420	518.32	5.6
Interest on General Debt	302,791	533.06	5.7
Public Safety	727,983	1,281.61	13.8
Social Services	1,606,811	2,828.78	30.4
Transportation	160,749	283.00	3.0
Utility/Liquor Store	101,997	179.57	1.9
Other	589,668	1,038.11	11.2

Note: (1) Payments to beneficiaries including withdrawal of contributions.
Source: U.S. Bureau of the Census, City Government Finances: 1993-94

Municipal Bond Ratings

Area	Moody's	S & P
Washington	Ba2	B

Note: n/a not available; n/r not rated
Source: Moody's Bond Record, 2/98; Statistical Abstract of the U.S., 1997; Governing Magazine, 9/97, 3/98

POPULATION

Population Growth

Area	1980	1990	% Chg. 1980-90	July 1996 Estimate	% Chg. 1990-96
City	638,333	606,900	-4.9	543,213	-10.5
MSA[1]	3,250,822	3,923,574	20.7	4,563,123	16.3
U.S.	226,545,805	248,765,170	9.8	265,179,411	6.6

Note: (1) Metropolitan Statistical Area - see Appendix A for areas included
Source: 1980/1990 Census of Housing and Population, Summary Tape File 3C; Census Bureau Population Estimates

Population Characteristics

Race	City 1980 Population	City 1980 %	City 1990 Population	City 1990 %	% Chg. 1980-90	MSA[1] 1990 Population	MSA[1] 1990 %
White	174,705	27.4	179,690	29.6	2.9	2,580,207	65.8
Black	448,370	70.2	399,751	65.9	-10.8	1,042,210	26.6
Amer Indian/Esk/Aleut	1,014	0.2	1,559	0.3	53.7	12,115	0.3
Asian/Pacific Islander	6,883	1.1	11,233	1.9	63.2	201,502	5.1
Other	7,361	1.2	14,667	2.4	99.3	87,540	2.2
Hispanic Origin[2]	17,679	2.8	31,358	5.2	77.4	218,256	5.6

Note: (1) Metropolitan Statistical Area - see Appendix A for areas included; (2) people of Hispanic origin can be of any race
Source: 1980/1990 Census of Housing and Population, Summary Tape File 3C

Ancestry

Area	German	Irish	English	Italian	U.S.	French	Polish	Dutch
City	6.5	5.7	5.6	1.9	1.9	1.4	1.6	0.6
MSA[1]	19.0	14.2	14.2	4.7	3.0	2.9	3.0	1.5
U.S.	23.3	15.6	13.1	5.9	5.3	4.2	3.8	2.5

Note: Figures are percentages and include persons that reported multiple ancestry (eg. if a person reported being Irish and Italian, they were included in both columns); (1) Metropolitan Statistical Area - see Appendix A for areas included
Source: 1990 Census of Population and Housing, Summary Tape File 3C

Age

Area	Median Age (Years)	Under 5	Under 18	18-24	25-44	45-64	65+	80+
		Age Distribution (%)						
City	33.4	6.0	19.2	13.4	35.9	18.7	12.8	2.8
MSA[1]	32.4	7.2	23.5	10.9	38.2	19.0	8.5	1.7
U.S.	32.9	7.3	25.6	10.5	32.6	18.7	12.5	2.8

Note: (1) Metropolitan Statistical Area - see Appendix A for areas included
Source: 1990 Census of Population and Housing, Summary Tape File 3C

Male/Female Ratio

Area	Number of males per 100 females (all ages)	Number of males per 100 females (18 years old+)
City	87.2	84.0
MSA[1]	94.8	92.2
U.S.	95.0	91.9

Note: (1) Metropolitan Statistical Area - see Appendix A for areas included
Source: 1990 Census of Population, General Population Characteristics

INCOME

Per Capita/Median/Average Income

Area	Per Capita ($)	Median Household ($)	Average Household ($)
City	18,881	30,727	44,413
MSA[1]	21,416	46,884	56,799
U.S.	14,420	30,056	38,453

Note: all figures are for 1989; (1) Metropolitan Statistical Area - see Appendix A for areas included
Source: 1990 Census of Population and Housing, Summary Tape File 3C

Household Income Distribution by Race

Income ($)	City (%) Total	White	Black	Other	Hisp.[1]	U.S. (%) Total	White	Black	Other	Hisp.[1]
Less than 5,000	8.7	3.5	11.7	10.2	8.1	6.2	4.8	15.2	8.6	8.8
5,000 - 9,999	7.8	3.6	10.2	8.8	8.0	9.3	8.6	14.2	9.9	11.1
10,000 - 14,999	7.2	4.4	8.7	8.5	11.2	8.8	8.5	11.0	9.8	11.0
15,000 - 24,999	17.3	12.3	20.2	19.2	19.5	17.5	17.3	18.9	18.5	20.5
25,000 - 34,999	14.7	13.4	15.3	18.0	19.6	15.8	16.1	14.2	15.4	16.4
35,000 - 49,999	15.6	16.5	15.0	16.5	15.3	17.9	18.6	13.3	16.1	16.0
50,000 - 74,999	14.4	18.6	12.2	10.5	10.3	15.0	15.8	9.3	13.4	11.1
75,000 - 99,999	6.4	10.4	4.3	3.5	4.0	5.1	5.5	2.6	4.7	3.1
100,000+	7.8	17.3	2.4	4.8	4.0	4.4	4.8	1.3	3.7	1.9

Note: all figures are for 1989; (1) people of Hispanic origin can be of any race
Source: 1990 Census of Population and Housing, Summary Tape File 3C

Effective Buying Income

Area	Per Capita ($)	Median Household ($)	Average Household ($)
City	22,282	37,361	52,736
MSA[1]	21,603	49,583	58,316
U.S.	15,444	33,201	41,849

Note: data as of 1/1/97; (1) Metropolitan Statistical Area - see Appendix A for areas included
Source: Standard Rate & Data Service, Newspaper Advertising Source, 2/98

Effective Household Buying Income Distribution

Area	% of Households Earning $10,000 -$19,999	$20,000 -$34,999	$35,000 -$49,999	$50,000 -$74,999	$75,000 -$99,000	$100,000 -$124,999	$125,000 and up
City	12.6	21.7	16.0	17.7	9.2	4.2	5.6
MSA[1]	8.1	17.8	18.9	26.0	13.2	5.3	5.0
U.S.	16.5	23.4	18.3	18.2	6.4	2.1	2.4

Note: data as of 1/1/97; (1) Metropolitan Statistical Area - see Appendix A for areas included
Source: Standard Rate & Data Service, Newspaper Advertising Source, 2/98

Poverty Rates by Race and Age

Area	Total (%)	By Race (%) White	Black	Other	Hisp.[2]	By Age (%) Under 5 years old	Under 18 years old	65 years and over
City	16.9	8.2	20.2	21.9	20.4	27.0	25.5	17.2
MSA[1]	6.4	3.6	12.6	9.9	12.0	8.3	7.9	8.6
U.S.	13.1	9.8	29.5	23.1	25.3	20.1	18.3	12.8

Note: figures show the percent of people living below the poverty line in 1989. The average poverty threshold was $12,674 for a family of four in 1989; (1) Metropolitan Statistical Area - see Appendix A for areas included; (2) people of Hispanic origin can be of any race
Source: 1990 Census of Population and Housing, Summary Tape File 3C

EMPLOYMENT

Labor Force and Employment

Area	Civilian Labor Force Dec. '95	Dec. '96	% Chg.	Workers Employed Dec. '95	Dec. '96	% Chg.
City	267,941	258,172	-3.6	246,885	238,292	-3.5
MSA[1]	2,534,687	2,560,910	1.0	2,448,378	2,480,243	1.3
U.S.	134,583,000	136,742,000	1.6	127,903,000	130,785,000	2.3

Note: Data is not seasonally adjusted and covers workers 16 years of age and older; (1) Metropolitan Statistical Area - see Appendix A for areas included
Source: Bureau of Labor Statistics, http://stats.bls.gov

Unemployment Rate

Area	1997											
	Jan.	Feb.	Mar.	Apr.	May	Jun.	Jul.	Aug.	Sep.	Oct.	Nov.	Dec.
City	8.1	7.8	7.7	6.8	6.9	7.8	8.0	7.9	7.7	8.1	7.7	7.7
MSA[1]	3.7	3.7	3.4	3.3	3.4	3.8	3.5	3.5	3.5	3.5	3.3	3.1
U.S.	5.9	5.7	5.5	4.8	4.7	5.2	5.0	4.8	4.7	4.4	4.3	4.4

Note: Data is not seasonally adjusted and covers workers 16 years of age and older; All figures are percentages; (1) Metropolitan Statistical Area - see Appendix A for areas included
Source: Bureau of Labor Statistics, http://stats.bls.gov

Employment by Industry

Sector	MSA[1]		U.S.
	Number of Employees	Percent of Total	Percent of Total
Services	966,600	38.3	29.0
Retail Trade	406,600	16.1	18.5
Government	592,900	23.5	16.1
Manufacturing	100,300	4.0	15.0
Finance/Insurance/Real Estate	134,500	5.3	5.7
Wholesale Trade	83,600	3.3	5.4
Transportation/Public Utilities	112,200	4.4	5.3
Construction	127,200	5.0	4.5
Mining	1,000	0.0	0.5

Note: Figures cover non-farm employment as of 12/97 and are not seasonally adjusted; (1) Metropolitan Statistical Area - see Appendix A for areas included
Source: Bureau of Labor Statistics, http://stats.bls.gov

Employment by Occupation

Occupation Category	City (%)	MSA[1] (%)	U.S. (%)
White Collar	71.1	73.2	58.1
Executive/Admin./Management	17.2	20.1	12.3
Professional	21.9	20.1	14.1
Technical & Related Support	4.9	5.1	3.7
Sales	6.7	9.7	11.8
Administrative Support/Clerical	20.4	18.1	16.3
Blue Collar	11.9	14.5	26.2
Precision Production/Craft/Repair	4.5	7.7	11.3
Machine Operators/Assem./Insp.	1.7	1.8	6.8
Transportation/Material Movers	3.3	2.7	4.1
Cleaners/Helpers/Laborers	2.4	2.3	3.9
Services	16.6	11.5	13.2
Farming/Forestry/Fishing	0.4	0.9	2.5

Note: figures cover employed persons 16 years old and over; (1) Metropolitan Statistical Area - see Appendix A for areas included
Source: 1990 Census of Population and Housing, Summary Tape File 3C

Occupational Employment Projections: 1994 - 2005

High Demand Occupations (ranked by annual openings)	Fast-Growing Occupations[1] (ranked by percent growth)
1. Janitors/cleaners/maids, ex. priv. hshld.	1. Child care workers, private household
2. Secretaries, except legal & medical	2. Residential counselors
3. General managers & top executives	3. Home health aides
4. Waiters & waitresses	4. Teachers, preschool and kindergarten
5. General office clerks	5. Human services workers
6. Lawyers	6. Personal and home care aides
7. Guards	7. Instructors, adult (nonvocational) educ.
8. Receptionists and information clerks	8. Janitors/cleaners/maids, ex. priv. hshld.
9. Clerical supervisors	9. Social workers, exc. med. & psych.
10. Food preparation, fast food	10. Artists and commercial artists

Projections cover District of Columbia.
Note: (1) Based on employment growth of 100 or more jobs
Source: Department of Employment Services, Occupational Employment Projections - Year 2005, District of Columbia

Average Wages

Occupation	Wage	Occupation	Wage
Professional/Technical/Clerical	$/Week	**Health/Protective Services**	$/Week
Accountants III	845	Corrections Officers	604
Attorneys III	1,265	Firefighters	684
Budget Analysts III	855	Nurses, Licensed Practical II	-
Buyers/Contracting Specialists II	677	Nurses, Registered II	-
Clerks, Accounting III	494	Nursing Assistants II	-
Clerks, General III	416	Police Officers I	698
Computer Operators II	456	**Hourly Workers**	$/Hour
Computer Programmers II	653	Forklift Operators	-
Drafters II	-	General Maintenance Workers	10.71
Engineering Technicians III	650	Guards I	-
Engineering Technicians, Civil III	597	Janitors	7.54
Engineers III	963	Maintenance Electricians	18.36
Key Entry Operators I	346	Maintenance Electronics Techs II	19.80
Personnel Assistants III	521	Maintenance Machinists	20.79
Personnel Specialists III	810	Maintenance Mechanics, Machinery	19.82
Secretaries III	586	Material Handling Laborers	-
Switchboard Operator-Receptionist	412	Motor Vehicle Mechanics	17.97
Systems Analysts II	928	Shipping/Receiving Clerks	11.76
Systems Analysts Supervisor/Mgr II	1,402	Tool and Die Makers	-
Tax Collectors II	557	Truckdrivers, Tractor Trailer	17.42
Word Processors II	486	Warehouse Specialists	-

Note: Wage data includes full-time workers only for 2/96 and cover the Metropolitan Statistical Area (see Appendix A for areas included). Dashes indicate that data was not available.
Source: Bureau of Labor Statistics, Occupational Compensation Survey, 8/96

TAXES

Major State and Local Tax Rates

State Corp. Income (%)	State Personal Income (%)	Residential Property (effective rate per $100)	Sales & Use State (%)	Sales & Use Local (%)	State Gasoline (cents/ gallon)	State Cigarette (cents/ 20-pack)
9.975	6.0 - 9.5	0.95	5.75	None	20	65

Note: Personal/corporate income tax rates as of 1/97. Sales, gasoline and cigarette tax rates as of 1/98.
Source: Federation of Tax Administrators, www.taxadmin.org; Washington D.C. Department of Finance and Revenue, Tax Rates and Tax Burdens in the District of Columbia: A Nationwide Comparison, June 1997; Chamber of Commerce

Total Taxes Per Capita and as a Percent of Income

Area	Per Capita Income ($)	Per Capita Taxes ($)			Taxes as Pct. of Income (%)		
		Total	Federal	State/ Local	Total	Federal	State/ Local
Dist. of Columbia	36,142	13,219	8,608	4,611	36.6	23.8	12.8
U.S.	26,187	9,205	6,127	3,078	35.2	23.4	11.8

Note: Figures are for 1997
Source: Tax Foundation, Web Site, www.taxfoundation.org

Estimated Tax Burden

Area	State Income	Local Income	Property	Sales	Total
Washington	4,166	0	1,800	489	6,455

Note: The numbers are estimates of taxes paid by a married couple with two kids and annual earnings of $65,000. Sales tax estimates assume they spend average amounts on food, clothing, household goods and gasoline. Property tax estimates assume they live in a $225,000 home.
Source: Kiplinger's Personal Finance Magazine, June 1997

COMMERCIAL REAL ESTATE

Office Market

Class/ Location	Total Space (sq. ft.)	Vacant Space (sq. ft.)	Vac. Rate (%)	Under Constr. (sq. ft.)	Net Absorp. (sq. ft.)	Rental Rates ($/sq.ft./yr.)
Class A						
CBD	44,685,681	3,158,610	7.1	1,419,070	n/a	n/a
Outside CBD	95,940,038	4,599,506	4.8	0	n/a	n/a
Class B						
CBD	42,289,693	4,283,483	10.1	1,364,393	169	n/a
Outside CBD	60,875,259	5,971,970	9.8	0	n/a	n/a

Note: Data as of 10/97 and covers the District of Columbia; CBD = Central Business District; n/a not available;
Source: Society of Industrial and Office Realtors, 1998 Comparative Statistics of Industrial and Office Real Estate Markets

"There were two substantial speculative redevelopment efforts under way in Washington at the end of 1997. The Garfinckel's building on 14th Street and historic Victor building on H Street will bring more than 400,000 sq. ft. of renovated space to the market. At the same time, 1.4 million sq. ft. of new Class 'A' space was under construction in the central business district. During the latter part of 1997 the Class 'A' vacancy rate in the CBD was 7.1 percent leading some market observers to expect a reduction in landlord concessions and a rise in rental rates. There is only one obstacle to this scenario. The Federal Government is still the biggest game in town and its agencies are not growing." *Society of Industrial and Office Realtors, 1998 Comparative Statistics of Industrial and Office Real Estate Markets*

Industrial Market

Location	Total Space (sq. ft.)	Vacant Space (sq. ft.)	Vac. Rate (%)	Under Constr. (sq. ft.)	Net Absorp. (sq. ft.)	Net Lease ($/sq.ft./yr.)
Central City	n/a	n/a	n/a	n/a	n/a	n/a
Suburban	56,400,000	4,000,000	7.1	500,000	5,200,000	4.25-7.75

Note: Data as of 10/97 and covers Washington, D.C.-Northern Virginia; n/a not available
Source: Society of Industrial and Office Realtors, 1998 Comparative Statistics of Industrial and Office Real Estate Markets

"With construction costs now generally lower than sales prices in every size and industrial category, some of next year's 750,000 to one million sq. ft. of new industrial space will be constructed on speculation. The once-sleepy Dulles Airport corridor remains the location of choice, National REITs, such as Security Capital, will be the most active speculative builders. But some of the strongest local developers with good banking relationships and stellar credit are also building this way. Well-located modern flex space will continue to draw tenants from older buildings in Northern Virginia. Our SIOR reporter indicates that all types of industrial space are in moderate shortage and expects that sales and lease prices will rise between six and 10 percent. With the continued downsizing of the federal government and on-going attraction of the area for high-tech firms, such as the rapidly deregulating telecommunications companies, there is a healthy possibility that telecommunications could take over as the new driver of Northern Virginia's economy." *Society of Industrial and Office Realtors, 1998 Comparative Statistics of Industrial and Office Real Estate Markets*

Retail Market

Shopping Center Inventory (sq. ft.)	Shopping Center Construction (sq. ft.)	Construction as a Percent of Inventory (%)	Torto Wheaton Rent Index[1] ($/sq. ft.)
84,389,000	1,162,000	1.4	16.67

Note: Data as of 1997 and covers the Metropolitan Statistical Area - see Appendix A for areas included; (1) Index is based on a model that predicts what the average rent should be for leases with certain characteristics, in certain locations during certain years.
Source: National Association of Realtors, 1997-1998 Market Conditions Report

"An easing of federal government cutbacks, coupled with a strong tourism industry, helped make 1997 a good year for the Washington D.C. area retail market. The area's retail rent index climbed 5.8% while shopping center completions remained robust. The addition of the new $200 million MCI Arena Downtown will be a boon to retailers in the area. Furthermore, Washington ranks near the top of the most eligible list in all of the most relevant demographic categories analyzed by restaurants. National retailers have recently stormed into the area, led by Minneapolis-based Target stores, which opened 15 stores between Baltimore and Washington. However, many brokers expect activity to level off in the near future." *National Association of Realtors, 1997-1998 Market Conditions Report*

COMMERCIAL UTILITIES

Typical Monthly Electric Bills

Area	Commercial Service ($/month)		Industrial Service ($/month)	
	12 kW demand 1,500 kWh	100 kW demand 30,000 kWh	1,000 kW demand 400,000 kWh	20,000 kW demand 10,000,000 kWh
City	175	3,549	35,997	781,446
U.S.	162	2,360	25,590	545,677

Note: Based on rates in effect July 1, 1997
Source: Edison Electric Institute, Typical Residential, Commercial and Industrial Bills, Summer 1997

TRANSPORTATION

Transportation Statistics

Avg. travel time to work (min.)	27.1
Interstate highways	I-66; I-95
Bus lines	
In-city	Washington Metropolitan Area TA, 1,337 vehicles
Inter-city	9
Passenger air service	
Airport	Dulles International; Washington National (now Reagan Airport)
Airlines	25
Aircraft departures	146,521 (1995)
Enplaned passengers	11,461,873 (1995)
Rail service	Amtrak; Metro (subway)
Motor freight carriers	n/a
Major waterways/ports	None

Source: OAG, Business Travel Planner, Summer 1997; Editor & Publisher Market Guide, 1998; FAA Airport Activity Statistics, 1996; Amtrak National Time Table, Northeast Timetable, Fall/Winter 1997-98; 1990 Census of Population and Housing, STF 3C; Chamber of Commerce/Economic Development 1997; Jane's Urban Transport Systems 1997-98; Transit Fact Book 1997

A survey of 90,000 airline passengers during the first half of 1997 ranked most of the largest airports in the U.S. Dulles International ranked #24 and Washington National #32 out of 36.

Criteria: cleanliness, quality of restaurants, attractiveness, speed of baggage delivery, ease of reaching gates, available ground transportation, ease of following signs and closeness of parking. *Plog Research Inc., First Half 1997*

Means of Transportation to Work

Area	Car/Truck/Van		Public Transportation			Bicycle	Walked	Other Means	Worked at Home
	Drove Alone	Car-pooled	Bus	Subway	Railroad				
City	35.0	12.0	22.3	12.9	0.2	0.8	11.8	2.0	3.0
MSA[1]	62.9	15.8	6.6	6.5	0.2	0.3	3.9	1.0	2.8
U.S.	73.2	13.4	3.0	1.5	0.5	0.4	3.9	1.2	3.0

Note: figures shown are percentages and only include workers 16 years old and over;
(1) Metropolitan Statistical Area - see Appendix A for areas included
Source: 1990 Census of Population and Housing, Summary Tape File 3C

BUSINESSES

Major Business Headquarters

Company Name	1997 Rankings	
	Fortune 500	Forbes 500
Fannie Mae	29	-
MCI Communications	59	-
Student Loan Marketing Assn.	376	-

Note: Companies listed are located in the city; Dashes indicate no ranking
Fortune 500: companies that produce a 10-K are ranked 1 - 500 based on 1996 revenue
Forbes 500: private companies are ranked 1 - 500 based on 1996 revenue
Source: Forbes 12/1/97; Fortune 4/28/97

Fast-Growing Businesses

Washington is home to one of *Business Week's* "hot growth" companies: Strayer Education. Criteria: sales and earnings, return on capital and stock price. *Business Week, 5/26/97*

Washington was ranked #20 out of 24 (#1 is best) in terms of the best-performing local stocks in 1996 according to the Money/Norby Cities Index. The index measures stocks of companies that have headquarters in 24 metro areas. *Money, 2/7/97*

Women-Owned Businesses: Number, Employment, Sales and Share

Area	Women-Owned Businesses in 1996				Share of Women-Owned Businesses in 1996	
	Number	Employment	Sales ($000)	Rank[2]	Percent (%)	Rank[3]
MSA[1]	167,500	299,400	37,307,900	5	39.5	6

Note: (1) Metropolitan Statistical Area - see Appendix A for areas included; (2) Calculated on an averaging of number of businesses, employment and sales and ranges from 1 to 50 where 1 is best; (3) Ranges from 1 to 50 where 1 is best
Source: The National Foundation for Women Business Owners, 1996 Facts on Women-Owned Businesses: Trends in the Top 50 Metropolitan Areas, March 26, 1997

Women-Owned Businesses: Growth

Area	Growth in Women-Owned Businesses (% change from 1987 to 1996)				Relative Growth in the Number of Women-Owned and All Businesses (% change from 1987 to 1996)			
	Num.	Empl.	Sales	Rank[2]	Women-Owned	All Firms	Absolute Difference	Relative Difference
MSA[1]	87.6	176.2	198.3	28	87.6	69.6	18.0	1.3:1

Note: (1) Metropolitan Statistical Area - see Appendix A for areas included; (2) Calculated on an averaging of the percent growth of number of businesses, employment and sales and ranges from 1 to 50 where 1 is best
Source: The National Foundation for Women Business Owners, 1996 Facts on Women-Owned Businesses: Trends in the Top 50 Metropolitan Areas, March 26, 1997

Minority Business Opportunity

Washington is home to two companies which are on the Black Enterprise Industrial/Service 100 list (largest based on gross sales): BET Holdings Inc. (cable TV network, magazine publishing); Dynamic Concepts Inc. (telecom. services, operations and maintenance support). Criteria: 1) operational in previous calendar year; 2) at least 51% black-owned; 3) manufactures/owns the product it sells or provides industrial or consumer services. Brokerages, real estate firms and firms that provide professional services are not eligible. *Black Enterprise, July 1997*

Seven of the 500 largest Hispanic-owned companies in the U.S. are located in Washington. *Hispanic Business, June 1997*

Washington is home to three companies which are on the Hispanic Business Fastest-Growing 100 list (greatest sales growth from 1992 to 1996): CSSI Inc. (system design & devel.), Lisboa Associates Inc. (mgmt. consulting svcs.), and Teleconsult Inc. (telecom. consulting svcs.) *Hispanic Business, July/August 1997*

Washington was listed among the top 25 metropolitan areas in terms of the number of Hispanic-owned companies. The city was ranked number 10 with 29,490 companies. *Hispanic Business, May 1997*

Small Business Opportunity

According to *Forbes*, Washington is home to one of America's 200 best small companies: BET Holdings. Criteria: companies must be publicly traded, U.S.-based corporations with latest 12-month sales of between $5 and $350 million. Earnings must be at least $1 million for the 12-month period. Limited partnerships, REITs and closed-end mutual funds were not considered. Banks, S&Ls and electric utilities were not included. *Forbes, November 3, 1997*

HOTELS & MOTELS

Hotels/Motels

Area	Hotels/ Motels	Rooms	Luxury-Level Hotels/Motels		Average Minimum Rates ($)		
			♦♦♦♦	♦♦♦♦♦	♦♦	♦♦♦	♦♦♦♦
City	85	20,780	12	1	103	148	230
Airport	45	11,792	2	0	n/a	n/a	n/a
Suburbs	127	22,607	2	0	n/a	n/a	n/a
Total	257	55,179	16	1	n/a	n/a	n/a

Note: n/a not available; Classifications range from one diamond (budget properties with basic amenities) to five diamond (luxury properties with the finest service, rooms and facilities).
Source: OAG, Business Travel Planner, Summer 1997

CONVENTION CENTERS

Major Convention Centers

Center Name	Meeting Rooms	Exhibit Space (sf)
District of Columbia Armory Board	n/a	66,000
Washington Convention Center	40	381,000

Note: n/a not available
Source: Trade Shows Worldwide 1997

Living Environment

COST OF LIVING

Cost of Living Index

Composite Index	Housing	Utilities	Groceries	Health Care	Trans- portation	Misc. Goods/ Services
122.1	151.8	92.7	109.6	119.8	124.9	109.8

Note: U.S. = 100; Figures are for the Metropolitan Statistical Area - see Appendix A for areas included
Source: ACCRA, Cost of Living Index, 3rd Quarter 1997

HOUSING

Median Home Prices and Housing Affordability

Area	Median Price[2] 3rd Qtr. 1997 ($)	HOI[3] 3rd Qtr. 1997	Afford- ability Rank[4]
MSA[1]	165,000	70.5	91
U.S.	127,000	63.7	–

Note: (1) Metropolitan Statistical Area - see Appendix A for areas included; (2) U.S. figures calculated from the sales of 625,000 new and existing homes in 195 markets; (3) Housing Opportunity Index - percent of homes sold that were within the reach of the median income household at the prevailing mortgage interest rate; (4) Rank is from 1-195 with 1 being most affordable
Source: National Association of Home Builders, Housing Opportunity Index, 3rd Quarter 1997

It is projected that the median price of existing single-family homes in the metro area will increase by 13.6% in 1998. Nationwide, home prices are projected to increase 6.6%. *Kiplinger's Personal Finance Magazine, January 1998*

Average New Home Price

Area	Price ($)
MSA[1]	206,783
U.S.	135,710

Note: Figures are based on a new home with 1,800 sq. ft. of living area on an 8,000 sq. ft. lot; (1) Metropolitan Statistical Area - see Appendix A for areas included
Source: ACCRA, Cost of Living Index, 3rd Quarter 1997

Average Apartment Rent

Area	Rent ($/mth)
MSA[1]	971
U.S.	569

Note: Figures are based on an unfurnished two bedroom, 1-1/2 or 2 bath apartment, approximately 950 sq. ft. in size, excluding all utilities except water; (1) Metropolitan Statistical Area - see Appendix A for areas included
Source: ACCRA, Cost of Living Index, 3rd Quarter 1997

RESIDENTIAL UTILITIES

Average Residential Utility Costs

Area	All Electric ($/mth)	Part Electric ($/mth)	Other Energy ($/mth)	Phone ($/mth)
MSA[1]	–	57.52	35.70	20.15
U.S.	109.40	55.25	43.64	19.48

Note: (1) (1) Metropolitan Statistical Area - see Appendix A for areas included
Source: ACCRA, Cost of Living Index, 3rd Quarter 1997

HEALTH CARE

Average Health Care Costs

Area	Hospital ($/day)	Doctor ($/visit)	Dentist ($/visit)
MSA[1]	454.50	60.33	71.33
U.S.	392.91	48.76	60.84

Note: Hospital - based on a semi-private room. Doctor - based on a general practitioner's routine exam of an established patient. Dentist - based on adult teeth cleaning and periodic oral exam; (1) Metropolitan Statistical Area - see Appendix A for areas included
Source: ACCRA, Cost of Living Index, 3rd Quarter 1997

Distribution of Office-Based Physicians

Area	Family/Gen. Practitioners	Specialists		
		Medical	Surgical	Other
MSA[1]	850	3,885	2,455	2,787

Note: Data as of 12/31/96; (1) Metropolitan Statistical Area - see Appendix A for areas included
Source: American Medical Assn., Physician Characteristics & Distribution in the U.S., 1997-1998

Hospitals

Washington has 11 general medical and surgical hospitals, 2 psychiatric, 1 obstetrics and gynecology, 1 rehabilitation, 1 children's general, 1 children's other specialty. *AHA Guide to the Healthcare Field 1997-98*

According to *U.S. News and World Report,* Washington has 3 of the best hospitals in the U.S.: **Georgetown University Hospital**, noted for cancer, gastroenterology, gynecology, neurology, pulmonology, rheumatology, urology; **Children's National Medical Center**, noted for pediatrics; **National Rehabilitation Hospital**, noted for rehabilitation; *U.S. News and World Report, "America's Best Hospitals", 7/28/97*

EDUCATION

Public School District Statistics

District Name	Num. Sch.	Enroll.	Classroom Teachers[1]	Pupils per Teacher	Minority Pupils (%)	Current Exp.[2] ($/pupil)
District of Columbia Pub Schls	186	79,802	n/a	n/a	96.0	9,187

Note: Data covers the 1995-1996 school year unless otherwise noted; (1) Excludes teachers reported as working in school district offices rather than in schools; (2) Based on 1993-94 enrollment collected by the Census Bureau, not the enrollment figure shown in column 3; SD = School District; ISD = Independent School District; n/a not available
Source: National Center for Education Statistics, Common Core of Data Survey; Bureau of the Census

Educational Quality

School District	Education Quotient[1]	Graduate Outcome[2]	Community Index[3]	Resource Index[4]
District of Columbia	93.0	52.0	95.0	131.0

Note: Nearly 1,000 secondary school districts were rated in terms of educational quality. The scores range from a low of 50 to a high of 150; (1) Average of the Graduate Outcome, Community and Resource indexes; (2) Based on graduation rates and college board scores (SAT/ACT); (3) Based on the surrounding community's average level of education and the area's average income level; (4) Based on teacher salaries, per-pupil expenditures and student-teacher ratios.
Source: Expansion Management, Ratings Issue 1997

Educational Attainment by Race

Area	High School Graduate (%)					Bachelor's Degree (%)				
	Total	White	Black	Other	Hisp.[2]	Total	White	Black	Other	Hisp.[2]
City	73.1	93.1	63.8	61.0	52.6	33.3	69.0	15.3	31.8	24.0
MSA[1]	85.2	90.1	74.5	75.7	64.5	38.5	45.3	19.9	38.4	23.8
U.S.	75.2	77.9	63.1	60.4	49.8	20.3	21.5	11.4	19.4	9.2

Note: figures shown cover persons 25 years old and over; (1) Metropolitan Statistical Area - see Appendix A for areas included; (2) people of Hispanic origin can be of any race
Source: 1990 Census of Population and Housing, Summary Tape File 3C

School Enrollment by Type

Area	Preprimary				Elementary/High School			
	Public		Private		Public		Private	
	Enrollment	%	Enrollment	%	Enrollment	%	Enrollment	%
City	5,532	61.8	3,425	38.2	67,278	83.9	12,882	16.1
MSA[1]	39,352	48.2	42,299	51.8	522,711	87.4	75,692	12.6
U.S.	2,679,029	59.5	1,824,256	40.5	38,379,689	90.2	4,187,099	9.8

Note: figures shown cover persons 3 years old and over;
(1) Metropolitan Statistical Area - see Appendix A for areas included
Source: 1990 Census of Population and Housing, Summary Tape File 3C

School Enrollment by Race

Area	Preprimary (%)				Elementary/High School (%)			
	White	Black	Other	Hisp.[1]	White	Black	Other	Hisp.[1]
City	25.0	71.2	3.8	3.4	12.6	82.2	5.2	6.5
MSA[2]	70.9	23.1	6.0	4.4	58.9	31.6	9.5	6.7
U.S.	80.4	12.5	7.1	7.8	74.1	15.6	10.3	12.5

Note: figures shown cover persons 3 years old and over; (1) people of Hispanic origin can be of any race; (2) Metropolitan Statistical Area - see Appendix A for areas included
Source: 1990 Census of Population and Housing, Summary Tape File 3C

SAT/ACT Scores

Area/District	1996 SAT				1996 ACT	
	Percent of Graduates Tested (%)	Average Math Score	Average Verbal Score	Average Combined Score	Percent of Graduates Tested (%)	Average Composite Score
District of Columbia	60	475	490	965	5	17.2
State	n/a	n/a	n/a	n/a	n/a	n/a
U.S.	41	508	505	1,013	35	20.9

Note: Math and verbal SAT scores are out of a possible 800; ACT scores are out of a possible 36
Caution: Comparing or ranking states/cities on the basis of SAT/ACT scores alone is invalid and strongly discouraged by the The College Board and The American College Testing Program as students who take the tests are self-selected and do not represent the entire student population. 1996 SAT scores cannot be compared to previous years due to recentering.
Source: American College Testing Program, 1997; College Board, 1997

Classroom Teacher Salaries in Public Schools

District	B.A. Degree		M.A. Degree		Ph.D. Degree	
	Min. ($)	Max ($)	Min. ($)	Max. ($)	Min. ($)	Max. ($)
Washington	25,937	40,221	28,531	46,382	31,140	49,131
Average[1]	26,120	39,270	28,175	44,667	31,643	49,825

Note: Salaries are for 1996-1997; (1) Based on all school districts covered
Source: American Federation of Teachers (unpublished data)

Higher Education

Two-Year Colleges		Four-Year Colleges		Medical Schools	Law Schools	Voc/ Tech
Public	Private	Public	Private			
0	0	2	11	3	6	10

Source: College Blue Book, Occupational Education 1997; Medical School Admission Requirements, 1998-99; Peterson's Guide to Two-Year Colleges, 1997; Peterson's Guide to Four-Year Colleges, 1997; Barron's Guide to Law Schools 1997

MAJOR EMPLOYERS

Major Employers

Children's Hospital Corp.	Federal Deposit Insurance Corp.
Federal National Mortgage Association	GEICO Corp.
Group Hospitalization & Medical Services	Inter-American Development Bank
International Bank for Reconstruction & Development	International Monetary Fund
Marriott International	National Geographic Society
Potomac Electric Power Co.	Providence Hospital
Smithsonian Institution	Bureau of National Affairs
Washington Metropolitan Area Transit Authority	News World Communications
National Railroad Passenger Corp.	

Note: companies listed are located in the city
Source: Dun's Business Rankings 1997; Ward's Business Directory, 1997

PUBLIC SAFETY

Crime Rate

Area	All Crimes	Violent Crimes				Property Crimes		
		Murder	Forcible Rape	Robbery	Aggrav. Assault	Burglary	Larceny -Theft	Motor Vehicle Theft
City	11,889.0	73.1	47.9	1,186.7	1,162.1	1,809.9	5,772.2	1,837.0
Suburbs[1]	4,567.9	5.7	24.8	177.0	226.7	598.2	2,980.2	555.3
MSA[2]	5,450.7	13.8	27.6	298.8	339.5	744.3	3,316.8	709.9
U.S.	5,078.9	7.4	36.1	202.4	388.2	943.0	2,975.9	525.9

Note: Crime rate is the number of crimes per 100,000 pop.; (1) defined as all areas within the MSA but located outside the central city; (2) Metropolitan Statistical Area - see Appendix A for areas incl.
Source: FBI Uniform Crime Reports 1996

RECREATION

Culture and Recreation

Museums	Symphony Orchestras	Opera Companies	Dance Companies	Professional Theatres	Zoos	Pro Sports Teams
45	4	4	3	9	1	3

Source: International Directory of the Performing Arts, 1996; Official Museum Directory, 1998; Chamber of Commerce/Economic Development 1997

Library System

The District of Columbia Public Library has 25 branches, holdings of 2,165,154 volumes and a budget of $n/a (1994-1995). Note: n/a means not available. *American Library Directory, 1997-1998*

MEDIA

Newspapers

Name	Type	Freq.	Distribution	Circulation
Aerospace Daily	n/a	5x/wk	International	22,000
B.E.T. Weekend Magazine	Black	1x/mo	n/a	1,000,000
Capital Spotlight Newspaper	Black	1x/wk	Area	50,000
City Paper	General	1x/wk	Area	94,100
The Georgetowner	General	17x/yr	Local	25,000
The InTowner	General	1x/mo	Regional	32,000
La Nacion	Hispanic	1x/wk	Area	22,000
News Dimensions	Black	1x/wk	Regional	25,000
The Rock Creek Current	General	1x/wk	Local	32,500
Roll Call: The Newspaper of Capitol Hill	General	2x/wk	National	17,027
The Washington Afro-American Newspaper	Black	1x/wk	Local	10,000
The Washington Blade	n/a	1x/wk	Area	44,000
Washington Hispanic	Hispanic	1x/wk	Area	20,000
Washington Informer	Black	1x/wk	Area	27,000
The Washington New Observer	Black	1x/wk	Area	20,000
Washington Post	n/a	7x/wk	Area	834,641
Washington Post Magazine	n/a	1x/wk	n/a	1,215,021
The Washington Post National Weekly	General	1x/wk	National	118,000
The Washington Times	General	7x/wk	Area	100,928
Washington Times (National Weekly Edition)	General	1x/wk	National	68,000

Note: Includes newspapers with circulations of 10,000 or more located in the city; n/a not available
Source: Burrelle's Media Directory, 1998 Edition

AM Radio Stations

Call Letters	Freq. (kHz)	Target Audience	Station Format	Music Format
WMAL	630	General	N/T	n/a
WYCB	1340	n/a	M/T	Christian
WTOP	1500	n/a	N	n/a

Note: Stations included broadcast in the Washington metro area; n/a not available
Station Format: E = Educational; M = Music; N = News; S = Sports; T = Talk
Source: Burrelle's Media Directory, 1998 Edition

FM Radio Stations

Call Letters	Freq. (mHz)	Target Audience	Station Format	Music Format
WAMU	88.5	n/a	M/N/T	Country
WETH	89.1	General	E/M/N	Classical
WPFW	89.3	General	E/M/N/T	Jazz/Oldies/R&B
WDCU	90.1	General	M	Christian/Jazz/R&B
WHUR	96.3	n/a	M	Adult Contemporary
WASH	97.1	General	M	Adult Contemporary
WMZQ	98.7	n/a	M	Country
WMMJ	102.3	Black	M	Adult Contemporary
WRQX	107.3	n/a	M	Adult Contemporary

Note: Stations included broadcast in the Washington metro area; n/a not available
Station Format: E = Educational; M = Music; N = News; S = Sports; T = Talk
Source: Burrelle's Media Directory, 1998 Edition

Television Stations

Name	Ch.	Affiliation	Type	Owner
WRC	4	NBC	Commercial	General Electric Company
WTTG	5	Fox	Commercial	Fox Television Stations Inc.
WJLA	7	ABC	Commercial	Allbritton Communications Company
WUSA	9	CBS	Commercial	Gannett Company Inc.
WHMM	32	PBS	Public	Howard University Board of Trustees
WBDC	50	Jasas Inc.	Commercial	Jasas Corporation

Note: Stations included broadcast in the Washington metro area
Source: Burrelle's Media Directory, 1998 Edition

CLIMATE

Average and Extreme Temperatures

Temperature	Jan	Feb	Mar	Apr	May	Jun	Jul	Aug	Sep	Oct	Nov	Dec	Ann
Extreme High (°F)	79	82	89	95	97	101	104	103	101	94	86	75	104
Average High (°F)	43	46	55	67	76	84	88	86	80	69	58	47	67
Average Temp. (°F)	36	38	46	57	66	75	79	78	71	60	49	39	58
Average Low (°F)	28	30	37	46	56	65	70	69	62	50	40	31	49
Extreme Low (°F)	-5	4	14	24	34	47	54	49	39	29	16	3	-5

Note: Figures cover the years 1945-1990
Source: National Climatic Data Center, International Station Meteorological Climate Summary, 3/95

Average Precipitation/Snowfall/Humidity

Precip./Humidity	Jan	Feb	Mar	Apr	May	Jun	Jul	Aug	Sep	Oct	Nov	Dec	Ann
Avg. Precip. (in.)	2.8	2.6	3.3	2.9	4.0	3.4	4.1	4.2	3.3	2.9	3.0	3.1	39.5
Avg. Snowfall (in.)	6	6	2	Tr	0	0	0	0	0	Tr	1	3	18
Avg. Rel. Hum. 7am (%)	71	70	70	70	74	75	77	80	82	80	76	72	75
Avg. Rel. Hum. 4pm (%)	54	50	46	45	51	52	53	54	54	53	53	55	52

Note: Figures cover the years 1945-1990; Tr = Trace amounts (<0.05 in. of rain; <0.5 in. of snow)
Source: National Climatic Data Center, International Station Meteorological Climate Summary, 3/95

Weather Conditions

Temperature			Daytime Sky			Precipitation		
10°F & below	32°F & below	90°F & above	Clear	Partly cloudy	Cloudy	0.01 inch or more precip.	0.1 inch or more snow/ice	Thunder-storms
2	71	34	84	144	137	112	9	30

Note: Figures are average number of days per year and covers the years 1945-1990
Source: National Climatic Data Center, International Station Meteorological Climate Summary, 3/95

AIR & WATER QUALITY

Maximum Pollutant Concentrations

	Particulate Matter (ug/m³)	Carbon Monoxide (ppm)	Sulfur Dioxide (ppm)	Nitrogen Dioxide (ppm)	Ozone (ppm)	Lead (ug/m³)
MSA[1] Level	57	5	0.048	0.026	0.12	0.02
NAAQS[2]	150	9	0.140	0.053	0.12	1.50
Met NAAQS?	Yes	Yes	Yes	Yes	Yes	Yes

Note: (1) Metropolitan Statistical Area - see Appendix A for areas included; (2) National Ambient Air Quality Standards; ppm = parts per million; ug/m³ = micrograms per cubic meter; n/a not available
Source: EPA, National Air Quality and Emissions Trends Report, 1996

Pollutant Standards Index

In the Washington MSA (see Appendix A for areas included), the Pollutant Standards Index (PSI) exceeded 100 on 2 days in 1996. A PSI value greater than 100 indicates that air quality would be in the unhealthful range on that day. *EPA, National Air Quality and Emissions Trends Report, 1996*

Drinking Water

Water System Name	Pop. Served	Primary Water Source Type	Number of Violations in Fiscal Year 1997	Type of Violation/ Contaminants
Water and Sewer Utility Admin	595,000	Purchased surface	None	None

Note: Data as of January 16, 1998
Source: EPA, Office of Ground Water and Drinking Water, Safe Drinking Water Information System

Washington tap water is slightly alkaline and medium soft.
Editor & Publisher Market Guide, 1998

Worcester, Massachusetts

Background

Known for its musical and dramatic civic events throughout the 19th century, Worcester now serves as a commercial, industrial and cultural center.

The city is located in eastcentral Massachusetts on the Blackstone River, 40 miles west of Boston.

After two previous attempts, the area was finally settled in 1713. A town charter was obtained in 1722 and a city charter in 1848. Worcester was a center of antislavery sentiment and Free Soilism from the 1830's through the 1850's. The Republican Party of Massachusetts was founded here in 1854 and National Women's Political Rights conventions were held in Worcester in 1850 and in 1851.

From 1880 to 1920 the population almost tripled. Irish, Canadian and Swedish immigrants settled in the city before 1900. The early 20th century witnessed an influx of Italian, Polish, Lithuanian, Greek, Armenian, Syrian and Lebanese settlers.

The 1960's were characterized by economic difficulty until the 1970's when an economic revival took place.

Worcester has a diversified economic base. Manufactures include abrasives, machine tools, heavy machinery, valves, forgings, apparel, data-processing accessories, and plastics. Banking, education, insurance and research are major areas of employment.

Joining a growing list of community outreach efforts by universities to clean up the neighborhoods surrounding their schools, Clark University in Worcester has started a secondary school for neighborhood children and is helping to develop a light industrial park to bring jobs to the local residents. *USA Today 11/12/97*

The proximity to the Atlantic Ocean, Long Island Sound, and the Berkshire Hills plays an important part in determining Worcester's climate. Winter-time cold snaps are quite frequent, but of short duration and temperatures are usually modified by the passage of air over land and mountains.

General Rankings and Evaluative Comments

- Worcester was ranked #77 out of 300 cities by *Money's* 1997 "Survey of the Best Places to Live." Criteria used: health services, crime, economy, housing, education, transportation, weather, leisure and the arts. The city was ranked #154 in 1996 and #178 in 1995. *Money, July 1997; Money, September 1996; Money, September 1995*

- *Ladies Home Journal* ranked America's 200 largest cities based on the qualities women care about most. Worcester ranked 38 out of 200. Criteria: low crime rate, good public schools, well-paying jobs, quality health and child care, the presence of women in government, proportion of women-owned businesses, size of the wage gap with men, local economy, divorce rates, the ratio of single men to single women, whether there are laws that require at least the same number of public toilets for women as men, and the probability of good hair days. *Ladies Home Journal, November 1997*

- Worcester was ranked #100 out of 219 cities in terms of children's health, safety, and economic well-being. Criteria: total population, percent population change, birth rate, child immunization rate, infant mortality rate, percent low birth weight infants, percent of births to teens, physician-to-population ratio, student-to-teacher ratio, dropout rate, unemployment rate, median family income, percent of children in poverty, violent and property crime rates, number of juvenile arrests for violent crimes as a percent of the total crime index, number of days with pollution standard index (PSI) over 100, pounds toxic releases per 1,000 people and number of superfund sites. *Zero Population Growth, Children's Environmental Index 1997*

- According to *Working Mother,* "Governor William Weld proposed increasing spending by $23 million this year, which would bring the total child care spending in Massachusetts to $283 million by 1998. Such funding is badly needed in the face of ever-increasing demand for child care across the state.

  The state also allocated $25 million to improve salaries for caregivers in many child care programs, a move that should help reduce turnover in centers. Other states should follow this example.

  As long as they hire an assistant, family child care providers here will soon be able to take in up to four more children (for a total of 10). This move increases the supply of care and also boosts its quality. In effect, the new assistants will improve the adult-to-child ratio in many homes. (Massachusetts is among the 10 best states for child care.)" *Working Mother, July/August 1997*

Business Environment

STATE ECONOMY

State Economic Profile

"...house prices have hit new highs in many areas and income growth is above the national average. The state's economy is strongest in the greater Boston area and markedly weaker, but strengthening, in western Massachusetts....

One of the largest new growth industries for the state is telecommunications, which has added more than 34,000 new jobs in the last three years. Internet-related companies alone have created nearly 30,000 new jobs since 1993, while telecommunications manufacturing, which includes network switching and fiber-optic devices, among others, created another 33,000 jobs. Of course, a good part of this growth is being offset by the continued downsizing of traditional telephone companies.

Construction is currently one of Massachusetts's fastest growing industries. Single-family permits issued rose nearly 15% in the first quarter of 1997, while multifamily permits rose a blistering 440%. While single-family activity is expected to moderate in the face of rising mortgage rates, the outlook for multifamily activity is very promising. Massachusetts' strong economy will increase household formation rates and decrease housing affordability. Rising rents will motivate developers to build additional units, and local towns have removed rent controls and anti-development laws.

Massachusetts has successfully replaced the shrinking minicomputer and defense industries with vibrant growth industries, such as money management, software, computer networking, Internet products, biotechnology, and business services. In addition, the state has enacted regulatory and tax reforms that have eased the state's high cost of doing business. Massachusetts' economy would be an even stronger performer if the state's migration flows and population growth were more favorable...." *National Association of Realtors, Economic Profiles: The Fifty States, July 1997*

IMPORTS/EXPORTS

Total Export Sales

Area	1993 ($000)	1994 ($000)	1995 ($000)	1996 ($000)	% Chg. 1993-96	% Chg. 1995-96
MSA[1]	1,017,883	603,793	757,553	685,676	-32.6	-9.5
U.S.	464,858,354	512,415,609	583,030,524	622,827,063	34.0	6.8

Note: (1) Metropolitan Statistical Area - see Appendix A for areas included
Source: U.S. Department of Commerce, International Trade Association, Metropolitan Area Exports: An Export Performance Report on Over 250 U.S. Cities, October 1997

Imports/Exports by Port

Type	Cargo Value			Share of U.S. Total	
	1995 (US$mil.)	1996 (US$mil.)	% Change 1995-1996	1995 (%)	1996 (%)
Imports	0	0	0	0	0
Exports	0	0	0	0	0

Source: Global Trade Information Services, WaterBorne Trade Atlas 1997

CITY FINANCES

City Government Finances

Component	FY92 ($000)	FY92 (per capita $)
Revenue	273,042	1,630.04
Expenditure	304,876	1,820.09
Debt Outstanding	160,029	955.36
Cash & Securities	54,792	327.10

Source: U.S. Bureau of the Census, City Government Finances: 1991-92

City Government Revenue by Source

Source	FY92 ($000)	FY92 (per capita $)	FY92 (%)
From Federal Government	21,468	128.16	7.9
From State Governments	105,831	631.80	38.8
From Local Governments	0	0.00	0.0
Property Taxes	102,588	612.44	37.6
General Sales Taxes	0	0.00	0.0
Selective Sales Taxes	390	2.33	0.1
Income Taxes	0	0.00	0.0
Current Charges	23,361	139.46	8.6
Utility/Liquor Store	12,598	75.21	4.6
Employee Retirement[1]	0	0.00	0.0
Other	6,806	40.63	2.5

Note: (1) Excludes "city contributions," classified as "nonrevenue," intragovernmental transfers.
Source: U.S. Bureau of the Census, City Government Finances: 1991-92

City Government Expenditures by Function

Function	FY92 ($000)	FY92 (per capita $)	FY92 (%)
Educational Services	127,705	762.39	41.9
Employee Retirement[1]	0	0.00	0.0
Environment/Housing	17,857	106.61	5.9
Government Administration	9,967	59.50	3.3
Interest on General Debt	7,196	42.96	2.4
Public Safety	35,976	214.77	11.8
Social Services	10,599	63.28	3.5
Transportation	13,958	83.33	4.6
Utility/Liquor Store	18,189	108.59	6.0
Other	63,429	378.67	20.8

Note: (1) Payments to beneficiaries including withdrawal of contributions.
Source: U.S. Bureau of the Census, City Government Finances: 1991-92

Municipal Bond Ratings

Area	Moody's	S & P
Worcester	Baa1	n/a

Note: n/a not available; n/r not rated
Source: Moody's Bond Record, 2/98; Statistical Abstract of the U.S., 1997; Governing Magazine, 9/97, 3/98

POPULATION

Population Growth

Area	1980	1990	% Chg. 1980-90	July 1996 Estimate	% Chg. 1990-96
City	161,799	169,759	4.9	166,350	-2.0
MSA[1]	402,918	436,941	8.4	485,229	11.1
U.S.	226,545,805	248,765,170	9.8	265,179,411	6.6

Note: (1) Metropolitan Statistical Area - see Appendix A for areas included
Source: 1980/1990 Census of Housing and Population, Summary Tape File 3C; Census Bureau Population Estimates

Population Characteristics

Race	City 1980 Population	City 1980 %	City 1990 Population	City 1990 %	City % Chg. 1980-90	MSA[1] 1990 Population	MSA[1] 1990 %
White	152,795	94.4	148,167	87.3	-3.0	408,725	93.5
Black	4,582	2.8	7,653	4.5	67.0	9,462	2.2
Amer Indian/Esk/Aleut	521	0.3	617	0.4	18.4	966	0.2
Asian/Pacific Islander	792	0.5	4,362	2.6	450.8	7,449	1.7
Other	3,109	1.9	8,960	5.3	188.2	10,339	2.4
Hispanic Origin[2]	6,468	4.0	15,868	9.3	145.3	19,435	4.4

Note: (1) Metropolitan Statistical Area - see Appendix A for areas included; (2) people of Hispanic origin can be of any race
Source: 1980/1990 Census of Housing and Population, Summary Tape File 3C

Ancestry

Area	German	Irish	English	Italian	U.S.	French	Polish	Dutch
City	5.4	24.9	9.8	13.5	2.4	15.1	6.9	0.5
MSA[1]	7.3	25.2	14.5	12.6	2.7	18.6	9.1	1.1
U.S.	23.3	15.6	13.1	5.9	5.3	4.2	3.8	2.5

Note: Figures are percentages and include persons that reported multiple ancestry (eg. if a person reported being Irish and Italian, they were included in both columns); (1) Metropolitan Statistical Area - see Appendix A for areas included
Source: 1990 Census of Population and Housing, Summary Tape File 3C

Age

Area	Median Age (Years)	Age Distribution (%) Under 5	Under 18	18-24	25-44	45-64	65+	80+
City	31.6	7.2	22.3	14.8	30.8	16.1	16.0	4.1
MSA[1]	33.2	7.3	23.8	11.5	32.7	17.8	14.2	3.4
U.S.	32.9	7.3	25.6	10.5	32.6	18.7	12.5	2.8

Note: (1) Metropolitan Statistical Area - see Appendix A for areas included
Source: 1990 Census of Population and Housing, Summary Tape File 3C

Male/Female Ratio

Area	Number of males per 100 females (all ages)	Number of males per 100 females (18 years old+)
City	91.1	87.3
MSA[1]	94.0	90.7
U.S.	95.0	91.9

Note: (1) Metropolitan Statistical Area - see Appendix A for areas included
Source: 1990 Census of Population, General Population Characteristics

INCOME

Per Capita/Median/Average Income

Area	Per Capita ($)	Median Household ($)	Average Household ($)
City	13,393	28,955	34,757
MSA[1]	15,657	35,977	41,796
U.S.	14,420	30,056	38,453

Note: all figures are for 1989; (1) Metropolitan Statistical Area - see Appendix A for areas included
Source: 1990 Census of Population and Housing, Summary Tape File 3C

Household Income Distribution by Race

Income ($)	City (%)					U.S. (%)				
	Total	White	Black	Other	Hisp.[1]	Total	White	Black	Other	Hisp.[1]
Less than 5,000	5.7	5.0	8.9	14.0	12.5	6.2	4.8	15.2	8.6	8.8
5,000 - 9,999	13.7	12.8	19.9	23.2	25.0	9.3	8.6	14.2	9.9	11.1
10,000 - 14,999	8.6	8.2	9.8	14.0	14.5	8.8	8.5	11.0	9.8	11.0
15,000 - 24,999	15.7	15.4	21.8	15.3	17.6	17.5	17.3	18.9	18.5	20.5
25,000 - 34,999	14.8	15.0	11.8	13.3	14.4	15.8	16.1	14.2	15.4	16.4
35,000 - 49,999	18.6	19.3	13.5	12.6	10.8	17.9	18.6	13.3	16.1	16.0
50,000 - 74,999	15.5	16.3	11.6	5.9	4.2	15.0	15.8	9.3	13.4	11.1
75,000 - 99,999	4.7	5.0	2.5	1.4	0.7	5.1	5.5	2.6	4.7	3.1
100,000+	2.6	2.8	0.2	0.4	0.3	4.4	4.8	1.3	3.7	1.9

Note: all figures are for 1989; (1) people of Hispanic origin can be of any race
Source: 1990 Census of Population and Housing, Summary Tape File 3C

Effective Buying Income

Area	Per Capita ($)	Median Household ($)	Average Household ($)
City	13,863	30,241	36,561
MSA[1]	18,900	42,850	50,561
U.S.	15,444	33,201	41,849

Note: data as of 1/1/97; (1) Metropolitan Statistical Area - see Appendix A for areas included
Source: Standard Rate & Data Service, Newspaper Advertising Source, 2/98

Effective Household Buying Income Distribution

Area	% of Households Earning						
	$10,000 -$19,999	$20,000 -$34,999	$35,000 -$49,999	$50,000 -$74,999	$75,000 -$99,000	$100,000 -$124,999	$125,000 and up
City	17.3	22.5	18.6	17.8	4.7	1.1	1.1
MSA[1]	12.1	18.3	18.1	23.6	10.5	3.8	3.6
U.S.	16.5	23.4	18.3	18.2	6.4	2.1	2.4

Note: data as of 1/1/97; (1) Metropolitan Statistical Area - see Appendix A for areas included
Source: Standard Rate & Data Service, Newspaper Advertising Source, 2/98

Poverty Rates by Race and Age

Area	Total (%)	By Race (%)				By Age (%)		
		White	Black	Other	Hisp.[2]	Under 5 years old	Under 18 years old	65 years and over
City	15.3	11.7	30.5	44.2	46.8	26.2	25.0	12.5
MSA[1]	8.7	7.0	27.5	35.4	41.0	13.6	12.6	10.2
U.S.	13.1	9.8	29.5	23.1	25.3	20.1	18.3	12.8

Note: figures show the percent of people living below the poverty line in 1989. The average poverty threshold was $12,674 for a family of four in 1989; (1) Metropolitan Statistical Area - see Appendix A for areas included; (2) people of Hispanic origin can be of any race
Source: 1990 Census of Population and Housing, Summary Tape File 3C

EMPLOYMENT

Labor Force and Employment

Area	Civilian Labor Force			Workers Employed		
	Dec. '95	Dec. '96	% Chg.	Dec. '95	Dec. '96	% Chg.
City	77,506	78,825	1.7	74,870	76,327	1.9
MSA[1]	248,116	252,805	1.9	240,450	245,117	1.9
U.S.	134,583,000	136,742,000	1.6	127,903,000	130,785,000	2.3

Note: Data is not seasonally adjusted and covers workers 16 years of age and older; (1) Metropolitan Statistical Area - see Appendix A for areas included
Source: Bureau of Labor Statistics, http://stats.bls.gov

Unemployment Rate

Area	1997											
	Jan.	Feb.	Mar.	Apr.	May	Jun.	Jul.	Aug.	Sep.	Oct.	Nov.	Dec.
City	4.4	4.1	4.2	4.0	4.4	4.6	4.2	4.3	4.4	3.4	3.4	3.2
MSA[1]	4.2	4.0	4.1	3.7	3.6	3.8	3.6	3.7	3.7	3.0	3.2	3.0
U.S.	5.9	5.7	5.5	4.8	4.7	5.2	5.0	4.8	4.7	4.4	4.3	4.4

Note: Data is not seasonally adjusted and covers workers 16 years of age and older; All figures are percentages; (1) Metropolitan Statistical Area - see Appendix A for areas included
Source: Bureau of Labor Statistics, http://stats.bls.gov

Employment by Industry

Sector	MSA[1]		U.S.
	Number of Employees	Percent of Total	Percent of Total
Services	66,700	29.1	29.0
Retail Trade	39,700	17.3	18.5
Government	35,500	15.5	16.1
Manufacturing	42,500	18.5	15.0
Finance/Insurance/Real Estate	15,000	6.5	5.7
Wholesale Trade	12,600	5.5	5.4
Transportation/Public Utilities	9,800	4.3	5.3
Construction	7,300	3.2	4.5
Mining	200	0.1	0.5

Note: Figures cover non-farm employment as of 12/97 and are not seasonally adjusted; (1) Metropolitan Statistical Area - see Appendix A for areas included
Source: Bureau of Labor Statistics, http://stats.bls.gov

Employment by Occupation

Occupation Category	City (%)	MSA[1] (%)	U.S. (%)
White Collar	60.5	62.5	58.1
Executive/Admin./Management	10.6	13.3	12.3
Professional	16.1	16.2	14.1
Technical & Related Support	4.3	4.3	3.7
Sales	10.9	11.0	11.8
Administrative Support/Clerical	18.6	17.6	16.3
Blue Collar	23.0	23.9	26.2
Precision Production/Craft/Repair	9.2	10.8	11.3
Machine Operators/Assem./Insp.	7.1	6.4	6.8
Transportation/Material Movers	3.1	3.4	4.1
Cleaners/Helpers/Laborers	3.6	3.3	3.9
Services	16.0	12.8	13.2
Farming/Forestry/Fishing	0.5	0.9	2.5

Note: figures cover employed persons 16 years old and over; (1) Metropolitan Statistical Area - see Appendix A for areas included
Source: 1990 Census of Population and Housing, Summary Tape File 3C

Occupational Employment Projections: 1994 - 2005

Occupations Expected to have the Largest Job Growth (ranked by numerical growth)	Fast-Growing Occupations (ranked by percent growth)
1. Systems analysts	1. Systems analysts
2. Registered nurses	2. Computer scientists
3. Salespersons, retail	3. Personal and home care aides
4. General managers & top executives	4. Home health aides
5. Janitors/cleaners/maids, ex. priv. hshld.	5. Human services workers
6. Waiters & waitresses	6. Electronic pagination systems workers
7. Home health aides	7. Manicurists
8. Cashiers	8. Computer engineers
9. Nursing aides/orderlies/attendants	9. Physical therapy assistants and aides
10. Computer engineers	10. Economists

Projections cover Massachusetts.
Source: U.S. Department of Labor, Employment and Training Administration, America's Labor Market Information System (ALMIS)

Average Wages

Occupation	Wage	Occupation	Wage
Professional/Technical/Clerical	$/Week	**Health/Protective Services**	$/Week
Accountants III	-	Corrections Officers	-
Attorneys III	-	Firefighters	-
Budget Analysts III	-	Nurses, Licensed Practical II	-
Buyers/Contracting Specialists II	-	Nurses, Registered II	776
Clerks, Accounting III	480	Nursing Assistants II	-
Clerks, General III	398	Police Officers I	-
Computer Operators II	418	**Hourly Workers**	$/Hour
Computer Programmers II	-	Forklift Operators	10.27
Drafters II	-	General Maintenance Workers	10.46
Engineering Technicians III	616	Guards I	8.22
Engineering Technicians, Civil III	-	Janitors	8.96
Engineers III	-	Maintenance Electricians	16.44
Key Entry Operators I	360	Maintenance Electronics Techs II	17.96
Personnel Assistants III	-	Maintenance Machinists	15.58
Personnel Specialists III	-	Maintenance Mechanics, Machinery	15.02
Secretaries III	529	Material Handling Laborers	12.08
Switchboard Operator-Receptionist	361	Motor Vehicle Mechanics	15.39
Systems Analysts II	832	Shipping/Receiving Clerks	9.98
Systems Analysts Supervisor/Mgr II	-	Tool and Die Makers	-
Tax Collectors II	-	Truckdrivers, Tractor Trailer	14.46
Word Processors II	-	Warehouse Specialists	10.74

Note: Wage data includes full-time workers only for 9/94 and cover the Metropolitan Statistical Area (see Appendix A for areas included). Dashes indicate that data was not available.
Source: Bureau of Labor Statistics, Occupational Compensation Survey

TAXES

Major State and Local Tax Rates

State Corp. Income (%)	State Personal Income (%)	Residential Property (effective rate per $100)	Sales & Use		State Gasoline (cents/ gallon)	State Cigarette (cents/ 20-pack)
			State (%)	Local (%)		
9.5[a]	5.95[b]	n/a	5.0	None	21	76

Note: Personal/corporate income tax rates as of 1/97. Sales, gasoline and cigarette tax rates as of 1/98; (b) A 12% rate applies to interest, capital gains and dividends; (a) Rate includes a 14% surtax, as does the following: an additional tax of $2.60 per $1,000 on taxable tangible property (or net worth allocable to state for intangible property corporations). Minimum tax is $456
Source: Federation of Tax Administrators, www.taxadmin.org; Washington D.C. Department of Finance and Revenue, Tax Rates and Tax Burdens in the District of Columbia: A Nationwide Comparison, June 1997; Chamber of Commerce

Total Taxes Per Capita and as a Percent of Income

Area	Per Capita Income ($)	Per Capita Taxes ($)			Taxes as Pct. of Income (%)		
		Total	Federal	State/ Local	Total	Federal	State/ Local
Massachusetts	31,617	11,027	7,600	3,427	34.9	24.0	10.8
U.S.	26,187	9,205	6,127	3,078	35.2	23.4	11.8

Note: Figures are for 1997
Source: Tax Foundation, Web Site, www.taxfoundation.org

Estimated Tax Burden

Area	State Income	Local Income	Property	Sales	Total
Worcester	3,162	0	2,025	425	5,612

Note: The numbers are estimates of taxes paid by a married couple with two kids and annual earnings of $65,000. Sales tax estimates assume they spend average amounts on food, clothing, household goods and gasoline. Property tax estimates assume they live in a $225,000 home.
Source: Kiplinger's Personal Finance Magazine, June 1997

COMMERCIAL REAL ESTATE

Data not available at time of publication.

COMMERCIAL UTILITIES

Typical Monthly Electric Bills

Area	Commercial Service ($/month)		Industrial Service ($/month)	
	12 kW demand 1,500 kWh	100 kW demand 30,000 kWh	1,000 kW demand 400,000 kWh	20,000 kW demand 10,000,000 kWh
City	180	2,785	33,012	779,284
U.S.	162	2,360	25,590	545,677

Note: Based on rates in effect July 1, 1997
Source: Edison Electric Institute, Typical Residential, Commercial and Industrial Bills, Summer 1997

TRANSPORTATION

Transportation Statistics

Avg. travel time to work (min.)	18.3
Interstate highways	I-90
Bus lines	
In-city	Worcester Regional TA
Inter-city	2
Passenger air service	
Airport	Worcester Regional
Airlines	2
Aircraft departures	n/a
Enplaned passengers	n/a
Rail service	Amtrak
Motor freight carriers	n/a
Major waterways/ports	None

Source: OAG, Business Travel Planner, Summer 1997; Editor & Publisher Market Guide, 1998; FAA Airport Activity Statistics, 1996; Amtrak National Time Table, Northeast Timetable, Fall/Winter 1997-98; 1990 Census of Population and Housing, STF 3C; Chamber of Commerce/Economic Development 1997; Jane's Urban Transport Systems 1997-98; Transit Fact Book 1997

Means of Transportation to Work

Area	Car/Truck/Van		Public Transportation			Bicycle	Walked	Other Means	Worked at Home
	Drove Alone	Car-pooled	Bus	Subway	Railroad				
City	71.0	13.2	4.1	0.0	0.0	0.2	8.8	1.1	1.7
MSA[1]	79.3	11.2	1.7	0.0	0.0	0.1	4.7	0.8	2.1
U.S.	73.2	13.4	3.0	1.5	0.5	0.4	3.9	1.2	3.0

Note: figures shown are percentages and only include workers 16 years old and over;
(1) Metropolitan Statistical Area - see Appendix A for areas included
Source: 1990 Census of Population and Housing, Summary Tape File 3C

BUSINESSES

Major Business Headquarters

Company Name	1997 Rankings	
	Fortune 500	Forbes 500
Allmerica Financial	412	-

Note: Companies listed are located in the city; Dashes indicate no ranking
Fortune 500: companies that produce a 10-K are ranked 1 - 500 based on 1996 revenue
Forbes 500: private companies are ranked 1 - 500 based on 1996 revenue
Source: Forbes 12/1/97; Fortune 4/28/97

HOTELS & MOTELS

Hotels/Motels

Area	Hotels/ Motels	Rooms	Luxury-Level Hotels/Motels		Average Minimum Rates ($)		
			♦♦♦♦	♦♦♦♦♦	♦♦	♦♦♦	♦♦♦♦
City	4	454	0	0	n/a	n/a	n/a
Airport	1	242	0	0	n/a	n/a	n/a
Suburbs	1	58	0	0	n/a	n/a	n/a
Total	6	754	0	0	n/a	n/a	n/a

Note: n/a not available; Classifications range from one diamond (budget properties with basic amenities) to five diamond (luxury properties with the finest service, rooms and facilities).
Source: OAG, Business Travel Planner, Summer 1997

CONVENTION CENTERS

Major Convention Centers

Center Name	Meeting Rooms	Exhibit Space (sf)
The Centrum	5	53,000
Mechanics Hall	4	14,945
Worcester Memorial Auditorium	5	22,000

Source: Trade Shows Worldwide 1997

Living Environment

COST OF LIVING

Cost of Living Index

Composite Index	Housing	Utilities	Groceries	Health Care	Trans-portation	Misc. Goods/ Services
96.7	89.5	110.5	98.8	107.5	97.5	96.2

Note: U.S. = 100
Source: ACCRA, Cost of Living Index, 1st Quarter 1997

HOUSING

Median Home Prices and Housing Affordability

Area	Median Price[2] 3rd Qtr. 1997 ($)	HOI[3] 3rd Qtr. 1997	Afford-ability Rank[4]
MSA[1]	124,000	69.6	97
U.S.	127,000	63.7	–

Note: (1) Metropolitan Statistical Area - see Appendix A for areas included; (2) U.S. figures calculated from the sales of 625,000 new and existing homes in 195 markets; (3) Housing Opportunity Index - percent of homes sold that were within the reach of the median income household at the prevailing mortgage interest rate; (4) Rank is from 1-195 with 1 being most affordable
Source: National Association of Home Builders, Housing Opportunity Index, 3rd Quarter 1997

Average New Home Price

Area	Price ($)
City	121,982
U.S.	133,782

Note: Figures are based on a new home with 1,800 sq. ft. of living area on an 8,000 sq. ft. lot.
Source: ACCRA, Cost of Living Index, 1st Quarter 1997

Average Apartment Rent

Area	Rent ($/mth)
City	509
U.S.	563

Note: Figures are based on an unfurnished two bedroom, 1-1/2 or 2 bath apartment, approximately 950 sq. ft. in size, excluding all utilities except water
Source: ACCRA, Cost of Living Index, 1st Quarter 1997

RESIDENTIAL UTILITIES

Average Residential Utility Costs

Area	All Electric ($/mth)	Part Electric ($/mth)	Other Energy ($/mth)	Phone ($/mth)
City	–	63.75	50.01	23.63
U.S.	110.19	56.83	45.14	19.36

Source: ACCRA, Cost of Living Index, 1st Quarter 1997

HEALTH CARE

Average Health Care Costs

Area	Hospital ($/day)	Doctor ($/visit)	Dentist ($/visit)
City	410.00	50.10	64.80
U.S.	385.60	47.34	59.26

Note: Hospital - based on a semi-private room. Doctor - based on a general practitioner's routine exam of an established patient. Dentist - based on adult teeth cleaning and periodic oral exam.
Source: ACCRA, Cost of Living Index, 1st Quarter 1997

Distribution of Office-Based Physicians

Area	Family/Gen. Practitioners	Specialists		
		Medical	Surgical	Other
MSA[1]	145	617	306	348

Note: Data as of 12/31/96; (1) Metropolitan Statistical Area - see Appendix A for areas included
Source: American Medical Assn., Physician Characteristics & Distribution in the U.S., 1997-1998

Hospitals

Worcester has 3 general medical and surgical hospitals, 1 psychiatric, 1 rehabilitation, 1 alcoholism and other chemical dependency. *AHA Guide to the Healthcare Field 1997-98*

EDUCATION

Public School District Statistics

District Name	Num. Sch.	Enroll.	Classroom Teachers[1]	Pupils per Teacher	Minority Pupils (%)	Current Exp.[2] ($/pupil)
Worcester School District	49	23,419	n/a	n/a	42.1	6,534
Worcester Trade Complex	2	854	n/a	n/a	n/a	n/a

Note: Data covers the 1995-1996 school year unless otherwise noted; (1) Excludes teachers reported as working in school district offices rather than in schools; (2) Based on 1993-94 enrollment collected by the Census Bureau, not the enrollment figure shown in column 3; SD = School District; ISD = Independent School District; n/a not available
Source: National Center for Education Statistics, Common Core of Data Survey; Bureau of the Census

Educational Quality

School District	Education Quotient[1]	Graduate Outcome[2]	Community Index[3]	Resource Index[4]
Worcester	95.0	78.0	112.0	94.0

Note: Nearly 1,000 secondary school districts were rated in terms of educational quality. The scores range from a low of 50 to a high of 150; (1) Average of the Graduate Outcome, Community and Resource indexes; (2) Based on graduation rates and college board scores (SAT/ACT); (3) Based on the surrounding community's average level of education and the area's average income level; (4) Based on teacher salaries, per-pupil expenditures and student-teacher ratios.
Source: Expansion Management, Ratings Issue 1997

Educational Attainment by Race

Area	High School Graduate (%)					Bachelor's Degree (%)				
	Total	White	Black	Other	Hisp.[2]	Total	White	Black	Other	Hisp.[2]
City	72.9	74.6	66.6	49.6	43.5	21.1	21.6	14.2	16.8	7.8
MSA[1]	78.1	78.8	70.6	59.2	49.6	23.4	23.3	19.7	27.5	12.3
U.S.	75.2	77.9	63.1	60.4	49.8	20.3	21.5	11.4	19.4	9.2

Note: figures shown cover persons 25 years old and over; (1) Metropolitan Statistical Area - see Appendix A for areas included; (2) people of Hispanic origin can be of any race
Source: 1990 Census of Population and Housing, Summary Tape File 3C

School Enrollment by Type

Area	Preprimary				Elementary/High School			
	Public		Private		Public		Private	
	Enrollment	%	Enrollment	%	Enrollment	%	Enrollment	%
City	1,871	63.6	1,073	36.4	20,873	88.4	2,738	11.6
MSA[1]	5,391	59.2	3,711	40.8	58,575	89.3	7,020	10.7
U.S.	2,679,029	59.5	1,824,256	40.5	38,379,689	90.2	4,187,099	9.8

Note: figures shown cover persons 3 years old and over;
(1) Metropolitan Statistical Area - see Appendix A for areas included
Source: 1990 Census of Population and Housing, Summary Tape File 3C

School Enrollment by Race

Area	Preprimary (%)				Elementary/High School (%)			
	White	Black	Other	Hisp.[1]	White	Black	Other	Hisp.[1]
City	80.2	8.8	11.0	10.7	76.8	7.2	16.0	19.4
MSA[2]	91.3	3.6	5.1	4.3	89.9	3.0	7.1	8.1
U.S.	80.4	12.5	7.1	7.8	74.1	15.6	10.3	12.5

Note: figures shown cover persons 3 years old and over; (1) people of Hispanic origin can be of any race; (2) Metropolitan Statistical Area - see Appendix A for areas included
Source: 1990 Census of Population and Housing, Summary Tape File 3C

SAT/ACT Scores

Area/District	1996 SAT				1996 ACT	
	Percent of Graduates Tested (%)	Average Math Score	Average Verbal Score	Average Combined Score	Percent of Graduates Tested (%)	Average Composite Score
Worcester SD	n/a	n/a	n/a	n/a	n/a	n/a
State	80	504	507	1,011	5	21.2
U.S.	41	508	505	1,013	35	20.9

Note: Math and verbal SAT scores are out of a possible 800; ACT scores are out of a possible 36
Caution: Comparing or ranking states/cities on the basis of SAT/ACT scores alone is invalid and strongly discouraged by the The College Board and The American College Testing Program as students who take the tests are self-selected and do not represent the entire student population. 1996 SAT scores cannot be compared to previous years due to recentering.
Source: American College Testing Program, 1996; College Board, 1996

Classroom Teacher Salaries in Public Schools

District	B.A. Degree		M.A. Degree		Ph.D. Degree	
	Min. ($)	Max ($)	Min. ($)	Max. ($)	Min. ($)	Max. ($)
Worcester	25,550	42,077	29,315	45,843	33,336	49,863
Average[1]	26,120	39,270	28,175	44,667	31,643	49,825

Note: Salaries are for 1996-1997; (1) Based on all school districts covered
Source: American Federation of Teachers (unpublished data)

Higher Education

Two-Year Colleges		Four-Year Colleges		Medical Schools	Law Schools	Voc/ Tech
Public	Private	Public	Private			
1	0	0	6	1	0	6

Source: College Blue Book, Occupational Education 1997; Medical School Admission Requirements, 1998-99; Peterson's Guide to Two-Year Colleges, 1997; Peterson's Guide to Four-Year Colleges, 1997; Barron's Guide to Law Schools 1997

MAJOR EMPLOYERS

Major Employers

First Allmerica Financial Life Ins.	Allegro Microsystems (semiconductors)
Deutsche Babcock Technologies	Medical Center of Central Massachusetts
Morgan Construction Co.	Neles-Jamesbury (industrial valves)
Norton Co. (abrasive products)	Paul Revere Corp.
Paul Revere Life Insurance	Paul Revere Variable Annuity Insurance
Memorial Health Care	

Note: companies listed are located in the city
Source: Dun's Business Rankings 1997; Ward's Business Directory, 1997

PUBLIC SAFETY

Crime Rate

Area	All Crimes	Violent Crimes				Property Crimes		
		Murder	Forcible Rape	Robbery	Aggrav. Assault	Burglary	Larceny -Theft	Motor Vehicle Theft
City	6,021.6	4.2	64.8	245.8	622.4	1,337.1	3,080.1	667.3
Suburbs[1]	2,035.0	0.0	17.8	17.8	364.0	399.3	1,092.4	143.7
MSA[2]	3,416.4	1.5	34.1	96.8	453.5	724.2	1,781.1	325.1
U.S.	5,078.9	7.4	36.1	202.4	388.2	943.0	2,975.9	525.9

Note: Crime rate is the number of crimes per 100,000 pop.; (1) defined as all areas within the MSA but located outside the central city; (2) Metropolitan Statistical Area - see Appendix A for areas incl.
Source: FBI Uniform Crime Reports 1996

RECREATION

Culture and Recreation

Museums	Symphony Orchestras	Opera Companies	Dance Companies	Professional Theatres	Zoos	Pro Sports Teams
7	1	1	1	1	0	0

Source: International Directory of the Performing Arts, 1996; Official Museum Directory, 1998; Chamber of Commerce/Economic Development 1997

Library System

The Worcester Public Library has three branches, holdings of 606,784 volumes and a budget of $3,300,128 (1994-1995). The Central Massachusetts Regional Library System has no branches, holdings of 119,548 volumes and a budget of $1,296,849 (1995-1996). Note: n/a means not available. *American Library Directory, 1997-1998*

MEDIA

Newspapers

Name	Type	Freq.	Distribution	Circulation
The Catholic Free Press	Religious	1x/wk	Local	18,319
Jewish Chronicle	Religious	2x/mo	Local	4,000
The Senior Advocate	Religious	2x/mo	State	102,000
The Telegram & Gazette	General	7x/wk	Area	113,000
Vocero Hispano	Hispanic	1x/wk	Area	12,500

Note: Includes newspapers with circulations of 1,000 or more located in the city; Source: Burrelle's Media Directory, 1998 Edition

AM Radio Stations

Call Letters	Freq. (kHz)	Target Audience	Station Format	Music Format
WTAG	580	General	N/S/T	n/a
WVNE	760	Religious	M/N/T	Christian
WGFP	940	General	N/S/T	n/a
WESO	970	General	M	Adult Standards/Big Band/Oldies
WARE	1250	General	M/N/S	Oldies
WEIM	1280	General	M/N/S	n/a
WORC	1310	n/a	M/N/S/T	Oldies
WWTM	1440	General	S/T	n/a
WMRC	1490	General	M/N/S/T	Adult Contemporary/Oldies

Note: Stations included broadcast in the Worcester metro area; n/a not available
Station Format: E = Educational; M = Music; N = News; S = Sports; T = Talk
Source: Burrelle's Media Directory, 1998 Edition

FM Radio Stations

Call Letters	Freq. (mHz)	Target Audience	Station Format	Music Format
WCHC	88.1	General	M/N/S	Alternative/Jazz/Urban Contemporary
WBPV	90.1	General	M	Alternative/Big Band/Classic Rock
WICN	90.5	General	E/M	Big Band/Classical/Jazz
WXPL	91.3	General	E/M	Alternative
WCUW	91.3	General	M	n/a
WMWC	91.7	General	M	Contemporary Top 40
WNRC	95.1	General	M/N/S	n/a
WSRS	96.1	General	M/N	Adult Contemporary
WINQ	97.7	General	M/N/S	Adult Contemporary
WXXW	98.9	n/a	n/a	n/a
WQVR	100.1	General	M	Country
WAAF	107.3	General	M	AOR

Note: Stations included broadcast in the Worcester metro area; n/a not available
Station Format: E = Educational; M = Music; N = News; S = Sports; T = Talk
Music Format: AOR = Album Oriented Rock; MOR = Middle-of-the-Road
Source: Burrelle's Media Directory, 1998 Edition

Television Stations

Name	Ch.	Affiliation	Type	Owner
No stations listed.				

Note: Stations included broadcast in the Worcester metro area
Source: Burrelle's Media Directory, 1998 Edition

CLIMATE

Average and Extreme Temperatures

Temperature	Jan	Feb	Mar	Apr	May	Jun	Jul	Aug	Sep	Oct	Nov	Dec	Ann
Extreme High (°F)	67	67	81	91	92	98	96	97	99	85	79	70	99
Average High (°F)	32	34	42	55	66	75	79	77	69	59	47	35	56
Average Temp. (°F)	24	26	34	45	56	65	70	68	60	51	40	28	47
Average Low (°F)	16	18	25	35	46	55	61	59	51	41	32	21	38
Extreme Low (°F)	-13	-12	-6	11	28	36	43	38	30	20	6	-13	-13

Note: Figures cover the years 1949-1992
Source: National Climatic Data Center, International Station Meteorological Climate Summary, 3/95

Average Precipitation/Snowfall/Humidity

Precip./Humidity	Jan	Feb	Mar	Apr	May	Jun	Jul	Aug	Sep	Oct	Nov	Dec	Ann
Avg. Precip. (in.)	3.6	3.4	4.1	4.0	4.3	3.7	3.7	4.1	4.0	4.1	4.5	4.1	47.6
Avg. Snowfall (in.)	16	16	11	3	Tr	0	0	0	Tr	1	4	13	62
Avg. Rel. Hum. 7am (%)	72	73	71	69	70	73	76	79	81	78	78	75	75
Avg. Rel. Hum. 4pm (%)	61	58	55	50	52	57	58	61	62	58	63	65	58

Note: Figures cover the years 1949-1992; Tr = Trace amounts (<0.05 in. of rain; <0.5 in. of snow)
Source: National Climatic Data Center, International Station Meteorological Climate Summary, 3/95

Weather Conditions

Temperature			Daytime Sky			Precipitation		
5°F & below	32°F & below	90°F & above	Clear	Partly cloudy	Cloudy	0.01 inch or more precip.	0.1 inch or more snow/ice	Thunderstorms
12	141	4	81	144	140	131	32	23

Note: Figures are average number of days per year and covers the years 1949-1992
Source: National Climatic Data Center, International Station Meteorological Climate Summary, 3/95

AIR & WATER QUALITY

Maximum Pollutant Concentrations

	Particulate Matter (ug/m³)	Carbon Monoxide (ppm)	Sulfur Dioxide (ppm)	Nitrogen Dioxide (ppm)	Ozone (ppm)	Lead (ug/m³)
MSA[1] Level	46	5	0.021	0.019	0.09	n/a
NAAQS[2]	150	9	0.140	0.053	0.12	1.50
Met NAAQS?	Yes	Yes	Yes	Yes	Yes	n/a

Note: (1) Metropolitan Statistical Area - see Appendix A for areas included; (2) National Ambient Air Quality Standards; ppm = parts per million; ug/m³ = micrograms per cubic meter; n/a not available
Source: EPA, National Air Quality and Emissions Trends Report, 1996

Pollutant Standards Index

Data not available. *EPA, National Air Quality and Emissions Trends Report, 1996*

Drinking Water

Water System Name	Pop. Served	Primary Water Source Type	Number of Violations in Fiscal Year 1997	Type of Violation/ Contaminants
Worcester DPW-Water Supply Div.	170,000	Surface	1	Failure to filter

Note: Data as of January 16, 1998
Source: EPA, Office of Ground Water and Drinking Water, Safe Drinking Water Information System

Worcester tap water is very soft, slightly acidic and not fluoridated.
Editor & Publisher Market Guide, 1998

Comparative Statistics

Population Growth: City

City	Population			% Change	
	1980	1990	1996[1]	1980-90	1990-96
Allentown	103,758	105,090	102,211	1.3	-2.7
Baltimore	786,775	736,014	675,401	-6.5	-8.2
Boston	562,994	574,283	558,394	2.0	-2.8
Bridgeport	142,546	141,686	137,990	-0.6	-2.6
Charlotte	314,447	396,003	441,297	25.9	11.4
Cincinnati	385,457	364,040	345,818	-5.6	-5.0
Cleveland	573,822	505,616	498,246	-11.9	-1.5
Durham	100,847	136,594	149,799	35.4	9.7
Greensboro	155,684	183,521	195,426	17.9	6.5
Lexington	204,165	225,366	0	10.4	-100.0
New York	7,071,639	7,322,564	7,380,906	3.5	0.8
Norfolk	266,979	261,229	233,430	-2.2	-10.6
Philadelphia	1,688,210	1,585,577	1,478,002	-6.1	-6.8
Pittsburgh	423,938	369,879	350,363	-12.8	-5.3
Raleigh	150,255	207,951	243,835	38.4	17.3
Richmond	219,214	203,056	198,267	-7.4	-2.4
Stamford	102,453	108,056	110,056	5.5	1.9
Washington	638,333	606,900	543,213	-4.9	-10.5
Worcester	161,799	169,759	166,350	4.9	-2.0
U.S.	**226,545,805**	**248,765,170**	**265,179,411**	**9.8**	**6.6**

Note: (1) Census Bureau estimate as of 7/96
Source: 1980 Census; 1990 Census of Population and Housing, Summary Tape File 3C

Population Growth: Metro Area

MSA[1]	Population			% Change	
	1980	1990	1996[2]	1980-90	1990-96
Allentown	635,481	686,688	614,304	8.1	-10.5
Baltimore	2,199,531	2,382,172	2,474,118	8.3	3.9
Boston	2,805,911	2,870,650	3,263,060	2.3	13.7
Bridgeport	438,557	443,722	443,637	1.2	-0.0
Charlotte	971,391	1,162,093	1,321,068	19.6	13.7
Cincinnati	1,401,491	1,452,645	1,597,352	3.6	10.0
Cleveland	1,898,825	1,831,122	2,233,288	-3.6	22.0
Durham	561,222	735,480	0	31.0	-100.0
Greensboro	851,444	942,091	1,141,238	10.6	21.1
Lexington	317,629	348,428	441,073	9.7	26.6
New York	8,274,961	8,546,846	8,643,437	3.3	1.1
Norfolk	1,160,311	1,396,107	1,540,252	20.3	10.3
Philadelphia	4,716,818	4,856,881	4,952,929	3.0	2.0
Pittsburgh	2,218,870	2,056,705	2,379,411	-7.3	15.7
Durham	561,222	735,480	1,025,253	31.0	39.4
Richmond	761,311	865,640	935,174	13.7	8.0
Stamford	198,854	202,557	331,767	1.9	63.8
Washington	3,250,822	3,923,574	4,563,123	20.7	16.3
Worcester	402,918	436,941	485,229	8.4	11.1
U.S.	**226,545,805**	**248,765,170**	**265,179,411**	**9.8**	**6.6**

Note: (1) Metropolitan Statistical Area - see Appendix A for areas included; (2) Census Bureau estimate as of 7/96
Source: 1980 Census; 1990 Census of Population and Housing, Summary Tape File 3C

Population Characteristics: City

City	1990 Percent of Total (%)					
	White	Black	American Indian/ Esk./Aleut.	Asian/ Pacific Islander	Other	Hispanic Origin[1]
Allentown	86.1	5.1	0.1	1.4	7.3	11.2
Baltimore	39.1	59.2	0.3	1.1	0.3	1.0
Boston	63.0	25.5	0.3	5.3	5.9	10.4
Bridgeport	58.7	26.6	0.2	2.1	12.3	25.3
Charlotte	65.6	31.9	0.4	1.7	0.5	1.3
Cincinnati	60.5	37.9	0.2	1.1	0.3	0.6
Cleveland	49.6	46.5	0.3	1.0	2.7	4.4
Durham	51.6	45.7	0.3	2.0	0.5	1.3
Greensboro	63.9	34.0	0.4	1.4	0.3	0.8
Lexington	84.7	13.4	0.2	1.5	0.3	1.0
New York	52.3	28.8	0.3	7.0	11.6	23.7
Norfolk	56.7	39.1	0.5	2.6	1.1	2.8
Philadelphia	53.5	39.9	0.2	2.7	3.6	5.3
Pittsburgh	72.1	25.9	0.2	1.6	0.3	0.9
Raleigh	69.3	27.5	0.3	2.5	0.4	1.2
Richmond	43.3	55.4	0.2	0.8	0.3	0.9
Stamford	76.5	17.9	0.1	2.1	3.4	9.1
Washington	29.6	65.9	0.3	1.9	2.4	5.2
Worcester	87.3	4.5	0.4	2.6	5.3	9.3
U.S.	**80.3**	**12.0**	**0.8**	**2.9**	**3.9**	**8.8**

Note: (1) People of Hispanic origin can be of any race
Source: 1990 Census of Population and Housing, Summary Tape File 3C

Population Characteristics: Metro Area

MSA[1]	1990 Percent of Total (%)					
	White	Black	American Indian/ Esk./Aleut.	Asian/ Pacific Islander	Other	Hispanic Origin[2]
Allentown	94.6	2.0	0.1	1.1	2.2	4.1
Baltimore	71.8	25.8	0.3	1.8	0.3	1.2
Boston	87.2	7.2	0.2	3.3	2.1	4.3
Bridgeport	84.0	10.3	0.1	1.3	4.3	9.6
Charlotte	78.5	19.9	0.4	0.9	0.3	0.8
Cincinnati	85.8	13.1	0.2	0.8	0.2	0.5
Cleveland	78.4	19.4	0.2	1.1	0.9	1.8
Durham	72.5	24.9	0.3	1.9	0.4	1.1
Greensboro	79.5	19.3	0.3	0.7	0.2	0.6
Lexington	87.8	10.7	0.2	1.1	0.2	0.9
New York	56.5	26.4	0.3	6.5	10.3	21.6
Norfolk	67.9	28.5	0.4	2.5	0.7	2.2
Philadelphia	76.6	19.1	0.2	2.1	2.0	3.4
Pittsburgh	90.8	8.2	0.1	0.7	0.2	0.5
Durham	72.5	24.9	0.3	1.9	0.4	1.1
Richmond	68.8	29.2	0.3	1.4	0.3	1.0
Stamford	85.1	10.3	0.1	2.5	2.0	6.4
Washington	65.8	26.6	0.3	5.1	2.2	5.6
Worcester	93.5	2.2	0.2	1.7	2.4	4.4
U.S.	**80.3**	**12.0**	**0.8**	**2.9**	**3.9**	**8.8**

Note: (1) Metropolitan Statistical Area - see Appendix A for areas included;
(2) People of Hispanic origin can be of any race
Source: 1990 Census of Population and Housing, Summary Tape File 3C

Age: City

City	Median Age (Years)	Age Distribution (%)						
		Under 5	Under 18	18-24	25-44	45-64	65+	80+
Allentown	33.7	7.2	21.9	11.3	31.9	18.0	17.0	4.1
Baltimore	32.5	7.7	24.5	11.1	32.9	17.9	13.7	3.0
Boston	30.2	6.2	19.1	17.3	36.8	15.3	11.5	2.9
Bridgeport	30.8	8.1	26.1	11.1	32.8	16.4	13.6	3.1
Charlotte	32.0	7.5	24.3	10.6	37.3	18.0	9.8	2.0
Cincinnati	30.8	8.4	25.0	12.8	32.6	15.7	13.9	3.7
Cleveland	31.8	8.7	27.0	10.4	30.7	18.0	13.9	3.0
Durham	30.6	7.3	22.1	14.9	37.0	14.8	11.2	2.8
Greensboro	32.2	6.4	21.6	14.8	33.8	18.0	11.8	2.5
Lexington	31.2	6.7	22.4	14.5	36.4	16.8	9.9	2.0
New York	33.6	6.9	23.0	10.3	33.9	19.8	13.0	3.1
Norfolk	27.2	8.3	23.0	21.6	31.8	13.1	10.5	2.1
Philadelphia	33.1	7.3	23.9	11.4	30.8	18.6	15.2	3.4
Pittsburgh	34.5	6.1	19.9	13.7	30.3	18.2	17.9	3.9
Raleigh	30.2	6.2	19.5	17.5	38.6	15.6	8.8	1.9
Richmond	33.1	6.9	20.8	12.9	33.9	17.1	15.3	3.7
Stamford	34.9	6.8	20.4	9.0	36.2	21.3	13.2	3.1
Washington	33.4	6.0	19.2	13.4	35.9	18.7	12.8	2.8
Worcester	31.6	7.2	22.3	14.8	30.8	16.1	16.0	4.1
U.S.	**32.9**	**7.3**	**25.6**	**10.5**	**32.6**	**18.7**	**12.5**	**2.8**

Source: 1990 Census of Population and Housing, Summary Tape File 3C

Age: Metro Area

MSA[1]	Median Age (Years)	Age Distribution (%)						
		Under 5	Under 18	18-24	25-44	45-64	65+	80+
Allentown	35.3	6.7	23.2	9.7	31.7	20.1	15.2	3.2
Baltimore	33.3	7.4	24.2	10.2	34.6	19.4	11.7	2.4
Boston	33.3	6.4	20.8	12.4	35.1	18.9	12.9	3.1
Bridgeport	34.6	7.0	23.3	9.8	32.2	20.0	14.7	3.1
Charlotte	32.7	7.2	24.8	10.9	34.2	19.3	10.9	2.2
Cincinnati	32.4	7.9	26.8	10.1	32.6	18.4	12.0	2.8
Cleveland	34.7	7.1	24.6	9.0	31.7	20.1	14.6	3.0
Durham	31.2	6.8	22.5	14.0	37.6	16.9	8.9	2.0
Greensboro	34.0	6.6	23.1	11.1	33.3	20.4	12.1	2.6
Lexington	31.7	6.8	23.9	13.1	35.1	17.6	10.3	2.2
New York	33.9	6.8	23.0	10.2	33.7	20.1	13.0	3.1
Norfolk	29.7	8.3	26.4	13.6	34.8	16.2	9.0	1.6
Philadelphia	33.7	7.3	24.4	10.3	32.4	19.5	13.5	2.9
Pittsburgh	36.9	6.2	21.7	9.2	30.6	21.0	17.4	3.5
Durham	31.2	6.8	22.5	14.0	37.6	16.9	8.9	2.0
Richmond	33.2	7.2	24.3	10.3	35.4	18.7	11.3	2.3
Stamford	36.9	6.5	21.0	8.1	33.2	23.7	14.0	3.2
Washington	32.4	7.2	23.5	10.9	38.2	19.0	8.5	1.7
Worcester	33.2	7.3	23.8	11.5	32.7	17.8	14.2	3.4
U.S.	**32.9**	**7.3**	**25.6**	**10.5**	**32.6**	**18.7**	**12.5**	**2.8**

Note: (1) Metropolitan Statistical Area - see Appendix A for areas included
Source: 1990 Census of Population and Housing, Summary Tape File 3C

Male/Female Ratio: City

City	Number of males per 100 females (all ages)	Number of males per 100 females (18 years old+)
Allentown	88.8	85.6
Baltimore	87.7	83.1
Boston	91.4	90.3
Bridgeport	90.1	85.8
Charlotte	90.2	86.7
Cincinnati	87.2	81.7
Cleveland	88.2	83.4
Durham	86.4	83.0
Greensboro	86.9	82.6
Lexington	91.7	88.2
New York	88.1	84.5
Norfolk	114.0	117.8
Philadelphia	86.8	82.6
Pittsburgh	86.8	82.9
Raleigh	93.6	92.8
Richmond	83.9	80.0
Stamford	91.2	88.7
Washington	87.2	84.0
Worcester	91.1	87.3
U.S.	**95.0**	**91.9**

Source: 1990 Census of Population, General Population Characteristics

Male/Female Ratio: Metro Area

MSA[1]	Number of males per 100 females (all ages)	Number of males per 100 females (18 years old+)
Allentown	93.3	90.2
Baltimore	93.5	90.2
Boston	92.0	89.2
Bridgeport	92.6	88.9
Charlotte	93.0	89.8
Cincinnati	92.1	87.8
Cleveland	90.1	85.9
Durham	92.9	90.5
Greensboro	91.7	87.9
Lexington	92.3	88.7
New York	88.6	85.0
Norfolk	100.4	99.4
Philadelphia	91.8	88.0
Pittsburgh	89.4	85.5
Durham	92.9	90.5
Richmond	90.7	87.1
Stamford	90.9	87.7
Washington	94.8	92.2
Worcester	94.0	90.7
U.S.	**95.0**	**91.9**

Note: (1) Metropolitan Statistical Area - see Appendix A for areas included
Source: 1990 Census of Population, General Population Characteristics

Educational Attainment by Race: City

City	High School Graduate (%)					Bachelor's Degree (%)				
	Total	White	Black	Other	Hisp.[1]	Total	White	Black	Other	Hisp.[1]
Allentown	69.4	71.4	65.8	41.7	41.8	15.3	16.0	9.6	8.1	5.0
Baltimore	60.7	64.4	57.3	72.5	66.7	15.5	23.5	8.6	32.7	25.3
Boston	75.7	81.5	66.7	55.8	52.8	30.0	36.7	14.0	20.3	13.9
Bridgeport	61.1	63.5	63.0	43.2	42.0	12.3	15.0	7.0	7.5	5.3
Charlotte	81.0	86.9	66.5	71.9	73.2	28.4	34.5	12.5	27.7	21.9
Cincinnati	69.6	74.7	59.4	83.5	76.4	22.2	28.9	7.9	56.6	42.0
Cleveland	58.8	61.9	55.6	49.3	44.7	8.1	10.2	5.0	13.9	6.2
Durham	78.5	85.6	68.1	89.7	75.0	35.4	45.1	20.8	60.9	40.9
Greensboro	79.2	83.3	70.6	63.6	75.0	29.9	35.0	17.7	35.1	29.3
Lexington	80.2	82.5	63.1	86.6	72.4	30.6	32.8	10.3	59.5	24.4
New York	68.3	74.2	64.1	54.6	47.9	23.0	29.2	12.4	17.7	8.2
Norfolk	72.7	80.7	58.8	77.8	84.2	16.8	21.8	7.9	23.5	16.0
Philadelphia	64.3	68.1	60.2	51.4	44.7	15.2	19.0	9.1	17.3	8.2
Pittsburgh	72.4	74.0	66.3	87.7	78.4	20.1	22.6	8.8	62.2	39.2
Raleigh	86.6	92.1	70.3	85.6	81.8	40.6	47.0	19.9	55.4	45.0
Richmond	68.1	80.1	56.3	76.2	75.1	24.2	39.4	9.5	33.2	26.9
Stamford	81.2	84.0	69.7	67.7	59.6	35.1	39.1	14.4	29.8	12.5
Washington	73.1	93.1	63.8	61.0	52.6	33.3	69.0	15.3	31.8	24.0
Worcester	72.9	74.6	66.6	49.6	43.5	21.1	21.6	14.2	16.8	7.8
U.S.	**75.2**	**77.9**	**63.1**	**60.4**	**49.8**	**20.3**	**21.5**	**11.4**	**19.4**	**9.2**

Note: Figures shown cover persons 25 years old and over; (1) people of Hispanic origin can be of any race
Source: 1990 Census of Population and Housing, Summary Tape File 3C

Educational Attainment by Race: Metro Area

MSA[1]	High School Graduate (%)					Bachelor's Degree (%)				
	Total	White	Black	Other	Hisp.[2]	Total	White	Black	Other	Hisp.[2]
Allentown	74.1	74.6	71.0	55.9	50.0	17.7	17.7	12.5	20.8	8.5
Baltimore	74.7	78.2	63.0	80.4	79.7	23.1	26.2	12.0	39.5	30.6
Boston	83.7	85.4	70.7	68.0	58.8	33.1	34.1	17.9	33.9	18.2
Bridgeport	75.8	78.0	65.1	51.9	47.5	23.0	24.7	9.2	16.0	8.0
Charlotte	72.5	74.8	61.7	68.7	69.5	19.6	21.4	10.5	24.5	19.9
Cincinnati	74.9	76.5	62.7	82.7	79.2	20.5	21.6	9.8	46.8	34.9
Cleveland	75.7	78.7	62.4	69.6	56.6	19.9	22.0	8.5	35.4	13.8
Durham	82.4	87.2	66.0	86.3	77.2	34.8	39.2	17.8	55.6	36.6
Greensboro	72.0	73.3	66.1	63.1	70.0	19.2	20.2	14.0	27.5	21.4
Lexington	75.9	77.3	61.8	84.6	72.5	25.3	26.7	9.2	55.8	22.9
New York	70.3	76.1	64.4	55.7	48.6	24.6	30.6	12.7	18.9	8.6
Norfolk	79.1	84.2	64.9	80.0	85.6	20.1	23.3	11.3	22.3	16.1
Philadelphia	75.9	79.2	63.8	62.6	51.8	22.8	25.2	10.9	26.5	11.7
Pittsburgh	77.4	78.0	68.6	86.1	80.6	19.5	19.9	10.1	56.1	30.0
Durham	82.4	87.2	66.0	86.3	77.2	34.8	39.2	17.8	55.6	36.6
Richmond	75.8	81.1	61.5	75.3	79.5	23.8	28.1	11.9	32.4	27.9
Stamford	85.7	87.7	69.6	76.2	63.8	43.7	46.6	14.3	42.0	16.6
Washington	85.2	90.1	74.5	75.7	64.5	38.5	45.3	19.9	38.4	23.8
Worcester	78.1	78.8	70.6	59.2	49.6	23.4	23.3	19.7	27.5	12.3
U.S.	**75.2**	**77.9**	**63.1**	**60.4**	**49.8**	**20.3**	**21.5**	**11.4**	**19.4**	**9.2**

Note: Figures shown cover persons 25 years old and over; (1) Metropolitan Statistical Area - see Appendix A for areas included; (2) people of Hispanic origin can be of any race
Source: 1990 Census of Population and Housing, Summary Tape File 3C

Per Capita/Median/Average Income: City

City	Per Capita ($)	Median Household ($)	Average Household ($)
Allentown	12,822	25,983	31,177
Baltimore	11,994	24,045	31,415
Boston	15,581	29,180	37,907
Bridgeport	13,156	28,704	34,679
Charlotte	16,793	31,873	41,578
Cincinnati	12,547	21,006	29,010
Cleveland	9,258	17,822	22,921
Durham	14,498	27,256	34,524
Greensboro	15,644	29,184	37,886
Lexington	14,962	28,056	36,979
New York	16,281	29,823	41,741
Norfolk	11,643	23,563	29,947
Philadelphia	12,091	24,603	31,208
Pittsburgh	12,580	20,747	29,587
Raleigh	16,896	32,451	40,243
Richmond	13,993	23,551	32,497
Stamford	27,092	49,787	69,312
Washington	18,881	30,727	44,413
Worcester	13,393	28,955	34,757
U.S.	**14,420**	**30,056**	**38,453**

Note: Figures are for 1989
Source: 1990 Census of Population and Housing, Summary Tape File 3C

Per Capita/Median/Average Income: Metro Area

MSA[1]	Per Capita ($)	Median Household ($)	Average Household ($)
Allentown	14,995	32,667	39,258
Baltimore	16,596	36,550	44,405
Boston	19,288	40,491	50,478
Bridgeport	18,611	40,874	50,037
Charlotte	14,611	31,125	38,214
Cincinnati	14,610	30,691	38,344
Cleveland	15,092	30,560	38,413
Durham	16,170	33,290	40,686
Greensboro	14,588	29,254	36,588
Lexington	13,945	27,558	35,698
New York	17,397	31,659	45,159
Norfolk	13,495	30,841	36,794
Philadelphia	16,386	35,437	44,191
Pittsburgh	14,052	26,700	34,902
Durham	16,170	33,290	40,686
Richmond	15,848	33,489	40,785
Stamford	37,044	57,876	96,804
Washington	21,416	46,884	56,799
Worcester	15,657	35,977	41,796
U.S.	**14,420**	**30,056**	**38,453**

Note: Figures are for 1989; (1) Metropolitan Statistical Area - see Appendix A for areas included
Source: 1990 Census of Population and Housing, Summary Tape File 3C

Household Income Distribution: City

City	% of Households Earning								
	Less than $5,000	$5,000 -$9,999	$10,000 -$14,999	$15,000 -$24,999	$25,000 -$34,999	$35,000 -$49,999	$50,000 -$74,999	$75,000 -$99,999	$100,000 and up
Allentown	5.3	11.2	9.8	21.7	18.0	18.9	10.7	2.7	1.8
Baltimore	11.7	11.6	9.5	18.7	15.7	15.9	11.3	3.2	2.4
Boston	8.0	12.5	7.4	15.8	14.6	16.2	15.3	5.4	4.8
Bridgeport	6.6	11.7	8.6	16.5	16.3	16.9	15.9	4.8	2.7
Charlotte	5.5	6.7	7.5	18.0	17.2	18.8	15.7	5.6	5.1
Cincinnati	13.5	13.6	10.7	19.3	14.7	14.1	8.8	2.7	2.6
Cleveland	16.7	15.5	11.5	19.5	14.8	13.0	7.0	1.3	0.7
Durham	8.1	8.7	9.4	18.9	17.2	16.4	13.9	4.1	3.2
Greensboro	5.9	8.4	9.2	19.2	16.9	18.1	13.8	4.2	4.4
Lexington	7.7	9.1	9.4	18.1	16.1	17.1	13.9	4.5	4.2
New York	8.9	11.3	7.5	15.2	14.1	15.9	14.6	6.0	6.4
Norfolk	9.3	9.7	10.7	23.2	17.5	15.4	9.3	2.7	2.2
Philadelphia	10.0	12.7	9.9	18.0	15.2	16.4	12.2	3.3	2.2
Pittsburgh	10.9	15.9	11.5	19.2	14.8	13.3	8.9	2.6	2.9
Raleigh	5.6	6.7	7.7	17.7	16.1	18.9	17.0	5.6	4.7
Richmond	10.6	11.1	10.9	19.8	15.5	15.1	10.1	3.4	3.4
Stamford	2.9	5.3	4.2	10.2	11.5	16.0	21.0	11.8	16.9
Washington	8.7	7.8	7.2	17.3	14.7	15.6	14.4	6.4	7.8
Worcester	5.7	13.7	8.6	15.7	14.8	18.6	15.5	4.7	2.6
U.S.	**6.2**	**9.3**	**8.8**	**17.5**	**15.8**	**17.9**	**15.0**	**5.1**	**4.4**

Note: Figures are for 1989
Source: 1990 Census of Population and Housing, Summary Tape File 3C

Household Income Distribution: Metro Area

MSA[1]	% of Households Earning								
	Less than $5,000	$5,000 -$9,999	$10,000 -$14,999	$15,000 -$24,999	$25,000 -$34,999	$35,000 -$49,999	$50,000 -$74,999	$75,000 -$99,999	$100,000 and up
Allentown	3.5	8.2	8.0	16.9	16.9	20.8	17.1	5.1	3.5
Baltimore	5.4	6.5	6.3	14.4	14.9	19.8	19.5	7.6	5.6
Boston	4.2	8.0	5.6	12.2	13.0	17.7	20.8	9.5	9.0
Bridgeport	3.5	7.2	6.0	12.6	13.4	17.8	21.7	9.6	8.3
Charlotte	5.2	7.9	8.0	18.1	17.1	19.2	15.9	4.9	3.6
Cincinnati	6.7	8.6	8.1	17.2	16.0	19.1	15.5	4.8	4.0
Cleveland	6.9	8.9	8.3	16.9	15.9	18.6	15.5	4.9	4.1
Durham	5.5	6.7	7.6	16.6	15.9	19.2	17.8	6.0	4.6
Greensboro	5.9	8.3	9.1	19.0	17.3	18.8	14.1	3.9	3.6
Lexington	7.7	9.5	9.6	18.3	16.3	17.3	13.6	4.1	3.6
New York	8.2	10.5	7.2	14.5	13.6	15.9	15.5	6.8	7.8
Norfolk	6.0	6.5	7.6	19.0	17.9	20.1	15.7	4.4	2.9
Philadelphia	5.2	7.8	7.0	14.7	14.6	19.2	18.6	6.9	5.9
Pittsburgh	6.3	11.7	10.1	18.8	16.1	16.9	12.8	3.9	3.4
Durham	5.5	6.7	7.6	16.6	15.9	19.2	17.8	6.0	4.6
Richmond	5.3	6.7	7.5	16.5	16.1	20.0	18.1	5.7	4.2
Stamford	2.3	4.2	3.5	8.8	10.1	13.9	18.8	11.7	26.6
Washington	3.2	3.4	3.8	10.9	13.0	19.2	23.7	12.0	10.7
Worcester	3.9	9.9	6.7	13.8	14.1	20.1	20.0	6.9	4.6
U.S.	**6.2**	**9.3**	**8.8**	**17.5**	**15.8**	**17.9**	**15.0**	**5.1**	**4.4**

Note: Figures are for 1989; (1) Metropolitan Statistical Area - see Appendix A for areas included
Source: 1990 Census of Population and Housing, Summary Tape File 3C

Effective Buying Income: City

City	Per Capita ($)	Median Household ($)	Average Household ($)
Allentown	15,238	30,984	37,439
Baltimore	12,562	25,842	33,519
Boston	17,607	34,523	44,905
Bridgeport	15,455	34,340	41,599
Charlotte	18,589	36,642	46,138
Cincinnati	14,779	25,127	34,610
Cleveland	10,685	20,931	26,848
Durham	16,255	31,409	39,243
Greensboro	16,710	32,101	40,890
Lexington	17,053	32,781	42,491
New York	16,875	32,417	44,604
Norfolk	12,710	25,356	36,375
Philadelphia	13,878	28,551	36,435
Pittsburgh	15,660	26,111	37,231
Raleigh	18,383	36,109	44,162
Richmond	14,164	24,224	33,076
Stamford	29,991	57,929	77,345
Washington	22,282	37,361	52,736
Worcester	13,863	30,241	36,561
U.S.	**15,444**	**33,201**	**41,849**

Note: Data as of 1/1/97
Source: Standard Rate & Data Service, Newspaper Advertising Source, 2/98

Effective Buying Income: Metro Area

MSA[1]	Per Capita ($)	Median Household ($)	Average Household ($)
Allentown	17,641	38,744	46,159
Baltimore	17,224	39,446	46,329
Boston	18,900	42,850	50,561
Bridgeport	24,668	50,028	65,683
Charlotte	16,599	35,921	43,456
Cincinnati	17,065	36,783	45,073
Cleveland	16,708	35,395	43,214
Durham	17,867	37,519	45,056
Greensboro	15,870	32,494	39,841
Lexington	15,830	32,322	41,331
New York	17,841	35,520	48,736
Norfolk	14,280	32,844	39,678
Philadelphia	19,160	42,422	52,092
Pittsburgh	17,668	34,352	43,998
Durham	17,867	37,519	45,056
Richmond	16,770	36,194	43,187
Stamford	24,668	50,028	65,683
Washington	21,603	49,583	58,316
Worcester	18,900	42,850	50,561
U.S.	**15,444**	**33,201**	**41,849**

Note: Data as of 1/1/97; (1) Metropolitan Statistical Area - see Appendix A for areas included; (2) Boston-Worcester-Lawrence-Lowell-Brockton; (3) New Haven-Bridgeport-Stamford-Danbury-Waterbury
Source: Standard Rate & Data Service, Newspaper Advertising Source, 2/98

Effective Household Buying Income Distribution: City

City	% of Households Earning $10,000 -$19,999	$20,000 -$34,999	$35,000 -$49,999	$50,000 -$74,999	$75,000 -$99,000	$100,000 -$124,999	$125,000 and up
Allentown	17.7	26.5	19.5	17.1	4.4	1.3	1.3
Baltimore	18.9	24.2	16.6	13.6	3.7	1.1	1.3
Boston	15.1	20.1	16.5	18.7	8.1	3.1	3.0
Bridgeport	15.9	21.3	17.3	19.5	8.0	2.6	1.7
Charlotte	13.6	24.2	19.2	19.8	7.6	2.7	3.1
Cincinnati	19.5	23.1	15.2	12.9	4.4	1.4	1.9
Cleveland	21.5	23.3	15.0	10.3	2.3	0.5	0.4
Durham	16.5	25.3	17.8	17.2	5.7	1.8	1.9
Greensboro	17.1	25.4	18.6	17.2	5.3	1.9	2.5
Lexington	16.4	23.5	17.4	17.6	6.6	2.3	2.8
New York	15.5	21.1	16.2	17.0	7.0	2.7	3.7
Norfolk	21.2	28.4	16.8	11.5	3.2	1.0	1.2
Philadelphia	18.3	22.3	16.8	16.1	5.3	1.5	1.4
Pittsburgh	20.8	22.4	15.2	13.2	4.9	1.6	2.5
Raleigh	14.5	23.6	18.7	20.5	7.2	2.5	2.5
Richmond	21.5	25.4	15.3	11.1	3.4	1.2	1.7
Stamford	8.0	14.1	14.1	22.1	14.6	7.7	13.2
Washington	12.6	21.7	16.0	17.7	9.2	4.2	5.6
Worcester	17.3	22.5	18.6	17.8	4.7	1.1	1.1
U.S.	**16.5**	**23.4**	**18.3**	**18.2**	**6.4**	**2.1**	**2.4**

Note: Data as of 1/1/97
Source: Standard Rate & Data Service, Newspaper Advertising Source, 2/98

Effective Household Buying Income Distribution: Metro Area

MSA[1]	% of Households Earning $10,000 -$19,999	$20,000 -$34,999	$35,000 -$49,999	$50,000 -$74,999	$75,000 -$99,000	$100,000 -$124,999	$125,000 and up
Allentown	14.0	22.3	19.8	22.3	8.1	2.5	2.4
Baltimore	12.5	21.4	20.2	22.7	8.4	2.5	2.5
Boston	12.1	18.3	18.1	23.6	10.5	3.8	3.6
Bridgeport	10.1	16.1	15.8	22.8	12.4	6.0	8.9
Charlotte	14.6	23.7	19.6	20.2	7.1	2.3	2.2
Cincinnati	14.3	21.8	18.6	20.4	7.9	2.6	2.8
Cleveland	15.0	22.1	18.9	19.6	7.3	2.3	2.5
Durham	13.9	22.3	18.9	21.4	8.0	2.6	2.5
Greensboro	16.8	25.4	19.5	17.8	5.2	1.7	2.0
Lexington	16.9	23.1	17.5	17.7	6.5	2.0	2.4
New York	14.4	19.9	16.1	18.2	8.2	3.4	4.7
Norfolk	15.7	26.9	20.7	18.2	4.9	1.3	1.3
Philadelphia	12.3	19.0	17.8	22.6	10.3	4.0	4.4
Pittsburgh	16.8	22.3	17.7	18.5	7.6	2.6	2.8
Durham	13.9	22.3	18.9	21.4	8.0	2.6	2.5
Richmond	14.5	23.5	20.1	21.0	6.6	1.9	2.1
Stamford	10.1	16.1	15.8	22.8	12.4	6.0	8.9
Washington	8.1	17.8	18.9	26.0	13.2	5.3	5.0
Worcester	12.1	18.3	18.1	23.6	10.5	3.8	3.6
U.S.	**16.5**	**23.4**	**18.3**	**18.2**	**6.4**	**2.1**	**2.4**

Note: Data as of 1/1/97; (1) Metropolitan Statistical Area - see Appendix A for areas included; (2) Boston-Worcester-Lawrence-Lowell-Brockton; (3) New Haven-Bridgeport-Stamford-Danbury-Waterbury
Source: Standard Rate & Data Service, Newspaper Advertising Source, 2/98

Poverty Rates by Race and Age: City

City	Total (%)	By Race (%) White	Black	Other	Hisp.[1]	By Age (%) Under 5 years old	Under 18 years old	65 years and over
Allentown	12.9	8.8	31.2	41.6	39.8	25.8	22.0	9.7
Baltimore	21.9	12.6	27.9	25.2	21.5	34.3	32.5	19.3
Boston	18.7	13.9	24.2	32.0	33.9	27.9	28.3	15.3
Bridgeport	17.1	12.7	20.7	27.7	30.7	30.9	29.1	11.2
Charlotte	10.8	5.1	22.5	12.2	9.9	18.4	16.0	13.8
Cincinnati	24.3	14.7	39.4	24.8	29.7	42.0	37.4	17.3
Cleveland	28.7	18.2	39.1	37.4	40.0	46.2	43.0	19.2
Durham	14.9	7.6	22.7	18.6	19.4	23.2	20.5	16.7
Greensboro	11.6	6.8	20.7	17.0	15.0	18.6	15.6	12.1
Lexington	14.1	10.9	34.0	22.1	26.4	19.9	18.8	13.2
New York	19.3	12.3	25.3	29.4	33.2	30.5	30.1	16.5
Norfolk	19.3	10.1	32.7	15.1	15.0	29.2	28.6	15.3
Philadelphia	20.3	11.1	29.0	41.6	45.3	31.9	30.3	16.3
Pittsburgh	21.4	14.0	40.9	38.1	23.6	37.0	32.5	14.4
Raleigh	11.8	7.4	21.7	24.4	17.4	17.4	14.7	13.0
Richmond	20.9	10.3	28.9	19.0	17.1	37.6	35.8	16.5
Stamford	6.3	3.9	15.2	9.9	12.3	10.4	10.3	7.5
Washington	16.9	8.2	20.2	21.9	20.4	27.0	25.5	17.2
Worcester	15.3	11.7	30.5	44.2	46.8	26.2	25.0	12.5
U.S.	**13.1**	**9.8**	**29.5**	**23.1**	**25.3**	**20.1**	**18.3**	**12.8**

Note: Figures show the percent of people living below the poverty line in 1989. The average poverty threshold was $12,674 for a family of four in 1989; (1) People of Hispanic origin can be of any race
Source: 1990 Census of Population and Housing, Summary Tape File 3C

Poverty Rates by Race and Age: Metro Area

MSA[1]	Total (%)	By Race (%) White	Black	Other	Hisp.[2]	By Age (%) Under 5 years old	Under 18 years old	65 years and over
Allentown	7.2	6.0	24.1	31.6	33.3	11.8	10.2	8.0
Baltimore	10.1	5.4	23.2	10.8	11.5	15.3	14.4	11.6
Boston	8.3	6.3	21.7	23.4	28.4	12.1	11.5	9.2
Bridgeport	7.8	5.4	18.8	23.6	26.9	14.9	13.2	7.3
Charlotte	9.6	6.2	22.9	11.6	11.1	14.3	12.9	15.2
Cincinnati	11.4	8.0	34.0	14.1	18.3	19.4	16.4	11.0
Cleveland	11.8	6.8	31.0	22.0	30.6	20.5	18.1	9.5
Durham	10.2	6.5	20.5	18.2	15.9	13.3	11.5	15.3
Greensboro	10.0	7.1	21.8	19.5	19.9	15.3	13.3	16.0
Lexington	14.2	11.9	32.7	20.9	24.3	21.1	18.9	16.3
New York	17.5	10.8	24.8	28.4	32.3	27.5	27.1	15.3
Norfolk	11.5	5.9	25.1	9.5	10.5	17.8	16.4	12.5
Philadelphia	10.4	5.6	25.5	30.1	35.2	15.9	15.0	10.4
Pittsburgh	12.2	10.0	35.9	23.2	19.4	20.4	17.9	10.5
Durham	10.2	6.5	20.5	18.2	15.9	13.3	11.5	15.3
Richmond	9.8	5.0	21.1	10.9	11.1	16.1	14.0	11.3
Stamford	4.6	3.2	14.6	8.4	11.3	6.9	6.5	5.7
Washington	6.4	3.6	12.6	9.9	12.0	8.3	7.9	8.6
Worcester	8.7	7.0	27.5	35.4	41.0	13.6	12.6	10.2
U.S.	**13.1**	**9.8**	**29.5**	**23.1**	**25.3**	**20.1**	**18.3**	**12.8**

Note: Figures show the percent of people living below the poverty line in 1989. The average poverty threshold was $12,674 for a family of four in 1989; (1) Metropolitan Statistical Area - see Appendix A for areas included; (2) People of Hispanic origin can be of any race
Source: 1990 Census of Population and Housing, Summary Tape File 3C

Major State and Local Tax Rates

City	State Corp. Income (%)	State Personal Income (%)	Residential Property (effective rate per $100)	Sales & Use State (%)	Sales & Use Local (%)	State Gasoline (cents/ gallon)	State Cigarette (cents/ 20-pack)
Allentown	9.99	2.8	n/a	6.0	None	25.9[a]	31
Baltimore	7.0	2.0 - 5.0	2.42	5.0	None	23.5	36
Boston	9.5[b]	5.95[c]	1.37	5.0	None	21	76
Bridgeport	10.5	3.0 - 4.5	3.96	6.0	None	36	50
Charlotte	7.5	6.0 - 7.75	1.12	4.0	2.0	22.6	5
Cincinnati	5.1 - 8.9[d]	0.693 - 7.004	n/a	5.0	1.0	22	24
Cleveland	5.1 - 8.9[d]	0.693 - 7.004	n/a	5.0	2.0	22	24
Durham	7.5	6.0 - 7.75	n/a	4.0	2.0	22.6	5
Greensboro	7.5	6.0 - 7.75	n/a	4.0	2.0	22.6	5
Lexington	4.0 - 8.25	2.0 - 6.0	n/a	6.0	None	16.4[e]	3
New York	9.0	4.0 - 6.85	0.86	4.0	4.25	8	56
Norfolk	6.0	2.0 - 5.75	n/a	3.5	1.0	17.5[f]	2.5[g]
Philadelphia	9.99	2.8	2.64	6.0	1.0	25.9[a]	31
Pittsburgh	9.99	2.8	n/a	6.0	1.0	25.9[a]	31
Raleigh	7.5	6.0 - 7.75	n/a	4.0	2.0	22.6	5
Richmond	6.0	2.0 - 5.75	n/a	3.5	1.0	17.5[f]	2.5[g]
Stamford	10.5	3.0 - 4.5	n/a	6.0	None	36	50
Washington	9.975	6.0 - 9.5	0.95	5.75	None	20	65
Worcester	9.5[b]	5.95[c]	n/a	5.0	None	21	76

Note: (a) Rate is comprised of 12 cents excise and 13.9 cent motor carrier tax; (b) Rate includes a 14% surtax, as does the following: an additional tax of $2.60 per $1,000 on taxable tangible property (or net worth allocable to state for intangible property corporations). Minimum tax is $456; (c) A 12% rate applies to interest, capital gains and dividends; (d) Or 5.82 mils times the value of the taxpayer's issued and outstanding share of stock. Minimum tax $50; (e) Rate is comprised of 15 cents excise and 1.4 cents motor carrier tax.; (f) Does not include a 2% local option tax; (g) Counties and cities may impose an additional tax of 2 - 15 cents per pack

Source: Source: Federation of Tax Administrators, www.taxadmin.org; Washington D.C. Department of Finance and Revenue, Tax Rates and Tax Burdens in the District of Columbia: A Nationwide Comparison, June 1997

Employment by Industry

MSA[1]	Services	Retail	Gov't.	Manuf.	Finance/ Ins./R.E.	Whole-sale	Transp./ Utilities	Constr.	Mining
Allentown	30.8	17.5	11.8	21.2	4.9	4.3	5.8	3.7	(a)
Baltimore	33.2	18.2	17.9	8.5	6.2	5.4	5.0	5.5	0.0
Boston	38.9	16.6	11.8	11.5	8.2	5.7	4.3	3.0	0.0
Bridgeport	31.4	17.6	11.3	21.4	5.6	5.3	3.9	3.5	0.0
Charlotte	24.5	17.3	12.1	18.9	7.0	7.1	6.9	6.2	(a)
Cincinnati	29.4	19.7	11.9	16.4	6.2	6.5	5.2	4.6	0.1
Cleveland	29.3	18.0	12.7	19.4	6.4	6.3	4.0	3.9	0.1
Durham	30.9	16.4	19.6	13.5	4.8	4.8	4.4	5.6	(a)
Greensboro	25.8	17.0	10.9	25.8	5.2	5.4	5.0	4.9	(a)
Lexington	26.5	18.6	20.5	17.3	3.7	4.6	4.0	4.8	0.1
New York	37.2	12.5	15.2	7.9	12.7	5.6	5.9	3.0	(a)
Norfolk	28.7	20.3	21.6	10.2	4.7	3.6	4.8	6.0	(a)
Philadelphia	35.6	17.0	13.0	13.3	6.9	5.5	4.8	3.9	(a)
Pittsburgh	34.1	19.1	11.9	12.8	5.8	5.4	6.1	4.5	0.4
Raleigh	30.9	16.4	19.6	13.5	4.8	4.8	4.4	5.6	(a)
Richmond	26.1	18.6	18.2	11.5	8.3	5.7	5.2	6.3	0.1
Stamford	35.5	17.0	8.7	13.0	12.1	5.9	4.8	2.9	(a)
Washington	38.3	16.1	23.5	4.0	5.3	3.3	4.4	5.0	0.0
Worcester	29.1	17.3	15.5	18.5	6.5	5.5	4.3	3.2	0.1
U.S.	**29.0**	**18.5**	**16.1**	**15.0**	**5.7**	**5.4**	**5.3**	**4.5**	**0.5**

Note: Figures cover non-farm employment as of 12/97 and are not seasonally adjusted; (1) Metropolitan Statistical Area - see Appendix A for areas included; (a) Mining is included with construction

Source: Bureau of Labor Statistics, http://stats.bls.gov

Labor Force, Employment and Job Growth: City

Area	Civilian Labor Force			Workers Employed		
	Dec. '95	Dec. '96	% Chg.	Dec. '95	Dec. '96	% Chg.
Allentown	51,604	52,185	1.1	48,990	49,717	1.5
Baltimore	319,737	318,809	-0.3	297,220	293,955	-1.1
Boston	289,851	295,561	2.0	279,622	285,759	2.2
Bridgeport	60,479	59,183	-2.1	54,281	54,624	0.6
Charlotte	267,762	263,588	-1.6	260,166	257,530	-1.0
Cincinnati	174,911	178,407	2.0	165,942	170,114	2.5
Cleveland	207,197	210,598	1.6	187,200	192,680	2.9
Durham	83,269	83,620	0.4	80,992	81,953	1.2
Greensboro	115,862	113,053	-2.4	112,322	110,208	-1.9
Lexington	138,982	146,439	5.4	135,791	143,495	5.7
New York	8,711,639	8,747,089	0.4	8,185,010	8,248,488	0.8
Norfolk	86,563	88,536	2.3	81,147	84,285	3.9
Philadelphia	654,379	665,513	1.7	617,097	629,699	2.0
Pittsburgh	163,794	164,810	0.6	157,253	158,320	0.7
Raleigh	153,644	154,918	0.8	150,408	152,192	1.2
Richmond	96,150	101,755	5.8	91,480	97,910	7.0
Stamford	63,912	63,940	0.0	61,111	61,790	1.1
Washington	267,941	258,172	-3.6	246,885	238,292	-3.5
Worcester	77,506	78,825	1.7	74,870	76,327	1.9
U.S.	**134,583,000**	**136,742,000**	**1.6**	**127,903,000**	**130,785,000**	**2.3**

Note: Data is not seasonally adjusted and covers workers 16 years of age and older
Source: Bureau of Labor Statistics, http://stats.bls.gov

Labor Force, Employment and Job Growth: Metro Area

Area	Civilian Labor Force			Workers Employed		
	Dec. '95	Dec. '96	% Chg.	Dec. '95	Dec. '96	% Chg.
Allentown	302,419	306,021	1.2	289,822	294,120	1.5
Baltimore	1,311,035	1,299,373	-0.9	1,251,836	1,238,084	-1.1
Boston	1,779,891	1,816,012	2.0	1,727,884	1,765,991	2.2
Bridgeport	218,542	216,238	-1.1	204,217	205,510	0.6
Charlotte	745,185	735,222	-1.3	720,854	717,807	-0.4
Cincinnati	820,118	840,782	2.5	789,609	812,683	2.9
Cleveland	1,111,117	1,132,800	2.0	1,051,656	1,082,447	2.9
Durham	587,379	591,986	0.8	575,408	582,236	1.2
Greensboro	640,560	626,638	-2.2	622,882	611,157	-1.9
Lexington	244,981	258,071	5.3	238,883	252,437	5.7
New York	3,969,059	3,988,748	0.5	3,654,143	3,701,557	1.3
Norfolk	709,006	728,929	2.8	676,602	702,316	3.8
Philadelphia	2,479,691	2,508,190	1.1	2,370,799	2,410,923	1.7
Pittsburgh	1,151,704	1,159,657	0.7	1,104,770	1,112,270	0.7
Raleigh	587,379	591,986	0.8	575,408	582,236	1.2
Richmond	481,057	510,458	6.1	463,897	496,502	7.0
Stamford	191,622	192,158	0.3	184,898	186,952	1.1
Washington	2,534,687	2,560,910	1.0	2,448,378	2,480,243	1.3
Worcester	248,116	252,805	1.9	240,450	245,117	1.9
U.S.	**134,583,000**	**136,742,000**	**1.6**	**127,903,000**	**130,785,000**	**2.3**

Note: Data is not seasonally adjusted and covers workers 16 years of age and older;
(1) Metropolitan Statistical Area - see Appendix A for areas included
Source: Bureau of Labor Statistics, http://stats.bls.gov

Unemployment Rate: City

Area	1997											
	Jan.	Feb.	Mar.	Apr.	May	Jun.	Jul.	Aug.	Sep.	Oct.	Nov.	Dec.
Allentown	6.3	6.5	6.4	6.5	6.7	6.4	6.5	6.1	6.2	5.6	5.5	4.7
Baltimore	7.8	7.9	7.8	7.7	8.2	9.2	8.5	8.3	10.7	8.7	8.4	7.8
Boston	4.4	4.0	4.1	3.9	4.1	4.5	4.4	4.7	4.6	3.7	3.8	3.3
Bridgeport	10.6	10.2	9.4	9.3	8.6	9.3	8.8	7.9	7.0	7.2	7.6	7.7
Charlotte	3.2	3.0	2.7	2.4	3.0	3.5	3.2	3.3	2.9	2.6	2.6	2.3
Cincinnati	6.1	6.0	5.2	4.8	4.9	5.1	4.5	4.6	5.1	5.0	5.0	4.6
Cleveland	11.1	11.0	10.1	9.4	9.0	8.6	7.8	8.0	8.8	8.5	8.7	8.5
Durham	3.0	3.2	2.7	2.2	2.4	3.1	2.9	3.0	2.6	2.5	2.3	2.0
Greensboro	3.5	4.0	3.6	2.3	2.9	3.3	3.6	3.4	3.1	2.9	2.8	2.5
Lexington	2.5	2.5	2.2	2.2	2.2	2.5	2.3	2.6	2.9	2.3	2.0	2.0
New York	7.1	7.1	7.0	6.4	6.3	6.3	6.6	6.2	6.1	6.1	5.9	5.7
Norfolk	6.5	6.6	6.7	6.9	7.5	8.6	7.5	7.4	7.3	6.0	5.5	4.8
Philadelphia	6.2	6.2	6.3	6.6	7.0	6.8	7.0	6.9	7.5	6.7	6.4	5.4
Pittsburgh	4.8	4.9	4.9	5.1	5.4	5.2	5.4	5.1	5.1	4.5	4.3	3.9
Raleigh	2.2	2.0	1.8	1.6	2.0	2.4	2.3	2.4	2.1	2.0	2.0	1.8
Richmond	5.1	5.0	4.6	4.6	5.1	5.9	5.3	5.4	5.5	4.5	4.2	3.8
Stamford	4.7	4.6	4.0	3.7	3.9	4.2	4.3	3.9	3.2	3.4	3.6	3.4
Washington	8.1	7.8	7.7	6.8	6.9	7.8	8.0	7.9	7.7	8.1	7.7	7.7
Worcester	4.4	4.1	4.2	4.0	4.4	4.6	4.2	4.3	4.4	3.4	3.4	3.2
U.S.	**5.9**	**5.7**	**5.5**	**4.8**	**4.7**	**5.2**	**5.0**	**4.8**	**4.7**	**4.4**	**4.3**	**4.4**

Note: All figures are percentages, are not seasonally adjusted and covers workers 16 years of age and older
Source: Bureau of Labor Statistics, http://stats.bls.gov

Unemployment Rate: Metro Area

Area	1997											
	Jan.	Feb.	Mar.	Apr.	May	Jun.	Jul.	Aug.	Sep.	Oct.	Nov.	Dec.
Allentown	5.3	5.3	5.2	5.1	5.2	5.2	5.4	5.1	5.0	4.5	4.3	3.9
Baltimore	5.2	5.4	5.1	4.9	5.1	5.7	5.4	5.0	5.7	5.2	5.0	4.7
Boston	3.8	3.5	3.6	3.3	3.3	3.6	3.4	3.5	3.6	2.9	3.0	2.8
Bridgeport	6.9	6.5	5.9	5.7	5.8	6.4	6.3	5.6	4.8	5.0	5.1	5.0
Charlotte	3.5	3.3	2.9	2.6	3.0	3.6	3.5	3.3	3.0	2.8	2.6	2.4
Cincinnati	4.7	4.8	4.0	3.7	3.5	3.6	3.3	3.3	3.5	3.6	3.4	3.3
Cleveland	6.1	6.4	5.5	5.0	4.4	4.3	4.1	3.9	4.4	4.2	4.6	4.4
Durham	2.3	2.1	1.9	1.6	1.9	2.3	2.1	2.2	1.9	1.8	1.8	1.6
Greensboro	3.2	3.2	2.9	2.3	2.7	3.1	3.2	3.1	2.7	2.6	2.7	2.5
Lexington	2.9	2.9	2.5	2.5	2.4	2.7	2.5	2.7	2.9	2.4	2.1	2.2
New York	8.9	8.9	9.0	8.6	8.4	8.8	8.9	8.5	8.1	8.2	7.7	7.2
Norfolk	5.0	4.9	4.6	4.7	5.3	6.1	5.4	5.3	5.2	4.3	4.1	3.7
Philadelphia	5.0	4.9	4.9	4.8	5.0	5.0	5.3	5.0	5.1	4.5	4.4	3.9
Pittsburgh	5.2	5.3	5.2	5.0	5.1	5.1	5.1	4.8	4.7	4.0	4.3	4.1
Raleigh	2.3	2.1	1.9	1.6	1.9	2.3	2.1	2.2	1.9	1.8	1.8	1.6
Richmond	3.8	3.7	3.3	3.4	3.8	4.3	3.6	3.8	3.9	3.3	3.1	2.7
Stamford	3.6	3.5	3.2	2.9	3.1	3.4	3.3	3.0	2.7	2.8	2.9	2.7
Washington	3.7	3.7	3.4	3.3	3.4	3.8	3.5	3.5	3.5	3.5	3.3	3.1
Worcester	4.2	4.0	4.1	3.7	3.6	3.8	3.6	3.7	3.7	3.0	3.2	3.0
U.S.	**5.9**	**5.7**	**5.5**	**4.8**	**4.7**	**5.2**	**5.0**	**4.8**	**4.7**	**4.4**	**4.3**	**4.4**

Note: All figures are percentages, are not seasonally adjusted and covers workers 16 years of age and older
(1) Metropolitan Statistical Area - see Appendix A for areas included
Source: Bureau of Labor Statistics, http://stats.bls.gov

Average Wages: Selected Professional Occupations

MSA[1] (Month/Year)	Accountant III	Attorney III	Computer Program. II	Engineer III	Systems Analyst II	Systems Analyst Supv./Mgr. II
Allentown	-	-	-	-	-	-
Baltimore (5/95)	755	1,267	597	922	861	-
Boston (6/96)	803	1,441	647	995	964	1,419
Bridgeport	-	-	-	-	-	-
Charlotte (10/95)	778	-	605	910	870	-
Cincinnati (5/96)	755	-	658	980	1,014	1,328
Cleveland (7/96)	787	1,293	613	931	899	1,306
Durham (5/95)	-	-	-	-	904	-
Greensboro (7/96)	-	-	619	-	963	-
Lexington (8/96)	-	-	-	-	882	-
New York (5/95)	831	1,289	675	972	991	1,569
Norfolk (4/96)	-	-	605	-	812	-
Philadelphia (11/96)	835	1,088	636	960	988	1,397
Pittsburgh (5/96)	790	1,194	597	909	894	1,321
Raleigh (5/95)	-	-	-	-	904	-
Richmond (8/96)	809	1,048	609	976	911	1,379
Stamford (1/94)	-	-	604	-	862	-
Washington (2/96)	845	1,265	653	963	928	1,402
Worcester (9/94)	-	-	-	-	832	-

Notes: Figures are average weekly earnings; Dashes indicate that data was not available;
(1) Metropolitan Statistical Area - see Appendix A for areas included
Source: Bureau of Labor Statistics, Occupational Compensation Surveys

Average Wages: Selected Technical and Clerical Occupations

MSA[1] (Month/Year)	Accounting Clerk III	General Clerk II	Computer Operator II	Key Entry Operator I	Secretary III	Switchboard Operator/ Receptionist
Allentown	-	-	-	-	-	-
Baltimore (5/95)	448	389	461	305	509	348
Boston (6/96)	491	438	466	380	581	402
Bridgeport	-	-	-	-	-	-
Charlotte (10/95)	448	397	467	334	526	352
Cincinnati (5/96)	445	414	488	330	545	337
Cleveland (7/96)	457	410	-	300	569	364
Durham (5/95)	443	-	383	289	492	359
Greensboro (7/96)	430	452	430	331	506	343
Lexington (8/96)	407	-	409	339	517	333
New York (5/95)	511	440	498	418	619	428
Norfolk (4/96)	424	420	425	-	492	294
Philadelphia (11/96)	459	402	445	366	538	370
Pittsburgh (5/96)	437	400	403	322	530	319
Raleigh (5/95)	443	-	383	289	492	359
Richmond (8/96)	444	-	-	-	570	-
Stamford (1/94)	452	387	419	345	536	379
Washington (2/96)	494	416	456	346	586	412
Worcester (9/94)	480	398	418	360	529	361

Notes: Figures are average weekly earnings; Dashes indicate that data was not available;
(1) Metropolitan Statistical Area - see Appendix A for areas included
Source: Bureau of Labor Statistics, Occupational Compensation Surveys

Average Wages: Selected Health and Protective Service Occupations

MSA[1] (Month/Year)	Corrections Officer	Firefighter	Lic. Prac. Nurse II	Registered Nurse II	Nursing Assistant II	Police Officer I
Allentown	-	-	-	-	-	-
Baltimore (5/95)	536	643	531	731	308	630
Boston (6/96)	-	639	-	-	-	638
Bridgeport	-	-	-	-	-	-
Charlotte (10/95)	404	569	-	-	-	557
Cincinnati (5/96)	465	719	-	-	-	682
Cleveland (7/96)	428	738	-	-	-	704
Durham (5/95)	-	-	-	-	-	-
Greensboro (7/96)	-	-	-	-	-	-
Lexington (8/96)	-	-	-	-	-	-
New York (5/95)	748	809	575	980	410	752
Norfolk (4/96)	-	-	-	-	-	-
Philadelphia (11/96)	653	701	-	-	-	729
Pittsburgh (5/96)	581	741	-	-	-	710
Raleigh (5/95)	-	-	-	-	-	-
Richmond (8/96)	-	-	-	-	-	643
Stamford (1/94)	-	-	-	-	-	-
Washington (2/96)	604	684	-	-	-	698
Worcester (9/94)	-	-	-	776	-	-

Notes: Figures are average weekly earnings; Dashes indicate that data was not available;
(1) Metropolitan Statistical Area - see Appendix A for areas included
Source: Bureau of Labor Statistics, Occupational Compensation Surveys

Average Wages: Selected Maintenance, Material Movement and Custodial Occupations

MSA[1] (Month/Year)	General Maintenance	Guard I	Janitor	Maintenance Electrician	Motor Vehicle Mechanic	Truckdriver (Trac. Trail.)
Allentown	-	-	-	-	-	-
Baltimore (5/95)	10.01	6.62	7.04	17.19	14.43	13.94
Boston (6/96)	11.95	8.04	9.08	19.10	17.52	14.71
Bridgeport	-	-	-	-	-	-
Charlotte (10/95)	9.44	6.39	6.54	14.54	14.69	12.91
Cincinnati (5/96)	10.63	7.04	7.59	19.19	16.14	-
Cleveland (7/96)	10.72	6.69	7.25	19.59	16.71	14.93
Durham (5/95)	8.84	-	5.58	17.51	15.05	13.89
Greensboro (7/96)	10.27	6.30	5.43	14.98	14.58	13.76
Lexington (8/96)	7.79	6.90	6.03	16.31	14.67	16.32
New York (5/95)	14.65	8.09	12.32	22.55	19.99	17.90
Norfolk (4/96)	8.71	5.58	5.81	17.60	13.53	10.04
Philadelphia (11/96)	11.19	7.53	11.84	17.67	15.44	13.29
Pittsburgh (5/96)	10.52	6.02	7.98	16.49	16.61	15.68
Raleigh (5/95)	8.84	-	5.58	17.51	15.05	13.89
Richmond (8/96)	9.62	-	6.44	20.05	13.73	15.37
Stamford (1/94)	11.43	7.00	6.49	17.47	16.07	14.73
Washington (2/96)	10.71	-	7.54	18.36	17.97	17.42
Worcester (9/94)	10.46	8.22	8.96	16.44	15.39	14.46

Notes: Figures are average hourly earnings; Dashes indicate that data was not available;
(1) Metropolitan Statistical Area - see Appendix A for areas included
Source: Bureau of Labor Statistics, Occupational Compensation Surveys

Means of Transportation to Work: City

City	Car/Truck/Van		Public Transportation			Bicycle	Walked	Other Means	Worked at Home
	Drove Alone	Car-pooled	Bus	Subway	Railroad				
Allentown	70.4	14.0	3.3	0.0	0.0	0.4	8.7	0.9	2.2
Baltimore	50.9	16.8	19.3	1.6	0.4	0.2	7.4	1.7	1.6
Boston	40.1	10.5	13.6	13.2	1.0	0.9	14.0	4.5	2.2
Bridgeport	69.4	16.6	5.2	0.0	1.0	0.1	5.1	1.2	1.3
Charlotte	77.2	12.9	4.3	0.0	0.0	0.2	2.2	1.0	2.2
Cincinnati	67.4	12.6	10.9	0.0	0.0	0.2	5.9	0.9	2.0
Cleveland	64.8	14.0	13.0	0.6	0.1	0.1	5.0	1.2	1.2
Durham	73.4	15.5	2.9	0.0	0.0	0.5	4.5	1.2	1.9
Greensboro	79.1	12.5	1.5	0.0	0.0	0.3	3.6	1.2	1.8
Lexington	78.4	11.6	1.5	0.0	0.0	0.3	5.1	0.6	2.4
New York	24.0	8.5	12.7	36.7	1.7	0.3	10.7	2.9	2.4
Norfolk	56.0	13.9	4.4	0.0	0.0	0.8	4.8	1.9	18.2
Philadelphia	44.7	13.2	18.5	7.0	1.8	0.6	10.4	2.1	1.8
Pittsburgh	48.9	13.5	21.1	0.3	0.0	0.4	12.6	1.3	1.8
Raleigh	79.0	11.3	2.7	0.0	0.0	0.4	3.5	1.1	2.0
Richmond	64.5	13.8	12.5	0.0	0.0	1.0	5.4	1.1	1.7
Stamford	70.2	10.0	3.4	0.2	7.3	0.2	4.6	1.0	3.2
Washington	35.0	12.0	22.3	12.9	0.2	0.8	11.8	2.0	3.0
Worcester	71.0	13.2	4.1	0.0	0.0	0.2	8.8	1.1	1.7
U.S.	**73.2**	**13.4**	**3.0**	**1.5**	**0.5**	**0.4**	**3.9**	**1.2**	**3.0**

Note: Figures shown are percentages and only include workers 16 years old and over
Source: 1990 Census of Population and Housing, Summary Tape File 3C

Means of Transportation to Work: Metro Area

MSA[1]	Car/Truck/Van		Public Transportation			Bicycle	Walked	Other Means	Worked at Home
	Drove Alone	Car-pooled	Bus	Subway	Railroad				
Allentown	77.9	12.6	1.2	0.0	0.0	0.2	4.9	0.7	2.4
Baltimore	70.9	14.2	6.2	0.8	0.3	0.2	4.0	1.1	2.3
Boston	65.8	9.8	5.4	5.9	1.4	0.5	6.5	2.0	2.6
Bridgeport	79.3	11.4	1.8	0.0	1.8	0.1	2.7	0.7	2.1
Charlotte	78.8	14.5	1.7	0.0	0.0	0.1	2.1	1.0	1.9
Cincinnati	78.6	11.6	4.1	0.0	0.0	0.1	2.8	0.7	2.1
Cleveland	77.7	10.5	5.5	0.4	0.1	0.1	2.9	0.8	2.0
Durham	78.0	13.3	1.8	0.0	0.0	0.4	3.1	1.0	2.3
Greensboro	79.1	14.5	1.0	0.0	0.0	0.1	2.3	0.8	2.1
Lexington	77.9	12.7	1.0	0.0	0.0	0.2	4.7	0.6	2.8
New York	30.7	8.9	11.4	30.9	3.0	0.3	9.7	2.6	2.5
Norfolk	72.7	14.1	2.0	0.0	0.0	0.5	3.7	1.6	5.3
Philadelphia	67.8	11.9	6.3	2.7	2.1	0.3	5.4	1.2	2.3
Pittsburgh	70.7	12.9	7.7	0.2	0.0	0.1	5.1	1.1	2.1
Durham	78.0	13.3	1.8	0.0	0.0	0.4	3.1	1.0	2.3
Richmond	77.2	13.4	3.5	0.0	0.0	0.3	2.5	0.9	2.1
Stamford	68.0	8.5	2.0	0.2	11.0	0.1	4.2	1.2	4.7
Washington	62.9	15.8	6.6	6.5	0.2	0.3	3.9	1.0	2.8
Worcester	79.3	11.2	1.7	0.0	0.0	0.1	4.7	0.8	2.1
U.S.	**73.2**	**13.4**	**3.0**	**1.5**	**0.5**	**0.4**	**3.9**	**1.2**	**3.0**

Note: Figures shown are percentages and only include workers 16 years old and over;
(1) Metropolitan Statistical Area - see Appendix A for areas included
Source: 1990 Census of Population and Housing, Summary Tape File 3C

Cost of Living Index

Area	Composite	Groceries	Health	Housing	Misc.	Transp.	Utilities
Allentown[1,4]	103.0	107.9	93.6	98.0	103.5	101.7	116.6
Baltimore	98.4	98.7	97.9	95.4	97.7	100.5	108.7
Boston[1]	138.5	110.2	135.8	194.5	108.5	121.6	143.4
Bridgeport	n/a	n/a	n/a	n/a	n/a	n/a	n/a
Charlotte	100.5	100.6	100.6	99.9	101.0	97.2	104.3
Cincinnati	98.9	101.2	95.7	96.1	100.5	99.3	99.2
Cleveland	104.5	104.0	109.0	104.9	99.4	102.3	124.6
Durham[2]	104.1	101.3	104.1	113.0	101.0	97.3	99.1
Greensboro[5]	94.9	94.4	79.4	93.1	96.2	98.6	104.7
Lexington[1]	97.3	99.2	100.9	95.4	101.3	97.8	80.5
New York[3]	226.9	137.8	191.2	445.3	131.3	122.3	179.4
Norfolk	n/a	n/a	n/a	n/a	n/a	n/a	n/a
Philadelphia	122.5	109.0	102.8	140.0	107.1	119.2	169.8
Pittsburgh[4]	108.4	102.6	98.8	111.0	103.8	112.6	132.5
Raleigh[2]	104.1	101.3	104.1	113.0	101.0	97.3	99.1
Richmond	104.8	99.2	106.1	103.8	102.9	106.5	124.4
Stamford	n/a	n/a	n/a	n/a	n/a	n/a	n/a
Washington[1]	122.1	109.6	119.8	151.8	109.8	124.9	92.7
Worcester[4]	96.7	98.8	107.5	89.5	96.2	97.5	110.5
U.S.	**100.0**	**100.0**	**100.0**	**100.0**	**100.0**	**100.0**	**100.0**

Note: n/a not available; (1) Metropolitan Statistical Area (MSA) - see Appendix A for areas included; (2) Raleigh-Durham; (3) Manhattan; (4) 1st Quarter 1997; (5) 2nd Quarter 1996
Source: ACCRA, Cost of Living Index, 3rd Quarter 1997 unless otherwise noted

Median Home Prices and Housing Affordability

MSA[1]	Median Price[2] 3rd Qtr. 1997 ($)	HOI[3] 3rd Qtr. 1997	Affordability Rank[4]
Allentown	103,000	76.3	45
Baltimore	135,000	67.3	111
Boston	151,000	67.5	109
Bridgeport	n/a	n/a	n/a
Charlotte	134,000	57.9	157
Cincinnati	106,000	72.6	71
Cleveland	106,000	71.0	89
Durham	143,000	61.3	138
Greensboro	118,000	61.4	137
Lexington	100,000	72.8	70
New York	158,000	47.3	177
Norfolk	104,000	70.5	91
Philadelphia	143,000	55.2	166
Pittsburgh	92,000	60.3	145
Raleigh	143,000	61.3	138
Richmond	118,000	71.9	80
Stamford	n/a	n/a	n/a
Washington	165,000	70.5	91
Worcester	124,000	69.6	97
U.S.	**127,000**	**63.7**	-

Note: (1) Metropolitan Statistical Area - see Appendix A for areas included; (2) U.S. figures calculated from the sales of 625,000 new and existing homes in 195 markets; (3) Housing Opportunity Index - percent of homes sold that were within the reach of the median income household at the prevailing mortgage interest rate; (4) Rank is from 1-195 with 1 being most affordable; n/a not available
Source: National Association of Home Builders, Housing News Service, 3rd Quarter 1997

Average Home Prices

Area	Price ($)
Allentown[1,4]	134,900
Baltimore	133,476
Boston[1]	264,200
Bridgeport	n/a
Charlotte	138,400
Cincinnati	130,868
Cleveland	137,683
Durham[2]	154,621
Greensboro[5]	126,400
Lexington[1]	123,280
New York[3]	584,333
Norfolk	n/a
Philadelphia	193,138
Pittsburgh[4]	151,450
Raleigh[2]	154,621
Richmond	135,500
Stamford	n/a
Washington[1]	206,783
Worcester[4]	121,982
U.S.	**135,710**

Note: Figures are based on a new home with 1,800 sq. ft. of living area on an 8,000 sq. ft. lot; n/a not available; (1) Metropolitan Statistical Area (MSA) - see Appendix A for areas included; (2) Raleigh-Durham; (3) Manhattan; (4) 1st Quarter 1997; (5) 2nd Quarter 1996
Source: ACCRA, Cost of Living Index, 3rd Quarter 1997 unless otherwise noted

Average Apartment Rent

Area	Rent ($/mth)
Allentown[1,4]	564
Baltimore	495
Boston[1]	1,106
Bridgeport	n/a
Charlotte	543
Cincinnati	581
Cleveland	690
Durham[2]	697
Greensboro[5]	505
Lexington[1]	666
New York[3]	2,920
Norfolk	n/a
Philadelphia	726
Pittsburgh[4]	598
Raleigh[2]	697
Richmond	749
Stamford	n/a
Washington[1]	971
Worcester[4]	509
U.S.	**569**

Note: Figures are based on an unfurnished two bedroom, 1-1/2 or 2 bath apartment, approximately 950 sq. ft. in size, excluding all utilities except water; n/a not available; (1) Metropolitan Statistical Area (MSA) - see Appendix A for areas included; (2) Raleigh-Durham; (3) Manhattan; (4) 1st Quarter 1997; (5) 2nd Quarter 1996
Source: ACCRA, Cost of Living Index, 3rd Quarter 1997 unless otherwise noted

Average Residential Utility Costs

Area	All Electric ($/mth)	Part Electric ($/mth)	Other Energy ($/mth)	Phone ($/mth)
Allentown[1,4]	125.94	-	-	17.85
Baltimore	-	65.23	45.47	22.01
Boston[1]	-	78.09	73.33	22.47
Bridgeport	n/a	n/a	n/a	n/a
Charlotte	109.12	-	-	17.51
Cincinnati	-	61.45	38.72	21.15
Cleveland	-	78.62	50.53	22.37
Durham[2]	102.74	-	-	17.86
Greensboro[5]	111.18	-	-	17.56
Lexington[1]	-	31.70	41.84	26.61
New York[3]	-	97.51	95.16	24.06
Norfolk	n/a	n/a	n/a	n/a
Philadelphia	187.42	-	-	16.51
Pittsburgh[4]	-	80.62	62.61	20.13
Raleigh[2]	102.74	-	-	17.86
Richmond	130.48	-	-	20.52
Stamford	n/a	n/a	n/a	n/a
Washington[1]	-	57.52	35.70	20.15
Worcester[4]	-	63.75	50.01	23.63
U.S.	**109.40**	**55.25**	**43.64**	**19.48**

Note: Dashes indicate data not applicable; n/a not available;
(1) Metropolitan Statistical Area (MSA) - see Appendix A for areas included; (2) Raleigh-Durham; (3) Manhattan; (4) 1st Quarter 1997; (5) 2nd Quarter 1996
Source: ACCRA, Cost of Living Index, 3rd Quarter 1997 unless otherwise noted

Average Health Care Costs

Area	Hospital ($/day)	Doctor ($/visit)	Dentist ($/visit)
Allentown[1,4]	470.00	36.75	55.80
Baltimore	536.60	44.00	53.60
Boston[1]	649.00	69.00	74.00
Bridgeport	n/a	n/a	n/a
Charlotte	367.00	52.80	58.60
Cincinnati	390.40	46.60	56.70
Cleveland	666.40	43.87	59.50
Durham[2]	316.00	56.50	64.62
Greensboro[5]	210.00	40.80	41.80
Lexington[1]	365.00	55.20	55.80
New York[3]	1,359.00	87.00	92.00
Norfolk	n/a	n/a	n/a
Philadelphia	447.00	47.50	61.25
Pittsburgh[4]	518.33	36.60	60.60
Raleigh[2]	316.00	56.50	64.62
Richmond	428.80	51.14	64.50
Stamford	n/a	n/a	n/a
Washington[1]	454.50	60.33	71.33
Worcester[4]	410.00	50.10	64.80
U.S.	**392.91**	**48.76**	**60.84**

Note: n/a not available; Hospital - based on a semi-private room. Doctor - based on a general practitioner's routine exam of an established patient. Dentist - based on adult teeth cleaning and periodic oral exam; (1) Metropolitan Statistical Area (MSA) - see Appendix A for areas included; (2) Raleigh-Durham; (3) Manhattan; (4) 1st Quarter 1997; (5) 2nd Quarter 1996
Source: ACCRA, Cost of Living Index, 3rd Quarter 1997 unless otherwise noted

Distribution of Office-Based Physicians

MSA[1]	General Practitioners	Specialists		
		Medical	Surgical	Other
Allentown	145	340	320	245
Baltimore	400	2,185	1,509	1,548
Boston	470	4,192	2,300	3,294
Bridgeport	122	848	542	476
Charlotte	279	667	622	514
Cincinnati	370	1,000	772	806
Cleveland	341	1,748	1,212	1,364
Durham	280	895	620	850
Greensboro	249	651	556	499
Lexington	135	370	284	363
New York	895	9,050	4,634	5,705
Norfolk	397	724	680	624
Philadelphia	903	3,861	2,571	3,202
Pittsburgh	577	1,721	1,265	1,403
Raleigh	280	895	620	850
Richmond	264	646	480	491
Stamford	122	848	542	476
Washington	850	3,885	2,455	2,787
Worcester	145	617	306	348

Note: Data as of 12/31/96; (1) Metropolitan Statistical Area - see Appendix A for areas included
Source: Physician Characteristics & Distribution in the U.S. 1997-98

Educational Quality

City	School District	Education Quotient[1]	Graduate Outcome[2]	Community Index[3]	Resource Index[4]
Allentown	Allentown City	108.0	66.0	110.0	148.0
Baltimore	Baltimore City	63.0	52.0	55.0	81.0
Boston	Boston	70.0	61.0	84.0	64.0
Bridgeport	Bridgeport	104.0	51.0	145.0	117.0
Charlotte	Charlotte-Mecklenburg	94.0	84.0	131.0	68.0
Cincinnati	Cincinnati City	90.0	64.0	100.0	105.0
Cleveland	Cleveland City	85.0	51.0	84.0	119.0
Durham	Durham Public	86.0	73.0	126.0	58.0
Greensboro	Guilford	85.0	79.0	115.0	60.0
Lexington	Fayette County	112.0	115.0	119.0	103.0
New York	New York	n/a	n/a	n/a	n/a
Norfolk	Norfolk City	81.0	55.0	65.0	122.0
Philadelphia	Philadelphia City	64.0	52.0	54.0	87.0
Pittsburgh	Pittsburgh	n/a	n/a	n/a	n/a
Raleigh	Wake County	119.0	106.0	143.0	108.0
Richmond	Richmond City	85.0	63.0	65.0	128.0
Stamford	Stamford	113.0	74.0	144.0	121.0
Washington	District of Columbia	93.0	52.0	95.0	131.0
Worcester	Worcester	95.0	78.0	112.0	94.0

Note: Nearly 1,000 secondary school districts were rated in terms of educational quality. The scores range from a low of 50 to a high of 150; (1) Average of the Graduate Outcome, Community and Resource indexes; (2) Based on graduation rates and college board scores (SAT/ACT); (3) Based on the surrounding community's average level of education and the area's average income level; (4) Based on teacher salaries, per-pupil expenditures and student-teacher ratios.
Source: Expansion Management, Ratings Issue 1997

School Enrollment by Type: City

City	Preprimary				Elementary/High School			
	Public		Private		Public		Private	
	Enrollment	%	Enrollment	%	Enrollment	%	Enrollment	%
Allentown	857	57.4	635	42.6	12,733	87.4	1,833	12.6
Baltimore	7,935	67.4	3,830	32.6	102,104	85.5	17,364	14.5
Boston	3,504	56.5	2,698	43.5	58,244	77.2	17,231	22.8
Bridgeport	1,453	70.8	600	29.2	20,451	81.7	4,577	18.3
Charlotte	4,071	53.5	3,540	46.5	55,638	89.3	6,640	10.7
Cincinnati	3,651	56.7	2,789	43.3	45,797	81.3	10,524	18.7
Cleveland	4,923	62.6	2,939	37.4	69,894	78.7	18,875	21.3
Durham	1,182	45.1	1,438	54.9	17,680	92.1	1,516	7.9
Greensboro	1,840	54.1	1,564	45.9	23,934	92.5	1,927	7.5
Lexington	1,718	45.0	2,100	55.0	29,574	90.0	3,284	10.0
New York	54,891	55.5	43,933	44.5	934,140	79.1	246,344	20.9
Norfolk	2,322	59.2	1,600	40.8	33,000	91.0	3,245	9.0
Philadelphia	13,314	55.4	10,702	44.6	179,728	70.8	74,032	29.2
Pittsburgh	3,400	58.5	2,412	41.5	36,244	75.8	11,549	24.2
Raleigh	1,680	44.8	2,074	55.2	24,478	93.2	1,782	6.8
Richmond	1,849	62.6	1,105	37.4	24,399	89.2	2,946	10.8
Stamford	1,053	47.9	1,147	52.1	12,000	84.1	2,270	15.9
Washington	5,532	61.8	3,425	38.2	67,278	83.9	12,882	16.1
Worcester	1,871	63.6	1,073	36.4	20,873	88.4	2,738	11.6
U.S.	**2,679,029**	**59.5**	**1,824,256**	**40.5**	**38,379,689**	**90.2**	**4,187,099**	**9.8**

Note: Figures shown cover persons 3 years old and over
Source: 1990 Census of Population and Housing, Summary Tape File 3C

School Enrollment by Type: Metro Area

MSA[1]	Preprimary				Elementary/High School			
	Public		Private		Public		Private	
	Enrollment	%	Enrollment	%	Enrollment	%	Enrollment	%
Allentown	7,056	54.8	5,827	45.2	91,613	88.3	12,092	11.7
Baltimore	25,147	55.8	19,929	44.2	320,507	86.2	51,108	13.8
Boston	27,026	49.3	27,803	50.7	331,757	85.6	55,619	14.4
Bridgeport	5,196	54.6	4,326	45.4	57,944	84.6	10,541	15.4
Charlotte	10,978	56.1	8,605	43.9	176,791	92.7	13,957	7.3
Cincinnati	15,601	53.0	13,831	47.0	206,692	81.4	47,137	18.6
Cleveland	19,818	55.4	15,951	44.6	241,493	80.6	58,046	19.4
Durham	6,751	46.9	7,652	53.1	99,864	92.8	7,735	7.2
Greensboro	8,849	58.2	6,354	41.8	136,757	93.7	9,199	6.3
Lexington	2,832	50.7	2,759	49.3	50,759	91.9	4,490	8.1
New York	66,531	53.1	58,729	46.9	1,086,038	79.3	283,106	20.7
Norfolk	14,319	54.5	11,942	45.5	218,089	92.8	16,852	7.2
Philadelphia	48,214	48.5	51,171	51.5	595,382	76.8	179,754	23.2
Pittsburgh	20,226	54.8	16,696	45.2	254,093	86.0	41,306	14.0
Durham	6,751	46.9	7,652	53.1	99,864	92.8	7,735	7.2
Richmond	9,730	59.5	6,628	40.5	130,034	93.0	9,840	7.0
Stamford	2,043	43.1	2,692	56.9	22,828	81.6	5,132	18.4
Washington	39,352	48.2	42,299	51.8	522,711	87.4	75,692	12.6
Worcester	5,391	59.2	3,711	40.8	58,575	89.3	7,020	10.7
U.S.	**2,679,029**	**59.5**	**1,824,256**	**40.5**	**38,379,689**	**90.2**	**4,187,099**	**9.8**

Note: Figures shown cover persons 3 years old and over;
(1) Metropolitan Statistical Area - see Appendix A for areas included
Source: 1990 Census of Population and Housing, Summary Tape File 3C

School Enrollment by Race: City

City	Preprimary (%)				Elementary/High School (%)			
	White	Black	Other	Hisp.[1]	White	Black	Other	Hisp.[1]
Allentown	76.7	6.7	16.6	22.7	74.2	8.0	17.8	23.6
Baltimore	34.8	63.7	1.4	1.4	26.1	72.4	1.5	1.1
Boston	50.0	37.8	12.2	11.7	39.1	42.1	18.8	17.4
Bridgeport	44.7	38.7	16.7	32.7	43.7	34.5	21.8	37.6
Charlotte	67.5	30.4	2.0	1.3	53.0	43.8	3.2	1.4
Cincinnati	58.4	39.9	1.7	0.9	45.6	53.0	1.4	0.6
Cleveland	43.5	53.1	3.4	5.4	37.6	57.0	5.4	6.5
Durham	53.8	43.1	3.1	0.6	35.5	62.1	2.4	1.2
Greensboro	66.1	30.7	3.2	0.2	54.1	43.1	2.9	1.0
Lexington	83.6	13.3	3.1	0.7	77.4	20.3	2.3	1.1
New York	47.4	35.6	17.1	21.2	38.6	36.8	24.6	32.6
Norfolk	60.5	35.6	3.9	3.4	41.5	54.4	4.1	2.5
Philadelphia	49.3	44.6	6.0	4.7	41.6	48.6	9.8	8.4
Pittsburgh	66.4	31.4	2.2	1.4	59.1	38.9	2.1	1.1
Raleigh	75.4	21.2	3.4	1.9	59.1	37.3	3.6	1.2
Richmond	34.4	63.4	2.2	0.7	20.0	79.0	1.0	1.0
Stamford	72.5	20.8	6.7	8.8	63.3	29.1	7.6	12.5
Washington	25.0	71.2	3.8	3.4	12.6	82.2	5.2	6.5
Worcester	80.2	8.8	11.0	10.7	76.8	7.2	16.0	19.4
U.S.	**80.4**	**12.5**	**7.1**	**7.8**	**74.1**	**15.6**	**10.3**	**12.5**

Note: Figures shown cover persons 3 years old and over; (1) People of Hispanic origin can be of any race
Source: 1990 Census of Population and Housing, Summary Tape File 3C

School Enrollment by Race: Metro Area

MSA[1]	Preprimary (%)				Elementary/High School (%)			
	White	Black	Other	Hisp.[2]	White	Black	Other	Hisp.[2]
Allentown	93.6	1.6	4.8	5.7	91.2	3.1	5.6	7.2
Baltimore	73.5	24.2	2.4	1.6	64.4	32.6	3.0	1.5
Boston	88.2	6.8	5.1	3.7	80.9	11.0	8.2	6.6
Bridgeport	83.4	11.1	5.5	9.4	75.6	15.1	9.3	15.8
Charlotte	78.5	19.9	1.6	0.8	71.2	26.7	2.0	1.0
Cincinnati	86.4	12.5	1.0	0.7	82.4	16.3	1.3	0.7
Cleveland	80.4	17.1	2.4	2.0	71.5	25.4	3.1	2.7
Durham	78.1	19.4	2.6	1.2	65.4	31.9	2.7	1.2
Greensboro	78.2	20.4	1.4	1.0	74.1	24.2	1.7	0.8
Lexington	86.2	11.1	2.7	0.7	83.7	14.7	1.7	0.9
New York	55.0	30.1	14.9	18.2	43.6	34.0	22.5	29.7
Norfolk	71.3	25.7	2.9	2.7	60.2	35.5	4.3	2.3
Philadelphia	79.3	16.9	3.8	3.0	69.7	23.9	6.4	5.3
Pittsburgh	89.5	9.1	1.4	0.8	87.5	11.3	1.3	0.6
Durham	78.1	19.4	2.6	1.2	65.4	31.9	2.7	1.2
Richmond	72.2	26.1	1.7	1.2	61.8	35.5	2.7	1.2
Stamford	84.8	10.1	5.1	5.1	77.1	15.9	7.0	8.5
Washington	70.9	23.1	6.0	4.4	58.9	31.6	9.5	6.7
Worcester	91.3	3.6	5.1	4.3	89.9	3.0	7.1	8.1
U.S.	**80.4**	**12.5**	**7.1**	**7.8**	**74.1**	**15.6**	**10.3**	**12.5**

Note: Figures shown cover persons 3 years old and over; (1) Metropolitan Statistical Area - see Appendix A for areas included; (2) People of Hispanic origin can be of any race
Source: 1990 Census of Population and Housing, Summary Tape File 3C

Crime Rate: City

City	All Crimes	Violent Crimes				Property Crimes		
		Murder	Forcible Rape	Robbery	Aggrav. Assault	Burglary	Larceny -Theft	Motor Vehicle Theft
Allentown	7,063.5	5.7	46.5	304.6	261.9	1,435.9	4,431.9	577.0
Baltimore	12,001.2	45.8	89.5	1,450.6	1,136.9	2,066.0	5,656.0	1,556.4
Boston	8,092.2	10.7	74.9	628.0	943.1	914.4	3,843.1	1,678.0
Bridgeport	8,300.6	33.1	45.9	712.7	792.4	1,863.7	3,065.1	1,787.8
Charlotte	9,659.1	12.8	55.2	468.2	1,072.8	1,845.8	5,450.4	753.9
Cincinnati	7,616.7	8.9	87.4	492.2	499.4	1,577.7	4,445.7	505.5
Cleveland	7,541.4	20.8	129.6	818.9	569.1	1,553.9	2,709.6	1,739.5
Durham	11,333.3	27.6	56.5	545.2	507.5	2,844.4	6,326.9	1,025.1
Greensboro	8,068.0	11.3	46.8	349.4	540.9	1,588.7	5,015.1	515.8
Lexington	6,356.2	5.8	50.6	240.1	532.0	1,199.7	3,948.6	379.4
New York	5,212.2	13.4	31.8	676.7	622.3	834.8	2,210.6	822.7
Norfolk	7,665.6	24.8	57.7	438.7	426.9	1,124.6	4,900.5	692.4
Philadelphia	6,920.0	27.1	46.1	1,013.1	442.6	1,060.2	2,817.6	1,513.4
Pittsburgh	5,296.0	13.3	58.1	441.7	290.7	860.6	2,838.5	793.1
Raleigh	6,966.4	10.2	36.7	298.6	514.7	1,280.3	4,264.7	561.2
Richmond	9,650.0	54.7	69.8	754.1	772.6	1,963.1	5,045.9	989.8
Stamford	4,623.7	5.6	16.8	197.8	191.3	656.9	3,109.2	446.0
Washington	11,889.0	73.1	47.9	1,186.7	1,162.1	1,809.9	5,772.2	1,837.0
Worcester	6,021.6	4.2	64.8	245.8	622.4	1,337.1	3,080.1	667.3
U.S.	**5,078.9**	**7.4**	**36.1**	**202.4**	**388.2**	**943.0**	**2,975.9**	**525.9**

Note: Crime rate is the number of crimes per 100,000 population; n/a not available;
Source: FBI Uniform Crime Reports 1996

Crime Rate: Suburbs

Suburbs[1]	All Crimes	Violent Crimes				Property Crimes		
		Murder	Forcible Rape	Robbery	Aggrav. Assault	Burglary	Larceny -Theft	Motor Vehicle Theft
Allentown	2,918.6	1.2	15.2	56.5	147.1	442.0	2,095.4	161.3
Baltimore	5,023.2	3.7	27.1	207.2	400.9	817.8	3,110.5	456.0
Boston	2,941.7	1.3	16.6	61.7	295.6	534.4	1,667.6	364.4
Bridgeport	3,260.1	1.6	18.8	53.8	80.7	678.6	2,067.1	359.6
Charlotte	4,753.3	6.0	31.6	113.4	361.7	1,044.4	2,971.6	224.8
Cincinnati	n/a	n/a	n/a	n/a	n/a	n/a	n/a	n/a
Cleveland	n/a	n/a	n/a	n/a	n/a	n/a	n/a	n/a
Durham	5,158.1	6.8	22.1	141.1	302.0	1,041.7	3,311.2	333.1
Greensboro	5,746.3	6.7	33.9	170.8	385.6	1,325.2	3,443.9	380.3
Lexington	n/a	n/a	n/a	n/a	n/a	n/a	n/a	n/a
New York	3,085.6	3.7	10.6	139.2	164.5	482.6	1,936.0	349.1
Norfolk	4,902.5	7.8	35.8	163.4	217.6	741.0	3,432.8	304.0
Philadelphia	3,613.2	2.7	21.1	130.0	225.8	586.1	2,223.5	423.9
Pittsburgh	2,211.6	1.8	16.9	51.0	147.2	372.7	1,411.4	210.5
Raleigh	5,787.0	9.8	24.1	169.5	273.3	1,319.4	3,595.5	395.3
Richmond	4,276.2	5.1	21.9	101.8	171.3	634.3	3,120.1	221.7
Stamford	3,302.8	3.1	12.5	90.9	64.2	623.1	2,272.7	236.2
Washington	4,567.9	5.7	24.8	177.0	226.7	598.2	2,980.2	555.3
Worcester	2,035.0	0.0	17.8	17.8	364.0	399.3	1,092.4	143.7
U.S.	**5,078.9**	**7.4**	**36.1**	**202.4**	**388.2**	**943.0**	**2,975.9**	**525.9**

Note: Crime rate is the number of crimes per 100,000 population; n/a not available; (1) Defined as all areas within the MSA but located outside the central city
Source: FBI Uniform Crime Reports 1996

Crime Rate: Metro Area

MSA[1]	All Crimes	Violent Crimes				Property Crimes		
		Murder	Forcible Rape	Robbery	Aggrav. Assault	Burglary	Larceny -Theft	Motor Vehicle Theft
Allentown	3,632.3	2.0	20.6	99.2	166.9	613.2	2,497.7	232.9
Baltimore	7,026.9	15.8	45.0	564.3	612.2	1,176.2	3,841.4	772.0
Boston	3,768.2	2.8	26.0	152.6	399.5	595.3	2,016.7	575.2
Bridgeport	4,740.9	10.8	26.7	247.4	289.8	1,026.8	2,360.3	779.2
Charlotte	6,841.0	8.9	41.6	264.4	664.3	1,385.4	4,026.4	449.9
Cincinnati	n/a	n/a	n/a	n/a	n/a	n/a	n/a	n/a
Cleveland	n/a	n/a	n/a	n/a	n/a	n/a	n/a	n/a
Durham	6,076.4	9.9	27.2	201.2	332.5	1,309.8	3,759.7	436.0
Greensboro	6,157.5	7.5	36.2	202.4	413.1	1,371.9	3,722.2	404.3
Lexington	n/a	n/a	n/a	n/a	n/a	n/a	n/a	n/a
New York	4,896.6	12.0	28.6	597.0	554.4	782.5	2,169.8	752.4
Norfolk	5,338.2	10.5	39.2	206.8	250.6	801.5	3,664.2	365.3
Philadelphia	4,630.8	10.2	28.8	401.8	292.5	732.0	2,406.3	759.2
Pittsburgh	2,665.1	3.4	23.0	108.5	168.3	444.5	1,621.2	296.2
Raleigh	6,076.4	9.9	27.2	201.2	332.5	1,309.8	3,759.7	436.0
Richmond	5,455.2	16.0	32.4	244.9	303.3	925.8	3,542.6	390.2
Stamford	3,729.8	3.9	13.9	125.5	105.3	634.0	2,543.1	304.1
Washington	5,450.7	13.8	27.6	298.8	339.5	744.3	3,316.8	709.9
Worcester	3,416.4	1.5	34.1	96.8	453.5	724.2	1,781.1	325.1
U.S.	**5,078.9**	**7.4**	**36.1**	**202.4**	**388.2**	**943.0**	**2,975.9**	**525.9**

Note: Crime rate is the number of crimes per 100,000 population; n/a not available;
(1) Metropolitan Statistical Area - see Appendix A for areas included
Source: FBI Uniform Crime Reports 1996

Temperature & Precipitation: Yearly Averages and Extremes

City	Extreme Low (°F)	Average Low (°F)	Average Temp. (°F)	Average High (°F)	Extreme High (°F)	Average Precip. (in.)	Average Snow (in.)
Allentown	-12	42	52	61	105	44.2	32
Baltimore	-7	45	56	65	105	41.2	21
Boston	-12	44	52	59	102	42.9	41
Bridgeport	-7	44	52	60	103	41.4	25
Charlotte	-5	50	61	71	104	42.8	6
Cincinnati	-25	44	54	64	103	40.9	23
Cleveland	-19	41	50	59	104	37.1	55
Durham	-9	48	60	71	105	42.0	8
Greensboro	-8	47	58	69	103	42.5	10
Lexington	-21	45	55	65	103	45.1	17
New York	-2	47	55	62	104	47.0	23
Norfolk	-3	51	60	68	104	45.0	8
Philadelphia	-7	45	55	64	104	41.4	22
Pittsburgh	-18	41	51	60	103	37.1	43
Raleigh	-9	48	60	71	105	42.0	8
Richmond	-8	48	58	69	105	43.0	13
Stamford	-7	44	52	60	103	41.4	25
Washington	-5	49	58	67	104	39.5	18
Worcester	-13	38	47	56	99	47.6	62

Note: Tr = Trace
Source: National Climatic Data Center, International Station Meteorological Climate Summary, 3/95

Weather Conditions

City	Temperature			Daytime Sky			Precipitation		
	10°F & below	32°F & below	90°F & above	Clear	Partly cloudy	Cloudy	.01 inch or more precip.	1.0 inch or more snow/ice	Thunder-storms
Allentown	(a)	123	15	77	148	140	123	20	31
Baltimore	6	97	31	91	143	131	113	13	27
Boston	(a)	97	12	88	127	150	253	48	18
Bridgeport	(a)	(b)	7	80	146	139	118	17	22
Charlotte	1	65	44	98	142	125	113	3	41
Cincinnati	14	107	23	80	126	159	127	25	39
Cleveland	(a)	123	12	63	127	175	157	48	34
Durham	(a)	(b)	39	98	143	124	110	3	42
Greensboro	3	85	32	94	143	128	113	5	43
Lexington	11	96	22	86	136	143	129	17	44
New York	(a)	(b)	18	85	166	114	120	11	20
Norfolk	< 1	54	32	89	149	127	115	6	37
Philadelphia	5	94	23	81	146	138	117	14	27
Pittsburgh	(a)	121	8	62	137	166	154	42	35
Raleigh	(a)	(b)	39	98	143	124	110	3	42
Richmond	3	79	41	90	147	128	115	7	43
Stamford	(a)	(b)	7	80	146	139	118	17	22
Washington	2	71	34	84	144	137	112	9	30
Worcester	(a)	141	4	81	144	140	131	32	23

Note: Figures are average number of days per year; (a) Figures for 10 degrees and below are not available; (b) Figures for 32 degrees and below are not available

Source: National Climatic Data Center, International Station Meteorological Climate Summary, 3/95

Air Quality

MSA[1]	PSI>100[2] (days)	Ozone (ppm)	Carbon Monoxide (ppm)	Sulfur Dioxide (ppm)	Nitrogen Dioxide (ppm)	PM10 (ug/m3)	Lead (ug/m3)
Allentown	0	0.11	3	0.035	0.024	65	0.08
Baltimore	4	0.13	4	0.028	0.027	75	0.03
Boston	0	0.11	5	0.037	0.031	80	n/a
Bridgeport	n/a	0.13	3	0.023	0.024	63	0.02
Charlotte	6	0.13	5	0.015	0.016	53	0.01
Cincinnati	2	0.12	3	0.045	0.029	72	0.22
Cleveland	5	0.12	9	0.049	0.026	123	0.04
Durham	0	0.11	6	0.010	n/a	49	n/a
Greensboro	2	0.12	4	0.026	0.016	58	n/a
Lexington	n/a	0.10	3	0.020	0.014	60	0.04
New York	7	0.12	6	0.055	0.042	87	0.16
Norfolk	0	0.10	6	0.025	0.018	50	0.03
Philadelphia	22	0.13	6	0.063	0.034	356	0.76
Pittsburgh	1	0.11	4	0.070	0.030	123	0.07
Raleigh	0	0.11	6	0.010	n/a	49	n/a
Richmond	0	0.11	3	0.027	0.022	69	0.01
Stamford	n/a	0.12	4	0.026	n/a	65	n/a
Washington	2	0.12	5	0.048	0.026	57	0.02
Worcester	n/a	0.09	5	0.021	0.019	46	n/a
NAAQS[3]	-	**0.12**	**9**	**0.140**	**0.053**	**150**	**1.50**

Note: (1) Metropolitan Statistical Area - see Appendix A for areas included; (2) Number of days the Pollutant Standards Index (PSI) exceeded 100 in 1996. A PSI value greater than 100 indicates that air quality would be in the unhealthful range on that day; (3) National Ambient Air Quality Standard; ppm = parts per million; ug/m^3 = micrograms per cubic meter; n/a not available

Source: EPA, National Air Quality and Emissions Trends Report, 1996

Water Quality

City	Tap Water
Allentown	Alkaline, hard and not fluoridated
Baltimore	Alkaline, very soft and fluoridated
Boston	The Metropolitan Water District (combined sources, Quabbin Reservoir and Wachusett Reservoir) supplies municipal Boston and the ABC City Zone. Water is soft and slightly acid
Bridgeport	Alkaline, very soft and fluoridated
Charlotte	Alkaline, very soft and fluoridated
Cincinnati	Alkaline, hard and fluoridated
Cleveland	Alkaline, hard and fluoridated
Durham	Alkaline, soft and fluoridated
Greensboro	Alkaline, soft
Lexington	Alkaline, medium and fluoridated
New York	New York City tap water has three major sources: the Catskills & Delaware subsytems (neutral, soft, average pH 7.0) and Croton subsystem (alkaline, moderately hard, average pH 7.1). All three supplies are fluoridated and chlorinated
Norfolk	Slightly soft, fluoridated and has low alkalinity
Philadelphia	Slightly acid, moderately hard (Schuykill River), moderately soft (Delaware River); fluoridated
Pittsburgh	Alkaline, soft 9 months, hard 3 months (June, July, August); fluoridated
Raleigh	Neutral, soft and fluoridated
Richmond	Alkaline, soft and fluoridated
Stamford	Slightly acid, moderately soft and fluoridated
Washington	Slightly alkaline and medium soft
Worcester	Very soft, slightly acidic and not fluoridated

Source: Editor & Publisher Market Guide 1998

Appendix A

Metropolitan Statistical Areas

Allentown–Bethlehem–Easton, PA

Includes Carbon, Lehigh and Northhampton Counties, PA (as of 6/30/93)

Includes Carbon, Lehigh and Northhampton Counties, PA; Warren County, NJ (prior to 6/30/93)

Baltimore, MD

Includes Baltimore City; Anne Arundel, Baltimore, Carroll, Harford, Howard, and Queen Anne's Counties

Boston, MA-NH

Includes parts of Bristol, Essex, Middlesex, Norfolk, Plymouth, and Worcester Counties, MA; and all of Suffolk County, MA; Part of Rockingham County, NH (as of 6/30/93)

Includes parts of Bristol, Essex, Middlesex, Norfolk, Plymouth, and Worcester Counties; and all of Suffolk County (prior to 6/30/93)

Bridgeport, CT

Includes parts of Fairfield and New Haven Counties

Charlotte-Gastonia-Rock Hill, NC-SC

Includes Cabarrus, Gaston, Lincoln, Mecklenburg, Rowan, and Union Counties, NC; York County, SC

Cincinnati, OH-KY-IN

Includes Brown, Clermont, Hamilton, and Warren Counties, OH; Boone, Campbell, Gallatin, Grant, Kenton and Pendleton Counties, KY; Dearborn and Ohio Counties, IN (as of 6/30/93)

Includes Clermont, Hamilton, and Warren Counties, OH; Boone, Campbell, and Kenton Counties, KY; Dearborn County, IN (prior to 6/30/93)

Cleveland, OH

Includes Ashtabula, Cuyahoga, Geauga, Lake, Lorain and Medina Counties (as of 6/30/93)

Includes Cuyahoga, Geauga, Lake, and Medina Counties (prior to 6/30/93)

Durham, NC

See Raleigh-Durham-Chapel Hill, NC

Greensboro–Winston-Salem–High Point, NC

Includes Alamance, Davidson, Davie, Forsyth, Guilford, Randolph, Stokes, and Yadkin Counties (as of 6/30/93)

Includes Davidson, Davie, Forsyth, Guilford, Randolph, Stokes, and Yadkin Counties (prior to 6/30/93)

Lexington, KY

Includes Bourbon, Clark, Fayette, Jessamine, Madison, Scott and Woodford Counties (as of 6/30/93)

Includes Bourbon, Clark, Fayette, Jessamine, Scott and Woodford Counties (prior to 6/30/93)

New York, NY

Includes Bronx, Kings, New York, Putnam, Queens, Richmond, Rockland, and Westchester Counties

Norfolk-Virginia Beach-Newport News, VA-NC

Includes Chesapeake, Hampton, Newport News, Norfolk, Poquoson, Portsmouth, Suffolk, Virginia Beach, and Williamsburg Cities, VA; Gloucester, Isle of Wright, James City, Mathews and York Counties, VA; Currituck County, NC (as of 6/30/93)

Includes Chesapeake, Hampton, Newport News, Norfolk, Poquoson, Portsmouth, Suffolk, Virginia Beach, and Williamsburg Cities; Gloucester, James City and York Counties (prior to 6/30/93)

Philadelphia, PA-NJ

Includes Bucks, Chester, Delaware, Montgomery and Philadelphia Counties, PA; Burlington, Camden, Gloucester and Salem Counties, NJ (as of 6/30/93)

Includes Bucks, Chester, Delaware, Montgomery and Philadelphia Counties, PA; Burlington, Camden and Gloucester Counties, NJ (prior to 6/30/93)

Pittsburgh, PA

Includes Allegheny, Beaver, Butler, Fayette, Washington and Westmoreland Counties (as of 6/30/93)

Includes Allegheny, Fayette, Washington and Westmoreland Counties (prior to 6/30/93)

Raleigh-Durham-Chapel Hill, NC

Includes Chatham, Durham, Franklin, Johnston, Orange, and Wake Counties (as of 6/30/93)

Includes Durham, Franklin, Orange, and Wake Counties (prior to 6/30/93)

Richmond-Petersburg, VA

Includes Colonial Heights, Hopewell, Petersburg, and Richmond Cities; Charles City, Chesterfield, Dinwiddie, Goochland, Hanover, Henrico, New Kent, Powhatan, and Prince George Counties

Stamford-Norwalk, CT

Includes part of Fairfield County

Washington, DC-MD-VA-WV

Includes District of Columbia; Calvert, Charles, Frederick, Montgomery and Prince George Counties, MD; Alexandria, Fairfax, Falls Church, Fredericksburg, Manassas and Manassas Park Cities, and Arlington, Clarke, Culpeper, Fairfax, Fauquier, King George, Loudoun, Prince William, Spotsylvania, Stafford and Warren Counties, VA; Berkeley and Jefferson Counties, WV (as of 6/30/93)

Includes District of Columbia; Calvert, Charles, Frederick, Montgomery and Prince George Counties, MD; Alexandria, Fairfax, Falls Church, Manassas and Manassas Park Cities, and Arlington, Fairfax, Loudoun, Prince William and Stafford Counties, VA (prior to 6/30/93)

Worcester, MA-CT

Includes parts of Hampden and Worcester Counties, MA; Part of Windham County, CT (as of 6/30/93)

Includes part of Worcester County (prior to 6/30/93)

Appendix B

Chambers of Commerce and Economic Development Organizations

Allentown

Lehigh Valley
Economic Devel. Corp.
P.O. Box 21750
Lehigh Valley, PA 18002
Phone: (610) 266-6775
Fax: (610) 266-7623

Baltimore

Baltimore City
Chamber of Commerce
204 E. Lombard Street, #300
Baltimore, MD 21202
Phone: (410) 837-7101
Fax: (410) 837-7104

City of Baltimore Development Corp.
36 S. Charles St. #1600
Baltimore, MD 21201
Phone: (410) 837-9305
Fax: (410) 547-7211

Boston

Greater Boston
Chamber of Commerce
One Beacon St.
Boston, MA 02108-3114
Phone: (617) 227-4500
Fax: (617) 227-7505

Bridgeport

Bridgeport Office of
Planning & Econ. Devel.
45 Lyon Terrace
Room 301
Bridgeport, CT 06604-4023
Phone: (203) 576-7221
Fax: (203) 332-5611

Charlotte

Charlotte Chamber of Commerce
P.O. Box 32785
Charlotte, NC 28232
Phone: (704) 377-6911
Fax: (704) 374-1903

Charlotte Region
Carolinas Partnership
112 S. Tryon St., Suite 510
Charlotte, NC 28284
Phone: (704) 347-8942
Fax: (704) 347-8981

Cincinnati

Dept. of Economic Development
Two Centennial Plaza
805 Central Ave. #710
Cincinnati, OH 45202
Phone: (513) 352-3950
Fax: (513) 352-6257

Greater Cincinnati
Chamber of Commerce
300 Carew Tower
441 Vine St.
Cincinnati, OH 45202
Phone: (513) 579-3100
Fax: (513) 579-3101

Cleveland

Cleveland Department of
Economic Development
601 Lakeside Ave.
Room 210 City Hall
Cleveland, OH 44114
Phone: (216) 664-2406
Fax: (216) 664-3681

Greater Cleveland Growth Assn.
200 Tower City Center
50 Public Square
Cleveland, OH 44113-2291
Phone: (216) 621-3300
Fax: (216) 621-6013

Durham

Greater Durham
Chamber of Commerce
P.O. Box 3829
300 W. Morgan Street, #1400
Durham, NC 27702
Phone: (919) 682-2133
Fax: (919) 688-8351

Greensboro

Greensboro Area
Chamber of Commerce
P.O. Box 3246
Greensboro, NC 27402-3246
Phone: (910) 275-8675
Fax: (910) 230-1867

Lexington

City of Lexington
Mayor's Office of Econ. Devel.
200 E. Main St.
Lexington, KY 40507
Phone: (606) 258-3131
Fax: (606) 258-3128

Greater Lexington Chamber of
Commerce
330 E. Main St. #100
P.O. Box 781
Lexington, KY 40587-0781
Phone: (606) 254-4447
Fax: (606) 233-3304

New York

New York City
Chamber of Commerce
One Battery Park Plaza
New York, NY 10004-1491
Phone: (212) 493-7500
Fax: (212) 344-3344

New York City Economic
Development Corp.
110 William St.
New York, NY 10038
Phone: (212) 619-5000

Norfolk

Forward Hampton Roads
555 Main Street
1214 First Virginia Bank Tower
Norfolk, VA 23510
Phone: (804) 627-2315
Fax: (804) 623-3081

Hampton Roads
Chamber of Commerce
420 Bank Street
P.O. Box 327
Norfolk, VA 23501
Phone: (804) 664-2526
Fax: (804) 622-5563

Philadelphia

Greater Philadelphia
Chamber of Commerce
200 South Broad Street, Suite 700
Philadelphia, PA 19102-3896
Phone: (215) 545-1234
Fax: (215) 972-3900

Greater Philadelphia First
1818 Market St., #3510
Philadelphia, PA 19103-3681

Pittsburgh

Allegheny County
Industrial Development Auth.
400 Fort Pitt Commons Rd.
Pittsburgh, PA 15219
Phone: (412) 644-1067
Fax: (412) 642-2217

Greater Pittsburgh
Chamber of Commerce
3 Gateway Center
Pittsburgh, PA 15222
Phone: (412) 392-4500
Fax: (412) 392-4520

Raleigh

Wake County
Economic Development
P.O. Box 2978
800 S. Salisbury St.
Raleigh, NC 27601-2978

Richmond

Greater Richmond
Chamber of Commerce
P. O. Box 12280
Richmond, VA 23241-2280
Phone: (804) 548-1234
Fax: (804) 780-0344

Greater Richmond Partnership
901 E. Byrd St., #801
Richmond, VA 23219-4070
Phone: (804) 643-3227
Fax: (804) 343-7167

Stamford

City of Stamford
Office of Economic Development
888 Washington Blvd.
Stamford, CT 06904
Phone: (203) 977-4150
Fax: (203) 977-5845

Stamford Chamber of Commerce
733 Summer St.
Stamform, CT 06901

Washington

District of Columbia
Chamber of Commerce
1301 Pennsylvania Ave NW
Suite 309
Washington, DC 20004
Phone: (202) 347-7201
Fax: (202) 347-3537

District of Columbia Office
of Business & Econ. Devel.
51 N. Street, NE
Washington, DC 20005
Phone: (202) 535-1970
Fax: (202) 535-1584

Worcester

Worcester Area
Chamber of Commerce
33 Waldo St.
Worcester, MA 01608-1581
Phone: (508) 753-2924
Fax: (508) 754-8560

Appendix C

State Departments of Labor and Employment

Connecticut

Connecticut Department of Labor
Employment Security Division
200 Folly Brook Boulevard
Wethersfield, CT 06109-1114

District of Columbia

District of Columbia
Department of Employment Services
500 C Street, NW
Washington, DC 20001

Kentucky

Kentucky Dept. for Employ. Services
Research and Statistics
275 E. Main Street
Frankfort, KY 40621

Maryland

Maryland Department of
Employment and Training
Research and Analysis Div.
1100 North Eutaw Street
Baltimore, MD 21201

Massachusetts

Massachusetts Department of
Employment & Training
Exec. Office of Econ. Affairs
19 Staniford Street
Boston, MA 02114

New York

New York State Department of Labor
Division of Research & Statistics
State Campus Bldg. 12, Room 488
Albany, NY 12214-0721

North Carolina

Employment Security Commission
Labor Market Information Division
PO Box 25903
Raleigh, NC 27611-5903

Ohio

Ohio Bureau of Employment Services
Labor Market Information Division
145 S. Front Street
PO Box 1618
Columbus, OH 43216-1618

Pennsylvania

Pennsylvania Department of
Labor & Industry
Employment Security
Harrisburg, PA 17121-0001

Virginia

Virginia Employment Commission
Economic Information Services
P.O. Box 1358
Richmond, VA 23211